# ABRAHAM LINCOLN

# SELECTED WRITINGS

# ABRAHAM LINCOLN

# SELECTED WRITINGS

**BARNES & NOBLE**

NEW YORK

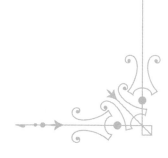

Cover design: Scott Russo
Lincoln photograph: Courtesy of Library of Congress
Endpapers: Courtesy of Library of Congress


Barnes & Noble, Inc.
122 Fifth Avenue
New York, NY 10011

ISBN: 978-1-4351-4771-3

Printed and bound in China

1 3 5 7 9 10 8 6 4 2

# Contents

## PRESIDENTIAL SPEECHES, WRITINGS, AND PROCLAMATIONS

## LETTERS

# Note on the Text

In the interest of historical authenticity, this volume retains the inconsistencies of spelling, punctuation, and grammar found in Abraham Lincoln's written documents, and in authoritative transcriptions by others of his speeches and addresses.

The text of the Lincoln-Douglas debates, and associated speeches, letters, and introductory material, is taken from *The Political Debates Between Abraham Lincoln and Stephen A. Douglas* (New York: G. P. Putnam's Sons, 1913).

# Chronology of Abraham Lincoln's Life

1809    Born on February 12, in a log cabin in Hardin County, Kentucky, the second child of Thomas Lincoln and Nancy Hanks Lincoln.

1818    Mother dies on October 5.

1819    Father remarries to Sarah (Sally) Bush Johnston, a widow with three children.

1827    Works as boatman and farmhand.

1830    Moves with family to Illinois, settling near Decatur.

1831    Moves to New Salem, Illinois, and briefly clerks in general store.

1832    Volunteers for Illinois militia during the Black Hawk Indian War. Loses election for Illinois House of Representatives.

1833    Appointed postmaster of New Salem, and later accepts appointment as deputy surveyor of Sangamon County.

1834    Elected to Illinois House of Representatives on the Whig ticket on August 4. Begins studying law.

1836    Receives license to practice law on September 9.

1842    Marries Mary Todd on November 4.

1843    Son Robert Todd Lincoln born on August 1.

1846    Second son, Edward Baker Lincoln, born on March 10. Elected to U.S. House of Representatives on August 3.

1849    Votes to abolish slave trade in District of Columbia.

1850    Son Edward dies on February 1. Third son, William Wallace Lincoln, born on December 21.

1853    Fourth son, Thomas Lincoln, born on April 4.

1854    Speaks against the Kansas-Nebraska Act, which repeals antislavery provisions of the Missouri Compromise, and appears before its principal author, Democrat Stephen A. Douglas.

1856    Helps to found the Republican Party of Illinois.

1857    Speaks against the Dred Scott decision—which denied Constitutional protection and citizenship to Africans brought into the United States as slaves—in Springfield on June 26.

1858    Endorsed at the Republican state convention for the Senate seat held by Stephen A. Douglas, and delivers "House Divided" speech on July 9. Debates Douglas in seven historic debates during the months of August through October.

1859    Loses Senate election to Douglas on January 5.

1860    Wins nomination for president at the Republican national convention on May 18. Elected first Republican president of the United States on November 6.

1861    Inaugurated president on March 4. Confederate forces fire on Fort Sumter on April 12, initiating the American Civil War. Appoints George B. McClellan commander of the Union army.

1862    Son William dies on February 20. Assumes direct command of the Union armies on March 11.

1863    More than five months after preliminary drafting, issues the Emancipation Proclamation on January 1, freeing slaves in Confederate territories. Signs act on military conscription on March 3. Delivers dedicatory address at Gettysburg Cemetery on November 19, commemorating the lives lost in the Confederate defeat on July 3.

1864    Re-elected president November 8. Appoints Salmon P. Chase chief justice of the U.S. Supreme Court on December 6.

1865    Begins mustering support from Democrats in the House of Representatives for proposed Thirteenth Amendment to abolish slavery (passed December 6). Makes last public speech on April 11. Shot by John Wilkes Booth at Ford's Theater in Washington, D.C. the evening of April 14 and dies the following morning. Buried in Oak Ridge Cemetery near Springfield, Illinois, on May 4.

# Introduction

SHORT AUTOBIOGRAPHY WRITTEN AT THE REQUEST OF A FRIEND
TO USE IN PREPARING A POPULAR CAMPAIGN BIOGRAPHY
IN THE ELECTION OF 1860

Abraham Lincoln was born Feb. 12, 1809, then in Hardin, now in the more recently formed county of Larue, Kentucky. His father, Thomas, & grand-father, Abraham, were born in Rockingham county Virginia, whither their ancestors had come from Berks county Pennsylvania. His lineage has been traced no farther back than this. The family were originally quakers, though in later times they have fallen away from the peculiar habits of that people. The grand-father, Abraham, had four brothers—Isaac, Jacob, John, & Thomas. So far as known, the descendants of Jacob and John are still in Virginia. Isaac went to a place near where Virginia, North Carolina, and Tennessee, join; and his descendants are in that region. Thomas came to Kentucky, and after many years, died there, whence his descendants went to Missouri. Abraham, grandfather of the subject of this sketch, came to Kentucky, and was killed by indians about the year 1784. He left a widow, three sons and two daughters. The eldest son, Mordecai, remained in Kentucky till late in life, when he removed to Hancock county, Illinois, where soon after he died, and where several of his descendants still remain. The second son, Josiah, removed at an early day to a place on Blue River, now within Harrison county, Indiana; but no recent information of him, or his family, has been obtained. The eldest sister, Mary, married Ralph Crume and some of her descendants are now known to be in Breckenridge county Kentucky. The second sister, Nancy, married William Brumfield, and her family are not known to have left Kentucky, but there is no recent information from them. Thomas, the youngest son, and father of the present subject, by the early death of his father, and very narrow circumstances of his mother, even in childhood was a wandering laboring boy, and grew up litterally without education. He never did more in the way of writing than to bunglingly sign his own name. Before he was grown, he passed one year as a hired hand with his uncle Isaac on Wataga, a branch of the Holsteen River. Getting back into Kentucky, and having reached his 28th. year, he married Nancy Hanks—mother of the present subject—in the year 1806. She also was born in Virginia; and relatives of hers of the name of Hanks, and of other names, now reside in Coles, in Macon, and in Adams counties, Illinois, and also in Iowa. The present subject has no brother or sister of the whole or half blood. He had a sister, older than himself, who was grown and married, but died many years ago, leaving no child. Also a brother, younger than himself, who died in infancy. Before leaving Kentucky he and his sister were sent for short periods, to A.B.C. schools, the first kept by Zachariah Riney, and the second by Caleb Hazel.

At this time his father resided on Knob-creek, on the road from Bardstown Ky. to Nashville Tenn. at a point three, or three and a half miles South or South-West of Atherton's ferry on the Rolling Fork. From this place he removed to what is now Spencer county Indiana, in the autumn of 1816, A. then being in his eigth year. This removal was partly on account of slavery; but chiefly on account of the difficulty in land titles in Ky. He settled in an unbroken forest; and the clearing away of surplus wood was the great task a head. A. though very young, was large of his age, and had an axe put into his hands at once; and from that till within his twentythird year, he was almost constantly handling that most useful instrument—less, of course, in plowing and harvesting seasons. At this place A. took an early start as a hunter, which was never much improved afterwards. (A few days before the completion of his eighth year, in the absence of his father, a flock of wild turkeys approached the new log-cabin, and A. with a rifle-gun, standing inside, shot through a crack, and killed one of them. He has never since pulled a trigger on any larger game.) In the autumn of 1818 his mother died; and a year afterwards his father married Mrs. Sally Johnston, at Elizabeth-Town, Ky—a widow, with three children of her first marriage. She proved a good and kind mother to A. and is still living in Coles Co. Illinois. There were no children of this second marriage. His father's residence continued at the same place in Indiana, till 1830. While here A. went to A.B.C. schools by littles, kept successively by Andrew Crawford, —— Sweeney, and Azel W. Dorsey. He does not remember any other. The family of Mr. Dorsey now reside in Schuyler Co. Illinois. A. now thinks that the aggregate of all his schooling did not amount to one year. He was never in a college or Academy as a student; and never inside of a college or academy building till since he had a law-license. What he has in the way of education, he has picked up. After he was twentythree, and had separated from his father, he studied English grammar, imperfectly of course, but so as to speak and write as well as he now does. He studied and nearly mastered the Six-books of Euclid, since he was a member of Congress. He regrets his want of education, and does what he can to supply the want. In his tenth year he was kicked by a horse, and apparently killed for a time. When he was nineteen, still residing in Indiana, he made his first trip upon a flat-boat to New-Orleans. He was a hired hand merely; and he and a son of the owner, without other assistance, made the trip. The nature of part of the cargo-load, as it was called—made it necessary for them to linger and trade along the Sugar coast—and one night they were attacked by seven negroes with intent to kill and rob them. They were hurt some in the melee, but succeeded in driving the negroes from the boat, and then "cut cable" "weighed anchor" and left.

March 1st. 1830—A. having just completed his 21st. year, his father and family, with the families of the two daughters and sons-in-law, of his step-mother, left the old homestead in Indiana, and came to Illinois. Their mode of conveyance was waggons drawn by ox-teams, or A. drove one of the teams. They reached the county of Macon, and stopped there some time within the same month of March. His father and family settled a new place on the North side of the Sangamon river, at the junction of the timber-land and prairie, about ten miles Westerly from Decatur. Here they built a log-cabin, into which they removed, and made sufficient of rails to fence ten acres of ground, fenced and broke the ground, and raised a crop of sown corn upon it the same year. These are, or are supposed to be, the rails about which so much is being said just now, though these are far from being the first or only rails ever made by A.

The sons-in-law, were temporarily settled at other places in the county. In the autumn all hands were greatly afflicted with ague and fever, to which they had not been used, and by which they were greatly discouraged—so much so that they determined on leaving the county. They remained however, through the succeeding winter, which was the winter of the very celebrated "deep snow" of Illinois. During that winter, A. together with his step-mother's son, John D. Johnston, and John Hanks, yet residing in Macon county, hired themselves to Denton Offutt, to take a flatboat from Beardstown Illinois to New-Orleans; and for that purpose were to join him—Offut—at Springfield, Ills., so soon as the snow should go off. When it did go off which was about the 1st. of March 1831—the county was so flooded, as to make traveling by land impracticable; to obviate which difficulty they purchased a large canoe and came down the Sangamon river in it. This is the time and the manner of A's first entrance into Sangamon County. They found Offutt at Springfield, but learned from him that he had failed in getting a boat at Beardstown. This led to their hiring themselves to him at $12 per month each; and getting the timber out of the trees and build-ing a boat at old Sangamon Town on the Sangamon river, seven miles N.W. of Springfield, which boat they took to New-Orleans, substantially upon the old contract. It was in connection with this boat that occurred the ludicrous incident of sewing up the hogs eyes. Offutt brought thirty odd large fat live hogs, but found difficulty in driving them from where he purchased them to the boat, and thereupon conceived the whim that he could sew up their eyes and drive them where he pleased. No sooner thought of than decided, he put his hands, including A. at the job, which they completed—all but the driving. In their blind condition they could not be driven out of the lot or field they were in. This expedient failing, they were tied and hauled on carts to the boat. It was near the Sangamon River, within what is now Menard county.

During this boat enterprize acquaintance with Offutt, who was previously an entire stranger, he conceived a liking for A. and believing he could turn him to account, he contracted with him to act as clerk for him, on his return from New-Orleans, in charge of a store and Mill at New-Salem, then in Sangamon, now in Menard county. Hanks had not gone to New-Orleans, but having a family, and being likely to be detained from home longer than at first expected, had turned back from St. Louis. He is the same John Hanks who now engineers the "rail enterprize" at Decatur; and is a first cousin to A's mother. A's father, with his own family & others mentioned, had, in pursuance of their intention, removed from Macon to Coles county. John D. Johnston, the step-mother's son, went to them; and A. stopped indefinitely, and, for the first time, as it were, by himself at New-Salem, before mentioned. This was in July 1831. Here he rapidly made acquaintances and friends. In less than a year Offutt's business was failing—had almost failed,—when the Black-Hawk war of 1832—broke out. A joined a volunteer company, and to his own surprise, was elected captain of it. He says he has not since had any success in life which gave him so much satisfaction. He went the campaign, served near three months, met the ordinary hardships of such an expedition, but was in no battle. He now owns in Iowa, the land upon which his own warrants for the service, were located. Returning from the campaign, and encouraged by his great popularity among his immediate neighbors, he, the same year, ran for the Legislature, and was beaten—his own precinct, however, casting it's votes 277 for and 7, against him. And this too while he was an avowed Clay man, and the precinct the autumn afterwards, giving a majority of 115 to Genl. Jackson over Mr. Clay. This was the only time A was ever beaten on a direct vote of the people. He was now without means and out of business, but was anxious to remain with his friends who had treated him with so much generosity, especially as he had nothing elsewhere to go to. He studied what he should do—thought of learning the black-smith trade—thought of trying to study law—rather thought he could not succeed at that without a better education. Before long, strangely enough, a man offered to sell and did sell, to A. and another as poor as himself, an old stock of goods, upon credit. They opened as merchants; and he says that was *the* store. Of course they did nothing but get deeper and deeper in debt. He was appointed Postmaster at New-Salem—the office being too insignificant, to make his politics an objection. The store winked out. The Surveyor of Sangamon, offered to depute to A that portion of his work which was within his part of the county. He accepted, procured a compass and chain, studied Flint, and Gibson a little, and went at it. This procured bread, and kept soul and body together. The election of 1834 came, and he was then elected to the Legislature by the highest vote cast for any candidate. Major John T. Stuart, then in full practice of the law, was also elected. During the canvass, in a private conversation he encouraged A. to study law. After the election he borrowed books of Stuart, took them home with him, and went at it in good earnest. He studied with nobody. He still mixed in the surveying to pay board and clothing bills. When the Legislature met, the law books were dropped, but were taken up again at the end of the session. He was re-elected in 1836, 1838, and 1840. In the autumn of 1836 he obtained a law licence, and on April 15, 1837 removed to Springfield, and commenced the practice, his old friend, Stuart taking him into partnership. March 3rd. 1837, by a protest entered upon the Ills. House Journal of that date, at pages 817, 818, A. with Dan Stone, another representative of Sangamon, briefly defined his position on the slavery question; and so far as it goes, it was then the same that it is now. The protest is as follows—(Here insert it) In 1838, & 1840 Mr. L's party in the Legislature voted for him as Speaker; but being in the minority, he was not elected. After 1840 he declined a re-election to the Legislature. He was on the Harrison electoral ticket in 1840, and on that of Clay in 1844, and spent much time and labor in both those canvasses. In Nov. 1842 he was married to Mary, daughter of Robert S. Todd, of Lexington, Kentucky. They have three living children, all sons—one born in 1843, one in 1850, and one in 1853. They lost one, who was born in 1846. In 1846, he was elected to the lower House of Congress, and served one term only, commencing in Dec. 1847 and ending with the inauguration of Gen. Taylor, in March 1849. All the battles of the Mexican war had been fought before Mr. L. took his seat in congress, but the American army was still in Mexico, and the treaty of peace was not fully and formally ratified till the June afterwards. Much has been said of his course in Congress in regard to this war. A careful examination of the Journals and Congressional Globe shows, that he voted for all the supply measures which came up, and for all the measures in any way favorable to the officers, soldiers, and their families, who conducted the war through; with this exception that some of these measures passed without yeas and nays, leaving no record as to how particular men voted. The Journals and Globe also show him voting that the war was unnecessarily and unconstitutionally begun by the President of the United States. This is the language of Mr. Ashmun's amendment, for which Mr. L. and nearly or quite all, other whigs of the H.R. voted.

Mr. L's reasons for the opinion expressed by this vote were briefly that the President had sent Genl. Taylor into an inhabited part of the country belonging to Mexico, and not to the U.S. and thereby had provoked the first act of hostility—in fact the commencement of the war; that the place, being the country bordering on the East bank of the Rio Grande, was inhabited by native Mexicans, born there under the Mexican government; and had never submitted to, nor been conquered by Texas, or the U.S. nor transferred to either by treaty—that although Texas claimed the Rio Grande as her boundary, Mexico had never recognized it, and neither Texas nor the U.S. had ever enforced it—that there was a broad desert between that, and the country over which Texas had actual control—that the country where hostilities commenced, having once belonged to Mexico, must remain so, until it was somehow legally transferred, which had never been done.

Mr. L. thought the act of sending an armed force among the Mexicans, was *unnecessary*, inasmuch as Mexico was in no way molesting, or menacing the U.S. or the people thereof; and that it was *unconstitutional*, because the power of levying war is vested in Congress, and not in the President. He thought the principal motive for the act, was to divert public attention from the surrender of "Fifty-four, forty, or fight" to Great Brittain, on the Oregon boundary question.

Mr. L. was not a candidate for re-election. This was determined upon, and declared before he went to Washington, in accordance with an understanding among whig friends, by which Col. Hardin, and Col. Baker had each previously served a single term in the same District.

In 1848, during his term in congress, he advocated Gen. Taylor's nomination for the Presidency, in opposition to all others, and also took an active part for his election after his nomination—speaking a few times in Maryland, near Washington, several times in Massachusetts, and canvassing quite fully his own district in Illinois, which was followed by a majority in the district of over 1500 for Gen. Taylor.

Upon his return from Congress he went to the practice of the law with greater earnestness than ever before. In 1852 he was upon the Scott electoral ticket, and did something in the way of canvassing, but owing to the hopelessness of the cause in Illinois, he did less than in previous presidential canvasses.

In 1854, his profession had almost superseded the thought of politics in his mind, when the repeal of the Missouri compromise aroused him as he had never been before.

In the autumn of that year he took the stump with no broader practical aim or object than to secure, if possible, the re-election of Hon Richard Yates to congress. His speeches at once attracted a more marked attention than they had ever before done. As the canvass proceeded, he was drawn to different parts of the state, outside of Mr. Yates' district. He did not abandon the law, but gave his attention, by turns, to that and politics. The State agricultural fair was at Springfield that year, and Douglas was announced to speak there.

In the canvass of 1856, Mr. L. made over fifty speeches, no one of which, so far as he remembers, was put in print. One of them was made at Galena, but Mr. L. has no recollection of any part of it being printed; nor does he remember whether in that speech he said anything about a Supreme court decision. He may have spoken upon that subject; and some of the newspapers may have reported him as saying what is now ascribed to him; but he thinks he could not have expressed himself as represented.

*c. June 1860*

# EARLY ADDRESSES, SPEECHES, *and* WRITINGS

# Address Before the Young Men's Lyceum
## of Springfield, Illinois

As a subject for the remarks of the evening, *the perpetuation of our political institutions,* is selected.

In the great journal of things happening under the sun, we, the American People, find our account running, under date of the nineteenth century of the Christian era. We find ourselves in the peaceful possession, of the fairest portion of the earth, as regards extent of territory, fertility of soil, and salubrity of climate. We find ourselves under the government of a system of political institutions, conducing more essentially to the ends of civil and religious liberty, than any of which the history of former times tells us. We, when mounting the stage of existence, found ourselves the legal inheritors of these fundamental blessings. We toiled not in the acquirement or establishment of them—they are a legacy bequeathed us, by a *once* hardy, brave, and patriotic, but *now* lamented and departed race of ancestors. Their's was the task (and nobly they performed it) to possess themselves, and through themselves, us, of this goodly land; and to uprear upon its hills and its valleys, a political edifice of liberty and equal rights; 'tis ours only, to transmit these, the former, unprofaned by the foot of an invader; the latter, undecayed by the lapse of time, and untorn by usurpation—to the latest generation that fate shall permit the world to know. This task of gratitude to our fathers, justice to ourselves, duty to posterity, and love for our species in general, all imperatively require us faithfully to perform.

How, then, shall we perform it? At what point shall we expect the approach of danger? By what means shall we fortify against it? Shall we expect some transatlantic military giant, to step the Ocean, and crush us at a blow? Never! All the armies of Europe, Asia and Africa combined, with all the treasure of the earth (our own excepted) in their military chest; with a Buonaparte for a commander, could not by force, take a drink from the Ohio, or make a track on the Blue Ridge, in a trial of a thousand years.

At what point then is the approach of danger to be expected? I answer, if it ever reach us, it must spring up amongst us. It cannot come from abroad. If destruction be our lot, we must ourselves be its author and finisher. As a nation of freemen, we must live through all time, or die by suicide.

I hope I am over wary; but if I am not, there is, even now, something of ill-omen amongst us. I mean the increasing disregard for law which pervades the country; the growing disposition to substitute the wild and furious passions, in lieu of the sober judgment of Courts; and the worse than savage mobs, for the executive ministers of justice. This disposition is awfully fearful in any community; and that it now exists in ours, though grating to our feelings to admit, it would be a violation of truth and an insult to our intelligence, to deny. Accounts of outrages committed by mobs, form the every-day news of the times. They have pervaded the country, from New England to Louisiana;—they are neither peculiar to the eternal snows of the former, nor the burning suns of the latter;—they are not the creature of climate—neither are they confined to the slaveholding, or the non-slaveholding States. Alike they spring up among the pleasure-hunting masters of Southern slaves, and the order loving citizens of the land of steady habits. Whatever, then, their cause may be, it is common to the whole country.

It would be tedious, as well as useless, to recount the horrors of all of them. Those happening in the State of Mississippi, and at St. Louis, are, perhaps, the most dangerous in example, and revolting to humanity. In the Mississippi case, they first commenced by hanging the regular gamblers: a set of men, certainly not following for a livelihood, a very useful, or very honest occupation; but one which, so far from being forbidden by the laws, was actually licensed by an act of the Legislature, passed but a single year before. Next, negroes, suspected of conspiring to raise an insurrection, were caught up and hanged in all parts of the State: then, white men, supposed to be leagued with the negroes; and finally, strangers, from neighboring States, going thither on business, were, in many instances, subjected to the same fate. Thus went on this process of hanging, from gamblers to negroes, from negroes to white citizens, and from these to strangers; till, dead men were seen literally dangling from the boughs of trees upon every road side; and in numbers almost sufficient, to rival the native Spanish moss of the country, as a drapery of the forest.

Turn, then, to that horror-striking scene at St. Louis. A single victim was only sacrificed there. His story is very short; and is, perhaps, the most highly tragic, of any thing of its length, that has ever been witnessed in real life. A mulatto man, by the name of McIntosh, was seized in the street, dragged to the suburbs of the city, chained to a tree, and actually burned to death; and all within a single hour from the time he had been a freeman, attending to his own business, and at peace with the world.

Such are the effects of mob law; and such are the scenes, becoming more and more frequent in this land so lately famed for love of law and order; and the stories of which, have even now grown too familiar, to attract any thing more, than an idle remark.

But you are, perhaps, ready to ask, "What has this to do with the perpetuation of our political institutions?" I answer, it has much to do with it. Its direct consequences are, comparatively speaking, but a small evil; and much of its danger consists in the proneness of our minds, to regard its direct, as its only consequences. Abstractly considered, the hanging of the gamblers at Vicksburg, was of but little consequence. They constitute a portion of population, that is worse than useless in any community; and their death, if no pernicious example be set by it, is never matter of reasonable regret with any one. If they were annually swept, from the stage of existence, by the plague or small pox, honest men would, perhaps, be much profited by the operation. Similar too, is the correct reasoning, in regard to the burning of the negro at St. Louis. He had forfeited his life, by the perpetration of an outrageous murder, upon one of the most worthy and respectable citizens of the city; and had he not died as he did, he must have died by the sentence of the law, in a very short time afterwards. As to him alone, it was as well the way it was, as it could otherwise have been. But the example in either case, was fearful. When men take it in their heads to day, to hang gamblers, or burn murderers, they should recollect, that, in the confusion usually attending such transactions, they will be as likely to hang or burn some one, who is neither a gambler nor a murderer as one who is; and that, acting upon the example they set, the mob of to-morrow, may, and probably will, hang or burn some of them, by the very same mistake. And not only so; the innocent, those who have ever set their faces against violations of law in every shape, alike with the guilty, fall victims to the ravages of mob law; and thus it goes up, step by step, till all the walls erected for the defence of the persons and property of individuals, are trodden down, and disregarded. But all this even, is not the full extent of the evil. By such examples, by instances of the perpetrators of such acts going unpunished, the lawless in spirit, are encouraged to become lawless in practice; and having been used to no restraint, but dread of punishment, they thus become, absolutely unrestrained. Having ever regarded Government as their deadliest bane, they make a jubilee of the suspension of its operations; and pray for nothing so much, as its total annihilation. While, on the other hand, good men, men who love tranquility, who desire to abide by the laws, and enjoy their benefits, who would gladly spill their blood in the defence of their country; seeing their property destroyed; their families insulted, and their lives endangered; their persons injured; and seeing nothing in prospect that forebodes a change for the better; become tired of, and disgusted with, a Government that offers them no protection; and are not much averse to a change in which they imagine they have nothing to lose. Thus, then, by the operation of this mobocratic spirit, which all must admit, is now abroad in the land, the strongest bulwark of any Government, and particularly of those constituted like ours, may effectually be broken down and destroyed—I mean the *attachment* of the People. Whenever this effect shall be produced among us; whenever the vicious portion of population shall be permitted to gather in bands of hundreds and thousands, and burn churches, ravage and rob provision stores, throw printing presses into rivers, shoot editors, and hang and burn obnoxious persons at pleasure, and with impunity, depend on it, this Government cannot last. By such things, the feelings of the best citizens will become more or less alienated from it; and thus it will be left without friends, or with too few, and those few too weak, to make their friendship effectual. At such a time and under such circumstances, men of sufficient talent and ambition will not be wanting to seize the opportunity, strike the blow, and overturn that fair fabric, which for the last half century, has been the fondest hope, of the lovers of freedom, throughout the world.

I know the American People are *much* attached to their Government;—I know they would suffer *much* for its sake;—I know they would endure evils long and patiently, before they would ever think of exchanging it for another. Yet, notwithstanding all this, if the laws be continually despised and disregarded, if their rights to be secure in their persons and property, are held by no better tenure than the caprice of a mob, the alienation of their affections from the Government is the natural consequence; and to that, sooner or later, it must come.

Here, then, is one point at which danger may be expected.

The question recurs "how shall we fortify against it?" The answer is simple. Let every American, every lover of liberty, every well wisher to his posterity, swear by the blood of the Revolution, never to violate in the least particular, the laws of the country; and never to tolerate their violation by others. As the patriots of seventy-six did to the support of the Declaration of Independence, so to the support of the Constitution and Laws, let every American pledge his life, his property, and his sacred honor;—let every man remember that to violate the law, is to trample on the blood of his father, and to tear the character of his own, and his children's liberty. Let reverence for the laws, be breathed by every American mother, to the lisping babe, that prattles on her lap—let it be taught in schools, in seminaries, and in colleges;—let it be written in Primmers, spelling books, and in Almanacs; let it be preached from the pulpit, proclaimed in legislative halls, and enforced in courts of justice. And, in short, let it become the *political religion* of the nation; and let the old and the young, the rich and the poor, the grave and the gay, of all sexes and tongues, and colors and conditions, sacrifice unceasingly upon its altars.

While ever a state of feeling, such as this, shall universally, or even, very generally prevail throughout the nation, vain will be every effort, and fruitless every attempt, to subvert our national freedom.

When I so pressingly urge a strict observance of all the laws, let me not be understood as saying there are no bad laws, or that grievances may not arise, for the redress of which, no legal provisions have been made. I mean to say no such thing. But I do mean to say, that, although bad laws, if they exist, should be repealed as soon as possible, still while they continue in force, for the sake of example, they should be religiously observed. So also in unprovided cases. If such arise, let proper legal provisions be made for them with the least possible delay; but, till then, let them if not too intolerable, be borne with.

There is no grievance that is a fit object of redress by mob law. In any case that arises, as for instance, the promulgation of abolitionism, one of two positions is necessarily true; that is, the thing is right within itself, and therefore deserves the protection of all law and all good citizens; or, it is wrong, and therefore proper to be prohibited by legal enactments; and in neither case, is the interposition of mob law, either necessary, justifiable, or excusable.

But, it may be asked, why suppose danger to our political institutions? Have we not preserved them for more than fifty years? And why may we not for fifty times as long?

We hope there is no *sufficient* reason. We hope all dangers may be overcome; but to conclude that no danger may ever arise, would itself be extremely dangerous. There are now, and will hereafter be, many causes, dangerous in their tendency, which have not existed heretofore; and which are not too insignificant to merit attention. That our government should have been maintained in its original form from its establishment until now, is not much to be wondered at. It had many props to support it through that period, which now are decayed, and crumbled away. Through that period, it was felt by all, to be an undecided experiment; now, it is understood to be a successful one. Then, all that sought celebrity and fame, and distinction, expected to find them in the success of that experiment. Their *all* was staked upon it:—their destiny was *inseparably* linked with it. Their ambition aspired to display before an admiring world, a practical demonstration of the truth of a proposition, which had hitherto been considered, at best no better, than problematical; namely, *the capability of a people to govern themselves.* If they succeeded, they were to be immortalized; their names were to be transferred to counties and cities, and rivers and mountains; and to be revered and sung, and toasted through all time. If they failed, they were to be called knaves and fools, and fanatics for a fleeting hour; then to sink and be forgotten. They succeeded. The experiment is successful; and thousands have won their deathless names in making it so. But the game is caught; and I believe it is true, that with the catching, end the pleasures of the chase. This field of glory is harvested, and the crop is already appropriated. But new reapers will arise, and *they*, too, will seek a field. It is to deny, what the history of the world tells us is true, to suppose that men of ambition and talents will not continue to spring up amongst us. And, when they do, they will as naturally seek the gratification of their ruling passion, as others have *so* done before them. The question then, is, can that gratification be found in supporting and maintaining an edifice that has been erected by others? Most certainly it cannot. Many great and good men sufficiently qualified for any task they should undertake, may ever be found, whose ambition would aspire to nothing beyond a seat in Congress, a gubernatorial or a presidential chair; *but such belong not to the family of the lion, or the tribe of the eagle.* What! think you these places would satisfy an Alexander, a Caesar, or a Napoleon? Never! Towering genius disdains a beaten path. It seeks regions hitherto unexplored. It sees *no distinction* in adding story to story, upon the monuments of fame, erected to the memory of others. It *denies* that it is glory enough to serve under any chief. It *scorns* to tread in the footsteps of *any* predecessor, however illustrious. It thirsts and burns for distinction; and, if possible, it will have it, whether at the expense of emancipating slaves, or enslaving freemen. Is it unreasonable then to expect, that some man possessed of the loftiest genius, coupled with ambition sufficient to push it to its utmost stretch, will at some time, spring up among us? And when such a one does, it will require the people to be united with each other, attached to the government and laws, and generally intelligent, to successfully frustrate his designs.

Distinction will be his paramount object; and although he would as willingly, perhaps more so, acquire it by doing good as harm; yet, that opportunity being past, and nothing left to be done in the way of building up, he would set boldly to the task of pulling down.

Here then, is a probable case, highly dangerous, and such a one as could not have well existed heretofore.

Another reason which *once was;* but which, to the same extent, is *now no more*, has done much in maintaining our institutions thus far. I mean the powerful influence which the interesting scenes of the Revolution had upon the *passions* of the people as distinguished from their judgment. By this influence, the jealousy, envy, and avarice incident to our nature, and so common to a state of peace, prosperity, and conscious strength, were, for the time, in a great measure smothered and rendered inactive; while the deep rooted principles of *hate*, and the powerful motive of *revenge*, instead of being turned against each other, were directed exclusively against the British nation. And thus, from the force of circumstances, the basest principles of our nature, were either made to lie dormant, or to become the active agents in the advancement of the noblest of causes—that of establishing and maintaining civil and religious liberty.

But this state of feeling *must fade, is fading, has faded*, with the circumstances that produced it.

I do not mean to say, that the scenes of the revolution *are now* or *ever will be* entirely forgotten; but that, like every thing else, they must fade upon the memory of the world, and grow more and more dim by the lapse of time. In history, we hope, they will be read of, and recounted, so long as the bible shall be read;—but even granting that they will, their influence *cannot be* what it heretofore has been. Even then, they *cannot be* so universally known, nor so vividly felt, as they were by the generation just gone to rest. At the close of that struggle, nearly every adult male had been a participator in some of its scenes. The consequence was, that of those scenes, in the form of a husband, a father, a son, or a brother, *a living history was* to be found in every family—a history bearing the indubitable testimonies of its own authenticity, in the limbs mangled, in the scars of wounds received, in the midst of the very scenes related—a history, too, that could be read and understood alike by all, the wise and the ignorant, the learned and the unlearned. But *those* histories are gone. They *can* be read no more forever. They *were* a fortress of strength; but, what invading foeman could *never do*, the silent artillery of time *has done*; the levelling of its walls. They are gone. They *were* a forest of giant oaks; but the all resistless hurricane has swept over them, and left only, here and there, a lonely trunk, despoiled of its verdure, shorn of its foliage; unshading and unshaded, to murmur in a few more gentle breezes, and to combat with its mutilated limbs, a few more ruder storms, then to sink, and be no more.

They *were* the pillars of the temple of liberty; and now, that they have crumbled away, that temple must fall, unless we, their descendants, supply their places with other pillars, hewn from the solid quarry of sober reason. Passion has helped us; but can do so no more. It will in future be our enemy. Reason, cold, calculating, unimpassioned reason, must furnish all the materials for our future support and defence. Let those materials be moulded into *general intelligence, sound morality* and, in particular, *a reverence for the constitution and laws*; and, that we improved to the last; that we remained free to the last; that we revered his name to the last; that, during his long sleep, we permitted no hostile foot to pass over or desecrate his resting place; shall be that which to learn the last trump shall awaken our WASHINGTON.

Upon these let the proud fabric of freedom rest, as the rock of its basis; and as truly as has been said of the only greater institution, *"the gates of hell shall not prevail against it."*

*January 27, 1838*

# Address Before the Springfield Washingtonian Temperance Society

Although the Temperance cause has been in progress for near twenty years, it is apparent to all, that it is, *just now,* being crowned with a degree of success, hitherto unparalleled.

The list of its friends is daily swelled by the additions of fifties, of hundreds, and of thousands. The cause itself seems suddenly transformed from a cold abstract theory, to a living, breathing, active, and powerful chieftain, going forth "conquering and to conquer." The citadels of his great adversary are daily being stormed and dismantled; his temples and his altars, where the rites of his idolatrous worship have long been performed, and where human sacrifices have long been wont to be made, are daily desecrated and deserted. The trump of the conqueror's fame is sounding from hill to hill, from sea to sea, and from land to land, and calling millions to his standard at a blast.

For this new and splendid success, we heartily rejoice. That that success is so much greater *now* than *heretofore,* is doubtless owing to rational causes; and if we would have it to continue, we shall do well to enquire what those causes are. The warfare heretofore waged against the demon of Intemperance, has, some how or other, been erroneous. Either the champions engaged, or the tactics they adopted, have not been the most proper. These champions for the most part, have been Preachers, Lawyers, and hired agents. Between these and the mass of mankind, there is a want of *approachability,* if the term be admissible, partially at least, fatal to their success. They are supposed to have no sympathy of feeling or interest, with those very persons whom it is their object to convince and persuade.

And again, it is so easy and so common to ascribe motives to men of these classes, other than those they profess to act upon. The *preacher,* it is said, advocates temperance because he is a fanatic, and desires a union of Church and State; the *lawyer,* from his pride and vanity of hearing himself speak; and the *hired agent,* for his salary. But when one, who has long been known as a victim of intemperance, bursts the fetters that have bound him, and appears before his neighbors "clothed, and in his right mind," a redeemed specimen of long lost humanity, and stands up with tears of joy trembling in eyes, to tell of the miseries *once* endured, *now* to be endured no more forever; of his once naked and starving children, now clad and fed comfortably; of a wife long weighed down with woe, weeping, and a broken heart, now restored to health, happiness, and renewed affection; and how easily it all is done, once it is resolved to be done; however simple his language, there is a logic, and an eloquence in it, that few, with human feelings, can resist. They cannot say that *he* desires a union of church and state, for he is not a church member; they can not say *he* is vain of hearing himself speak, for his whole demeanor shows, he would gladly avoid speaking at all; they cannot say *he* speaks for pay for he receives none, and asks for none. Nor can his sincerity in any way be doubted; or his sympathy for those he would persuade to imitate his example, be denied.

In my judgment, it is to the battles of this new class of champions that our late success is greatly, perhaps chiefly, owing. But, had the old school champions themselves, been of the most wise selecting, was their *system* of tactics, the most judicious? It seems to me, it was not. Too much denunciation against dram sellers and dram-drinkers was indulged in. This, I think, was both impolitic and unjust. It was *impolitic*, because, it is not much in the nature of man to be driven to any thing; still less to be driven about that which is exclusively his own business; and least of all, where such driving is to be submitted to, at the expense of pecuniary interest, or burning appetite. When the dram-seller and drinker, were incessantly told, not in the accents of entreaty and persuasion, diffidently addressed by erring man to an erring brother; but in the thundering tones of anathema and denunciation, with which the lordly Judge often groups together all the crimes of the felon's life, and thrusts them in his face just ere he passes sentence of death upon him, that *they* were the authors of all the vice and misery and crime in the land; that *they* were the manufacturers and material of all the thieves and robbers and murderers that infested the earth; that *their* houses were the workshops of the devil; and that *their persons* should be shunned by all the good and virtuous, as moral pestilences—I say, when they were told all this, and in this way, it is not wonderful that they were slow, *very slow,* to acknowledge the truth of such denunciations, and to join the ranks of their denouncers, in a hue and cry against themselves.

To have expected them to do otherwise than as they did—to have expected them not to meet denunciation with denunciation, crimination with crimination, and anathema with anathema, was to expect a reversal of human nature, which is God's decree, and never can be reversed. When the conduct of men is designed to be influenced, *persuasion*, kind, unassuming persuasion, should ever be adopted. It is an old and a true maxim, that a "drop of honey catches more flies than a gallon of gall." So with men. If you would win a man to your cause, *first* convince him that you are his sincere friend. Therein is a drop of honey that catches his heart, which, say what he will, is the great high road to his reason, and which, when once gained, you will find but little trouble in convincing his judgment of the justice of your cause, if indeed that cause really be a just one. On the contrary, assume to dictate to his judgment, or to command his action, or to mark him as one to be shunned and despised, and he will retreat within himself, close all the avenues to his head and his heart; and tho' your cause be naked truth itself, transformed to the heaviest lance, harder than steel, and sharper than steel can be made, and tho' you throw it with more than Herculean force and precision, you shall no more be able to pierce him, than to penetrate the hard shell of a tortoise with a rye straw.

Such is man, and so *must* he be understood by those who would lead him, even to his own best interest.

On this point, the Washingtonians greatly excel the temperance advocates of former times. Those whom *they* desire to convince and persuade, are their old friends and companions. They know they are not demons, nor even the worst of men. *They* know that generally, they are kind, generous and charitable, even beyond the example of their more staid and sober neighbors. *They* are practical philanthropists; and *they* glow with a generous and brotherly zeal, that mere theorizers are incapable of feeling. Benevolence and charity possess *their* hearts entirely; and out of the abundance of their hearts, their tongues give utterance. "Love through all their actions runs, and all their words are mild." In this spirit they speak and act, and in the same, they are heard and regarded. And when such is the temper of the advocate, and such of the audience, no good cause can be unsuccessful.

But I have said that denunciations against dram-sellers and dram-drinkers, are *unjust* as well as impolitic. Let us see. ·

I have not enquired at what period of time the use of intoxicating drinks commenced; nor is it important to know. It is sufficient that to all of us who now inhabit the world, the practice of drinking them, is just as old as the world itself,—that is, we have seen the one, just as long as we have seen the other. When all such of us, as have now reached the years of maturity, first opened our eyes upon the stage of existence, we found intoxicating liquor, recognized by every body, used by every body, and repudiated by nobody. It commonly entered into the first draught of the infant, and the last draught of the dying man. From the sideboard of the parson, down to the ragged pocket of the houseless loafer, it was constantly found. Physicians prescribed it in this, that, and the other disease. Government provided it for its soldiers and sailors; and to have a rolling or rais-ing, a husking or hoe-down, any where without it, was *positively insufferable.*

So too, it was every where a respectable article of manufacture and of mer-chandize. The making of it was regarded as an honorable livelihood; and he who could make most, was the most enterprising and respectable. Large and small manufactories of it were every where erected, in which all the earthly goods of their owners were invested. Wagons drew it from town to town—boats bore it from clime to clime, and the winds wafted it from nation to nation; and merchants bought and sold it, by wholesale and by retail, with precisely the same feelings, on the part of seller, buyer, and bystander, as are felt at the selling and buying of flour, beef, bacon, or any other of the real necessaries of life. Universal public opinion not only tolerated, but recognized and adopted its use.

It is true, that even *then,* it was known and acknowledged, that many were greatly injured by it; but none seemed to think the injury arose from the *use* of a *bad thing,* but from the *abuse* of a *very good thing.* The victims to it were pitied, and compassionated, just as now are, the heirs of consumptions, and other hereditary diseases. Their failing was treated as a *misfortune,* and not as a *crime,* or even as a *disgrace.*

If, then, what I have been saying be true, is it wonderful, that *some* should think and act *now,* as *all* thought and acted *twenty years ago?* And is it *just* to assail, *contemn,* or despise them, for doing so? The universal *sense* of mankind, on any subject, is an argument, or at least an *influence* not easily overcome. The success of the argument in favor of the existence of an over-ruling Providence, mainly depends upon that sense; and men ought not, in justice, to be denounced for yielding to it, in any case, or for giving it up slowly, *especially*, where they are backed by interest, fixed habits, or burning appetites.

Another error, as it seems to me, into which the old reformers fell, was, the position that all habitual drunkards were utterly incorrigible, and therefore, must be turned adrift, and damned without remedy, in order that the grace of temperance might abound to the temperate *then,* and to all mankind some hundred years *thereafter.* There is in this something so repugnant to humanity, so uncharitable, so cold-blooded and feelingless, that it never did, nor ever can enlist the enthusiasm of a popular cause. We could not love the man who taught it—we could not hear him with patience. The heart could not throw open its portals to it. The generous man could not adopt it. It could not mix with his blood. It looked so fiendishly selfish, so like throwing fathers and brothers overboard, to lighten the boat for our security—that the noble minded shrank from the manifest meanness of the thing.

And besides this, the benefits of a reformation to be effected by such a system, were too remote in point of time, to warmly engage many in its behalf. Few can be induced to labor exclusively for posterity; and none will do it enthusiastically. Posterity has done nothing for us; and theorise on it as we may, practically we shall do very little for it, unless we are made to think, we are, at the same time, doing something for ourselves. What an ignorance of human nature does it exhibit, to ask or expect a whole community to rise up and labor for the *temporal* happiness of *others* after *themselves* shall be consigned to the dust, a majority of which community take no pains whatever to secure their own eternal welfare, at a no greater distant day? Great distance, in either time or space, has wonderful power to lull and render quiescent the human mind. Pleasures to be enjoyed, or pains to be endured, *after* we shall be dead and gone, are but little regarded, even in our *own* cases, and much less in the cases of others.

Still, in addition to this, there is something so ludicrous in *promises* of good, or *threats* of evil, a great way off, as to render the whole subject with which they are connected, easily turned into ridicule. "Better lay down that spade you're stealing, Paddy,—if you don't you'll pay for it at the day of judgment." "By the powers, if ye'll credit me so long, I'll take another, jist."

By the Washingtonians, this system of consigning the habitual drunkard to hopeless ruin, is repudiated. *They* adopt a more enlarged philanthropy. *They* go for present as well as future good. *They* labor for all *now* living, as well as all *hereafter* to live. *They* teach *hope* to all—*despair* to none. As applying to *their* cause, *they* deny the doctrine of unpardonable sin. As in Christianity it is taught, so in this *they* teach, that

> While the lamp holds out to burn,
> The vilest sinner may return.

And, what is matter of the most profound gratulation, they, by experiment upon experiment, and example upon example, prove the maxim to be no less true in the one case than in the other. On every hand we behold those, who but yesterday, were the chief of sinners, now the chief apostles of the cause. Drunken devils are cast out by ones, by sevens, and by legions; and their unfortunate victims, like the poor possessed, who was redeemed from his long and lonely wanderings in the tombs, are publishing to the ends of the earth, how great things have been done for them.

To these *new champions,* and this new system of tactics, our late success is mainly owing; and to *them* we must chiefly look for the final consummation. The ball is now rolling gloriously on, and none are so able as *they* to increase its speed, and its bulk—to add to its momentum, and its magnitude. Even though unlearned in letters, for this task, none others are so well educated. To fit them for this work, they have been taught in the true school. *They* have been in *that* gulf, from which they would teach others the means of escape. *They* have passed that prison wall, which others have long declared impassable; and who that has not, shall dare to weigh opinions with *them,* as to the mode of passing.

But if it be true, as I have insisted, that those who have suffered by intemperance *personally,* and have reformed, are the most powerful and efficient instruments to push the reformation to ultimate success, it does not follow, that those who have not suffered, have no part left them to perform. Whether or not the world would be vastly benefitted by a total and final banishment from it of all intoxicating drinks, seems to me not *now* to be an open question. Three-fourths of mankind confess the affirmative with their *tongues,* and, I believe, all the rest acknowledge it in their *hearts.*

Ought *any,* then, to refuse their aid in doing what the good of the *whole* demands? Shall he, who cannot do *much,* be, for that reason, excused if he do *nothing?* "But," says one, "what good can I do by signing the pledge? I never drink even without signing." This question has already been asked and answered more than millions of times. Let it be answered once more. For the man to suddenly, or in any other way, to break off from the use of drams, who has indulged in them for a long course of years, and until his appetite for them has become ten or a hundred fold stronger, and more craving, than any natural appetite can be, requires a most powerful moral effort. In such an undertaking, he needs every moral support and influence, that can possibly be brought to his aid, and thrown around him. And not only so; but every moral prop, should be taken *from* whatever argument might rise in his mind to lure him to his backsliding. When he casts his eyes around him, he should be able to see, all that he respects, all that he admires, and all that he loves, kindly and anxiously pointing him onward; and none beckoning him back, to his former miserable "wallowing in the mire."

But it is said by some, that men will *think* and *act* for themselves; that none will disuse spirits or any thing else, merely because his neighbors do; and that *moral influence* is not that powerful engine contended for. Let us examine this. Let me ask the man who would maintain this position most stiffly, what compensation he will accept to go to church some Sunday and sit during the sermon with his wife's bonnet upon his head? Not a trifle, I'll venture. And why not? There would be nothing irreligious in it: nothing immoral, nothing uncomfortable. Then why not? Is it not because there would be something egregiously unfashionable in it? Then it is the influence of *fashion*; and what is the influence of fashion, but the influence that *other* people's actions have on our own actions, the strong inclination each of us feels to do as we see all our neighbors do? Nor is the influence of fashion confined to any particular thing or class of things. It is just as strong on one subject as another. Let us make it as unfashionable to with-hold our names from the temperance pledge as for husbands to wear their wives bonnets to church, and instances will be just as rare in the one case as the other.

"But," say some, "we are no drunkards; and we shall not acknowledge ourselves such by joining a reformed drunkard's society, whatever our influence might be." Surely no Christian will adhere to this objection. If they believe, as they profess, that Omnipotence condescended to take on himself the form of sinful man, and, as such, to die an ignominious death for their sakes, surely they will not refuse sub-mission to the infinitely lesser condescension, for the temporal, and perhaps eternal salvation, of a large, erring, and unfortunate class of their own fellow creatures. Nor is the condescension very great.

In my judgment, such of us as have never fallen victims, have been spared more from the absence of appetite, than from any mental or moral superiority over those who have. Indeed, I believe, if we take habitual drunkards as a class, their heads and their hearts will bear an advantageous comparison with those of any other class. There seems ever to have been a proneness in the brilliant, and the warm-blooded, to fall into this vice. The demon of intemperance ever seems to have delighted in sucking the blood of genius and of generosity. What one of us but can call to mind some dear relative, more promising in youth than all his fellows, who has fallen a sacrifice to his rapacity? He ever seems to have gone forth, like the Egyptian angel of death, commissioned to slay if not the first, the fairest born of every family. Shall he now be arrested in his desolating career? In that arrest, all can give aid that will; and who shall be excused that *can*, and will not? Far around as human breath has ever blown, he keeps our fathers, our broth-ers, our sons, and our friends, prostrate in the chains of moral death. To all the living every where, we cry, "come sound the moral resurrection trump, that these may rise and stand up, an exceeding great army"—"Come from the four winds, O breath! and breathe upon these slain, that they may live."

If the relative grandeur of revolutions shall be estimated by the great amount of human misery they alleviate, and the small amount they inflict, then, indeed, will this be the grandest the world shall ever have seen. Of our political revolu-tion of '76, we all are justly proud. It has given us a degree of political freedom, far exceeding that of any other of the nations of the earth. In it the world has found a solution of that long mooted problem, as to the capability of man to govern himself. In it was the germ which has vegetated, and still is to grow and expand into the universal liberty of mankind.

But with all these glorious results, past, present, and to come, it had its evils too. It breathed forth famine, swam in blood and rode on fire; and long, long after, the orphan's cry, and the widow's wail, continued to break the sad silence that ensued. These were the price, the inevitable price, paid for the blessings it bought.

Turn now, to the temperance revolution. In *it,* we shall find a stronger bondage broken; a viler slavery, manumitted; a greater tyrant deposed. In *it,* more of want supplied, more disease healed, more sorrow assuaged. By *it* no orphans starving, no widows weeping. By *it,* none wounded in feeling, none injured in interest. Even the dram-maker, and dram seller, will have glided into other occupations *so* gradually, as never to have felt the shock of change; and will stand ready to join all others in the universal song of gladness.

And what a noble ally this, to the cause of political freedom. With such an aid, its march cannot fail to be on and on, till every son of earth shall drink in rich fruition, the sorrow quenching draughts of perfect liberty. Happy day, when, all appetites controled, all passions subdued, all matters subjected, *mind,* all conquering *mind,* shall live and move the monarch of the world. Glorious consummation! Hail fall of Fury! Reign of Reason, all hail!

And when the victory shall be complete—when there shall be neither a slave nor a drunkard on the earth—how proud the title of that *Land,* which may truly claim to be the birth-place and the cradle of both those revolutions, that shall have ended in that victory. How nobly distinguished that People, who shall have planted, and nurtured to maturity, both the political and moral freedom of their species.

This is the one hundred and tenth anniversary of the birth-day of Washington. We are met to celebrate this day. Washington is the mightiest name of earth—*long since* mightiest in the cause of civil liberty; *still* mightiest in moral reformation. On that name, an eulogy is expected. It cannot be. To add brightness to the sun, or glory to the name of Washington, is alike impossible. Let none attempt it. In solemn awe pronounce the name, and in its naked deathless splendor, leave it shining on.

*February 22, 1842*

# Speech in the U.S. House of Representatives on the War with Mexico

Mr. Chairman:

Some, if not all the gentlemen on, the other side of the House, who have addressed the committee within the last two days, have spoken rather complainingly, if I have rightly understood them, of the vote given a week or ten days ago, declaring that the war with Mexico was unnecessarily and unconstitutionally commenced by the President. I admit that such a vote should not be given, in mere party wantonness, and that the one given, is justly censurable, if it have no other, or better foundation. I am one of those who joined in that vote; and I did so under my best impression of the *truth* of the case. How I got this impression, and how it may possibly be removed, I will now try to show. When the war began, it was my opinion that all those who, because of knowing too *little,* or because of knowing too *much,* could not conscientiously approve the conduct of the President, in the beginning of it, should, nevertheless, as good citizens and patriots, remain silent on that point, at least till the war should be ended. Some leading democrats, including Ex President Van Buren, have taken this same view, as I understand them; and I adhered to it, and acted upon it, until since I took my seat here; and I think I should still adhere to it, were it not that the President and his friends will not allow it to be so. Besides the continual effort of the President to argue every silent vote given for supplies, into an endorsement of the justice and wisdom of his conduct—besides that singularly candid paragraph, in his late message in which he tells us that Congress, with great unanimity, only two in the Senate and fourteen in the House dissenting, had declared that, "by the act of the Republic of Mexico, a state of war exists between that Government and the United States," when the same journals that informed him of this, also informed him, that when that declaration stood disconnected from the question of supplies, sixtyseven in the House, and not fourteen merely, voted against it—besides this open attempt to prove, by telling the *truth,* what he could not prove by telling the *whole truth*—demanding of all who will not submit to be misrepresented, in justice to themselves, to speak out—besides all this, one of my colleagues (Mr. Richardson) at a very early day in the session brought in a set of resolutions, expressly endorsing the original justice of the war on the part of the President. Upon these resolutions, when they shall be put on their passage I shall be *compelled* to vote; so that I can not be silent, if I would. Seeing this, I went about preparing myself to give the vote understandingly when it should come. I carefully examined the President's messages, to ascertain what he himself had said and proved upon the point. The result of this examination was to make the impression, that taking for true, all the President states as facts, he falls far short of proving his justification; and that the President would have gone farther with his proof, if it had not been for the small matter, that the *truth* would not permit him. Under the impression thus made, I gave the vote before mentioned. I propose now to give, concisely, the process of the examination I made, and how I reached the conclusion I did. The President, in his first war message of May 1846, declares that the soil was *ours* on which hostilities were commenced by Mexico; and he repeats that declaration, almost in the same language, in each successive annual message, thus showing that he esteems that point, a highly essential one. In the importance of that point, I entirely agree with the President. To my judgment, it is the *very point,* upon which he should be justified, or condemned. In his message of Decr. 1846, it seems to have occurred to him, as is certainly true, that title—ownership—to soil, or any thing else, is not a simple fact; but is a conclusion following one or more simple facts; and that it was incumbent upon him, to present the facts, from which he concluded, the soil was ours, on which the first blood of the war was shed.

Accordingly a little below the middle of page twelve in the message last referred to, he enters upon that task; forming an issue, and introducing testimony, extending the whole, to a little below the middle of page fourteen. Now I propose to try to show, that the whole of this,—issue and evidence—is, from beginning to end, the sheerest deception. The issue, as he presents it, is in these words "But there are those who, conceding all this to be true, assume the ground that the true western boundary of Texas is the Nueces, instead of the Rio Grande; and that, therefore, in marching our army to the east bank of the latter river, we passed the Texan line, and invaded the teritory of Mexico." Now this issue, is made up of two affirmatives and no negative. The main deception of it is, that it assumes as true, that *one* river or the *other* is necessarily the boundary; and cheats the superficial thinker entirely out of the idea, that *possibly* the boundary is somewhere *between* the two, and not actually at either. A further deception is, that it will let in *evidence,* which a true issue would exclude. A true issue, made by the President, would be about as follows "I say, the soil *was ours,* on which the first blood was shed; there are those who say it was not."

I now proceed to examine the Presidents evidence, as applicable to such an issue. When that evidence is analized, it is all included in the following propositions:

1.  That the Rio Grande was the Western boundary of Louisiana as we purchased it of France in 1803.
2.  That the Republic of Texas always *claimed* the Rio Grande, as her Western boundary.
3.  That by various acts, she had claimed it *on paper*.
4.  That Santa Anna, in his treaty with Texas, recognised the Rio Grande, as her boundary.
5.  That Texas *before*, and the U.S. *after*, annexation had *exercised* jurisdiction *beyond* the Nueces—*between* the two rivers.
6.  That our Congress, *understood* the boundary of Texas to extend beyond the Nueces.

Now for each of these in it's turn.

His first item is, that the Rio Grande was the Western boundary of Louisiana, as we purchased it of France in 1803; and seeming to expect this to be disputed, he argues over the amount of nearly a page, to prove it true; at the end of which he lets us know, that by the treaty of 1819, we sold to Spain the whole country from the Rio Grande eastward, to the Sabine. Now, admitting for the present, that the Rio Grande, was the boundary of Louisiana, what, under heaven, had that to do with the *present* boundary between us and Mexico? How, Mr. Chairman, the line, that once divided your land from mine, can *still* be the boundary between us, *after* I have sold my land to you, is, to me, beyond all comprehension. And how any man, with an honest purpose only, of proving the truth, could ever have *thought* of introducing such a fact to prove such an issue, is equally incomprehensible. His next piece of evidence is that "The Republic of Texas always *claimed* this river (Rio Grande) as her western boundary." That is not true, in fact. Texas *has* claimed it, but she has not *always* claimed it. There is, at least, one distinguished exception. Her state constitution,—the republic's most solemn, and well considered act—that which may, without impropriety, be called her last will and testament revoking all others—makes no such claim. But suppose she had always claimed it. Has not Mexico always claimed the contrary? so that there is but *claim* against *claim,* leaving nothing proved, until we get back of the claims, and find which has the better *foundation.* Though not in the order in which the President presents his evidence, I now consider that class of his statements, which are, in substance, nothing more than that Texas has, by various acts of her convention and congress, claimed the Rio Grande, as her boundary, *on paper.* I mean here what he says about the fixing of the Rio Grande as her boundary in her old constitution (not her state constitution) about forming congressional districts, counties &c &c. Now all of this is but naked *claim;* and what I have already said about claims is strictly applicable to this. If I should claim your land, by word of mouth, that certainly would not make it mine; and if I were to claim it by a deed which I had made myself, and with which, you had had nothing to do, the claim would be quite the same, in substance—or rather, in utter nothingness. I next consider the President's statement that Santa Anna in his *treaty* with Texas, recognised the Rio Grande, as the western boundary of Texas. Besides the position, so often taken that Santa Anna, while a prisoner of war—a captive—*could* not bind Mexico by a treaty, which I deem conclusive—besides this, I wish to say something in relation to this treaty, so called by the President, with Santa Anna. If any man would like to be amused by a sight of that *little* thing, which the President calls by that *big* name, he can have it, by turning to Niles' Register volume 50, page 336. And if any one should suppose that Niles' Register is a curious repository of so mighty a document, as a solemn treaty between nations, I can only say that I learned, to a tolerable degree of certainty, by enquiry at the State Department, that the President himself, never saw it any where else. By the way, I believe I should not err, if I were to declare, that during the first ten years of the existence of that document, it was never, by any body, *called* a treaty—that it was never so called, till the President, in his extremity, attempted, by so calling it, to wring something from it in justification of himself in connection with the Mexican war. It has none of the distinguishing features of a treaty. It does not call itself a treaty. Santa Anna does not therein, assume to bind Mexico; he assumes only to act as the President-Commander-in-chief of the Mexican Army and Navy; stipulates that the then present hostilities should cease, and that he would not *himself* take up arms, nor *influence* the Mexican people to take up arms, against Texas during the existence of the war of independence. He did not recognise the independence of Texas; he did not assume to put an end to the war; but clearly indicated his expectation of it's continuance; he did not say one word about boundary, and, most probably, never thought of it. It *is* stipulated therein that the Mexican forces should evacuate the teritory of Texas, *passing to the other side of the Rio Grande;* and in another article, it is stipulated that, to prevent collisions between the armies, the Texan army should not approach nearer than within five leagues—of *what* is not said—but clearly, from the object stated it is—of the Rio Grande. Now, if this is a treaty, recognising the Rio Grande, as the boundary of Texas, it contains the singular feauture, of stipulating, that Texas shall not go within five leagues of *her own* boundary.

Next comes the evidence of Texas before annexation, and the United States, afterwards, *exercising* jurisdiction *beyond* the Nueces, and *between* the two rivers. This actual *exercise* of jurisdiction, is the very class or quality of evidence we want. It is excellent so far as it goes; but does it go far enough? He tells us it went *beyond* the Nueces; but he does not tell us it went to the Rio Grande. He tells us, jurisdiction was exercised *between* the two rivers, but he does not tell us it was exercised over *all* the teritory between them. Some simple minded people, think it is *possible,* to cross one river and go *beyond* it without going *all the way* to the next—that jurisdiction may be exercised *between* two rivers without covering *all* the country between them. I know a man, not very unlike myself, who exercises jurisdiction over a piece of land between the Wabash and the Mississippi; and yet so far is this from being *all* there is between those rivers, that it is just one hundred and fifty two feet long by fifty wide, and no part of it much within a hundred miles of either. He has a neighbour between him and the Mississippi,— that is, just across the street, in that direction—whom, I am sure, he could nei- ther *persuade* nor *force* to give up his habitation; but which nevertheless, he could certainly annex, if it were to be done, by merely standing on his own side of the street and *claiming* it, or even, sitting down, and writing a *deed* for it.

But next the President tells us, the Congress of the United States *understood* the state of Texas they admitted into the union, to extend *beyond* the Nueces. Well, I suppose they did. *I* certainly so understood it. But how *far* beyond? That Congress did *not* understand it to extend clear to the Rio Grande, is quite certain by the fact of their joint resolutions, for admission, expressly leaving all questions of boundary to future adjustment. And it may be added, that Texas herself, is proved to have had the same understanding of it, that our Congress had, by the fact of the exact conformity of her new constitution, to those resolutions.

I am now through the whole of the President's evidence; and it is a singular fact, that if any one should declare the President sent the army into the midst of a settlement of Mexican people, who had never submited, by consent or by force, to the authority of Texas or of the United States, and that *there*, and *thereby*, the first blood of the war was shed, there is not one word in all the President has said, which would either admit or deny the declaration. This strange omission, it does seem to me, could not have occurred but by design. My way of living leads me to be about the courts of justice; and there, I have sometimes seen a good lawyer, struggling for his client's neck, in a desperate case, employing every artifice to work round, befog, and cover up, with many words, some point arising in the case, which he *dared* not admit, and yet *could* not deny. Party bias may help to make it appear so; but with all the allowance I can make for such bias, it still does appear, to me, that just such, and from just such necessity, is the President's struggle in this case.

Some time after my colleague (Mr. Richardson) introduced the resolutions I have mentioned, I introduced a preamble, resolution, and interrogatories, intended to draw the President out, if possible, on this hitherto untrodden ground. To show their relevancy, I propose to state my understanding of the true rule for ascertaining the boundary between Texas and Mexico. It is, that *wherever* Texas was *exercising* jurisdiction, was hers; and *wherever Mexico* was exercising jurisdiction, was hers; and that *whatever* separated the actual exercise of jurisdiction of the one, from that of the other, was the true boundary between them. If, as is probably true, Texas was exercising jurisdiction along the western bank of the Nueces, and Mexico was exercising it along the eastern bank of the Rio Grande, then *neither* river was the boundary; but the uninhabited country between the two, was. The extent of our teritory in that region depended, not on any *treaty-fixed* boundary (for no treaty had attempted it) but on revolution. Any people anywhere, being inclined and having the power, have the *right* to rise up, and shake off the existing government, and form a new one that suits them better. This is a most valuable,—a most sacred right—a right, which we hope and believe, is to liberate the world. Nor is this right confined to cases in which the whole people of an existing government, may choose to exercise it. Any portion of such people that *can, may* revolutionize, and make their *own*, of so much of the teritory as they inhabit. More than this, a *majority* of any portion of such people may revolutionize, putting down a *minority,* intermingled with, or near about them, who may oppose their movement. Such minority, was precisely the case, of the tories of our own revolution. It is a quality of revolutions not to go by *old* lines, or *old* laws; but to break up both, and make new ones. As to the country now in question, we bought it of France in 1803, and sold it to Spain in 1819, according to the President's statements. After this, all Mexico, including Texas, revolutionized against Spain; and still later, Texas revolutionized against Mexico. In my view, just so far as she carried her revolution, by obtaining the *actual,* willing or unwilling, submission of the people, *so far,* the country was hers, and no farther. Now sir, for the purpose of obtaining the very best evidence, as to whether Texas had actually carried her revolution, to the place where the hostilities of the present war commenced, let the President answer the interrogatories, I proposed, as before mentioned, or some other similar ones. Let him answer, fully, fairly, and candidly. Let him answer with *facts,* and not with arguments. Let him remember he sits where Washington sat, and so remembering, let him answer, as Washington would answer. As a nation *should* not, and the Almighty *will* not, be evaded, so let him attempt no envasion—no equivocation. And if, so answering, he can show that the soil was ours, where the first blood of the war was shed—that it was not within an inhabited country, or, if within such, that the inhabitants had submitted themselves to the civil authority of Texas, or of the United States, and that the same is true of the site of Fort

Brown, then I am with him for his justification. In that case I, shall be most happy to reverse the vote I gave the other day. I have a selfish motive for desiring that the President may do this. I expect to give some votes, in connection with the war, which, without his so doing, will be of doubtful propriety in my own judgment, but which will be free from the doubt if he does so. But if he *can* not, or *will* not do this—if on any pretence, or no pretence, he shall refuse or omit it, then I shall be fully convinced, of what I more than suspect already, that he is deeply conscious of being in the wrong—that he feels the blood of this war, like the blood of Abel, is crying to Heaven against him. That originally having some strong motive—what, I will not stop now to give my opinion concerning—to involve the two countries in a war, and trusting to escape scrutiny, by fixing the public gaze upon the exceeding brightness of military glory—that attractive rainbow, that rises in showers of blood—that serpent's eye, that charms to destroy—he plunged into it, and has swept, *on* and *on,* till, disappointed in his calculation of the ease with which Mexico might be subdued, he now finds himself, he knows not where. How like the half insane mumbling of a fever-dream, is the whole war part of his late message! At one time telling us that Mexico has nothing whatever, that we can get, but territory; at another, showing us how we can support the war, by levying contributions on Mexico. At one time, urging the national honor, the security of the future, the prevention of foreign interference, and even, the good of Mexico herself, as among the objects of the war; at another, telling us, that "to reject indemnity, by refusing to accept a cession of teritory, would be to abandon all our just demands, and to wage the war, bearing all it's expenses, *without a purpose or definite object.*" So then, the national honor, security of the future, and every thing but teritorial indemnity, may be considered the *no-purposes*, and *indefinite,* objects of the war! But, having it now settled that teritorial indemnity is the only object, we are urged to seize, by legislation here, all that he was content to take, a few months ago, and the whole province of lower California to boot, and to still carry on the war—to take *all* we are fighting for, and *still* fight on. Again, the President is resolved, under all circumstances, to have full teritorial indemnity for the expenses of the war; but he forgets to tell us how we are to get the *excess,* after those expenses shall have surpassed the value of the *whole* of the Mexican teritory. So again, he insists that the separate national existence of Mexico, shall be maintained; but he does not tell us *how* this can be done, after we shall have taken *all* her teritory. Lest the questions, I here suggest, be considered speculative merely, let me be indulged a moment in trying to show they are not. The war has gone on some twenty months; for the expenses of which, together with an inconsiderable old score, the President now claims about one half of the Mexican teritory; and that, by far the better half, so far as concerns our ability to make any thing out of it. *It* is comparatively uninhabited; so that we could establish land offices in it, and raise some money in that way. But the other half is already inhabited, as I understand it, tolerably densely for the nature of the country; and all it's lands, or all that are valuable, already appropriated as private property. How then are we to make any thing out of these lands with this incumbrance on them? or how, remove the incumbrance? I suppose no one will say we should kill the people, or drive them out, or make slaves of them, or even confiscate their property. How then can we make much out of this part of the teritory? If the prossecution of the war has, in expenses, already equalled the *better* half of the country, how long it's future prosecution, will be in equalling, the less valuable half, is not a *speculative,* but a *practical* question, pressing closely upon us. And yet it is a question which the President seems to never have thought of. As to the mode of terminating the war, and securing peace, the President is equally wandering and indefinite. First, it is to be done by a more vigorous prossecution of the war in the vital parts of the enemies country; and, after apparently, talking himself tired, on this point, the President drops down into a half despairing tone, and tells us that "with a people distracted and divided by contending factions, and a government subject to constant changes, by successive revolutions, *the continued success of our arms may fail to secure a satisfactory peace.*" Then he suggests the propriety of wheedling the Mexican people to desert the counsels of their own leaders, and trusting in our protection, to set up a government from which we can secure a satisfactory peace; telling us, that *"this may become the only mode of obtaining such a peace."* But soon he falls into doubt of this too; and then drops back on to the already half abandoned ground of "more vigorous prossecution." All this shows that the President is, in no wise, satisfied with his own positions. First he takes up one, and in attempting to argue us *into* it, he argues himself *out* of it; then seizes another, and goes through the same process; and then, confused at being able to think of nothing new, he snatches up the old one again, which he has some time before cast off. His mind, tasked beyond it's power, is running hither and thither, like some tortured creature, on a burning surface, finding no position, on which it can settle down, and be at ease.

Again, it is a singular omission in this message, that it, no where intimates *when* the President expects the war to terminate. At it's beginning, Genl. Scott was, by this same President, driven into disfavor, if not disgrace, for intimating that peace could not be conquered in less than three or four months. But now, at the end of about twenty months, during which time our arms have given us the most splendid successes—every department, and every part, land and water, officers and privates, regulars and volunteers, doing all that men *could* do, and hundreds of things which it had ever before been thought men could *not* do,— after all this, this same President gives us a long message, without showing us, that, *as to the end,* he himself, has, even an imaginary conception. As I have before said, he knows not where he is. He is a bewildered, confounded, and miserably perplexed man. God grant he may be able to show, there is not something about his conscience, more painful than all his mental perplexity!

*January 12, 1848*

# Notes on the Practice of Law

I am not an accomplished lawyer. I find quite as much material for a lecture, in those points wherein I have failed, as in those wherein I have been moderately successful.

The leading rule for a lawyer, as for the man, of every other calling, is *diligence*. Leave nothing for to-morrow, which can be done to-day. Never let your correspondence fall behind. Whatever piece of business you have in hand, before stopping, do all the labor pertaining to it which can *then* be done. When you bring a common-law suit, if you have the facts for doing so, write the declaration at once. If a law point be involved, examine the books, and note the authority you rely on, upon the declaration itself, where you are sure to find it when wanted. The same of defences and pleas. In business not likely to be litigated—ordinary collection cases, foreclosures, partitions, and the like,—make all examinations of titles, and note them, and even draft orders and decrees in advance. This course has a tripple advantage; it avoids omissions and neglect, *saves* your labor, when once done; performs the labor out of court when you *have* leisure, rather than in court, when you have not. Extemporaneous speaking should be practiced and cultivated. It is the lawyer's avenue to the public. However able and faithful he may be in other respects, people are slow to bring him business, if he cannot make a speech. And yet there is not a more fatal error to young lawyers, than relying too much on speech-making. If any one, upon his rare powers of speaking, shall claim exemption from the drudgery of the law, his case is a failure in advance.

Discourage litigation. Persuade your neighbors to compromise whenever you can. Point out to them how the *nominal* winner is often a *real* loser—in fees, expenses, and waste of time. As a peace-maker the lawyer has a superior opportunity of being a good man. There will still be business enough.

Never stir up litigation. A worse man can scarcely be found than one who does this. Who can be more nearly a fiend than he who habitually overhauls the Register of deeds in search of defects in titles, whereon to stir up strife, and put money in his pocket? A moral tone ought to be infused into the profession, which should drive such men out of it.

The matter of fees is important far beyond the mere question of bread and butter involved. Properly attended to fuller justice is done to both lawyer and client. An exorbitant fee should never be claimed. As a general rule, never take your whole fee in advance, nor any more than a small retainer. When fully paid before hand, you are more than a common mortal if you can feel the same interest in the case, as if something was still in prospect for you, as well as for your client. And when you lack interest in the case, the job will very likely lack skill and diligence in the performance. Settle the *amount* of fee, and take a note in advance. Then you will feel that you are working for something, and you are sure to do your work faithfully and well. Never sell a fee-note—at least, not before the consideration service is performed. It leads to negligence and dishonesty—negligence, by losing interest in the case, and dishonesty in refusing to refund, when you have allowed the consideration to fail.

There is a vague popular belief that lawyers are necessarily dishonest. I say *vague*, because when we consider to what extent *confidence*, and *honors* are reposed in, and conferred upon lawyers by the people, it appears improbable that their *impression* of dishonesty is very distinct and vivid. Yet the impression, is common—almost universal. Let no young man, choosing the law for a calling, for a moment yield to the popular belief. Resolve to be honest at all events; and if, in your own judgment, you can not be an honest lawyer, resolve to be honest without being a lawyer. Choose some other occupation, rather than one in the choosing of which you do, in advance, consent to be a knave.

*ca. 1850*

# On the Life and Services of Zachary Taylor, the Late President of the United States

General Zachary Taylor, the eleventh elected President of the United States, is dead. He was born Nov. 2nd, 1784, in Orange county, Virginia; and died July the 9th 1850, in the sixty-sixth year of his age, at the White House in Washington City. He was the second son of Richard Taylor, a Colonel in the army of the revolution. His youth was passed among the pioneers of Kentucky, whither his parents emigrated soon after his birth; and where his taste for military life, probably inherited, was greatly stimulated. Near the commencement of our last war with Great Britain, he was appointed by President Jefferson, a lieutenant in the 7th regiment of Infantry. During the war, he served under Gen. Harrison in his North Western campaign against the Indians; and, having been promoted to a captaincy, was intrusted with the defence of Fort Harrison, with fifty men, half of them unfit for duty. A strong party of Indians, under the Prophet, brother of Tecumseh, made a midnight attack on the Fort; but Taylor, though weak in his force, and without preparation, was resolute, and on the alert; and, after a battle, which lasted till after daylight, completely repulsed them. Soon after, he took a prominent part in the expedition under Major Gen. Hopkins against the Prophet's town; and, on his return, found a letter from President Madison, who had succeeded Mr. Jefferson, conferring on him a major's brevet for his gallant defence of Fort Harrison.

After the close of the British war, he remained in the frontier service of the West, till 1818. He was then transferred to the Southern frontier, where he remained, most of the time in active service till 1826. In 1819, and during his service in the South, he was promoted to the rank of lieutenant colonel. In 1826 he was again sent to the North West, where he continued until 1836. In 1832, he was promoted to the rank of a colonel. In 1836 he was ordered to the South to engage in what is well known as the Florida War. In the autumn of 1837, he fought and conquered in the memorable battle of Okeechobee, one of the most desperate struggles known to the annals of Indian warfare. For this, he was honored with the rank of Brigadier General; and, in 1838 was appointed to succeed Gen. Jessup in command of the forces in Florida. In 1841 he was ordered to Fort Gibson to take command of the Second Military department of the United States; and in September, 1844, was directed to hold the troops between the Red River and the

Sabine in readiness to march as might be indicated by the Charge of the United States, near Texas. In 1845 his forces were concentrated at Corpus Christi.

In obedience to orders, in March 1846, he planted his troops on the Rio Grande opposite Mattamoras. Soon after this, and near this place, a small detachment of Gen. Taylor's forces, under Captain Thornton, was cut to pieces by a party of Mexicans. Open hostilities being thus commenced, and Gen. Taylor being constantly menaced by Mexican forces vastly superior to his own, in numbers, his position became exceedingly critical. Having erected a fort, he might defend himself against great odds while he could remain within it; but his provisions had failed, and there was no supply nearer than Point Isabel, between which and the new fort, the country was open to, and full of, armed Mexicans. His resolution was at once taken. He garrisoned Fort Brown, (the new fort) with a force of about four hundred; and, putting himself at the head of the main body of his troops, marched forthwith for Point Isabel. He met no resistance on his march. Having obtained his supplies, he began his return march, to the relief of Fort Brown, which he at first knew, would be, and then knew had been besieged by the enemy, immediately upon his leaving it. On the first or second day of this return march, the Mexican General, Arista, met General Taylor in front, and offered battle. The Mexicans numbered six or eight thousand, opposed to whom were about two thousand Americans. The moment was a trying one. Comparatively, Taylor's forces were but a handful; and few, of either officers or men, had ever been under fire. A brief council was held; and the result was, the battle commenced. The issue of that contest all remember—remember with mingled sensations of pride and sorrow, that then, American valor and powers triumphed, and then the gallant and accomplished, and noble Ringgold fell.

The Americans passed the night on the field. The General knew the enemy was still in his fort; and the question rose upon him, whether to advance or retreat. A council was again held; and, it is said, the General overruled the majority, and resolved to advance. Accordingly in the morning, he moved rapidly forward. At about four or five miles from Fort Brown he again met the enemy in force, who had selected his position, and made some hasty fortification. Again the battle commenced, and raged till toward nightfall, when the Mexicans were entirely routed, and the General with his fatigued and bleeding, and reduced battalions marched into Fort Brown. There was a joyous meeting. A brief hour before, whether all *within* the fort had perished, all *without* feared, but none could tell—while the incessant roar of artillery, wrought those *within* to the highest pitch of apprehension, that their brethren *without* were being massacred to the last man. And now the din of battle nears the fort and sweeps obliquely by; a gleam of hope flies through the half imprisoned few; they fly to the wall; every eye is strained—it is—it is—the stars and stripes are still aloft! Anon the anxious brethren meet; and while hand strikes hand, the heavens are rent with a loud, long, glorious, gushing cry of victory! victory!! victory!!!

Soon after these two battles, Gen. Taylor was breveted a Major General in the U.S. Army.

In the mean time, war having been declared to exist between the United States and Mexico, provisions were made to reinforce Gen. Taylor; and he was ordered to march into the interior of Mexico. He next marched upon Monterey, arriving there on the 19th of September. He commenced an assault upon the city, on the 21st, and on the 23d was about carrying it at the point of the bayonet, when Gen. Ampudia capitulated. Taylor's forces consisted of 425 officers, and 9,220 men. His artillery consisted of one 10 inch mortar, two 24 pound Howitzers, and four light field batteries of four guns—the mortar being the only piece serviceable for the siege. The Mexican works were armed with forty-two pieces of cannon, and manned with a force of at least 7000 troops of the line, and from 2000 to 3000 irregulars.

Next we find him advancing farther into the interior of Mexico, at the head of 5,400 men, not more than 600 being regular troops.

At Agua Nueva he received intelligence that Santa Anna, the greatest military chieftain of Mexico, was advancing after him; and he fell back to Buena Vista, a strong position a few miles in advance of Saltillo. On the 22nd of Feb., 1847, the battle, now called the battle of Buena Vista, was commenced by Santa Anna at the head of 20,000 well appointed soldiers. This was Gen. Taylor's great battle. The particulars of it are familiar to all. It continued through the 23d; and although Gen. Taylor's defeat seemed to be inevitable, yet he succeeded by skill, and by the courage and devotion of his officers and men, in repulsing the overwhelming forces of the enemy, and throwing them back into the desert. This was the battle of the chiefest interest fought during the Mexican war. At the time it was fought, and for some weeks after, Gen. Taylor's communication with the United States was cut off; and the road was in possession of parties of the enemy. For many days after full intelligence of it, should have been in all parts of this country, nothing certain, concerning it, was known, while vague and painful rumors were afloat, that a great battle had been fought, and that Gen. Taylor, and his whole force had been annihilated.

At length the truth came, with its thrilling details of victory and blood—of glory and grief. A bright and glowing page was added to our Nation's history; but then too, in eternal silence, lay Clay, and Mc'Kee, and Yell, and Lincoln, and our own beloved Hardin.

This also was Gen. Taylor's *last* battle. He remained in active service in Mexico, till the autumn of the same year, when he returned to the United States.

Passing in review, Gen. Taylor's military history, some striking peculiarities will appear. No one of the six battles which he fought, excepting perhaps, that of Monterey, presented a field, which would have been selected by an ambitious captain upon which to gather laurels. So far as fame was concerned, the prospect—the promise in advance, was, "you may lose, but you can not win." Yet Taylor, in his blunt business-like view of things, seems never to have thought of this.

It did not happen to Gen. Taylor once in his life, to fight a battle on equal terms, or on terms advantageous to himself—and yet he was never beaten, and never retreated. In *all,* the odds was greatly against him; in each, defeat seemed inevitable; and yet *in all,* he triumphed. Wherever he has led, while the battle still raged, the issue was painfully doubtful; yet in *each* and *all,* when the din had ceased, and the smoke had blown away, our country's flag was still seen, fluttering in the breeze.

Gen. Taylor's battles were not distinguished for brilliant military manoeuvers; but in all, he seems rather to have conquered by the exercise of a sober and steady judgment, coupled with a dogged incapacity to understand that defeat was possible. His rarest military trait, was a combination of negatives—absence of *excitement* and absence of *fear.* He could not be *flurried,* and he could not be *scared.*

In connection with Gen. Taylor's military character, may be mentioned his relations with his brother officers, and his soldiers. Terrible as he was to his country's enemies, no man was so little disposed to have difficulty with his friends. During the period of his life, *duelling* was a practice not quite uncommon among gentlemen in the peaceful avocations of life, and still more common, among the officers of the Army and Navy. Yet, so far as I can learn, a *duel* with Gen. Taylor, has never been talked of.

He was alike averse to *sudden,* and to *startling* quarrels; and he pursued no man with *revenge.* A notable, and a noble instance of this, is found in his conduct to the gallant and now lamented Gen. Worth. A short while before the battles of the 8th and 9th of May, some questions of precedence arose between Worth, (then a colonel) and some other officer, which question it seems Gen. Taylor's duty to decide. He decided against Worth. Worth was greatly offended, left the Army, came to the United States, and tendered his resignation to the authorities at Washington. It is said, that in his passionate feeling, he hesitated not to speak harshly and disparagingly of Gen. Taylor. He was an officer of the highest character; and his word, on military subjects, and about military men, could not, with the country, pass for nothing. In this absence from the army of Col. Worth, the unexpected turn of things brought on the battles of the 8th and 9th. He was deeply mortified—in almost absolute desperation—at having lost the opportunity of being present, and taking part in those battles. The laurels won by his previous service, in his own eyes, seemed withering away. The Government, both *wisely* and *generously*, I think, declined accepting his resignation; and he returned to Gen. Taylor. Then came Gen. Taylor's *opportunity* for revenge. The battle of Monterey was approaching, and even at hand. Taylor *could* if he *would,* so place Worth in that battle, that his name would scarcely be noticed in the report. But no. He felt it was due to the service, to assign the real post of honor to some one of the best officers; he knew Worth was one of the best, and he felt that it was *generous* to allow him, then and there, to retrieve his secret loss. Accordingly he assigned to Col. Worth in that assault, what was *par excellence*, the post of honor; and, the duties of which, he executed so well, and so brilliantly, as to eclipse, in that battle, even Gen. Taylor himself.

As to Gen. Taylor's relations with his soldiers, details would be endless. It is perhaps enough to say—and it is far from the *least* of his honors that we can *truly* say—that of the many who served with him through the long course of forty years, all testify to the uniform kindness, and his constant care for, and hearty sympathy with, their every want and every suffering; while none can be found to declare, that he was ever a tyrant anywhere, in anything.

Going back a little in point of time, it is proper to say that so soon as the news of the battles of the 8th and 9th of May 1846, had fairly reached the United States, Gen. Taylor began to be named for the next Presidency, by letter writers, newspapers, public meetings and conventions in various parts of the country.

These nominations were generally put forth as being of a no-party character. Up to this time I think it highly probable—nay, almost certain, that Gen. Taylor had never thought of the Presidency in connection with himself. And there is reason for believing that the first intelligence of these nominations rather *amused* than *seriously* interested him. Yet I should be insincere, were I not to confess, that in my opinion, the repeated, and steady manifestations in his favor, *did* beget in his mind a laudable ambition to reach the high distinction of the Presidential chair.

As the time for the Presidential canvass approached, it was seen that general nominations, combining anything near the number of votes necessary to an election, could not be made without some pretty strong and decided reference to party politics. Accordingly, in the month of May, 1848, the great Democratic party nominated as their candidate, an able and distinguished member of their own party, on strictly party grounds. Almost immediately following this, the Whig party, in general convention, nominated Gen. Taylor as their candidate.

The election came off in the November following; and though there was also a third candidate, the two former only, received any vote in the electoral college. Gen. Taylor, having the majority of them was duly elected; and he entered on the duties of that high and responsible office, March 5th, 1849. The incidents of his administration up to the time of his death, are too familiar and too fresh to require any direct repetition.

The Presidency, even to the most experienced politicians, is no bed of roses; and Gen. Taylor like others, found thorns within it. No human being can fill that station and escape censure. Still I hope and believe when Gen. Taylor's official conduct shall come to be viewed in the calm light of history, he will be found to have *deserved* as little as any who have succeeded him.

Upon the death of Gen. Taylor, as it would in the case of the death of any President, we are naturally led to consider what will be its effect, politically, upon the country. I will not pretend to believe that all the wisdom, or all the patriotism of the country, died with Gen. Taylor. But we know that *wisdom* and *patriotism*, in a public office, under institutions like ours, are wholly inefficient and worthless, unless they are sustained by the confidence and devotion of the people. And I confess my apprehensions, that in the death of the late President, we have lost a degree of that confidence and devotion, which will not soon again pertain to any successor. Between public measures regarded as antagonistic, there is often less real difference in its bearing on the public weal, than there is between the dispute being *kept up,* or being *settled* either way. I fear the one *great* question of the day, is not now so likely to be partially acquiesced in by the different sections of the Union, as it would have been, could Gen. Taylor have been spared to us. Yet, under all circumstances, trusting to our Maker, and through his wisdom and beneficence, to the great body of our people, we will not despair, nor despond.

In Gen. Taylor's general public relation to his country, what will strongly impress a close observer, was his unostentatious, self-sacrificing, long enduring devotion to his *duty.* He indulged in no recreations, he visited no public places, seeking applause; but quietly, as the earth in its orbit, he was always at his post. Along our whole Indian frontier, thro' summer and winter, in sunshine and storm, like a sleepless sentinel, *he* has *watched,* while *we* have *slept* for forty long years. How well might the dying hero say at last, "I have done my duty, I am ready to go."

Nor can I help thinking that the American people, in electing Gen. Taylor to the presidency, thereby showing their high appreciation, of his sterling, but unobtrusive qualities, did their *country* a service, and *themselves* an imperishable honor. It is *much* for the young to know, that treading the hard path of duty, as he trod it, *will* be noticed, and *will* lead to high places.

But he is gone. The conqueror at last is conquered. The fruits of his labor, his name, his memory and example, are all that is left us—his example, verifying the great truth, that "he that humbleth himself, shall be exalted" teaching, that to serve one's country with a singleness of purpose, gives assurance of that country's gratitude, secures its best honors, and makes "a dying bed, soft as downy pillows are."

The death of the late President may not be without its use, in reminding us, that we, too, must die. Death, abstractly considered, is the same with the high as with the low; but practically, we are not so much aroused to the contemplation of our own mortal natures, by the fall of *many* undistinguished, as that of *one* great, and well known, name. By the latter, we are forced to muse, and ponder, sadly.

"Oh, why should the spirit of mortal be proud"

So the multitude goes, like the flower or the weed,
That withers away to let others succeed;
So the multitude comes, even those we behold,
To repeat every tale that has often been told.

For we are the same, our fathers have been,
We see the same sights our fathers have seen;
We drink the same streams and see the same sun
And run the same course our fathers have run.

*They* loved; but the story *we* cannot unfold;
They scorned, but the heart of the haughty is cold;
They grieved, but no wail from their slumbers will come,
They joyed, but the tongue of their gladness is dumb.

They died! Aye, they died; we things that are now;
That work on the turf that lies on their brow,
And make in their dwellings a transient abode,
Meet the things that they met on their pilgrimage road.

Yea! hope and despondency, pleasure and pain,
Are mingled together in sun-shine and rain;
And the smile and the tear, and the song and the dirge,
Still follow each other, like surge upon surge.

'Tis the wink of an eye, 'tis the draught of a breath,
From the blossoms of health, to the paleness of death.
From the gilded saloon, to the bier and the shroud.
Oh, why should the spirit of mortal be proud!

*July 25th, 1850*

# Eulogy on Henry Clay

On the fourth day of July, 1776, the people of a few feeble and oppressed colonies of Great Britain, inhabiting a portion of the Atlantic coast of North America, publicly declared their national independence, and made their appeal to the justice of their cause, and to the God of battles, for the maintainance of that declaration. That people were few in numbers, and without resources, save only their own wise heads and stout hearts. Within the first year of that declared independence, and while its maintainance was yet problematical—while the bloody struggle between those resolute rebels, and their haughty would-be-masters, was still waging, of undistinguished parents, and in an obscure district of one of those colonies, Henry Clay was born. The infant nation, and the infant child began the race of life together. For three quarters of a century they have travelled hand in hand. They have been companions ever. The nation has passed its perils, and is free, prosperous, and powerful. The child has reached his manhood, his middle age, his old age, and is dead. In all that has concerned the nation the man ever sympathised; and now the nation mourns for the man.

The day after his death, one of the public Journals, opposed to him politically, held the following pathetic and beautiful language, which I adopt, partly because such high and exclusive eulogy, originating with a political friend, might offend good taste, but chiefly, because I could not, in any language of my own, so well express my thoughts—

"Alas! who can realize that Henry Clay is dead! Who can realize that never again that majestic form shall rise in the council-chambers of his country to beat back the storms of anarchy which may threaten, or pour the oil of peace upon the troubled billows as they rage and menace around? Who can realize, that the workings of that mighty mind have ceased—that the throbbings of that gallant heart are stilled—that the mighty sweep of that graceful arm will be felt no more, and the magic of that eloquent tongue, which spake as spake no other tongue besides, is hushed—hushed forever! Who can realize that freedom's champion—the champion of a civilized world, and of all tongues and kindreds and people, has indeed fallen! Alas, in those dark hours, which, as they come in the history of all nations, must come in ours—those hours of peril and dread which our land has experienced, and which she may be called to experience again—to whom now may her people look up for that council and advice, which only wisdom and experience and patriotism can give, and which only the undoubting confidence of a nation will receive? Perchance, in the whole circle of the great and gifted of our land, there remains but one on whose shoulders the mighty mantle of the departed statesman may fall—one, while we now write, is doubtless pouring his tears over the bier of his brother and his friend—brother, friend ever, yet in political senti-ment, as far apart as party could make them. Ah, it is at times like these, that the petty distinctions of mere party disappear. We see only the great, the grand, the noble features of the departed statesman; and we do not even beg permission to bow at his feet and mingle our tears with those who have ever been his political adherents—we do not beg this permission—we claim it as a right, though we feel it as a privilege. Henry Clay belonged to his country—to the world, mere party cannot claim men like him. His career has been national—his fame has filled the earth—his memory will endure to 'the last syllable of recorded time.'

"Henry Clay is dead!—He breathed his last on yesterday at twenty minutes after eleven, in his chamber at Washington. To those who followed his lead in pub-lic affairs, it more appropriately belongs to pronounce his eulogy, and pay specific honors to the memory of the illustrious dead—but all Americans may show the grief which his death inspires, for, his character and fame are national property. As on a question of liberty, he knew no North, no South, no East, no West, but only the Union, which held them all in its sacred circle, so now his countrymen will know no grief, that is not as wide-spread as the bounds of the confederacy. The career of Henry Clay was a public career. From his youth he has been devoted to the public service, at a period too, in the world's history justly regarded as a remark-able era in human affairs. He witnessed in the beginning the throes of the French Revolution. He saw the rise and fall of Napoleon. He was called upon to legislate for America, and direct her policy when all Europe was the battle-field of contend-ing dynasties, and when the struggle for supremacy imperilled the rights of all neutral nations. His voice, spoke war and peace in the contest with Great Britain.

"When Greece rose against the Turks and struck for liberty, his name was mingled with the battle-cry of freedom. When South America threw off the thral-dom of Spain, his speeches were read at the head of her armies by Bolivar. His name has been, and will continue to be, hallowed in two hemispheres, for it is—

'One of the few the immortal names
That were not born to die,'

"To the ardent patriot and profound statesman, he added a quality possessed by few of the gifted on earth. His eloquence has not been surpassed. In the effective power to move the heart of man, Clay was without an equal, and the heaven born endowment, in the spirit of its origin, has been most conspicuously exhibited against intestine feud. On at least three important occasions, he has quelled our civil commotions, by a power and influence, which belonged to no other statesman of his age and times. And in our last internal discord, when this Union trembled to its center—in old age, he left the shades of private life and gave the death blow to fraternal strife, with the vigor of his earlier years in a series of Senatorial efforts, which in themselves would bring immortality, by challenging comparison with the efforts of any statesman in any age. He exorcised the demon which possessed the body politic, and gave peace to a distracted land. Alas! the achievement cost him his life! He sank day by day to the tomb—his pale, but noble brow, bound with a triple wreath, put there by a grateful country. May his ashes rest in peace, while his spirit goes to take its station among the great and good men who preceded him!"

While it is customary, and proper, upon occasions like the present, to give a brief sketch of the life of the deceased; in the case of Mr. Clay, it is less necessary than most others; for his biography has been written and re-written, and read, and re-read, for the last twenty-five years; so that, with the exception of a few of the latest incidents of his life, all is as well known, as it can be. The short sketch which I give is, therefore merely to maintain the connection of this discourse.

Henry Clay was born on the 12th of April 1777, in Hanover county, Virginia. Of his father, who died in the fourth or fifth year of Henry's age, little seems to be known, except that he was a respectable man, and a preacher of the baptist persuasion. Mr. Clay's education, to the end of his life, was comparatively limited. I say *"to the end of his life,"* because I have understood that, from time to time, he added something to his education during the greater part of his whole life. Mr. Clay's lack of a more perfect early education, however it may be regretted generally, teaches at least one profitable lesson; it teaches that in this country, one can scarcely be so poor, but that, if he *will*, he *can* acquire sufficient education to get through the world respectably. In his twenty-third year Mr. Clay was licenced to practice law, and emigrated to Lexington, Kentucky. Here he commenced and continued the practice till the year 1803, when he was first elected to the Kentucky Legislature. By successive elections he was continued in the Legislature till the latter part of 1806, when he was elected to fill a vacancy, of a single session, in the United States Senate. In 1807 he was again elected to the Kentucky House of Representatives, and by that body, chosen its speaker. In 1808 he was re-elected to the same body. In 1809 he was again chosen to fill a vacancy of two years in the United States Senate. In 1811 he was elected to the

United States House of Representatives, and on the first day of taking his seat in that body, he was chosen its speaker. In 1813 he was again elected Speaker. Early in 1814, being the period of our last British war, Mr. Clay was sent as commissioner, with others, to negotiate a treaty of peace, which treaty was concluded in the latter part of the same year. On his return from Europe he was again elected to the lower branch of Congress, and on taking his seat in December 1815 was called to his old post—the speaker's chair, a position in which he was retained, by successive elections, with one brief intermission, till the inauguration of John Q. Adams in March 1825. He was then appointed Secretary of State, and occupied that important station till the inauguration of Gen. Jackson in March 1829. After this he returned to Kentucky, resumed the practice of the law, and continued it till the Autumn of 1831, when he was by the Legislature of Kentucky, again placed in the United States Senate. By a re-election he was continued in the Senate till he resigned his seat, and retired, in March 1842. In December 1849 he again took his seat in the Senate, which he again resigned only a few months before his death.

By the foregoing it is perceived that the period from the beginning of Mr. Clay's official life, in 1803, to the end of it in 1852, is but one year short of half a century; and that the sum of all the intervals in it, will not amount to ten years. But mere duration of time in office, constitutes the smallest part of Mr. Clay's history. Throughout that long period, he has constantly been the most loved, and most implicitly followed by friends, and the most dreaded by opponents, of all living American politicians. In all the great questions which have agitated the country, and particularly in those great and fearful crises, the Missouri question—the Nullification question, and the late slavery question, as connected with the newly acquired territory, involving and endangering the stability of the Union, his has been the leading and most conspicuous part. In 1824 he was first a candidate for the Presidency, and was defeated; and, although he was successively defeated for the same office in 1832, and in 1844, there has never been a moment since 1824 till after 1848 when a very large portion of the American people did not cling to him with an enthusiastic hope and purpose of still elevating him to the Presidency. With other men, to be defeated, was to be forgotten; but to him, defeat was but a trifling incident, neither changing him, or the world's estimate of him. Even those of both political parties, who have been preferred to him for the highest office, have run far briefer courses than he, and left him, still shining, high in the heavens of the political world. Jackson, Van Buren, Harrison, Polk, and Taylor, all rose *after,* and set long before him. The spell—the long enduring spell—with which the souls of men were bound to him, is a miracle. Who can compass it? It is probably true he owed his pre-eminence to no one quality, but to a fortunate combination of several. He was surpassingly eloquent; but many eloquent men fail utterly; and they are not, as a class, generally successful. His judgment was excellent; but many men of good judgment, live and die unnoticed. His will was indomitable; but this quality often secures to its owner nothing better than a character for useless obstinacy. These then were Mr. Clay's leading qualities. No one of them is very uncommon; but all taken together are rarely combined in a single individual; and this is probably the reason why such men as Henry Clay are so rare in the world.

Mr. Clay's eloquence did not consist, as many fine specimens of eloquence does, of types and figures—of antithesis, and elegant arrangement of words and sentences; but rather of that deeply earnest and impassioned tone, and manner, which can proceed only from great sincerity and a thorough conviction, in the speaker of the justice and importance of his cause. This it is, that truly touches the chords of human sympathy; and those who heard Mr. Clay, never failed to be moved by it, or ever afterwards, forgot the impression. All his efforts were made for practical effect. He never spoke merely to be heard. He never delivered a Fourth of July Oration, or an eulogy on an occasion like this. As a politician or statesman, no one was so habitually careful to avoid all sectional ground. Whatever he did, he did for the whole country. In the construction of his measures he ever carefully surveyed every part of the field, and duly weighed every conflicting interest. Feeling, as he did, and as the truth surely is, that the world's best hope depended on the continued Union of these States, he was ever jealous of, and watchful for, whatever might have the slightest tendency to separate them.

Mr. Clay's predominant sentiment, from first to last, was a deep devotion to the cause of human liberty—a strong sympathy with the oppressed every where, and an ardent wish for their elevation. With him, this was a primary and all controlling passion. Subsidiary to this was the conduct of his whole life. He loved his country partly because it was his own country, but mostly because it was a free country; and he burned with a zeal for its advancement, prosperity and glory, because he saw in such, the advancement, prosperity and glory, of human liberty, human right and human nature. He desired the prosperity of his countrymen partly because they were his countrymen, but chiefly to show to the world that freemen could be prosperous.

That his views and measures were always the wisest, needs not to be affirmed; nor should it be, on this occasion, where so many, thinking differently, join in doing honor to his memory. A free people, in times of peace and quiet—when pressed by no common danger—naturally divide into parties. At such times, the man who is of neither party, is not—cannot be, of any consequence. Mr. Clay, therefore, was of a party. Taking a prominent part, as he did, in all the great political questions of his country for the last half century, the wisdom of his course on many, is doubted and denied by a large portion of his countrymen; and of such it is not now proper to speak particularly. But there are many others, about his course upon which, there is little or no disagreement amongst intelligent and patriotic Americans. Of these last are the War of 1812, the Missouri question, Nullification, and the now recent compromise measures. In 1812 Mr. Clay, though not unknown, was still a young man. Whether we should go to war with Great Britain, being the question of the day, a minority opposed the declaration of war by Congress, while the majority, though apparently inclining to war, had, for years, wavered, and hesitated to act decisively. Meanwhile British aggressions multiplied, and grew more daring and aggravated. By Mr. Clay, more than any other man, the struggle was brought to a decision in Congress. The question, being now fully before congress, came up, in a variety of ways, in rapid succession, on most of which occasions Mr. Clay spoke. Adding to all the logic, of which the subject was susceptible, that noble inspiration, which came to him as it came to no other, he aroused, and nerved, and inspired his friends, and confounded and bore-down all opposition. Several of his speeches, on these occasions, were reported, and are still extant; but the best of these all never was. During its delivery the reporters forgot their vocations, dropped their pens, and sat enchanted from near the beginning to quite the close. The speech now lives only in the memory of a few old men; and the enthusiasm with which they cherish their recollection of it is absolutely astonishing. The precise language of this speech we shall never know; but we do know—we cannot help knowing, that, with deep pathos, it pleaded the cause of the injured sailor—that it invoked the genius of the revolution—that it apostrophised the names of Otis, of Henry and of Washington—that it appealed to the interest, the pride, the honor and the glory of the nation—that it shamed and taunted the timidity of friends—that it scorned, and scouted, and withered the temerity of domestic foes—that it bearded and defied the British Lion—and rising, and swelling, and maddening in its course, it sounded the onset, till the charge, the shock, the steady struggle, and the glorious victory, all passed in vivid review before the entranced hearers.

Important and exciting as was the War question, of 1812, it never so alarmed the sagacious statesmen of the country for the safety of the republic, as afterwards did the Missouri question. This sprang from that unfortunate source of discord—negro slavery. When our Federal Constitution was adopted, we owned no territory beyond the limits or ownership of the states, except the territory

North-West of the River Ohio, and East of the Mississippi. What has since been formed into the States of Maine, Kentucky, and Tennessee, was, I believe, within the limits of or owned by Massachusetts, Virginia, and North Carolina. As to the North Western Territory, provision had been made, even before the adoption of the Constitution, that slavery should never go there. On the admission of the States into the Union carved from the territory we owned before the constitution, no question—or at most, no considerable question—arose about slavery— those which were within the limits of or owned by the old states, following, respectively, the condition of the parent state, and those within the North West territory, following the previously made provision. But in 1803 we purchased Louisiana of the French; and it included with much more, what has since been formed into the State of Missouri. With regard to it, nothing had been done to forestall the question of slavery. When, therefore, in 1819, Missouri, having formed a State constitution, without excluding slavery, and with slavery already actually existing within its limits, knocked at the door of the Union for admission, almost the entire representation of the non-slaveholding states, objected. A fearful and angry struggle instantly followed. This alarmed thinking men, more than any previous question, because, unlike all the former, it divided the country by geographical lines. Other questions had their opposing partizans in all localities of the country and in almost every family; so that no division of the Union could follow such, without a separation of friends, to quite as great an extent, as that of opponents. Not so with the Missouri question. On this a geographical line could be traced which, in the main, would separate opponents only. This was the danger. Mr. Jefferson, then in retirement wrote:

"I had for a long time ceased to read newspapers, or to pay any attention to public affairs, confident they were in good hands, and content to be a passenger in our bark to the shore from which I am not distant. But this momentous question, like a fire bell in the night, awakened, and filled me with terror. I considered it at once as the knell of the Union. It is hushed, indeed, for the moment. But this is a reprieve only, not a final sentence. A geographical line, co-inciding with a marked principle, moral and political, once conceived, and held up to the angry passions of men, will never be obliterated; and every irritation will mark it deeper and deeper. I can say, with conscious truth, that there is not a man on earth who would sacrifice more than I would to relieve us from this heavy reproach, in any *practicable* way. The cession of that kind of property, for so it is misnamed, is a bagatelle which would not cost me a second thought, if, in that way, a general emancipation, and *expatriation* could be effected; and, gradually, and with due sacrifices I think it might be. But as it is, we have the wolf by the ears and we can neither hold him, nor safely let him go. Justice is in one scale, and self-preservation in the other."

Mr. Clay was in congress, and, perceiving the danger, at once engaged his whole energies to avert it. It began, as I have said, in 1819; and it did not terminate till 1821. Missouri would not yield the point; and congress—that is, a majority in congress—by repeated votes, showed a determination to not admit the state unless it should yield. After several failures, and great labor on the part of Mr. Clay to so present the question that a majority could consent to the admission, it was, by a vote, rejected, and as all seemed to think, finally. A sullen gloom hung over the nation. All felt that the rejection of Missouri, was equivalent to a dissolution of the Union: because those states which already had, what Missouri was rejected for refusing to relinquish, would go with Missouri. All deprecated and deplored this, but none saw how to avert it. For the judgment of Members to be convinced of the necessity of yielding, was not the whole difficulty; each had a constituency to meet, and to answer to. Mr. Clay, though worn down, and exhausted, was appealed to by members, to renew his efforts at compromise. He did so, and by some judicious modifications of his plan, coupled with laborious efforts with individual members, and his own over-mastering eloquence upon the floor, he finally secured the admission of the State. Brightly, and captivating as it had previously shown, it was now perceived that his great eloquence, was a mere embellishment, or, at most, but a helping hand to his inventive genius, and his devotion to his country in the day of her extreme peril.

After the settlement of the Missouri question, although a portion of the American people have differed with Mr. Clay, and a majority even, appear generally to have been opposed to him on questions of ordinary administration, he seems constantly to have been regarded by all, as *the* man for a crisis. Accordingly, in the days of Nullification, and more recently in the re-appearance of the slavery question, connected with our territory newly acquired of Mexico, the task of devising a mode of adjustment, seems to have been cast upon Mr. Clay, by common consent—and his performance of the task, in each case, was little else than a literal fulfilment of the public expectation.

Mr. Clay's efforts in behalf of the South Americans, and afterwards, in behalf of the Greeks, in the times of their respective struggles for civil liberty are among the finest on record, upon the noblest of all themes; and bear ample corroboration of what I have said was his ruling passion—a love of liberty and right, unselfishly, and for their own sakes.

Having been led to allude to domestic slavery so frequently already, I am unwilling to close without referring more particularly to Mr. Clay's views and conduct in regard to it. He ever was, on principle and in feeling, opposed to slavery. The very earliest, and one of the latest public efforts of his life, separated by a period of more than fifty years, were both made in favor of gradual emancipation of the slaves in Kentucky. He did not perceive, that on a question of human right, the negroes were to be excepted from the human race. And yet Mr. Clay was the owner of slaves. Cast into life where slavery was already widely spread and deeply seated, he did not perceive, as I think no wise man has perceived, how it could be at *once* eradicated, without producing a greater evil, even to the cause of human liberty itself. His feeling and his judgment, therefore, ever led him to oppose both extremes of opinion on the subject. Those who would shiver into fragments the Union of these States; tear to tatters its now venerated constitution; and even burn the last copy of the Bible, rather than slavery should continue a single hour, together with all their more halting sympathisers, have received, and are receiving their just execration; and the name, and opinions, and influence of Mr. Clay, are fully, and, as I trust, effectually and enduringly, arrayed against them. But I would also, if I could, array his name, opinions, and influence against the opposite extreme—against a few, but an increasing number of men, who, for the sake of perpetuating slavery, are beginning to assail and to ridicule the white-man's charter of freedom—the declaration that "all men are created free and equal." So far as I have learned, the first American, of any note, to do or attempt this, was the late John C. Calhoun; and if I mistake not, it soon after found its way into some of the messages of the Governors of South Carolina. We, however, look for, and are not much shocked by, political eccentricities and heresies in South Carolina. But, only last year, I saw with astonishment, what purported to be a letter of a very distinguished and influential clergyman of Virginia, copied, with apparent approbation, into a St. Louis newspaper, containing the following, to me, very extraordinary language—

"I am fully aware that there is a text in some Bibles that is not in mine. Professional abolitionists have made more use of it, than of any passage in the Bible. It came, however, as I trace it, from Saint Voltaire, and was baptized by Thomas Jefferson, and since almost universally regarded as canonical authority *'All men are born free and equal.'*

"This is a genuine coin in the political currency of our generation. I am sorry to say that I have never seen two men of whom it is true. But I must admit I never saw the Siamese twins, and therefore will not dogmatically say that no man ever saw a proof of this sage aphorism."

This sounds strangely in republican America. The like was not heard in the fresher days of the Republic. Let us contrast with it the language of that truly national man, whose life and death we now commemorate and lament. I quote from a speech of Mr. Clay delivered before the American Colonization Society in 1827.

"We are reproached with doing mischief by the agitation of this question. The society goes into no household to disturb its domestic tranquility; it addresses itself to no slaves to weaken their obligations of obedience. It seeks to affect no man's property. It neither has the power nor the will to affect the property of any one contrary to his consent. The execution of its scheme would augment instead of diminishing the value of the property left behind. The society, composed of free men, concerns itself only with the free. Collateral consequences we are not responsible for. It is not this society which has produced the great moral revolution which the age exhibits. What would they, who thus reproach us, have done? If they would repress all tendencies towards liberty, and ultimate emancipation, they must do more than put down the benevolent efforts of this society. They must go back to the era of our liberty and independence, and muzzle the cannon which thunders its annual joyous return. They must renew the slave trade with all its train of atrocities. They must suppress the workings of British philanthropy, seeking to meliorate the condition of the unfortunate West Indian slave. They must arrest the career of South American deliverance from thraldom. They must blow out the moral lights around us, and extinguish that greatest torch of all which America presents to a benighted world—pointing the way to their rights, their liberties, and their happiness. And when they have achieved all those purposes their work will be yet incomplete. They must penetrate the human soul, and eradicate the light of reason, and the love of liberty. Then, and not till then, when universal darkness and despair prevail, can you perpetuate slavery, and repress all sympathy, and all humane, and benevolent efforts among free men, in behalf of the unhappy portion of our race doomed to bondage."

The American Colonization Society was organized in 1816. Mr. Clay, though not its projector, was one of its earliest members; and he died, as for the many preceding years he had been, its President. It was one of the most cherished objects of his direct care and consideration; and the association of his name with it has probably been its very greatest collateral support. He considered it no demerit in the society, that it tended to relieve slave-holders from the troublesome presence of the free negroes; but this was far from being its whole merit in his estimation. In the same speech from which I have quoted he says: "There is a moral fitness in the idea of returning to Africa her children, whose ancestors have been torn from her by the ruthless hand of fraud and violence. Transplanted in a foreign land, they will carry back to their native soil the rich fruits of religion, civilization, law and liberty. May it not be one of the great designs of the Ruler of the universe, (whose ways are often inscrutable by short-sighted mortals,) thus to transform an original crime, into a signal blessing to that most unfortunate portion of the globe?" This suggestion of the possible ultimate redemption of the African race and African continent, was made twenty-five years ago. Every succeeding year has added strength to the hope of its realization. May it indeed be realized! Pharaoh's country was cursed with plagues, and his hosts were drowned in the Red Sea for striving to retain a captive people who had already served them more than four hundred years. May like disasters never befall us! If as the friends of colonization hope, the present and coming generations of our countrymen shall by any means, succeed in freeing our land from the dangerous presence of slavery; and, at the same time, in restoring a captive people to their long-lost father-land, with bright prospects for the future; and this too, so gradually, that neither races nor individuals shall have suffered by the change, it will indeed be a glorious consummation. And if, to such a consummation, the efforts of Mr. Clay shall have contributed, it will be what he most ardently wished, and none of his labors will have been more valuable to his country and his kind.

But Henry Clay is dead. His long and eventful life is closed. Our country is prosperous and powerful; but could it have been quite all it has been, and is, and is to be, without Henry Clay? Such a man the times have demanded, and such, in the providence of God was given us. But he is gone. Let us strive to deserve, as far as mortals may, the continued care of Divine Providence, trusting that, in future national emergencies, He will not fail to provide us the instruments of safety and security.

*July 6, 1852*

# Address Before the Springfield Scott Club, in Reply to Judge Douglas's Richmond Speech

GENTLEMEN:

Unlike our young friend who has just taken his seat, I do not appear before you on a flattering invitation, or on any invitation at all; but, on the contrary I am about to address you, by your permission, given me at my own special request. Soon after the Democratic nomination for President and vice-President in June last at Baltimore, it was announced somewhat ostentatiously, as it seemed to me, that Judge Douglas would, previous to the election, make speeches in favor of those nominations, in twenty-eight of the thirty-one States. Since then, and as I suppose, in part performance of this undertaking, he has actually made one speech at Richmond, Virginia. This speech has been published, with high commendations, in at least one of the democratic papers in this state, and I suppose it has been, and will be, in most of the others. When I first saw it, and read it, I was reminded of old times—of the times when Judge Douglas was not so much greater man than all the rest of us, as he now is—of the Harrison campaign, twelve years ago, when I used to hear, and *try* to answer many of his speeches; and believing that the Richmond speech though marked with the same species of "shirks and quirks" as the old ones, was not marked with any greater ability, I was seized with a strong inclination to attempt an answer to it; and this inclination it was that prompted me to seek the privilege of addressing you on this occasion. In the speech, so far as I propose noticing it now, the Judge rebukes the whigs for calling Gen. Pierce "a fainting General;" eulogizes Gen. Scott's military character; denounces the whig platform, except as to the slavery question, which he says is a plank stolen from the democratic platform; charges that Gen. Scott's nomination was forced on the South by the North on a sectional issue; charges Gen. Scott with duplicity, and intent to deceive in his letter of acceptance; attempts to ridicule Gen. Scott's views on naturalization; charges that Gen. Scott, in his letter of acceptance, has pledged himself to proscription; denounces as dangerous the election of military men to the Presidency; says the hand of Providence saved us from our first and only military administration; speaks of Mr. Fillmore and his administration. In addition to these specific points, a constant repetition of something more than insinuations and yet something less than direct charges, that Gen. Scott is wholly under the control of Seward of New York; and that abolitionism is controlling the whole whig party, forms a sort of key-note to the whole speech. As a further characteristic of the speech, it may be noted that a very small portion of it is devoted to Pierce, and almost the whole of it to attacks upon Scott.

As I desire to say something on each of these matters, and as the evening is already partially spent, I propose going only about halfway through, reserving the remainder for a subsequent meeting. As to the Judge's rebuke of the whigs for calling Pierce "a fainting General," in which he insists that they mean to impute cowardice to Gen. Pierce, and that it is cowardly and false in them to cast such an imputation, I have only to say that, Gen. Pierce's history being as it is, the attempt to set him up as a great General, is simply ludicrous and laughable; and that the free merry people of the country have laughed at it, and will continue to laugh at it, in spite of the querulous scolding of Judge Douglas or of anybody else; and further, that if the Judge has any real honest indignation against unjust imputations of cowardice, he will find a much ampler field for the indulgence of it against his own friends, who are everywhere seeking by reference to an old affair with Gen. Jackson, to throw such an imputation upon Gen. Scott.

As to the Judge's eulogy on Gen. Scott's military character, in which he says "I will not depreciate his merits as a soldier, because truth and honor forbid it," I have but to remark that whoever will read the speech through and carefully note the imputations implying ignorance and stupidity, and duplicity and knavery, against Gen. Scott in almost every paragraph, will I think, conclude that the eulogy on his military character, was dictated quite as much by the Judge's view of the party impolicy of assailing that character, as by a love of truth and honor.

In denouncing the whig platform generally, the Judge gives no reason other than that it is "a whig concern" and that all democrats are presumed to be opposed to it. This needs no answer other than that for the same reason all whigs are presumed to be in favor of it. But as to the slavery question, the Judge says it was a plank stolen from the democratic platform. On what authority does he make this declaration? Upon what fact, or what reasoning from facts does he base it? I had understood and now understand, as the indelibly written history of the country, that the compromise measures were not party measures—that for praise or blame, they belonged to neither party to the exclusion of the other; but that the chief leaders in their origin and adoption were whigs and not democrats. I had thought that the pen of history had written, acknowledged, and recorded it as facts, that Henry Clay, more than any other man, or perhaps more than any other ten men, was the originator of that system of measures; and that he together with Webster and Pearce of Maryland, (not Gen. Pierce,) were its most efficient supporters in its progress. I knew, or supposed I knew, that democrats, numerous and distinguished, gave it able and efficient support; and I have not sought, or known of any whig seeking to deprive them of the credit of it. Among these last Judge Douglas himself was not the least. After the close of the session of Congress at which these measures were passed, Judge Douglas visited Chicago, in this State, and the measures, if not the Judge himself, were there clamorously assailed. He succeeded in getting a hearing at a public meeting, and made a speech which silenced his adversaries, and gave him a triumph most complete. It was afterwards written out and published. I saw a copy, and read it once hastily, and glanced over it a second time. I do not now remember seeing anything in it to condemn, and I do remember that I considered it a very able production—by far superior to any thing I had ever seen from Judge Douglas, and comparing favorably with any thing from any source, which I had seen, on that general subject. The reading of it afforded me a good deal of pleasure; and I never said, or inclined to say any thing in disparagement of it. But as the Judge, in his Richmond speech, has thought fit to speak so confidently, and, in my judgment so unjustly, of stealing, I will venture to suggest that if he had stolen none of the ideas of Henry Clay and Daniel Webster, and other whigs, which he had been listening to for the last preceding six or eight months, he might not have been able to get up quite so creditable a speech at Chicago as he did.

But the Judge asserts in substance, that the nomination of Scott was forced on the south by the north, on a sectional issue; and he argues that such a nomination is exceedingly perilous to the safety of the Union. As evidence that the nomination was forced on the south by the north, the Judge says, "every southern delegation voted against him more than fifty times, day after day, and night after night." This is not quite correct, for one, two, or more of the Virginia delegation voted for Scott every ballot after the first; but call it substantially correct to say that the Southern delegations did not vote for Scott, does it follow, in the sense the Judge would have us to understand, that they voted *against* Scott? If so, then, by the same rule, in the democratic Convention, every delegation north and south, voted against Gen. Pierce thirty-four times.

Now, according to the Judge's logic, the nomination of Pierce was *forced* on the whole country by some mysterious and invisible agency, "a defiance of the thirty-four times repeated protest and remonstrance of the delegates from ALL the States of the Union represented in the Convention." Still the Judge thinks the nomination of Scott, made in compliance with the original preference of nearly half the whig convention, is extremely perilous to the safety of the Union; but that the nomination of Pierce, made contrary to the original preference of every man in the democratic Convention (and every man out of it, I presume) is to be the very salvation of the Union!!! It may be said that although every member of the democratic convention preferred some other man, finally they all honorably surrendered their preferences and united on Pierce. Very well, if the whole democratic convention could honorably, and without being forced, go over to Pierce, why could not HALF the whig convention, as honorably and as free from force, go over to Scott?

But, according to the Judge's view, Scott's nomination was not only forced upon the south, but was forced upon it, *on a sectional issue.* Now, in point of fact, at the time the nomination was made, there was no issue, except as to who should be the *men* to lead the campaign upon a set of principles previously put in writing and acquiesced in by the whole convention; and those principles, too, being precisely such as the south demanded. When the platform, which I understand to be just such as the south desired, was voted upon by the convention—the whole south, and more than half the north voted for, and adopted it, by a vote of 226 to 66; those who voted against it made no further opposition to it. On the adoption of the platform arose the only sectional issue which came before the convention, and by the vote it passed from an issue into a decision, and left no issue before the convention, except as to men. It is proper to notice too, that on the first ballot for a candidate for the presidency, Scott's vote only lacked one of doubling the numbers of all the votes cast against the platform; so that of Scott's original friends in the convention, more than half *may* have been, and within one of half *must* have been original platform men. If Scott should throw himself into the hands exclusively of those who originally preferred him, to be controlled by the majority of them, in utter disregard of all those who originally preferred others, it is still probable that the majority would lead him to adopt the platform or union view of the slavery question.

But the gist of all the Judge's views is, that Scott's nomination, made as it was, is more perilous to the safety of the Union, than all the scenes through which we have recently passed in connection with the slavery question. Well, we ought all to be startled at the view of "peril to the Union," but it may be a little difficult for some shortsighted mortals to perceive such peril in the *nomination of* Scott. Mark you, it is the *nomination* and not the *election,* which produces the peril. The Judge does not say the election, and he cannot mean the election, because he constantly assures us there is no prospect of Scott's election. He could not be so alarmed at what he is so sure will never happen. In plain truth I suppose he did mean the election, so far as he meant anything; but feeling that his whole proposition was mere nonsense, he did not think of it distinctly enough to enable him to speak with any precision.

As one point in support of his charge of duplicity against Gen. Scott, Judge Douglas attempts to show that Gen. Scott in his letter of acceptance, framed language studiously for the purpose of enabling men north and south to read it one way or the other, as the public pulse should beat in their particular localities, and he insists that the language so designed will be so used. He quotes Scott's language as follows, "I accept the nomination, with the resolutions annexed," and then he criticises it as follows: "Now gentlemen I desire to know what is the meaning of the words 'with the resolutions annexed.' Does he mean that he approves the resolutions? If so, why did he not say so, as the candidate for the Vice Presidency, Mr. Graham, did in his letter of acceptance? Or why did he not do as that gallant and honest man, Frank Pierce did, and say, 'I accept the nomination upon the platform adopted by the convention, not because this is expected of me as a candidate, but because the principles *it* embraces command the approbation of my judgement.'

"There you have (continues the Judge) an honest man speaking from an honest heart, without any equivocation, dissimulation, or mental reservation. Here you find that Gen. Scott accepts the nomination with the resolution annexed— that is to say, using language susceptible of two constructions—one at the North, and another at the South. In the North it will be said he accepts the nomination notwithstanding the platform; that he accepts it although he defies the platform; that he accepts it although he spits upon the platform. At the South it will be said he accepts it with the approval of the platform. I submit the question to you whether that language was not framed studiously for the purpose of enabling men, North and South to read it one way or the other as the public pulse should beat in their particular localities. Again, I submit to you, was it the General-in-chief of the armies who fought the battles in Mexico, that conceived this part of the letter, or was it his commander-in-chief, Gen. Seward, who dictated it?" [Great applause.]

What wonderful acumen the Judge displays on the construction of language!!! According to this criticism of his, the word "with" is equivalent to the word "notwithstanding," and also to the phrases, "although I defy," and "although I spit upon." Verily these are wonderful substitutes for the word "with." When the builders of the tower of Babel got into difficulty about language, if they had just called on Judge Douglas, he would, at once, have construed away the difficulty, and enabled them to finish the structure, upon the truly democratic platform on which they were building. Suppose, gentlemen, you were to amuse yourselves some leisure hour, by selecting sentences, from well known compositions, each containing the word "with" and by striking it out, and inserting alternately, the Judge's substitutes, and then testing whether the sense is changed.

As an example, take a sentence from an old and well known book, not much suspected for duplicity, or equivocal language; which sentence is as follows:

"And Enoch walked *with* God; and he was not, for God took him."

Try, for yourselves, how Judge Douglas' substitutes for the word "with" will affect this sentence. Let Judge Douglas be brought to understand that he can advance the interest of a locofoco candidate for the presidency by criticising this sentence; and forthwith he will hie away to the African church in Richmond, Virginia, and make a great speech, in which he will find great difficulty in understanding the meaning of the words "walked with God." He will contrast it, greatly to its disadvantage, with the language of that *gallant* and *honest* man, Frank Pierce! He will show that it is, and was designed to be, susceptible of two constructions, one at the North, and another at the South; that at the North the word "with" will be read "NOTWITHSTANDING," "ALTHOUGH HE DEFIES," "ALTHOUGH HE SPITS UPON;" and finally he will thrill, and electrify, and throw into spasms of ecstasy his African church auditors by suggesting that such monstrous duplicity could not have been conceived by Enoch or Moses, but must have been dictated by Gen. Seward!!!

As another example, take from Judge Douglas' ratification speech a sentence in relation to the democratic platform and the democratic ticket, Pierce and King, which is as follows:

"With such a platform, and with such a ticket, a glorious victory awaits us."

Now according to the Judge's rule of criticising Gen. Scott's language, the above sentence of his will, without perversion of meaning admit of being read in each of the following ways:

"NOTWITHSTANDING such a platform, and notwithstanding such a ticket, a glorious victory awaits us."

"ALTHOUGH WE DEFY such a platform, and although we defy such a ticket, a glorious victory awaits us."

"ALTHOUGH WE SPIT UPON such a platform, and although we spit upon such a ticket, a glorious victory awaits us."

Similar examples might be found without end; but the foregoing are enough, if indeed anything was wanting to show the utter absurdity of the Judge's criticism. Can any two fair minded men differ about the meaning of this part of Gen. Scott's letter? Do his friends, north and south, read it differently, as Judge Douglas asserts they will? Nothing is too absurd for the malice of his fault finding enemies; but where among his millions of friends can a single one be found who is supporting him because he understands him to defy, and spit upon the Whig platform?

Judge Douglas also perceives the same duplicity in Gen. Scott's language about the Public Lands, and about Naturalization; but his criticisms upon it, are so similar to that which I have already reviewed, that I am willing to trust my review of the one, to stand as answer to the whole.

But, in addition to the charge of duplicity, the Judge also seizes upon what Gen. Scott says about naturalization, on which to base a charge of ignorance and stupidity against Gen. Scott. Scott, in his letter of acceptance, suggests the propriety of so altering the naturalization laws as to admit to the rights of citizenship, such foreigners as may serve one year in time of war, in the land or naval service of the United States. The Judge insists that it is uncertain whether the General means this to be an *addition* to the present laws on the subject, or *a substitute* for them; but by a few brief dashes, he argues himself into the belief that the General means his proposition to be a substitute—to embrace the *only* law on naturalization; and then the Judge bewails the supposed condition of things, when the numbers of the army and navy must either be swelled to a million, or the bulk of the foreigners must remain unnaturalized, and without rights of citizenship among us. He admits the General does not say that he intends his proposition to embrace the only law; but inasmuch as he does not say the contrary, he must so mean it, because, the Judge argues, to maintain the present laws, and such as Scott proposes, *together,* would be unconstitutional. He quotes from the constitution, and shows that there can be but *one* uniform rule of naturalization; and swelling with indignation, he grows severe on Gen. Scott, and asks, "Is it possible that this candidate for the presidency never read the constitution?" He insists that to add Scott's proposition to the present laws, would establish *two* rules because it would admit one person on one set of reasons and another person on another; and hence the unconstitutionality. Now it so happens that the first Congress which ever sat under the constitution, composed in a great part of the same men who made the constitution, passed a naturalization law, in which it was provided that adult aliens should come in on one set of reasons; that their minor children should come in on another set; and that such particular foreigners as had been proscribed by any State, should come in, if at all, on still another set. Will Judge Douglas sneeringly ask if the framers of *this law* never read the Constitution? Since the passage of the first law, there have been some half a dozen acts modifying, adding to, and substituting, the preceding acts; and there has never been a moment from that day to this, when, by the existing system, different persons might not have become naturalized on different sets of reasons.

Would it be discourteous to Judge Douglas to retort his question upon him, and ask, "Is it possible that this candidate for a nomination to the Presidency never read the naturalization laws?" Cases under these laws, have frequently arisen in the courts, and some of them have gone to and passed through, the Supreme Court of the United States. Certainly in some, probably in every one of these cases, one of the parties could have gained his suit by establishing that the laws were unconstitutional; and yet I believe Judge Douglas is the first man who has been found wise enough or enough otherwise, as the case may be, to even suggest their unconstitutionality.

Even those adopted citizens, whose votes have given Judge Douglas all his consequence, came in under these very laws. Would not the Judge have considered the holding those laws unconstitutional, and those particular votes illegal, as more deplorable, than even an army and navy, a million strong?

If the Judge finds no cause to regret this part of his assault, upon the General, I certainly think that the General needs not.

> The man recovered of the bite,
> The dog it was that died.

[The Club adjourned to Wednesday evening August 26, on which evening the Speech was concluded as follows:]

When I spoke on a previous evening, I was not aware of what I have since learned, that Mr. Edwards, in his address to you, had, to some extent, reviewed Judge Douglas' Richmond speech. Had I known this, I probably should have abstained from selecting it as the subject of my remarks; because I dislike the appearance of unfairness of two attacking one. After all, however, as the Judge is a giant, and Edwards and I are but common mortals, it may not be very unfair. And then it is to be considered too, that in attempting to answer the Judge, we do not assail him personally; but we are only trying to meet his mode of conducting the assault which the whole party are making upon Gen. Scott.

Taking up the Richmond speech at the point where I left it, the next charge is that Gen. Scott has pledged himself to a course of proscription. This charge the Judge makes in the following language—

"Gen. Scott, in his letter of acceptance,—in cunning and adroit language— solemnly pledges himself that no democrat shall ever hold office under his administration; but that abolition whigs may do so without the slightest hindrance."

Upon this the Judge indulges himself in a long comment, in the course of which he falls into a strain of wailing pathos which Jeremiah in his last days might envy, for the old soldier democrats to be turned out of office by Gen. Scott. And finally he winds up with the use of Clayton's name in such connection, as to insinuate that he, as Secretary of State under Gen. Taylor, had been exceedingly proscriptive.

In the first place, I think it will be in vain, any fair minded man will search for any such solemn pledge in the letter of acceptance, as Judge Douglas attributes to it. Indeed, the Judge himself seems to have thought it would not be quite safe to his reputation to leave his allegation without furnishing it the means of escape from a charge which might be brought against it; for he immediately adds, "This is my translation of that part of his letter." He then quotes from the letter, as follows—

"In regard to the general policy of the administration, if elected I should, of course, look among those who may approve that policy for the agents to carry it into execution; and I should seek to cultivate harmony and fraternal sentiments throughout the whig party, without attempting to reduce its members by proscription to exact conformity to my own views."

Now it appears to me the Judge's translation of this may be called a very *free* translation—a translation enjoying a perfect freedom from all the restraint of justice and fair dealing. So far from having solemnly pledged himself that no democrat should ever hold office, the evident sense of the sentence shows that he was not speaking or thinking of the democrats at all—that he was merely giving an assurance that difference of opinion among whigs should not be regarded, except in the higher offices through which the general policy of the administration is to be conducted.

But suppose the translation is correct, I still should like to hear from the Judge where are the democratic office holders who are to be made to "walk the plank" by Gen. Scott, after having told us in this very speech that the Taylor and Fillmore administrations have proscribed nearly every democrat in office. The Judge's pathos on this subject reminds me of a little rumor I heard at Washington about the time of Gen. Taylor's inauguration. The Senate was democratic and could reject all the nominations. The rumor was that the democratic clerks from Illinois, appealed to our democratic delegation to save them their places if possible; but that the delegation told them no; "we prefer your heads should fall; the sight of your blood will aid us to regain our lost power." Judge Douglas was then at the head of our delegation, and will know better than I whether the rumor was true.

A word now about Clayton, and his proscriptive disposition and practices, as insinuated by Judge Douglas. It is matter of public history, that on Saturday night before Taylor was inaugurated Monday, Mr. Polk nominated Edward Hannegan, a democrat, as minister to Prussia, and that the Senate confirmed the nomination; and that Clayton, a few days after becoming Secretary of State, to which department such appointments belong, allowed him to go, and receive the outfit and salary of $18,000. This is public history, about which there is no disputing. But the more private history, as I have heard and believe it, and as I believe Judge Douglas, knows it, is still more favorable to Clayton's character for generosity. It is that Mr.

Clayton induced Mr. Polk to make the appointment, by an assurance that the new administration would not revoke it. Hannegan had been a Senator from Indiana six years, and, in that time, had done his state some credit, and gained some reputation for himself; but in the end, was undermined and superseded by a man who will never do either. He was the son of an Irishman, with a bit of the brogue still lingering on his tongue; and with a very large share of that sprightliness and generous feeling, which generally characterize Irishmen who have had anything of a fair chance in the world. He was personally a great favorite with Senators, and particularly so with Mr. Clayton, although of opposite politics. He was now broken down politically and pecuniarily; and Mr. Clayton, disregarding the ties of party came to his relief. With a knowledge of the exact truth on this subject, how could Judge Douglas find it in his heart to so try to prejudice the nation against John M. Clayton? Poor Hannegan! Since his return, in a heated, and unguarded moment, he spilled the life of a favorite brother-in-law, and for which he is now enduring the tortures of deepest mental agony; yet I greatly mistake his nature, if, ever to be released from his extreme misery, he could be induced to assail John M. Clayton, as one wanting in liberality and generosity.

Next Judge Douglas runs a tilt at Gen. Scott as a military politician, commencing with the interrogatory "Why has the whig party forgotten with an oblivion so complete all that it once said about military politicians?" I retort the question, and ask, why has the *democratic* party forgotten with an oblivion so complete all that it once said about military politicians?

But the Judge proceeds to contrast Scott with General Pierce and with all our General presidents, except Taylor; and he succeeds in showing that Scott differs from them, in having held a military commission longer than any of them; in holding such a commission when nominated for the presidency, in not having been a physician or farmer and in not having held civil office. He does not stop to point *how* any of these differences is material to the question of his qualification for the presidency; but he seems to assume that disqualification must necessarily follow from these facts. Let us not adopt this conclusion too hastily. Let us examine the premises. He has held a military commission a long time—over forty years. If you assert that this has bred in him a thirst for war, and a distaste for peace, "the known incidents of a long public life" abundantly prove the contrary. Among them are his successful efforts for peace and against war in the South Carolina Nullification question, on the burning of the Caroline, and on the Maine boundary question. The mere fact that he held a military commission when he was nominated, I presume no one will seriously contend proves anything to the point. Nor is it perceived how the being a physician or farmer, should qualify a man for office. Whatever of sound views of government is acquired by the physician and farmer, is acquired not in their regular occupations, but by reading and reflection in the hours of relaxation from their regular occupations. It is probable that the leisure time for such reading and reflection would, in time of peace, be quite as abundant with an officer of the army, as with a physician or farmer.

But Gen. Scott has not held civil office, and General Pierce has; and this is the great point. Well, let us examine this too. Gen. Pierce has been in the State Legislature and in congress; and I misread his history if it does not show him to have had just sufficient capacity, and no more, of setting his foot down in the track, as his partizan leader lifted his out of it—and so trudging along in the party team without a single original tho't or independent action. Scott, on the contrary, has on many occasions, been placed in the lead, when originality of thought and independence of action, both of the highest order, have been indispensable to success; and yet he failed in none. What he has performed in these stations bears much stronger resemblance to the duties he would have to perform as president, than any thing Gen. Pierce has ever done. Indeed they were literally, in every instance, executive duties—functions delegated to Gen. Scott by the president, because the president could not perform them in person. Is it not great folly to suppose that the manner of performing them is any less a test of his capacity for civil administration than it would be if he had held a civil office at the time? They say we rely solely on Gen. Scott's military reputation. Throw it aside then. In comparing the candidates let no consideration be given to military reputations. Let it be alike forgotten that Gen. Pierce ever fainted, or that Gen. Scott ever made a "fuss" or wore a "feather." Let them be placed in the scales solely on what they have done, giving evidence of capacity for civil administration; and let him kick the beam who is found lightest.

But, we cannot help observing the fact, that the democrats, with all their present horror of military candidates, have themselves put a general on the track. Why is this? It must have been by *accident* or by *design*; and it could not have been by accident, because I understand the party has become very philosophical, and it would be very unphilosophical to do such a thing by *accident*. It was by design, then. Let us try to trace it. They made their nomination before we made ours; but they knew we *ought,* and therefore concluded we *would,* not nominate Gen. Scott, and they shaped their course accordingly. They said "confound these old generals, is there no way of beating them? In 1840 we thought it would be mere sport to beat Harrison. We charged that his friends kept him in a cage; that he was an abolitionist, so far as he had sense enough to be anything; and we called him a petticoat general, and an old granny; but the election showed we had not hit upon the true philosophy. Again when Taylor was put up, we did not venture to call him an old granny, but we insisted he was not a whig; and, to help along, we put up a general against him, relying on our accustomed confidence in the capacity of the people to *not see* the difference between one who *is* a general, and one who is *called* a general, but we failed again. History is philosophy teaching by example, and if we regard the examples it has given us, we must try something new, before we can succeed in beating a general for the presidency."

Accordingly they nominated Pierce. It soon came to light that the first thing ever urged in his favor as a candidate was his having given a strange boy a cent to buy candy with. An examination of the official reports of his doings as a general in Mexico, showed him to have been the victim of a most extraordinary scene of mishap, which though it might by possibility have so happened with a brave and skillful general, left no considerable evidence that he was such. Forthwith also appears a biographical sketch of him, in which he is represented, at the age of seventeen, to have spelled "but" for his father, who was unable to spell it for himself. By the way I *do* wish Frank had not been present on that trying occasion. I have a great curiosity to know how "old dad" would have spelled that difficult word, if he had been left entirely to himself. But the biography also represents him as cutting at the enemy's flying cannon balls with his sword in the battles of Mexico, and calling out, "Boys there's a game of ball for you;" and finally that he added enough to a balance due him to raise the whole to three hundred dollars, and treated his men.

When I first saw these things I suspected they had been put forward by mischievous whigs; but very soon I saw the biography published at length in a veritable democratic paper, conducted by a man whose party fidelity and intelligent co-operation with his party, I know to be beyond suspicion. Then I was puzzled. But now we have a letter from Gen. Shields, in which, speaking of Pierce and himself, he says, "As we approached the enemy's position, directly under his fire, we encountered a deep ditch, or rather a deep narrow, slimy canal, which had been previously used for the purpose of irrigation. It was no time to hesitate, so we both plunged in. The horse I happened to ride that day was a light active Mexican horse. This circumstance operated in my favor, and enabled me to extricate myself and horse after considerable difficulty. Pierce, on the contrary, was mounted on a large, heavy American horse, and man and horse both sank down and rolled over in the ditch. There I was compelled to leave him . . . After struggling there, I cannot say how long, he extricated himself from his horse, and hurried on foot to join his command, &c."

Now, what right had a brigadier general, when approaching the enemy's position, and directly under his fire, to sink down and roll over in a deep slimy canal and struggle there before he got out, how long, another brigadier general cannot tell, when the whole of both their brigades got across that same "slimy canal," without any difficulty worth mentioning? I say, Judge Douglas, "Is *this* manoeuvre sanctioned by Scott's Infantry Tactics as adopted in the army?" This ludicrous scene in Gen. Pierce's career had not been told of before; and the telling of it by Gen. Shields, looks very much like a pertinacious purpose to "pile up" the ridiculous. This explains the new plan or system of tactics adopted by the democracy. It is to ridicule and burlesque the whole military character out of credit; and this to kill Gen. Scott with vexation. Being philosophical and literary men, they have read, and remembered, how the institution of chivalry was ridiculed out of existence by its fictitious votary Don Quixote. They also remember how our own "militia trainings" have been "laughed to death" by fantastic parades and caricatures upon them. We remember one of these parades ourselves here, at the head of which, on horse-back, figured our old friend Gordon Abrams, with a pine wood sword, about nine feet long, and a paste-board cocked hat, from front to rear about the length of an ox yoke, and very much the shape of one turned bottom upwards; and with spurs having rowels as large as the bottom of a teacup, and shanks a foot and a half long. That was the last militia muster here. Among the rules and regulations, no man is to wear more than five pounds of cod-fish for epaulets, or more than thirty yards of bologna sausages for a sash; and no two men are to dress alike, and if any two should dress alike the one that dresses most alike is to be fined, (I forget how much). Flags they had too, with devices and mottoes, one of which latter is, "We'll fight till we run, and we'll run till we die."

Now, in the language of Judge Douglas, "I submit to you gentlemen," whether there is not great cause to fear that on some occasion when Gen. Scott suspects no danger, suddenly Gen. Pierce will be discovered charging upon him, holding a huge roll of candy in one hand for a spy-glass; with B U T labelled on some appropriate part of his person; with Abrams' long pine sword cutting in the air at imaginary cannon balls, and calling out "boys there's a game of ball for you," and over all streaming the flag, with the motto, "We'll fight till we faint, and I'll treat when it's over."

It is calculated that such opposition will take "Old Fuss and Feathers" by surprise. He has thought of, and prepared himself for, all the ordinary modes of assault—for over-reachings, and underminings; for fires in front and fires in the rear; but I guess this would be a fire on the "blind side"—totally unlooked for by him. Unless the opposition should, once more sink down, and roll over, in that deep slimy canal, I cannot conceive what is to save Gen. Scott.

But Judge Douglas alluding to the death of General Taylor says it was the hand of Providence which saved us from our first and only military administration. This reminds me of Judge Douglas' so much wanted confidence in the people. The people had elected Gen. Taylor; and, as is appointed to all men once to do, he died. Douglas chooses to consider this a special interference of Providence, against the people, and in favor of Locofocoism. After all, his confidence in the people seems to go no farther than this, that they may be safely trusted with their own affairs, provided Providence retains, and exercises a sort of veto upon their acts, whenever they fall into the "marvelous hallucination," as the Judge calls it, of electing some one to office contrary to the dictation of a democratic convention. The people have fallen into this hallucination in two of the presidential elections of the four since the retirement of Gen. Jackson. The present struggle is for the best three in five. Let us stand by our candidate as faithfully as he has always stood by our country, and I much doubt if we do not perceive a slight abatement in Judge Douglas' confidence in Providence, as well as in the people. I suspect that confidence is not more firmly fixed with the Judge than it was with the old woman, whose horse ran away with her in a buggy. She said she trusted in Providence till the britchen broke; and then she didn't know what on airth *to* do. The chance is the Judge will see the breechen break, and then he can at his leisure, bewail the fate of locofocoism, as the victim of misplaced confidence.

Speaking of Mr. Fillmore, the Judge calls him, "a man who, previous to that time (his accession to the presidency) had never furnished such proofs of superiority of statesmanship as to cause him to be looked to as a candidate for the first office." O ho! Judge; it is you, is it, that thinks a man should furnish *proof of superiority of statesmanship*, before he is looked to as a candidate for the first office? Do please show us those proofs in the case of your "gallant and honest man, Frank Pierce." Do please name a single one that you consider such. What good thing, or even *part* of good thing has the country ever enjoyed, which originated with him? What evil thing has ever been averted by him? Compare his proofs of statesmanship with those of Mr. Fillmore, up to the times respectively when their names were first connected with presidential elections. Mr. Fillmore, if I remember rightly, had not been in Congress so long as Mr. or Gen. Pierce; yet he did acquire the distinction of being placed at the head of one of the most important Committees; and as its Chairman, was the principal member of the H.R. in manturing the tariff of 1842. On the other hand, Gen. Pierce was in Congress six whole years, without being the chairman of any committee at all; and it was at the beginning of his seventh year when he was first placed at the head of one; and then it was a comparatively unimportant one. To show by comparison, to the people of Illinois, the estimate in which Mr. Pierce was held, let me mention, that Douglas and McClernand were each, placed at the head of an important committee, at the commencement of their second term; while it was not till the commencement of Pierce's fourth term, or rather of the fourth congress of which he had been a member, that he was admitted to the head of a less important one. I have no doubt that Col. McClernand is as much the superior of Pierce as this difference in the estimation in which they were held in Congress, would indicate. I have glanced over the Journals a little to ascertain if I could, what it is, or was, that Gen. Pierce had originated; and the most noted of any thing I could see, was a proposition to plead the Statute of Limitations against certain Revolutionary claims; and even this I believe he did not succeed in having adopted. There is one good democrat in our town who I apprehend would turn against Pierce if he only knew of this; for I have several times heard him insist that there is nothing but unmitigated rascality in Statutes of Limitation.

Judge Douglas says Mr. Fillmore, as president, "did no harm to the country," and he says this in such connection as to show that he regards it a disparagement to an administration to be able to say no more for it, than that it "did no harm to the country." And please Judge, is not an administration that "does no harm," the very *beau ideal* of a democratic administration? Is not the very idea of *beneficence,* unjust, inexpedient, and unconstitutional, in your view? Take the present democratic platform, and it does not propose to do a single thing. It is full of declarations as to what ought *not* to be done, but names no one to be done. If there is in it, even an inference in favor of any positive action by the democracy, should they again get into power, it only extends to the collecting a sufficient revenue to pay their own salaries, including perhaps, constructive mileage to Senators. Propose a course of policy that shall ultimately supplant the monstrous folly of bringing untold millions of iron, thousands of miles across water and land, which our own hills and mountains are groaning with the best quality in the world, and in quantity sufficient for ten such worlds, and the cry instantly is "no." Propose to remove a snag, a rock, or a sand-bar from a lake or river, and the cry still is "no."

I have seen in a dirty little democratic issue, called "papers for the people," what is there called a "democratic Battle Hymn." The first stanza of the delectable production runs as follows:

> Sturdy and strong, we march along,
>     Millions on millions of freemen bold;
> Raising the dead, with our iron tread—
>     The noble dead, of the days of old!

Now I do not wish to disturb the poet's delicious reverie, but I will thank him to inform me, at his earliest convenience, whether among the "noble dead" he saw "stirred up" there were any from the hulls of flats and keels, and brigs, and steam boats, which had gone to the bottom on questions of constitutionality?

After speaking rather kindly of Mr. Fillmore, the Judge proceeds to find fault with "certain features" of his administration, for which, he says, the Whig party is responsible, even more than Mr. Fillmore. This is palpably absurd. The Whigs hold no department of the government but the executive, and that is in the hands of Mr. Fillmore. What can they be responsible for which he is not? What led the Judge to make this absurd declaration is equally plain. He knew the Whigs of Virginia were partial to Mr. Fillmore, and he supposed to hold him up as a good man sacrificed, might excite his friends against Scott; but suddenly it occurs to him it will not do to leave the thing in such shape, as that the Whig party may claim it as an indorsement, to any extent, of a Whig administration. It was with some regret, that the Judge could do no more for lack of time than merely glance at these "certain features." He had before, in his ratification speech at Washington, glanced at the same features, not having sufficient *time* to consider them at length. It is to be hoped that in some one of the twenty-seven speeches yet to come, he will find *time* to be a little more specific.

One of these "certain features" is that the proper satisfaction was not insisted upon, for the shooting of the Americans in Cuba last year. He says that, whether they were right or wrong, they were, by a treaty stipulation, entitled to a trial, which was not given them. Now whether there is a treaty stipulation that American citizens shall not be punished in the Spanish dominions, without a fair trial, I know not; but it strikes me as most remarkable that there should be. Without any express treaty stipulation, it would seem to me to be a plain principle of public law. The question is, did the principle apply to these fifty men? Were they "American citizens" in the sense of that principle? The position they had assumed was, that they were oppressed Spanish subjects, and as such, had a right to revolutionize the Spanish government in Cuba. They had renounced our authority and our protection; and we had no more legal right to demand satisfaction for their treatment, than if they had been native born Cubans. Their butchery was, as it seemed to me, most unnecessary, and inhuman. They were fighting against one of the worst governments in the world; but their fault was, that the real people of Cuba had not asked for their assistance; were neither desirous of, nor fit for civil liberty.

But suppose I am mistaken, and that satisfaction should have been demanded of Spain for the shooting of the fifty in Cuba. What should have been the nature of the satisfaction? Not pecuniary certainly? A disavowal of the act by the government, with the punishment of perpetrators? The very nature of the case made this impossible. The satisfaction, if sought at all, must have been sought in war. If

Judge Douglas thought it cause for war, upon him rests the responsibility of not bringing a proposition before the Senate to declare war. I suppose he knows that under the constitution, Congress, and not the president, declares war. Does not his omission to move in the matter, in Congress, coupled with his greediness to agitate it before ratification meetings, and African church audiences, prove that he feels much greater concern for a presidential election, than he does to vindicate the honor of the nation, or to avenge the blood of its citizens?

The extravagant expenditures of the present administration is another of the Judge's "certain features." On this subject his language is very general, for want of *time* no doubt. At the "ratification" he says, "You find the expenditures nearly doubled, running up to about sixty millions of dollars a year, in times of profound peace." At Richmond he says, "I should like to know why a whig administration costs more in a profound peace than a democratic administration does during a great war." I have not had the opportunity to investigate this subject as I would like to do before undertaking to speak upon it; but I have learned enough to feel confident that the expenditures (of 1850-51 for instance) have not, by any plausible mode of estimating them, amounted to sixty millions, or to more than the expenditures of a "democratic administration in a great war," by at least ten millions of dollars.

I take the following from a paper which, is not often misled, and never intentionally misleads others—the National Intelligencer:—

"In the discussions which have taken place, in the newspaper and elsewhere, on the financial question, an attempt has been made to hold the present administration responsible for an alleged large *increase* of the expenditures of the Government. With the growth of the Government, and the additional cost of governing newly acquired and distant territories, it could not well be otherwise than that the expenses of the Government must be somewhat increased, but not to anything like the amount at which it has been stated; as, for example in the 'Union' of a few days ago, in which the expenditures of Government were charged to have reached fifty two millions of dollars, instead of the thirty seven millions which they had reached at one period of the Van Buren administration.

"Let us briefly analyze this sweeping charge. It is not true, in the first place, that the expenditures of the Government last year amounted so high as fifty millions. In so large an expenditure, however, a few millions more or less would by some persons be thought to make little difference. But the *actual* payments during the year amounted to only forty eight millions of dollars, instead of fifty two millions (or fifty millions, as estimated by others,) as will be seen by the following statement, made up from authentic materials:

The *payment* (net expenses) of the Government
 for fiscal year 1850 and 1851 were . . . . . . . . . .$48,005,878

From which *deduct*—

One Mexican instalment . . . . . . . . . . . . . . . . . . . .$3,242,400

Mexican indemnity claims . . . . . . . . . . . . . . . . . . .2,516,691

              5,759,091

             42,246,787

Duties *refunded* on sugar and molasses wrongfully
 collected (see decisions of Supreme Court). . . . . . $513,850

Debentures . . . . . . . . . . . . . . . . . . . . . . . . . . . . . . 867,268

Excess of duties . . . . . . . . . . . . . . . . . . . . . . . . . . . 896,024

Expenses of collecting the revenues and
 sales of lands. . . . . . . . . . . . . . . . . . . . . . . . . . . . .2,051,708

              4,328,845

             38,917,936

Census expenses . . . . . . . . . . . . . . . . . . . . . . . . . . 672,500

Three and five per cent. funds to states,
 and repayment of lands erroneously sold . . . . . . . . . 74,345

Smithsonian Institution . . . . . . . . . . . . . . . . . . . . . . . . 30,910

              777,755

             37,140,177

And mail service—Navy Department. . . . . . . . . . .1,303,365

             35,837,812

Payments to volunteers . . . . . . . . . . . . . . . . . . . . . 635,380

            $35,201,432

"Of the expenditures of the last year nearly six millions of dollars, it will be seen, went to pay in part for our little property in California.

"The duties refunded, and the expenses of collecting the revenues, &c., amounting to more than four millions of dollars, would, under *former Administrations*, according to the then existing laws, have been paid by and deducted from the revenue by collectors. Now every thing is paid into the Treasury and repaid to the employees, &c.

"The items under the third division of the above statement are surely not 'ordinary expenses' of Government.

"The revenue from the Ocean Mail Steamers not appearing in the *receipts* of the Treasury, the fourth item of the above should not be added to the expenses.

"The volunteers (comprising the fifth item) ought to have been paid years ago. Why, then, does that hold a place in the account of 'ordinary expenses' of the Government?

"A just computation of the 'ordinary' expenditures of the Government for the year 1851 is, therefore, by this analysis, reduced to little more than thirty five millions of dollars, being a less annual amount, as before stated, than the Government expenditure had risen to before the Whigs had ever had any effective share in the administration of the General Government."

By this it appears that in this twice made assault upon the administration, Judge Douglas is only mistaken about twenty five millions of dollars—a mere trifle for a giant!

I come now to the key-notes of the Richmond speech—Seward—Abolition— free soil, &c. &c. It is amusing to observe what a "Raw Head and Bloody Bones" Seward is to universal Locofocoism. That they do really hate him there is no mistake; but that they do not choose to tell the true reason of their hatred, is manifest from the vagueness of their attacks upon him. His supposed proclamation of a "higher law" is the only specific charge I have seen for a long time. I never read the speech in which that proclamation is said to have been made; so that I cannot by its connection, judge of its import and purpose; and I therefore have only to say of it now, that in so far as it may attempt to foment a disobedience to the constitution, or to the constitutional laws of the country, it has my unqualified condemnation. But this is not the true ground of democratic hatred to Seward; else they would not so fondly cherish so many "higher law" men in their own ranks. The real secret is this: whoever does not get the State of New York will not be elected president. In 1848, in New York, Taylor had 218 538 votes—Cass 114 319, and free soilism, under Van Buren 120 497, Taylor only lacking 16 234 of beating them both. Now in 1852, the free soil organization is broken up, Van Buren has gone back to Locofocoism, and his 120 thousand votes are the stakes for which the game in New York is being played. If Scott can get nine thousand of them he carries the State, and is elected; while Pierce is beaten unless he can get about one hundred and eleven thousand of them. Pierce has all the leaders, and can carry a majority; but that won't do—he cannot live unless he gets nearly all. Standing in the way of this Seward is thought to be the greatest obstacle. In this division of free soil effects, they greatly fear he may be able to get as many as nine out of each hundred, which is more than they can bear; and hence their insane malice against him. The indispensable necessity with the democrats of getting these New York free soil votes, to my mind, explains why they nominated a man who "loathes the Fugitive Slave Law." In December or January last Gen. Pierce made a speech, in which, according to two different news paper reports, published at the time in his vicinity and never questioned by him or any one else till after the nomination, he publicly declared his loathing of the Slave law. Now we shall allow ourselves to be very green, if we conclude the democratic convention did not know of this when they nominated him. On the contrary, its suposed efficacy to win free soil votes, was the very thing that secured his nomination. His Southern allies will continue to bluster and pretend to disbelieve the report, but they would not, for any consideration, have him to contradict it. And he will not contradict it—mark me, *he will not contradict it.* I see by the despatches he has already written a letter on the subject; but I have not seen the letter, or any quotation from it. When we shall see it, we shall also see it does not contradict the report—that is, it will not specifically deny the charge that he declared his loathing for the Fugitive Slave Law. I know it will not, because I know the *necessity* of the party will not permit it to be done. The letter will deal in generalities, and will be framed with a view of having it to pass at the South for a denial; but the specific point will not be made and met.

And this being the necessity of the party, and its action and attitude in relation to it, is it not particularly bright—in Judge Douglas to stand up before a slave-holding audience, and make flings at the Whigs about free soil and abolition! Why Pierce's only chance for presidency, is to be born into it, as a cross between New York old hunkerism, and free soilism, the latter predominating in the offspring. Marryat, in some one of his books, describes the sailors, weighing anchor, and singing:

> Sally is a bright Mullatter,
>> Oh Sally Brown—
> Pretty gal, but can't get at her,
>> Oh, Sally Brown.

Now, should Pierce ever be President, he will, politically speaking, not only be a mulatto; but he will be a good deal darker one than Sally Brown.

*August 14, 26, 1852*

# Fragments on Government

The legitimate object of government, is to do for a community of people, whatever they need to have done, but can not do, *at all*, or can not, *so well do*, for themselves—in their separate, and individual capacities.

In all that the people can individually do as well for themselves, government ought not to interfere.

The desirable things which the individuals of a people can not do, or can not well do, for themselves, fall into two classes: those which have relation to *wrongs*, and those which have not. Each of these branch off into an infinite variety of subdivisions.

The first—that in relation to wrongs—embraces all crimes, misdemeanors, and non-performance of contracts. The other embraces all which, in its nature, and without wrong, requires combined actions, as public roads and highways, public schools, charities, pauperism, orphanage, estates of the deceased, and the machinery of government itself.

From this it appears that if all men were just, there still would be *some*, though not *so much*, need of government.

Government is a combination of the people of a country to effect certain objects by joint effort. The best framed and best administered governments are necessarily expensive; while by errors in frame and maladministration most of them are more onerous than they need be, and some of them very oppressive. Why, then, should we have government? Why not each individual take to himself the whole fruit of his labor, without having any of it taxed away, in services, corn, or money? Why not take just so much land as he can cultivate with his own hands, without buying it of any one?

The legitimate object of government is "to do for the people what needs to be done, but which they can not, by individual effort, do at all, or do so well, for themselves." There are many such things—some of them exist independently of the injustice in the world. Making and maintaining roads, bridges, and the like; providing for the helpless young and afflicted; common schools; and disposing of deceased men's property, are instances.

But a far larger class of objects springs from the injustice of men. If one people will make war upon another, it is a necessity with that other to unite and coöperate for defense. Hence the military department. If some men will kill, or beat, or constrain others, or despoil them of property, by force, fraud, or non-compliance with contracts, it is a common object with peaceful and just men to prevent it. Hence the criminal and civil departments.

*ca. July 1, 1854*

# Editorial on the Kansas-Nebraska Act

The following is the 14th section of the Kansas-Nebraska law. It repeals the Missouri Compromise; and then puts in a declaration that it is not intended by this repeal to legislate slavery in or exclude it therefrom, the territory.

> SEC. 14. That the constitution, and all the laws of the United States which are not locally inapplicable, shall have the same force and effect within said territory of Nebraska as elsewhere in the United States, except the 8th section of the act preparatory to the admission of Missouri into the Union, approved March sixth, eighteen hundred and twenty, which being inconsistent with the principles of non-intervention by congress with slavery in the States and Territories as recognized by the legislation of eighteen hundred and fifty, commonly called the compromise measures, is hereby declared inoperative and void; it being the true intent and meaning of this act not to legislate slavery into any territory or State, nor to exclude it therefrom, but to leave the people thereof perfectly free to form and regulate their domestic institutions in their own way, subject only to the constitution of the United States: Provided, that nothing herein contained shall be construed to revive or put in force any law or regulation which may have existed prior to the act of sixth of March, eighteen hundred and twenty, either protecting, establishing, prohibiting, or abolishing slavery.

The state of the case in a few words, is this: The Missouri Compromise excluded slavery from the Kansas-Nebraska territory. The repeal opened the territories to slavery. If there is any meaning to the declaration in the 14th section, that it does not mean to legislate slavery into the territories, it is this: that it does not require slaves to be sent there. The Kansas and Nebraska territories are now as open to slavery as Mississippi or Arkansas were when they were territories.

To illustrate the case—Abraham Lincoln has a fine meadow, containing beautiful springs of water, and well fenced, which John Calhoun had agreed with

Abraham (originally owning the land in common) should be his, and the agreement had been consummated in the most solemn manner, regarded by both as sacred. John Calhoun, however, in the course of time, had become owner of an extensive herd of cattle—the prairie grass had become dried up and there was no convenient water to be had. John Calhoun then looks with a longing eye on Lincoln's meadow, and goes to it and throws down the fences, and exposes it to the ravages of his starving and famishing cattle. "You rascal," says Lincoln, "what have you done? what do you do this for?" "Oh," replies Calhoun, "everything is right. I have taken down your fence; but nothing more. It is my true intent and meaning not to drive my cattle into your meadow, nor to exclude them therefrom, but to leave them perfectly free to form their own notions of the feed, and to direct their movements in their own way!"

Now would not the man who committed this outrage be deemed both a knave and a fool,—a knave in removing the restrictive fence, which he had solemnly pledged himself to sustain;—and a fool in supposing that there could be one man found in the country to believe that he had not pulled down the fence for the purpose of opening the meadow for his cattle?

*September 11, 1854*

# Speech on the Kansas-Nebraska Act

The repeal of the Missouri Compromise, and the propriety of its restoration, constitute the subject of what I am about to say.

As I desire to present my own connected view of this subject, my remarks will not be, specifically, an answer to Judge Douglas; yet, as I proceed, the main points he has presented will arise, and will receive such respectful attention as I may be able to give them.

I wish further to say, that I do not propose to question the patriotism, or to assail the motives of any man, or class of men; but rather to strictly confine myself to the naked merits of the question.

I also wish to be no less than National in all the positions I may take; and whenever I take ground which others have thought, or may think, narrow, sectional and dangerous to the Union, I hope to give a reason, which will appear sufficient, at least to some, why I think differently.

And, as this subject is no other, than part and parcel of the larger general question of domestic-slavery, I wish to MAKE and to KEEP the distinction between the EXISTING institution, and the EXTENSION of it, so broad, and so clear, that no honest man can misunderstand me, and no dishonest one, successfully misrepresent me.

In order to [get] a clear understanding of what the Missouri Compromise is, a short history of the preceding kindred subjects will perhaps be proper. When we established our independence, we did not own, or claim, the country to which this compromise applies. Indeed, strictly speaking, the confederacy then owned no country at all; the States respectively owned the country within their limits; and some of them owned territory beyond their strict State limits. Virginia thus owned the North-Western territory—the country out of which the principal part of Ohio, all Indiana, all Illinois, all Michigan and all Wisconsin, have since been formed. She also owned (perhaps within her then limits) what has since been formed into the State of Kentucky. North Carolina thus owned what is now the State of Tennessee; and South Carolina and Georgia, in separate parts, owned what are now Mississippi and Alabama. Connecticut, I think, owned the little remaining part of Ohio—being the same where they now send Giddings to Congress, and beat all creation at making cheese. These territories, together with the States themselves, constituted all the country over which the confederacy then claimed any sort of jurisdiction. We were then living under the Articles of Confederation, which were superceded by the Constitution several years afterwards. The question of ceding these territories to the general government was set on foot. Mr. Jefferson, the author of the Declaration of Independence, and otherwise a chief actor in the revolution; then a delegate in Congress; afterwards twice President; who was, is, and perhaps will continue to be, the most distinguished politician of our history; a Virginian by birth and continued residence, and withal, a slave-holder; conceived the idea of taking that occasion, to prevent slavery ever going into the north-western territory. He prevailed on the Virginia Legislature to adopt his views, and to cede the territory, making the prohibition of slavery therein, a condition of the deed. Congress accepted the cession, with the condition; and in the first Ordinance (which the acts of Congress were then called) for the government of the territory, provided that slavery should never be permitted therein. This is the famed ordinance of '87 so often spoken of. Thenceforward, for sixty-one years, and until in 1848, the last scrap of this territory came into the Union as the State of Wisconsin, all parties acted in quiet obedience to this ordinance. It is now what Jefferson foresaw and intended—the happy home of teeming millions of free, white, prosperous people, and no slave amongst them.

Thus, with the author of the declaration of Independence, the policy of prohibiting slavery in new territory originated. Thus, away back of the constitution, in the pure fresh, free breath of the revolution, the State of Virginia, and the National congress put that policy in practice. Thus through sixty odd of the best years of the republic did that policy steadily work to its great and beneficent end. And thus, in those five states, and five millions of free, enterprising people, we have before us the rich fruits of this policy. But *now* new light breaks upon us. Now congress declares this ought never to have been; and the like of it, must never be again. The sacred right of self government is grossly violated by it! We even find some men, who drew their first breath, and every other breath of their lives, under this very restriction, now live in dread of absolute suffocation, if they should be restricted in the "sacred right" of taking slaves to Nebraska. That *per-fect* liberty they sigh for—the liberty of making slaves of other people—Jefferson never thought of; their own father never thought of; they never thought of them-selves, a year ago. How fortunate for them, they did not sooner become sensible of their great misery! Oh, how difficult it is to treat with respect, such assaults upon all we have ever really held sacred.

But to return to history. In 1803 we purchased what was then called Louisiana, of France. It included the now states of Louisiana, Arkansas, Missouri, and Iowa; also the territory of Minnesota, and the present bone of contention, Kansas and

Nebraska. Slavery already existed among the French at New Orleans; and, to some extent, at St. Louis. In 1812 Louisiana came into the Union as a slave state, without controversy. In 1818 or '19, Missouri showed signs of a wish to come in with slavery. This was resisted by northern members of Congress; and thus began the first great slavery agitation in the nation. This controversy lasted several months, and became very angry and exciting; the House of Representatives voting steadily for the prohibition of slavery in Missouri, and the Senate voting as steadily against it. Threats of breaking up the Union were freely made; and the ablest public men of the day became seriously alarmed. At length a compromise was made, in which, like all compromises, both sides yielded something. It was a law passed on the 6th day of March, 1820, providing that Missouri might come into the Union *with* slavery, but that in all the remaining part of the territory purchased of France, which lies north of 36 degrees and 30 minutes north latitude, slavery should never be permitted. This provision of law, *is the Missouri Compromise*. In excluding slavery North of the line, the same language is employed as in the Ordinance of '87. It directly applied to Iowa, Minnesota, and to the present bone of contention, Kansas and Nebraska. Whether there should or should not, be slavery south of that line, nothing was said in the law; but Arkansas constituted the principal remaining part, south of the line; and it has since been admitted as a slave state without serious controversy. More recently, Iowa, north of the line, came in as a free state without controversy. Still later, Minnesota, north of the line, had a territorial organization without controversy. Texas principally south of the line, and West of Arkansas; though originally within the purchase from France, had, in 1819, been traded off to Spain, in our treaty for the acquisition of Florida. It had thus become a part of Mexico. Mexico revolutionized and became independent of Spain. American citizens began settling rapidly, with their slaves in the southern part of Texas. Soon they revolutionized against Mexico, and established an independent government of their own, adopting a constitution, with slavery, strongly resembling the constitutions of our slave states. By still another rapid move, Texas, claiming a boundary much further West, than when we parted with her in 1819, was brought back to the United States, and admitted into the Union as a slave state. There then was little or no settlement in the northern part of Texas, a considerable portion of which lay north of the Missouri line; and in the resolutions admitting her into the Union, the Missouri restriction was expressly extended westward across her territory. This was in 1845, only nine years ago.

Thus originated the Missouri Compromise; and thus has it been respected down to 1845. And even four years later, in 1849, our distinguished Senator, in a public address, held the following language in relation to it:

"The Missouri Compromise had been in practical operation for about a quarter of a century, and had received the sanction and approbation of men of all parties in every section of the Union. It had allayed all sectional jealousies and irritations growing out of this vexed question, and harmonized and tranquilized the whole country. It had given to Henry Clay, as its prominent champion, the proud sobriquet of the *"Great Pacificator"* and by that title and for that service, his political friends had repeatedly appealed to the people to rally under his standard, as a presidential candidate, as the man who had exhibited the patriotism and the power to suppress, an unholy and treasonable agitation, and preserve the Union. He was not aware that any man or any party from any section of the Union, had ever urged as an objection to Mr. Clay, that he was the great champion of the Missouri Compromise. On the contrary, the effort was made by the opponents of Mr. Clay, to prove that he was not entitled to the exclusive merit of that great patriotic measure, and that the honor was equally due to others as well as to him, for securing its adoption—that it had its origin in the hearts of all patriotic men, who desired to preserve and perpetuate the blessings of our glorious Union—an origin akin that of the constitution of the United States, conceived in the same spirit of fraternal affection, and calculated to remove forever, the only danger, which seemed to threaten, at some distant day, to sever the social bond of union. All the evidences of public opinion at that day, seemed to indicate that this Compromise had been canonized in the hearts of the American people, as a sacred thing which no ruthless hand would ever be reckless enough to disturb."

I do not read this extract to involve Judge Douglas in an inconsistency. If he afterwards thought he had been wrong, it was right for him to change. I bring this forward merely to show the high estimate placed on the Missouri Compromise by all parties up to so late as the year 1849.

But, going back a little, in point of time, our war with Mexico broke out in 1846. When Congress was about adjourning that session, President Polk asked them to place two millions of dollars under his control, to be used by him in the recess, if found practicable and expedient, in negociating a treaty of peace with Mexico, and acquiring some part of her territory. A bill was duly got up, for the purpose, and was progressing swimmingly, in the House of Representatives, when a member by the name of David Wilmot, a democrat from Pennsylvania, moved as an amendment "Provided that in any territory thus acquired, there shall never be slavery."

This is the origin of the far-famed "Wilmot Proviso." It created a great flutter; but it stuck like wax, was voted into the bill, and the bill passed with it through the House. The Senate, however, adjourned without final action on it and so both appropriation and proviso were lost, for the time. The war continued, and at the next session, the president renewed his request for the appropriation, enlarging the amount, I think, to three million. Again came the proviso; and defeated the measure. Congress adjourned again, and the war went on. In Dec., 1847, the new congress assembled. I was in the lower House that term. The "Wilmot Proviso" or the principle of it, was constantly coming up in some shape or other, and I think I may venture to say I voted for it at least forty times; during the short term I was there. The Senate, however, held it in check, and it never became law. In the spring of 1848 a treaty of peace was made with Mexico; by which we obtained that portion of her country which now constitutes the territories of New Mexico and Utah, and the now state of California. By this treaty the Wilmot Proviso was defeated, as so far as it was intended to be, a condition of the acquisition of territory. Its friends however, were still determined to find some way to restrain slavery from getting into the new country. This new acquisition lay directly West of our old purchase from France, and extended west to the Pacific ocean—and was so situated that if the Missouri line should be extended straight West, the new country would be divided by such extended line, leaving some North and some South of it. On Judge Douglas' motion a bill, or provision of a bill, passed the Senate to so extend the Missouri line. The Proviso men in the House, including myself, voted it down, because by implication, it gave up the Southern part to slavery, while we were bent on having it *all* free.

In the fall of 1848 the gold mines were discovered in California. This attracted people to it with unprecedented rapidity, so that on, or soon after, the meeting of the new congress in Dec., 1849, she already had a population of nearly a hundred thousand, had called a convention, formed a state constitution, excluding slavery, and was knocking for admission into the Union. The Proviso men, of course were for letting her in, but the Senate, always true to the other side would not consent to her admission. And there California stood, kept *out* of the Union, because she would not let slavery *into* her borders. Under all the circumstances perhaps this was not wrong. There were other points of dispute, connected with the general question of slavery, which equally needed adjustment. The South clamored for a more efficient fugitive slave law. The North clamored for the abolition of a peculiar species of slave trade in the District of Columbia, in connection with which, in view from the windows of the capitol, a sort of negro-livery stable, where droves of negroes were collected, temporarily kept, and finally taken to Southern markets, precisely like droves of horses, had been openly maintained for fifty years. Utah and New Mexico needed territorial governments; and whether slavery should or should not be prohibited within them, was another question.

The indefinite Western boundary of Texas was to be settled. She was received a slave state; and consequently the farther West the slavery men could push her boundary, the more slave country they secured. And the farther East the slavery opponents could thrust the boundary back, the less slave ground was secured. Thus this was just as clearly a slavery question as any of the others.

These points all needed adjustment; and they were all held up, perhaps wisely to make them help to adjust one another. The Union, now, as in 1820, was thought to be in danger; and devotion to the Union rightfully inclined men to yield somewhat, in points where nothing else could have so inclined them. A compromise was finally effected. The south got their new fugitive-slave law; and the North got California, (the far best part of our acquisition from Mexico,) as a free State. The south got a provision that New Mexico and Utah, *when admitted as States,* may come in *with* or *without* slavery as they may then choose; and the north got the slave-trade abolished in the District of Columbia. The north got the western boundary of Texas, thence further back eastward than the south desired; but, in turn, they gave Texas ten millions of dollars, with which to pay her old debts. This is the Compromise of 1850.

Preceding the Presidential election of 1852, each of the great political parties, democrats and whigs, met in convention, and adopted resolutions endorsing the compromise of '50; as a "finality," a final settlement, so far as these parties could make it so, of all slavery agitation. Previous to this, in 1851, the Illinois Legislature had indorsed it.

During this long period of time Nebraska had remained, substantially an uninhabited country, but now emigration to, and settlement within it began to take place. It is about one third as large as the present United States, and its importance so long overlooked, begins to come into view. The restriction of slavery by the Missouri Compromise directly applies to it; in fact, was first made, and has since been maintained, expressly for it. In 1853, a bill to give it a territorial government passed the House of Representatives, and, in the hands of Judge Douglas, failed of passing the Senate only for want of time. This bill contained no repeal of the Missouri Compromise. Indeed, when it was assailed because it did not contain such repeal, Judge Douglas defended it in its existing form. On January 4th, 1854, Judge Douglas introduces a new bill to give Nebraska territorial government. He accompanies this bill with a report, in which last, he expressly recommends that the Missouri Compromise shall neither be affirmed nor repealed.

Before long the bill is so modified as to make two territories instead of one; calling the Southern one Kansas.

Also, about a month after the introduction of the bill, on the judge's own motion, it is so amended as to declare the Missouri Compromise inoperative and void; and, substantially, that the People who go and settle there may establish slavery, or exclude it, as they may see fit. In this shape the bill passed both branches of congress, and became a law.

This is the *repeal* of the Missouri Compromise. The foregoing history may not be precisely accurate in every particular; but I am sure it is sufficiently so, for all the uses I shall attempt to make of it, and in it, we have before us, the chief material enabling us to correctly judge whether the repeal of the Missouri Compromise is right or wrong.

I think, and shall try to show, that it is wrong; wrong in its direct effect, letting slavery into Kansas and Nebraska—and wrong in its prospective principle, allowing it to spread to every other part of the wide world, where men can be found inclined to take it.

This *declared* indifference, but as I must think, covert *real* zeal for the spread of slavery, I can not but hate. I hate it because of the monstrous injustice of slavery itself. I hate it because it deprives our republican example of its just influence in the world—enables the enemies of free institutions, with plausibility, to taunt us as hypocrites—causes the real friends of freedom to doubt our sincerity, and especially because it forces so many really good men amongst ourselves into an open war with the very fundamental principles of civil liberty—criticising the Declaration of Independence, and insisting that there is no right principle of action but *self-interest*.

Before proceeding, let me say I think I have no prejudice against the Southern people. They are just what we would be in their situation. If slavery did not now exist amongst them, they would not introduce it. If it did now exist amongst us, we should not instantly give it up. This I believe of the masses north and south. Doubtless there are individuals, on both sides, who would not hold slaves under any circumstances; and others who would gladly introduce slavery anew, if it were out of existence. We know that some southern men do free their slaves, go north, and become tip-top abolitionists; while some northern ones go south, and become most cruel slave-masters.

When southern people tell us they are no more responsible for the origin of slavery, than we; I acknowledge the fact. When it is said that the institution exists; and that it is very difficult to get rid of it, in any satisfactory way, I can understand and appreciate the saying. I surely will not blame them for not doing what I should not know how to do myself. If all earthly power were given me, I should not know what to do, as to the existing institution. My first impulse would be to free all the slaves, and send them to Liberia,—to their own native land. But a moment's reflection would convince me, that whatever of high hope, (as I think there is) there may be in this, in the long run, its sudden execution is impossible. If they were all landed there in a day, they would all perish in the next ten days; and there are not surplus shipping and surplus money enough in the world to carry them there in many times ten days. What then? Free them all, and keep them among us as underlings? Is it quite certain that this betters their condition? I think I would not hold one in slavery, at any rate; yet the point is not clear enough for me to denounce people upon. What next? Free them, and make them politically and socially, our equals? My own feelings will not admit of this; and if mine would, we well know that those of the great mass of white people will not. Whether this feeling accords with justice and sound judgment, is not the sole question, if indeed, it is any part of it. A universal feeling, whether well or ill-founded, can not be safely disregarded. We can not, then, make them equals. It does seem to me that systems of gradual emancipation might be adopted; but for their tardiness in this, I will not undertake to judge our brethren of the south.

When they remind us of their constitutional rights, I acknowledge them, not grudgingly, but fully, and fairly; and I would give them any legislation for the reclaiming of their fugitives, which should not, in its stringency, be more likely to carry a free man into slavery, than our ordinary criminal laws are to hang an innocent one.

But all this, to my judgment, furnishes no more excuse for permitting slavery to go into our own free territory, than it would for reviving the African slave trade by law. The law which forbids the bringing of slaves *from* Africa; and that which has so long forbid the taking them *to* Nebraska, can hardly be distinguished on any moral principle; and the repeal of the former could find quite as plausible excuses as that of the latter.

The arguments by which the repeal of the Missouri Compromise is sought to be justified, are these:

First, that the Nebraska country needed a territorial government.

Second, that in various ways, the public had repudiated it, and demanded the repeal; and therefore should not now complain of it.

And lastly, that the repeal establishes a principle, which is intrinsically right.

I will attempt an answer to each of them in its turn.

First, then, if that country was in need of a territorial organization, could it not have had it as well without as with the repeal? Iowa and Minnesota, to both of which the Missouri restriction applied, had, without its repeal, each in succession, territorial organizations. And even, the year before, a bill for Nebraska itself, was within an ace of passing, without the repealing clause; and this in the hands of the same men who are now the champions of repeal. Why no necessity then for the repeal? But still later, when this very bill was first brought in, it contained no repeal. But, say they, because the public had demanded, or rather commanded the repeal, the repeal was to accompany the organization, whenever that should occur.

Now I deny that the public ever demanded any such thing—ever repudiated the Missouri Compromise—ever commanded its repeal. I deny it, and call for the proof. It is not contended, I believe, that any such command has ever been given in express terms. It is only said that it was done *in principle*. The support of the Wilmot Proviso, is the first fact mentioned, to prove that the Missouri restriction was repudiated in *principle*, and the second is, the refusal to extend the Missouri line over the country acquired from Mexico. These are near enough alike to be treated together. The one was to exclude the chances of slavery from the *whole* new acquisition by the lump; and the other was to reject a division of it, by which one *half* was to be given up to those chances. Now whether this was a repudiation of the Missouri line, in *principle*, depends upon whether the Missouri law contained any *principle* requiring the line to be extended over the country acquired from Mexico. I contend it did not. I insist that it contained no general principle, but that it was, in every sense, specific. That its terms limit it to the country purchased from France, is undenied and undeniable. It could have no principle beyond the intention of those who made it. They did not intend to extend the line to country which they did not own. If they intended to extend it, in the event of acquiring additional territory, why did they not say so? It was just as easy to say, that "in all the country west of the Mississippi, which we now own, *or may hereafter acquire* there shall never be slavery," as to say, what they did say; and they would have said it if they had meant it. An intention to extend the law is not only not mentioned in the law, but is not mentioned in any contemporaneous history. Both the law itself, and the history of the times are a blank as to any *principle* of extension; and by neither the known rules for construing statutes and contracts, nor by common sense, can any such *principle* be inferred.

Another fact showing the *specific* character of the Missouri law—showing that it intended no more than it expressed—showing that the line was not intended as a universal dividing line between free and slave territory, present and prospective— north of which slavery could never go—is the fact that by that very law, Missouri came in as a slave state, *north* of the line. If that law contained any prospective *principle*, the whole law must be looked to in order to ascertain what the *principle* was. And by this rule, the south could fairly contend that inasmuch as they got one slave state north of the line at the inception of the law, they have the right to have another given them *north* of it occasionally—now and then in the indefinite westward extension of the line. This demonstrates the absurdity of attempting to deduce a prospective *principle* from the Missouri Compromise line.

When we voted for the Wilmot Proviso, we were voting to keep slavery *out* of the whole Mexican acquisition; and little did we think we were thereby voting, to let it *into* Nebraska, laying several hundred miles distant. When we voted against extending the Missouri line, little did we think we were voting to destroy the old line, then of near thirty years standing. To argue that we thus repudiated the Missouri Compromise is no less absurd than it would be to argue that because we have, so far, forborne to acquire Cuba, we have thereby, *in principle,* repudiated our former acquisitions, and determined to throw them out of the Union! No less absurd than it would be to say that because I may have refused to build an addition to my house, I thereby have decided to destroy the existing house! And if I catch you setting fire to my house, you will turn upon me and say I INSTRUCTED you to do it! The most conclusive argument, however, that, while voting for the Wilmot Proviso, and while voting against the EXTENSION of the Missouri line, we never thought of disturbing the original Missouri Compromise, is found in the facts, that there was then, and still is, an unorganized tract of fine country, nearly as large as the state of Missouri, lying immediately west of Arkansas, and south of the Missouri Compromise line; and that we never attempted to prohibit slavery as to it. I wish particular attention to this. It adjoins the original Missouri Compromise line, by its northern boundary; and consequently is part of the country, into which, by implication, slavery was permitted to go, by that compromise. There it has lain open ever since, and there it still lies. And yet no effort has been made at any time to wrest it from the south. In all our struggles to prohibit slavery within our Mexican acquisitions, we never so much as lifted a finger to prohibit it, as to this tract. Is not this entirely conclusive that at all times, we have held the Missouri Compromise as a sacred thing; even when against ourselves, as well as when for us?

Senator Douglas sometimes says the Missouri line itself was, *in principle*, only an extension of the line of the ordinance of '87—that is to say, an extension of the Ohio river. I think this is weak enough on its face. I will remark, however that, as a glance at the map will show, the Missouri line is a long way farther South than the Ohio; and that if our Senator, in proposing his extension, had stuck to the *principle* of jogging southward, perhaps it might not have been voted down so readily.

But next it is said that the compromises of '50 and the ratification of them by both political parties, in '52, established a *new principle*, which required the repeal of the Missouri Compromise. This again I deny. I deny it, and demand the proof. I have already stated fully what the compromises of '50 are. The particular part of those measures, for which the virtual repeal of the Missouri compromise is sought to be inferred (for it is admitted they contain nothing about it, in express terms) is the provision in the Utah and New Mexico laws, which permits them when they seek admission into the Union as States, to come in with or without slavery as they shall then see fit. Now I insist this provision was made for Utah and New Mexico, and for no other place whatever. It had no more direct reference to Nebraska than it had to the territories of the moon. But, say they, it had reference to Nebraska, *in principle.* Let us see. The North consented to this provision, not because they considered it right in itself; but because they were compensated—paid for it. They, at the same time, got California into the Union as a free State. This was far the best part of all they had struggled for by the Wilmot Proviso. They also got the area of slavery somewhat narrowed in the settlement of the boundary of Texas. Also, they got the slave trade abolished in the District of Columbia. For all these desirable objects the North could afford to yield something; and they did yield to the South the Utah and New Mexico provision. I do not mean that the whole North, or even a majority, yielded, when the law passed; but enough yielded, when added to the vote of the South, to carry the measure. Now can it be pretended that the *principle* of this arrangement requires us to permit the same provision to be applied to Nebraska, *without any equivalent at all?* Give us another free State; press the boundary of Texas still further back, give us another step toward the destruction of slavery in the District, and you present us a similar case. But ask us not to repeat, for nothing, what you paid for in the first instance. If you wish the thing again, pay again. That is the *principle* of the compromises of '50, if indeed they had any principles beyond their specific terms—it was the system of equivalents.

Again, if Congress, at that time, intended that all future territories should, when admitted as States, come in with or without slavery, at their own option, why did it not say so? With such an universal provision, all know the bills could not have passed. Did they, then—could they—establish a *principle* contrary to their own intention? Still further, if they intended to establish the principle that wherever Congress had control, it should be left to the people to do as they thought fit with slavery why did they not authorize the people of the District of Columbia at their adoption to abolish slavery within these limits? I personally know that this has not been left undone, because it was unthought of. It was frequently spoken of by members of Congress and by citizens of Washington six years ago; and I heard no one express a doubt that a system of gradual emancipation, with compensation to owners, would meet the approbation of a large majority of the white people of the District. But without the action of Congress they could say nothing; and Congress said "no." In the measures of 1850 Congress had the subject of slavery in the District expressly in hand. If they were then establishing the *principle* of allowing the people to do as they please with slavery, why did they not apply the *principle* to that people?

Again, it is claimed that by the Resolutions of the Illinois Legislature, passed in 1851, the repeal of the Missouri compromise was demanded. This I deny also. Whatever may be worked out by a criticism of the language of those resolutions, the people have never understood them as being any more than an endorsement of the compromises of 1850; and a release of our Senators from voting for the Wilmot Proviso. The whole people are living witnesses, that this only, was their view. Finally, it is asked "If we did not mean to apply the Utah and New Mexico provision, to all future territories, what did we mean, when we, in 1852, endorsed the compromises of '50?"

For myself, I can answer this question most easily. I meant not to ask a repeal, or modification of the fugitive slave law. I meant not to ask for the abolition of slavery in the District of Columbia. I meant not to resist the admission of Utah and New Mexico, even should they ask to come in as slave States. I meant nothing about additional territories, because, as I understood, we then had no territory whose character as to slavery was not already settled. As to Nebraska, I regarded its character as being fixed, by the Missouri compromise, for thirty years—as unalterably fixed as that of my own home in Illinois. As to new acquisitions I said "sufficient unto the day is the evil thereof." When we make new acquisitions, we will, as heretofore, try to manage them some how. That is my answer. That is what I meant and said; and I appeal to the people to say, each for himself, whether that was not also the universal meaning of the free States.

And now, in turn, let me ask a few questions. If by any, or all these matters, the repeal of the Missouri Compromise was commanded, why was not the command sooner obeyed? Why was the repeal omitted in the Nebraska bill of 1853? Why was it omitted in the original bill of 1854? Why, in the accompanying report, was such a repeal characterized as a *departure* from the course pursued in 1850? and its continued omission recommended?

I am aware Judge Douglas now argues that the subsequent express repeal is no substantial alteration of the bill. This argument seems wonderful to me. It is as if one should argue that white and black are not different. He admits, however, that there is a literal change in the bill; and that he made the change in deference to other Senators, who would not support the bill without. This proves that those other Senators thought the change a substantial one; and that the Judge thought their opinions worth deferring to. His own opinions, therefore, seem not to rest on a very firm basis even in his own mind—and I suppose the world believes, and will continue to believe, that precisely on the substance of that change this whole agitation has arisen.

I conclude then, that the public never demanded the repeal of the Missouri compromise.

I now come to consider whether the repeal, with its avowed principle, is intrinsically right. I insist that it is not. Take the particular case. A controversy had arisen between the advocates and opponents of slavery, in relation to its establishment within the country we had purchased of France. The southern, and then best part of the purchase, was already in as a slave State. The controversy was settled by also letting Missouri in as a slave State; but with the agreement that within all the remaining part of the purchase, North of a certain line, there should never be slavery. As to what was to be done with the remaining part south of the line, nothing was said; but perhaps the fair implication was, that it should come in with slavery if it should so choose. The southern part, except a portion heretofore mentioned, afterwards did come in with slavery, as the State of Arkansas. All these many years since 1820, the Northern part had remained a wilderness. At length settlements began in it also. In due course, Iowa, came in as a free State, and Minnesota was given a territorial government, without removing the slavery restriction. Finally the sole remaining part, North of the line, Kansas and Nebraska, was to be organized; and it is proposed, and carried, to blot out the old dividing line of thirty-four years standing, and to open the whole of that country to the introduction of slavery. Now, this, to my mind, is manifestly unjust. After an angry and dangerous controversy, the parties made friends by dividing the bone of contention. The one party first appropriates her own share, beyond all power to be disturbed in the possession of it; and then seizes the share of the other party. It is as if two starving men had divided their only loaf; the one had hastily swallowed his half, and then grabbed the other half just as he was putting it to his mouth!

Let me here drop the main argument, to notice what I consider rather an inferior matter. It is argued that slavery will not go to Kansas and Nebraska, *in any event*. This is a *palliation*—a *lullaby*. I have some hope that it will not; but let us not be too confident. As to climate, a glance at the map shows that there are five slave States—Delaware, Maryland, Virginia, Kentucky, and Missouri—and also the District of Columbia, all north of the Missouri compromise line. The census returns of 1850 show that, within these, there are 867,276 slaves—being more than one-fourth of all the slaves in the nation.

It is not climate, then, that will keep slavery out of these territories. Is there any thing in the peculiar nature of the country? Missouri adjoins these territories, by her entire western boundary, and slavery is already within every one of her western counties. I have even heard it said that there are more slaves, in proportion to whites, in the north western county of Missouri, than within any county of the State. Slavery pressed entirely up to the old western boundary of the State, and when, rather recently, a part of that boundary, at the northwest was moved out a little farther west, slavery followed on quite up to the new line. Now, when the restriction is removed, what is to prevent it from going still further? Climate will not. No peculiarity of the country will—nothing in *nature* will. Will the disposition of the people prevent it? Those nearest the scene, are all in favor of the extension. The yankees, who are opposed to it may be more numerous; but in military phrase, the battle-field is too far from *their* base of operations.

But it is said, there now is *no* law in Nebraska on the subject of slavery; and that, in such case, taking a slave there, operates his freedom. That *is* good book-law; but is not the rule of actual practice. Wherever slavery is, it has been first introduced without law. The oldest laws we find concerning it, are not laws introducing it; but *regulating* it, as an already existing thing. A white man takes his slave to Nebraska now; who will inform the negro that he is free? Who will take him before court to test the question of his freedom? In ignorance of his legal emancipation, he is kept chopping, splitting and plowing. Others are brought, and move on in the same track. At last, if ever the time for voting comes, on the question of slavery, the institution already in fact exists in the country, and cannot well be removed. The facts of its presence, and the difficulty of its removal will carry the vote in its favor. Keep it out until a vote is taken, and a vote in favor of it, can not be got in any population of forty thousand, on earth, who have been drawn together by the ordinary motives of emigration and settlement. To get slaves into the country simultaneously with the whites, in the incipient stages of settlement, is the precise stake played for, and won in this Nebraska measure.

The question is asked us, "If slaves will go in, notwithstanding the general principle of law liberates them, why would they not equally go in against positive statute law?—go in, even if the Missouri restriction were maintained?" I answer, because it takes a much bolder man to venture in, with his property, in the latter case, than in the former—because the positive congressional enactment is known to, and respected by all, or nearly all; whereas the negative principle that *no* law is free law, is not much known except among lawyers. We have some experience of this practical difference. In spite of the Ordinance of '87, a few negroes were brought into Illinois, and held in a state of quasi slavery; not enough, however to carry a vote of the people in favor of the institution when they came to form a constitution. But in the adjoining Missouri country, where there was no ordinance of '87—was no restriction—they were carried ten times, nay a hundred times, as fast, and actually made a slave State. This is fact—naked fact.

Another LULLABY argument is, that taking slaves to new countries does not increase their number—does not make any one slave who otherwise would be free. There is some truth in this, and I am glad of it, but it is not WHOLLY true. The African slave trade is not yet effectually suppressed; and if we make a reasonable deduction for the white people amongst us, who are foreigners, and the descendants of foreigners, arriving here since 1808, we shall find the increase of the black population out-running that of the white, to an extent unaccountable, except by supposing that some of them too, have been coming from Africa. If this be so, the opening of new countries to the institution, increases the demand for, and augments the price of slaves, and so does, in fact, make slaves of freemen by causing them to be brought from Africa, and sold into bondage.

But, however this may be, we know the opening of new countries to slavery, tends to the perpetuation of the institution, and so does KEEP men in slavery who otherwise would be free. This result we do not FEEL like favoring, and we are under no legal obligation to suppress our feelings in this respect.

Equal justice to the south, it is said, requires us to consent to the extending of slavery to new countries. That is to say, inasmuch as you do not object to my taking my hog to Nebraska, therefore I must not object to you taking your slave. Now, I admit this is perfectly logical, if there is no difference between hogs and negroes. But while you thus require me to deny the humanity of the negro, I wish to ask whether you of the south yourselves, have ever been willing to do as much? It is kindly provided that of all those who come into the world, only a small percentage are natural tyrants. That percentage is no larger in the slave States than in the free. The great majority, south as well as north, have human sympathies, of which they can no more divest themselves than they can of their sensibility to physical pain. These sympathies in the bosoms of the southern people, manifest in many ways, their sense of the wrong of slavery, and their consciousness that, after all, there is humanity in the negro. If they deny this, let me address them a few plain questions. In 1820 you joined the north, almost unanimously, in declaring the African slave trade piracy, and in annexing to it the punishment of death. Why did you do this? If you did not feel that it was wrong, why did you join in providing that men should be hung for it? The practice was no more than bringing wild negroes from Africa, to sell to such as would buy them. But you never thought of hanging men for catching and selling wild horses, wild buffaloes or wild bears.

Again, you have amongst you, a sneaking individual, of the class of native tyrants, known as the "SLAVE-DEALER." He watches your necessities, and crawls up to buy your slave, at a speculating price. If you cannot help it, you sell to him; but if you can help it, you drive him from your door. You despise him utterly. You do not recognize him as a friend, or even as an honest man. Your children must not play with his; they may rollick freely with the little negroes, but not with the "slave-dealers" children. If you are obliged to deal with him, you try to get through the job without so much as touching him. It is common with you to join hands with the men you meet; but with the slave dealer you avoid the ceremony—instinctively shrinking from the snaky contact. If he grows rich and retires from business, you still remember him, and still keep up the ban of non-intercourse upon him and his family. Now why is this? You do not so treat the man who deals in corn, cattle or tobacco.

And yet again; there are in the United States and territories, including the District of Columbia, 433,643 free blacks. At $500 per head they are worth over two hundred millions of dollars. How comes this vast amount of property to be running about without owners? We do not see free horses or free cattle running at large. How is this? All these free blacks are the descendants of slaves, or have been slaves themselves, and they would be slaves now, but for SOMETHING which has operated on their white owners, inducing them, at vast pecuniary sacrifices, to liberate them. What is that SOMETHING? Is there any mistaking it? In all these cases it is your sense of justice, and human sympathy, continually telling you, that the poor negro has some natural right to himself—that those who deny it, and make mere merchandise of him, deserve kickings, contempt and death.

And now, why will you ask us to deny the humanity of the slave? and estimate him only as the equal of the hog? Why ask us to do what you will not do yourselves? Why ask us to do for *nothing*, what two hundred million of dollars could not induce you to do?

But one great argument in the support of the repeal of the Missouri Compromise, is still to come. That argument is "the sacred right of self government." It seems our distinguished Senator has found great difficulty in getting his antagonists, even in the Senate to meet him fairly on this argument—some poet has said

Fools rush in where angels fear to tread.

At the hazzard of being thought one of the fools of this quotation, I meet that argument—I rush in, I take that bull by the horns.

I trust I understand, and truly estimate the right of self-government. My faith in the proposition that each man should do precisely as he pleases with all which is exclusively his own, lies at the foundation of the sense of justice there is in me. I extend the principles to communities of men, as well as to individuals. I so extend it, because it is politically wise, as well as naturally just: politically wise, in saving us from broils about matters which do not concern us. Here, or at Washington, I would not trouble myself with the oyster laws of Virginia, or the cranberry laws of Indiana.

The doctrine of self government is right—absolutely and eternally right— but it has no just application, as here attempted. Or perhaps I should rather say that whether it has such just application depends upon whether a negro is *not* or *is* a man. If he is *not* a man, why in that case, he who *is* a man may, as a matter of self-government, do just as he pleases with him. But if the negro *is* a man, is it not to that extent, a total destruction of self-government, to say that he too shall not govern *himself?* When the white man governs himself that is self-government; but when he governs himself, and also governs *another* man, that is *more* than self-government—that is despotism. If the negro is a *man,* why then my ancient faith teaches me that "all men are created equal"; and that there can be no moral right in connection with one man's making a slave of another.

Judge Douglas frequently, with bitter irony and sarcasm, paraphrases our argument by saying "The white people of Nebraska are good enough to govern themselves, *but they are not good enough to govern a few miserable negroes!!*"

Well I doubt not that the people of Nebraska are, and will continue to be as good as the average of people elsewhere. I do not say the contrary. What I do say is, that no man is good enough to govern another man, *without that other's consent.* I say this is the leading principle—the sheet anchor of American republicanism. Our Declaration of Independence says:

"We hold these truths to be self evident: that all men are created equal; that they are endowed by their Creator with certain inalienable rights; that among these are life, liberty and the pursuit of happiness. That to secure these rights, governments are instituted among men, DERIVING THEIR JUST POWERS FROM THE CONSENT OF THE GOVERNED."

I have quoted so much at this time merely to show that according to our ancient faith, the just powers of governments are derived from the consent of the governed. Now the relation of masters and slaves is, PRO TANTO, a total violation of this principle. The master not only governs the slave without his consent;

but he governs him by a set of rules altogether different from those which he prescribes for himself. Allow ALL the governed an equal voice in the government, and that, and that only is self government.

Let it not be said I am contending for the establishment of political and social equality between the whites and blacks. I have already said the contrary. I am not now combating the argument of NECESSITY, arising from the fact that the blacks are already amongst us; but I am combating what is set up as MORAL argument for allowing them to be taken where they have never yet been—arguing against the EXTENSION of a bad thing, which where it already exists, we must of necessity, manage as we best can.

In support of his application of the doctrine of self-government, Senator Douglas has sought to bring to his aid the opinions and examples of our revolutionary fathers. I am glad he has done this. I love the sentiments of those old-time men; and shall be most happy to abide by their opinions. He shows us that when it was in contemplation for the colonies to break off from Great Britain, and set up a new government for themselves, several of the states instructed their delegates to go for the measure PROVIDED EACH STATE SHOULD BE ALLOWED TO REGULATE ITS DOMESTIC CONCERNS IN ITS OWN WAY. I do not quote; but this in substance. This was right. I see nothing objectionable in it. I also think it probable that it had some reference to the existence of slavery amongst them. I will not deny that it had. But had it, in any reference to the carrying of slavery into NEW COUNTRIES? That is the question; and we will let the fathers themselves answer it.

This same generation of men, and mostly the same individuals of the generation, who declared this principle—who declared independence—who fought the war of the revolution through—who afterwards made the constitution under which we still live—these same men passed the ordinance of '87, declaring that slavery should never go to the north-west territory. I have no doubt Judge Douglas thinks they were very inconsistent in this. It is a question of discrimination between them and him. But there is not an inch of ground left for his claiming that their opinions—their example—their authority—are on his side in this controversy.

Again, is not Nebraska, while a territory, a part of us? Do we not own the country? And if we surrender the control of it, do we not surrender the right of self-government? It is part of ourselves. If you say we shall not control it because it is ONLY part, the same is true of every other part; and when all the parts are gone, what has become of the whole? What is then left of us? What use for the general government, when there is nothing left for it to govern?

But you say this question should be left to the people of Nebraska, because they are more particularly interested. If this be the rule, you must leave it to each individual to say for himself whether he will have slaves. What better moral right have thirty-one citizens of Nebraska to say, that the thirty-second shall not hold slaves, than the people of the thirty-one States have to say that slavery shall not go into the thirty-second State at all?

But if it is a sacred right for the people of Nebraska to take and hold slaves there, it is equally their sacred right to buy them where they can buy them cheapest; and that undoubtedly will be on the coast of Africa; provided you will consent to not hang them for going there to buy them. You must remove this restriction too, from the sacred right of self-government. I am aware you say that taking slaves from the States of Nebraska, does not make slaves of freemen; but the African slave-trader can say just as much. He does not catch free negroes and bring them here. He finds them already slaves in the hands of their black captors, and he honestly buys them at the rate of about a red cotton handkerchief a head. This is very cheap, and it is a great abridgement of the sacred right of self-government to hang men for engaging in this profitable trade!

Another important objection to this application of the right of self-government, is that it enables the first FEW, to deprive the succeeding MANY, of a free exercise of the right of self-government. The first few may get slavery IN, and the subsequent many cannot easily get it OUT. How common is the remark now in the slave States—"If we were only clear of our slaves, how much better it would be for us." They are actually deprived of the privilege of governing themselves as they would, by the action of a very few, in the beginning. The same thing was true of the whole nation at the time our constitution was formed.

Whether slavery shall go into Nebraska, or other new territories, is not a matter of exclusive concern to the people who may go there. The whole nation is interested that the best use shall be made of these territories. We want them for the homes of free white people. This they cannot be, to any considerable extent, if slavery shall be planted within them. Slave States are places for poor white people to remove FROM; not to remove TO. New free States are the places for poor people to go to and better their condition. For this use, the nation needs these territories.

Still further; there are constitutional relations between the slave and free States, which are degrading to the latter. We are under legal obligations to catch and return their runaway slaves to them—a sort of dirty, disagreeable job, which I believe, as a general rule the slave-holders will not perform for one another. Then again, in the control of the government—the management of the partnership affairs—they have greatly the advantage of us. By the constitution, each State has two Senators—each has a number of Representatives; in proportion to the number of its people—and each has a number of presidential electors, equal to the whole number of its Senators and Representatives together. But in ascertaining the number of the people, for this purpose, five slaves are counted as being equal to three whites. The slaves do not vote; they are only counted and so used, as to swell the influence of the white people's votes. The practical effect of this is more aptly shown by a comparison of the States of South Carolina and Maine. South Carolina has six representatives, and so has Maine; South Carolina has eight presidential electors, and so has Maine. This is precise equality so far; and, of course they are equal in Senators, each having two. Thus in the control of the government, the two States are equals precisely. But how are they in the number of their white people? Maine has 581,813—while South Carolina has 274,567. Maine has twice as many as South Carolina, and 32,679 over. Thus each white man in South Carolina is more than the double of any man in Maine. This is all because South Carolina, besides her free people, has 384,984 slaves. The South Carolinian has precisely the same advantage over the white man in every other free State, as well as in Maine. He is more than the double of any one of us in this crowd. The same advantage, but not to the same extent, is held by all the citizens of the slave States, over those of the free; and it is an absolute truth, without an exception, that there is no voter in any slave State, but who has more legal power in the government, than any voter in any free State. There is no instance of exact equality; and the disadvantage is against us the whole chapter through. This principle, in the aggregate, gives the slave States, in the present Congress, twenty additional representatives—being seven more than the whole majority by which they passed the Nebraska bill.

Now all this is manifestly unfair; yet I do not mention it to complain of it, in so far as it is already settled. It is in the constitution; and I do not, for that cause, or any other cause, propose to destroy, or alter, or disregard the constitution. I stand to it, fairly, fully, and firmly.

But when I am told I must leave it altogether to OTHER PEOPLE to say whether new partners are to be bred up and brought into the firm, on the same degrading terms against me, I respectfully demur. I insist, that whether I shall be a whole man, or only, the half of one, in comparison with others, is a question in which I am somewhat concerned; and one which no other man can have a sacred right of deciding for me. If I am wrong in this—if it really be a sacred right of self-government, in the man who shall go to Nebraska, to decide whether he will be the EQUAL of me or the DOUBLE of me, then after he shall have exercised that right, and thereby shall have reduced me to a still smaller fraction of a man than I already am, I should like for some gentleman deeply skilled in the mysteries of sacred rights, to provide himself with a microscope, and peep about, and find out, if he can, what has become of my sacred rights! They will surely be too small for detection with the naked eye.

Finally, I insist, that if there is ANY THING which it is the duty of the WHOLE PEOPLE to never entrust to any hands but their own, that thing is the preservation and perpetuity, of their own liberties, and institutions. And if they shall think, as I do, that the extension of slavery endangers them, more than any, or all other causes, how recreant to themselves, if they submit the question, and with it, the fate of their country, to a mere hand-full of men, bent only on temporary self-interest. If this question of slavery extension were an insignificant one—one having no power to do harm—it might be shuffled aside in this way. But being, as it is, the great Behemoth of danger, shall the strong gripe of the nation be loosened upon him, to entrust him to the hands of such feeble keepers?

I have done with this mighty argument, of self-government. Go, sacred thing! Go in peace.

But Nebraska is urged as a great Union-saving measure. Well I too, go for saving the Union. Much as I hate slavery, I would consent to the extension of it rather than see the Union dissolved, just as I would consent to any GREAT evil, to avoid a GREATER one. But when I go to Union saving, I must believe, at least, that the means I employ has some adaptation to the end. To my mind, Nebraska has no such adaptation.

It hath no relish of salvation in it.

It is an aggravation, rather, of the only one thing which ever endangers the Union. When it came upon us, all was peace and quiet. The nation was looking to the forming of new bonds of Union; and a long course of peace and prosperity seemed to lie before us. In the whole range of possibility, there scarcely appears to me to have been any thing, out of which the slavery agitation could have been revived, except the very project of repealing the Missouri compromise. Every inch of territory we owned, already had a definite settlement of the slavery question, and by which, all parties were pledged to abide. Indeed, there was no uninhabited country on the continent, which we could acquire; if we except some extreme northern regions, which are wholly out of the question. In this state of case, the genius of Discord himself, could scarcely have invented a way of again getting us by the ears, but by turning back and destroying the peace measures of the past. The councils of that genius seem to have prevailed, the Missouri compromise was repealed; and here we are, in the midst of a new slavery agitation, such, I think, as we have never seen before. Who is responsible for this? Is it those who resist the measure; or those who, causelessly, brought it forward, and pressed it through, having reason to know, and, in fact, knowing it must and would be so resisted? It could not but be expected by its author, that it would be looked upon as a measure for the extension of slavery, aggravated by a gross breach of faith. Argue as you will, and long as you will, this is the naked FRONT and ASPECT, of the measure. And in this aspect, it could not but produce agitation. Slavery is founded in the selfishness of man's nature—opposition to it, is his love of justice. These principles are an eternal antagonism; and when brought into collision so fiercely, as slavery extension brings them, shocks, and throes, and convulsions must ceaselessly follow. Repeal the Missouri compromise—repeal all compromises—repeal the declaration of independence—repeal all past history, you still can not repeal human nature. It still will be the abundance of man's heart, that slavery extension is wrong; and out of the abundance of his heart, his mouth will continue to speak.

The structure, too, of the Nebraska bill is very peculiar. The people are to decide the question of slavery for themselves; but WHEN they are to decide; or HOW they are to decide; or whether, when the question is once decided, it is to remain so, or is it to be subject to an indefinite succession of new trials, the law does not say, Is it to be decided by the first dozen settlers who arrive there? or is it to await the arrival of a hundred? Is it to be decided by a vote of the people? or a vote of the legislature? or, indeed by a vote of any sort? To these questions, the law gives no answer. There is a mystery about this; for when a member proposed to give the legislature express authority to exclude slavery, it was hooted down by the friends of the bill. This fact is worth remembering. Some yankees, in the east, are sending emigrants to Nebraska, to exclude slavery from it; and, so far as I can judge, they expect the question to be decided by voting, in some way or other. But the Missourians are awake too. They are within a stone's throw of the contested ground. They hold meetings, and pass resolutions, in which not the slightest allusion to voting is made. They resolve that slavery already exists in the territory; that more shall go there; that they, remaining in Missouri will protect it; and that abolitionists shall be hung, or driven away. Through all this, bowie-knives and six-shooters are seen plainly enough; but never a glimpse of the ballot-box. And, really, what is to be the result of this? Each party WITHIN, having numerous and determined backers WITHOUT, is it not probable that the contest will come to blows, and bloodshed? Could there be a more apt invention to bring about collision and violence, on the slavery question, than this Nebraska project is? I do not charge, or believe, that such was intended by Congress; but if they had literally formed a ring, and placed champions within it to fight out the controversy, the fight could be no more likely to come off, than it is. And if this fight should begin, is it likely to take a very peaceful, Union-saving turn? Will not the first drop of blood so shed, be the real knell of the Union?

The Missouri Compromise ought to be restored. For the sake of the Union, it ought to be restored. We ought to elect a House of Representatives which will vote its restoration. If by any means, we omit to do this, what follows? Slavery may or may not be established in Nebraska. But whether it be or not, we shall have repudiated—discarded from the councils of the Nation—the SPIRIT OF COMPROMISE; for who after this will ever trust in a national compromise? The spirit of mutual concession—that spirit which first gave us the constitution, and which has thrice saved the Union—we shall have strangled and cast from us forever. And what shall we have in lieu of it? The South flushed with triumph and tempted to excesses; the North, betrayed, as they believe, brooding on wrong and burning for revenge. One side will provoke; the other resent. The one will taunt, the other defy; one aggresses, the other retaliates. Already a few in the North, defy all constitutional restraints, resist the execution of the fugitive slave law, and even menace the institution of slavery in the states where it exists.

Already a few in the South, claim the constitutional right to take to and hold slaves in the free states—demand the revival of the slave trade; and demand a treaty with Great Britain by which fugitive slaves may be reclaimed from Canada. As yet they are but few on either side. It is a grave question for the lovers of the Union, whether the final destruction of the Missouri Compromise, and with it the spirit of all compromise will or will not embolden and embitter each of these, and fatally increase the numbers of both.

But restore the compromise, and what then? We thereby restore the national faith, the national confidence, the national feeling of brotherhood. We thereby reinstate the spirit of concession and compromise—that spirit which has never failed us in past perils, and which may be safely trusted for all the future. The south ought to join in doing this. The peace of the nation is as dear to them as to us. In memories of the past and hopes of the future, they share as largely as we. It would be on their part, a great act—great in its spirit, and great in its effect. It would be worth to the nation a hundred years' purchase of peace and prosperity. And what of sacrifice would they make? They only surrender to us, what they gave us for a consideration long, long ago; what they have not now, asked for, struggled or cared for; what has been thrust upon them, not less to their own astonishment than to ours.

But it is said we cannot restore it; that though we elect every member of the lower house, the Senate is still against us. It is quite true, that of the Senators who passed the Nebraska bill, a majority of the whole Senate will retain their seats in spite of the elections of this and the next year. But if at these elections, their several constituencies shall clearly express their will against Nebraska, will these senators disregard their will? Will they neither obey, nor make room for those who will?

But even if we fail to technically restore the compromise, it is still a great point to carry a popular vote in favor of the restoration. The moral weight of such a vote can not be estimated too highly. The authors of Nebraska are not at all satisfied with the destruction of the compromise—an endorsement of this PRINCIPLE, they proclaim to be the great object. With them, Nebraska alone is a small matter—to establish a principle, for FUTURE USE, is what they particularly desire.

That future use is to be the planting of slavery wherever in the wide world, local and unorganized opposition can not prevent it. Now if you wish to give them this endorsement—if you wish to establish this principle—do so. I shall regret it; but it is your right. On the contrary if you are opposed to the principle—intend to give it no such endorsement—let no wheedling, no sophistry, divert you from throwing a direct vote against it.

Some men, mostly whigs, who condemn the repeal of the Missouri Compromise, nevertheless hesitate to go for its restoration, lest they be thrown in company with the abolitionist. Will they allow me as an old whig to tell them good humoredly, that I think this is very silly? Stand with anybody that stands RIGHT. Stand with him while he is right and PART with him when he goes wrong. Stand WITH the abolitionist in restoring the Missouri Compromise; and stand AGAINST him when he attempts to repeal the fugitive slave law. In the latter case you stand with the southern disunionist. What of that? you are still right. In both cases you are right. In both cases you oppose the dangerous extremes. In both you stand on middle ground and hold the ship level and steady. In both you are national and nothing less than national. This is good old whig ground. To desert such ground, because of any company, is to be less than a whig—less than a man—less than an American.

I particularly object to the NEW position which the avowed principle of this Nebraska law gives to slavery in the body politic. I object to it because it assumes that there CAN be MORAL RIGHT in the enslaving of one man by another. I object to it as a dangerous dalliance for a free people—a sad evidence that, feeling prosperity we forget right—that liberty, as a principle, we have ceased to revere. I object to it because the fathers of the republic eschewed, and rejected it. The argument of "Necessity" was the only argument they ever admitted in favor of slavery; and so far, and so far only as it carried them, did they ever go. They found the institution existing among us, which they could not help; and they cast blame upon the British King for having permitted its introduction. BEFORE the constitution, they prohibited its introduction into the north-western Territory—the only country we owned, then free from it. AT the framing and adoption of the constitution, they forbore to so much as mention the word "slave" or "slavery" in the whole instrument. In the provision for the recovery of fugitives, the slave is spoken of as a "PERSON HELD TO SERVICE OR LABOR." In that prohibiting the abolition of the African slave trade for twenty years, that trade is spoken of as "The migration or importation of such persons as any of the States NOW EXISTING, shall think proper to admit," &c. These are the only provisions alluding to slavery. Thus, the thing is hid away, in the constitution, just as an afflicted man hides away a wen or a cancer, which he dares not cut out at once, lest he bleed to death; with the promise, nevertheless, that the cutting may begin at the end of a given time. Less than this our fathers COULD not do; and MORE they WOULD not do. Necessity drove them so far, and farther, they would not go. But this is not all. The earliest Congress, under the constitution, took the same view of slavery. They hedged and hemmed it in to the narrowest limits of necessity.

In 1794, they prohibited an out-going slave-trade—that is, the taking of slaves FROM the United States to sell.

In 1798, they prohibited the bringing of slaves from Africa, INTO the Mississippi Territory—this territory then comprising what are now the States of Mississippi and Alabama. This was TEN YEARS before they had the authority to do the same thing as to the States existing at the adoption of the constitution.

In 1800 they prohibited AMERICAN CITIZENS from trading in slaves between foreign countries—as, for instance, from Africa to Brazil.

In 1803 they passed a law in aid of one or two State laws, in restraint of the internal slave trade.

In 1807, in apparent hot haste, they passed the law, nearly a year in advance to take effect the first day of 1808—the very first day the constitution would permit—prohibiting the African slave trade by heavy pecuniary and corporal penalties.

In 1820, finding these provisions ineffectual, they declared the trade piracy, and annexed to it, the extreme penalty of death. While all this was passing in the general government, five or six of the original slave States had adopted systems of gradual emancipation; and by which the institution was rapidly becoming extinct within these limits.

Thus we see, the plain unmistakable spirit of that age, towards slavery, was hostility to the PRINCIPLE, and toleration, ONLY BY NECESSITY.

But NOW it is to be transformed into a "sacred right." Nebraska brings it forth, places it on the high road to extension and perpetuity; and, with a pat on its back, says to it, "Go, and God speed you." Henceforth it is to be the chief jewel of the nation—the very figure-head of the ship of State. Little by little, but steadily as man's march to the grave, we have been giving up the OLD for the NEW faith. Near eighty years ago we began by declaring that all men are created equal; but now from that beginning we have run down to the other declaration, that for SOME men to enslave OTHERS is a "sacred right of self-government." These principles can not stand together. They are as opposite as God and mammon; and whoever holds to the one, must despise the other. When Pettit, in connection with his support of the Nebraska bill, called the Declaration of Independence "a self-evident lie" he only did what consistency and candor require all other Nebraska men to do. Of the forty odd Nebraska Senators who sat present and heard him, no one rebuked him. Nor am I apprized that any Nebraska newspaper, or any Nebraska orator, in the whole nation, has ever yet rebuked him. If this had been said among Marion's men, Southerners though they were, what would have become of the man who said it? If this had been said to the men who captured André, the man who said it, would probably have been hung sooner than André was. If it had been said in old Independence Hall, seventy-eight years ago, the very door-keeper would have throttled the man, and thrust him into the street.

Let no one be deceived. The spirit of seventy-six and the spirit of Nebraska, are utter antagonisms; and the former is being rapidly displaced by the latter.

Fellow countrymen—Americans south, as well as north, shall we make no effort to arrest this? Already the liberal party throughout the world, express the apprehension "that the one retrograde institution in America, is undermining the principles of progress, and fatally violating the noblest political system the world ever saw." This is not the taunt of enemies, but the warning of friends. Is it quite safe to disregard it—to despise it? Is there no danger to liberty itself, in discarding the earliest practice, and first precept of our ancient faith? In our greedy chase to make profit of the negro, let us beware, lest we "cancel and tear to pieces" even the white man's charter of freedom.

Our republican robe is soiled, and trailed in the dust. Let us repurify it. Let us turn and wash it white, in the spirit, if not the blood, of the Revolution. Let us turn slavery from its claims of "moral right," back upon its existing legal rights, and its arguments of "necessity." Let us return it to the position our fathers gave it; and there let it rest in peace. Let us re-adopt the Declaration of Independence, and with it, the practices, and policy, which harmonize with it. Let north and south—let all Americans—let all lovers of liberty everywhere—join in the great and good work. If we do this, we shall not only have saved the Union; but we shall have so saved it, as to make, and to keep it, forever worthy of the saving. We shall have so saved it, that the succeeding millions of free happy people, the world over, shall rise up, and call us blessed, to the latest generations.

At Springfield, twelve days ago, where I had spoken substantially as I have here, Judge Douglas replied to me—and as he is to reply to me here, I shall attempt to anticipate him, by noticing some of the points he made there.

He commenced by stating I had assumed all the way through, that the principle of the Nebraska bill, would have the effect of extending slavery. He denied that this was INTENDED, or that this EFFECT would follow.

I will not re-open the argument upon this point. That such was the intention, the world believed at the start, and will continue to believe. This was the COUNTENANCE of the thing; and, both friends and enemies, instantly recognized it as such. That countenance can not now be changed by argument. You can as easily argue the color out of the negroes' skin. Like the "bloody hand" you may wash it, and wash it, the red witness of guilt still sticks, and stares horribly at you.

Next he says, congressional intervention never prevented slavery, any where—that it did not prevent it in the north west territory, nor in Illinois—that in fact, Illinois came into the Union as a slave State—that the principle of the Nebraska bill expelled it from Illinois, from several old States, from every where.

Now this is mere quibbling all the way through. If the ordinance of '87 did not keep slavery out of the north west territory, how happens it that the north west shore of the Ohio river is entirely free from it; while the south east shore, less than a mile distant, along nearly the whole length of the river, is entirely covered with it?

If that ordinance did not keep it out of Illinois, what was it that made the difference between Illinois and Missouri? They lie side by side, the Mississippi river only dividing them; while their early settlements were within the same latitude. Between 1810 and 1820 the number of slaves in Missouri INCREASED 7,211; while in Illinois, in the same ten years, they DECREASED 51. This appears by the census returns. During nearly all of that ten years, both were territories—not States. During this time, the ordinance forbid slavery to go into Illinois; and NOTHING forbid it to go into Missouri. It DID go into Missouri, and did NOT go into Illinois. That is the fact. Can any one doubt as to the reason of it?

But, he says, Illinois came into the Union as a slave State. Silence, perhaps, would be the best answer to this flat contradiction of the known history of the country. What are the facts upon which this bold assertion is based? When we first acquired the country, as far back as 1787, there were some slaves within it, held by the French inhabitants at Kaskaskia. The territorial legislation, admitted a few negroes, from the slave States, as indentured servants. One year after the adoption of the first State constitution the whole number of them was—what do you think? just 117—while the aggregate free population was 55,094—about 470 to one. Upon this state of facts, the people framed their constitution prohibiting the further introduction of slavery, with a sort of guaranty to the owners of the few indentured servants, giving freedom to their children to be born thereafter, and making no mention whatever, of any supposed slave for life. Out of this small matter, the Judge manufactures his argument that Illinois came into the Union as a slave State. Let the facts be the answer to the argument.

The principles of the Nebraska bill, he says, expelled slavery from Illinois? The principle of that bill first planted it here—that is, it first came, because there was no law to prevent it—first came before we owned the country; and finding it here, and having the ordinance of '87 to prevent its increasing, our people struggled along, and finally got rid of it as best they could.

But the principle of the Nebraska bill abolished slavery in several of the old States. Well, it is true that several of the old States, in the last quarter of the last century, did adopt systems of gradual emancipation, by which the institution has finally become extinct within their limits; but it MAY or MAY NOT be true that the principle of the Nebraska bill was the cause that led to the adoption of these measures. It is now more than fifty years, since the last of these States adopted its system of emancipation. If Nebraska bill is the real author of these benevolent works, it is rather deplorable, that he has, for so long a time, ceased working all together. Is there not some reason to suspect that it was the principle of the REVOLUTION, and not the principle of Nebraska bill, that led to emancipation in these old States? Leave it to the people of those old emancipating States, and I am quite sure they will decide, that neither that, nor any other good thing, ever did, or ever will come of Nebraska bill.

In the course of my main argument, Judge Douglas interrupted me to say, that the principle of the Nebraska bill was very old; that it originated when God made man and placed good and evil before him, allowing him to choose for himself, being responsible for the choice he should make. At the time I thought this was merely playful; and I answered it accordingly. But in his reply to me he renewed it, as a serious argument. In seriousness then, the facts of this proposition are not true as stated. God did not place good and evil before man, telling him to make his choice. On the contrary, he did tell him there was one tree, of the fruit of which, he should not eat, upon pain of certain death. I should scarcely wish so strong a prohibition against slavery in Nebraska.

But this argument strikes me as not a little remarkable in another particular— in its strong resemblance to the old argument for the "Divine right of Kings." By the latter, the King is to do just as he pleases with his white subjects, being responsible to God alone. By the former the white man is to do just as he pleases with his black slaves, being responsible to God alone. The two things are precisely alike; and it is but natural that they should find similar arguments to sustain them.

I had argued, that the application of the principle of self-government, as contended for, would require the revival of the African slave trade—that no argument could be made in favor of a man's right to take slaves to Nebraska, which could not be equally well made in favor of his right to bring them from the coast of Africa. The Judge replied, that the constitution requires the suppression of the foreign slave trade; but does NOT require the prohibition of slavery in the territories. That is a mistake, in point of fact. The constitution does NOT require the action of Congress in either case; and it does AUTHORIZE it in both. And so, there is still no difference between the cases.

In regard to what I had said, the advantage the slave States have over the free, in the matter of representation, the Judge replied that we, in the free States, count five free negroes as five white people, while in the slave States, they count five slaves as three whites only; and that the advantage, at last, was on the side of the free States.

Now, in the slave States, they count free negroes just as we do; and it so happens that besides their slaves, they have as many free negroes as we have, and thirty-three thousand over. Thus their free negroes more than balance ours; and their advantage over us, in consequence of their slaves, still remains as I stated it.

In reply to my argument, that the compromise measures of 1850, were a system of equivalents; and that the provisions of no one of them could fairly be carried to other subjects, without its corresponding equivalent being carried with it, the Judge denied out-right, that these measures had any connection with, or dependence upon, each other. This is mere desperation. If they have no connection, why are they always spoken of in connection? Why has he so spoken of them, a thousand times? Why has he constantly called them a SERIES of measures? Why does everybody call them a compromise? Why was California kept out of the Union, six or seven months, if it was not because of its connection with the other measures? Webster's leading definition of the verb "to compromise" is "to adjust and settle a difference, by mutual agreement with concessions of claims by the parties." This conveys precisely the popular understanding of the word compromise. We knew, before the Judge told us, that these measures passed separately, and in distinct bills; and that no two of them were passed by the votes of precisely the same members. But we also know, and so does he know, that no one of them could have passed both branches of Congress but for the understanding that the others were to pass also. Upon this understanding each got votes, which it could have got in no other way. It is this fact, that gives to the measures their true character; and it is the universal knowledge of this fact, that has given them the name of compromise so expressive of that true character.

I had asked "If in carrying the provisions of the Utah and New Mexico laws to Nebraska, you could clear away other objection, how can you leave Nebraska "perfectly free" to introduce slavery BEFORE she forms a constitution—during her territorial government?—while the Utah and New Mexico laws only authorize it WHEN they form constitutions, and are admitted into the Union?" To this Judge Douglas answered that the Utah and New Mexico laws, also authorized it BEFORE; and to prove this, he read from one of their laws, as follows: "That the legislative power of said territory shall extend to all rightful subjects of legislation consistent with the constitution of the United States and the provisions of this act."

Now it is perceived from the reading of this, that there is nothing express upon the subject; but that the authority is sought to be implied merely, for the general provision of "all rightful subjects of legislation." In reply to this, I insist, as a legal rule of construction, as well as the plain popular view of the matter, that the EXPRESS provision for Utah and New Mexico coming in with slavery if they choose, when they shall form constitutions, is an EXCLUSION of all implied authority on the same subject—that Congress, having the subject distinctly in their minds, when they made the express provision, they therein expressed their WHOLE meaning on that subject.

The Judge rather insinuated that I had found it convenient to forget the Washington territorial law passed in 1853. This was a division of Oregon, organizing the northern part, as the territory of Washington. He asserted that, by this act, the ordinance of '87 theretofore existing in Oregon, was repealed; that nearly all the members of Congress voted for it, beginning in the H.R., with Charles Allen of Massachusetts, and ending with Richard Yates, of Illinois; and that he could not understand how those who now oppose the Nebraska bill, so voted then, unless it was because it was then too soon after both the great political parties had ratified the compromises of 1850, and the ratification therefore too fresh, to be then repudiated.

Now I had seen the Washington act before; and I have carefully examined it since; and I aver that there is no repeal of the ordinance of '87, or of any prohibition of slavery, in it. In express terms, there is absolutely nothing in the whole law upon the subject—in fact, nothing to lead a reader to THINK of the subject. To my judgment, it is equally free from every thing from which such repeal can be legally implied; but however this may be, are men now to be entrapped by a legal implication, extracted from covert language, introduced perhaps, for the very purpose of entrapping them? I sincerely wish every man could read this law quite through, carefully watching every sentence, and every line, for a repeal of the ordinance of '87 or any thing equivalent to it.

Another point on the Washington act. If it was intended to be modelled after the Utah and New Mexico acts, as Judge Douglas, insists, why was it not inserted in it, as in them, that Washington was to come in with or without slavery as she may choose at the adoption of her constitution? It has no such provision in it; and I defy the ingenuity of man to give a reason for the omission, other than that it was not intended to follow the Utah and New Mexico laws in regard to the question of slavery.

The Washington act not only differs vitally from the Utah and New Mexico acts; but the Nebraska act differs vitally from both. By the latter act the people are left "perfectly free" to regulate their own domestic concerns, &c.; but in all the former, all their laws are to be submitted to Congress, and if disapproved are to be null. The Washington act goes even further; it absolutely prohibits the territorial legislation, by very strong and guarded language, from establishing banks, or borrowing money on the faith of the territory. Is this the sacred right of self-government we hear vaunted so much? No sir, the Nebraska bill finds no model in the acts of '50 or the Washington act. It finds no model in any law from Adam till today. As Phillips says of Napoleon, the Nebraska act is grand, gloomy, and peculiar; wrapped in the solitude of its own originality; without a model, and without a shadow upon the earth.

In the course of his reply, Senator Douglas remarked, in substance, that he had always considered this government was made for the white people and not for the negroes. Why, in point of mere fact, I think so too. But in this remark of the Judge, there is a significance, which I think is the key to the great mistake (if there is any such mistake) which he has made in this Nebraska measure. It shows that the Judge has no very vivid impression that the negro is a human; and consequently has no idea that there can be any moral question in legislating about him. In his view, the question of whether a new country shall be slave or free, is a matter of as utter indifference, as it is whether his neighbor shall plant his farm with tobacco, or stock it with horned cattle. Now, whether this view is right or wrong, it is very certain that the great mass of mankind take a totally different view. They consider slavery a great moral wrong; and their feelings against it, is not evanescent, but eternal. It lies at the very foundation of their sense of justice; and it cannot be trifled with. It is a great and durable element of popular action, and, I think, no statesman can safely disregard it.

Our Senator also objects that those who oppose him in this measure do not entirely agree with one another. He reminds me that in my firm adherence to the constitutional rights of the slave States, I differ widely from others who are co-operating with me in opposing the Nebraska bill; and he says it is not quite fair to oppose him in this variety of ways. He should remember that he took us by surprise—astounded us—by this measure. We were thunderstruck and stunned; and we reeled and fell in utter confusion. But we rose each fighting, grasping whatever he could first reach—a scythe—a pitchfork—a chopping axe, or a butcher's cleaver. We struck in the direction of the sound; and we are rapidly closing in upon him. He must not think to divert us from our purpose, by showing us that our drill, our dress, and our weapons, are not entirely perfect and uniform. When the storm shall be past, he shall find us still Americans; no less devoted to the continued Union and prosperity of the country than heretofore.

Finally, the Judge invokes against me, the memory of Clay and of Webster. They were great men; and men of great deeds. But where have I assailed them? For what is it, that their life-long enemy, shall now make profit, by assuming to defend them against me, their life-long friend? I go against the repeal of the Missouri compromise; did they ever go for it? They went for the compromise of 1850; did I ever go against them? They were greatly devoted to the Union; to the small measure of my ability, was I ever less so? Clay and Webster were dead before this question arose; by what authority shall our Senator say they would espouse his side of it, if alive? Mr. Clay was the leading spirit in making the Missouri compromise; is it very credible that if now alive, he would take the lead in the breaking of it? The truth is that some support from whigs is now a necessity with the Judge, and for thus it is, that the names of Clay and Webster are now invoked. His old friends have deserted him in such numbers as to leave too few to live by. He came to his own, and his own received him not, and Lo! he turns unto the Gentiles.

A word now as to the Judge's desperate assumption that the compromises of '50 had no connection with one another; that Illinois came into the Union as a slave state, and some other similar ones. This is no other than a bold denial of the history of the country. If we do not know that the Compromises of '50 were dependent on each other; if we do not know that Illinois came into the Union as a free state—we do not know any thing. If we do not know these things, we do not know that we ever had a revolutionary war, or such a chief as Washington. To deny these things is to deny our national axioms, or dogmas, at least; and it puts an end to all argument. If a man will stand up and assert, and repeat, and re-assert, that two and two do not make four, I know nothing in the power of argument that can stop him. I think I can answer the Judge so long as he sticks to the premises; but when he flies from them, I can not work an argument into the consistency of a maternal gag, and actually close his mouth with it. In such a case I can only commend him to the seventy thousand answers just in from Pennsylvania, Ohio and Indiana.

*October 16, 1854*

# Fragment on Sectionalism

It is constantly objected to Fremont & Dayton, that they are supported by a *sectional* party, who, by their *sectionalism*, endanger the National Union. This objection, more than all others, causes men, really opposed to slavery extension, to hesitate. Practically, it is the most difficult objection we have to meet.

For this reason, I now propose to examine it, a little more carefully than I have heretofore done, or seen it done by others.

First, then, what is the question between the parties, respectively represented by Buchanan and Fremont?

Simply this: "*Shall slavery be allowed to extend into U.S. territories, now legally free?*" Buchanan says it *shall*; and Fremont says it shall *not*.

That is the *naked* issue, and the *whole* of it. Lay the respective platforms side by side; and the difference between them, will be found to amount to precisely that.

True, each party charges upon the other, *designs* much beyond what is involved in the issue, as stated; but as these charges cannot be fully proved either way, it is probably better to reject them on both sides, and stick to the naked issue, as it is clearly made up on the record.

And now to restate the question "*Shall slavery be allowed to extend into U.S. territories, now legally free?*" I beg to know *how one* side of that question is more sectional than the other? Of course I expect to effect nothing with the man who makes the charge of sectionalism, without caring whether it is just or not. But of the *candid, fair,* man who has been puzzled with this charge, I do ask how is *one* side of this question, more *sectional*, than the other? I beg of him to consider well, and answer calmly.

If one side be as sectional as the other, nothing is gained, as to sectionalism, by changing sides; so that each must choose sides of the question on some other ground—as I should think, according, as the one side or the other, shall appear nearest right.

If he shall really think slavery *ought* to be extended, let him go to Buchanan; if he think it ought *not* let him go to Fremont.

But, Fremont and Dayton, are both residents of the free-states; and this fact has been vaunted, in high places, as excessive *sectionalism*.

While interested individuals become *indignant* and *excited*, against this manifestation of *sectionalism*, I am very happy to know, that the Constitution remains calm—keeps cool—upon the subject. It does say that President and Vice President shall be resident of different states; but it does not say that one must live in a *slave*, and the other in a *free* state.

It has been a *custom* to take one from a slave, and the other from a free state; but the custom has not, at all been uniform. In 1828 Gen. Jackson and Mr. Calhoun, both from slave-states, were placed on the same ticket; and Mr. Adams and Dr. Rush both from free-states, were pitted against them. Gen. Jackson and Mr. Calhoun were elected; and qualified and served under the election; yet the whole thing never suggested the idea of sectionalism.

In 1841, the President, Gen. Harrison, died, by which Mr. Tyler, the Vice-President & a slave-state man, became President. Mr. Mangum, another slave-state man, was placed in the Vice Presidential chair, served out the term, and no fuss about it—no sectionalism thought of.

In 1853 the present president came into office. He is a free-state man. Mr. King, the new Vice President elect, was a slave state man; but he died without entering on the duties of his office. At first, his vacancy was filled by Atchison, another slave-state man; but he soon resigned, and the place was supplied by Bright, a free-state man. So that right now, and for the year and a half last past, our president and vice-president are both actually free-state men.

But, it is said, the friends of Fremont, avow the purpose of electing him exclusively by free-state votes, and that this is unendurable *sectionalism*.

This statement of fact, is not exactly true. With the friends of Fremont, it is an *expected necessity*, but it is not an "*avowed purpose*," to elect him, if at all, principally, by free-state votes; but it is, with equal intensity, true that Buchanan's friends expect to elect him, if at all, chiefly by slave-state votes.

Here, again, the sectionalism is just as much on one side as the other.

The thing which gives most color to the charge of Sectionalism, made against those who oppose the spread of slavery into free territory, is the fact that *they* can get no votes in the slave-states, while their opponents get all, or nearly so, in the slave-states, and also a large number in the free States. To state it in another way, the Extensionists, can get votes all over the Nation, while the Restrictionists can get them only in the free states.

This being the fact, *why* is it so ? It is not because one *side* of the question dividing them, is more sectional than the *other*; nor because of any difference in the mental or moral structure of the people North and South. It is because, in that question, the people of the South have an immediate palpable and immensely great pecuniary interest; while, with the people of the North, it is merely an abstract question of moral right, with only *slight*, and *remote* pecuniary interest added.

The slaves of the South, at a moderate estimate, are worth a thousand millions of dollars. Let it be permanently settled that this property may extend to new territory, without restraint, and it greatly *enhances*, perhaps quite *doubles*, its value at once. This immense, palpable pecuniary interest, on the question of extending slavery, unites the Southern people, as one man. But it can not be demonstrated that the *North* will gain a dollar by restricting it.

Moral principle is all, or nearly all, that unites us of the North. Pity 'tis, it is so, but this is a looser bond, than pecuniary interest. Right here is the plain cause of *their perfect* union and *our want* of it. And see how it works. If a Southern man aspires to be president, they choke him down instantly, in order that the glittering prize of the presidency, may be held up, on Southern terms, to the greedy eyes of Northern ambition. With this they tempt us, and break in upon us.

The democratic party, in 1844, elected a Southern president. Since then, they have neither had a Southern candidate for *election,* or *nomination*. Their Conventions of 1848–1852 and 1856, have been struggles exclusively among *Northern* men, each vying to out-bid the other for the Southern vote—the South standing calmly by to finally cry going, going, gone, to the highest bidder; and, at the same time, to make its power more distinctly seen, and thereby to secure a still higher bid at the next succeeding struggle.

"Actions speak louder than words" is the maxim; and, if true, the South now distinctly says to the North "Give us the *measures*, and you take the *men*."

The total withdrawal of Southern aspirants, for the presidency, multiplies the number of Northern ones. These last, in competing with each other, commit themselves to the utmost verge that, through their own greediness, they have the least hope their Northern supporters will bear. Having got committed, in a race of competition, necessity drives them into union to sustain themselves. Each, at first secures all he can, on personal attachments to him, and through *hopes* resting on him personally. Next, they unite with one another, and with the perfectly banded South, to make the offensive position they have got into, "a party measure." This done, large additional numbers are secured.

When the repeal of the Missouri compromise was first proposed, at the North there was literally "*nobody*" in favor of it. In February 1854 our Legislature met in call, or extra, session. From them Douglas sought an indorsement of his then pending measure of Repeal. In our Legislature were about 70 democrats to 30 whigs. The former held a caucus, in which it was resolved to give Douglas the desired indorsement. Some of the members of the caucus bolted—would not stand it—and they now divulge the secrets. They say that the caucus fairly confessed that the Repeal was wrong; and they placed their determination to indorse it, solely on the ground that it was *necessary* to sustain Douglas. Here we have the direct evidence of how the Nebraska-bill obtained it's strength in Illinois. It was given, not in a sense of right, but in the teeth of a sense of wrong, to *sustain Douglas*. So Illinois was divided. So New England, for Pierce; Michigan for Cass, Pennsylvania for Buchanan, and all for the Democratic party.

And when, by such means, they have got a large portion of the Northern people into a position contrary to their own honest impulses, and sense of right; they have the impudence to turn upon those who do stand firm, and call them *sectional*.

Were it not too serious a matter, this cool impudence would be laughable, to say the least.

Recurring to the question *"Shall slavery be allowed to extend into U.S. territory now legally free?"*

This *is* a sectional question—that is to say, it is a question, in its nature calculated to divide the American people geographically. Who is to *blame* for that? *who* can help it? Either side *can* help it; but how? Simply by *yielding* to the other side. There is no other way. In the whole range of *possibility*, there is no other way. Then, which side shall yield? To this again, there can be but one answer—the side which is in the *wrong*. True, we differ, as to which side *is* wrong; and we boldly say, let all who really think slavery ought to be spread into free territory, openly go over against us. There is where they rightfully belong.

But why should any go, who really think slavery ought not to spread? Do they really think the *right* ought to yield to the *wrong*? Are they afraid to stand by the *right*? Do they fear that the constitution is too weak to sustain them in the right? Do they really think that by right surrendering to wrong the hopes of our constitution, our Union, and our liberties, can possibly be bettered?

*ca. July, 1856*

# Speech at Kalamazoo, Michigan

FELLOW COUNTRYMEN:—

Under the Constitution of the U.S. another Presidential contest approaches us. All over this land—that portion at least, of which I know much—the people are assembling to consider the proper course to be adopted by them. One of the first considerations is to learn what the people differ about. If we ascertain what we differ about, we shall be better able to decide. The question of slavery, at the present day, should be not only the greatest question, but very nearly the sole question. Our opponents, however, prefer that this should not be the case. To get at this question, I will occupy your attention but a single moment. The question is simply this:—Shall slavery be spread into the new Territories, or not? This is the naked question. If we should support Fremont successfully in this, it may be charged that we will not be content with restricting slavery in the new territories. If we should charge that James Buchanan, by his platform, is bound to extend slavery into the territories, and that he is in favor of its being thus spread, we should be puzzled to prove it. We believe it, nevertheless. By taking the issue as I present it, whether it shall be permitted as an issue, is made up between the parties. Each takes his own stand. This is the question: Shall the Government of the United States prohibit slavery in the United States.

We have been in the habit of deploring the fact that slavery exists amongst us. We have ever deplored it. Our forefathers did, and they declared, as we have done in later years, the blame rested on the mother Government of Great Britain. We constantly condemn Great Britain for not preventing slavery from coming amongst us. She would not interfere to prevent it, and so individuals were enabled to introduce the institution without opposition. I have alluded to this, to ask you if this is not exactly the policy of Buchanan and his friends, to place this government in the attitude then occupied by the government of Great Britain—placing the nation in the position to authorize the territories to reproach it, for refusing to allow them to hold slaves. I would like to ask your attention, any gentleman to tell me when the people of Kansas are going to decide. When are they to do it? How are they to do it? I asked that question two years ago—when, and how are they to do it? Not many weeks ago, our new Senator from Illinois, (Mr. Trumbull) asked Douglas how it could be done. Douglas is a great man—at keeping from answering questions he don't want to answer. He would not answer. He said it was a question for the Supreme Court to decide. In the North, his friends argue that the people can decide it at any time. The Southerners say there is no power in the people, whatever. We know that from the time that white people have been allowed in the territory, they have brought slaves with them. Suppose the people come up to vote as freely, and with as perfect protection as we could do it here. Will they be at liberty to vote their sentiments? If they can, then all that has ever been said about our provincial ancestors is untrue, and they could have done so, also. We know our Southern friends say that the General Government cannot interfere. The people, say they, have no right to interfere. They could as truly say,—"It is amongst us—we cannot get rid of it."

But I am afraid I waste too much time on this point. I take it as an illustration of the principle, that slaves are admitted into the territories. And, while I am speaking of Kansas, how will that operate? Can men vote truly? We will suppose that there are ten men who go into Kansas to settle. Nine of these are opposed to slavery. One has ten slaves. The slaveholder is a good man in other respects; he is a good neighbor, and being a wealthy man, he is enabled to do the others many neighborly kindnesses. They like the man, though they don't like the system by which he holds his fellow-men in bondage. And here let me say, that in intellectual and physical structure, our Southern brethren do not differ from us. They are, like us, subject to passions, and it is only their odious institution of slavery, that makes the breach between us. These ten men of whom I was speaking, live together three or four years; they intermarry; their family ties are strengthened. And who wonders that in time, the people learn to look upon slavery with complacency? This is the way in which slavery is planted, and gains so firm a foothold. I think this is a strong card that the Nebraska party have played, and won upon, in this game.

I suppose that this crowd are opposed to the admission of slavery into Kansas, yet it is true that in all crowds there are some who differ from the majority. I want to ask the Buchanan men, who are against the spread of slavery, if there be any present, why not vote for the man who is against it? I understand that Mr. Fillmore's position is precisely like Buchanan's. I understand that, by the Nebraska bill, a door has been opened for the spread of slavery in the Territories. Examine, if you please, and see if they have ever done any such thing as try to shut the door. It is true that Fillmore tickles a few of his friends with the notion that he is not the cause of the door being opened. Well; it brings him into this position: he tries to get both sides, one by denouncing those who opened the door, and the other by hinting that he doesn't care a fig for its being open. If he were President, he would have one side or the other—he would either restrict slavery or not. Of course it would be so. There could be no middle way. You who hate slavery and love freedom, why not, as Fillmore and Buchanan are on the same ground, vote for Fremont? Why not vote for the man who takes your side of the question? "Well," says Buchanier, "it is none of our business." But is it not *our* business? There are several reasons why I think it is our business. But let us see how it is. Others have urged these reasons before, but they are still of use. By our Constitution we are represented in Congress in proportion to numbers, and in counting the numbers that give us our representatives, three slaves are counted as two people. The State of Maine has six representatives in the lower house of Congress. In strength South Carolina is equal to her. But stop! Maine has *twice as many* white people, and 32,000 to boot! And is that fair? I don't complain of it. This regulation was put in force when the exigencies of the times demanded it, and could not have been avoided. Now, one man in South Carolina is the same as two men here. Maine should have twice as many men in Congress as South Carolina. It is a fact that any man in South Carolina has more influence and power in Congress today than any two now before me. The same thing is true of all slave States, though it may not be in the same proportion. It is a truth that cannot be denied, that in all the free States no white man is the equal of the white man of the slave States. But this is in the Constitution, and we must stand up to it. The question, then is, "Have we no interest as to whether the white man of the North shall be the equal of the white man of the South?" Once when I used this argument in the presence of Douglas, he answered that in the North the black man was counted as a full man, and had an equal vote with the white, while at the South they were counted at but three-fifths. And Douglas, when he had made this reply, doubtless thought he had forever silenced the objection.

Have we no interest in the free Territories of the United States—that they should be kept open for the homes of free white people? As our Northern States are growing more and more in wealth and population, we are continually in want of an outlet, through which it may pass out to enrich our country. In this we have an interest—a deep and abiding interest. There is another thing, and that is the mature knowledge we have—the greatest interest of all. It is the doctrine, that the people are to be driven from the maxims of our free Government, that despises the spirit which for eighty years has celebrated the anniversary of our national independence.

We are a great empire. We are eighty years old. We stand at once the wonder and admiration of the whole world, and we must enquire what it is that has given us so much prosperity, and we shall understand that to give up that one thing, would be to give up all future prosperity. This cause is that every man can make himself. It has been said that such a race of prosperity has been run nowhere else. We find a people on the North-east, who have a different government from ours, being ruled by a Queen. Turning to the South, we see a people who, while they boast of being free, keep their fellow beings in bondage. Compare our Free States with either, shall we say here that we have no interest in keeping that principle alive? Shall we say—"Let it be." No—we have an interest in the maintenance of the principles of the Government, and without this interest, it is worth nothing. I have noticed in Southern newspapers, particularly the Richmond *Enquirer*, the Southern view of the Free States. They insist that slavery has a right to spread. They defend it upon principle. They insist that their slaves are far better off than Northern freemen. What a mistaken view do these men have of Northern laborers! They think that men are always to remain laborers here—but there is no such class. The man who labored for another last year, this year labors for himself, and next year he will hire others to labor for him. These men don't understand when they think in this manner of Northern free labor. When these reasons can be introduced, tell me not that we have no interest in keeping the Territories free for the settlement of free laborers.

I pass, then, from this question. I think we have an ever growing interest in maintaining the free institutions of our country.

It is said that our party is a sectional party. It has been said in high quarters that if Fremont and Dayton were elected the Union would be dissolved. The South do not think so. I believe it! I believe it! It is a shameful thing that the subject is talked of so much. Did we not have a Southern President and Vice-President at one time? And yet the Union has not yet been dissolved. Why, at this very moment, there is a Northern President and Vice-President. Pierce and King were elected, and King died without ever taking his seat. The Senate elected a Northern man from their own numbers, to perform the duties of the Vice-President. He resigned his seat, however, as soon as he got the job of making a slave State out of Kansas. Was not that a great mistake?

A VOICE: "He didn't mean that!"

Then why didn't he speak what he did mean? Why did not he speak what he ought to have spoken? That was the very thing. He should have spoken manly, and we should then have known where to have found him. It is said we expect to elect Fremont by Northern votes. Certainly we do not think the South will elect him. But let us ask the question differently. Does not Buchanan expect to be elected by Southern votes? Fillmore, however, will go out of this contest the most national man we have. He has no prospect of having a single vote on either side of Mason and Dixon's line, to trouble his poor soul about. (Laughter and cheers.)

We believe that it is right that slavery should not be tolerated in the new territories, yet we cannot get support for this doctrine, except in one part of the country. Slavery is looked upon by men in the light of dollars and cents. The estimated worth of the slaves at the South is $1,000,000,000, and in a very few years, if the institution shall be admitted into the territories, they will have increased fifty per cent in value.

Our adversaries charge Fremont with being an abolitionist. When pressed to show proof, they frankly confess that they can show no such thing. They then run off upon the assertion that his supporters are abolitionists. But this they have never attempted to prove. I know of no word in the language that has been used so much as that one "abolitionist," having no definition. It has no meaning unless taken as designating a person who is abolishing something. If that be its signification, the supporters of Fremont are not abolitionists. In Kansas all who come there are perfectly free to regulate their own social relations. There has never been a man there who was an abolitionist—for what was there to be abolished? People there had perfect freedom to express what they wished on the subject, when the Nebraska bill was first passed. Our friends in the South, who support Buchanan, have five disunion men to one at the North. This disunion is a sectional question. Who is to blame for it? Are we? I don't care how you express it. This government is sought to be put on a new track. Slavery is to be made a ruling element in our government. The question can be avoided in but two ways. By the one, we must submit, and allow slavery to triumph, or, by the other, we must triumph over the black demon. We have chosen the latter manner. If you of the North wish to get rid of this question, you must decide between these two ways—submit and vote for Buchanan, submit and vote that slavery is a just and good thing and immediately get rid of the question; or unite with us, and help us to triumph. We would all like to have the question done away with, but we cannot submit.

They tell us that we are in company with men who have long been known as abolitionists. What care we how many may feel disposed to labor for our cause? Why do not you, Buchanan men, come in and use your influence to make our party respectable? (Laughter.) How is the dissolution of the Union to be consummated? They tell us that the Union is in danger. Who will divide it? Is it those who make the charge? Are they themselves the persons who wish to see this result? A majority will never dissolve the Union. Can a minority do it? When this Nebraska bill was first introduced into Congress, the sense of the Democratic party was outraged. That party has ever prided itself, that it was the friend of individual, universal freedom. It was that principle upon which they carried their measures. When the Kansas scheme was conceived, it was natural that this respect and sense should have been outraged. Now I make this appeal to the Democratic citizens here. Don't you find yourself making arguments in support of these measures, which you never would have made before? Did you ever do it before this Nebraska bill compelled you to do it? If you answer this in the affirmative, see how a whole party have been turned away from their love of liberty! And now, my Democratic friends, come forward. Throw off these things, and come to the rescue of this great principle of equality. Don't interfere with anything in the Constitution. That must be maintained, for it is the only safeguard of our liberties. And not to Democrats alone do I make this appeal, but to all who love these great and true principles. Come, and keep coming! Strike, and strike again! So sure as God lives, the victory shall be yours. (Great cheering.)

*August 27, 1856*

# Speech on the Dred Scott Decision

Fellow citizens:—

I am here to-night, partly by the invitation of some of you, and partly by my own inclination. Two weeks ago Judge Douglas spoke here on the several subjects of Kansas, the Dred Scott decision, and Utah. I listened to the speech at the time, and have read the report of it since. It was intended to controvert opinions which I think just, and to assail (politically, not personally,) those men who, in common with me, entertain those opinions. For this reason I wished then, and still wish, to make some answer to it, which I now take the opportunity of doing.

I begin with Utah. If it prove to be true, as is probable, that the people of Utah are in open rebellion to the United States, then Judge Douglas is in favor of repealing their territorial organization, and attaching them to the adjoining States for judicial purposes. I say, too, if they are in rebellion, they ought to be somehow coerced to obedience; and I am not now prepared to admit or deny that the Judge's mode of coercing them is not as good as any. The Republicans can fall in with it without taking back anything they have ever said. To be sure, it would be a considerable backing down by Judge Douglas from his much vaunted doctrine of self-government for the territories; but this is only additional proof of what was very plain from the beginning, that that doctrine was a mere deceitful pretense for the benefit of slavery. Those who could not see that much in the Nebraska act itself, which forced Governors, and Secretaries, and Judges on the people of the territories, without their choice or consent, could not be made to see, though one should rise from the dead to testify.

But in all this, it is very plain the Judge evades the only question the Republicans have ever pressed upon the Democracy in regard to Utah. That question the Judge well knows to be this: "If the people of Utah shall peacefully form a State Constitution tolerating polygamy, will the Democracy admit them into the Union?" There is nothing in the United States Constitution or law against polygamy; and why is it not a part of the Judge's "sacred right of self-government" for that people to have it, or rather to *keep* it, if they choose? These questions, so far as I know, the Judge never answers. It might involve the Democracy to answer them either way, and they go unanswered.

As to Kansas. The substance of the Judge's speech on Kansas is an effort to put the free State men in the wrong for not voting at the election of delegates to the Constitutional Convention. He says: *"There is every reason to hope and believe that the law will be fairly interpreted and impartially executed, so as to insure to every bona fide inhabitant the free and quiet exercise of the elective franchise."*

It appears extraordinary that Judge Douglas should make such a statement. He knows that, by the law, no one can vote who has not been registered; and he knows that the free State men place their refusal to vote on the ground that but few of them have been registered. It is *possible* this is not true, but Judge Douglas knows it is asserted to be true in letters, newspapers and public speeches, and borne by every mail, and blown by every breeze to the eyes and ears of the world. He knows it is boldly declared that the people of many whole counties, and many whole neighborhoods in others, are left unregistered; yet, he does not venture to contradict the declaration, nor to point out how they *can* vote without being registered; but he just slips along, not seeming to know there is any such question of fact, and complacently declares: "There is every reason to hope and believe that the law will be fairly and impartially executed, so as to insure to every *bona fide* inhabitant the free and quiet exercise of the elective franchise."

I readily agree that if all had a chance to vote, they ought to have voted. If, on the contrary, as they allege, and Judge Douglas ventures not to particularly contradict, few only of the free State men had a chance to vote, they were perfectly right in staying from the polls in a body.

By the way since the Judge spoke, the Kansas election has come off. The Judge expressed his confidence that all the Democrats in Kansas would do their duty—including "free state Democrats" of course. The returns received here as yet are very incomplete; but so far as they go, they indicate that only about one sixth of the registered voters, have really voted; and this too, when not more, perhaps, than one half of the rightful voters have been registered, thus showing the thing to have been altogether the most exquisite farce ever enacted. I am watching with considerable interest, to ascertain what figure "the free state Democrats" cut in the concern. Of course they voted—all democrats do their duty—and of course they did not vote for slave-state candidates. We soon shall know how many delegates *they* elected, how many candidates they had, pledged for a free state; and how many votes were cast for them.

Allow me to barely whisper my suspicion that there were no such things in Kansas "as free state Democrats"—that they were altogether mythical, good only to figure in newspapers and speeches in the free states. If there should prove to be one real living free state Democrat in Kansas, I suggest that it might be well to catch him, and stuff and preserve his skin, as an interesting specimen of that soon to be extinct variety of the genus, Democrat.

And now as to the Dred Scott decision. That decision declares two propositions—first, that a negro cannot sue in the U.S. Courts; and secondly, that Congress cannot prohibit slavery in the Territories. It was made by a divided court—dividing differently on the different points. Judge Douglas does not discuss the merits of the decision; and, in that respect, I shall follow his example, believing I could no more improve on McLean and Curtis, than he could on Taney.

He denounces all who question the correctness of that decision, as offering violent resistance to it. But who resists it? Who has, in spite of the decision, declared Dred Scott free, and resisted the authority of his master over him?

Judicial decisions have two uses—first, to absolutely determine the case decided, and secondly, to indicate to the public how other similar cases will be decided when they arise. For the latter use, they are called "precedents" and "authorities."

We believe, as much as Judge Douglas, (perhaps more) in obedience to, and respect for the judicial department of government. We think its decisions on Constitutional questions, when fully settled, should control, not only the particular cases decided, but the general policy of the country, subject to be disturbed only by amendments of the Constitution as provided in that instrument itself. More than this would be revolution. But we think the Dred Scott decision is erroneous. We know the court that made it, has often over-ruled its own decisions, and we shall do what we can to have it to over-rule this. We offer no *resistance* to it.

Judicial decisions are of greater or less authority as precedents, according to circumstances. That this should be so, accords both with common sense, and the customary understanding of the legal profession.

If this important decision had been made by the unanimous concurrence of the judges, and without any apparent partisan bias, and in accordance with legal public expectation, and with the steady practice of the departments throughout our history, and had been in no part, based on assumed historical facts which are not really true; or, if wanting in some of these, it had been before the court more than once, and had there been affirmed and re-affirmed through a course of years, it then might be, perhaps would be, factious, nay, even revolutionary, to not acquiesce in it as a precedent.

But when, as it is true we find it wanting in all these claims to the public confidence, it is not resistance, it is not factious, it is not even disrespectful, to treat it as not having yet quite established a settled doctrine for the country—But Judge Douglas considers this view awful. Hear him:

"The courts are the tribunals prescribed by the Constitution and created by the authority of the people to determine, expound and enforce the law. Hence, whoever resists the final decision of the highest judicial tribunal, aims a deadly blow to our whole Republican system of government—a blow, which if success-ful would place all our rights and liberties at the mercy of passion, anarchy and violence. I repeat, therefore, that if resistance to the decisions of the Supreme Court of the United States, in a matter like the points decided in the Dred Scott case, clearly within their jurisdiction as defined by the Constitution, shall be forced upon the country as a political issue, it will become a distinct and naked issue between the friends and the enemies of the Constitution—the friends and the enemies of the supremacy of the laws."

Why this same Supreme court once decided a national bank to be constitu-tional; but Gen. Jackson, as President of the United States, disregarded the deci-sion, and vetoed a bill for a re-charter, partly on constitutional ground, declaring that each public functionary must support the Constitution, *"as he understands it."* But hear the General's own words. Here they are, taken from his veto message:

"It is maintained by the advocates of the bank, that its constitutionality, in all its features, ought to be considered as settled by precedent, and by the deci-sion of the Supreme Court. To this conclusion I cannot assent. Mere precedent is a dangerous source of authority, and should not be regarded as deciding ques-tions of constitutional power, except where the acquiescence of the people and the States can be considered as well settled. So far from this being the case on this subject, an argument against the bank might be based on precedent. One Congress in 1791, decided in favor of a bank; another in 1811, decided against it. One Congress in 1815 decided against a bank; another in 1816 decided in its favor. Prior to the present Congress, therefore the precedents drawn from that source were equal. If we resort to the States, the expressions of legislative, judicial and executive opinions against the bank have been probably to those in its favor as four to one. There is nothing in precedent, therefore, which if its authority were admitted, ought to weigh in favor of the act before me."

I drop the quotations merely to remark that all there ever was, in the way of precedent up to the Dred Scott decision, on the points therein decided, had been against that decision. But hear Gen. Jackson further—

"If the opinion of the Supreme court covered the whole ground of this act, it ought not to control the co-ordinate authorities of this Government. The Congress, the executive and the court, must each for itself be guided by its own opinion of the Constitution. Each public officer, who takes an oath to support the Constitution, swears that he will support it as he understands it, and not as it is understood by others."

Again and again have I heard Judge Douglas denounce that bank decision, and applaud Gen. Jackson for disregarding it. It would be interesting for him to look over his recent speech, and see how exactly his fierce philippics against us for resisting Supreme Court decisions, fall upon his own head. It will call to his mind a long and fierce political war in this country, upon an issue which, in his own language, and, of course, in his own changeless estimation, was "a distinct and naked issue between the friends and the enemies of the Constitution," and in which war he fought in the ranks of the enemies of the Constitution.

I have said, in substance, that the Dred Scott decision was, in part, based on assumed historical facts which were not really true; and I ought not to leave the subject without giving some reasons for saying this; I therefore give an instance or two, which I think fully sustain me. Chief Justice Taney, in delivering the opinion of the majority of the Court, insists at great length that negroes were no part of the people who made, or for whom was made, the Declaration of Independence, or the Constitution of the United States.

On the contrary, Judge Curtis, in his dissenting opinion, shows that in five of the then thirteen states, to wit, New Hampshire, Massachusetts, New York, New Jersey and North Carolina, free negroes were voters, and, in proportion to their numbers, had the same part in making the Constitution that the white people had. He shows this with so much particularity as to leave no doubt of its truth; and, as a sort of conclusion on that point, holds the following language:

"The Constitution was ordained and established by the people of the United States, through the action, in each State, of those persons who were qualified by its laws to act thereon in behalf of themselves and all other citizens of the State. In some of the States, as we have seen, colored persons were among those qualified by law to act on the subject. These colored persons were not only included in the body of 'the people of the United States,' by whom the Constitution was ordained and established; but in at least five of the States they had the power to act, and, doubtless, did act, by their suffrages, upon the question of its adoption."

Again, Chief Justice Taney says: "It is difficult, at this day to realize the state of public opinion in relation to that unfortunate race, which prevailed in the civilized and enlightened portions of the world at the time of the Declaration of Independence, and when the Constitution of the United States was framed and adopted." And again, after quoting from the Declaration, he says: "The general words above quoted would seem to include the whole human family, and if they were used in a similar instrument at this day, would be so understood."

In these the Chief Justice does not directly assert, but plainly assumes, as a fact, that the public estimate of the black man is more favorable *now* than it was in the days of the Revolution. This assumption is a mistake. In some trifling particulars, the condition of that race has been ameliorated; but, as a whole, in this country, the change between then and now is decidedly the other way; and their ultimate destiny has never appeared so hopeless as in the last three or four years. In two of the five States—New Jersey and North Carolina—that then gave the free negro the right of voting, the right has since been taken away; and in a third—New York—it has been greatly abridged; while it has not been extended, so far as I know, to a single additional State, though the number of the States has more than doubled. In those days, as I understand, masters could, at their own pleasure, emancipate their slaves; but since then, such legal restraints have been made upon emancipation, as to amount almost to prohibition. In those days, Legislatures held the unquestioned power to abolish slavery in their respective States; but now it is becoming quite fashionable for State Constitutions to with-hold that power from the Legislatures. In those days, by common consent, the spread of the black man's bondage to new countries was prohibited; but now, Congress decides that it *will* not continue the prohibition, and the Supreme Court decides that it *could* not if it would. In those days, our Declaration of Independence was held sacred by all, and thought to include all; but now, to aid in making the bondage of the negro universal and eternal, it is assailed, and sneered at, and construed, and hawked at, and torn, till, if its framers could rise from their graves, they could not at all recognize it. All the powers of earth seem rapidly combining against him. Mammon is after him; ambition follows, and philosophy follows, and the Theology of the day is fast joining the cry. They have him in his prison house; they have searched his person, and left no prying instrument with him. One after another they have closed the heavy iron doors upon him, and now they have him, as it were, bolted in with a lock of a hundred keys, which can never be unlocked without the concurrence of every key; the keys in the hands of a hundred different men, and they scattered to a hundred different and distant places; and they stand musing as to what invention, in all the dominions of mind and matter, can be produced to make the impossibility of his escape more complete than it is.

It is grossly incorrect to say or assume, that the public estimate of the negro is more favorable now than it was at the origin of the government.

Three years and a half ago, Judge Douglas brought forward his famous Nebraska bill. The country was at once in a blaze. He scorned all opposition, and carried it through Congress. Since then he has seen himself superseded in a Presidential nomination, by one indorsing the general doctrine of his mea-sure, but at the same time standing clear of the odium of its untimely agita-tion, and its gross breach of national faith; and he has seen that successful rival Constitutionally elected, not by the strength of friends, but by the division of adversaries, being in a popular minority of nearly four hundred thousand votes. He has seen his chief aids in his own State, Shields and Richardson, politically speaking, successively tried, convicted, and executed, for an offense not their own, but his. And now he sees his own case, standing next on the docket for trial.

There is a natural disgust in the minds of nearly all white people, to the idea of an indiscriminate amalgamation of the white and black races; and Judge Douglas evidently is basing his chief hope, upon the chances of being able to appropriate the benefit of this disgust to himself. If he can, by much drumming and repeating, fasten the odium of that idea upon his adversaries, he thinks he can struggle through the storm. He therefore clings to this hope, as a drowning man to the last plank. He makes an occasion for lugging it in from the opposition to the Dred Scott decision. He finds the Republicans insisting that the Declaration of Independence includes ALL men, black as well as white; and forthwith he boldly denies that it includes negroes at all, and proceeds to argue gravely that all who contend it does, do so only because they want to vote, and eat, and sleep, and marry with negroes! He will have it that they cannot be consistent else. Now I protest against that counterfeit logic which concludes that, because I do not want a black woman for a *slave* I must necessarily want her for a *wife*. I need not have her for either, I can just leave her alone. In some respects she certainly is not my equal; but in her natural right to eat the bread she earns with her own hands without asking leave of any one else, she is my equal, and the equal of all others.

Chief Justice Taney, in his opinion in the Dred Scott case, admits that the language of the Declaration is broad enough to include the whole human family, but he and Judge Douglas argue that the authors of that instrument did not intend to include negroes, by the fact that they did not at once, actually place them on an equality with the whites. Now this grave argument comes to just nothing at all, by the other fact, that they did not at once, *or ever afterwards*, actually place all white people on an equality with one or another. And this is the staple argument of both the Chief Justice and the Senator, for doing this obvious violence to the plain unmistakable language of the Declaration. I think the authors of that notable instrument intended to include *all* men, but they did not intend to declare all men equal *in all respects*. They did not mean to say all were equal in color, size, intellect, moral developments, or social capacity. They defined with tolerable distinctness, in what respects they did consider all men created equal—equal in "certain inalienable rights, among which are life, liberty, and the pursuit of happiness." This they said, and this meant. They did not mean to assert the obvious untruth, that all were then actually enjoying that equality, nor yet, that they were about to confer it immediately upon them. In fact they had no power to confer such a boon. They meant

simply to declare the *right*, so that the *enforcement* of it might follow as fast as circumstances should permit. They meant to set up a standard maxim for free society,
which should be familiar to all, and revered by all; constantly looked to, constantly
labored for, and even though never perfectly attained, constantly approximated,
and thereby constantly spreading and deepening its influence, and augmenting the
happiness and value of life to all people of all colors everywhere. The assertion that
"all men are created equal" was of no practical use in effecting our separation from
Great Britain; and it was placed in the Declaration, not for that, but for future use.
Its authors meant it to be, thank God, it is now proving itself, a stumbling block to
those who in after times might seek to turn a free people back into the hateful paths
of despotism. They knew the proneness of prosperity to breed tyrants, and they
meant when such should re-appear in this fair land and commence their vocation
they should find left for them at least one hard nut to crack.

I have now briefly expressed my view of the *meaning* and *objects* of that part of
the Declaration of Independence which declares that "all men are created equal."

Now let us hear Judge Douglas' view of the same subject, as I find it in the
printed report of his late speech. Here it is:

"No man can vindicate the character, motives and conduct of the signers of
the Declaration of Independence, except upon the hypothesis that they referred
to the white race alone, and not to the African, when they declared all men to
have been created equal—that they were speaking of British subjects on this continent being equal to British subjects born and residing in Great Britain—that
they were entitled to the same inalienable rights, and among them were enumerated life, liberty and the pursuit of happiness. The Declaration was adopted for
the purpose of justifying the colonists in the eyes of the civilized world in withdrawing their allegiance from the British crown, and dissolving their connection
with the mother country."

My good friends, read that carefully over some leisure hour, and ponder well
upon it—see what a mere wreck—mangled ruin—it makes of our once glorious
Declaration.

"They were speaking of British subjects on this continent being equal to
British subjects born and residing in Great Britain!" Why, according to this, not
only negroes but white people outside of Great Britain and America are not
spoken of in that instrument. The English, Irish and Scotch, along with white
Americans, were included to be sure, but the French, Germans and other white
people of the world are all gone to pot along with the Judge's inferior races.

I had thought the Declaration promised something better than the condition of British subjects; but no, it only meant that we should be *equal* to them in

their own oppressed and *unequal* condition. According to that, it gave no promise that having kicked off the King and Lords of Great Britain, we should not at once be saddled with a King and Lords of our own.

I had thought the Declaration contemplated the progressive improvement in the condition of all men everywhere; but no, it merely "was adopted for the purpose of justifying the colonists in the eyes of the civilized world in withdrawing their allegiance from the British crown, and dissolving their connection with the mother country." Why, that object having been effected some eighty years ago, the Declaration is of no practical use now—mere rubbish—old wadding left to rot on the battle-field after the victory is won.

I understand you are preparing to celebrate the "Fourth," to-morrow week. What for? The doings of that day had no reference to the present; and quite half of you are not even descendants of those who were referred to at that day. But I suppose you will celebrate; and will even go so far as to read the Declaration. Suppose after you read it once in the old fashioned way, you read it once more with Judge Douglas' version. It will then run thus: "We hold these truths to be self-evident that all British subjects who were on this continent eighty-one years ago, were created equal to all British subjects born and *then* residing in Great Britain."

And now I appeal to all—to Democrats as well as others,—are you really willing that the Declaration shall be thus frittered away?—thus left no more at most, than an interesting memorial of the dead past? thus shorn of its vitality, and practical value; and left without the *germ* or even the *suggestion* of the individual rights of man in it?

But Judge Douglas is especially horrified at the thought of the mixing blood by the white and black races: agreed for once—a thousand times agreed. There are white men enough to marry all the white women, and black men enough to marry all the black women; and so let them be married. On this point we fully agree with the Judge; and when he shall show that his policy is better adapted to prevent amalgamation than ours we shall drop ours, and adopt his. Let us see. In 1850 there were in the United States, 405,751, mulattoes. Very few of these are the offspring of whites and *free* blacks; nearly all have sprung from black *slaves* and white masters. A separation of the races is the only perfect preventive of amalgamation but as all immediate separation is impossible the next best thing is to *keep* them apart *where* they are not already together. If white and black people never get together in Kansas, they will never mix blood in Kansas. That is at least one self-evident truth. A few free colored persons may get into the free States, in any event; but their number is too insignificant to amount to much in the way of mixing blood. In 1850 there were in the free states, 56,649 mulattoes; but for the most part they were not born there—they came from the slave States, ready made up. In the same year the slave States had 348,874 mulattoes all of home production. The proportion of free mulattoes to free blacks—the only colored classes in the free states—is much greater in the slave than in the free states. It is worthy of note too, that among the free states those which make the colored man the nearest to equal the white, have, proportionally the fewest mulattoes the least of amalgamation. In New Hampshire, the State which goes farthest towards equality between the races, there are just 184 Mulattoes while there are in Virginia—how many do you think? 79,775, being 23,126 more than in all the free States together.

These statistics show that slavery is the greatest source of amalgamation; and next to it, not the elevation, but the degeneration of the free blacks. Yet Judge Douglas dreads the slightest restraints on the spread of slavery, and the slightest human recognition of the negro, as tending horribly to amalgamation.

This very Dred Scott case affords a strong test as to which party most favors amalgamation, the Republicans or the dear Union-saving Democracy. Dred Scott, his wife and two daughters were all involved in the suit. We desired the court to have held that they were citizens so far at least as to entitle them to a hearing as to whether they were free or not; and then, also, that they were in fact and in law really free. Could we have had our way, the chances of these black girls, ever mixing their blood with that of white people, would have been diminished at least to the extent that it could not have been without their consent. But Judge Douglas is delighted to have them decided to be slaves, and not human enough to have a hearing, even if they were free, and thus left subject to the forced concubinage of their masters, and liable to become the mothers of mulattoes in spite of themselves—the very state of case that produces nine tenths of all the mulattoes—all the mixing of blood in the nation.

Of course, I state this case as an illustration only, not meaning to say or intimate that the master of Dred Scott and his family, or any more than a per centage of masters generally, are inclined to exercise this particular power which they hold over their female slaves.

I have said that the separation of the races is the only perfect preventive of amalgamation. I have no right to say all the members of the Republican party are in favor of this, nor to say that as a party they are in favor of it. There is nothing in their platform directly on the subject. But I can say a very large proportion of its members are for it, and that the chief plank in their platform—opposition to the spread of slavery—is most favorable to that separation.

Such separation, if ever effected at all, must be effected by colonization; and no political party, as such, is now doing anything directly for colonization. Party operations at present only favor or retard colonization incidentally. The enterprise is a difficult one; but "when there is a will there is a way;" and what colonization needs most is a hearty will. Will springs from the two elements of moral sense and self-interest. Let us be brought to believe it is morally right, and, at the same time, favorable to, or, at least, not against, our interest, to transfer the African to his native clime, and we shall find a way to do it, however great the task may be. The children of Israel, to such numbers as to include four hundred thousand fighting men, went out of Egyptian bondage in a body.

How differently the respective courses of the Democratic and Republican parties incidentally bear on the question of forming a will—a public sentiment—for colonization, is easy to see. The Republicans inculcate, with whatever of ability they can, that the negro is a man; that his bondage is cruelly wrong, and that the field of his oppression ought not to be enlarged. The Democrats deny his manhood; deny, or dwarf to insignificance, the wrong of his bondage; so far as possible, crush all sympathy for him, and cultivate and excite hatred and disgust against him; compliment themselves as Union-savers for doing so; and call the indefinite outspreading of his bondage "a sacred right of self-government."

The plainest print cannot be read through a gold eagle; and it will be ever hard to find many men who will send a slave to Liberia, and pay his passage while they can send him to a new country, Kansas for instance, and sell him for fifteen hundred dollars, and the rise.

*June 26, 1857*

*The*
# POLITICAL DEBATES
*between*
# ABRAHAM LINCOLN
*and*
# STEPHEN A. DOUGLAS,
*for the*
# ILLINOIS SENATORIAL
# CAMPAIGN *of* 1858

# Introduction

In 1854, Douglas carried through Congress the Kansas-Nebraska Bill. This bill repealed the Missouri Compromise of 1820, and cancelled also the provisions of the series of compromises of 1850. Its purpose was to throw open for settlement and for later organization as Slave States the whole territory of the North-west from which, under the Missouri Compromise, slavery had been excluded. The Kansas-Nebraska Bill not only threw open a great territory to slavery but re-opened the whole slavery discussion. The issues that were brought to the front in the discussions about this bill, and in the still more bitter contests after the passage of the bill in regard to the admission of Kansas as a Slave State, were the immediate precursors of the Civil War. The larger causes lay farther back, but the war would have been postponed for an indefinite period if it had not been for the pressing on the part of the South for the right to make Slave States throughout the entire territory of the country, and for the readiness on the part of certain Democratic leaders of the North, of whom Douglas was the chief, to accept this contention, and through such expedients to gain, or to retain, political control for the Democratic party.

In one of the long series of debates in Congress on the question of the right to take slaves into free territory, a planter from South Carolina drew an affecting picture of his relations with his old colored foster-mother, the "Mammy" of the plantation. "Do you tell me," he said, addressing himself to a Free-soil opponent, "that I, a free American citizen, am not to be permitted, if I want to go across the Missouri River, to take with me my whole home circle? Do you say that I must leave my old 'Mammy' behind in South Carolina?" "Oh!" replied the Westerner, "the trouble with you is not that you cannot take your 'Mammy' into this free territory, but that you are not to be at liberty to sell her when you get her there."

Lincoln threw himself with full earnestness of conviction and ardor into the fight to preserve for freedom the territory belonging to the nation. In common with the majority of the Whig party, he held the opinion that if slavery could be restricted to the States in which it was already in existence, if no further States should be admitted into the Union, with the burden of slavery, the institution must, in the course of a generation or two, die out. He was clear in his mind that slavery was an enormous evil for the whites as well as for the blacks, for the individual as for the nation. He had, himself, as a young man, been brought up to do toilsome manual labor. He would not admit that there was anything in manual labor that ought to impair the respect of the community for the laborer or the worker's respect for himself. Not the least of the evils of slavery was, in his judgment, its inevitable influence in bringing degradation upon labor and the laborer.

The passage of the Kansas-Nebraska Act made clear to the North that the South would accept no limitations for slavery. The position of the Southern leaders, in which they had the substantial backing of their constituents, was that slaves were property and that the Constitution, having guaranteed the protection of property to all the citizens of the commonwealth, a slaveholder was deprived of his constitutional rights as a citizen if his control of this portion of his property was in any way interfered with or restricted. The argument in behalf of this extreme Southern claim had been shaped most eloquently and most forcibly by John C. Calhoun during the years between 1830 and 1850. The Calhoun opinion was represented a few years later in the Presidential candidacy of John C. Breckinridge. The contention of the more extreme of the Northern opponents of slavery voters, whose spokesmen were William Lloyd Garrison, Wendell Phillips, James G. Birney, Owen Lovejoy, and others, was that the Constitution in so far as it recognized slavery (which it did only by implication) was a compact with evil. They held that the Fathers had been led into this compact unwittingly and without full realization of the responsibilities that they were assuming for the perpetuation of a great wrong. They refused to accept the view that later generations of American citizens were to be bound for an indefinite period by this error of judgment on the part of the Fathers. They proposed to get rid of slavery, as an institution incompatible with the principles on which the Republic was founded. They pointed out that under the Declaration of Independence all men had an equal right to "life, liberty, and the pursuit of happiness," and that there was no limitation of this claim to men of white race. If it was not going to be possible to argue slavery out of existence, these men preferred to have the Union dissolved rather than to bring upon States like Massachusetts a share of the responsibility for the wrong done to mankind and to justice under the laws of South Carolina.

The Whig party, whose great leader, Henry Clay, had closed his life in 1852, just at the time when Lincoln was becoming prominent in politics, held that all citizens were bound by the compact entered into by their ancestors, first under the Articles of Confederation of 1783, and later under the Constitution of 1789. Our ancestors had for the purpose of bringing about the organization of the Union, agreed to respect the institution of slavery in the States in which it existed. The Whigs of 1850, held, therefore, that in such of the Slave States as had been part of the original thirteen, slavery was an institution to be recognized and protected under the law of the land. They admitted, further, that what their grandfathers had done in 1789 had been in a measure confirmed by the action of their fathers in 1820. The Missouri Compromise of 1820, in making clear that all States thereafter organized north of the line thirty-six, thirty were to be Free States, made clear also that States south of that line had the privilege of coming into the Union with the institution of slavery, and that the citizens in these newer Slave States should be assured of the same recognition and rights as had been accorded to those of the original thirteen.

The Missouri Compromise permitted also the introduction of Missouri itself into the Union as a Slave State (as a counterpoise to the State of Maine admitted the same year), although almost the entire territory of the State of Missouri was north of the latitude 36° 30'.

We may recall that, under the Constitution, the States of the South, while denying the suffrage to the negro, had secured the right to include the negro population as a basis for their representation in the lower House. In apportioning the representatives to the population, five negroes were to be counted as the equivalent of three white men. The passage, in 1854, of the Kansas-Nebraska Act, the purpose of which was to confirm the existence of slavery and to extend the institution throughout the country, was carried in the House by thirteen votes. The House contained at that time no less than twenty members representing the negro population. The negroes were, therefore, in this instance involuntarily made the instruments for strengthening the chains of their own serfdom.

It was in 1854 that Lincoln first propounded the famous question, "Can the nation endure half slave and half free?" This question, slightly modified, became the keynote four years later of Lincoln's contention against the Douglas theory of "squatter sovereignty." The organization of the Republican party dates from 1856. Various claims have been made concerning the precise date and place at which was first presented the statement of principles that constituted the final platform of the party and in regard to the men who were responsible for such statement. At a meeting held as far back as July, 1854, at Jackson, Michigan, a platform was adopted by a convention which had been brought together to formulate opposition to any extension of slavery, and this Jackson platform did contain the substance of the conclusions and certain of the phrases which later were included in the Republican platform. In January, 1856, Parke Godwin published in *Putnam's Monthly*, of which he was political editor, an article outlining the necessary constitution of the new party. This article gave a fuller expression than had thus far been made of the views of the men who were later accepted as the leaders of the Republican party. In May, 1856, Lincoln made a speech at Bloomington,

Illinois, setting forth the principles for the antislavery campaign as they were understood by his group of Whigs. In this speech, Lincoln speaks of "that perfect liberty for which our Southern fellow-citizens are sighing, the liberty of making slaves of other people"; and again: "It is the contention of Mr. Douglas, in his claim for the rights of American citizens, that if *A* sees fit to enslave *B*, no other man shall have the right to object." Of this Bloomington speech, Herndon says: "It was logic; it was pathos; it was enthusiasm; it was justice, integrity, truth, and right. The words seemed to be set ablaze by the divine fires of a soul maddened by a great wrong. The utterance was hard, knotty, gnarly, backed with wrath."

Lincoln's correspondence has been preserved with what is probably substantial completeness. The letters written by him to friends, acquaintances, political correspondents, individual men of one kind or another, have been gathered together and have been brought into print not, as is most frequently the case, under the discretion or judgment of a friendly biographer, but by a great variety of more or less sympathetic people. It would seem as if but very few of Lincoln's letters could have been mislaid or destroyed. One can but be impressed, in reading these letters, with the absolute honesty of purpose and of statement that characterizes them. There are very few men, particularly those whose active lives have been passed in a period of political struggle and civil war, whose correspondence could stand such a test. There never came to Lincoln requirement to say to his correspondent, "Burn this letter."

In 1856, the Supreme Court, under the headship of Judge Taney, gave out the decision in the Dred Scott case. The purport of this decision was that a negro was not to be considered as a person but as a chattel; and that the taking of such negro chattel into free territory did not cancel or impair the property rights of the master. It appeared to the men of the North as if under this decision the entire country, including in addition to the national territories the independent States which had excluded slavery, was to be thrown open to the invasion of the institution. The Dred Scott decision, taken in connection with the repeal of the Missouri Compromise (and the two acts were doubtless a part of one thoroughly considered policy), foreshadowed as their logical and almost inevitable consequence the bringing of the entire nation under this control of slavery. The men of the future State of Kansas made during 1856–57 a plucky fight to keep slavery out of their borders. The so-called Lecompton Constitution undertook to force slavery upon Kansas. This constitution was declared by the administration (that of President Buchanan) to have been adopted, but the fraudulent character of the voting was so evident that Walker, the Democratic Governor, although a sympathizer with slavery, felt compelled to repudiate it. This constitution was repudiated also by

Douglas, although Douglas had declared that the State ought to be thrown open to slavery. Jefferson Davis, at that time Secretary of War, declared that "Kansas was in a state of rebellion and that the rebellion must be crushed." Armed bands from Missouri crossed the river to Kansas for the purpose of casting fraudulent votes and for the further purpose of keeping the Free-soil settlers away from the polls.

This fight for freedom in Kansas gave a further basis for Lincoln's statement that "a house divided against itself cannot stand; this government cannot endure half slave and half free." It was with this statement as his starting-point that Lincoln entered into his famous Senatorial campaign with Douglas. Douglas had already represented Illinois in the Senate for two terms and had, therefore, the advantage of possession and of a substantial control of the machinery of the State. He had the repute at the time of being the leading political debater in the country. He was shrewd, forcible, courageous, and, in the matter of convictions, unprincipled. He knew admirably how to cater to the prejudices of the masses. His career thus far had been one of unbroken success. His Senatorial fight was, in his hope and expectation, to be but a step towards the Presidency. The Democratic party, with an absolute control south of Mason and Dixon's Line and with a very substantial support in the Northern States, was in a position, if unbroken, to control with practical certainty the Presidential election of 1860. Douglas seemed to be the natural leader of the party. It was necessary for him, however, while retaining the support of the Democrats of the North, to make clear to those of the South that his influence would work for the maintenance and for the extension of slavery.

The South was well pleased with the purpose and with the result of the Dred Scott decision and with the repeal of the Missouri Compromise. It is probable, however, that if the Dred Scott decision had not given to the South so full a measure of satisfaction, the South would have been more ready to accept the leadership of a Northern Democrat like Douglas. Up to a certain point in the conflict, they had felt the need of Douglas and had realized the importance of the support that he was in a position to bring from the North. When, however, the Missouri Compromise had been repealed and the Supreme Court had declared that slaves must be recognized as property throughout the entire country, the Southern claims were increased to a point to which certain of the followers of Douglas were not willing to go. It was a large compliment to the young lawyer of Illinois to have placed upon him the responsibility of leading, against such a competitor as Douglas, the contest of the Whigs, and of the Free-soilers back of the Whigs, against any further extension of slavery, a contest which was really a fight for the continued existence of the nation.

Lincoln seems to have gone into the fight with full courage, the courage of his convictions. He felt that Douglas was a trimmer, and he believed that the issue had now been brought to a point at which the trimmer could not hold support on both sides of Mason and Dixon's Line. He formulated at the outset of the debate a question which was pressed persistently upon Douglas during the succeeding three weeks. This question was worded as follows: "Can the people of a United States territory, prior to the formation of a State constitution or against the protest of any citizen of the United States, exclude slavery?" Lincoln's campaign advisers were of opinion that this question was inadvisable. They took the ground that Douglas would answer the question in such way as to secure the approval of the voters of Illinois and that in so doing he would win the Senatorship. Lincoln's response was in substance: "That may be. I hold, however, that if Douglas answers this question in a way to satisfy the Democrats of the North, he will inevitably lose the support of the more extreme, at least, of the Democrats of the South. We may lose the Senatorship as far as my personal candidacy is concerned. If, however, Douglas fails to retain the support of the South, he cannot become President in 1860. The line will be drawn directly between those who are willing to accept the extreme claims of the South and those who resist these claims. A right decision is the essential thing for the safety of the nation." The question gave no little perplexity to Douglas. He finally, however, replied that in his judgment the people of a United States territory had the right to exclude slavery. When asked again by Lincoln how he brought this decision into accord with the Dred Scott decision, he replied in substance: "Well, they have not the right to take constitutional measures to exclude slavery, but they can by local legislation render slavery practically impossible." The Dred Scott decision had in fact itself overturned the Douglas theory of popular sovereignty or "squatter sovereignty." Douglas was only able to say that his sovereignty contention made provision for such control of domestic or local regulations as would make slavery impossible.

The South, rendered autocratic by the authority of the Supreme Court, was not willing to accept the possibility of slavery being thus restricted out of existence in any part of the country. The Southerners repudiated Douglas as Lincoln had prophesied they would do. Douglas had been trying the impossible task of carrying water on both shoulders. He gained the Senatorship by a narrow margin; he secured in the vote in the Legislature a majority of eight, but Lincoln had even in this fight won the support of the people. His majority on the popular vote was four thousand.

The series of debates between these two leaders came to be of national importance. It was not merely a question of the representation in the Senate from the

State of Illinois, but of the presentation of arguments, not only to the voters of Illinois but to citizens throughout the entire country, in behalf of the restriction of slavery on the one hand or of its indefinite expansion and protection on the other. The debate was educational not merely for the voters who listened, but for the thousands of other voters who read the reports.

It would be an enormous advantage for the political education of candidates and for the education of voters if such debates could become the routine in Congressional and Presidential campaigns. Under the present routine, we have, in place of an assembly of voters representing the conflicting views of the two parties or of the several political groups, a homogeneous audience of one way of thinking, and speakers who have no opponent present to check the temptation to launch forth into wild statements, personal abuse, and irresponsible conclusions. An interruption of the speaker is considered to be a disturbance of order, and the man who is not fully in sympathy with the views of the audience is likely to be put out as an interloper. With a system of joint debates, the speakers would be under an educational repression. False or exaggerated statements would not be made, or would not be made consciously, because they would be promptly corrected by the other fellow. There would of necessity come to be a better understanding and a larger respect for the positions of the opponent. The men selected as leaders or speakers to enforce the contentions of the party, would have to possess some reasoning faculty as well as oratorical fluency. The voters, instead of being shut in with one group of arguments more or less reasonable, would be brought into touch with the arguments of other groups of citizens. I can conceive of no better method than the institution of joint debates, for bringing representative government on to a higher plane and for making an election what it ought to be, a reasonable decision by reasoning voters.

—George Haven Putnam
*New York, April, 1910*

# "A House Divided" Speech of Abraham Lincoln

*Delivered at Springfield, Ill., June 17, 1858*

[The following speech was delivered at Springfield, Ill., at the close of the Republican State Convention held at that time and place, and by which Convention MR. LINCOLN had been named as their candidate for United States Senator. MR. DOUGLAS was not present.]

MR. PRESIDENT AND GENTLEMEN OF THE CONVENTION: If we could first know where we are, and whither we are tending, we could better judge what to do, and how to do it. We are now far into the fifth year since a policy was initiated with the avowed object and confident promise of putting an end to slavery agitation. Under the operation of that policy, that agitation has not only not ceased, but has constantly augmented. In my opinion, it will not cease until a crisis shall have been reached and passed. "A house divided against itself cannot stand." I believe this government cannot endure permanently half slave and half free. I do not expect the Union to be dissolved; I do not expect the house to fall; but I do expect it will cease to be divided. It will become all one thing, or all the other. Either the opponents of slavery will arrest the further spread of it, and place it where the public mind shall rest in the belief that it is in the course of ultimate extinction, or its advocates will push it forward till it shall become alike lawful in all the States, old as well as new, North as well as South.

Have we no tendency to the latter condition?

Let any one who doubts, carefully contemplate that now almost complete legal combination—piece of machinery, so to speak—compounded of the Nebraska doctrine and the Dred Scott decision. Let him consider, not only what work the machinery is adapted to do, and how well adapted, but also let him study the history of its construction, and trace, if he can, or rather fail, if he can, to trace the evidences of design, and concert of action, among its chief architects, from the beginning.

The new year of 1854 found slavery excluded from more than half the States by State Constitutions, and from most of the National territory by Congressional prohibition. Four days later, commenced the struggle which ended in repealing that Congressional prohibition. This opened all the National territory to slavery, and was the first point gained.

But, so far, Congress only had acted, and an indorsement by the people, real or apparent, was indispensable to save the point already gained, and give chance for more.

This necessity had not been overlooked, but had been provided for, as well as might be, in the notable argument of "squatter sovereignty," otherwise called "sacred right of self-government," which latter phrase, though expressive of the only rightful basis of any government, was so perverted in this attempted use of it as to amount to just this: That if any *one* man choose to enslave *another,* no *third* man shall be allowed to object. That argument was incorporated into the Nebraska Bill itself, in the language which follows: "It being the true intent and meaning of this Act not to legislate slavery into any Territory or State, nor to exclude it therefrom, but to leave the people thereof perfectly free to form and regulate their domestic institutions in their own way, subject only to the Constitution of the United States." Then opened the roar of loose declamation in favor of "squatter sovereignty," and "sacred right of self-government." "But," said opposition members, "let us amend the bill so as to expressly declare that the people of the Territory may exclude slavery." "Not we," said the friends of the measure, and down they voted the amendment.

While the Nebraska Bill was passing through Congress, a *law case,* involving the question of a negro's freedom, by reason of his owner having voluntarily taken him first into a free State, and then into a territory covered by the Congressional prohibition, and held him as a slave for a long time in each, was passing through the United States Circuit Court for the District of Missouri; and both Nebraska Bill and lawsuit were brought to a decision in the same month of May, 1854. The negro's name was "Dred Scott," which name now designates the decision finally made in the case. Before the then next Presidential election, the law case came to, and was argued in, the Supreme Court of the United States; but the decision of it was deferred until after the election. Still, before the election, Senator Trumbull, on the floor of the Senate, requested the leading advocate of the Nebraska Bill to state *his opinion* whether the people of a Territory can constitutionally exclude slavery from their limits; and the latter answers: "That is a question for the Supreme Court."

The election came. Mr. Buchanan was elected, and the indorsement, such as it was, secured. That was the second point gained. The indorsement, however, fell short of a clear popular majority by nearly four hundred thousand votes, and so, perhaps, was not overwhelmingly reliable and satisfactory. The outgoing President, in his last annual message, as impressively as possible echoed back upon the people the weight and authority of the indorsement. The Supreme

Court met again, did not announce their decision, but ordered a reargument. The Presidential inauguration came, and still no decision of the court; but the incoming President, in his inaugural address, fervently exhorted the people to abide by the forthcoming decision, whatever it might be. Then, in a few days, came the decision.

The reputed author of the Nebraska Bill finds an early occasion to make a speech at this capital indorsing the Dred Scott decision, and vehemently denouncing all opposition to it. The new President, too, seizes the early occasion of the Silliman letter to indorse and strongly construe that decision, and to express his astonishment that any different view had ever been entertained!

At length a squabble springs up between the President and the author of the Nebraska Bill, on the mere question of *fact,* whether the Lecompton Constitution was or was not in any just sense made by the people of Kansas; and in that quarrel the latter declares that all he wants is a fair vote for the people, and that he cares not whether slavery be voted *down* or voted *up.* I do not understand his declaration, that he cares not whether slavery be voted down or voted up, to be intended by him other than as an apt definition of the policy he would impress upon the public mind,—the principle for which he declares he has suffered so much, and is ready to suffer to the end. And well may he cling to that principle! If he has any parental feeling, well may he cling to it. That principle is the only shred left of his original Nebraska doctrine. Under the Dred Scott decision "squatter sovereignty" squatted out of existence, tumbled down like temporary scaffolding; like the mould at the foundry, served through one blast, and fell back into loose sand; helped to carry an election, and then was kicked to the winds. His late joint struggle with the Republicans, against the Lecompton Constitution, involves nothing of the original Nebraska doctrine. That struggle was made on a point—the right of a people to make their own constitution—upon which he and the Republicans have never differed.

The several points of the Dred Scott decision, in connection with Senator Douglas's "care not" policy, constitute the piece of machinery, in its present state of advancement. This was the third point gained. The working points of that machinery are:

Firstly, That no negro slave, imported as such from Africa, and no descendant of such slave, can ever be a citizen of any State, in the sense of that term as used in the Constitution of the United States. This point is made in order to deprive the negro, in every possible event, of the benefit of that provision of the United States Constitution which declares that "The citizens of each State shall be entitled to all privileges and immunities of citizens in the several States."

Secondly, That, "subject to the Constitution of the United States," neither Congress nor a Territorial Legislature can exclude slavery from any United States Territory. This point is made in order that individual men may fill up the Territories with slaves, without danger of losing them as property, and thus to enhance the chances of permanency to the institution through all the future.

Thirdly, That whether the holding a negro in actual slavery in a free State makes him free, as against the holder, the United States courts will not decide, but will leave to be decided by the courts of any slave State the negro may be forced into by the master. This point is made, not to be pressed immediately; but, if acquiesced in for a while, and apparently indorsed by the people at an election, then to sustain the logical conclusion that what Dred Scott's master might lawfully do with Dred Scott, in the free State of Illinois, every other master may lawfully do with any other one, or one thousand slaves, in Illinois, or in any other free State.

Auxiliary to all this, and working hand in hand with it, the Nebraska doctrine, or what is left of it, is to educate and mould public opinion, at least Northern public opinion, not to care whether slavery is voted down or voted up. This shows exactly where we now are; and partially, also, whither we are tending.

It will throw additional light on the latter, to go back and run the mind over the string of historical facts already stated. Several things will now appear less dark and mysterious than they did when they were transpiring. The people were to be left "perfectly free," "subject only to the Constitution." What the Constitution had to do with it, outsiders could not then see. Plainly enough now,—it was an exactly fitted niche, for the Dred Scott decision to afterward come in, and declare the perfect freedom of the people to be just no freedom at all. Why was the amendment, expressly declaring the right of the people, voted down? Plainly enough now,—the adoption of it would have spoiled the niche for the Dred Scott decision. Why was the court decision held up? Why even a Senator's individual opinion withheld, till after the Presidential election? Plainly enough now,—the speaking out then would have damaged the "perfectly free" argument upon which the election was to be carried. Why the outgoing President's felicitation on the indorsement? Why the delay of a reargument? Why the incoming President's advance exhortation in favor of the decision? These things look like the cautious patting and petting of a spirited horse preparatory to mounting him, when it is dreaded that he may give the rider a fall. And why the hasty after-indorsement of the decision by the President and others?

We cannot absolutely know that all these exact adaptations are the result of preconcert. But when we see a lot of framed timbers, different portions of which we know have been gotten out at different times and places and by different

workmen,—Stephen, Franklin, Roger, and James, for instance,—and when we
see these timbers joined together, and see they exactly make the frame of a house
or a mill, all the tenons and mortises exactly fitting, and all the lengths and proportions of the different pieces exactly adapted to their respective places, and not
a piece too many or too few,—not omitting even scaffolding,—or, if a single piece
be lacking, we see the place in the frame exactly fitted and prepared yet to bring
such piece in,—in such a case, we find it impossible not to believe that Stephen
and Franklin and Roger and James all understood one another from the beginning, and all worked upon a common plan or draft drawn up before the first blow
was struck.

It should not be overlooked that by the Nebraska Bill the people of a *State* as
well as Territory were to be left "perfectly free," "subject only to the Constitution."
Why mention a State? They were legislating for Territories, and not for or
about States. Certainly the people of a State are and ought to be subject to the
Constitution of the United States; but why is mention of this lugged into this
merely Territorial law? Why are the people of a Territory and the people of a State
therein lumped together, and their relation to the Constitution therein treated
as being precisely the same? While the opinion of the court, by Chief Justice
Taney, in the Dred Scott case, and the separate opinions of all the concurring
Judges, expressly declare that the Constitution of the United States neither permits Congress nor a Territorial Legislature to exclude slavery from any United
States Territory, they all omit to declare whether or not the same Constitution permits a State, or the people of a State, to exclude it. *Possibly,* this is a mere omission;
but who can be quite sure, if McLean or Curtis had sought to get into the opinion
a declaration of unlimited power in the people of a State to exclude slavery from
their limits, just as Chase and Mace sought to get such declaration, in behalf of the
people of a Territory, into the Nebraska Bill,—I ask, who can be quite sure that
it would not have been voted down in the one case as it had been in the other?
The nearest approach to the point of declaring the power of a State over slavery is
made by Judge Nelson. He approaches it more than once, using the precise idea,
and almost the language, too, of the Nebraska Act. On one occasion, his exact language is, "Except in cases where the power is restrained by the Constitution of the
United States, the law of the State is supreme over the subject of slavery within its
jurisdiction." In what cases the power of the States is so restrained by the United
States Constitution, is left an open question, precisely as the same question, as
to the restraint on the power of the Territories, was left open in the Nebraska
Act. Put this and that together, and we have another nice little niche, which we
may, ere long, see filled with another Supreme Court decision, declaring that the

Constitution of the United States does not permit a *State* to exclude slavery from its limits. And this may especially be expected if the doctrine of "care not whether slavery be voted down or voted up" shall gain upon the public mind sufficiently to give promise that such a decision can be maintained when made.

Such a decision is all that slavery now lacks of being alike lawful in all the States. Welcome or unwelcome, such decision is probably coming, and will soon be upon us, unless the power of the present political dynasty shall be met and overthrown. We shall lie down pleasantly dreaming that the people of Missouri are on the verge of making their State free, and we shall awake to the reality instead that the Supreme Court has made Illinois a slave State. To meet and overthrow the power of that dynasty is the work now before all those who would prevent that consummation. That is what we have to do. How can we best do it?

There are those who denounce us openly to their own friends, and yet whisper us softly that Senator Douglas is the aptest instrument there is with which to effect that object. They wish us to *infer* all, from the fact that he now has a little quarrel with the present head of the dynasty, and that he has regularly voted with us on a single point, upon which he and we have never differed. They remind us that he is a great man, and that the largest of us are very small ones. Let this be granted. But "a living dog is better than a dead lion." Judge Douglas, if not a dead lion, for this work is at least a caged and toothless one. How can he oppose the advances of slavery? He don't care anything about it. His avowed mission is impressing the "public heart" to *care nothing about it*. A leading Douglas Democrat newspaper thinks Douglas's superior talent will be needed to resist the revival of the African slave trade. Does Douglas believe an effort to revive that trade is approaching? He has not said so. Does he really think so? But if it is, how can he resist it? For years he has labored to prove it a sacred right of white men to take negro slaves into the new Territories. Can he possibly show that it is less a sacred right to buy them where they can be bought cheapest? And unquestionably they can be bought cheaper in Africa than in Virginia. He has done all in his power to reduce the whole question of slavery to one of a mere right of property; and, as such, how can he oppose the foreign slave trade,—how can he refuse that trade in that "property" shall be "perfectly free,"—unless he does it as a protection to the home production? And as the home producers will probably not ask the protection, he will be wholly without a ground of opposition.

Senator Douglas holds, we know, that a man may rightfully be wiser to-day than he was yesterday; that he may rightfully change when he finds himself wrong. But can we, for that reason, run ahead, and infer that he will make any particular change, of which he himself has given no intimation? Can we safely base our action upon any such vague inference? Now, as ever, I wish not to misrepresent Judge Douglas's position, question his motives, or do aught that can be personally offensive to him. Whenever, if ever, he and we can come together on principle so that our cause may have assistance from his great ability, I hope to have interposed no adventitious obstacles. But clearly he is not now with us; he does not pretend to be,—he does not promise ever to be.

Our cause, then, must be intrusted to, and conducted by, its own undoubted friends,—those whose hands are free, whose hearts are in the work, who *do care* for the result. Two years ago the Republicans of the nation mustered over thirteen hundred thousand strong. We did this under the single impulse of resistance to a common danger, with every external circumstance against us. Of strange, discordant, and even hostile elements we gathered from the four winds, and formed and fought the battle through, under the constant hot fire of a disciplined, proud, and pampered enemy. Did we brave all then to falter now,—now, when that same enemy is wavering, dissevered, and belligerent? The result is not doubtful. We shall not fail; if we stand firm, we *shall not fail.* Wise counsels may accelerate, or mistakes delay it, but, sooner or later, the victory is sure to come.

# Speech of Senator Douglas

*On the Occasion of his Public Reception at Chicago, Ill.,*
*Delivered Friday Evening, July 9, 1858.*
(Mr. Lincoln was Present.)

MR. DOUGLAS said,—

MR. CHAIRMAN AND FELLOW-CITIZENS: I can find no language which can adequately express my profound gratitude for the magnificent welcome which you have extended to me on this occasion. This vast sea of human faces indicates how deep an interest is felt by our people in the great questions which agitate the public mind, and which underlie the foundations of our free institutions. A reception like this, so great in numbers that no human voice can be heard to its countless thousands,—so enthusiastic that no one individual can be the object of such enthusiasm,—clearly shows that there is some great principle which sinks deep in the heart of the masses, and involves the rights and the liberties of a whole people, that has brought you together with a unanimity and a cordiality never before excelled, if, indeed, equalled, on any occasion. I have not the vanity to believe that it is any personal compliment to me.

It is an expression of your devotion to that great principle of self-government, to which my life for many years past has been, and in the future will be, devoted. If there is any one principle dearer and more sacred than all others in free governments, it is that which asserts the exclusive right of a free people to form and adopt their own fundamental law, and to manage and regulate their own internal affairs and domestic institutions.

When I found an effort being made during the recent session of Congress to force a constitution upon the people of Kansas against their will, and to force that State into the Union with a constitution which her people had rejected by more than ten thousand, I felt bound as a man of honor and a representative of Illinois, bound by every consideration of duty, of fidelity, and of patriotism, to resist to the utmost of my power the consummation of that fraud. With others, I did resist it, and resisted it successfully until the attempt was abandoned. We forced them to refer that constitution back to the people of Kansas, to be accepted or rejected as they shall decide at an election which is fixed for the first Monday in August next. It is true that the mode of reference, and the form of the submission, was not such as I could sanction with my vote, for the reason that it discriminated between free States and slave States; providing that if Kansas consented to come in under the Lecompton Constitution it should be received with a population of thirty-five thousand; but that if she demanded another constitution, more consistent with the sentiments of her people and their feelings, that it should not be received into the Union until she had 93,420 inhabitants. I did not consider that mode of submission fair, for the reason that any election is a mockery which is not free, that any election is a fraud upon the rights of the people which holds out inducements for affirmative votes, and threatens penalties for negative votes. But whilst I was not satisfied with the mode of submission, whilst I resisted it to the last, demanding a fair, a just, a free mode of submission, still, when the law passed placing it within the power of the people of Kansas at that election to reject the Lecompton Constitution, and then make another in harmony with their principles and their opinions, I did not believe that either the penalties on the one hand, or the inducements on the other, would force that people to accept a constitution to which they are irreconcilably opposed. All I can say is, that if their votes can be controlled by such considerations all the sympathy which has been expended upon them has been misplaced, and all the efforts that have been made in defence of their right to self-government have been made in an unworthy cause.

Hence, my friends, I regard the Lecompton battle as having been fought, and the victory won, because the arrogant demand for the admission of Kansas under the Lecompton Constitution unconditionally, whether her people wanted it or not, has been abandoned, and the principle which recognizes the right of the people to decide for themselves has been submitted in its place.

Fellow-citizens, while I devoted my best energies—all my energies, mental and physical—to the vindication of the great principle, and whilst the result has been such as will enable the people of Kansas to come into the Union with such a constitution as they desire, yet the credit of this great moral victory is to be divided among a large number of men of various and different political creeds. I was rejoiced when I found in this great contest the Republican party coming up manfully and sustaining the principle that the people of each Territory, when coming into the Union, have the right to decide for themselves whether slavery shall or shall not exist within their limits. I have seen the time when that principle was controverted. I have seen the time when all parties did not recognize the right of a people to have slavery or freedom, to tolerate or prohibit slavery as they deemed best, but claimed that power for the Congress of the United States, regardless of the wishes of the people to be affected by it; and when I found upon the Crittenden-Montgomery bill the Republicans and Americans of the North, and I may say, too, some glorious Americans and old-line Whigs from the

South, like Crittenden and his patriotic associates, joined with a portion of the Democracy to carry out and vindicate the right of the people to decide whether slavery should or should not exist within the limits of Kansas, I was rejoiced within my secret soul, for I saw an indication that the American people, when they came to understand the principle, would give it their cordial support.

The Crittenden-Montgomery bill was as fair and as perfect an exposition of the doctrine of popular sovereignty as could be carried out by any bill that man ever devised. It proposed to refer the Lecompton Constitution back to the people of Kansas, and give them the right to accept or reject it as they pleased, at a fair election, held in pursuance of law, and in the event of their rejecting it, and forming another in its stead, to permit them to come into the Union on an equal footing with the original States. It was fair and just in all of its provisions. I gave it my cordial support, and was rejoiced when I found that it passed the House of Representatives, and at one time I entertained high hope that it would pass the Senate.

I regard the great principle of popular sovereignty as having been vindicated and made triumphant in this land as a permanent rule of public policy in the organization of Territories and the admission of new States. Illinois took her position upon this principle many years ago. You all recollect that in 1850, after the passage of the Compromise measures of that year, when I returned to my home there was great dissatisfaction expressed at my course in supporting those measures. I appeared before the people of Chicago at a mass meeting, and vindicated each and every one of those measures; and by reference to my speech on that occasion, which was printed and circulated broadcast throughout the State at the time, you will find that I then and there said that those measures were all founded upon the great principle that every people ought to possess the right to form and regulate their own domestic institutions in their own way, and that, that right being possessed by the people of the States, I saw no reason why the same principle should not be extended to all of the Territories of the United States. A general election was held in this State a few months afterwards, for members of the Legislature, pending which all these questions were thoroughly canvassed and discussed, and the nominees of the different parties instructed in regard to the wishes of their constituents upon them. When that election was over, and the Legislature assembled, they proceeded to consider the merits of those Compromise measures, and the principles upon which they were predicated. And what was the result of their action? They passed resolutions, first repealing the Wilmot Proviso instructions, and in lieu thereof adopted another resolution, in which they declared the great principle which asserts the right of the people to make their own form of government and establish their own institutions. That resolution is as follows:

> *Resolved,* That our liberty and independence are based upon the right of the people to form for themselves such a government as they may choose; that this great principle, the birthright of freemen, the gift of Heaven, secured to us by the blood of our ancestors, ought to be secured to future generations, and no limitation ought to be applied to this power in the organization of any Territory of the United States, of either Territorial Government or State Constitution, provided the Government so established shall be republican, and in conformity with the Constitution of the United States.

That resolution, declaring the great principle of self-government as applicable to the Territories and new States, passed the House of Representatives of this State by a vote of sixty-one in the affirmative, to only four in the negative. Thus you find that an expression of public opinion—enlightened, educated, intelligent public opinion—on this question, by the representatives of Illinois in 1851, approaches nearer to unanimity than has ever been obtained on any controverted question. That resolution was entered on the journal of the Legislature of the State of Illinois, and it has remained there from that day to this, a standing instruction to her Senators, and a request to her Representatives, in Congress to carry out that principle in all future cases. Illinois, therefore, stands pre-eminent as the State which stepped forward early and established a platform applicable to this slavery question, concurred in alike by Whigs and Democrats, in which it was declared to be the wish of our people that thereafter the people of the Territories should be left perfectly free to form and regulate their domestic institutions in their own way, and that no limitation should be placed upon that right in any form.

Hence what was my duty in 1854, when it became necessary to bring forward a bill for the organization of the Territories of Kansas and Nebraska? Was it not my duty, in obedience to the Illinois platform, to your standing instructions to your Senators, adopted with almost entire unanimity, to incorporate in that bill the great principle of self-government, declaring that it was "the true intent and meaning of the Act not to legislate slavery into any State or Territory, or to exclude it therefrom, but to leave the people thereof perfectly free to form and regulate their domestic institutions in their own way, subject only to the Constitution of the United States"? I did incorporate that principle in the Kansas-Nebraska Bill, and perhaps I did as much as any living man in the enactment of that bill, thus establishing the doctrine in the public policy of the country. I then defended that principle against assaults from one section of the Union. During this last winter it became my duty to vindicate it against assaults from the other section of the Union. I vindicated it boldly and fearlessly, as the people of Chicago can bear witness, when it was assailed by Free-soilers; and during this winter I vindicated and defended it as boldly and fearlessly when it was attempted to be violated by the almost united South. I pledged myself to you on every stump in Illinois in 1854, 1 pledged myself to the people of other States north and south, wherever I spoke; and in the United States Senate and elsewhere, in every form in which I could reach the public mind or the public ear, I gave the pledge that I, so far as the power should be in my hands, would vindicate the principle of the right of the people to form their own institutions, to establish free States or slave States as they chose, and that that principle should never be violated either by fraud, by violence, by circumvention, or by any other means, if it was in my power to prevent it. I now submit to you, my fellow-citizens, whether I have not redeemed that pledge in good faith. Yes, my friends, I have redeemed it in good faith; and it is a matter of heartfelt gratification to me to see these assembled thousands here to-night bearing their testimony to the fidelity with which I have advocated that principle, and redeemed my pledges in connection with it.

I will be entirely frank with you. My object was to secure the right of the people of each State and of each Territory, north or south, to decide the question for themselves, to have slavery or not, just as they chose; and my opposition to the Lecompton Constitution was not predicated upon the ground that it was a pro-slavery constitution, nor would my action have been different had it been a Free-soil constitution. My speech against the Lecompton fraud was made on the 9th of December, while the vote on the slavery clause in that constitution was not taken until the 21st of the same month, nearly two weeks after. I made my speech against the Lecompton monstrosity solely on the ground that it was a violation of the fundamental principles of free government; on the ground that it was not the act and deed of the people of Kansas; that it did not embody their will; that they were averse to it; and hence I denied the right of Congress to force it upon them, either as a free State or a slave State. I deny the right of Congress to force a slaveholding State upon an unwilling people. I deny their right to force a free State upon an unwilling people. I deny their right to force a good thing upon a people who are unwilling to receive it. The great principle is the right of every community to judge and decide for itself whether a thing is right or wrong, whether it would be good or evil for them to adopt it; and the right of free action, the right of free thought, the right of free judgment, upon the question is dearer to every true American than any other under a free government. My objection to the Lecompton contrivance was that it undertook to put a constitution on the people of Kansas against their will, in opposition to their wishes, and thus violated the great principle upon which all our institutions rest. It is no answer to this argument to say that slavery is an evil, and hence should not be tolerated. You must allow the people to decide for themselves whether it is a good or an evil. You allow them to decide for themselves whether they desire a Maine liquor law or not; you allow them to decide for themselves what kind of common schools they will have, what system of banking they will adopt, or whether they will adopt any at all; you allow them to decide for themselves the relations between husband and wife, parent and child, guardian and ward,—in fact, you allow them to decide for themselves all other questions: and why not upon this question? Whenever you put a limitation upon the right of any people to decide what laws they want, you have destroyed the fundamental principle of self-government.

In connection with this subject, perhaps, it will not be improper for me on this occasion to allude to the position of those who have chosen to arraign my conduct on this same subject. I have observed from the public prints that but a few days ago the Republican party of the State of Illinois assembled in Convention at Springfield, and not only laid down their platform, but nominated a candidate for the United States Senate, as my successor. I take great pleasure in saying that I have known, personally and intimately, for about a quarter of a century, the worthy gentleman who has been nominated for my place, and I will say that I regard him as a kind, amiable, and intelligent gentleman, a good citizen and an honorable opponent; and whatever issue I may have with him will be of principle, and not involving personalities. Mr. Lincoln made a speech before that Republican Convention which unanimously nominated him for the Senate,—a speech evidently well prepared and carefully written,—in which he states the basis upon which he proposes to carry on the campaign during this summer. In it he lays down two distinct propositions which I shall notice, and upon which I shall take a direct and bold issue with him.

His first and main proposition I will give in his own language, Scripture quotations and all [laughter]; I give his exact language: " 'A house divided against itself cannot stand.' I believe this government cannot endure, permanently, half *slave* and half *free*. I do not expect the Union to be *dissolved*, I do not expect the house to *fall*; but I do expect it to cease to be divided. It will become *all* one thing, or *all* the other."

In other words, Mr. Lincoln asserts, as a fundamental principle of this government, that there must be uniformity in the local laws and domestic institutions of each and all the States of the Union; and he therefore invites all the non-slaveholding States to band together, organize as one body, and make war upon slavery in Kentucky, upon slavery in Virginia, upon the Carolinas, upon slavery in all of the slaveholding States in this Union, and to persevere in that war until it shall be exterminated. He then notifies the slaveholding States to stand together as a unit and make an aggressive war upon the free States of this Union with a view of establishing slavery in them all; of forcing it upon Illinois, of forcing it upon New York, upon New England, and upon every other free State, and that they shall keep up the warfare until it has been formally established in them all. In other words, Mr. Lincoln advocates boldly and clearly a war of sections, a war of the North against the South, of the free States against the slave States,—a war of extermination, to be continued relentlessly until the one or the other shall be subdued, and all the States shall either become free or become slave.

Now, my friends, I must say to you frankly that I take bold, unqualified issue with him upon that principle. I assert that it is neither desirable nor possible that there should be uniformity in the local institutions and domestic regulations of the different States of the Union. The framers of our government never contemplated uniformity in its internal concerns. The fathers of the Revolution and the sages who made the Constitution well understood that the laws and domestic institutions which would suit the granite hills of New Hampshire would be totally unfit for the rice plantations of South Carolina; they well understood that the laws which would suit the agricultural districts of Pennsylvania and New York would be totally unfit for the large mining regions of the Pacific, or the lumber regions of Maine. They well understood that the great varieties of soil, of production, and of interests in a republic as large as this, required different local and domestic regulations in each locality, adapted to the wants and interests of each separate State; and for that reason it was provided in the Federal Constitution that the thirteen original States should remain sovereign and supreme within their own limits in regard to all that was local and internal and domestic, while the Federal Government should have certain specified powers which were general and national, and could be exercised only by Federal authority.

The framers of the Constitution well understood that each locality, having separate and distinct interests, required separate and distinct laws, domestic institutions, and police regulations adapted to its own wants and its own condition; and they acted on the presumption, also, that these laws and institutions would be as diversified and as dissimilar as the States would be numerous, and that no two would be precisely alike, because the interests of no two would be precisely the same. Hence I assert that the great fundamental principle which underlies our complex system of State and Federal governments contemplated diversity and dissimilarity in the local institutions and domestic affairs of each and every State then in the Union, or thereafter to be admitted into the Confederacy. I therefore conceive that my friend Mr. Lincoln has totally misapprehended the great principles upon which our government rests. Uniformity in local and domestic affairs would be destructive of State rights, of State sovereignty, of personal liberty and personal freedom. Uniformity is the parent of despotism the world over, not only in politics, but in religion. Wherever the doctrine of uniformity is proclaimed, that all the States must be free or all slave, that all labor must be white or all black, that all the citizens of the different States must have the same privileges or be governed by the same regulations, you have destroyed the greatest safeguard which our institutions have thrown around the rights of the citizen.

How could this uniformity be accomplished, if it was desirable and possible? There is but one mode in which it could be obtained, and that must be by abolishing the State legislatures, blotting out State sovereignty, merging the rights and sovereignty of the States in one consolidated empire, and vesting Congress with the plenary power to make all the police regulations, domestic and local laws, uniform throughout the limits of the Republic. When you shall have done this, you will have uniformity. Then the States will all be slave or all be free; then negroes will vote everywhere or nowhere; then you will have a Maine liquor law in every State or none; then you will have uniformity in all things, local and domestic, by the authority of the Federal Government. But when you attain that uniformity, you will have converted these thirty-two sovereign, independent States into one consolidated empire, with the uniformity of despotism reigning triumphant throughout the length and breadth of the land.

From this view of the case, my friends, I am driven irresistibly to the conclusion that diversity, dissimilarity, variety, in all our local and domestic institutions is the great safeguard of our liberties, and that the framers of our institutions were wise, sagacious, and patriotic when they made this government a confederation of sovereign States, with a legislature for each, and conferred upon each legislature the power to make all local and domestic institutions to suit the people it represented, without interference from any other State or from the general Congress of the Union. If we expect to maintain our liberties, we must preserve the rights and sovereignty of the States; we must maintain and carry out that great principle of self-government incorporated in the Compromise measures of 1850, indorsed by the Illinois Legislature in 1851, emphatically embodied and carried out in the Kansas-Nebraska Bill, and vindicated this year by the refusal to bring Kansas into the Union with a constitution distasteful to her people.

The other proposition discussed by Mr. Lincoln in his speech consists in a crusade against the Supreme Court of the United States on account of the Dred Scott decision. On this question also I desire to say to you unequivocally that I take direct and distinct issue with him. I have no warfare to make on the Supreme Court of the United States, either on account of that or any other decision which they have pronounced from that bench. The Constitution of the United States has provided that the powers of government (and the constitution of each State has the same provision) shall be divided into three departments,— executive, legislative, and judicial. The right and the province of expounding the Constitution and construing the law is vested in the judiciary established by the Constitution. As a lawyer, I feel at liberty to appear before the court and controvert any principle of law while the question is pending before the tribunal; but when the decision is made, my private opinion, your opinion, all other opinions, must yield to the majesty of that authoritative adjudication. I wish you to bear in mind that this involves a great principle, upon which our rights, our liberty, and our property all depend. What security have you for your property, for your reputation, and for your personal rights, if the courts are not upheld, and their decisions respected when once fairly rendered by the highest tribunal known to the Constitution? I do not choose, therefore, to go into any argument with Mr. Lincoln in reviewing the various decisions which the Supreme Court has made, either upon the Dred Scott case or any other. I have no idea of appealing from the decision of the Supreme Court upon a constitutional question to the decisions of a tumultuous town meeting. I am aware that once an eminent lawyer of this city, now no more, said that the State of Illinois had the most perfect judicial system in the world, subject to but one exception, which could be cured by a slight amendment, and that amendment was to so change the law as to allow an appeal from the decisions of the Supreme Court of Illinois, on all constitutional questions, to justices of the peace.

My friend Mr. Lincoln, who sits behind me, reminds me that that proposition was made when I was judge of the Supreme Court. Be that as it may, I do not think that fact adds any greater weight or authority to the suggestion. It matters not with me who was on the bench, whether Mr. Lincoln or myself, whether a Lockwood or a Smith, a Taney or a Marshall; the decision of the highest tribunal known to the Constitution of the country must be final till it has been reversed by an equally high authority. Hence, I am opposed to this doctrine of Mr. Lincoln by which he proposes to take an appeal from the decision of the Supreme Court of the United States, upon this high constitutional question, to a Republican caucus sitting in the country. Yes, or any other caucus or town meeting, whether it be Republican, American, or Democratic. I respect the decisions of that august tribunal; I shall always bow in deference to them. I am a law-abiding man. I will sustain the Constitution of my country as our fathers have made it. I will yield obedience to the laws, whether I like them or not, as I find them on the statute book. I will sustain the judicial tribunals and constituted authorities in all matters within the pale of their jurisdiction as defined by the Constitution.

But I am equally free to say that the reason assigned by Mr. Lincoln for resisting the decision of the Supreme Court in the Dred Scott case does not in itself meet my approbation. He objects to it because that decision declared that a negro descended from African parents, who were brought here and sold as slaves, is not and cannot be a citizen of the United States. He says it is wrong because it deprives the negro of the benefits of that clause of the Constitution which says that citizens of one State shall enjoy all the privileges and immunities of citizens of the several States; in other words, he thinks it wrong because it deprives the negro of the privileges, immunities, and rights of citizenship, which pertain, according to that decision, only to the white man. I am free to say to you that in my opinion this government of ours is founded on the white basis. It was made by the white man, for the benefit of the white man, to be administered by white men, in such manner as they should determine. It is also true that a negro, an Indian, or any other man of inferior race to a white man should be permitted to enjoy, and humanity requires that he should have, all the rights, privileges, and immunities which he is capable of exercising consistent with the safety of society. I would give him every right and every privilege which his capacity would enable him to enjoy, consistent with the good of the society in which he lived. But you ask me, What are these rights and these privileges? My answer is, that each State must decide for itself the nature and extent of these rights. Illinois has decided for herself. We have decided that the negro shall not be a slave, and we have at the same time decided that he shall not vote, or serve on juries, or enjoy political privileges. I am content with that system of policy which we have adopted for ourselves. I deny the right of any other State to complain of our policy in that respect, or to interfere with it, or to attempt to change it. On the other hand, the State of Maine has decided that in that State a negro man may vote on an equality with the white man. The sovereign power of Maine had the right to prescribe that rule for herself. Illinois has no right to complain of Maine for conferring the right of negro suffrage, nor has Maine any right to interfere with or complain of Illinois because she has denied negro suffrage.

The State of New York has decided by her constitution that a negro may vote, provided that he own $250 worth of property, but not otherwise. The rich negro can vote, but the poor one cannot. Although that distinction does not commend itself to my judgment, yet I assert that the sovereign power of New York had a right to prescribe that form of the elective franchise. Kentucky, Virginia, and other States have provided that negroes, or a certain class of them in those States, shall be slaves, having neither civil nor political rights. Without indorsing the wisdom of that decision, I assert that Virginia has the same power, by virtue of her sovereignty, to protect slavery within her limits as Illinois has to banish it forever from our own borders. I assert the right of each State to decide for itself on all these questions, and I do not subscribe to the doctrine of my friend Mr. Lincoln, that uniformity is either desirable or possible. I do not acknowledge that the States must all be free or must all be slave.

I do not acknowledge that the negro must have civil and political rights everywhere or nowhere. I do not acknowledge that the Chinese must have the same rights in California that we would confer upon him here. I do not acknowledge that the coolie imported into this country must necessarily be put upon an equality with the white race. I do not acknowledge any of these doctrines of uniformity in the local and domestic regulations in the different States.

Thus you see, my fellow-citizens, that the issues between Mr. Lincoln and myself, as respective candidates for the United States Senate, as made up, are direct, unequivocal, and irreconcilable. He goes for uniformity in our domestic institutions, for a war of sections, until one or the other shall be subdued. I go for the great principle of the Kansas-Nebraska Bill,—the right of the people to decide for themselves.

On the other point, Mr. Lincoln goes for a warfare upon the Supreme Court of the United States because of their judicial decision in the Dred Scott case. I yield obedience to the decisions in that court,—to the final determination of the highest judicial tribunal known to our Constitution. He objects to the Dred Scott decision because it does not put the negro in the possession of the rights of citizenship on an equality with the white man. I am opposed to negro equality. I repeat that this nation is a white people,—a people composed of European descendants, a people that have established this government for themselves and their posterity,—and I am in favor of preserving, not only the purity of the blood, but the purity of the government from any mixture or amalgamation with inferior races. I have seen the effects of this mixture of superior and inferior races, this amalgamation of white men and Indians and negroes; we have seen it in Mexico, in Central America, in South America, and in all the Spanish-American States;

and its result has been degeneration, demoralization, and degradation below the capacity for self-government.

I am opposed to taking any step that recognizes the negro man or the Indian as the equal of the white man. I am opposed to giving him a voice in the administration of the government. I would extend to the negro and the Indian and to all dependent races every right, every privilege, and every immunity consistent with the safety and welfare of the white races; but equality they never should have, either political or social, or in any other respect whatever.

My friends, you see that the issues are distinctly drawn. I stand by the same platform that I have so often proclaimed to you and to the people of Illinois heretofore. I stand by the Democratic organization, yield obedience to its usages, and support its regular nominations. I indorse and approve the Cincinnati platform, and I adhere to and intend to carry out, as part of that platform, the great principle of self-government, which recognizes the right of the people in each State and Territory to decide for themselves their domestic institutions. In other words, if the Lecompton issue shall arise again, you have only to turn back and see where you have found me during the last six months, and then rest assured that you will find me in the same position, battling for the same principle, and vindicating it from assault from whatever quarter it may come, so long as I have the power to do it.

Fellow-citizens, you now have before you the outlines of the propositions which I intend to discuss before the people of Illinois during the pending campaign. I have spoken without preparation and in a very desultory manner, and may have omitted some points which I desired to discuss, and may have been less explicit on others than I could have wished. I have made up my mind to appeal to the people against the combination which has been made against me. The Republican leaders have formed an alliance—an unholy, unnatural alliance—with a portion of the unscrupulous Federal officeholders. I intend to fight that allied army wherever I meet them. I know they deny the alliance, while avoiding the common purpose; but yet these men who are trying to divide the Democratic party for the purpose of electing a Republican Senator in my place are just as much the agents, the tools, the supporters of Mr. Lincoln as if they were avowed Republicans, and expect their reward for their services when the Republicans come into power. I shall deal with these allied forces just as the Russians dealt with the Allies at Sebastopol. The Russians, when they fired a broadside at the common enemy, did not stop to inquire whether it hit a Frenchman, an Englishman, or a Turk, nor will I stop, nor shall I stop to inquire whether my blows hit the Republican leaders or their allies, who are holding the Federal offices and yet acting in concert with the Republicans to defeat the Democratic party and its nominees. I do not include all of the Federal officeholders in this remark. Such of them as are Democrats and show their Democracy by remaining inside of the Democratic organization and supporting its nominees, I recognize as Democrats; but those who, having been defeated inside of the organization, go outside and attempt to divide and destroy the party in concert with the Republican leaders, have ceased to be Democrats, and belong to the allied army, whose avowed object is to elect the Republican ticket by dividing and destroying the Democratic party.

My friends, I have exhausted myself, and I certainly have fatigued you, in the long and desultory remarks which I have made. It is now two nights since I have been in bed, and I think I have a right to a little sleep. I will, however, have an opportunity of meeting you face to face, and addressing you on more than one occasion before the November election. In conclusion, I must again say to you, justice to my own feelings demands it, that my gratitude for the welcome you have extended to me on this occasion knows no bounds, and can be described by no language which I can command. I see that I am literally at home when among my constituents. This welcome has amply repaid me for every effort that I have made in the public service during nearly twenty-five years that I have held office at your hands. It not only compensates me for the past, but it furnishes an inducement and incentive for future efforts which no man, no matter how patriotic, can feel who has not witnessed the magnificent reception you have extended to me to-night on my return.

# Speech of Abraham Lincoln

*In Reply to Senator Douglas.*
*Delivered at Chicago, Ill., Saturday Evening, July 10, 1858.*
(Mr. Douglas was not present.)

Mr. Lincoln was introduced by C. L. Wilson, Esq., and as he made his appearance he was greeted with a perfect storm of applause. For some moments the enthusiasm continued unabated. At last, when by a wave of his hand partial silence was restored, Mr. Lincoln said,—

My Fellow-Citizens: On yesterday evening, upon the occasion of the reception given to Senator Douglas, I was furnished with a seat very convenient for hearing him, and was otherwise very courteously treated by him and his friends, and for which I thank him and them. During the course of his remarks my name was mentioned in such a way as, I suppose, renders it at least not improper that I should make some sort of reply to him. I shall not attempt to follow him in the precise order in which he addressed the assembled multitude upon that occasion, though I shall perhaps do so in the main.

There was one question to which he asked the attention of the crowd, which I deem of somewhat less importance—at least of propriety—for me to dwell upon than the others, which he brought in near the close of his speech, and which I think it would not be entirely proper for me to omit attending to, and yet if I were not to give some attention to it now, I should probably forget it altogether. While I am upon this subject, allow me to say that I do not intend to indulge in that inconvenient mode sometimes adopted in public speaking, of reading from documents; but I shall depart from that rule so far as to read a little scrap from his speech, which notices this first topic of which I shall speak,—that is, provided I can find it in the paper:

> I have made up my mind to appeal to the people against the combination that has been made against me; the Republican leaders having formed an alliance—an unholy and unnatural alliance—with a portion of unscrupulous Federal office-holders. I intend to fight that allied army wherever I meet them. I know they deny the alliance; but yet these men who are trying to divide the Democratic party for the purpose of electing a Republican

Senator in my place are just as much the agents and tools of the supporters of Mr. Lincoln. Hence I shall deal with this allied army just as the Russians dealt with the Allies at Sebastopol,— that is, the Russians did not stop to inquire, when they fired a broadside, whether it hit an Englishman, a Frenchman, or a Turk. Nor will I stop to inquire, nor shall I hesitate, whether my blows shall hit the Republican leaders or their allies, who are holding the Federal offices, and yet acting in concert with them.

Well, now, gentlemen, is not that very alarming? Just to think of it! right at the outset of his canvass, I, a poor, kind, amiable, intelligent gentleman,—I am to be slain in this way! Why, my friend the Judge is not only, as it turns out, not a dead lion, nor even a living one,—he is the rugged Russian Bear!

But if they will have it—for he says that we deny it—that there is any such alliance, as he says there is,—and I don't propose hanging very much upon this question of veracity,—but if he will have it that there is such an alliance, that the Administration men and we are allied, and we stand in the attitude of English, French, and Turk, he occupying the position of the Russian, in that case I beg that he will indulge us while we barely suggest to him that these allies took Sebastopol.

Gentlemen, only a few more words as to this alliance. For my part, I have to say that whether there be such an alliance depends, so far as I know, upon what may be a right definition of the term " alliance." If for the Republican party to see the other great party to which they are opposed divided among themselves, and not try to stop the division, and rather be glad of it,—if that is an alliance, I confess I am in; but if it is meant to be said that the Republicans had formed an alliance going beyond that, by which there is contribution of money or sacrifice of principle on the one side or the other, so far as the Republican party is concerned,—if there be any such thing, I protest that I neither know anything of it, nor do I believe it. I will, however, say,—as I think this branch of the argument is lugged in,—I would before I leave it state, for the benefit of those concerned, that one of those same Buchanan men did once tell me of an argument that he made for his opposition to Judge Douglas. He said that a friend of our Senator Douglas had been talking to him, and had, among other things, said to him: "Why, you don't want to beat Douglas?" "Yes," said he, "I do want to beat him, and I will tell you why. I believe his original Nebraska Bill was right in the abstract, but it was wrong in the time that it was brought forward. It was wrong in the application to a Territory in regard to which the question had been settled; it was brought forward at a time when nobody asked him; it was tendered to the South when the South had not asked for it, but when they could not well refuse it; and for this same reason he forced that question upon our party. It has sunk the best men all over the nation, everywhere; and now, when our President, struggling with the difficulties of this man's getting up, has reached the very hardest point to turn in the case, he deserts him and I am for putting him where he will trouble us no more."

Now, gentlemen, that is not my argument; that is not my argument at all. I have only been stating to you the argument of a Buchanan man. You will judge if there is any force in it.

Popular sovereignty! everlasting popular sovereignty! Let us for a moment inquire into this vast matter of popular sovereignty. What is popular sovereignty? We recollect that at an early period in the history of this struggle there was another name for the same thing,—"squatter sovereignty." It was not exactly popular sovereignty, but squatter sovereignty. What do those terms mean? What do those terms mean when used now? And vast credit is taken by our friend the Judge in regard to his support of it, when he declares the last years of his life have been, and all the future years of his life shall be, devoted to this matter of popular sovereignty. What is it? Why, it is the sovereignty of the people! What was squatter sovereignty? I suppose, if it had any significance at all, it was the right of the people to govern themselves, to be sovereign in their own affairs while they were squatted down in a country not their own, while they had squatted on a Territory that did not belong to them, in the sense that a State belongs to the people who inhabit it,—when it belonged to the nation; such right to govern themselves was called "squatter sovereignty."

Now, I wish you to mark: What has become of that squatter sovereignty? What has become of it? Can you get anybody to tell you now that the people of a Territory have any authority to govern themselves, in regard to this mooted question of slavery, before they form a State constitution? No such thing at all; although there is a general running fire, and although there has been a hurrah made in every speech on that side, assuming that policy had given the people of a Territory the right to govern themselves upon this question, yet the point is dodged. To-day it has been decided—no more than a year ago it was decided— by the Supreme Court of the United States, and is insisted upon to-day that the people of a Territory have no right to exclude slavery from a Territory; that if any one man chooses to take slaves into a Territory, all the rest of the people have no right to keep them out. This being so, and this decision being made one of the points that the Judge approved, and one in the approval of which he says he means to keep me down,—put me down I should not say, for I have never been up,—he says he is in favor of it, and sticks to it, and expects to win his battle on that decision, which says that there is no such thing as squatter sovereignty, but that any one man may take slaves into a Territory, and all the other men in the Territory may be opposed to it, and yet by reason of the Constitution they cannot prohibit it. When that is so, how much is left of this vast matter of squatter sovereignty, I should like to know?

When we get back, we get to the point of the right of the people to make a constitution. Kansas was settled, for example, in 1854. It was a Territory yet, without having formed a constitution, in a very regular way, for three years. All this time negro slavery could be taken in by any few individuals, and by that decision of the Supreme Court, which the Judge approves, all the rest of the people cannot keep it out; but when they come to make a constitution, they may say they will not have slavery. But it is there; they are obliged to tolerate it some way, and all experience shows it will be so, for they will not take the negro slaves and absolutely deprive the owners of them. All experience shows this to be so. All that space of time that runs from the beginning of the settlement of the Territory until there is sufficiency of people to make a State constitution,—all that portion of time popular sovereignty is given up. The seal is absolutely put down upon it by the court decision, and Judge Douglas puts his own upon the top of that; yet he is appealing to the people to give him vast credit for his devotion to popular sovereignty.

Again, when we get to the question of the right of the people to form a State constitution as they please, to form it with slavery or without slavery,—if that is anything new, I confess I don't know it. Has there ever been a time when anybody said that any other than the people of a Territory itself should form a constitution? What is now in it that Judge Douglas should have fought several years of his life, and pledge himself to fight all the remaining years of his life for? Can Judge Douglas find anybody on earth that said that anybody else should form a constitution for a people? [A voice, "Yes."] Well, I should like you to name him; I should like to know who he was. [Same voice, "John Calhoun."]

MR. LINCOLN: No, sir, I never heard of even John Calhoun saying such a thing. He insisted on the same principle as Judge Douglas; but his mode of applying it, in fact, was wrong. It is enough for my purpose to ask this crowd whenever a Republican said anything against it. They never said anything against it, but they have constantly spoken for it; and whoever will undertake to examine the platform, and the speeches of responsible men of the party, and of irresponsible men, too, if you please, will be unable to find one word from anybody in the Republican ranks opposed to that popular sovereignty which Judge Douglas thinks that he has invented. I suppose that Judge Douglas will claim, in a little while, that he is the inventor of the idea that the people should govern themselves; that nobody ever thought of such a thing until he brought it forward. We do not remember that in that old Declaration of Independence it is said that "We hold these truths to be self-evident, that all men are created equal; that they are endowed by their Creator with certain inalienable rights; that among these are life, liberty, and the pursuit of happiness; that to secure these rights, governments are instituted among men, deriving their just powers from the consent of the governed." There is the origin of popular sovereignty. Who, then, shall come in at this day and claim that he invented it?

The Lecompton Constitution connects itself with this question, for it is in this matter of the Lecompton Constitution that our friend Judge Douglas claims such vast credit. I agree that in opposing the Lecompton Constitution, so far as I can perceive, he was right. I do not deny that at all; and, gentlemen, you will readily see why I could not deny it, even if I wanted to. But I do not wish to; for all the Republicans in the nation opposed it, and they would have opposed it just as much without Judge Douglas's aid as with it. They had all taken ground against it long before he did. Why, the reason that he urges against that constitution I urged against him a year before. I have the printed speech in my hand. The argument that he makes, why that constitution should not be adopted, that the people were not fairly represented nor allowed to vote, I pointed out in a speech a year ago, which I hold in my hand now, that no fair chance was to be given to the people. ["Read it, Read it."] I shall not waste your time by trying to read it. ["Read it, Read it."] Gentlemen, reading from speeches is a very tedious business, particularly for an old man that has to put on spectacles, and more so if the man be so tall that he has to bend over to the light.

A little more, now, as to this matter of popular sovereignty and the Lecompton Constitution. The Lecompton Constitution, as the Judge tells us, was defeated. The defeat of it was a good thing or it was not. He thinks the defeat of it was a good thing, and so do I, and we agree in that. Who defeated it?

A VOICE: Judge Douglas.

MR. LINCOLN: Yes, he furnished himself, and if you suppose he controlled the other Democrats that went with him, he furnished *three* votes; while the Republicans furnished *twenty*.

That is what he did to defeat it. In the House of Representatives he and his friends furnished some twenty votes, and the Republicans furnished *ninety odd*. Now, who was it that did the work?

A VOICE: Douglas.

MR. LINCOLN: Why, yes, Douglas did it! To be sure he did.

Let us, however, put that proposition another way. The Republicans could not have done it without Judge Douglas. Could he have done it without them? Which could have come the nearest to doing it without the other?

A VOICE: Who killed the bill?

ANOTHER VOICE: Douglas.

MR. LINCOLN: Ground was taken against it by the Republicans long before Douglas did it. The proportion of opposition to that measure is about five to one.

A VOICE: Why don't they come out on it?

MR. LINCOLN: You don't know what you are talking about, my friend. I am quite willing to answer any gentleman in the crowd who asks an *intelligent* question.

Now, who in all this country has ever found any of our friends of Judge Douglas's way of thinking, and who have acted upon this main question, that has ever thought of uttering a word in behalf of Judge Trumbull?

A VOICE: We have.

MR. LINCOLN: I defy you to show a printed resolution passed in a Democratic meeting—I take it upon myself to defy any man to show a printed resolution of a Democratic meeting, large or small—in favor of Judge Trumbull, or any of the five to one Republicans who beat that bill. Everything must be for the Democrats! They did everything, and the five to the one that really did the thing they snub over, and they do not seem to remember that they have an existence upon the face of the earth.

Gentlemen, I fear that I shall become tedious. I leave this branch of the subject to take hold of another. I take up that part of Judge Douglas's speech in which he respectfully attended to me.

Judge Douglas made two points upon my recent speech at Springfield. He says they are to be the issues of this campaign. The first one of these points he bases upon the language in a speech which I delivered at Springfield, which I believe I can quote correctly from memory. I said there that "we are now far into the fifth year since a policy was instituted for the avowed object, and with the confident promise, of putting an end to slavery agitation; under the operation of that policy, that agitation has not only not ceased, but has constantly augmented." "I believe it will not cease until a crisis shall have been reached and passed. 'A house divided against itself cannot stand.' I believe this government cannot endure permanently half slave and half free." "I do not expect the Union to be dissolved,"—I am quoting from my speech,—"I do not expect the house to fall, but I do expect it will cease to be divided. It will become all one thing or all the other. Either the opponents of slavery will arrest the spread of it and place it where the public mind shall rest in the belief that it is in the course of ultimate extinction, or its advocates will push it forward until it shall become alike lawful in all the States, north as well as south."

What is the paragraph? In this paragraph, which I have quoted in your hearing, and to which I ask the attention of all, Judge Douglas thinks he discovers great political heresy. I want your attention particularly to what he has inferred from it. He says I am in favor of making all the States of this Union uniform in all their internal regulations; that in all their domestic concerns I am in favor of making them entirely uniform. He draws this inference from the language I have quoted to you. He says that I am in favor of making war by the North upon the South for the extinction of slavery; that I am also in favor of inviting (as he expresses it) the South to a war upon the North for the purpose of nationalizing slavery. Now, it is singular enough, if you will carefully read that passage over, that I did not say that I was in favor of anything in it. I only said what I expected would take place. I made a prediction only,—it may have been a foolish one, perhaps. I did not even say that I desired that slavery should be put in course of ultimate extinction. I do say so now, however, so there need be no longer any difficulty about that. It may be written down in the great speech.

Gentlemen, Judge Douglas informed you that this speech of mine was probably carefully prepared. I admit that it was. I am not master of language; I have not a fine education; I am not capable of entering into a disquisition upon dialectics, as I believe you call it; but I do not believe the language I employed bears any such construction as Judge Douglas puts union it. But I don't care about a quibble in regard to words. I know what I meant, and I will not leave this crowd in doubt, if I can explain it to them, what I really meant in the use of that paragraph.

I am not, in the first place, unaware that this government has endured eighty-two years half slave and half free. I know that. I am tolerably well acquainted with the history of the country, and I know that it has endured eighty-two years half slave and half free. I *believe*—and that is what I meant to allude to there— I *believe* it has endured because during all that time, until the introduction of the Nebraska Bill, the public mind did rest all the time in the belief that slavery was in course of ultimate extinction. That was what gave us the rest that we had through that period of eighty-two years,—at least, so I believe. I have always hated slavery, I think, as much as any Abolitionist,—I have been an Old Line Whig,—I have always hated it; but I have always been quiet about it until this new era of the introduction of the Nebraska Bill began. I always believed that everybody was against it, and that it was in course of ultimate extinction.

[Pointing to Mr. Browning, who stood near by.] Browning thought so; the great mass of the nation have rested in the belief that slavery was in course of ultimate extinction. They had reason so to believe.

The adoption of the Constitution and its attendant history led the people to believe so; and that such was the belief of the framers of the Constitution itself, why did those old men, about the time of the adoption of the Constitution, decree that slavery should not go into the new Territory, where it had not already gone? Why declare that within twenty years the African slave trade, by which slaves are supplied, might be cut off by Congress? Why were all these acts? I might enumerate more of these acts; but enough. What were they but a clear indication that the framers of the Constitution intended and expected the ultimate extinction of that institution? And now, when I say, as I said in my speech that Judge Douglas has quoted from, when I say that I think the opponents of slavery will resist the farther spread of it, and place it where the public mind shall rest with the belief that it is in course of ultimate extinction, I only mean to say that they will place it where the founders of this government originally placed it.

I have said a hundred times, and I have now no inclination to take it back, that I believe there is no right, and ought to be no inclination, in the people of the free States to enter into the slave States and interfere with the question of slavery at all. I have said that always; Judge Douglas has heard me say it, if not quite a hundred times, at least as good as a hundred times; and when it is said that I am in favor of interfering with slavery where it exists, I know it is unwarranted by anything I have ever *intended,* and, as I believe, by anything I have ever *said.* If, by any means, I have ever used language which could fairly be so construed (as, however, I believe I never have), I now correct it.

So much, then, for the inference that Judge Douglas draws, that I am in favor of setting the sections at war with one another. I know that I never meant any such thing, and I believe that no fair mind can infer any such thing from anything I have ever said.

Now, in relation to his inference that I am in favor of a general consolidation of all the local institutions of the various States. I will attend to that for a little while, and try to inquire, if I can, how on earth it could be that any man could draw such an inference from anything I said. I have said, very many times, in Judge Douglas's hearing, that no man believed more than I in the principle of self-government; that it lies at the bottom of all my ideas of just government, from beginning to end. I have denied that his use of that term applies properly. But for the thing itself, I deny that any man has ever gone ahead of me in his devotion to the principle, whatever he may have done in efficiency in advocating it. I think that I have said it in your hearing, that I believe each individual is naturally enti- tled to do as he pleases with himself and the fruit of his labor, so far as it in no wise interferes with any other man's rights; that each community as a State has a right to do exactly as it pleases with all the concerns within that State that interfere with the right of no other State; and that the General Government, upon principle, has no right to interfere with anything other than that general class of things that does concern the whole. I have said that at all times. I have said, as illustrations, that I do not believe in the right of Illinois to interfere with the cranberry laws of Indiana, the oyster laws of Virginia, or the liquor laws of Maine. I have said these things over and over again, and I repeat them here as my sentiments.

How is it, then, that Judge Douglas infers, because I hope to see slavery put where the public mind shall rest in the belief that it is in the course of ultimate extinction, that I am in favor of Illinois going over and interfering with the cran- berry laws of Indiana? What can authorize him to draw any such inference? I sup- pose there might be one thing that at least enabled *him* to draw such an inference that would not be true with me or many others: that is, because he looks upon all this matter of slavery as an exceedingly little thing,—this matter of keeping one sixth of the population of the whole nation in a state of oppression and tyranny unequalled in the world. He looks upon it as being an exceedingly little thing,— only equal to the question of the cranberry laws of Indiana; as something having no moral question in it; as something on a par with the question of whether a man shall pasture his land with cattle, or plant it with tobacco; so little and so small a thing that he concludes, if I could desire that anything should be done to bring about the ultimate extinction of that little thing, I must be in favor of bringing about an amalgamation of all the other little things in the Union. Now, it so happens—and there, I presume, is the foundation of this mistake—that the Judge thinks thus; and it so happens that there is a vast portion of the American people that do *not* look upon that matter as being this very little thing. They look upon it as a vast moral evil; they can prove it as such by the writings of those who gave us the blessings of liberty which we enjoy, and that they so looked upon it, and not as an evil merely confining itself to the States where it is situated; and while we agree that, by the Constitution we assented to, in the States where it exists, we have no right to interfere with it, because it is in the Constitution; and we are by both duty and inclination to stick by that Constitution, in all its letter and spirit, from beginning to end.

So much, then, as to my disposition—my wish—to have all the State legis- latures blotted out, and to have one consolidated government, and a uniformity of domestic regulations in all the States, by which I suppose it is meant, if we raise corn here, we must make sugar-cane grow here too, and we must make those which grow North grow in the South. All this I suppose he understands I am in favor of doing. Now, so much for all this nonsense; for I must call it so. The Judge can have no issue with me on a question of establishing uniformity in the domestic regulations of the States.

A little now on the other point,—the Dred Scott decision. Another of the issues he says that is to be made with me is upon his devotion to the Dred Scott decision, and my opposition to it.

I have expressed heretofore, and I now repeat, my opposition to the Dred Scott decision; but I should be allowed to state the nature of that opposition, and I ask your indulgence while I do so. What is fairly implied by the term Judge Douglas has used, "resistance to the decision"? I do not resist it. If I wanted to take Dred Scott from his master, I would be interfering with property, and that terrible difficulty that Judge Douglas speaks of, of interfering with property, would arise. But I am doing no such thing as that, but all that I am doing is refusing to obey it as a political rule. If I were in Congress, and a vote should come up on a question whether slavery should be prohibited in a new Territory, in spite of the Dred Scott decision, I would vote that it should.

That is what I should do. Judge Douglas said last night that before the decision he might advance his opinion, and it might be contrary to the decision when it was made; but after it was made he would abide by it until it was reversed. Just so! We let this property abide by the decision, but we will try to reverse that decision. We will try to put it where Judge Douglas would not object, for he says he will obey it until it is reversed. Somebody has to reverse that decision, since it is made, and we mean to reverse it, and we mean to do it peaceably.

What are the uses of decisions of courts? They have two uses. As rules of property they have two uses. First, they decide upon the question before the court. They decide in this case that Dred Scott is a slave. Nobody resists that. Not only that, but they say to everybody else that persons standing just as Dred Scott stands are as he is. That is, they say that when a question comes up upon another person, it will be so decided again, unless the court decides in another way, unless the court overrules its decision. Well, we mean to do what we can to have the court decide the other way. That is one thing we mean to try to do.

The sacredness that Judge Douglas throws around this decision is a degree of sacredness that has never been before thrown around any other decision. I have never heard of such a thing. Why, decisions apparently contrary to that decision, or that good lawyers thought were contrary to that decision, have been made by that very court before. It is the first of its kind; it is an astonisher in legal history. It is a new wonder of the world. It is based upon falsehood in the main as to the facts; allegations of facts upon which it stands are not facts at all in many instances, and no decision made on any question—the first instance of a decision made under so many unfavorable circumstances—thus placed, has ever been held by the profession as law, and it has always needed confirmation before the lawyers regarded it as settled law. But Judge Douglas will have it that all hands must take this extraordinary decision, made under these extraordinary circumstances, and give their vote in Congress in accordance with it, yield to it, and obey it in every possible sense. Circumstances alter cases. Do not gentlemen here remember the case of that same Supreme Court some twenty-five or thirty years ago deciding that a National Bank was constitutional? I ask, if somebody does not remember that a National Bank was declared to be constitutional? Such is the truth, whether it be remembered or not. The Bank charter ran out, and a recharter was granted by Congress. That recharter was laid before General Jackson. It was urged upon him, when he denied the constitutionality of the Bank, that the Supreme Court had decided that it was constitutional; and General Jackson then said that the Supreme Court had no right to lay down a rule to govern a coordinate branch of the government, the members of which had sworn to support the Constitution; that each member had sworn to support that Constitution as he understood it. I will venture here to say that I have heard Judge Douglas say that he approved of General Jackson for that act. What has now become of all his tirade about "resistance of the Supreme Court"?

My fellow-citizens, getting back a little,—for I pass from these points,—when Judge Douglas makes his threat of annihilation upon the "alliance," he is cautious to say that that warfare of his is to fall upon the leaders of the Republican party. Almost every word he utters, and every distinction he makes, has its significance. He means for the Republicans who do not count themselves as leaders, to be his friends; he makes no fuss over them; it is the leaders that he is making war upon. He wants it understood that the mass of the Republican party are really his friends. It is only the leaders that are doing something that are intolerant, and that require extermination at his hands. As this is clearly and unquestionably the light in which he presents that matter, I want to ask your attention, addressing myself to the Republicans here, that I may ask you some questions as to where you, as the Republican party, would be placed if you sustained Judge Douglas in his present position by a re-election? I do not claim, gentlemen, to be unselfish; I do not pretend that I would not like to go to the United States Senate,—I make no such hypocritical pretence; but I do say to you that in this mighty issue it is nothing to you—nothing to the mass of the people of the nation,—whether or not Judge Douglas or myself shall ever be heard of after this night; it may be a trifle to either of us, but in connection with this mighty question, upon which hang the destinies of the nation, perhaps, it is absolutely nothing: but where will you be placed if you reindorse Judge Douglas? Don't you know how apt he is, how exceedingly anxious he is at all times, to seize upon anything and everything to persuade you that something *he* has done *you* did yourselves? Why, he tried to persuade you last night that our Illinois Legislature instructed him to introduce the Nebraska Bill. There was nobody in that Legislature ever thought of such a thing; and when he first introduced the bill, he never thought of it; but still he fights furiously for the proposition, and that he did it because there was a standing instruction to our Senators to be always introducing Nebraska bills. He tells you he is for the Cincinnati platform, he tells you he is for the Dred Scott decision. He tells you, not in his speech last night, but substantially in a former speech, that he cares not if slavery is voted up or down; he tells you the struggle on Lecompton is past; it may come up again or not, and if it does, he stands where he stood when, in spite of him and his opposition, you built up the Republican party. If you indorse him, you tell him you do not care whether slavery be voted up or down, and he will close or try to close your mouths with his declaration, repeated by the day, the week, the month, and the year. Is that what you mean? [Cries of "No," one voice "Yes."] Yes, I have no doubt you who have always been for him, if you mean that. No doubt of that, soberly I have said, and I repeat it. I think, in the position in which Judge Douglas stood in opposing the Lecompton Constitution, he was right; he does not know that it will return, but if it does we may know where to find him, and if it does not, we may know where to look for him, and that is on the Cincinnati platform. Now, I could ask the Republican party, after all the hard names that Judge Douglas has called them by all his repeated charges of their inclination to marry with and hug negroes; all his declarations of Black Republicanism,—by the way, we are improving, the black has got rubbed off,— but with all that, if he be indorsed by Republican votes, where do you stand? Plainly, you stand ready saddled, bridled, and harnessed, and waiting to be driven over to the slavery extension camp of the nation,—just ready to be driven over, tied together in a lot, to be driven over, every man with a rope around his neck, that halter being held by Judge Douglas. That is the question. If Republican men have been in earnest in what they have done, I think they had better not do it; but I think that the Republican party is made up of those who, as far as they can peaceably, will oppose the extension of slavery, and who will hope for its ultimate extinction. If they believe it is wrong in grasping up the new lands of the conti-nent and keeping them from the settlement of free white laborers, who want the land to bring up their families upon; if they are in earnest, although they may make a mistake, they will grow restless, and the time will come when they will come back again and reorganize, if not by the same name, at least upon the same principles as their party now has. It is better, then, to save the work while it is begun. You have done the labor; maintain it, keep it. If men choose to serve you, go with them; but as you have made up your organization upon principle, stand by it; for, as surely as God reigns over you, and has inspired your mind, and given you a sense of propriety, and continues to give you hope, so surely will you still cling to these ideas, and you will at last come back again after your wanderings, merely to do your work over again.

We were often,—more than once, at least,—in the course of Judge Douglas's speech last night, reminded that this government was made for white men; that he believed it was made for white men. Well, that is putting it into a shape in which no one wants to deny it; but the Judge then goes into his passion for draw-ing inferences that are not warranted. I protest, now and forever, against that counterfeit logic which presumes that because I did not want a negro woman for a slave, I do necessarily want her for a wife. My understanding is that I need not have her for either, but, as God made us separate, we can leave one another alone, and do one another much good thereby. There are white men enough to marry all the white women, and enough black men to marry all the black women; and in God's name let them be so married. The Judge regales us with the terrible enormities that take place by the mixture of races; that the inferior race bears the superior down. Why, Judge, if we do not let them get together in the Territories, they won't mix there.

A VOICE: Three cheers for Lincoln. (The cheers were given with a hearty good-will.)

MR. LINCOLN: I should say at least that that is a self-evident truth.

Now, it happens that we meet together once every year, sometimes about the 4th of July, for some reason or other. These 4th of July gatherings I suppose have their uses. If you will indulge me, I will state what I suppose to be some of them.

We are now a mighty nation; we are thirty or about thirty millions of people, and we own and inhabit about one fifteenth part of the dry land of the whole earth. We run our memory back over the pages of history for about eighty-two years, and we discover that we were then a very small people in point of numbers, vastly inferior to what we are now, with a vastly less extent of country, with vastly less of everything we deem desirable among men; we look upon the change as exceedingly advantageous to us and to our posterity, and we fix upon something that happened away back, as in some way or other being connected with this rise of prosperity. We find a race of men living in that day whom we claim as our fathers and grandfathers; they were iron men; they fought for the principle that they were contending for; and we understood that by what they then did it has followed that the degree of prosperity which we now enjoy has come to us. We hold this annual celebration to remind ourselves of all the good done in this process of time, of how it was done and who did it, and how we are historically connected with it; and we go from these meetings in better humor with ourselves, we feel more attached the one to the other, and more firmly bound to the country we inhabit. In every way we are better men in the age and race and country in which we live, for these celebrations. But after we have done all this we have not yet reached the whole. There is something else connected with it. We have—besides these, men descended by blood from our ancestors—among us perhaps half our people who are not descendants at all of these men; they are men who have come from Europe,—German, Irish, French, and Scandinavian,—men that have come from Europe themselves, or whose ancestors have come hither and settled here, finding themselves our equals in all things. If they look back through this history to trace their connection with those days by blood, they find they have none, they cannot carry themselves back into that glorious epoch and make themselves feel that they are part of us; but when they look through that old Declaration of Independence, they find that those old men say that "We hold these truths to be self-evident, that all men are created equal"; and then they feel that that moral sentiment, taught in that day, evidences their relation to those men, that it is the father of all moral principle in them, and that they have a right to claim it as though they were blood of the blood, and flesh of the flesh, of the men who wrote that Declaration; and so they are. That is the electric cord in that Declaration that links the hearts of patriotic and liberty-loving men together, that will link those patriotic hearts as long as the love of freedom exists in the minds of men throughout the world.

Now, sirs, for the purpose of squaring things with this idea of "don't care if slavery is voted up or voted down," for sustaining the Dred Scott decision, for holding that the Declaration of Independence did not mean anything at all, we have Judge Douglas giving his exposition of what the Declaration of Independence means, and we have him saying that the people of America are equal to the people of England. According to his construction, you Germans are not connected with it. Now, I ask you in all soberness if all these things, if indulged in, if ratified, if confirmed and indorsed, if taught to our children, and repeated to them, do not tend to rub out the sentiment of liberty in the country, and to transform this government into a government of some other form. Those arguments that are made, that the inferior race are to be treated with as much allowance as they are capable of enjoying; that as much is to be done for them as their condition will allow,—what are these arguments? They are the arguments that kings have made for enslaving the people in all ages of the world. You will find that all the arguments in favor of kingcraft were of this class; they always bestrode the necks of the people not that they wanted to do it, but because the people were better off for being ridden. That is their argument, and this argument of the Judge is the same old serpent that says, You work, and I eat; you toil, and I will enjoy the fruits of it. Turn in whatever way you will, whether it come from the mouth of a king, an excuse for enslaving the people of his country, or from the mouth of men of one race as a reason for enslaving the men of another race, it is all the same old serpent; and I hold, if that course of argumentation that is made for the purpose of convincing the public mind that we should not care about this should be granted, it does not stop with the negro. I should like to know, if taking this old Declaration of Independence, which declares that all men are equal upon principle, and making exceptions to it, where will it stop? If one man says it does not mean a negro, why not another say it does not mean some other man? If that Declaration is not the truth, let us get the statute book, in which we find it, and tear it out! Who is so bold as to do it? If it is not true, let us tear it out! [Cries of "No, no."] Let us stick to it, then; let us stand firmly by it, then.

It may be argued that there are certain conditions that make necessities and impose them upon us; and to the extent that a necessity is imposed upon a man, he must submit to it. I think that was the condition in which we found ourselves when we established this government. We had slavery among us, we could not get our Constitution unless we permitted them to remain in slavery, we could not secure the good we did secure if we grasped for more; and having by necessity submitted to that much, it does not destroy the principle that is the charter of our liberties. Let that charter stand as our standard.

My friend has said to me that I am a poor hand to quote Scripture. I will try it again, however. It is said in one of the admonitions of our Lord, "As your Father in heaven is perfect, be ye also perfect." The Saviour, I suppose, did not expect that any human creature could be perfect as the Father in heaven; but he said, "As your Father in heaven is perfect, be ye also perfect." He set that up as a standard; and he who did most towards reaching that standard attained the highest degree of moral perfection. So I say in relation to the principle that all men are created equal, let it be as nearly reached as we can. If we cannot give freedom to every creature, let us do nothing that will impose slavery upon any other creature. Let us then turn this government back into the channel in which the framers of the Constitution originally placed it. Let us stand firmly by each other. If we do not do so, we are turning in the contrary direction, that our friend Judge Douglas proposes—not intentionally—as working in the traces tends to make this one universal slave nation. He is one that runs in that direction, and as such I resist him.

My friends, I have detained you about as long as I desired to do, and I have only to say: Let us discard all this quibbling about this man and the other man; this race and that race and the other race being inferior, and therefore they must be placed in an inferior position; discarding our standard that we have left us. Let us discard all these things, and unite as one people throughout this land, until we shall once more stand up declaring that all men are created equal.

My friends, I could not, without launching off upon some new topic, which would detain you too long, continue to-night. I thank you for this most extensive audience that you have furnished me to-night. I leave you, hoping that the lamp of liberty will burn in your bosoms until there shall no longer be a doubt that all men are created free and equal.

# Speech of Senator Douglas

*Delivered at Bloomington, Ill., July 16, 1858.*
(Mr. Lincoln was present.)

Senator Douglas said:

Mr. Chairman and Fellow-citizens of McLean County: To say that I am profoundly touched by the hearty welcome you have extended me, and by the kind and complimentary sentiments you have expressed toward me, is but a feeble expression of the feelings of my heart.

I appear before you this evening for the purpose of vindicating the course which I have felt it my duty to pursue in the Senate of the United States upon the great public questions which have agitated the country since I last addressed you. I am aware that my senatorial course has been arraigned, not only by political foes, but by a few men pretending to belong to the Democratic party, and yet acting in alliance with the enemies of that party, for the purpose of electing Republicans to Congress in this State, in place of the present Democratic delegation. I desire your attention whilst I address you, and then I will ask your verdict whether I have not in all things acted in entire good faith, and honestly carried out the principles, the professions, and the avowals which I made before my constituents previous to my going to the Senate.

During the last session of Congress the great question of controversy has been the admission of Kansas into the Union under the Lecompton Constitution. I need not inform you that from the beginning to the end I took bold, determined, and unrelenting ground in opposition to that Lecompton Constitution. My reason for that course is contained in the fact that that instrument was not the act and deed of the people of Kansas, and did not embody their will. I hold it to be a fundamental principle in all free governments—a principle asserted in the Declaration of Independence, and underlying the Constitution of the United States, as well as the Constitution of every State of the Union—that every people ought to have the right to form, adopt, and ratify the constitution under which they are to live. When I introduced the Nebraska Bill in the Senate of the United States, in 1854, I incorporated in it the provision that it was the true intent and meaning of the bill not to legislate slavery into any Territory or State, or to exclude it therefrom, but to leave the people thereof perfectly free to form and regulate their own domestic institutions in their own way, subject only to the

Constitution of the United States. In that bill the pledge was distinctly made that the people of Kansas should be left not only free, but perfectly free to form and regulate their own domestic institutions to suit themselves; and the question arose, when the Lecompton Constitution was sent into Congress, and the admission of Kansas not only asked, but attempted to be forced under it, whether or not that Constitution was the free act and deed of the people of Kansas. No man pretends that it embodied their will. Every man in America knows that it was rejected by the people of Kansas, by a majority of over ten thousand, before the attempt was made in Congress to force the Territory into the Union under that Constitution, I resisted, therefore, the Lecompton Constitution because it was a violation of the great principle of self-government, upon which all our institutions rest. I do not wish to mislead you, or to leave you in doubt as to the motives of my action. I did not oppose the Lecompton Constitution upon the ground of the slavery clause contained in it. I made my speech against that instrument before the vote was taken on the slavery clause. At the time I made it I did not know whether that clause would be voted in or out; whether it would be included in the Constitution, or excluded from it; and it made no difference with me what the result of the vote was, for the reason that I was contending for a principle, under which you have no more right to force a free State upon a people against their will than you have to force a slave State upon them without their consent. The error consisted in attempting to control the free action of the people of Kansas in any respect whatever. It is no argument with me to say that such and such a clause of the Constitution was not palatable, that you did not like it; it is a matter of no consequence whether you in Illinois like any clause in the Kansas Constitution or not; it is not a question for you, but it is a question for the people of Kansas. They have the right to make a constitution in accordance with their own wishes, and if you do not like it, you are not bound to go there and live under it. We in Illinois have made a constitution to suit ourselves, and we think we have a tolerably good one; but whether we have or not, it is nobody's business but our own. If the people of Kentucky do not like it, they need not come here to live under it. If the people of Indiana are not satisfied with it, what matters it to us? We, and we alone, have the right to a voice in its adoption or rejection. Reasoning thus, my friends, my efforts were directed to the vindication of the great principle involving the right of the people of each State and each Territory to form and regulate their own domestic institutions to suit themselves, subject only to the Constitution of our common country. I am rejoiced to be enabled to say to you that we fought that battle until we forced the advocates of the Lecompton instrument to abandon the attempt of inflicting it upon the people of Kansas without first giving them an opportunity of rejecting it. When we compelled them to abandon that effort, they resorted to a scheme. They agreed to refer the Constitution back to the people of Kansas, thus conceding the correctness of the principle for which I had contended, and granting all I had desired, provided the mode of that reference and the mode of submission to the people had been just, fair, and equal. I did not consider the mode of submission provided in what is known as the "English" bill a fair submission, and for this simple reason, among others: It provided, in effect, that if the people of Kansas would accept the Lecompton Constitution, that they might come in with 35,000 inhabitants; but that if they rejected it, in order that they might form a constitution agreeable to their own feelings, and conformable to their own principles, that they should not be received into the Union until they had 93,420 inhabitants. In other words, it said to the people,—If you will come into the Union as a slaveholding State, you shall be admitted with 35,000 inhabitants; but if you insist on being a free State, you shall not be admitted until you have 93,420. I was not willing to discriminate between free States and slave States in this Confederacy. I will not put a restriction upon a slave State that I would not put upon a free State, and I will not permit, if I can prevent it, a restriction being put upon a free State which is not applied with the same force to the slaveholding States. Equality among the States is a cardinal and fundamental principle in our Confederacy, and cannot be violated without overturning our system of government. Hence I demanded that the free States and the slaveholding States should be kept on an exact equality, one with the other, as the Constitution of the United States had placed them. If the people of Kansas want a slaveholding State, let them have it; and if they want a free State they have a right to it; and it is not for the people of Illinois, or Missouri, or New York, or Kentucky, to complain, whatever the decision of the people of Kansas may be upon that point.

But while I was not content with the mode of submission contained in the English bill, and while I could not sanction it for the reason that, in my opinion, it violated the great principle of equality among the different States, yet when it became the law of the land, and under it the question was referred back to the people of Kansas for their decision, at an election to be held on the first Monday in August next, I bowed in deference, because whatever decision the people shall make at that election must be final, and conclusive of the whole question. If the people of Kansas accept the proposition submitted by Congress, from that moment Kansas will become a State of the Union, and there is no way of keeping her out if you should try. The act of admission would become irrepealable; Kansas would be a State, and there would be an end of the controversy. On the other hand, if at that election the people of Kansas shall reject the proposition, as is now generally thought will be the case, from that moment the Lecompton Constitution is dead, and again there is an end of the controversy. So you see that either way, on the 3d of August next, the Lecompton controversy ceases and terminates forever; and a similar question can never arise unless some man shall attempt to play the Lecompton game over again. But, my fellow-citizens, I am well convinced that that game will never be attempted again; it has been so solemnly and thoroughly rebuked during the last session of Congress that it will find but few advocates in the future. The President of the United States, in his annual message, expressly recommends that the example of the Minnesota case, wherein Congress required the Constitution to be submitted to the vote of the people for ratification or rejection, shall be followed in all future cases; and all we have to do is to sustain as one man that recommendation, and the Kansas controversy can never again arise.

My friends, I do not desire you to understand me as claiming for myself any special merit for the course I have pursued on this question. I simply did my duty,—a duty enjoined by fidelity, by honor, by patriotism; a duty which I could not have shrunk from, in my opinion, without dishonor and faithlessness to my constituency. Besides, I only did what it was in the power of any one man to do. There were others, men of eminent ability, men of wide reputation, renowned all over America, who led the van, and are entitled to the greatest share of the credit. Foremost among them all, as he was head and shoulders above them all, was Kentucky's great and gallant statesman, John J. Crittenden. By his course upon this question he has shown himself a worthy successor of the immortal Clay, and well may Kentucky be proud of him. I will not withhold, either, the meed of praise due the Republican party in Congress for the course which they pursued. In the language of the *New York Tribune*, they came to the Douglas platform, abandoning their own, believing that under the peculiar circumstances they would in that mode best subserve the interests of the country. My friends, when I am battling for a great principle, I want aid and support from whatever quarter I can get it, in order to carry out that principle. I never hesitate in my course when I find those who on all former occasions differed from me upon the principle finally coming to its support. Nor is it for me to inquire into the motives which animated the Republican members of Congress in supporting the Crittenden-Montgomery bill. It is enough for me that in that case they came square up and indorsed the great principle of the Kansas-Nebraska Bill, which declared that Kansas should be received into the Union, with slavery or without, as its Constitution should prescribe. I was the more rejoiced at the action of the Republicans on that occasion for another reason. I could not forget, you will not soon forget, how unanimous that party was, in 1854, in declaring that never should another slave State be admitted into this Union under any circumstances whatever: and yet we find that during this last winter they came up and voted, to a man, declaring that Kansas should come in as a State with slavery under the Lecompton Constitution, if her people desired it, and that if they did not, they might form a new constitution, with slavery or without, just as they pleased. I do not question the motive when men do a good act; I give them credit for the act; and if they will stand by that principle in the future, and abandon their heresy of "no more slave States even if the people want them," I will then give them still more credit. I am afraid, though, that they will not stand by it in the future. If they do, I will freely forgive them all the abuse they heaped upon me in 1854 for having advocated and carried out that same principle in the Kansas-Nebraska Bill.

Illinois stands proudly forward as a State which early took her position in favor of the principle of popular sovereignty as applied to the Territories of the United States. When the Compromise measures of 1850 passed, predicated upon that principle, you recollect the excitement which prevailed throughout the northern portion of this State. I vindicated those measures then, and defended myself for having voted for them, upon the ground that they embodied the principle that every people ought to have the privilege of forming and regulating their own institutions to suit themselves; that each State had that right, and I saw no reason why it should not be extended to the Territories. When the people of Illinois had an opportunity of passing judgment upon those measures, they indorsed them by a vote of their representatives in the Legislature,—sixty-one in the affirmative, and only four in the negative,—in which they asserted that the principle embodied in the measures was the birthright of freemen, the gift of Heaven, a principle vindicated by our revolutionary fathers, and that no limitation should ever be placed upon it, either in the organization of a territorial government or the admission of a State into the Union. That resolution still stands unrepealed on the journals of the Legislature of Illinois. In obedience to it, and in exact conformity with the principle, I brought in the Kansas-Nebraska Bill, requiring that the people should be left perfectly free in the formation of their institutions and in the organization of their government. I now submit to you whether I have not in good faith redeemed that pledge, that the people of Kansas should be left perfectly free to form and regulate their institutions to suit themselves. And yet, while no man can arise in any crowd and deny that I have been faithful to my principles and redeemed my pledge, we find those who are struggling to crush and defeat me, for the very reason that I have been faithful in carrying out those measures. We find the Republican leaders forming an alliance with professed Lecompton men to defeat every Democratic nominee and elect Republicans in their places, and aiding and defending them in order to help them break down Anti-Lecompton men, who they acknowledge did right in their opposition to Lecompton. The only hope that Mr. Lincoln has of defeating me for Senator rests in the fact that I was faithful to my principles and that he may be able in consequence of that fact to form a coalition with Lecompton men who wish to defeat me for that fidelity.

This is one element of strength upon which he relies to accomplish his object. He hopes he can secure the few men claiming to be friends of the Lecompton Constitution, and for that reason you will find he does not say a word against the Lecompton Constitution or its supporters. He is as silent as the grave upon that subject. Behold Mr. Lincoln courting Lecompton votes, in order that he may go to the Senate as the representative of Republican principles! You know that the alliance exists. I think you will find that it will ooze out before the contest is over.

Every Republican paper takes ground with my Lecompton enemies, encouraging them, stimulating them in their opposition to me, and styling my friends bolters from the Democratic party, and their Lecompton allies the true Democratic party of the country. If they think that they can mislead and deceive the people of Illinois, or the Democracy of Illinois, by that sort of an unnatural and unholy alliance, I think they show very little sagacity, or give the people very little credit for intelligence. It must be a contest of principle. Either the radical Abolition principles of Mr. Lincoln must be maintained, or the strong, constitutional, national Democratic principles with which I am identified must be carried out.

There can be but two great political parties in this country. The contest this year and in 1860 must necessarily be between the Democracy and the Republicans, if we can judge from present indications. My whole life has been identified with the Democratic party. I have devoted all of my energies to advocating its principles and sustaining its organization. In this State the party was never better united or more harmonious than at this time. The State Convention which assembled on the 2d of April, and nominated Fondey and French, was regularly called by the State Central Committee, appointed by the previous State Convention for that purpose. The meetings in each county in the State for the appointment of delegates to the Convention were regularly called by the county committees, and the proceedings in every county in the State, as well as in the State Convention, were regular in all respects. No convention was ever more harmonious in its action, or showed a more tolerant and just spirit toward brother Democrats. The leaders of the party there assembled declared their unalterable attachment to the time-honored principles and organization of the Democratic party, and to the Cincinnati platform. They declared that that platform was the only authoritative exposition of Democratic principles, and that it must so stand until changed by another National Convention; that in the mean time they would make no new tests, and submit to none; that they would proscribe no Democrat nor permit the proscription of Democrats because of their opinion upon Lecomptonism, or upon any other issue which has arisen, but would recognize all men as Democrats who remained inside of the organization, preserved the usages of the party, and supported its nominees. These bolting Democrats who now claim to be the peculiar friends of the National Administration, and have formed an alliance with Mr. Lincoln and the Republicans for the purpose of defeating the Democratic party, have ceased to claim fellowship with the Democratic organization, have entirely separated themselves from it, and are endeavoring to build up a faction in the State, not with the hope or expectation of electing any one man who professes to be a Democrat to office in any county in the State, but merely to secure the defeat of the Democratic nominees and the election of Republicans in their places. What excuse can any honest Democrat have for abandoning the Democratic organization and joining with the Republicans to defeat our nominees, in view of the platform established by the State Convention? They cannot pretend that they were proscribed because of their opinions upon Lecompton or any other question, for the Convention expressly declared that they recognized all as good Democrats who remained inside of the organization and abided by the nominations. If the question is settled or is to be considered as finally disposed of by the votes on the 3d of August, what possible excuse can any good Democrat make for keeping up a division for the purpose of prostrating his party, after that election is over and the controversy has terminated? It is evident that all who shall keep up this warfare for the purpose of dividing and destroying the party have made up their minds to abandon the Democratic organization forever, and to join those for whose benefit they are now trying to distract our party, and elect Republicans in the place of the Democratic nominees.

I submit the question to you whether I have been right or wrong in the course I have pursued in Congress. And I submit, also, whether I have not redeemed in good faith every pledge I have made to you. Then, my friends, the question recurs, whether I shall be sustained or rejected? If you are of opinion that Mr. Lincoln will advance the interests of Illinois better than I can; that he will sustain her honor and her dignity higher than it has been in my power to do; that your interests and the interests of your children require his election instead of mine, it is your duty to give him your support. If, on the contrary, you think that my adherence to these great fundamental principles upon which our government is founded is the true mode of sustaining the peace and harmony of the country, and maintaining the perpetuity of the Republic, I then ask you to stand by me in the efforts I have made to that end.

And this brings me to the consideration of the two points at issue between Mr. Lincoln and myself. The Republican Convention, when it assembled at Springfield, did me and the country the honor of indicating the man who was to be their standard-bearer, and the embodiment of their principles, in this State. I owe them my gratitude for thus making up a direct issue between Mr. Lincoln and myself I shall have no controversies of a personal character with Mr. Lincoln. I have known him well for a quarter of a century. I have known him, as you all know him, a kind-hearted, amiable gentleman, a right good fellow, a worthy citizen, of eminent ability as a lawyer, and, I have no doubt, sufficient ability to make a good Senator. The question, then, for you to decide is whether his principles are more in accordance with the genius of our free institutions, the peace and harmony of the Republic, than those which I advocate. He tells you, in his speech made at Springfield, before the Convention which gave him his unanimous nomination, that—

"A house divided against itself cannot stand."

"I believe this government cannot endure permanently half slave and half free."

"I do not expect the Union to be dissolved, I don't expect the house to fall; but I do expect it will cease to be divided."

"It will become all one thing or all the other."

That is the fundamental principle upon which he sets out in this campaign. Well, I do not suppose you will believe one word of it when you come to examine it carefully, and see its consequences. Although the Republic has existed from 1789 to this day divided into free States and slave States, yet we are told that in the future it cannot endure unless they shall become all free or all slave. For that reason, he says, as the gentleman in the crowd says, that they must be all free. He wishes to go to the Senate of the United States in order to carry out that line of public policy, which will compel all the States in the South to become free. How is he going to do it? Has Congress any power over the subject of slavery in Kentucky, or Virginia, or any other State of this Union? How, then, is Mr. Lincoln going to carry out that principle which he says is essential to the existence of this Union, to wit, that slavery must be abolished in all the States of the Union, or must be established in them all? You convince the South that they must either establish slavery in Illinois, and in every other free State, or submit to its abolition in every Southern State, and you invite them to make a warfare upon the Northern States in order to establish slavery, for the sake of perpetuating it at home. Thus, Mr. Lincoln invites by his proposition a war of sections, a war between Illinois and Kentucky, a war between the free States and the slave States, a war between the North and the South, for the purpose of either exterminating slavery in every Southern State or planting it in every Northern State. He tells you that the safety of this Republic, that the existence of this Union, depends upon that warfare being carried on until one section or the other shall be entirely subdued. The States must all be free or slave, for a house divided against itself cannot stand. That is Mr. Lincoln's argument upon that question. My friends, is it possible to preserve peace between the North and the South if such a doctrine shall prevail in either section of the Union? Will you ever submit to a warfare waged by the Southern States to establish slavery in Illinois? What man in Illinois would not lose the last drop of his heart's blood before he would submit to the institution of slavery being forced upon us by other States, against our will? And if that be true of us, what Southern man would not shed the last drop of his heart's blood to prevent Illinois, or any other Northern State, from interfering to abolish slavery in his State? Each of these States is sovereign under the Constitution; and if we wish to preserve our liberties, the reserved rights and sovereignty of each and every State must be maintained. I have said on a former occasion, and I here repeat, that it is neither desirable nor possible to establish uniformity in the local and domestic institutions of all the States of this Confederacy. And why? Because the Constitution of the United States rests upon the right of every State to decide all its local and domestic institutions for itself. It is not possible, therefore, to make them conform to each other, unless we subvert the Constitution of the United States. No, sir, that cannot be done. God forbid that any man should ever make the attempt! Let that Constitution ever be trodden under foot and destroyed, and there will not be wisdom and patriotism enough left to make another that will work half so well. Our safety, our liberty, depends upon preserving the Constitution of the United States as our fathers made it, inviolate, at the same time maintaining the reserved rights and the sovereignty of each State over its local and domestic institutions, against Federal authority, or any outside interference.

The difference between Mr. Lincoln and myself upon this point is, that he goes for a combination of the Northern States, or the organization of a sectional political party in the free States, to make war on the domestic institutions of the Southern States, and to prosecute that war until they shall all be subdued, and made to conform to such rules as the North shall dictate to them. I am aware that Mr. Lincoln, on Saturday night last, made a speech at Chicago for the purpose, as he said, of explaining his position on this question. I have read that speech with great care, and will do him the justice to say that it is marked by eminent ability, and great success in concealing what he did mean to say in his Springfield speech. His answer to this point, which I have been arguing, is, that he never did mean, and that I ought to know that he never intended to convey the idea, that he wished the "people of the free States to *enter into* the Southern States, and interfere with slavery." Well, I never did suppose that he ever dreamed of entering into Kentucky to make war upon her institutions; nor will any Abolitionist ever enter into Kentucky to wage such war. Their mode of making war is not to enter into those States where slavery exists, and there interfere, and render themselves responsible for the consequences. Oh, no! They stand on this side of the Ohio River and shoot across. They stand in Bloomington, and shake their fists at the people of Lexington; they threaten South Carolina from Chicago. And they call that bravery! But they are very particular, as Mr. Lincoln says, not to enter into those States for the purpose of interfering with the institution of slavery there. I am not only opposed to entering into the Slave States, for the purpose of interfering with their institutions, but I am opposed to a sectional agitation to control the institutions of other States. I am opposed to organizing a sectional party, which appeals to Northern pride, and Northern passion and prejudice, against Southern institutions, thus stirring up ill-feeling and hot blood between brethren of the same Republic. I am opposed to that whole system of sectional agitation, which can produce nothing but strife, but discord, but hostility, and, finally, disunion. And yet Mr. Lincoln asks you to send him to the Senate of the United States, in order that he may carry out that great principle of his, that all the States must be slave, or all must be free. I repeat, how is he to carry it out when he gets to the Senate? Does he intend to introduce a bill to abolish slavery in Kentucky? Does he intend to introduce a bill to interfere with slavery in Virginia? How is he to accomplish what he professes must be done in order to save the Union? Mr. Lincoln is a lawyer, sagacious and able enough to tell you how he proposes to do it. I ask Mr. Lincoln how it is that he proposes ultimately to bring about this uniformity in each and all the States of the Union. There is but one possible mode which I can see, and perhaps Mr. Lincoln intends to pursue it; that is, to introduce a proposition into the Senate to change the Constitution of the United States, in order that all the State legislatures may be abolished, State sovereignty blotted out, and the power conferred upon Congress to make local laws and establish the domestic institutions and police regulations uniformly throughout the United States. Are you prepared for such a change in the institutions of your country? Whenever you shall have blotted out the State sovereignties, abolished the State legislatures, and consolidated all the power in the Federal Government, you will have established a consolidated empire as destructive to the liberties of the people and the rights of the citizen as that of Austria, or Russia, or any other despotism that rests upon the necks of the people. How is it possible for Mr. Lincoln to carry out his cherished principle of abolishing slavery everywhere or establishing it everywhere, except by the mode which I have pointed out,—by an amendment to the Constitution to the effect that I have suggested? There is no other possible mode. Mr. Lincoln intends resorting to that, or else he means nothing by the great principle upon which he desires to be elected. My friends, I trust that we will be able to get him to define what he does mean by this scriptural quotation that "A house divided against itself cannot stand"; that the government cannot endure permanently half slave and half free; that it must be all one thing, or all the other. Who among you expects to live, or have his children live, until slavery shall be established in Illinois or abolished in South Carolina? Who expects to see that occur during the lifetime of ourselves or our children?

There is but one possible way in which slavery can be abolished, and that is by leaving a State, according to the principle of the Kansas-Nebraska Bill, perfectly free to form and regulate its institutions in its own way. That was the principle upon which this Republic was founded, and it is under the operation of that principle that we have been able to preserve the Union thus far. Under its operations, slavery disappeared from New Hampshire, from Rhode Island, from Connecticut, from New York, from New Jersey, from Pennsylvania, from six of the twelve original slaveholding States; and this gradual system of emancipation went on quietly, peacefully, and steadily, so long as we in the free States minded our own business and left our neighbors alone. But the moment the abolition societies were organized throughout the North, preaching a violent crusade against slavery in the Southern States, this combination necessarily caused a counter-combination in the South, and a sectional line was drawn which was a barrier to any further emancipation. Bear in mind that emancipation has not taken place in any one State since the Free-soil party was organized as a political party in this country. Emancipation went on gradually in State after State so long as the free States were content with managing their own affairs and leaving the South perfectly free to do as they pleased; but the moment the North said, We are powerful enough to control you of the South, the moment the North proclaimed itself the determined master of the South, that moment the South combined to resist the attack, and thus sectional parties were formed, and gradual emancipation ceased in all the Northern slaveholding States. And yet Mr. Lincoln, in view of these historical facts, proposes to keep up this sectional agitation, band all the Northern States together in one political party, elect a President by Northern votes alone, and then, of course, make a cabinet composed of Northern men, and administer the government by Northern men only, denying all the Southern States of this Union any participation in the administration of affairs whatsoever. I submit to you, my fellow-citizens, whether such a line of policy is consistent with the peace and harmony of the country? Can the Union endure under such a system of policy? He has taken his position in favor of sectional agitation and sectional warfare. I have taken mine in favor of securing peace, harmony, and good-will among all the States, by permitting each to mind its own business, and discountenancing any attempt at interference on the part of one State with the domestic concerns of the others.

Mr. Lincoln makes another issue with me, and he wishes to confine the contest to these two issues. I accept the other as readily as the one to which I have already referred. The other issue is a crusade against the Supreme Court of the United States, because of its decision in the Dred Scott case. My fellow-citizens, I have no issue to make with the Supreme Court. I have no crusade to preach against that august body. I have no warfare to make upon it. I receive the decision of the Judges of that Court, when pronounced, as the final adjudication upon all questions within their jurisdiction. It would be perfectly legitimate and proper for Mr. Lincoln, myself, or any other lawyer, to go before the Supreme Court and argue any question that might arise there, taking either side of it, and enforcing it with all our ability, zeal, and energy; but when the decision is pronounced, that decision becomes the law of the land, and he, and you, and myself, and every other good citizen, must bow to it, and yield obedience to it. Unless we respect and bow in deference to the final decisions of the highest judicial tribunal in our country, we are driven at once to anarchy, to violence, to mob law, and there is no security left for our property or our own civil rights. What protects your property but the law? and who expounds the law but the judicial tribunals? and if an appeal is to be taken from the decisions of the Supreme Court of the United States in all cases where a person does not like the adjudication, to whom is that appeal to be taken? Are we to appeal from the Supreme Court to a county meeting like this? And shall we here reargue the question and reverse the decision? If so, how are we to enforce our decrees after we have pronounced them? Does Mr. Lincoln intend to appeal from the Supreme Court to a Republican caucus, or a town meeting? To whom is he going to appeal? ["To Lovejoy," and shouts of laughter.] Why, if I understand aright, Lincoln and Lovejoy are co-appellants in a joint suit, and inasmuch as they are so, he would not, certainly, appeal from the Supreme Court to his own partner to decide the case for him.

Mr. Lincoln tells you that he is opposed to the decision of the Supreme Court in the Dred Scott case. Well, suppose he is; what is he going to do about it? I never got beat in a lawsuit in my life that I was not opposed to the decision; and if I had it before the Circuit Court I took it up to the Supreme Court, where, if I got beat again, I thought it better to say no more about it, as I did not know of any lawful mode of reversing the decision of the highest tribunal on earth. To whom is Mr. Lincoln going to appeal? Why, he says he is going to appeal to Congress. Let us see how he will appeal to Congress. He tells us that on the 8th of March, 1820, Congress passed a law called the Missouri Compromise, prohibiting slavery forever in all the territory west of the Mississippi and north of the Missouri line of thirty-six degrees and thirty minutes; that Dred Scott, a slave in Missouri, was taken by his master to Fort Snelling, in the present State of Minnesota, situated on the west bank of the Mississippi River, and consequently in the Territory where slavery was prohibited by the Act of 1820; and that when Dred Scott appealed for his freedom in consequence of having been taken into a free Territory, the Supreme Court of the United States decided that Dred Scott did not become free by being taken into that Territory, but that, having been carried back to Missouri, he was yet a slave. Mr. Lincoln is going to appeal from that decision and reverse it. He does not intend to reverse it as to Dred Scott. Oh, no! But he will reverse it so that it shall not stand as a rule in the future. How will he do it? He says that if he is elected to the Senate he will introduce and pass a law just like the Missouri Compromise, prohibiting slavery again in all the Territories. Suppose he does re-enact the same law which the Court has pronounced unconstitutional, will that make it constitutional? If the Act of 1820 was unconstitutional, in consequence of Congress having no power to pass it, will Mr. Lincoln make it constitutional by passing it again? What clause of the Constitution of the United States provides for an appeal from the decision of the Supreme Court to Congress? If my reading of that instrument is correct, it is to the effect that that Constitution and all laws made in pursuance of it are of the supreme law of the land, anything in the constitution or laws of a State to the contrary notwithstanding. Hence, you will find that only such Acts of Congress are laws as are made in pursuance of the Constitution. When Congress has passed an act, and put it on the statute book as law, who is to decide whether that act is in conformity with the Constitution or not? The Constitution of the United States tells you. It has provided that the judicial power of the United States shall be vested in a Supreme Court, and such inferior courts as Congress may from time to time ordain and establish. Thus, by the Constitution, the Supreme Court is declared, in so many words, to be the tribunal, and the only tribunal, which is competent to adjudicate upon the constitutionality of an Act of Congress. He tells you that that Court has adjudicated the question, and decided that an Act of Congress prohibiting slavery in the Territory is unconstitutional and void; and yet he says he is going to pass another like it. What for? Will it be any more valid? Will he be able to convince the Court that the second act is valid when the first is invalid and void? What good does it do to pass a second act? Why, it will have the effect to arraign the Supreme Court before the people, and to bring them into all the political discussions of the country. Will that do any good? Will it inspire any more confidence in the judicial tribunals of the country? What good can it do to wage this war upon the Court, arraying it against Congress, and Congress against the Court? The Constitution of the United States has said that this government shall be divided into three separate and distinct branches—the executive, the legislative, and the judicial; and of course each one is supreme and independent of the other within the circle of its own powers. The functions of Congress are to enact the statutes, the province of the Court is to pronounce upon their validity, and the duty of the executive is to carry the decision into effect when rendered by the Court. And yet, notwithstanding the Constitution makes the decision of the Court final in regard to the validity of an Act of Congress, Mr. Lincoln is going to reverse that decision by passing another Act of Congress,

When he has become convinced of the folly of the proposition, perhaps he will resort to the same subterfuge that I have found others of his party resort to, which is to agitate and agitate until he can change the Supreme Court and put other men in the places of the present incumbents. I wonder whether Mr. Lincoln is right sure that he can accomplish that reform. He certainly will not be able to get rid of the present Judges until they die, and from present appearances I think they have as good security of life as he has himself. I am afraid that my friend Lincoln would not accomplish this task during his own lifetime, and yet he wants to go to Congress to do all this in six years. Do you think that he can persuade nine Judges, or a majority of them, to die in that six years, just to accommodate him? They are appointed Judges for life, and according to the present organization, new ones cannot be appointed during that time; but he is going to agitate until they die, and then have the President appoint good Republicans in their places. He had better be quite sure that he gets a Republican President at the same time to appoint them. He wants to have a Republican President elected by Northern votes, not a Southern man participating, and elected for the purpose of placing none but Republicans on the bench; and, consequently, if he succeeds in electing that President, and succeeds in persuading the present Judges to die, in order that their vacancies may be filled, that the President will then appoint their successors. And by what process will he appoint them? He first looks for a man who has the legal qualifications; perhaps he takes Mr. Lincoln, and says, "Mr. Lincoln, would you not like to go on the Supreme bench?" "Yes," replies Mr. Lincoln. "Well," returns the Republican President, "I cannot appoint you until you give me a pledge as to how you will decide in the event of a particular question coming before you." What would you think of Mr. Lincoln if he would consent to give that pledge? And yet he is going to prosecute a war until he gets the present Judges out, and then catechise each man and require a pledge before his appointment as to how he will decide each question that may arise upon points affecting the Republican party.

Now, my friends, suppose this scheme was practical, I ask you what confidence you would have in a court thus constituted,—a court composed of partisan judges, appointed on political grounds, selected with a view to the decision of questions in a particular way, and pledged in regard to a decision before the argument, and without reference to the peculiar state of the facts. Would such a court command the respect of the country? If the Republican party cannot trust Democratic judges, how can they expect us to trust Republican judges, when they have been selected in advance for the purpose of packing a decision in the event of a case arising? My fellow-citizens, whenever partisan politics shall be carried on to the bench; whenever the judges shall be arraigned upon the stump, and their judicial conduct reviewed in town meetings and caucuses; whenever the independence and integrity of the judiciary shall be tampered with to the extent of rendering them partial, blind, and suppliant tools, what security will you have for your rights and your liberties? I therefore take issue with Mr. Lincoln directly in regard to this warfare upon the Supreme Court of the United States. I accept the decision of that Court as it was pronounced. Whatever my individual opinions may be, I, as a good citizen, am bound by the laws of the land, as the Legislature makes them, as the Court expounds them, and as the executive officers administer them. I am bound by our Constitution as our fathers made it, and as it is our duty to support it. I am bound, as a good citizen, to sustain the constituted authorities, and to resist, discourage, and beat down, by all lawful and peaceful means, all attempts at exciting mobs, or violence, or any other revolutionary proceedings against the Constitution and the constituted authorities of the country.

Mr. Lincoln is alarmed for fear that, under the Dred Scott decision, slavery will go into all the Territories of the United States. All I have to say is that, with or without that decision, slavery will go just where the people want it, and not one inch further. You have had experience upon that subject in the case of Kansas. You have been told by the Republican party that, from 1854, when the Kansas-Nebraska Bill passed, down to last winter, that slavery was sustained and supported in Kansas by the laws of what they called a "bogus" Legislature. And how many slaves were there in the Territory at the end of last winter? Not as many at the end of that period as there were on the day the Kansas-Nebraska Bill passed. There was quite a number of slaves in Kansas, taken there under the Missouri Compromise, and in spite of it, before the Kansas-Nebraska Bill passed; and now it is asserted that there are not as many there as there were before the passage of the bill, notwithstanding that they had local laws sustaining and encouraging it, enacted, as the Republicans say, by a "bogus" Legislature, imposed upon Kansas by an invasion from Missouri. Why has not slavery obtained a foothold in Kansas under these circumstances? Simply because there was a majority of her people opposed to slavery, and every slaveholder knew that if he took his slaves there, the moment that majority got possession of the ballot-boxes, and a fair election was held, that moment slavery would be abolished, and he would lose them. For that reason, such owners as took their slaves there brought them back to Missouri, fearing that if they remained they would be emancipated. Thus you see that under the principle of popular sovereignty slavery has been kept out of Kansas, notwithstanding the fact that for the first three years they had a Legislature in that Territory favorable to it. I tell you, my friends, it is impossible under our institutions to force slavery on an unwilling people. If this principle of popular sovereignty asserted in the Nebraska Bill be fairly carried out, by letting the people decide the question for themselves, by a fair vote, at a fair election, and with honest returns, slavery will never exist one day, or one hour, in any Territory against the unfriendly legislation of an unfriendly people. I care not how the Dred Scott decision may have settled the abstract question so far as the practical result is concerned; for, to use the language of an eminent Southern Senator on this very question:

> I do not care a fig which way the decision shall be, for it is
> of no particular consequence; slavery cannot exist a day or an
> hour, in any Territory or State, unless it has affirmative laws
> sustaining and supporting it, furnishing police regulation and
> remedies; and an omission to furnish them would be as fatal as a
> constitutional prohibition. Without affirmative legislation in its
> favor, slavery could not exist any longer than a new-born infant
> could survive under the heat of the sun, on a barren rock, without protection. It would wilt and die for the want of support.

Hence, if the people of a Territory want slavery, they will encourage it by passing affirmatory laws, and the necessary police regulations, patrol laws, and slave code; if they do not want it, they will withhold that legislation, and by with-holding it slavery is as dead as if it was prohibited by a constitutional prohibition, especially if, in addition, their legislation is unfriendly, as it would be if they were opposed to it. They could pass such local laws and police regulations as would drive slavery out in one day, or one hour, if they were opposed to it; and there-fore, so far as the question of slavery in the Territories is concerned, so far as the principle of popular sovereignty is concerned, in its practical operation, it matters not how the Dred Scott case may be decided with reference to the Territories. My own opinion on that law point is well known. It is shown by my votes and speeches in Congress. But be it as it may, the question was an abstract question, inviting no practical results; and whether slavery shall exist or shall not exist in any State or Territory will depend upon whether the people are for or against it; and whichever way they shall decide it in any Territory or in any State will be entirely satisfactory to me.

But I must now bestow a few words upon Mr. Lincoln's main objection to the Dred Scott decision. He is not going to submit to it. Not that he is going to make war upon it with force of arms, but he is going to appeal and reverse it in some way; he cannot tell us how. I reckon not by a writ of error, because I do not know where he would prosecute that, except before an Abolition Society. And when he appeals, he does not exactly tell us to whom he will appeal—except it be the Republican party, and I have yet to learn that the Republican party, under the Constitution, has judicial powers—but he is going to appeal from it and reverse it, either by an Act of Congress, or by turning out the judges, or in some other way. And why? Because he says that that decision deprives the negro of the benefits of that clause of the Constitution of the United States which entitles the citizens of each State to all the privileges and immunities of citizens of the several States. Well, it is very true that the decision does have that effect. By deciding that a negro is not a citizen, of course it denies to him the rights and privileges awarded to citizens of the United States. It is this that Mr. Lincoln will not sub-mit to. Why? For the palpable reason that he wishes to confer upon the negro all the rights, privileges, and immunities of citizens of the several States. I will not quarrel with Mr. Lincoln for his views on that subject. I have no doubt he is conscientious in them. I have not the slightest idea but that he conscientiously believes that a negro ought to enjoy and exercise all the rights and privileges given to white men; but I do not agree with him, and hence I cannot concur with him. I believe that this government of ours was founded on the white basis. I believe that it was established by white men, by men of European birth, or descended of European races, for the benefit of white men and their posterity in all time to come. I do not believe that it was the design or intention of the signers of the Declaration of Independence or the framers of the Constitution to include negroes, Indians, or other inferior races, with white men, as citizens. Our fathers had at that day seen the evil consequences of conferring civil and political rights upon the Indian and negro in the Spanish and French colonies on the American continent and the adjacent islands. In Mexico, in Central America, in South America and in the West India Islands, where the Indian, the negro, and men of all colors and all races are put on an equality by law, the effect of political amalgamation can be seen. Ask any of those gallant young men in your own county who went to Mexico to fight the battles of their country, in what friend Lincoln considers an unjust and unholy war, and hear what they will tell you in regard to the amalgamation of races in that country. Amalgamation there, first political, then social, has led to demoralization and degradation, until it has reduced that people below the point of capacity for self-government. Our fathers knew what the effect of it would be, and from the time they planted foot on the American continent, not only those who landed at Jamestown, but at Plymouth Rock and all other points on the coast, they pursued the policy of confining civil and political rights to the white race, and excluding the negro in all cases. Still, Mr. Lincoln conscientiously believes that it is his duty to advocate negro citizenship. He wants to give the negro the privilege of citizenship. He quotes Scripture again, and says: "As your Father in heaven is perfect, be ye also perfect." And he applies that Scriptural quotation to all classes; not that he expects us all to be as perfect as our Master, but as nearly perfect as possible. In other words, he is willing to give the negro an equality under the law, in order that he may approach as near perfection, or an equality with the white man, as possible. To this same end he quotes the Declaration of Independence in these words: "We hold these truths to be self-evident, that all men were created equal, and endowed by their Creator with certain inalienable rights, among which are life, liberty, and the pursuit of happiness"; and goes on to argue that the negro was included, or intended to be included, in that Declaration, by the signers of the paper. He says that, by the Declaration of Independence, therefore, all kinds of men, negroes included, were created equal and endowed by their Creator with certain inalienable rights, and, further, that the right of the negro to be on an equality with the white man is a divine right, conferred by the Almighty, and rendered inalienable according to the Declaration of Independence. Hence no human law or constitution can deprive the negro of that equality with the white man to which he is entitled by the divine law. ["Higher law."] Yes, higher law. Now, I do not question Mr. Lincoln's sincerity on this point. He believes that the negro, by the divine law, is created the equal of the white man, and that no human law can deprive him of that equality, thus secured; and he contends that the negro ought, therefore, to have all the rights and privileges of citizenship on an equality with the white man. In order to accomplish this, the first thing that would have to be done in this State would be to blot out of our State Constitution that clause which prohibits negroes from coming into this State and making it an African colony, and permit them to come and spread over these charming prairies until in midday they shall look black as night. When our friend Lincoln gets all his colored brethren around him here, he will then raise them to perfection as fast as possible, and place them on an equality with the white man, first removing all legal restrictions, because they are our equals by divine law, and there should be no such restrictions. He wants them to vote. I am opposed to it. If they had a vote, I reckon they would all vote for him in preference to me, entertaining the views I do. But that matters not. The position he has taken on this question not only presents him as claiming for them the right to vote, but their right, under the divine law and the Declaration of Independence, to be elected to office, to become members of the Legislature, to go to Congress, to become Governors, or United States Senators, or Judges of the Supreme Court; and I suppose that when they control that court they will probably reverse the Dred Scott decision. He is going to bring negroes here, and give them the right of citizenship, the right of voting, and the right of holding office and sitting on juries; and what else? Why, he would permit them to marry, would he not? And if he gives them that right, I suppose he will let them marry whom they please, provided they marry their equals. If the divine law declares that the white man is the equal of the negro woman, that they are on a perfect equality, I suppose he admits the right of the negro woman to marry the white man. In other words, his doctrine that the negro, by divine law, is placed on a perfect equality with the white man, and that that equality is recognized by the Declaration of Independence, leads him necessarily to establish negro equality under the law; but whether even then they would be so in fact would depend upon the degree of virtue and intelligence they possessed, and certain other qualities that are matters of taste rather than of law. I do not understand Mr. Lincoln as saying that he expects to make them our equals socially, or by intelligence, nor in fact as citizens, but that he wishes to make them our equals under the law, and then say to them, "As your Master in heaven is perfect, be ye also perfect."

Well, I confess to you, my fellow-citizens, that I am utterly opposed to that system of Abolition philosophy. I do not believe that the signers of the Declaration of Independence had any reference to negroes when they used the expression that all men were created equal, or that they had any reference to the Chinese or Coolies, the Indians, the Japanese, or any other inferior race. They were speaking of the white race, the European race on this continent, and their descendants, and emigrants who should come here. They were speaking only of the white race, and never dreamed that their language would be construed to include the negro. And now for the evidence of that fact: At the time the Declaration of Independence was put forth, declaring the equality of all men, every one of the thirteen colonies was a slaveholding colony, and every man who signed that Declaration represented a slaveholding constituency. Did they intend, when they put their signatures to that instrument, to declare that their own slaves were on an equality with them; that they were made their equals by divine law, and that any human law reducing them to an inferior position was void, as being in violation of divine law? Was that the meaning of the signers of the Declaration of Independence? Did Jefferson and Henry and Lee,—did any of the signers of that instrument, or all of them, on the day they signed it, give their slaves freedom? History records that they did not. Did they go further, and put the negro on an equality with the white man throughout the country? They did not. And yet if they had understood that Declaration as including the negro, which Mr. Lincoln holds they did, they would have been bound, as conscientious men, to have restored the negroes to that equality which he thinks the Almighty intended they should occupy with the white man. They did not do it. Slavery was abolished in only one State before the adoption of the Constitution in 1789, and then in others gradually, down to the time this Abolition agitation began; and it has not been abolished in one since. The history of the country shows that neither the signers of the Declaration, nor the framers of the Constitution, ever supposed it possible that their language would be used in an attempt to make this nation a mixed nation of Indians, negroes, whites, and mongrels. I repeat that our whole history confirms the proposition that, from the earliest settlement of the colonies down to the Declaration of Independence and the adoption of the Constitution of the United States, our fathers proceeded on the white basis, making the white people the governing race, but conceding to the Indian and negro, and all inferior races, all the rights and all the privileges they could enjoy consistent with the safety of the society in which they lived. That is my opinion now. I told you that humanity, philanthropy, justice, and sound policy required that we should give the negro every right, every privilege, every immunity, consistent with the safety and welfare of the State. The question then naturally arises, What are those rights and privileges, and What is the nature and extent of them? My answer is, that that is a question which each State and each Territory must decide for itself. We have decided that question. We have said that in this State the negro shall not be a slave, but that he shall enjoy no political rights; that negro equality shall not exist. I am content with that position. My friend Lincoln is not. He thinks that our policy and our laws on that subject are contrary to the Declaration of Independence. He thinks that the Almighty made the negro his equal and his brother. For my part, I do not consider the negro any kin to me, nor to any other white man; but I would still carry my humanity and my philanthropy to the extent of giving him every privilege and every immunity that he could enjoy, consistent with our own good. We in Illinois have the right to decide upon that question for ourselves, and we are bound to allow every other State to do the same. Maine allows the negro to vote on an equality with the white man. I do not quarrel with our friends in Maine for that. If they think it wise and proper in Maine to put the negro on an equality with the white man, and allow him to go to the polls and negative the vote of a white man, it is their business, and not mine. On the other hand, New York permits a negro to vote provided he owns $250 worth of property. New York thinks that a negro ought to be permitted to vote provided he is rich, but not otherwise. They allow the aristocratic negro to vote there. I never saw the wisdom, the propriety, or the justice of that decision on the part of New York, and yet it never occurred to me that I had a right to find fault with that State. It is her business; she is a sovereign State, and has a right to do as she pleases; and if she will take care of her own negroes, making such regulations concerning them as suit her, and let us alone, I will mind my business, and not interfere with her. In Kentucky they will not give a negro any political or any civil rights. I shall not argue the question whether Kentucky in so doing has decided right or wrong, wisely or unwisely. It is a question for Kentucky to decide for herself. I believe that the Kentuckians have consciences as well as ourselves; they have as keen a perception of their religious, moral, and social duties as we have; and I am willing that they shall decide this slavery question for themselves, and be accountable to their God for their action. It is not for me to arraign them for what they do. I will not judge them, lest I shall be judged. Let Kentucky mind her own business and take care of her negroes, and us attend to our own affairs and take care of our negroes, and we will be the best of friends; but if Kentucky attempts to interfere with us, or we with her, there will be strife, there will be discord, there will be relentless hatred, there will be everything but fraternal feeling and brotherly love. It is not necessary that you should enter Kentucky and interfere in that State, to use the language of Mr. Lincoln. It is just as offensive to interfere from this State, or send your missiles over there. I care not whether an enemy, if he is going to assault us, shall actually come into our State, or come along the line, and throw his bombshells over to explode in our midst. Suppose England should plant a battery on the Canadian side of the Niagara River, opposite Buffalo, and throw bombshells over, which would explode in Main Street, in that city, and destroy the buildings, and that, when we protested, she would say, in the language of Mr. Lincoln, that she never dreamed of coming into the United States to interfere with us, and that she was just throwing her bombs over the line from her own side, which she had a right to do. Would that explanation satisfy us? So it is with Mr. Lincoln. He is not going into Kentucky, but he will plant his batteries on this side of the Ohio, where he is safe and secure for a retreat, and will throw his bombshells—his Abolition documents—over the river, and will carry on a political warfare, and get up strife between the North and the South, until he elects a sectional President, reduces the South to the condition of dependent colonies, raises the negro to an equality, and forces the South to submit to the doctrine that a house divided against itself cannot stand; that the Union divided into half slave States and half free cannot endure; that they must all be slave or they must all be free; and that as we in the North are in the majority, we will not permit them to be all slave, and therefore they in the South must consent to the States all being free. Now, fellow-citizens, I submit to you whether these doctrines are consistent with the peace and harmony of this Union? I submit to you whether they are consistent with our duties as citizens of a common confederacy; whether they are consistent with the principles which ought to govern brethren of the same family? I recognize all the people of these States, North and South, East and West, old or new, Atlantic or Pacific, as our brethren, flesh of our flesh, and I will do no act unto them that I would not be willing they should do unto us. I would apply the same Christian rule to the States of this Union that we are taught to apply to individuals,—"Do unto others as you would have others do unto you"; and this would secure peace. Why should this slavery agitation be kept up? Does it benefit the white man, or the slave? Whom does it benefit, except the Republican politicians, who use it as their hobby to ride into office? Why, I repeat, should it be continued? Why cannot we be content to administer this government as it was made,—a confederacy of sovereign and independent States? Let us recognize the sovereignty and independence of each State, refrain from interfering with the domestic institutions and regulations of other States, permit the Territories and new States to decide their institutions for themselves, as we did when we were in their condition; blot out these lines of North and South, and resort back to these lines of State boundaries which the Constitution has marked out and engraved upon the face of the country; have no other dividing lines but these, and we will be one united, harmonious people, with fraternal feelings, and no discord or dissension.

These are my views, and these are the principles to which I have devoted all my energies since 1850, when I acted side by side with the immortal Clay and the godlike Webster in that memorable struggle, in which Whigs and Democrats united upon a common platform of patriotism and the Constitution, throwing aside partisan feelings in order to restore peace and harmony to a distracted country. And when I stood beside the death-bed of Mr. Clay, and heard him refer, with feelings and emotions of the deepest solicitude, to the welfare of the country, and saw that he looked upon the principle embodied in the great Compromise measures of 1850, the principle of the Nebraska Bill, the doctrine of leaving each State and Territory free to decide its institutions for itself, as the only means by which the peace of the country could be preserved and the Union perpetuated,—I pledged him, on that death-bed of his, that so long as I lived, my energies should be devoted to the vindication of that principle, and of his fame as connected with it. I gave the same pledge to the great expounder of the Constitution, he who has been called the "godlike Webster." I looked up to Clay and to him as a son would to a father, and I call upon the people of Illinois, and the people of the whole Union, to bear testimony that never since the sod has been laid upon the graves of these eminent statesmen have I failed, on any occasion, to vindicate the principle with which the last great crowning acts of their lives were identified, or to vindicate their names whenever they have been assailed; and now my life and energy are devoted to this great work as the means of preserving this Union. This Union can only be preserved by maintaining the fraternal feeling between the North and the South, the East and the West. If that good feeling can be preserved, the Union will be as perpetual as the fame of its great founders. It can be maintained by preserving the sovereignty of the States, the right of each State and each Territory to settle its domestic concerns for itself, and the duty of each to refrain from interfering with the other in any of its local or domestic institutions. Let that be done, and the Union will be perpetual; let that be done, and this Republic, which began with thirteen States, and which now numbers thirty-two, which, when it began, only extended from the Atlantic to the Mississippi, but now reaches to the Pacific, may yet expand, north and south, until it covers the whole continent, and becomes one vast ocean-bound confederacy. Then, my friends, the path of duty of honor, of patriotism, is plain. There are a few simple principles to be preserved. Bear in mind the dividing line between State rights and Federal authority; let us maintain the great principle of popular sovereignty, of State rights, and of the Federal Union as the Constitution has made it, and this Republic will endure forever.

I thank you kindly for the patience with which you have listened to me. I fear I have wearied you. I have a heavy day's work before me to-morrow. I have several speeches to make. My friends, in whose hands I am, are taxing me beyond human endurance; but I shall take the helm and control them hereafter. I am profoundly grateful to the people of McLean for the reception they have given me, and the kindness with which they have listened to me. I remember when I first came among you here, twenty-five years ago, that I was prosecuting attorney in this district, and that my earliest efforts were made here, when my deficiencies were too apparent, I am afraid, to be concealed from any one. I remember the courtesy and kindness with which I was uniformly treated by you all; and whenever I can recognize the face of one of your old citizens, it is like meeting an old and cherished friend. I come among you with a heart filled with gratitude for past favors. I have been with you but little for the past few years, on account of my official duties. I intend to visit you again before the campaign is over. I wish to speak to your whole people. I wish them to pass judgment upon the correctness of my course, and the soundness of the principles which I have proclaimed. If you do not approve my principles, I cannot ask your support. If you believe that the election of Mr. Lincoln would contribute more to preserve the harmony of the country, to perpetuate the Union, and more to the prosperity and the honor and glory of the State, then it is your duty to give him the preference. If, on the contrary, you believe that I have been faithful to my trust, and that by sustaining me you will give greater strength and efficiency to the principles which I have expounded, I shall then be grateful for your support. I renew my profound thanks for your attention.

# Speech of Senator Douglas

*Delivered July 17, 1858, at Springfield, Ill.*
(Mr. Lincoln was not present.)

MR. CHAIRMAN AND FELLOW-CITIZENS OF SPRINGFIELD AND OLD SANGAMON: My heart is filled with emotions at the allusions which have been so happily and so kindly made in the welcome just extended to me,—a welcome so numerous and so enthusiastic, bringing me to my home among my old friends, that language cannot express my gratitude. I do feel at home whenever I return to old Sangamon and receive those kind and friendly greetings which have never failed to meet me when I have come among you; but never before have I had such occasion to be grateful and to be proud of the manner of the reception as at the present. While I am willing, sir, to attribute a part of this demonstration to those kind and friendly personal relations to which you have referred, I cannot conceal from myself that the controlling and prevailing element in this great mass of human beings is devotion to that principle of self-government to which so many years of my life have been devoted; and rejoice more in considering it an approval of my support of a cardinal principle than I would if I could appropriate it to myself as a personal compliment.

You but speak rightly when you assert that during the last session of Congress there was an attempt to violate one of the fundamental principles upon which our free institutions rest. The attempt to force the Lecompton Constitution upon the people of Kansas against her will would have been, if successful, subversive of the great fundamental principles upon which all our institutions rest. If there is any one principle more sacred and more vital to the existence of a free government than all others, it is the right of the people to form and ratify the constitution under which they are to live. It is the corner-stone of the temple of liberty; it is the foundation upon which the whole structure rests; and whenever it can be successfully evaded, self-government has received a vital stab. I deemed it my duty, as a citizen and as a representative of the State of Illinois, to resist, with all my energies and with whatever of ability I could command, the consummation of that effort to force a constitution upon an unwilling people.

I am aware that other questions have been connected, or attempted to be connected, with that great struggle; but they were mere collateral questions, not affecting the main point. My opposition to the Lecompton Constitution rested solely upon the fact that it was not the act and deed of that people, and that it did not embody their will, I did not object to it upon the ground of the slavery clause contained in it. I should have resisted it with the same energy and determination even if it had been a free State instead of a slaveholding State; and as an evidence of this fact I wish you to bear in mind that my speech against that Lecompton Act was made on the 9th day of December, nearly two weeks before the vote was taken on the acceptance or rejection of the slavery clause. I did not then know, I could not have known, whether the slavery clause would be accepted or rejected; the general impression was that it would be rejected, and in my speech I assumed that impression to be true, that probably it would be voted down; and then I said to the United States Senate, as I now proclaim to you, my constituents, that you have no more right to force a free State upon an unwilling people than you have to force a slave State upon them against their will. You have no right to force either a good or a bad thing upon a people who do not choose to receive it. And then, again, the highest privilege of our people is to determine for themselves what kind of institutions are good and what kind of institutions are bad; and it may be true that the same people, situated in a different latitude and different climate, and with different productions and different interests, might decide the same question one way in the North and another way in the South, in order to adapt their institutions to the wants and wishes of the people to be affected by them.

You all are familiar with the Lecompton struggle, and I will occupy no more time upon the subject, except to remark that when we drove the enemies of the principle of popular sovereignty from the effort to force the Lecompton Constitution upon the people of Kansas, and when we compelled them to abandon the attempt and to refer that Constitution to that people for acceptance or rejection, we obtained a concession of the principle for which I had contended throughout the struggle. When I saw that the principle was conceded, and that the Constitution was not to be forced upon Kansas against the wishes of the people, I felt anxious to give the proposition my support; but when I examined it, I found that the mode of reference to the people and the form of submission, upon which the vote was taken, was so objectionable as to make it unfair and unjust.

Sir, it is an axiom with me that in every free government an unfair election is no election at all. Every election should be free, should be fair, with the same privileges and the same inducements for a negative as for an affirmative vote. The objection to what is called the "English" proposition, by which the Lecompton Constitution was referred back to the people of Kansas, was this: that if the people chose to accept the Lecompton Constitution they could come in with only 35,000 inhabitants; while if they determined to reject it, in order to form another more in accordance with their wishes and sentiments, they were compelled to stay out until they should have 93,420 inhabitants. In other words, it was making a distinction and discrimination between free States and slave States under the Federal Constitution. I deny the justice, I deny the right, of any distinction or discrimination between the States north and south, free or slave. Equality among the States is a fundamental principle of this government. Hence, while I will never consent to the passage of a law that a slave State may come in with 35,000, while a free State shall not come in unless it have 93,000, on the other hand, I shall not consent to admit a free State with a population of 35,000, and require 93,000 in a slaveholding State.

My principle is to recognize each State of the Union as independent, sovereign, and equal in its sovereignty. I will apply that principle, not only to the original thirteen States, but to the States which have since been brought into the Union, and also to every State that shall hereafter be received, "as long as water shall run, and grass grow." For these reasons I felt compelled, by a sense of duty, by a conviction of principle, to record my vote against what is called the English bill; but yet the bill became a law, and under that law an election has been ordered to be held on the first Monday in August, for the purpose of determining the question of the acceptance or rejection of the proposition submitted by Congress. I have no hesitation in saying to you, as the chairman of your committee has justly said in his address, that whatever the decision of the people of Kansas may be at that election, it must be final and conclusive of the whole subject; for if at that election a majority of the people of Kansas shall vote for the acceptance of the Congressional proposition, Kansas from that moment becomes a State of the Union, the law admitting her becomes irrepealable, and thus the controversy terminates forever; if, on the other hand, the people of Kansas shall vote down that proposition, as it is now generally admitted they will, by a large majority, then from that instant the Lecompton Constitution is *dead*,—dead beyond the power of resurrection; and thus the controversy terminates. And when the monster shall die, I shall be willing, and trust that all of you will be willing, to acquiesce in the death of the Lecompton Constitution. The controversy may now be considered as terminated, for in three weeks from now it will be finally settled, and all the ill-feeling, all the embittered feeling which grew out of it shall cease, unless an attempt should be made in the future to repeat the same outrage upon popular rights. I need not tell you that my past course is a sufficient guaranty that if the occasion shall ever arise again while I occupy a seat in the United States Senate, you will find me carrying out the same principle that I have this winter with all the energy and all the power I may be able to command. I have the gratification of saying to you that I do not believe that that controversy will ever arise again: firstly, because the fate of Lecompton is a *warning* to the people of every Territory and of every State to be cautious how the example is repeated; and, secondly, because the President of the United States, in his annual message, has said that he trusts the example in the Minnesota case, wherein Congress passed a law, called an Enabling Act, requiring the Constitution to be submitted to the people for acceptance or rejection, will be followed in all future cases. ["That was right."] I agree with you that it was right. I said so on the day after the message was delivered in my speech in the Senate on the Lecompton Constitution, and I have frequently in the debate tendered to the President and his friends, tendered to the Lecomptonites, my voluntary pledge, that if he will stand by that recommendation, and they will stand by it, that they will find me working hand in hand with them in the effort to carry it out. All we have to do, therefore, is to adhere firmly in future, as we have done in the past, to the principle contained in the recommendation of the President in his annual message, that the example in the Minnesota case shall be carried out in all future cases of the admission of Territories into the Union as States. Let that be done, and the principle of popular sovereignty will be maintained in all of its vigor and all of its integrity. I rejoice to know that Illinois stands prominently and proudly forward among the States which first took their position firmly and immovably upon this principle of popular sovereignty, applied to the Territories as well as the States. You all recollect when, in 1850, the peace of the country was disturbed in consequence of the agitation of the slavery question, and the effort to force the Wilmot Proviso upon all the Territories, that it required all the talent and all the energy, all the wisdom, all the patriotism, of a Clay and a Webster, united with other great party leaders, to devise a system of measures by which peace and harmony could be restored to our distracted country. Those compromise measures eventually passed, and were recorded on the statute book, not only as the settlement of the then existing difficulties, but as furnishing a rule of action which should prevent in all future time the recurrence of like evils, if they were firmly and fairly carried out. Those compromise measures rested, as I said in my speech at Chicago on my return home that year, upon the principle that every people ought to have the right to form and regulate their own domestic institutions in their own way, subject only to the Constitution. They were founded upon the principle that while every State possessed that right under the Constitution, that the same right ought to be extended to and exercised by the people of the Territories. When the Illinois Legislature assembled, a few months after the adoption of these measures, the first thing the members did was to review their action upon this slavery agitation, and to correct the errors into which their predecessors had fallen. You remember that their first act was to repeal the Wilmot Proviso instructions to our United States Senators, which had been previously passed, and in lieu of them to record another resolution upon the journal, with which you must all be familiar,—a resolution brought forward by Mr. Ninian Edwards, and adopted by the House of Representatives by a vote of 61 in the affirmative to 4 in the negative. That resolution I can quote to you in almost its precise language. It declared that the great principle of self-government was the birthright of free-men, was the gift of Heaven, was achieved by the blood of our revolutionary fathers, and must be continued and carried out in the organization of all the Territories and the admission of all new States. That became the Illinois platform by the united voices of the Democratic party and of the Whig party in 1851; all the Whigs and all the Democrats in the Legislature uniting in an affirmative vote upon it, and there being only four votes in the negative,—of Abolitionists, of course. That resolution stands upon the journal of your Legislature to this day and hour unrepealed, as a standing, living, perpetual instruction to the Senators from Illinois in all time to come to carry out that principle of self-government, and allow no limitation upon it in the organization of any Territories or the admission of any new States. In 1854, when it became my duty as the chairman of the committee on Territories to bring forward a bill for the organization of Kansas and Nebraska, I incorporated that principle in it, and Congress passed it, thus carrying the principle into practical effect. I will not recur to the scenes which took place all over the country in 1854, when that Nebraska Bill passed. I could then travel from Boston to Chicago by the light of my own effigies, in consequence of having stood up for it. I leave it to you to say how I met that storm, and whether I quailed under it; whether I did not "face the music," justify the principle, and pledge my life to carry it out.

A friend here reminds me, too, that when making speeches then, justifying the Nebraska Bill and the great principle of self-government, that I predicted that in less than five years you would have to get out a search-warrant to find an anti-Nebraska man. Well, I believe I did make that prediction. I did not claim the power of a prophet, but it occurred to me that among a free people, and an honest people, and an intelligent people, that five years was long enough for them to come to an understanding that the great principle of self-government was right, not only in the States, but in the Territories. I rejoiced this year to see my prediction, in that respect, carried out and fulfilled by the unanimous vote, in one form or another, of both Houses of Congress. If you will remember that pending this Lecompton controversy that gallant old Roman, Kentucky's favorite son, the worthy successor of the immortal Clay,—I allude, as you know, to the gallant John J. Crittenden—brought forward a bill, now known as the Crittenden-Montgomery bill, in which it was proposed that the Lecompton Constitution should be referred back to the people of Kansas, to be decided for or against it, at a fair election, and if a majority were in favor of it, that Kansas should come into the Union as a slaveholding State, but that if a majority were against it, that they should make a new constitution, and come in with slavery or without it, as they thought proper. ["That was right."] Yes, my dear sir, it was not only right, but it was carrying out the principle of the Nebraska Bill in its letter and in its spirit. Of course I voted for it, and so did every Republican Senator and Representative in Congress. I have found some Democrats so perfectly straight that they blame me for voting for the principle of the Nebraska Bill because the Republicans voted the same way. [Great laughter. "What did they say?"]

What did they say? Why, many of them said that Douglas voted with the Republicans. Yes, not only that, but with the *black* Republicans. Well, there are different modes of stating that proposition. The New York *Tribune* says that Douglas did not vote with the Republicans, but that on that question the Republicans went over to Douglas and voted with him.

My friends, I have never yet abandoned a principle because of the support I found men yielding to it, and I shall never abandon my Democratic principles merely because Republicans come to them. For what do we travel over the country and make speeches in every political canvass, if it is not to enlighten the minds of these Republicans, to remove the scales from their eyes, and to impart to them the light of Democratic vision, so that they may be able to carry out the Constitution of our country as our fathers made it? And if by preaching our principles to the people we succeed in convincing the Republicans of the errors of their ways, and bring them over to us, are we bound to turn traitors to our principles merely because they give them their support? All I have to say is that I hope the Republican party will stand firm, in the future, by the vote they gave on the Crittenden-Montgomery bill. I hope we will find, in the resolutions of their county and Congressional conventions, no declarations of "no more Slave States to be admitted into this Union," but in lieu of that declaration that we will find the principle that the people of every State and every Territory shall come into the Union with slavery or without it, just as they please, without any interference on the part of Congress.

My friends, whilst I was at Washington, engaged in this great battle for sound constitutional principles, I find from the newspapers that the Republican party of this State assembled in this capital in State Convention, and not only nominated, as it was wise and proper for them to do, a man for my successor in the Senate, but laid down a platform, and their nominee made a speech, carefully written and prepared, and well delivered, which that Convention accepted as containing the Republican creed. I have no comment to make on that part of Mr. Lincoln's speech in which he represents me as forming a conspiracy with the Supreme Court, and with the late President of the United States and the present chief magistrate, having for my object the passage of the Nebraska Bill, the Dred Scott decision, and the extension of slavery,—a scheme of political tricksters, composed of Chief Justice Taney and his eight associates, two Presidents of the United States, and one Senator of Illinois. If Mr. Lincoln deems me a conspirator of that kind, all I have to say is that I do not think so badly of the President of the United States, and the Supreme Court of the United States, the highest judicial tribunal on earth, as to believe that they were capable in their action and decision of entering into political intrigues for partisan purposes. I therefore shall only notice those parts of Mr. Lincoln's speech in which he lays down his platform of principles, and tells you what he intends to do if he is elected to the Senate of the United States.

[An old gentleman here rose on the platform and said: "Be particular now, Judge, be particular."]

MR. DOUGLAS: My venerable friend here says that he will be gratified if I will be particular; and in order that I may be so, I will read the language of Mr. Lincoln as reported by himself and published to the country. Mr. Lincoln lays down his main proposition in these words:

> "A house divided against itself cannot stand." I believe this Union cannot endure permanently half free and half slave. I do not expect the Union will be dissolved, I do not expect the house to fall; but I do expect it to cease to be divided. It will become all one thing or all the other.

Mr. Lincoln does not think this Union can continue to exist composed of half slave and half free States; they must all be free, or all slave. I do not doubt that this is Mr. Lincoln's conscientious conviction. I do not doubt that he thinks it is the highest duty of every patriotic citizen to preserve this glorious Union, and to adopt these measures as necessary to its preservation. He tells you that the only mode to preserve the Union is to make all the States free, or all slave. It must be the one, or it must be the other. Now, that being essential, in his estimation, to the preservation of this glorious Union, how is he going to accomplish it? He says that he wants to go to the Senate in order to carry out this favorite patriotic policy of his, of making all the States free, so that the house shall no longer be divided against itself. When he gets to the Senate, by what means is he going to accomplish it? By an Act of Congress? Will he contend that Congress has any power under the Constitution to abolish slavery in any State of this Union, or to interfere with it directly or indirectly? Of course he will not contend that. Then what is to be his mode of carrying out his principle, by which slavery shall be abolished in all of the States? Mr. Lincoln certainly does not speak at random. He is a lawyer,—an eminent lawyer,—and his profession is to know the remedy for every wrong. What is his remedy for this imaginary wrong which he supposes to exist? The Constitution of the United States provides that it may be amended by Congress passing an amendment by a two-thirds majority of each house, which shall be ratified by three fourths of the States; and the inference is that Mr. Lincoln intends to carry this slavery agitation into Congress with the view of amending the Constitution so that slavery can be abolished in all the States of the Union. In other words, he is not going to allow one portion of the Union to be slave and another portion to be free; he is not going to permit the house to be divided against itself. He is going to remedy it by lawful and constitutional means. What are to be these means? How can he abolish slavery in those States where it exists? There is but one mode by which a political organization, composed of men in the free States, can abolish slavery in the slaveholding States, and that would be to abolish the State legislatures, blot out of existence the State sovereignties, invest Congress with full and plenary power over all the local and domestic and police regulations of the different States of this Union. Then there would be uniformity in the local concerns and domestic institutions of the different States; then the house would be no longer divided against itself; then the States would all be free, or they would all be slave; then you would have uniformity prevailing throughout this whole land in the local and domestic institutions: but it would be a uniformity, not of liberty, but a uniformity of despotism that would triumph. I submit to you, my fellow-citizens, whether this is not the logical consequence of Mr. Lincoln's proposition? I have called on Mr. Lincoln to explain what he did mean, if he did not mean this, and he has made a speech at Chicago in which he attempts to explain. And how does he explain? I will give him the benefit of his own language, precisely as it was reported in the Republican papers of that city, after undergoing his revision:

> I have said a hundred times, and have now no inclination to take it back, that I believe there is no right and ought to be no inclination in the people of the free States to enter into the slave States and interfere with the question of slavery at all.

He believes there is no right on the part of the free people of the free States to enter the slave States and interfere with the question of slavery; hence he does not propose to go into Kentucky and stir up a civil war and a servile war between the blacks and the whites. All he proposes is to invite the people of Illinois and every other free State to band together as one sectional party, governed and divided by a geographical line, to make war upon the institution of slavery in the slaveholding States. He is going to carry it out by means of a political party that has its adherents only in the free States—a political party that does not pretend that it can give a solitary vote in the slave States of the Union; and by this sectional vote he is going to elect a President of the United States, form a cabinet, and administer the government on sectional grounds, being the power of the North over that of the South. In other words, he invites a war of the North against the South, a warfare of the free States against the slaveholding States. He asks all men in the free States to conspire to exterminate slavery in the Southern States, so as to make them all free, and then he notifies the South that, unless they are going to submit to our efforts to exterminate their institutions, they must band together and plant slavery in Illinois and every Northern State. He says that the States must all be free or must all be slave. On this point I take issue with him directly. I assert that Illinois has a right to decide the slavery question for herself. We have decided it, and I think we have done it wisely; but whether wisely or unwisely, it is our business, and the people of no other State have any right to interfere with us, directly or indirectly. Claiming as we do this right for ourselves, we must concede it to every other State, to be exercised by them respectively.

Now, Mr. Lincoln says that he will not enter into Kentucky to abolish slavery there, but that all he will do is to fight slavery in Kentucky from Illinois. He will not go over there to set fire to the match. I do not think he would. Mr. Lincoln is a very prudent man. He would not deem it wise to go over into Kentucky to stir up this strife, but he would do it from this side of the river. Permit me to inquire whether the wrong, the outrage, of interference by one State with the local concerns of another is worse when you actually invade them than it would be if you carried on the warfare from another State? For the purpose of illustration, suppose the British Government should plant a battery on the Niagara River, opposite Buffalo, and throw their shells over into Buffalo, where they should explode and blow up the houses and destroy the town. We call the British Government to an account, and they say, in the language of Mr. Lincoln, We did not enter into the limits of the United States to interfere with you; we planted the battery on our own soil, and had a right to shoot from our own soil; and if our shells and balls fell in Buffalo and killed your inhabitants, why, it is your lookout, not ours. Thus,

Mr. Lincoln is going to plant his Abolition batteries all along the banks of the Ohio River, and throw his shells into Virginia and Kentucky and into Missouri, and blow up the institution of slavery; and when we arraign him for his unjust interference with the institutions of the other States, he says, Why, I never did enter into Kentucky to interfere with her; I do not propose to do it; I only propose to take care of my own head by keeping on this side of the river, out of harm's way. But yet he says he is going to persevere in this system of sectional warfare, and I have no doubt he is sincere in what he says. He says that the existence of the Union depends upon his success in firing into these slave States until he exterminates them. He says that unless he shall play his batteries successfully, so as to abolish slavery in every one of the States, that the Union shall be dissolved; and he says that a dissolution of the Union would be a terrible calamity. Of course it would. We are all friends of the Union. We all believe—I do—that our lives, our liberties, our hopes in the future, depend upon the preservation and perpetuity of this glorious Union. I believe that the hopes of the friends of liberty throughout the world depend upon the perpetuity of the American Union. But while I believe that my mode of preserving the Union is a very different one from that of Mr. Lincoln: I believe that the Union can only be preserved by maintaining inviolate the Constitution of the United States as our fathers have made it. That Constitution guarantees to the people of every State the right to have slavery or not have it; to have negroes or not have them; to have Maine liquor laws or not have them; to have just such institutions as they choose, each State being left free to decide for itself. The framers of that Constitution never conceived the idea that uniformity in the domestic institutions of the different States was either desirable or possible. They well understood that the laws and institutions which would be well adapted to the granite hills of New Hampshire would be unfit for the rice plantations of South Carolina; they well understood that each one of the thirteen States had distinct and separate interests, and required distinct and separate local laws and local institutions. And in view of that fact they provided that each State should retain its sovereign power within its own limits, with the right to make just such laws and just such institutions as it saw proper, under the belief that no two of them would be alike. If they had supposed that uniformity was desirable and possible, why did they provide for a separate Legislature for each State? Why did they not blot out State sovereignty and State legislatures, and give all the power to Congress, in order that the laws might be uniform? For the very reason that uniformity, in their opinion, was neither desirable nor possible. We have increased from thirteen States to thirty-two States; and just in proportion as the number of States increases and our territory expands, there will be a still greater variety and dissimilarity of climate, of production, and of interest, requiring a corresponding dissimilarity and variety in the local laws and institutions adapted thereto. The laws that are necessary in the mining regions of California would be totally useless and vicious on the prairies of Illinois; the laws that would suit the lumber regions of Maine or of Minnesota would be totally useless and valueless in the tobacco regions of Virginia and Kentucky; the laws which would suit the manufacturing districts of New England would be totally unsuited to the planting regions of the Carolinas, of Georgia, and of Louisiana. Each State is supposed to have interests separate and distinct from each and every other; and hence must have laws different from each and every other State, in order that its laws shall be adapted to the condition and necessities of the people. Hence I insist that our institutions rest on the theory that there shall be dissimilarity and variety in the local laws and institutions of the different States, instead of all being uniform; and you find, my friends, that Mr. Lincoln and myself differ radically and totally on the fundamental principles of this government. He goes for consolidation, for uniformity in our local institutions, for blotting out State rights and State sovereignty, and consolidating all the power in the Federal Government, for converting these thirty-two sovereign States into one empire, and making uniformity throughout the length and breadth of the land. On the other hand, I go for maintaining the authority of the Federal Government within the limits marked out by the Constitution, and then for maintaining and preserving the sovereignty of each and all of the States of the Union, in order that each State may regulate and adopt its own local institutions in its own way, without interference from any power whatsoever. Thus you find there is a distinct issue of principles—principles irreconcilable—between Mr. Lincoln and myself. He goes for consolidation and uniformity in our government; I go for maintaining the confederation of the sovereign States under the Constitution as our fathers made it, leaving each State at liberty to manage its own affairs and own internal institutions.

Mr. Lincoln makes another point upon me, and rests his whole case upon these two points. His last point is, that he will wage a warfare upon the Supreme Court of the United States because of the Dred Scott decision. He takes occasion, in his speech made before the Republican Convention, in my absence, to arraign me, not only for having expressed my acquiescence in that decision, but to charge me with being a conspirator with that court in devising that decision three years before Dred Scott ever thought of commencing a suit for his freedom. The object of his speech was to convey the idea to the people that the court could not be trusted, that the late President could not be trusted, that the present one could not be trusted, and that Mr. Douglas could not be trusted; that they were all conspirators in bringing about that corrupt decision, to which Mr. Lincoln is determined he will never yield a willing obedience.

He makes two points upon the Dred Scott decision. The first is that he objects to it because the court decided that negroes descended of slave parents are not citizens of the United States; and, secondly, because they have decided that the Act of Congress passed 8th of March, 1820, prohibiting slavery in all of the Territories north of 36° 30', was unconstitutional and void, and hence did not have effect in emancipating a slave brought into that Territory. And he will not submit to that decision. He says that he will not fight the judges or the United States marshals in order to liberate Dred Scott, but that he will not respect that decision, as a rule of law binding on this country, in the future. Why not? Because, he says, it is unjust. How is he going to remedy it? Why, he says he is going to reverse it. How? He is going to take an appeal. To whom is he going to appeal? The Constitution of the United States provides that the Supreme Court is the ultimate tribunal, the highest judicial tribunal on earth; and Mr. Lincoln is going to appeal from that. To whom? I know he appealed to the Republican State Convention of Illinois, and I believe that Convention reversed the decision; but I am not aware that they have yet carried it into effect. How are they going to make that reversal effectual? Why, Mr. Lincoln tells us in his late Chicago speech. He explains it as clear as light. He says to the people of Illinois that if you elect him to the Senate he will introduce a bill to re-enact the law which the court pronounced unconstitutional. [Shouts of laughter, and voices, "*Spot* the law."] Yes, he is going to spot the law. The court pronounces that law, prohibiting slavery, unconstitutional and void, and Mr. Lincoln is going to pass an act reversing that decision and making it valid. I never heard before of an appeal being taken from the Supreme Court to the Congress of the United States to reverse its decision. I have heard of appeals being taken from Congress to the Supreme Court to declare a statute void. That has been done from the earliest days of Chief Justice Marshall down to the present time.

The Supreme Court of Illinois do not hesitate to pronounce an Act of the Legislature void, as being repugnant to the Constitution, and the Supreme Court of the United States is vested by the Constitution with that very power. The Constitution says that the judicial power of the United States shall be vested in the Supreme Court and such inferior courts as Congress shall, from time to time, ordain and establish. Hence it is the province and duty of the Supreme Court to pronounce judgment on the validity and constitutionality of an Act of Congress. In this case they have done so, and Mr. Lincoln will not submit to it, and he is going to reverse it by another Act of Congress of the same tenor. My opinion is that Mr. Lincoln ought to be on the Supreme Bench himself, when the Republicans get into power, if that kind of law knowledge qualifies a man for the bench. But Mr. Lincoln intimates that there is another mode by which he can reverse the Dred Scott decision. How is that? Why, he is going to appeal to the people to elect a President who will appoint judges who will reverse the Dred Scott decision. Well, let us see how that is going to be done. First, he has to carry on his sectional organization, a party confined to the free States, making war upon the slaveholding States until he gets a Republican President elected. ["He never will, sir."] I do not believe he ever will. But suppose he should; when that Republican President shall have taken his seat (Mr. Seward, for instance), will he then proceed to appoint judges? No! he will have to wait until the present judges die before he can do that; and perhaps his four years would be out before a majority of these judges found it agreeable to die; and it is very possible, too, that Mr. Lincoln's senatorial term would expire before these judges would be accommodating enough to die. If it should so happen I do not see a very great prospect for Mr. Lincoln to reverse the Dred Scott decision. But suppose they should die, then how are the new judges to be appointed? Why, the Republican President is to call upon the candidates and catechise them, and ask them, "How will you decide this case if I appoint you judge?" Suppose, for instance, Mr. Lincoln to be a candidate for a vacancy on the Supreme Bench to fill Chief Justice Taney's place, and when he applied to Seward, the latter would say, "Mr. Lincoln, I cannot appoint you until I know how you will decide the Dred Scott case?" Mr. Lincoln tells him, and he then asks him how he will decide Tom Jones's case, and Bill Wilson's case, and thus catechises the judge as to how he will decide any case which may arise before him. Suppose you get a Supreme Court composed of such judges, who have been appointed by a partisan President upon their giving pledges how they would decide a case before it arose,—what confidence would you have in such a court? Would not your court be prostituted beneath the contempt of all mankind? What man would feel that his liberties were safe, his right of person or property was secure, if the Supreme Bench, that august tribunal, the highest on earth, was brought down to that low, dirty pool wherein the judges are to give pledges in advance how they will decide all the questions which may be brought before them? It is a proposition to make that court the corrupt, unscrupulous tool of a political party. But Mr. Lincoln cannot conscientiously submit, he thinks, to the decision of a court composed of a majority of Democrats. If he cannot, how can he expect us to have confidence in a court composed of a majority of Republicans, selected for the purpose of deciding against the Democracy, and in favor of the Republicans? The very proposition carries with it the demoralization and degradation destructive of the judicial department of the Federal Government.

I say to you, fellow-citizens, that I have no warfare to make upon the Supreme Court because of the Dred Scott decision. I have no complaints to make against that court because of that decision. My private opinions on some points of the case may have been one way, and on other points of the case another; in some things concurring with the court, and in others dissenting; but what have my private opinions in a question of law to do with the decision after it has been pronounced by the highest judicial tribunal known to the Constitution? You, sir [addressing the chairman], as an eminent lawyer, have a right to entertain your opinions on any question that comes before the court, and to appear before the tribunal and maintain them boldly and with tenacity until the final decision shall have been pronounced; and then, sir, whether you are sustained or over-ruled, your duty as a lawyer and a citizen is to bow in deference to that decision. I intend to yield obedience to the decisions of the highest tribunals in the land in all cases, whether their opinions are in conformity with my views as a lawyer or not. When we refuse to abide by judicial decisions, what protection is there left for life and property? To whom shall you appeal? To mob law, to partisan caucuses, to town meetings, to revolution? Where is the remedy when you refuse obedience to the constituted authorities? I will not stop to inquire whether I agree or disagree with all the opinions expressed by Judge Taney or any other judge. It is enough for me to know that the decision has been made. It has been made by a tribunal appointed by the Constitution to make it; it was a point within their jurisdiction, and I am bound by it.

But, my friends, Mr. Lincoln says that this Dred Scott decision destroys the doctrine of popular sovereignty, for the reason that the court has decided that Congress had no power to prohibit slavery in the Territories, and hence he infers that it would decide that the Territorial legislatures could not prohibit slavery there. I will not stop to inquire whether the court will carry the decision that far or not. It would be interesting as a matter of theory, but of no importance in practice; for this reason, that if the people of a Territory want slavery they will have it, and if they do not want it they will drive it out, and you cannot force it on them. Slavery cannot exist a day in the midst of an unfriendly people with unfriendly laws. There is truth and wisdom in a remark made to me by an eminent Southern senator, when speaking of this technical right to take slaves into the Territories. Said he:

> I do not care a fig which way the decision shall be, for it is of no particular consequence; slavery cannot exist a day or an hour in any Territory or State unless it has affirmative laws sustaining and supporting it, furnishing police regulations and

remedies; and an omission to furnish them would be as fatal as a constitutional prohibition. Without affirmative legislation in its favor, slavery could not exist any longer than a new-born infant could survive under the heat of the sun, on a barren rock, without protection. It would wilt and die for the want of support.

So it would be in the Territories. See the illustration in Kansas. The Republicans have told you, during the whole history of that Territory, down to last winter, that the pro-slavery party in the Legislature had passed a pro-slavery code, establishing and sustaining slavery in Kansas, but that this pro-slavery Legislature did not truly represent the people, but was imposed upon them by an invasion from Missouri; and hence the Legislature were one way, and the people another. Granting all this, and what has been the result? With laws supporting slavery, but the people against, there are not as many slaves in Kansas today as there were on the day the Nebraska Bill passed and the Missouri Compromise was repealed. Why? Simply because slaveowners knew that if they took their slaves into Kansas, where a majority of the people were opposed to slavery, that it would soon be abolished, and they would lose their right of property in consequence of taking them there. For that reason they would not take or keep them there. If there had been a majority of the people in favor of slavery, and the climate had been favorable, they would have taken them there; but the climate not being suitable, the interest of the people being opposed to it, and a majority being against it, the slaveowner did not find it profitable to take his slaves there, and consequently there are not as many slaves there to-day as on the day the Missouri Compromise was repealed. This shows clearly that if the people do not want slavery they will keep it out; and if they do want it, they will protect it.

You have a good illustration of this in the Territorial history of this State. You all remember that by the Ordinance of 1787 slavery was prohibited in Illinois; yet you all know, particularly you old settlers who were here in Territorial times, that the Territorial Legislature, in defiance of that Ordinance, passed a law allowing you to go into Kentucky, buy slaves, and bring them into the Territory, having them sign indentures to serve you and your posterity ninety-nine years, and their posterity thereafter to do the same. This hereditary slavery was introduced in defiance of the Act of Congress. That was the exercise of popular sovereignty,—the right of a Territory to decide the question for itself in defiance of the Act of Congress. On the other hand, if the people of a Territory are hostile to slavery, they will drive it out. Consequently, this theoretical question raised upon the Dred Scott decision is worthy of no consideration whatsoever, for it is only brought into these political discussions and used as a hobby upon which to ride into office, or out of which to manufacture political capital.

But Mr. Lincoln's main objection to the Dred Scott decision I have reserved for my conclusion. His principal objection to that decision is that it was intended to deprive the negro of the rights of citizenship in the different States of the Union. Well, suppose it was,—and there is no doubt that that was its legal effect,—what is his objection to it? Why, he thinks that a negro ought to be permitted to have the rights of citizenship. He is in favor of negro citizenship, and opposed to the Dred Scott decision, because it declares that a negro is not a citizen, and hence is not entitled to vote. Here I have a direct issue with Mr. Lincoln. I am not in favor of negro citizenship. I do not believe that a negro is a citizen or ought to be a citizen. I believe that this government of ours was founded, and wisely founded, upon the white basis. It was made by white men for the benefit of white men and their posterity, to be executed and managed by white men. I freely concede that humanity requires us to extend all the protection, all the privileges, all the immunities, to the Indian and the negro which they are capable of enjoying consistent with the safety of society. You may then ask me what are those rights, what is the nature and extent of the rights which a negro ought to have? My answer is that this is a question for each State and each Territory to decide for itself. In Illinois we have decided that a negro is not a slave, but we have at the same time determined that he is not a citizen and shall not enjoy any political rights. I concur in the wisdom of that policy, and am content with it. I assert that the sovereignty of Illinois had a right to determine that question as we have decided it, and I deny that any other State has a right to interfere with us or call us to account for that decision. In the State of Maine they have decided by their constitution that the negro shall exercise the elective franchise and hold office on an equality with the white man. Whilst I do not concur in the good sense or correct taste of that decision on the part of Maine, I have no disposition to quarrel with her. It is her business, and not ours. If the people of Maine desire to be put on an equality with the negro, I do not know that anybody in this State will attempt to prevent it. If the white people of Maine think a negro their equal, and that he has a right to come and kill their vote by a negro vote, they have a right to think so, I suppose, and I have no disposition to interfere with them. Then, again, passing over to New York, we find in that State they have provided that a negro may vote provided he holds $250 worth of property, but that he shall not unless he does; that is to say, they will allow a negro to vote if he is rich, but a poor fellow they will not allow to vote. In New York they think a rich negro is equal to a white man. Well, that is a matter of taste with them. If they think so in that State, and do not carry the doctrine outside of it and propose to interfere with us, I have no quarrel to make with them. It is their business. There is a great deal of philosophy and good sense in a saying of Fridley of Kane. Fridley had a lawsuit before a justice of the peace, and the justice decided it against him. This he did not like; and standing up and looking at the justice for a moment, "Well, Squire," said he, "if a man chooses to make a darnation fool of himself, I suppose there is no law against it." That is all I have to say about these negro regulations and this negro voting in other States where they have systems different from ours. If it is their wish to have it so, be it so. There is no cause to complain. Kentucky has decided that it is not consistent with her safety and her prosperity to allow a negro to have either political rights or his freedom, and hence she makes him a slave. That is her business, not mine. It is her right under the Constitution of the country. The sovereignty of Kentucky, and that alone, can decide that question; and when she decides it, there is no power on earth to which you can appeal to reverse it. Therefore, leave Kentucky as the Constitution has left her, a sovereign, independent State, with the exclusive right to have slavery or not, as she chooses; and so long as I hold powder I will maintain and defend her rights against any assaults, from whatever quarter they may come.

I will never stop to inquire whether I approve or disapprove of the domestic institutions of a State. I maintain her sovereign rights. I defend her sovereignty from all assault, in the hope that she will join in defending us when we are assailed by any outside power. How are we to protect our sovereign rights, to keep slavery out, unless we protect the sovereign rights to every other State to decide the question for itself? Let Kentucky, or South Carolina, or any other State attempt to interfere in Illinois, and tell us that we shall establish slavery, in order to make it uniform, according to Mr. Lincoln's proposition, throughout the Union; let them come here and tell us that we must and shall have slavery,—and I will call on you to follow me, and shed the last drop of our heart's blood in repelling the invasion and chastising their insolence. And if we would fight for our reserved rights and sovereign power in our own limits, we must respect the sovereignty of each other State.

Hence, you find that Mr. Lincoln and myself come to a direct issue on this whole doctrine of slavery. He is going to wage a war against it everywhere, not only in Illinois, but in his native State of Kentucky. And why? Because he says that the Declaration of Independence contains this language: "We hold these truths to be self-evident—that all men are created equal; that they are endowed by their Creator with certain inalienable rights; that among these are life, liberty, and the pursuit of happiness"; and he asks whether that instrument does not declare that all men are created equal. Mr. Lincoln then goes on to say that that clause of the Declaration of Independence includes negroes. ["I say not."] Well, if you say not, I do not think you will vote for Mr. Lincoln. Mr. Lincoln goes on to argue that the language "all men" included the negroes, Indians, and all inferior races.

In his Chicago speech he says, in so many words, that it includes the negroes, that they were endowed by the Almighty with the right of equality with the white man, and therefore that that right is divine,—a right under the higher law; that the law of God makes them equal to the white man, and therefore that the law of the white man cannot deprive them of that right. This is Mr. Lincoln's argument. He is conscientious in his belief. I do not question his sincerity; I do not doubt that he, in his conscience, believes that the Almighty made the negro equal to the white man. He thinks that the negro is his brother. I do not think that the negro is any kin of mine at all. And here is the difference between us. I believe that the Declaration of Independence, in the words "all men are created equal," was intended to allude only to the people of the United States, to men of European birth or descent, being white men; that they were created equal, and hence that Great Britain had no right to deprive them of their political and religious privileges; but the signers of that paper did not intend to include the Indian or the negro in that Declaration; for if they had, would they not have been bound to abolish slavery in every State and colony from that day? Remember, too, that at the time the Declaration was put forth, every one of the thirteen colonies were slaveholding colonies; every man who signed that Declaration represented slaveholding constituents. Did those signers mean by that act to charge themselves and all their constituents with having violated the law of God, in holding the negro in an inferior condition to the white man? And yet, if they included negroes in that term, they were bound, as conscientious men, that day and that hour, not only to have abolished slavery throughout the land, but to have conferred political rights and privileges on the negro, and elevated him to an equality with the white man. ["They did not do it."] I know they did not do it; and the very fact that they did not shows that they did not understand the language they used to include any but the white race. Did they mean to say that the Indian, on this continent, was created equal to the white man, and that he was endowed by the Almighty with inalienable rights,—rights so sacred that they could not be taken away by any constitution or law that man could pass? Why, their whole action toward the Indian showed that they never dreamed that they were bound to put him on an equality. I am not only opposed to negro equality, but I am opposed to Indian equality. I am opposed to putting the coolies, now importing into this country, on an equality with us, or putting the Chinese or any inferior race on an equality with us. I hold the white race, the European race, I care not whether Irish, German, French, Scotch, English, or to what nation they belong, so they are the white race, to be our equals. And I am for placing them, as our fathers did, on an equality with us. Emigrants from Europe, and their descendants, constitute the people of the United States. The Declaration of Independence only included the white people of the United States. The Constitution of the United States was framed by the white people; it ought to be administered by them, leaving each State to make such regulations concerning the negro as it chooses, allowing him political rights or not, as it chooses, and allowing him civil rights or not, as it may determine for itself.

Let us only carry out those principles, and we will have peace and harmony in the different States. But Mr. Lincoln's conscientious scruples on this point govern his actions, and I honor him for following them, although I abhor the doctrine which he preaches. His conscientious scruples lead him to believe that the negro is entitled by divine right to the civil and political privileges of citizenship on an equality with the white man.

For that reason he says he wishes the Dred Scott decision reversed. He wishes to confer those privileges of citizenship on the negro. Let us see how he will do it. He will first be called upon to strike out of the Constitution of Illinois that clause which prohibits free negroes and slaves from Kentucky or any other State coming into Illinois. When he blots out that clause, when he lets down the door or opens the gate for all the negro population to flow in and cover our prairies, until in midday they will look dark and black as night,—when he shall have done this, his mission will yet be unfulfilled. Then it will be that he will apply his principles of negro equality; that is, if he can get the Dred Scott decision reversed in the mean time. He will then change the Constitution again, and allow negroes to vote and hold office, and will make them eligible to the Legislature, so that thereafter they can have the right men for United States Senators. He will allow them to vote to elect the Legislature, the judges, and the Governor, and will make them eligible to the office of judge or Governor, or to the Legislature. He will put them on an equality with the white man. What then? Of course, after making them eligible to the judiciary, when he gets Cuffee elevated to the bench, he certainly will not refuse his judge the privilege of marrying any woman he may select! I submit to you whether these are not the legitimate consequences of his doctrine? If it be true, as he says, that by the Declaration of Independence and by divine law the negro is created the equal of the white man; if it be true that the Dred Scott decision is unjust and wrong, because it deprives the negro of citizenship and equality with the white man,—then does it not follow that if he had the power he would make negroes citizens, and give them all the rights and all the privileges of citizenship on an equality with white men? I think that is the inevitable conclusion. I do not doubt Mr. Lincoln's conscientious conviction on the subject, and I do not doubt that he will carry out that doctrine if he ever has the power; but I resist it because I am utterly opposed to any political amalgamation or any other amalgamation on this continent. We are witnessing the result of giving civil and political rights to inferior races in Mexico, in Central America, in South America, and in the West India Islands. Those young men who went from here to Mexico to fight the battles of their country in the Mexican war can tell you the fruits of negro equality with the white man. They will tell you that the result of that equality is social amalgamation, demoralization, and degradation below the capacity for self-government.

My friends, if we wish to preserve this government we must maintain it on the basis on which it was established; to wit, the white basis. We must preserve the purity of the race not only in our politics, but in our domestic relations. We must then preserve the sovereignty of the States, and we maintain the Federal Union by preserving the Federal Constitution inviolate. Let us do that, and our Union will not only be perpetual, but may extend until it shall spread over the entire continent.

Fellow-citizens, I have already detained you too long. I have exhausted myself and wearied you, and owe you an apology for the desultory manner in which I have discussed these topics. I will have an opporttinity of addressing you again before the November election comes off. I come to you to appeal to your judgment as American citizens, to take your verdict of approval or disapproval upon the discharge of my public duty and my principles as compared with those of Mr. Lincoln. If you conscientiously believe that his principles are more in harmony with the feelings of the American people and the interests and honor of the Republic, elect him. If, on the contrary, you believe that my principles are more consistent with those great principles upon which our fathers framed this government, then I shall ask you to so express your opinion at the polls. I am aware that it is a bitter and severe contest, but I do not doubt what the decision of the people of Illinois will be. I do not anticipate any personal collision between Mr. Lincoln and myself. You all know I am an amiable, goodnatured man, and I take great pleasure in bearing testimony to the fact that Mr. Lincoln is a kindhearted, amiable, good-natured gentleman, with whom no man has a right to pick a quarrel, even if he wanted one. He is a worthy gentleman. I have known him for twenty-five years, and there is no better citizen and no kinder-hearted man. He is a fine lawyer, possesses high ability, and there is no objection to him, except the monstrous revolutionary doctrines with which he is identified and which he conscientiously entertains, and is determined to carry out if he gets the power.

He has one element of strength upon which he relies to accomplish his object, and that is his alliance with certain men in this State claiming to be Democrats, whose avowed object is to use their power to prostrate the Democratic nominees. He hopes he can secure the few men claiming to be friends of the Lecompton Constitution, and for that reason you will find he does not say a word against the Lecompton Constitution or its supporters. He is as silent as the grave upon that subject. Behold Mr. Lincoln courting Lecompton votes, in order that he may go to the Senate as the representative of Republican principles! You know that that alliance exists. I think you will find that it will ooze out before the contest is over. It must be a contest of principle. Either the radical Abolition principles of Mr. Lincoln must be maintained, or the strong, constitutional, national Democratic principles with which I am identified must be carried out. I shall be satisfied whatever way you decide. I have been sustained by the people of Illinois with a steadiness, a firmness, and an enthusiasm which makes my heart overflow with gratitude. If I was now to be consigned to private life I would have nothing to complain of. I would even then owe you a debt of gratitude which the balance of my life could not repay. But, my friends, you have discharged every obligation you owe to me. I have been a thousand times paid by the welcome you have extended to me since I have entered the State on my return home this time. Your reception not only discharges all obligations, but it furnishes inducement to renewed efforts to serve you in the future. If you think Mr. Lincoln will do more to advance the interests and elevate the character of Illinois than myself, it is your duty to elect him; if you think he would do more to preserve the peace of the country and perpetuate the Union than myself, then elect him. I leave the question in your hands, and again tender you my profound thanks for the cordial and heartfelt welcome tendered to me this evening.

# Speech of Abraham Lincoln

*Delivered at Springfield, Ill., Saturday Evening, July 17, 1858.*
(Mr. Douglas was not present.)

FELLOW-CITIZENS: Another election, which is deemed an important one, is approaching, and, as I suppose, the Republican party will, without much difficulty, elect their State ticket. But in regard to the Legislature, we, the Republicans, labor under some disadvantages. In the first place, we have a Legislature to elect upon an apportionment of the representation made several years ago, when the proportion of the population was far greater in the South (as compared with the North) than it now is; and inasmuch as our opponents hold almost entire sway in the South, and we a correspondingly large majority in the North, the fact that we are now to be represented as we were years ago, when the population was different, is to us a very great disadvantage. We had in the year 1855, according to law, a census, or enumeration of the inhabitants, taken for the purpose of a new apportionment of representation. We know what a fair apportionment of representation upon that census would give us. We know that it could not, if fairly made, fail to give the Republican party from six to ten more members of the Legislature than they can probably get as the law now stands. It so happened at the last session of the Legislature that our opponents, holding the control of both branches of the Legislature, steadily refused to give us such an apportionment as we were rightly entitled to have upon the census already taken. The Legislature steadily refused to give us such an apportionment as we were rightfully entitled to have upon the census taken of the population of the State. The Legislature would pass no bill upon that subject, except such as was at least as unfair to us as the old one, and in which, in some instances, two men in the Democratic regions were allowed to go as far toward sending a member to the Legislature as three were in the Republican regions. Comparison was made at the time as to representative and senatorial districts, which completely demonstrated that such was the fact. Such a bill was passed and tendered to the Republican Governor for his signature; but, principally for the reasons I have stated, he withheld his approval, and the bill fell without becoming a law.

Another disadvantage under which we labor is that there are one or two Democratic Senators who will be members of the next Legislature, and will vote for the election of Senator, who are holding over in districts in which we could, on all reasonable calculation, elect men of our own, if we only had the chance of an election. When we consider that there are but twenty-five Senators in the Senate, taking two from the side where they rightfully belong, and adding them to the other, is to us a disadvantage not to be lightly regarded. Still, so it is; we have this to contend with. Perhaps there is no ground of complaint on our part. In attending to the many things involved in the last general election for President, Governor, Auditor, Treasurer, Superintendent of Public Instruction, Members of Congress, of the Legislature, County Officers, and so on, we allowed these things to happen by want of sufficient attention, and we have no cause to complain of our adversaries, so far as this matter is concerned. But we have some cause to complain of the refusal to give us a fair apportionment.

There is still another disadvantage under which we labor, and to which I will ask your attention. It arises out of the relative positions of the two persons who stand before the State as candidates for the Senate. Senator Douglas is of world-wide renown. All the anxious politicians of his party, or who have been of his party for years past, have been looking upon him as certainly, at no distant day, to be the President of the United States. They have seen in his round, jolly, fruitful face post-offices, land-offices, marshalships, and cabinet appointments, chargéships and foreign missions bursting and sprouting out in wonderful exuberance, ready to be laid hold of by their greedy hands. And as they have been gazing upon this attractive picture so long, they cannot, in the little distraction that has taken place in the party, bring themselves to give up the charming hope; but with greedier anxiety they rush about him, sustain him, and give him marches, triumphal entries, and receptions beyond what even in the days of his highest prosperity they could have brought about in his favor. On the contrary, nobody has ever expected me to be President. In my poor, lean, lank face, nobody has ever seen that any cabbages were sprouting out. These are disadvantages all, taken together, that the Republicans labor under. *We* have to fight this battle upon principle, and upon principle alone. I am, in a certain sense, made the standard-bearer in behalf of the Republicans. I was made so merely because there had to be some one so placed,—I being in nowise preferable to any other one of twenty-five, perhaps a hundred, we have in the Republican ranks. Then I say I wish it to be distinctly understood and borne in mind that we have to fight this battle without many—perhaps without any—of the external aids which are brought to bear against us. So I hope those with whom I am surrounded have principle enough to nerve themselves for the task, and leave nothing undone that can be fairly done to bring about the right result.

After Senator Douglas left Washington, as his movements were made known by the public prints, he tarried a considerable time in the city of New York; and it was heralded that, like another Napoleon, he was lying by and framing the plan of his campaign. It was telegraphed to Washington City, and published in the *Union*, that he was framing his plan for the purpose of going to Illinois to pounce upon and annihilate the treasonable and disunion speech which Lincoln had made here on the 16th of June. Now, I do suppose that the Judge really spent some time in New York maturing the plan of the campaign, as his friends heralded for him. I have been able, by noting his movements since his arrival in Illinois, to discover evidences confirmatory of that allegation. I think I have been able to see what are the material points of that plan. I will, for a little while, ask your attention to some of them. What I shall point out, though not showing the whole plan, are, nevertheless, the main points, as I suppose.

They are not very numerous. The first is popular sovereignty. The second and third are attacks upon my speech made on the 16th of June. Out of these three points—drawing within the range of popular sovereignty the question of the Lecompton Constitution—he makes his principal assault. Upon these his successive speeches are substantially one and the same. On this matter of popular sovereignty I wish to be a little careful. Auxiliary to these main points, to be sure, are their thimderings of cannon, their marching and music, their fizzlegigs and fireworks; but I will not waste time with them. They are but the little trappings of the campaign.

Coming to the substance,—the first point,—"popular sovereignty." It is to be labelled upon the cars in which he travels; put upon the hacks he rides in; to be flaunted upon the arches he passes under, and the banners which wave over him. It is to be dished up in as many varieties as a French cook can produce soups from potatoes. Now, as this is so great a staple of the plan of the campaign, it is worth while to examine it carefully; and if we examine only a very little, and do not allow ourselves to be misled, we shall be able to see that the whole thing is the most arrant Quixotism that was ever enacted before a community. What is the matter of popular sovereignty? The first thing, in order to understand it, is to get a good definition of what it is, and after that to see how it is applied.

I suppose almost every one knows that, in this controversy, whatever has been said has had reference to the question of negro slavery. We have not been in a controversy about the right of the people to govern themselves in the *ordinary* matters of domestic concern in the States and Territories. Mr. Buchanan, in one of his late messages (I think when he sent up the Lecompton Constitution) urged that the main point to which the public attention had been directed was not in regard to the great variety of small domestic matters, but was directed to the question of negro slavery; and he asserts that if the people had had a fair chance to vote on that question there was no reasonable ground of objection in regard to minor questions. Now, while I think that the people had *not* had given, or offered, them a fair chance upon that slavery question, still, if there had been a fair submission to a vote upon that main question, the President's proposition would have been true to the utmost. Hence, when hereafter I speak of popular sovereignty, I wish to be understood as applying what I say to the question of slavery only, not to other minor domestic matters of a Territory or a State.

Does Judge Douglas, when he says that several of the past years of his life have been devoted to the question of "popular sovereignty," and that all the remainder of his life shall be devoted to it, does he mean to say that he has been devoting his life to securing to the people of the Territories the right to exclude slavery from the Territories? If he means so to say he means to deceive; because he and every one knows that the decision of the Supreme Court, which he approves and makes especial ground of attack upon me for disapproving, forbids the people of a Territory to exclude slavery. This covers the whole ground, from the settlement of a Territory till it reaches the degree of maturity entitling it to form a State Constitution. So far as all that ground is concerned, the Judge is not sustaining popular sovereignty, but absolutely opposing it. He sustains the decision which declares that the popular will of the Territory has no constitutional power to exclude slavery during their territorial existence. This being so, the period of time from the first settlement of a Territory till it reaches the point of forming a State Constitution is not the thing that the Judge has fought for or is fighting for, but, on the contrary, he has fought for, and is fighting for, the thing that annihilates and crushes out that same popular sovereignty.

Well, so much being disposed of, what is left? Why, he is contending for the right of the people, when they come to make a State Constitution, to make it for themselves, and precisely as best suits themselves. I say again, that is quixotic. I defy contradiction when I declare that the Judge can find no one to oppose him on that proposition. I repeat, there is nobody opposing that proposition on *principle*. Let me not be misunderstood. I know that, with reference to the Lecompton Constitution, I may be misunderstood; but when you understand me correctly, my proposition will be true and accurate. Nobody is opposing, or has opposed, the right of the people, when they form a constitution, to form it for themselves. Mr. Buchanan and his friends have not done it; they, too, as well as the Republicans and the Anti-Lecompton Democrats, have not done it; but on the contrary, they together have insisted on the right of the people to form a constitution for themselves. The difference between the Buchanan men on the one hand, and the Douglas men and the Republicans on the other, has not been on a question of principle, but on a question of *fact.*

The dispute was upon the question of fact, whether the Lecompton Constitution had been fairly formed by the people or not. Mr. Buchanan and his friends have not contended for the contrary principle any more than the Douglas men or the Republicans. They have insisted that whatever of small irregularities existed in getting up the Lecompton Constitution were such as happen in the settlement of all new Territories. The question was, Was it a fair emanation of the people? It was a question of fact, and not of principle. As to the principle, all were agreed. Judge Douglas voted with the Republicans upon that matter of fact.

He and they, by their voices and votes, denied that it was a fair emanation of the people. The Administration affirmed that it was. With respect to the evidence bearing upon that question of fact, I readily agree that Judge Douglas and the Republicans had the right on their side, and that the Administration was wrong. But I state again that, as a matter of principle, there is no dispute upon the right of a people in a Territory, merging into a State, to form a constitution for themselves without outside interference from any quarter. This being so, what is Judge Douglas going to spend his life for? Is he going to spend his life in maintaining a principle that nobody on earth opposes? Does he expect to stand up in majestic dignity, and go through his *apotheosis* and become a god in the maintaining of a principle which neither man nor mouse in all God's creation is opposing? Now something in regard to the Lecompton Constitution more specially; for I pass from this other question of popular sovereignty as the most arrant humbug that has ever been attempted on an intelligent community.

As to the Lecompton Constitution, I have already said that on the question of fact, as to whether it was a fair emanation of the people or not, Judge Douglas, with the Republicans and some Americans, had greatly the argument against the Administration; and while I repeat this, I wish to know what there is in the opposition of Judge Douglas to the Lecompton Constitution that entitles him to be considered the only opponent to it,—as being *par excellence* the very *quintessence* of that opposition. I agree to the rightfulness of his opposition. He in the Senate and his class of men there formed the number *three,* and no more. In the House of Representatives his class of men—the Anti-Lecompton Democrats— formed a number of about twenty. It took one hundred and twenty to defeat the measure, against one hundred and twelve. Of the votes of that one hundred and twenty, Judge Douglas's friends furnished twenty, to add to which there were six Americans and ninety-four Republicans. I do not say that I am precisely accurate in their numbers, but I am sufficiently so for any use I am making of it.

Why is it that twenty shall be entitled to all the credit of doing that work, and the hundred none of it? Why, if, as Judge Douglas says, the honor is to be divided and due credit is to be given to other parties, why is just so much given as is consonant with the wishes, the interests, and advancement of the twenty? My understanding is, when a common job is done, or a common enterprise prosecuted, if I put in five dollars to your one, I have a right to take out five dollars to your one. But he does not so understand it. He declares the dividend of credit for defeating Lecompton upon a basis which seems unprecedented and incomprehensible.

Let us see. Lecompton in the raw was defeated. It afterward took a sort of cooked-up shape, and was passed in the English bill. It is said by the Judge that the defeat was a good and proper thing. If it was a good thing, why is he entitled to more credit than others for the performance of that good act, unless there was something in the antecedents of the Republicans that might induce every one to expect them to join in that good work, and at the same time something leading them to doubt that he would? Does he place his superior claim to credit on the ground that he performed a good act which was never expected of him? He says I have a proneness for quoting Scripture. If I should do so now, it occurs that perhaps he places himself somewhat upon the ground of the parable of the lost sheep which went astray upon the mountains, and when the owner of the hundred sheep found the one that was lost, and threw it upon his shoulders and came home rejoicing, it was said that there was more rejoicing over the one sheep that was lost and had been found than over the ninety and nine in the fold. The application is made by the Saviour in this parable, thus: "Verily, I say unto you, there is more rejoicing in heaven over one sinner that repenteth, than over ninety and nine just persons that need no repentance."

And now, if the Judge claims the benefit of this parable, *let him repent*. Let him not come up here and say: "I am the only just person; and you are the ninety-nine sinners! *Repentance* before *forgiveness* is a provision of the Christian system, and on that condition alone will the Republicans grant his forgiveness.

How will he prove that we have ever occupied a different position in regard to the Lecompton Constitution or any principle in it? He says he did not make his opposition on the ground as to whether it was a free or slave constitution, and he would have you understand that the Republicans made their opposition because it ultimately became a slave constitution. To make proof in favor of himself on this point, he reminds us that he opposed Lecompton before the vote was taken declaring whether the State was to be free or slave. But he forgets to say that our Republican Senator, Trumbull, made a speech against Lecompton even before he did.

Why did he oppose it? Partly, as he declares, because the members of the convention who framed it were not fairly elected by the people; that the people were not allowed to vote unless they had been registered; and that the people of whole counties, in some instances, were not registered. For these reasons he declares the Constitution was not an emanation, in any true sense, from the people. He also has an additional objection as to the mode of submitting the Constitution back to the people. But bearing on the question of whether the delegates were fairly elected, a speech of his, made something more than twelve months ago, from this stand, becomes important. It was made a little while before the election of the delegates who made Lecompton. In that speech he declared there was every reason to hope and believe the election would be fair; and if any one failed to vote, it would be his own culpable fault.

I, a few days after, made a sort of answer to that speech. In that answer I made, substantially, the very argument with which he combated his Lecompton adversaries in the Senate last winter. I pointed to the facts that the people could not vote without being registered, and that the time for registering had gone by. I commented on it as wonderful that Judge Douglas could be ignorant of these facts, which every one else in the nation so well knew.

I now pass from popular sovereignty and Lecompton. I may have occasion to refer to one or both.

When he was preparing his plan of campaign, Napoleon-like, in New York, as appears by two speeches I have heard him deliver since his arrival in Illinois, he gave special attention to a speech of mine, delivered here on the 16th of June last. He says that he carefully read that speech. He told us that at Chicago a week ago last night, and he repeated it at Bloomington last night. Doubtless, he repeated it again to-day, though I did not hear him. In the first two places—Chicago and Bloomington—I heard him; to-day I did not. He said he had carefully examined that speech,—*when,* he did not say; but there is no reasonable doubt it was when he was in New York preparing his plan of campaign. I am glad he did read it carefully. He says it was evidently prepared with great care. I freely admit it was prepared with care. I claim not to be more free from errors than others,—perhaps scarcely so much; but I was very careful not to put anything in that speech as a matter of fact, or make any inferences, which did not appear to me to be true and fully warrantable. If I had made any mistake, I was willing to be corrected; if I had drawn any inference in regard to Judge Douglas or any one else which was not warranted, I was fully prepared to modify it as soon as discovered. I planted myself upon the truth and the truth only, so far as I knew it, or could be brought to know it.

Having made that speech with the most kindly feelings toward Judge Douglas, as manifested therein, I was gratified when I found that he had carefully examined it, and had detected no error of fact, nor any inference against him, nor any misrepresentations of which he thought fit to complain. In neither of the two speeches I have mentioned did he make any such complaint. I will thank any one who will inform me that he, in his speech to-day, pointed out anything I had stated respecting him as being erroneous. I presume there is no such thing. I have reason to be gratified that the care and caution used in that speech left it so that he, most of all others interested in discovering error, has not been able to point out one thing against him which he could say was wrong. He seizes upon the doctrines he supposes to be included in that speech, and declares that upon them will turn the issues of this campaign. He then quotes, or attempts to quote, from my speech. I will not say that he wilfully misquotes, but he does fail to quote accurately. His attempt at quoting is from a passage which I believe I can quote accurately from memory. I shall make the quotation now, with some comments upon it, as I have already said, in order that the Judge shall be left entirely without excuse for misrepresenting me. I do so now, as I hope, for the last time. I do this in great caution, in order that if he repeats his misrepresentation it shall be plain to all that he does so wilfully. If, after all, he still persists, I shall be compelled to reconstruct the course I have marked out for myself, and draw upon such humble resources, as I have, for a new course, better suited to the real exigencies of the case. I set out in this campaign with the intention of conducting it strictly as a gentleman, in substance at least, if not in the outside polish. The latter I shall never be; but that which constitutes the inside of a gentleman I hope I understand, and am not less inclined to practise than others. It was my purpose and expectation that this canvass would be conducted upon principle, and with fairness on both sides, and it shall not be my fault if this purpose and expectation shall be given up.

He charges, in substance, that I invite a war of sections; that I propose all the local institutions of the different States shall become consolidated and uniform. What is there in the language of that speech which expresses such purpose or bears such construction? I have again and again said that I would not enter into any of the States to disturb the institution of slavery. Judge Douglas said, at Bloomington, that I used language most able and ingenious for concealing what I really meant; and that while I had protested against entering into the slave States, I nevertheless did mean to go on the banks of the Ohio and throw missiles into Kentucky, to disturb them in their domestic institutions.

I said in that speech, and I meant no more, that the institution of slavery ought to be placed in the very attitude where the framers of this government placed it and left it. I do not understand that the framers of our Constitution left the people of the free States in the attitude of firing bombs or shells into the slave States. I was not using that passage for the purpose for which he infers I did use it. I said:

> We are now far advanced into the fifth year since a policy was created for the avowed object and with the confident promise of putting an end to slavery agitation. Under the operation of that policy that agitation has not only not ceased, but has constantly augmented. In my opinion it will not cease till a crisis shall have been reached and passed. 'A house divided against itself cannot stand.' I believe that this government cannot endure permanently half slave and half free; it will become all one thing or all the other. Either the opponents of slavery will arrest the further spread of it, and place it where the public mind shall rest in the belief that it is in the course of ultimate extinction, or its advocates will push it forward till it shall become alike lawful in all the States, old as well as new. North as well as South.

Now, you all see, from that quotation, I did not express my *wish* on anything. In that passage I indicated no wish or purpose of my own; I simply expressed my *expectation*. Cannot the Judge perceive a distinction between a *purpose* and an *expectation?* I have often expressed an expectation to die, but I have never expressed a *wish* to die. I said at Chicago, and now repeat, that I am quite aware this government has endured, half slave and, half free, for eighty-two years. I understand that little bit of history. I expressed the opinion I did because I perceived—or thought I perceived—a new set of causes introduced. I did say at Chicago, in my speech there, that I do wish to see the spread of slavery arrested, and to see it placed where the public mind shall rest in the belief that it is in the course of ultimate extinction. I said that because I supposed, when the public mind shall rest in that belief, we shall have peace on the slavery question. I have believed—and now believe—the public mind did rest on that belief up to the introduction of the Nebraska Bill.

Although I have ever been opposed to slavery, so far I rested in the hope and belief that it was in the course of ultimate extinction. For that reason it had been a minor question with me. I might have been mistaken; but I had believed, and now believe, that the whole public mind, that is, the mind of the great majority, had rested in that belief up to the repeal of the Missouri Compromise. But upon that event I became convinced that either I had been resting in a delusion, or the institution was being placed on a new basis, a basis for making it perpetual, national, and universal. Subsequent events have greatly confirmed me in that belief. I believe that bill to be the beginning of a conspiracy for that purpose. So believing, I have since then considered that question a paramount one. So believing, I thought the public mind will never rest till the power of Congress to restrict the spread of it shall again be acknowledged and exercised on the one hand or, on the other, all resistance be entirely crushed out. I have expressed that opinion, and I entertain it to-night. It is denied that there is any tendency to the nationalization of slavery in these States.

Mr. Brooks, of South Carolina, in one of his speeches, when they were presenting him canes, silver plate, gold pitchers, and the like, for assaulting Senator Sumner, distinctly affirmed his opinion that when this Constitution was formed it was the belief of no man that slavery would last to the present day. He said, what I think, that the framers of our Constitution placed the institution of slavery where the public mind rested in the hope that it was in the course of ultimate extinction. But he went on to say that the men of the present age, by their experience, have become wiser than the framers of the Constitution, and the invention of the cotton gin had made the perpetuity of slavery a necessity in this country.

As another piece of evidence tending to this same point: Quite recently in Virginia, a man—the owner of slaves—made a will providing that after his death certain of his slaves should have their freedom if they should so choose, and go to Liberia, rather than remain in slavery. They chose to be liberated. But the persons to whom they would descend as property claimed them as slaves. A suit was instituted, which finally came to the Supreme Court of Virginia, and was therein decided against the slaves upon the ground that a negro cannot make a choice; that they had no legal power to choose,—could not perform the condition upon which their freedom depended.

I do not mention this with any purpose of criticising it, but to connect it with the arguments as affording additional evidence of the change of sentiment upon this question of slavery in the direction of making it perpetual and national. I argue now as I did before, that there is such a tendency; and I am backed, not merely by the facts, but by the open confession in the slave States.

And now as to the Judge's inference that because I wish to see slavery placed in the course of ultimate extinction—placed where our fathers originally placed it,—I wish to annihilate the State Legislatures, to force cotton to grow upon the tops of the Green Mountains, to freeze ice in Florida, to cut lumber on the broad Illinois prairie,—that I am in favor of all these ridiculous and impossible things.

It seems to me it is a complete answer to all this to ask if, when Congress did have the fashion of restricting slavery from free territory; when courts did have the fashion of deciding that taking a slave into a free country made him free,—I say it is a sufficient answer to ask if any of this ridiculous nonsense about consolidation and uniformity did actually follow. Who heard of any such thing because of the Ordinance of '87? because of the Missouri restriction? because of the numerous court decisions of that character?

Now, as to the Dred Scott decision; for upon that he makes his last point at me. He boldly takes ground in favor of that decision.

This is one half the onslaught, and one third of the entire plan of the campaign. I am opposed to that decision in a certain sense, but not in the sense which he puts it. I say that in so far as it decided in favor of Dred Scott's master, and against Dred Scott and his family, I do not propose to disturb or resist the decision.

I never have proposed to do any such thing. I think that in respect for judicial authority my humble history would not suffer in comparison with that of Judge Douglas. He would have the citizen conform his vote to that decision; the member of Congress, his; the President, his use of the veto power. He would make it a rule of political action for the people and all the departments of the government. I would not. By resisting it as a political rule, I disturb no right of property, create no disorder, excite no mobs.

When he spoke at Chicago, on Friday evening of last week, he made this same point upon me. On Saturday evening I replied, and reminded him of a Supreme Court decision which he opposed for at least several years. Last night, at Bloomington, he took some notice of that reply, but entirely forgot to remember that part of it.

He renews his onslaught upon me, forgetting to remember that I have turned the tables against himself on that very point. I renew the effort to draw his attention to it. I wish to stand erect before the country, as well as Judge Douglas, on this question of judicial authority; and therefore I add something to the authority in favor of my own position. I wish to show that I am sustained by authority, in addition to that heretofore presented. I do not expect to convince the Judge. It is part of the plan of his campaign, and he will cling to it with a desperate grip. Even turn it upon him,—the sharp point against him, and gaff him through,— he will still cling to it till he can invent some new dodge to take the place of it.

In public speaking it is tedious reading from documents; but I must beg to indulge the practice to a limited extent. I shall read from a letter written by Mr. Jefferson in 1820, and now to be found in the seventh volume of his correspondence, at page 177. It seems he had been presented by a gentleman of the name of Jarvis with a book, or essay, or periodical, called the *Republican*, and he was writing in acknowledgment of the present, and noting some of its contents. After expressing the hope that the work will produce a favorable effect upon the minds of the young, he proceeds to say:

> That it will have this tendency may be expected, and for that reason I feel an urgency to note what I deem an error in it, the more requiring notice as your opinion is strengthened by that of many others. You seem, in pages 84 and 148, to consider the judges as the ultimate arbiters of all constitutional questions,—a very dangerous doctrine indeed, and one which would place us under the despotism of an oligarchy. Our judges are as honest as other men, and not more so. They have, with others, the same passions for party, for power, and the privilege of their corps. Their maxim is, "Boni judicis est ampliare jurisdictionem"; and their power is the more dangerous as they are in office for life, and not responsible, as the other functionaries are, to the elective control. The Constitution has erected no such single tribunal, knowing that, to whatever hands confided, with the corruptions of time and party, its members would become despots. It has more wisely made all the departments co-equal and co-sovereign with themselves.

Thus we see the power claimed for the Supreme Court by Judge Douglas, Mr. Jefferson holds, would reduce us to the despotism of an oligarchy.

Now, I have said no more than this,—in fact, never quite so much as this; at least I am sustained by Mr. Jefferson.

Let us go a little further. You remember we once had a National Bank. Some one owed the bank a debt; he was sued, and sought to avoid payment on the ground that the bank was unconstitutional. The case went to the Supreme Court, and therein it was decided that the bank was constitutional. The whole Democratic party revolted against that decision. General Jackson himself asserted that he, as President, would not be bound to hold a National Bank to be constitutional, even though the court had decided it to be so. He fell in precisely with the view of Mr. Jefferson, and acted upon it under his official oath, in vetoing a charter for a National Bank. The declaration that Congress does not possess this constitutional power to charter a bank has gone into the Democratic platform, at their National Conventions, and was brought forward and reaffirmed in their last Convention at Cincinnati. They have contended for that declaration, in the very teeth of the Supreme Court, for more than a quarter of a century. In fact, they have reduced the decision to an absolute nullity. That decision, I repeat, is repudiated in the Cincinnati platform; and still, as if to show that effrontery can go no further, Judge Douglas vaunts in the very speeches in which he denounces me for opposing the Dred Scott decision that he stands on the Cincinnati platform.

Now, I wish to know what the Judge can charge upon me, with respect to decisions of the Supreme Court, which does not lie in all its length, breadth, and proportions at his own door. The plain truth is simply this: Judge Douglas is *for* Supreme Court decisions when he likes and against them when he does not like them. He is for the Dred Scott decision because it tends to nationalize slavery; because it is part of the original combination for that object. It so happens, singularly enough, that I never stood opposed to a decision of the Supreme Court till this. On the contrary, I have no recollection that he was ever particularly in favor of one till this. He never was in favor of any nor opposed to any, till the present one, which helps to nationalize slavery.

Free men of Sangamon, free men of Illinois, free men everywhere, judge ye between him and me upon this issue.

He says this Dred Scott case is a very small matter at most,—that it has no practical effect; that at best, or rather, I suppose, at worst, it is but an abstraction. I submit that the proposition that the thing which determines whether a man is free or a slave is rather *concrete* than *abstract*. I think you would conclude that it was, if your liberty depended upon it, and so would Judge Douglas, if his liberty depended upon it. But suppose it was on the question of spreading slavery over the new Territories that he considers it as being merely an abstract matter, and one of no practical importance. How has the planting of slavery in new countries always been effected? It has now been decided that slavery cannot be kept out of our new Territories by any legal means. In what do our new Territories now differ in this respect from the old Colonies when slavery was first planted within them? It was planted, as Mr. Clay once declared, and as history proves true, by individual men, in spite of the wishes of the people; the Mother Government refusing to prohibit it, and withholding from the people of the Colonies the authority to prohibit it for themselves. Mr. Clay says this was one of the great and just causes of complaint against Great Britain by the Colonies, and the best apology we can now make for having the institution amongst us. In that precise condition our Nebraska politicians have at last succeeded in placing our own new Territories; the government will not prohibit slavery within them, nor allow the people to prohibit it.

I defy any man to find any difference between the policy which originally planted slavery in these Colonies and that policy which now prevails in our new Territories. If it does not go into them, it is only because no individual wishes it to go. The Judge indulged himself doubtless to-day with the question as to what I am going to do with or about the Dred Scott decision. Well, Judge, will you please tell me what you did about the bank decision? Will you not graciously allow us to do with the Dred Scott decision precisely as you did with the bank decision? You succeeded in breaking down the moral effect of that decision: did you find it necessary to amend the Constitution, or to set up a court of negroes in order to do it?

There is one other point. Judge Douglas has a very affectionate leaning toward the Americans and Old Whigs. Last evening, in a sort of weeping tone, he described to us a death-bed scene. He had been called to the side of Mr. Clay, in his last moments, in order that the genius of "popular sovereignty" might duly descend from the dying man and settle upon him, the living and most worthy successor. He could do no less than promise that he would devote the remainder of his life to "popular sovereignty"; and then the great statesman departs in peace. By this part of the "plan of the campaign" the Judge has evidently promised himself that tears shall be drawn down the cheeks of all Old Whigs, as large as half-grown apples.

Mr. Webster, too, was mentioned; but it did not quite come to a death-bed scene as to him. It would be amusing, if it were not disgusting, to see how quick these compromise-breakers administer on the political effects of their dead adversaries, trumping up claims never before heard of, and dividing the assets among themselves. If I should be found dead to-morrow morning, nothing but my insignificance could prevent a speech being made on my authority, before the end of next week. It so happens that in that "popular sovereignty" with which Mr. Clay was identified, the Missouri Compromise was expressly reversed; and it was a little singular if Mr. Clay cast his mantle upon Judge Douglas on purpose to have that compromise repealed.

Again, the Judge did not keep faith with Mr. Clay when he first brought in his Nebraska Bill. He left the Missouri Compromise unrepealed, and in his report accompanying the bill he told the world he did it on purpose. The manes of Mr. Clay must have been in great agony till thirty days later, when "popular sovereignty" stood forth in all its glory.

One more thing. Last night Judge Douglas tormented himself with horrors about my disposition to make negroes perfectly equal with white men in social and political relations. He did not stop to show that I have said any such thing, or that it legitimately follows from anything I have said, but he rushes on with his assertions. I adhere to the Declaration of Independence. If Judge Douglas and his friends are not willing to stand by it, let them come up and amend it. Let them make it read that all men are created equal except negroes. Let us have it decided whether the Declaration of Independence, in this blessed year of 1858, shall be thus amended. In his construction of the Declaration last year, he said it only meant that Americans in America were equal to Englishmen in England. Then, when I pointed out to him that by that rule he excludes the Germans, the Irish, the Portuguese, and all the other people who have come among us since the Revolution, he reconstructs his construction. In his last speech he tells us it meant Europeans.

I press him a little further, and ask if it meant to include the Russians in Asia; or does he mean to exclude that vast population from the principles of our Declaration of Independence? I expect ere long he will introduce another amendment to his definition. He is not at all particular. He is satisfied with anything which does not endanger the nationalizing of negro slavery. It may draw white men down, but it must not lift negroes up. Who shall say, "I am the superior, and you are the inferior"?

My declarations upon this subject of negro slavery may be misrepresented, but cannot be misunderstood. I have said that I do not understand the Declaration to mean that all men were created equal in all respects. They are not our equal in color; but I suppose that it does mean to declare that all men are equal in some respects; they are equal in their right to "life, liberty, and the pursuit of happiness." Certainly the negro is not our equal in color,—perhaps not in many other respects; still, in the right to put into his mouth the bread that his own hands have earned, he is the equal of every other man, white or black. In pointing out that more has been given you, you cannot be justified in taking away the little which has been given him. All I ask for the negro is that if you do not like him, let him alone. If God gave him but little, that little let him enjoy.

When our government was established we had the institution of slavery among us. We were in a certain sense compelled to tolerate its existence. It was a sort of necessity. We had gone through our struggle and secured our own independence. The framers of the Constitution found the institution of slavery amongst their own institutions at the time. They found that by an effort to eradicate it they might lose much of what they had already gained. They were obliged to bow to the necessity. They gave power to Congress to abolish the slave trade at the end of twenty years. They also prohibited it in the Territories where it did not exist. They did what they could, and yielded to the necessity for the rest. I also yield to all which follows from that necessity. What I would most desire would be the separation of the white and black races.

One more point on this Springfield speech which Judge Douglas says he has read so carefully. I expressed my belief in the existence of a conspiracy to perpetuate and nationalize slavery. I did not profess to know it, nor do I now. I showed the part Judge Douglas had played in the string of facts constituting to my mind the proof of that conspiracy. I showed the parts played by others.

I charged that the people had been deceived into carrying the last Presidential election, by the impression that the people of the Territories might exclude slavery if they chose, when it was known in advance by the conspirators that the court was to decide that neither Congress nor the people could so exclude slavery. These charges are more distinctly made than anything else in the speech.

Judge Douglas has carefully read and reread that speech. He has not, so far as I know, contradicted those charges. In the two speeches which I heard he certainly did not. On this own tacit admission, I renew that charge. I charge him with having been a party to that conspiracy and to that deception for the sole purpose of nationalizing slavery.

# Correspondence Between Lincoln and Douglas Before the Debates

The following is the correspondence between the two rival candidates for the United States Senate:

## MR. LINCOLN TO MR. DOUGLAS

Chicago, Ill., July 24, 1858

HON. S. A. DOUGLAS: My dear Sir,—Will it be agreeable to you to make an arrangement for you and myself to divide time, and address the same audiences the present canvass? Mr. Judd, who will hand you this, is authorized to receive your answer; and, if agreeable to you, to enter into the terms of such arrangement.

Your obedient servant,

A. LINCOLN

## MR. DOUGLAS TO MR. LINCOLN

Chicago, July 24, 1858

HON. A. LINCOLN: Dear Sir,—Your note of this date, in which you inquire if it would be agreeable to me to make an arrangement to divide the time and address the same audiences during the present canvass, was handed me by Mr. Judd. Recent events have interposed difficulties in the way of such an arrangement.

I went to Springfield last week for the purpose of conferring with the Democratic State Central Committee upon the mode of conducting the canvass, and with them, and under their advice, made a list of appointments covering the entire period until late in October. The people of the several localities have been notified of the times and places of the meetings. Those appointments have all been made for Democratic meetings, and arrangements have been made by which the Democratic candidates for Congress, for the Legislature, and other offices, will be present and address the people. It is evident, therefore, that these various candidates, in connection with myself, will occupy the whole time of the day and evening, and leave no opportunity for other speeches.

Besides, there is another consideration which should be kept in mind. It has been suggested recently that an arrangement had been made to bring out a third candidate for the United States Senate, who, with yourself, should canvass the State in opposition to me, with no other purpose than to insure my defeat, by dividing the Democratic party for your benefit. If I should make this arrangement with you, it is more than probable that this other candidate, who has a common object with you, would desire to become a party to it, and claim the right to speak from the same stand; so that he and you, in concert, might be able to take the opening and closing speech in every case.

I cannot refrain from expressing my surprise, if it was your original intention to invite such an arrangement, that you should have waited until after I had made my appointments, inasmuch as we were both here in Chicago together for several days after my arrival, and again at Bloomington, Atlanta, Lincoln, and Springfield, where it was well known I went for the purpose of consulting with the State Central Committee, and agreeing upon the plan of the campaign.

While, under these circumstances, I do not feel at liberty to make any arrangements which would deprive the Democratic candidates for Congress, State offices, and the Legislature from participating in the discussion at the various meetings designated by the Democratic State Central Committee, I will, in order to accommodate you as far as it is in my power to do so, take the responsibility of making an arrangement with you for a discussion between us at one prominent point in each Congressional District in the State, except the Second and Sixth districts, where we have both spoken, and in each of which cases you had the concluding speech. If agreeable to you, I will indicate the following places as those most suitable in the several Congressional districts at which we should speak, to wit: Freeport, Ottawa, Galesburg, Quincy, Alton, Jonesboro, and Charleston. I will confer with you at the earliest convenient opportunity in regard to the mode of conducting the debate, the times of meeting at the several places, subject to the condition that where appointments have already been made by the Democratic State Central Committee at any of those places, I must insist upon you meeting me at the times specified.

Very respectfully, your most obedient servant,

S. A. DOUGLAS

## Mr. Lincoln to Mr. Douglas

Springfield, July 29, 1858

HON. S. A. DOUGLAS: Dear Sir,—Yours of the 24th in relation to an arrangement to divide time, and address the same audiences, is received; and, in apology for not sooner replying, allow me to say, that when I sat by you at dinner yesterday, I was not aware that you had answered my note, nor, certainly, that my own note had been presented to you. An hour after, I saw a copy of your answer in the Chicago *Times,* and reaching home, I found the original awaiting me. Protesting that your insinuations of attempted unfairness on my part are unjust, and with the hope that you did not very considerately make them, I proceed to reply. To your statement that "It has been suggested, recently, that an arrangement had been made to bring out a third candidate for the United States Senate, who, with your-self, should canvass the state in opposition to me," etc., I can only say, that such suggestion must have been made by yourself, for certainly none such has been made by or to me, or otherwise, to my knowledge. Surely you did not *deliberately* conclude, as you insinuate, that I was expecting to draw you into an arrangement of terms, to be agreed on by yourself, by which a third candidate and myself, "in concert, might be able to take the opening and closing speech in every case."

As to your surprise that I did not sooner make the proposal to divide time with you, I can only say, I made it as soon as I resolved to make it. I did not know but that such proposal would come from you; I waited, respectfully, to see. It may have been well known to you that you went to Springfield for the purpose of agreeing on the plan of campaign; but it was not so known to me. When your appointments were announced in the papers, extending only to the 21st of August, I for the first time considered it certain that you would make no proposal to me, and then resolved that, if my friends concurred, I would make one to you. As soon thereafter as I could see and consult with friends satisfactorily, I did make the proposal. It did not occur to me that the proposed arrangement could derange your plans after the latest of your appointments already made. After that, there was, before the election, largely over two months of clear time.

For you to say that we have already spoken at Chicago and Springfield, and that on both occasions I had the concluding speech, is hardly a fair statement. The truth rather is this: At Chicago, July 9th, you made a carefully prepared con-clusion on my speech of June 16th. Twenty-four hours after, I made a hasty con-clusion on yours of the 9th. You had six days to prepare, and concluded on me again at Bloomington on the 16th. Twenty-four hours after, I concluded again on you at Springfield. In the mean time, you had made another conclusion on me at

Springfield, which I did not hear, and of the contents of which I knew nothing when I spoke; so that your speech made in daylight, and mine at night, of the 17th, at Springfield, were both made in perfect independence of each other. The dates of making all these speeches will show, I think, that in the matter of time for preparation the advantage has all been on your side, and that none of the external circumstances have stood to my advantage.

I agree to an arrangement for us to speak at the seven places you have named, and at your own times, provided you name the times at once, so that I as well as you can have to myself the time not covered by the arrangement. As to the other details, I wish perfect reciprocity and no more. I wish as much time as you, and that conclusions shall alternate. That is all.

Your obedient servant,

A. LINCOLN

P.S.—As matters now stand, I shall be at no more of your exclusive meetings, and for about a week from to-day a letter from you will reach me at Springfield.

A.L.

### MR. DOUGLAS TO MR. LINCOLN

Bement, Piatt Co., Ill., July 30, 1858

Dear Sir,—Your letter dated yesterday, accepting my proposition for a joint discussion at one prominent point in each Congressional District, as stated in my previous letter, was received this morning.

The times and places designated are as follows

| | | | |
|---|---|---|---|
| Ottawa, La Salle County | August | 21st, | 1858 |
| Freeport, Stephenson County | " | 27th, | " |
| Jonesboro, Union County | September | 15th, | " |
| Charleston, Coles County | " | 18th, | " |
| Galesburgh, Knox County | October | 7th, | 1858 |
| Quincy, Adams County | " | 13th, | " |
| Alton, Madison County | " | 15th, | " |

I agree to your suggestion that we shall alternately open and close the discussion. I will speak at Ottawa one hour, you can reply, occupying an hour and a half, and I will then follow for half an hour. At Freeport, you shall open the discussion and speak one hour; I will follow for an hour and a half, and you can then reply for half an hour. We will alternate in like manner in each successive place.

Very respectfully, your obedient servant,

S. A. Douglas

Hon. A. Lincoln, Springfield, Ill.

Mr. Lincoln to Mr. Douglas

Springfield, July 31, 1858

Hon. S. A. Douglas: Dear Sir,—Yours of yesterday, naming places, times, and terms for joint discussions between us, was received this morning. Although, by the terms, as you propose, you take *four* openings and closes, to my *three*, I accede, and thus close the arrangement. I direct this to you at Hillsboro, and shall try to have both your letter and this appear in the *Journal* and *Register* of Monday morning.

Your obedient servant,

A. Lincoln

# First Joint Debate, at Ottawa

*August 21, 1858*

### Mr. Douglas's Opening Speech

Ladies and Gentlemen: I appear before you to-day for the purpose of discussing the leading political topics which now agitate the public mind. By an arrangement between Mr. Lincoln and myself we are present here to-day for the purpose of having a joint discussion, as the representatives of the two great political parties of the State and Union, upon the principles in issue between those parties; and this vast concourse of people shows the deep feeling which pervades the public mind in regard to the questions dividing us.

Prior to 1854 this country was divided into two great political parties, known as the Whig and Democratic parties. Both were national and patriotic, advocating principles that were universal in their application. An old line Whig could proclaim his principles in Louisiana and Massachusetts alike. Whig principles had no boundary sectional line; they were not limited by the Ohio River, nor by the Potomac, nor by the line of the free and slave States, but applied and were proclaimed wherever the Constitution ruled or the American flag waved over the American soil. So it was, and so it is with the great Democratic party, which, from the days of Jefferson until this period, has proven itself to be the historic party of this nation. While the Whig and Democratic parties differed in regard to a bank, the tariff, distribution, the specie circular, and the sub-treasury, they agreed on the great slavery question which now agitates the Union. I say that the Whig party and the Democratic party agreed on this slavery question, while they differed on those matters of expediency to which I have referred. The Whig party and the Democratic party jointly adopted the Compromise measures of 1850 as the basis of a proper and just solution of this slavery question in all its forms. Clay was the great leader, with Webster on his right and Cass on his left, and sustained by the patriots in the Whig and Democratic ranks who had devised and enacted the Compromise measures of 1850.

In 1851 the Whig party and the Democratic party united in Illinois in adopting resolutions indorsing and approving the principles of the Compromise measures of 1850, as the proper adjustment of that question. In 1852, when the Whig party assembled in convention at Baltimore for the purpose of nominating a candidate for the presidency, the first thing it did was to declare the Compromise measures of 1850, in substance and in principle, a suitable adjustment of that question. [Here the speaker was interrupted by loud and long-continued applause.] My friends, silence will be more acceptable to me in the discussion of these questions than applause. I desire to address myself to your judgment, your understanding, and your consciences, and not to your passions or your enthusiasm. When the Democratic Convention assembled in Baltimore in the same year, for the purpose of nominating a Democratic candidate for the presidency, it also adopted the Compromise measures of 1850 as the basis of Democratic action. Thus you see that up to 1853–'54, the Whig party and the Democratic party both stood on the same platform with regard to the slavery question. That platform was the right of the people of each State and each Territory to decide their local and domestic institutions for themselves, subject only to the Federal Constitution.

During the session of Congress of 1853–'54, I introduced into the Senate of the United States a bill to organize the Territories of Kansas and Nebraska on that principle which had been adopted in the Compromise measures of 1850, approved by the Whig party and the Democratic party in Illinois in 1851, and indorsed by the Whig party and the Democratic party in National Convention in 1852. In order that there might be no misunderstanding in relation to the principle involved in the Kansas and Nebraska Bill, I put forth the true intent and meaning of this Act in these words: "It is the true intent and meaning of this Act not to legislate slavery into any State or Territory, or to exclude it therefrom, but to leave the people thereof perfectly free to form and regulate their domestic institutions in their own way, subject only to the Federal Constitution." Thus you see that up to 1854, when the Kansas and Nebraska Bill was brought into Congress for the purpose of carrying out the principles which both parties had up to that time indorsed and approved, there had been no division in this country in regard to that principle except the opposition of the Abolitionists. In the House of Representatives of the Illinois Legislature, upon a resolution asserting that principle, every Whig and every Democrat in the House voted in the affirmative, and only four men voted against it, and those four were old line Abolitionists.

In 1854, Mr. Abraham Lincoln and Mr. Trumbull entered into an arrangement, one with the other, and each with his respective friends, to dissolve the old Whig party on the one hand, and to dissolve the old Democratic party on the other, and to connect the members of both into an Abolition party, under the name and disguise of a Republican party. The terms of that arrangement between Mr. Lincoln and Mr. Trumbull have been published to the world by Mr. Lincoln's special friend James H. Matheny, Esq., and they were, that Lincoln should have Shields's place in the United States Senate, which was then about to become vacant, and that Trumbull should have my seat when my term expired. Lincoln went to work to Abolitionize the old Whig party all over the State, pretending that he was then as good a Whig as ever; and Trumbull went to work in his part of the State preaching Abolitionism in its milder and lighter form, and trying to Abolitionize the Democratic party, and bring old Democrats handcuffed and bound hand and foot into the Abolition camp. In pursuance of the arrangement, the parties met at Springfield in October, 1854, and proclaimed their new platform. Lincoln was to bring into the Abolition camp the old line Whigs, and transfer them over to Giddings, Chase, Fred Douglass, and Parson Lovejoy, who were ready to receive them and christen them in their new faith. They laid down on that occasion a platform for their new Republican party, which was to be thus constructed. I have the resolutions of their State Convention then held, which was the first mass State Convention ever held in Illinois by the Black Republican party, and I now hold them in my hands, and will read a part of them, and cause the others to be printed. Here are the most important and material resolutions of this Abolition platform:

1. *Resolved,* That we believe this truth to be self-evident, that when parties become subversive of the ends for which they are established, or incapable of restoring the government to the true principles of the Constitution, it is the right and duty of the people to dissolve the political bands by which they may have been connected therewith, and to organize new parties, upon such principles and with such views as the circumstances and exigencies of the nation may demand.

2. *Resolved,* That the times imperatively demand the reorganization of parties, and, repudiating all previous party attachments, names and predilections, we unite ourselves in defence of the liberty and Constitution of the country, and will hereafter co-operate as the Republican party, pledged to the accomplishment of the following purposes: To bring the administration of the government back to the control of first principles; to restore Nebraska and Kansas to the position of free Territories; that, as the Constitution of the United States vests in the States, and not in Congress, the power to legislate for the extradition of fugitives from labor, to repeal and entirely abrogate the Fugitive Slave law; to restrict slavery to those States in which it exists; to prohibit the admission of any more Slave States into the Union; to abolish slavery in the District of Columbia; to exclude slavery from all the Territories over which the General Government has exclusive juris-

diction; and to resist the acquirement of any more Territories, unless the practice of slavery therein forever shall have been prohibited.

3. *Resolved,* That in furtherance of these principles we will use such constitutional and lawful means as shall seem best adapted to their accomplishment, and that we will support no man for office, under the General or State Government, who is not positively and fully committed to the support of these principles, and whose personal character and conduct is not a guarantee that he is reliable, and who shall not have abjured old party allegiance and ties.

Now, gentlemen, your Black Republicans have cheered every one of those propositions, and yet I venture to say that you cannot get Mr. Lincoln to come out and say that he is now in favor of each one of them. That these propositions, one and all, constitute the platform of the Black Republican party of this day, I have no doubt; and when you were not aware for what purpose I was reading them, your Black Republicans cheered them as good Black Republican doctrines. My object in reading these resolutions was to put the question to Abraham Lincoln this day, whether he now stands and will stand by each article in that creed and carry it out. I desire to know whether Mr. Lincoln to-day stands, as he did in 1854, in favor of the unconditional repeal of the Fugitive Slave law, I desire him to answer whether he stands pledged to-day, as he did in 1854, against the admission of any more slave States into the Union, even if the people want them. I want to know whether he stands pledged against the admission of a new State into the Union with such a constitution as the people of that State may see fit to make. I want to know whether he stands to-day pledged to the abolition of slavery in the District of Columbia. I desire him to answer whether he stands pledged to the prohibition of the slave trade between the different States. I desire to know whether he stands pledged to prohibit slavery in all the Territories of the United States, north as well as south of the Missouri Compromise line. I desire him to answer whether he is opposed to the acquisition of any more territory, unless slavery is prohibited therein. I want his answer to these questions. Your affirmative cheers in favor of this Abolition platform is not satisfactory. I ask Abraham Lincoln to answer these questions, in order that, when I trot him down to lower Egypt, I may put the same questions to him. My principles are the same everywhere. I can proclaim them alike in the North, the South, the East, and the West. My principles will apply wherever the Constitution prevails and the American flag waves. I desire to know whether Mr. Lincoln's principles will bear transplanting from Ottawa to Jonesboro? I put these questions to him to-day distinctly and ask an answer. I have a right to an answer, for I quote from the platform of the Republican party, made by himself and others at the time that party was formed, and the bargain made by Lincoln to dissolve and kill the old Whig party, and transfer its members, bound hand and foot, to the Abolition party, under the direction of Giddings and Fred Douglass. In the remarks I have made on this platform, and the position of Mr. Lincoln upon it, I mean nothing personally disrespectful or unkind to that gentleman. I have known him for nearly twenty-five years. There were many points of sympathy between us when we first got acquainted. We were both comparatively boys, and both struggling with poverty in a strange land. I was a school-teacher in the town of Winchester, and he a flourishing grocery-keeper in the town of Salem. He was more successful in his occupation than I was in mine, and hence more fortunate in this world's goods. Lincoln is one of those peculiar men who perform with admirable skill everything which they undertake. I made as good a school-teacher as I could, and when a cabinet-maker I made a good bedstead and tables, although my old boss said I succeeded better with bureaus and secretaries than anything else; but I believe that Lincoln was always more successful in business than I, for his business enabled him to get into the Legislature. I met him there, however, and had a sympathy with him, because of the up-hill struggle we both had in life. He was then just as good at telling an anecdote as now. He could beat any of the boys wrestling, or running a foot-race, in pitching quoits or tossing a copper; could ruin more liquor than all the boys of the town together; and the dignity and impartiality with which he presided at a horse-race or fist-fight excited the admiration and won the praise of everybody that was present and participated. I sympathized with him because he was struggling with difficulties and so was I. Mr. Lincoln served with me in the Legislature in 1836, when we both retired, and he subsided, or became submerged, and he was lost sight of as a public man for some years. In 1846, when Wilmot introduced his celebrated proviso, and the Abolition tornado swept over the country, Lincoln again turned up as a member of Congress from the Sangamon district. I was then in the Senate of the United States, and was glad to welcome my old friend and companion. Whilst in Congress, he distinguished himself by his opposition to the Mexican war, taking the side of the common enemy against his own country; and when he returned home he found that the indignation of the people followed him everywhere, and he was again submerged, or obliged to retire into private life, forgotten by his former friends. He came up again in 1854, just in time to make this Abolition or Black Republican platform, in company with Giddings, Lovejoy, Chase, and Fred Douglass, for the Republican party to stand upon. Trumbull, too, was one of our own contemporaries. He was born and raised in old Connecticut, was bred a Federalist, but, removing to Georgia, turned

Nullifier when Nullification was popular, and as soon as he disposed of his clocks and wound up his business, migrated to Illinois, turned politician and lawyer here, and made his appearance in 1841 as a member of the Legislature. He became noted as the author of the scheme to repudiate a large portion of the State debt of Illinois, which, if successful, would have brought infamy and disgrace upon the fair escutcheon of our glorious State. The odium attached to that measure consigned him to oblivion for a time. I helped to do it. I walked into a public meeting in the hall of the House of Representatives, and replied to his repudiating speeches, and resolutions were carried over his head denouncing repudiation, and asserting the moral and legal obligation of Illinois to pay every dollar of the debt she owed, and every bond that bore her seal. Trumbull's malignity has followed me since I thus defeated his infamous scheme.

These two men having formed this combination to Abolitionize the old Whig party and the old Democratic party, and put themselves into the Senate of the United States, in pursuance of their bargain, are now carrying out that arrangement. Matheny states that Trumbull broke faith; that the bargain was that Lincoln should be the Senator in Shields's place, and Trumbull was to wait for mine; and the story goes that Trumbull cheated Lincoln: having control of four or five Abolitionized Democrats who were holding over in the Senate, he would not let them vote for Lincoln, and which obliged the rest of the Abolitionists to support him in order to secure an Abolition Senator. There are a number of authorities for the truth of this besides Matheny, and I suppose that even Mr. Lincoln will not deny it.

Mr. Lincoln demands that he shall have the place intended for Trumbull, as Trumbull cheated him and got his, and Trumbull is stumping the State traducing me for the purpose of securing the position for Lincoln, in order to quiet him. It was in consequence of this arrangement that the Republican Convention was empanelled to instruct for Lincoln and nobody else, and it was on this account that they passed resolutions that he was their first, their last, and their only choice. Archy Williams was nowhere, Browning was nobody, Wentworth was not to be considered; they had no man in the Republican party for the place except Lincoln, for the reason that he demanded that they should carry out the arrangement.

Having formed this new party for the benefit of deserters from Whiggery, and deserters from Democracy, and having laid down the Abolition platform which I have read, Lincoln now takes his stand and proclaims his Abolition doctrines. Let me read a part of them. In his speech at Springfield to the convention which nominated him for the Senate, he said:

In my opinion it will not cease until a crisis shall have been reached and passed. "A house divided against itself cannot stand." I believe this government *cannot endure permanently half slave and half free.* I do not expect the Union to be dissolved,— I do not expect the house to fall; *but I do expect it will cease to be divided.* It will become all one thing, or all the other. Either the opponents of slavery *will arrest the further spread of it,* and place it where the public mind shall rest in the belief *that it is in the course of ultimate extinction,* or its advocates *will push it forward till it shall become alike lawful in all the States,*—old as well as new, North as well as South.

["Good," "Good," and cheers.]

I am delighted to hear you Black Republicans say "good." I have no doubt that doctrine expresses your sentiments, and I will prove to you now, if you will listen to me, that it is revolutionary, and destructive of the existence of this government. Mr. Lincoln, in the extract from which I have read, says that this government cannot endure permanently in the same condition in which it was made by its framers,— divided into free and slave States. He says that it has existed for about seventy years thus divided, and yet he tells you that it cannot endure permanently on the same principles and in the same relative condition in which our fathers made it. Why can it not exist divided into free and slave States? Washington, Jefferson, Franklin, Madison, Hamilton, Jay, and the great men of that day, made this government divided into free and slave States, and left each State perfectly free to do as it pleased on the subject of slavery. Why can it not exist on the same principles on which our fathers made it? They knew when they framed the Constitution that in a country as wide and broad as this, with such a variety of climate, production, and interest, the people necessarily required different laws and institutions in different localities. They knew that the laws and regulations which would suit the granite hills of New Hampshire would be unsuited to the rice plantations of South Carolina, and they therefore provided that each State should retain its own Legislature and its own sovereignty, with the full and complete power to do as it pleased within its own limits, in all that was local and not national. One of the reserved rights of the States was the right to regulate the relations between master and servant on the slavery question. At the time the Constitution was framed, there were thirteen States in the Union, twelve of which were slaveholding States and one a free State. Suppose this doctrine of uniformity preached by Mr. Lincoln, that the States should all be free or all be slave, had prevailed, and what would have been the result? Of course, the twelve slaveholding States would have overruled the one free State, and slavery would have been fastened by a constitutional provision on every inch of the American Republic, instead of being left, as our fathers wisely left it, to each State to decide for itself. Here I assert that uniformity in the local laws and institutions of the different States is neither possible nor desirable. If uniformity had been adopted when the government was established, it must inevitably have been the uniformity of slavery everywhere, or else the uniformity of negro citizenship and negro equality everywhere.

We are told by Lincoln that he is utterly opposed to the Dred Scott decision, and will not submit to it, for the reason that he says it deprive the negro of the rights and privileges of citizenship. That is the first and main reason which he assigns for his warfare on the Supreme Court of the United States and its decision. I ask you, are you in favor of conferring upon the negro the rights and privileges of citizenship? Do you desire to strike out of our State Constitution that clause which keeps slaves and free negroes out of the State, and allow the free negroes to flow in, and cover your prairies with black settlements? Do you desire to turn this beautiful State into a free negro colony, in order that when Missouri abolishes slavery she can send one hundred thousand emancipated slaves into Illinois, to become citizens and voters, on an equality with yourselves? If you desire negro citizenship, if you desire to allow them to come into the State and settle with the white man, if you desire them to vote on an equality with yourselves, and to make them eligible to office, to serve on juries, and to adjudge your rights, then support Mr. Lincoln and the Black Republican party, who are in favor of the citizenship of the negro. For one, I am opposed to negro citizenship in any and every form, I believe this government was made on the white basis. I believe it was made by white men, for the benefit of white men and their posterity forever, and I am in favor of confining citizenship to white men, men of European birth and descent, instead of conferring it upon negroes, Indians, and other inferior races.

Mr. Lincoln, following the example and lead of all the little Abolition orators, who go around and lecture in the basements of schools and churches, reads from the Declaration of Independence that all men were created equal, and then asks, How can you deprive a negro of that equality which God and the Declaration of Independence award to him? He and they maintain that negro equality is guaranteed by the laws of God, and that it is asserted in the Declaration of Independence. If they think so, of course they have a right to do so, and so vote. I do not question Mr. Lincoln's conscientious belief that the negro was made his equal, and hence is his brother, but for my own part, I do not regard the negro as my equal, and positively deny that he is my brother, or any kin to me whatever. Lincoln has evidently learned by heart Parson Lovejoy's catechism. He can repeat it as well as Farnsworth, and he is worthy of a medal from Father Giddings and Fred Douglass for his Abolitionism. He holds that the negro was born his equal and yours, and that he was endowed with equality by the Almighty, and that no human law can deprive him of these rights, which were guaranteed to him by the Supreme Ruler of the Universe. Now I do not believe that the Almighty ever intended the negro to be the equal of the white man. If He did, He has been a long time demonstrating the fact. For thousands of years the negro has been a race upon the earth, and during all that time, in all latitudes and climates, wherever he has wandered or been taken, he has been inferior to the race which he has there met. He belongs to an inferior race, and must always occupy an inferior position. I do not hold that because the negro is our inferior that therefore he ought to be a slave. By no means can such a conclusion be drawn from what I have said. On the contrary, I hold that humanity and Christianity both require that the negro shall have and enjoy every right, every privilege, and every immunity consistent with the safety of the society in which he lives. On that point, I presume, there can be no diversity of opinion. You and I are bound to extend to our inferior and dependent beings every right, every privilege, every facility and immunity consistent with the public good.

The question then arises, What rights and privileges are consistent with the public good? This is a question which each State and each Territory must decide for itself. Illinois has decided it for herself. We have provided that the negro shall not be a slave and we have also provided that he shall not be a citizen, but protect him in his civil rights, in his life, his person and his property, only depriving him of all political rights whatsoever, and refusing to put him on an equality with the white man. That policy of Illinois is satisfactory to the Democratic party and to me; and if it were to the Republicans, there would then be no question upon the subject. But the Republicans say that he ought to be made a citizen, and when he becomes a citizen he becomes your equal, with all your rights and privileges. They assert the Dred Scott decision to be monstrous because it denies that the negro is or can be a citizen under the Constitution. Now, I hold that Illinois had a right to abolish and prohibit slavery as she did, and I hold that Kentucky has the same right to continue and protect slavery that Illinois had to abolish it. I hold that New York had as much right to abolish slavery as Virginia has to continue it, and that each and every State of this Union is a sovereign power, with the right to do as it pleases upon this question of slavery, and upon all its domestic institutions. Slavery is not the only question which comes up in this controversy. There is a far more important one to you, and that is,—What shall be done with the free negro? We have settled the slavery question as far as we are concerned; we have prohibited it in Illinois forever;

and in doing so, I think we have done wisely, and there is no man in the State who would be more strenuous in his opposition to the introduction of slavery than I would. But when we settled it for ourselves, we exhausted all our power over that subject. We have done our whole duty, and can do no more. We must leave each and every other State to decide for itself the same question. In relation to the policy to be pursued toward the free negroes, we have said that they shall not vote; whilst Maine, on the other hand, has said that they shall vote. Maine is a sovereign State, and has the power to regulate the qualifications of voters within her limits. I would never consent to confer the right of voting and of citizenship upon a negro; but still I am not going to quarrel with Maine for differing from me in opinion. Let Maine take care of her own negroes, and fix the qualifications of her own voters to suit herself, without interfering with Illinois, and Illinois will not interfere with Maine. So with the State of New York. She allows the negro to vote, provided he owns two hundred and fifty dollars' worth of property but not otherwise. While I would not make any distinction whatever between a negro who held property and one who did not, yet if the sovereign State of New York chooses to make that distinction, it is her business and not mine, and I will not quarrel with her for it. She can do as she pleases on this question if she minds her own business, and we will do the same thing. Now, my friends, if we will only act conscientiously and rigidly upon this great principle of popular sovereignty, which guarantees to each State and Territory the right to do as it pleases on all things, local and domestic, instead of Congress interfering, we will continue at peace one with another. Why should Illinois be at war with Missouri, or Kentucky with Ohio, or Virginia with New York, merely because their institutions differ? Our fathers intended that our institutions should differ. They knew that the North and the South, having different climates, productions, and interests, required different institutions. This doctrine of Mr. Lincoln, of uniformity among the institutions of the different States, is a new doctrine, never dreamed of by Washington, Madison, or the framers of this government. Mr. Lincoln and the Republican party set themselves up as wiser than these men who made this government, which has flourished for seventy years under the principle of popular sovereignty, recognizing the right of each State to do as it pleased. Under that principle, we have grown from a nation of three or four millions to a nation of about thirty millions of people; we have crossed the Alleghany Mountains and filled up the whole Northwest, turning the prairie into a garden, and building up churches and schools, thus spreading civilization and Christianity where before there was nothing but savage barbarism. Under that principle we have become, from a feeble nation, the most powerful on the face of the earth; and if we only adhere to that principle, we can go forward increasing in territory, in power, in strength, and in glory until the Republic of America shall be the North Star that shall guide the friends of freedom throughout the civilized world. And why can we not adhere to the great principle of self-government, upon which our institutions were originally based? I believe that this new doctrine preached by Mr. Lincoln and his party will dissolve the Union if it succeeds. They are trying to array all the Northern States in one body against the South, to excite a sectional war between the free States and the slave States, in order that the one or the other may be driven to the wall.

I am told that my time is out. Mr. Lincoln will now address you for an hour and a half, and I will then occupy an half hour in replying to him.

## MR. LINCOLN'S REPLY

MY FELLOW-CITIZENS: When a man hears himself somewhat misrepresented, it provokes him,—at least, I find it so with myself; but when misrepresentation becomes very gross and palpable, it is more apt to amuse him. The first thing I see fit to notice is the fact that Judge Douglas alleges, after running through the history of the old Democratic and the old Whig parties, that Judge Trumbull and myself made an arrangement in 1854, by which I was to have the place of General Shields in the United States Senate, and Judge Trumbull was to have the place of Judge Douglas. Now, all I have to say upon that subject is that I think no man—not even Judge Douglas—can prove it, *because it is not true*. I have no doubt he is "*conscientious*" in saying it. As to those resolutions that he took such a length of time to read, as being the platform of the Republican party in 1854, I say I never had anything to do with them, and I think Trumbull never had. Judge Douglas cannot show that either of us ever did have anything to do with them. I believe *this* is true about those resolutions: There was a call for a convention to form a Republican party at Springfield, and I think that my friend Mr. Lovejoy, who is here upon this stand, had a hand in it. I think this is true, and I think if he will remember accurately he will be able to recollect that he tried to get me into it, and I would not go in. I believe it is also true that I went away from Springfield when the convention was in session, to attend court in Tazewell County. It is true they did place my name, though without authority, upon the committee, and afterward wrote me to attend the meeting of the committee; but I refused to do so, and I never had anything to do with that organization. This is the plain truth about all that matter of the resolutions.

Now, about this story that Judge Douglas tells of Trumbull bargaining to sell out the old Democratic party, and Lincoln agreeing to sell out the old Whig party, I have the means of *knowing* about that: Judge Douglas cannot have; and

I know there is no substance to it whatever. Yet I have no doubt he is "*conscientious*" about it. I know that after Mr. Lovejoy got into the Legislature that winter, he complained of me that I had told all the old Whigs of his district that the old Whig party was good enough for them, and some of them voted against him because I told them so. Now, I have no means of totally disproving such charges as this which the Judge makes. A man cannot prove a negative; but he has a right to claim that when a man makes an affirmative charge, he must offer some proof to show the truth of what he says. I certainly cannot introduce testimony to show the negative about things, but I have a right to claim that if a man says he *knows* a thing, then he must show *how* he knows it. I always have a right to claim this, and it is not satisfactory to me that he may be "conscientious" on the subject.

Now, gentlemen, I hate to waste my time on such things; but in regard to that general Abolition tilt that Judge Douglas makes, when he says that I was engaged at that time in selling out and Abolitionizing the old Whig party, I hope you will permit me to read a part of a printed speech that I made then at Peoria, which will show altogether a different view of the position I took in that contest of 1854.

A VOICE: "Put on your specs."

MR. LINCOLN: Yes, sir, I am obliged to do so; I am no longer a young man.

> This is the *repeal* of the Missouri Compromise.* The foregoing history may not be precisely accurate in every particular, but I am sure it is sufficiently so for all the uses I shall attempt to make of it, and in it we have before us the chief materials enabling us to correctly judge whether the repeal of the Missouri Compromise is right or wrong.
>
> I think, and shall try to show, that it is wrong—wrong in its direct effect, letting slavery into Kansas and Nebraska, and wrong in its prospective principle, allowing it to spread to every other part of the wide world where men can be found inclined to take it.
>
> This *declared* indifference, but, as I must think, covert *real* zeal for the spread of slavery, I cannot but hate. I hate it because of the monstrous injustice of slavery itself. I hate it because it deprives our republican example of its just influence in the

---

* This extract from Mr. Lincoln's Peoria speech of 1854 was read by him in the Ottawa debate, but was not reported fully or accurately in either the *Times* or *Press and Tribune*. It is inserted now as necessary to a complete report of the debate.

world,—enables the enemies of free institutions, with plausibility, to taunt us as hypocrites; causes the real friends of freedom to doubt our sincerity, and especially because it forces so many really good men amongst ourselves into an open war with the very fundamental principles of civil liberty,—criticising the Declaration of Independence, and insisting that there is no right principle of action but *self-interest.*

Before proceeding, let me say I think I have no prejudice against the Southern people. They are just what we would be in their situation. If slavery did not now exist among them, they would not introduce it. If it did now exist among us, we should not instantly give it up. This I believe of the masses north and south. Doubtless there are individuals on both sides who would not hold slaves under any circumstances; and others who would gladly introduce slavery anew, if it were out of existence. We know that some Southern men do free their slaves, go north, and become tip-top Abolitionists; while some Northern ones go south and become most cruel slave-masters.

When Southern people tell us they are no more responsible for the origin of slavery than we, I acknowledge the fact. When it is said that the institution exists, and that it is very difficult to get rid of it, in any satisfactory way, I can understand and appreciate the saying. I will not blame them for not doing what I should not know how to do myself. If all earthly power were given me, I should not know what to do, as to the existing institution. My first impulse would be to free all the slaves and send them to Liberia,—to their own native land. But a moment's reflection would convince me that whatever of high hope (as I think there is), there may be in this in the long run, its sudden execution is impossible. If they were all landed there in a day, they would all perish in the next ten days; and there are not surplus shipping and surplus money enough in the world to carry them there in many times ten days. What then? Free them all and keep them among us as underlings? Is it quite certain that this betters their condition? I think I would not hold one in slavery, at any rate; yet the point is not clear enough to me to denounce people upon. What next? Free them, and make them politically and socially our equals? My own feelings will not admit of this; and if mine would, we well know that those of the great mass of white people will not. Whether this feeling accords with justice and sound judgment, is not the sole question, if, indeed, it is any part of it. A universal feeling, whether well or ill founded, cannot be safely disregarded. We cannot, then, make them equals. It does seem to me that systems of gradual emancipation might be adopted; but for their tardiness in this I will not undertake to judge our brethren of the South.

When they remind us of their constitutional rights, I acknowledge them, not grudgingly, but fully and fairly; and I would give them any legislation for the reclaiming of their fugitives, which should not, in its stringency, be more likely to carry a free man into slavery than our ordinary criminal laws are to hang an innocent one.

But all this, to my judgment, furnishes no more excuse for permitting slavery to go into our own free territory than it would for reviving the African slave-trade by law. The law which forbids the bringing of slaves *from* Africa, and that which has so long forbid the taking of them *to* Nebraska, can hardly be distinguished on any moral principle; and the repeal of the former could find quite as plausible excuses as that of the latter.

I have reason to know that Judge Douglas *knows* that I said this. I think he has the answer here to one of the questions he put to me. I do not mean to allow him to catechise me unless he pays back for it in kind. I will not answer questions one after another, unless he reciprocates; but as he has made this inquiry, and I have answered it before, he has got it without my getting anything in return. He has got my answer on the Fugitive Slave law.

Now, gentlemen, I don't want to read at any greater length; but this is the true complexion of all I have ever said in regard to the institution of slavery and the black race. This is the whole of it; and anything that argues me into his idea of perfect social and political equality with the negro is but a specious and fantastic arrangement of words, by which a man can prove a horse-chestnut to be a chestnut horse. I will say here, while upon this subject, that I have no purpose, directly or indirectly, to interfere with the institution of slavery in the States where it exists. I believe I have no lawful right to do so, and I have no inclination to do so. I have no purpose to introduce political and social equality between the white and the black races. There is a physical difference between the two which, in my judgment, will probably forever forbid their living together upon the footing of perfect equality; and inasmuch as it becomes a necessity that there must be a difference, I, as well as Judge Douglas, am in favor of the race to which I belong having the superior position. I have never said anything to the contrary, but I hold that, notwithstanding all this, there is no reason in the world why the negro is not entitled to all the natural rights enumerated in the Declaration of Independence,—the right to life, liberty, and the pursuit of happiness. I hold that he is as much entitled to these as the white man. I agree with Judge Douglas he is not my equal in many respects,—certainly not in color, perhaps not in moral or intellectual endowment. But in the right to eat the bread, without the leave of anybody else, which his own hand earns, *he is my equal, and the equal of Judge Douglas, and the equal of every living man.*

Now I pass on to consider one or two more of these little follies. The Judge is wofully at fault about his early friend Lincoln being a "grocery-keeper." I don't know as it would be a great sin, if I had been; but he is mistaken. Lincoln never kept a grocery anywhere in the world. It is true that Lincoln did work the latter part of one winter in a little stillhouse, up at the head of a hollow. And so I think my friend the Judge is equally at fault when he charges me at the time when I was in Congress of having opposed our soldiers who were fighting in the Mexican war. The Judge did not make his charge very distinctly, but I can tell you what he can prove, by referring to the record. You remember I was an old Whig, and whenever the Democratic party tried to get me to vote that the war had been righteously begun by the President, I would not do it. But whenever they asked for any money, or landwarrants, or anything to pay the soldiers there, during all that time, I gave the same vote that Judge Douglas did. You can think as you please as to whether that was consistent. Such is the truth; and the Judge has the right to make all he can out of it. But when he, by a general charge, conveys the idea that I withheld supplies from the soldiers who were fighting in the Mexican war, or did anything else to hinder the soldiers, he is, to say the least, grossly and altogether mistaken, as a consultation of the records will prove to him.

As I have not used up so much of my time as I had supposed, I will dwell a little longer upon one or two of these minor topics upon which the Judge has spoken. He has read from my speech in Springfield, in which I say that "a house divided against itself cannot stand." Does the Judge say it *can* stand? I don't know whether he does or not. The Judge does not seem to be attending to me just now, but I would like to know if it is his opinion that a house divided against itself *can stand.* If he does, then there is a question of veracity, not between him and me, but between the Judge and an Authority of a somewhat higher character.

Now, my friends, I ask your attention to this matter for the purpose of say-ing something seriously. I know that the Judge may readily enough agree with me that the maxim which was put forth by the Saviour is true, but he may allege that I misapply it; and the Judge has a right to urge that, in my application, I do misapply it, and then I have a right to show that I do *not* misapply it. When he undertakes to say that because I think this nation, so far as the question of slavery is concerned, will all become one thing or all the other, I am in favor of bringing about a dead uniformity in the various States, in all their institutions, he argues erroneously. The great variety of the local institutions in the States, springing from differences in the soil, differences in the face of the country, and in the cli-mate, are bonds of Union. They do not make "a house divided against itself," but they make a house united. If they produce in one section of the country what is called for by the wants of another section, and this other section can supply the wants of the first, they are not matters of discord, but bonds of union, true bonds of union. But can this question of slavery be considered as among *these* varieties in the institutions of the country? I leave it to you to say whether, in the history of our government, this institution of slavery has not always failed to be a bond of union, and, on the contrary, been an apple of discord and an element of division in the house. I ask you to consider whether, so long as the moral constitution of men's minds shall continue to be the same, after this generation and assemblage shall sink into the grave, and another race shall arise, with the same moral and intellectual development we have,—whether, if that institution is standing in the same irritating position in which it now is, it will not continue an element of divi-sion? If so, then I have a right to say that, in regard to this question, the Union is a house divided against itself; and when the Judge reminds me that I have often said to him that the institution of slavery has existed for eighty years in some States, and yet it does not exist in some others, I agree to the fact, and I account for it by looking at the position in which our fathers originally placed it—restricting it from the new Territories where it had not gone, and legislating to cut off its source by the abrogation of the slave-trade, thus putting the seal of legislation *against its spread*. The public mind *did* rest in the belief that it was in the course of ultimate extinction. But lately, I think—and in this I charge nothing on the Judge's motives—lately, I think that he, and those acting with him, have placed that institution on a new basis, which looks to the *perpetuity and nationalization of slavery*. And while it is placed upon this new basis, I say, and I have said, that I believe we shall not have peace upon the question until the opponents of slavery arrest the further spread of it, and place it where the public mind shall rest in the belief that it is in the course of ultimate extinction; or, on the other hand, that its advocates will push it forward until it shall become alike lawful in all the States, old as well as new, North as well as South. Now, I believe if we could arrest the spread, and place it where Washington and Jefferson and Madison placed it, it *would be* in the course of ultimate extinction, and the public mind *would,* as for eighty years past, believe that it was in the course of ultimate extinction. The crisis would be past, and the institution might be let alone for a hundred years, if it should live so long, in the States where it exists; yet it would be going out of existence in the way best for both the black and the white races.

A VOICE: "Then do you repudiate popular sovereignty?"

MR. LINCOLN: Well, then, let us talk about popular sovereignty! What is popular sovereignty? Is it the right of the people to have slavery or not have it, as they see fit, in the Territories? I will state—and I have an able man to watch me—my understanding is that popular sovereignty, as now applied to the question of slavery, does allow the people of a Territory to have slavery if they want to, but does not allow them *not* to have it if they *do not* want it. I do not mean that if this vast concourse of people were in a Territory of the United States, any one of them would be obliged to have a slave if he did not want one; but I do say that, as I understand the Dred Scott decision, if any one man wants slaves, all the rest have no way of keeping that one man from holding them.

When I made my speech at Springfield, of which the Judge complains, and from which he quotes, I really was not thinking of the things which he ascribes to me at all. I had no thought in the world that I was doing anything to bring about a war between the free and slave states. I had no thought in the world that I was doing anything to bring about a political and social equality of the black and white races. It never occurred to me that I was doing anything or favoring anything to reduce to a dead uniformity all the local institutions of the various States. But I must say, in all fairness to him, if he thinks I am doing something which leads to these bad results, it is none the better that I did not mean it. It is just as fatal to the country, if I have any influence in producing it, whether I intend it or not. But can it be true that placing this institution upon the original basis—the basis upon which our fathers placed it—can have any tendency to set the Northern and the Southern States at war with one another, or that it can have any tendency to make the people of Vermont raise sugar-cane, because they raise it in Louisiana, or that it can compel the people of Illinois to cut pine logs on the Grand Prairie, where they will not grow, because they cut pine logs in Maine, where they do grow? The Judge says this is a new principle started in regard to this question. Does the Judge claim that he is working on the plan of the founders of government? I think he says in some of his speeches—indeed, I have one here now—that he saw evidence of a policy to allow slavery to be south of a certain line, while north of it it should be excluded, and he saw an indisposition on the part of the country to stand upon that policy, and therefore he set about studying the subject upon *original principles*, and upon *original principles* he got up the Nebraska Bill! I am fighting it upon these "original principles,"—fighting it in the Jeffersonian, Washingtonian, and Madisonian fashion.

Now, my friends, I wish you to attend for a little while to one or two other things in that Springfield speech. My main object was to show, so far as my humble ability was capable of showing, to the people of this country what I believed was the truth,—that there was a *tendency*, if not a conspiracy, among those who have engineered this slavery question for the last four or five years, to make slavery perpetual and universal in this nation. Having made that speech principally for that object, after arranging the evidences that I thought tended to prove my proposition, I concluded with this bit of comment:

> We cannot absolutely know that these exact adaptations are the result of preconcert; but when we see a lot of framed timbers, different portions of which we know have been gotten out at different times and places, and by different workmen—Stephen, Franklin, Roger, and James, for instance,—and when we see these timbers joined together, and see they exactly make the frame of a house or a mill, all the tenons and mortises exactly fitting, and all the lengths and proportions of the different pieces exactly adapted to their respective places, and not a piece too many or too few,—not omitting even the scaffolding,—or if a single piece be lacking, we see the place in the frame exactly fitted and prepared yet to bring such piece in,—in such a case we feel it impossible not to believe that Stephen and Franklin and Roger and James all understood one another from the beginning, and all worked upon a common plan or draft drawn before the first blow was struck.

When my friend Judge Douglas came to Chicago on the 9th of July, this speech having been delivered on the 16th of June, he made an harangue there, in which he took hold of this speech of mine, showing that he had carefully read it; and while he paid no attention to *this* matter at all, but complimented me as being a "kind, amiable, and intelligent gentleman," notwithstanding I had said this, he goes on and eliminates, or draws out, from my speech this tendency of mine to set the States at war with one another, to make all the institutions uniform, and set

the niggers and white people to marrying together. Then, as the Judge had complimented me with these pleasant titles (I must confess to my weakness), I was a little
"taken," for it came from a great man. I was not very much accustomed to flattery,
and it came the sweeter to me. I was rather like the Hoosier, with the gingerbread,
when he said he reckoned he loved it better than any other man, and got less of
it. As the Judge had so flattered me, I could not make up my mind that he meant
to deal unfairly with me; so I went to work to show him that he misunderstood
the whole scope of my speech, and that I really never intended to set the people at
war with one another. As an illustration, the next time I met him, which was at
Springfield, I used this expression, that I claimed no right under the Constitution,
nor had I any inclination, to enter into the slave States and interfere with the institutions of slavery. He says upon that: Lincoln will not enter into the slave States,
but will go to the banks of the Ohio, on this side, and shoot over! He runs on, step
by step, in the horse-chestnut style of argument, until in the Springfield speech
he says: "Unless he shall be successful in firing his batteries until he shall have extinguished slavery in all the States the Union shall be dissolved." Now, I don't think
that was exactly the way to treat "a kind, amiable, intelligent gentleman." I know if
I had asked the Judge to show when or where it was I had said that, if I didn't succeed in firing into the slave States until slavery should be extinguished, the Union
should be dissolved, he could not have shown it. I understand what he would do.
He would say: I don't mean to quote from you, but this was the *result* of what you
say. But I have the right to ask, and I do ask now. Did you not put it in such a form
that an ordinary reader or listener would take it as an expression *from me?*

In a speech at Springfield, on the night of the 17th, I thought I might as well
attend to my own business a little, and I recalled his attention as well as I could
to this charge of conspiracy to nationalize slavery. I called his attention to the
fact that he had acknowledged in my hearing twice that he had carefully read the
speech, and, in the language of the lawyers, as he had twice read the speech, and
still had put in no plea or answer, I took a default on him. I insisted that I had a
right then to renew that charge of conspiracy. Ten days afterward I met the Judge
at Clinton,—that is to say, I was on the ground, but not in the discussion,—and
heard him make a speech. Then he comes in with his plea to this charge, for the
first time; and his plea when put in, as well as I can recollect it, amounted to
this: that he never had any talk with Judge Taney or the President of the United
States with regard to the Dred Scott decision before it was made. I (Lincoln)
ought to know that the man who makes a charge without knowing it to be true
falsifies as much as he who knowingly tells a falsehood; and, lastly, that he would
pronounce the whole thing a falsehood; but, he would make no personal appli-

cation of the charge of falsehood, not because of any regard for the "kind, amiable, intelligent gentleman," but because of his own personal self-respect! I have understood since then (but [turning to Judge Douglas] will not hold the Judge to it if he is not willing) that he has broken through the "self-respect," and has got to saying the thing *out*. The Judge nods to me that it is so. It is fortunate for me that I can keep as good-humored as I do, when the Judge acknowledges that he has been trying to make a question of veracity with me. I know the Judge is a great man, while I am only a small man, but *I feel that I have got him.* I demur to that plea. I waive all objections that it was not filed till after default was taken, and demur to it upon the merits. What if Judge Douglas never did talk with Chief Justice Taney and the President before the Dred Scott decision was made, does it follow that he could not have had as perfect an understanding without talking as with it? I am not disposed to stand upon my legal advantage. I am disposed to take his denial as being like an answer in chancery, that he neither had any knowledge, information, or belief in the existence of such a conspiracy. I am disposed to take his answer as being as broad as though he had put it in these words. And now, I ask, even if he had done so, have not I a right to *prove it on him*, and to offer the evidence of more than two witnesses, by whom to prove it; and if the evidence proves the existence of the conspiracy, does his broader answer denying all knowledge, information, or belief, disturb the fact? It can only show that he was *used* by conspirators, and was not a *leader* of them.

Now, in regard to his reminding me of the moral rule that persons who tell what they do not know to be true falsify as much as those who knowingly tell falsehoods. I remember the rule, and it must be borne in mind that in what I have read to you, I do not say that I *know* such a conspiracy to exist. To that I reply, *I believe it.* If the Judge says that I do *not* believe it, then *he* says what *he* does not know, and falls within his own rule, that he who asserts a thing which he does not know to be true, falsifies as much as he who knowingly tells a falsehood. I want to call your attention to a little discussion on that branch of the case, and the evidence which brought my mind to the conclusion which I expressed as my *belief.* If, in arraying that evidence I had stated anything which was false or erroneous, it needed but that Judge Douglas should point it out, and I would have taken it back, with all the kindness in the world. I do not deal in that way. If I have brought forward anything not a fact, if he will point it out, it will not even ruffle me to take it back. But if he will not point out anything erroneous in the evidence, is it not rather for him to show, by a comparison of the evidence, that I have *reasoned* falsely, than to call the "kind, amiable, intelligent gentleman" a liar? If I have reasoned to a false conclusion, it is the vocation of an able debater to show by argument that I have wandered to an erroneous conclusion. I want to ask your attention to a portion of the Nebraska Bill, which Judge Douglas has quoted: "It being the true intent and meaning of this Act, not to legislate slavery into any Territory or State, nor to exclude it therefrom, but to leave the people thereof perfectly free to form and regulate their domestic institutions in their own way, subject only to the Constitution of the United States." Thereupon Judge Douglas and others began to argue in favor of "popular sovereignty,"—the right of the people to have slaves if they wanted them, and to exclude slavery if they did not want them. "But," said, in substance, a Senator from Ohio (Mr. Chase, I believe), "we more than suspect that you do not mean to allow the people to exclude slavery if they wish to; and if you do mean it, accept an amendment which I propose, expressly authorizing the people to exclude slavery." I believe I have the amendment here before me, which was offered, and under which the people of the Territory, through their representatives, might, if they saw fit, prohibit the existence of slavery therein. And now I state it as a *fact,* to be taken back if there is any mistake about it, that Judge Douglas and those acting with him *voted that amendment down.* I now think that those men who voted it down had a *real reason* for doing so. They know what that reason was. It looks to us, since we have seen the Dred Scott decision pronounced, holding that "under the Constitution" the people cannot exclude slavery,—I say it looks to outsiders, poor, simple, "amiable, intelligent gentlemen," as though the niche was left as a place to put that Dred Scott decision in,—a niche which would have been spoiled by adopting the amendment. And now, I say again, if *this* was not the reason, it will avail the Judge much more to calmly and good-humoredly point out to these people what that *other* reason was for voting the amendment down, than, swelling himself up, to vociferate that he may be provoked to call somebody a liar.

Again: There is in that same quotation from the Nebraska Bill this clause: "It being the true intent and meaning of this bill not to legislate slavery into any Territory or *State.*" I have always been puzzled to know what business the word "State" had in that connection. Judge Douglas knows. *He put it there.* He knows what he put it there for. We outsiders cannot say what he put it there for. The law they were passing was not about States, and was not making provisions for States. What was it placed there for? After seeing the Dred Scott decision, which holds that the people cannot exclude slavery from a *Territory,* if another Dred Scott decision shall come, holding that they cannot exclude it from a *State,* we shall discover that when the word was originally put there, it was in view of something which was to come in due time, we shall see that it was the *other half* of something. I now say again, if there is any different reason for putting it there. Judge Douglas, in a good-humored way, without calling anybody a liar, *can tell what the reason was.*

When the Judge spoke at Clinton, he came very near making a charge of falsehood against me. He used, as I found it printed in a newspaper, which, I remember, was very nearly like the real speech, the following language:

> I did not answer the charge [of conspiracy] before, for the reason that I did not suppose there was a man in America with a heart so corrupt as to believe such a charge could be true. I have too much respect for Mr. Lincoln to suppose he is serious in making the charge.

I confess this is rather a curious view, that out of respect for me he should consider I was making what I deemed rather a grave charge in fun. I confess it strikes me rather strangely. But I let it pass. As the Judge did not for a moment believe that there was a man in America whose heart was so "corrupt" as to make such a charge, and as he places me among the "men in America" who have hearts base enough to make such a charge, I hope he will excuse me if I hunt out another charge very like this; and if it should turn out that in hunting I should find that other, and it should turn out to be Judge Douglas himself who made it, I hope he will reconsider this question of the deep corruption of heart he has thought fit to ascribe to me. In Judge Douglas's speech of March 22, 1858, which I hold in my hand, he says:

> In this connection there is another topic to which I desire to allude. I seldom refer to the course of newspapers, or notice the articles which they publish in regard to myself; but the course of the Washington *Union* has been so extraordinary for the last two or three months, that I think it well enough to make some allusion to it. It has read me out of the Democratic party every other day, at least for two or three months, and keeps reading me out, and, as if it had not succeeded, still continues to read me out, using such terms as "traitor," "renegade," "deserter," and other kind and polite epithets of that nature. Sir, I have no vindication to make of my Democracy against the Washington *Union*, or any other newspapers. I am willing to allow my history and action for the last twenty years to speak for themselves as to my political principles and my fidelity to political obligations. The Washington *Union* has a personal grievance. When its editor was nominated for public printer, I declined to vote for him, and stated that at some time I might give my reasons

for doing so. Since I declined to give that vote, this scurrilous abuse, these vindictive and constant attacks have been repeated almost daily on me. Will my friend from Michigan read the article to which I allude?

This is a part of the speech. You must excuse me from reading the entire article of the Washington *Union*, as Mr. Stuart read it for Mr. Douglas. The Judge goes on and sums up, as I think, correctly:

Mr. President, you here find several distinct propositions advanced boldly by the Washington *Union* editorially, and apparently *authoritatively*; and any man who questions any of them is denounced as an Abolitionist, a Free-soiler, a fanatic. The propositions are, first, that the primary object of all government at its original institution is the protection of person and property; second, that the Constitution of the United States declares that the citizens of each State shall be entitled to all the privileges and immunities of citizens in the several States; and that, therefore, thirdly, all State laws, whether organic or otherwise, which prohibit the citizens of one State from settling in another with their slave property, and especially declaring it forfeited, are direct violations of the original intention of the government and Constitution of the United States; and, fourth, that the emancipation of the slaves of the Northern States was a gross outrage of the rights of property, inasmuch as it was involuntarily done on the part of the owner.

Remember that this article was published in the *Union* on the 17th of November, and on the 18th appeared the first article giving the adhesion of the *Union* to the Lecompton Constitution. It was in these words:

"KANSAS AND HER CONSTITUTION.—The vexed question is settled. The problem is solved. The dead point of danger is passed. All serious trouble to Kansas affairs is over and gone"—

And a column nearly of the same sort. Then, when you come to look into the Lecompton Constitution, you find the same doctrine incorporated in it which was put forth editorially in the *Union*. What is it?

"ARTICLE 7, *Section* I. The right of property is before and higher than any constitutional sanction; and the right of the owner of a slave to such slave and its increase is the same and as inviolable as the right of the owner of any property whatever."

Then in the schedule is a provision that the Constitution may be amended after 1864 by a two-thirds vote:

"But no alteration shall be made to affect the right of property in the ownership of slaves."

It will be seen by these clauses in the Lecompton Constitution that they are identical in spirit with the *authoritative* article in the Washington *Union* of the day previous to its indorsement of this Constitution.

I pass over some portions of the speech, and I hope that any one who feels interested in this matter will read the entire section of the speech, and see whether I do the Judge injustice. He proceeds:

> When I saw that article in the *Union* of the 17th of November, followed by the glorification of the Lecompton Constitution on the 18th of November, and this clause in the Constitution asserting the doctrine that a State has no right to prohibit slavery within its limits, I saw that there was a *fatal blow* being struck at the sovereignty of the States of this Union.

I stop the quotation there, again requesting that it may all be read. I have read all of the portion I desire to comment upon. What is this charge that the Judge thinks I must have a very corrupt heart to make? It was a purpose on the part of certain high functionaries to make it impossible for the people of one State to prohibit the people of any other State from entering it with their "property," so called, and making it a slave State. In other words, it was a charge implying a design to make the institution of slavery national. And now I ask your attention to what Judge Douglas has himself done here. I know he made that part of the speech as a reason why he had refused to vote for a certain man for public printer; but when we get at it, the charge itself is the very one I made against him, that he thinks I am so corrupt for uttering. Now, whom does he make that charge against? Does he make it against that newspaper editor merely? No; he says it is identical in spirit with the Lecompton Constitution, and so the framers of that Constitution are brought in with the editor of the newspaper in that "fatal blow being struck," He did not call it a "conspiracy." In his language, it is a "fatal blow being struck." And if the words carry the meaning better when changed from a "conspiracy" into a "fatal blow being struck," I will change *my* expression, and call it "fatal blow being struck." We see the charge made not merely against the editor of the *Union*, but all the framers of the Lecompton Constitution; and not only so, but the article was an *authoritative* article. By whose authority? Is there any question but he means it was by the authority of the President and his Cabinet,—the Administration?

Is there any sort of question but he means to make that charge? Then there are the editors of the *Union*, the framers of the Lecompton Constitution, the President of the United States and his Cabinet, and all the supporters of the Lecompton Constitution, in Congress and out of Congress, who are all involved in this "fatal blow being struck." I com mend to Judge Douglas's consideration the question of *how corrupt a man's heart must be to make such a charge!*

Now, my friends, I have but one branch of the subject, in the little time I have left, to which to call your attention; and as I shall come to a close at the end of that branch, it is probable that I shall not occupy quite all the time allotted to me. Although on these questions I would like to talk twice as long as I have, I could not enter upon another head and discuss it properly without running over my time. I ask the attention of the people here assembled and elsewhere to the course that Judge Douglas is pursuing every day as bearing upon this question of making slavery national. Not going back to the records, but taking the speeches he makes, the speeches he made yesterday and day before, and makes constantly all over the country,—I ask your attention to them. In the first place, what is necessary to make the institution national? Not war. There is no danger that the people of Kentucky will shoulder their muskets, and, with a young nigger stuck on every bayonet, march into Illinois and force them upon us. There is no danger of our going over there and making war upon them. Then what is necessary for the nationalization of slavery? It is simply the next Dred Scott decision. It is merely for the Supreme Court to decide that no *State* under the Constitution can exclude it, just as they have already decided that under the Constitution neither Congress nor the Territorial Legislature can do it. When that is decided and acquiesced in, the whole thing is done. This being true, and this being the way, as I think, that slavery is to be made national, let us consider what Judge Douglas is doing every day to that end. In the first place, let us see what influence he is exerting on public sentiment. In this and like communities, public sentiment is everything. With public sentiment, nothing can fail; without it, nothing can succeed. Consequently, he who moulds public sentiment goes deeper then he who enacts statutes or pronounces decisions. He makes statutes and decisions possible or impossible to be executed. This must be borne in mind, as also the additional fact that Judge Douglas is a man of vast influence, so great that it is enough for many men to profess to believe anything when they once find out Judge Douglas professes to believe it. Consider also the attitude he occupies at the head of a large party,—a party which he claims has a majority of all the voters in the country. This man sticks to a decision which forbids the people of a Territory from excluding slavery, and he does so, not because he says it is right in itself,—he does not give any opinion on that,—but because it has been *decided by the court;* and being decided by the court, he is, and you are, bound to take it in your political action as *law,* not that he judges at all of its merits, but because a decision of the court is to him a "Thus saith the Lord." He places it on that ground alone; and you will bear in mind that thus committing himself unreservedly to this decision *commits him to the next one* just as firmly as to this. He did not commit himself on account of the merit or demerit of the decision, but it is a "Thus saith the Lord." The next decision, as much as this, will be a "Thus saith the Lord." There is nothing that can divert or turn him away from this decision. It is nothing that I point out to him that his great prototype, General Jackson, did not believe in the binding force of decisions. It is nothing to him that Jefferson did not so believe. I have said that I have often heard him approve of Jackson's course in disregarding the decision of the Supreme Court pronouncing a National Bank constitutional. He says I did not hear him say so. He denies the accuracy of my recollection. I say he ought to know better than I, but I will make no question about this thing, though it still seems to me that I heard him say it twenty times. I will tell him, though, that he now claims to stand on the Cincinnati platform, which affirms that Congress *cannot* charter a National Bank, in the teeth of that old standing decision that Congress *can* charter a bank. And I remind him of another piece of history on the question of respect for judicial decisions, and it is a piece of Illinois history belonging to a time when the large party to which Judge Douglas belonged were displeased with a decision of the Supreme Court of Illinois, because they had decided that a Governor could not remove a Secretary of State. You will find the whole story in Ford's *History of Illinois,* and I know that Judge Douglas will not deny that he was then in favor of over-slaughing that decision by the mode of adding five new judges, so as to vote down the four old ones. Not only so, but it ended in *the Judge's sitting down on that very bench as one of the five new judges to break down the four old ones.* It was in this way precisely that he got his title of judge. Now, when the Judge tells me that men appointed conditionally to sit as members of a court will have to be catechised beforehand upon some subject, I say, "You know, Judge; you have tried it." When he says a court of this kind will lose the confidence of all men, will be prostituted and disgraced by such a proceeding, I say, "You know best, Judge; you have been through the mill." But I cannot shake

Judge Douglas's teeth loose from the Dred Scott decision. Like some obstinate animal (I mean no disrespect) that will hang on when he has once got his teeth fixed, you may cut off a leg, or you may tear away an arm, still he will not relax his hold. And so I may point out to the Judge, and say that he is bespattered all over, from the beginning of his political life to the present time, with attacks upon judicial decisions; I may cut off limb after limb of his public record, and strive to wrench him from a single dictum of the court,—yet I cannot divert him from it. He hangs, to the last, to the Dred Scott decision. These things show there is a purpose *strong as death and eternity* for which he adheres to this decision, and for which he will adhere to *all other decisions* of the same court.

A HIBERNIAN: "Give us something besides Dred Scott."

MR. LINCOLN: Yes; no doubt you want to hear something that don't hurt. Now, having spoken of the Dred Scott decision, one more word, and I am done. Henry Clay, my *beau-ideal* of a statesman, the man for whom I fought all my humble life,—Henry Clay once said of a class of men who would repress all tendencies to liberty and ultimate emancipation that they must, if they would do this, go back to the era of our Independence, and muzzle the cannon which thunders its annual joyous return; they must blow out the moral lights around us; they must penetrate the human soul, and eradicate there the love of liberty; and then, and not till then, could they perpetuate slavery in this country! To my thinking, Judge Douglas is, by his example and vast influence, doing that very thing in this community, when he says that the negro has nothing in the Declaration of Independence. Henry Clay plainly understood the contrary. Judge Douglas is going back to the era of our Revolution, and, to the extent of his ability, muzzling the cannon which thunders its annual joyous return. When he invites any people, willing to have slavery, to establish it, he is blowing out the moral lights around us. When he says he "cares not whether slavery is voted down or up,"—that it is a sacred right of self-government,—he is, in my judgment, penetrating the human soul and eradicating the light of reason and the love of liberty in this American people. And now I will only say that when, by all these means and appliances, Judge Douglas shall succeed in bringing public sentiment to an exact accordance with his own views; when these vast assemblages shall echo back all these sentiments; when they shall come to repeat his views and to avow his principles, and to say all that he says on these mighty questions,— then it needs only the formality of the second Dred Scott decision, which he indorses in advance, to make slavery alike lawful in all the States, old as well as new, North as well as South.

My friends, that ends the chapter. The Judge can take his half -hour.

## MR. DOUGLAS'S REJOINDER

FELLOW-CITIZENS: I will now occupy the half-hour allotted to me in replying to Mr. Lincoln. The first point to which I will call your attention is as to what I said about the organization of the Republican party in 1854, and the platform that was formed on the 5th of October of that year, and I will then put the question to Mr. Lincoln, whether or not he approves of each article in that platform, and ask for a specific answer. I did not charge him with being a member of the committee which reported that platform. I charged that that platform was the platform of the Republican party adopted by them. The fact that it was the platform of the Republican party is not denied; but Mr. Lincoln now says that, although his name was on the committee which reported it, that he does not think he was there, but thinks he was in Tazewell, holding court. Now, I want to remind Mr. Lincoln that he was at Springfield when that Convention was held and those resolutions adopted.

The point I am going to remind Mr. Lincoln of is this: that after I had made my speech in 1854, during the fair, he gave me notice that he was going to reply to me the next day. I was sick at the time, but I stayed over in Springfield to hear his reply and to reply to him. On that day this very Convention, the resolutions adopted by which I have read, was to meet in the Senate chamber. He spoke in the hall of the House; and when he got through his speech—my recollection is distinct, and I shall never forget it—Mr. Codding walked in as I took the stand to reply, and gave notice that the Republican State Convention would meet instantly in the Senate chamber, and called upon the Republicans to retire there and go into this very Convention, instead of remaining and listening to me.

In the first place, Mr. Lincoln was selected by the very men who made the Republican organization, on that day, to reply to me. He spoke for them and for that party, and he was the leader of the party; and on the very day he made his speech in reply to me, preaching up this same doctrine of negro equality under the Declaration of Independence, this Republican party met in Convention. Another evidence that he was acting in concert with them is to be found in the fact that that Convention waited an hour after its time of meeting to hear Lincoln's speech, and Codding, one of their leading men, marched in the moment Lincoln got through, and gave notice that they did not want to hear me, and would proceed with the business of the Convention. Still another fact: I have here a newspaper printed at Springfield, Mr. Lincoln's own town, in October, 1854, a few days afterward, publishing these resolutions, charging Mr. Lincoln with entertaining these sentiments, and trying to prove that they were also the sentiments of Mr. Yates, their candidate for Congress. This has been published on Mr. Lincoln over and over again, and never before has he denied it.

But, my friends, this denial of his that he did not act on the committee is a miserable quibble to avoid the main issue, which is, that this Republican platform declares in favor of the unconditional repeal of the Fugitive Slave law. Has Lincoln answered whether he indorsed that or not? I called his attention to it when I first addressed you, and asked him for an answer, and I then predicted that he would not answer. How does he answer? Why, that he was not on the committee that wrote the resolutions. I then repeated the next proposition contained in the resolutions, which was to restrict slavery in those States in which it exists, and asked him whether he indorsed it. Does he answer yes, or no? He says in reply, "I was not on the committee at the time; I was up in Tazewell." The next question I put to him was, whether he was in favor of prohibiting the admission of any more slave States into the Union. I put the question to him distinctly, whether, if the people of the Territory, when they had sufficient population to make a State, should form their constitution recognizing slavery, he would vote for or against its admission. He is a candidate for the United States Senate, and it is possible, if he should be elected, that he would have to vote directly on that question, I asked him to answer me and you, whether he would vote to admit a State into the Union, with slavery or without it, as its own people might choose. He did not answer that question. He dodges that question also, under the cover that he was not on the committee at the time, that he was not present when the platform was made. I want to know if he should happen to be in the Senate when a State applied for admission, with a constitution acceptable to her own people, he would vote to admit that State, if slavery was one of its institutions. He avoids the answer.

It is true he gives the Abolitionists to understand by a hint that he would not vote to admit such a State. And why? He goes on to say that the man who would talk about giving each State the right to have slavery or not, as it pleased, was akin to the man who would muzzle the guns which thundered forth the annual joyous return of the day of our Independence. He says that that kind of talk is casting a blight on the glory of this country. What is the meaning of that? That he is not in favor of each State to have the right of doing as it pleases on the slavery question? I will put the question to him again and again, and I intend to force it out of him.

Then, again, this platform, which was made at Springfield by his own party when he was its acknowledged head, provides that Republicans will insist on the abolition of slavery in the District of Columbia, and I asked Lincoln specifically whether he agreed with them in that? ["Did you get an answer?"] He is afraid to answer it. He knows I would trot him down to Egypt. I intend to make him answer there, or I will show the people of Illinois that he does not intend to answer these questions. The Convention to which I have been alluding goes a little further, and pledges itself to exclude slavery from all the Territories over which the General Government has exclusive jurisdiction north of 36 deg. 30 min., as well as south. Now, I want to know whether he approves that provision. I want him to answer, and when he does, I want to know his opinion on another point, which is, whether he will redeem the pledge of this platform, and resist the acquirement of any more territory unless slavery therein shall be forever prohibited. I want him to answer this last question. Each of the questions I have put to him are practical questions,— questions based upon the fundamental principles of the Black Republican party; and I want to know whether he is the first, last, and only choice of a party with whom he does not agree in principle. He does not deny but that that principle was unanimously adopted by the Republican party; he does not deny that the whole Republican party is pledged to it; he does not deny that a man who is not faithful to it is faithless to the Republican party; and now I want to know whether that party is unanimously in favor of a man who does not adopt that creed and agree with them in their principles; I want to know whether the man who does not agree with them, and who is afraid to avow his differences, and who dodges the issue, is the first, last, and only choice of the Republican party.

A VOICE: "How about the conspiracy?"

MR. DOUGLAS: Never mind, I will come to that soon enough. But the platform which I have read to you not only lays down these principles, but it adds:

> *Resolved,* That in furtherance of these principles, we will use such constitutional and lawful means as shall seem best adapted to their accomplishment, and that we will support no man for office, under the General or State Government, who is not positively and fully committed to the support of these principles, and whose personal character and conduct is not a guarantee that he is reliable, and who shall not have abjured old party allegiance and ties.

The Black Republican party stands pledged that they will never support Lincoln until he has pledged himself to that platform; but he cannot devise his answer, he has not made up his mind whether he will or not. He talked about everything else he could think of to occupy his hour and a half, and when he could not think of anything more to say, without an excuse for refusing to answer these questions, he sat down long before his time was out.

In relation to Mr. Lincoln's charge of conspiracy against me, I have a word to say. In his speech to-day he quotes a playful part of his speech at Springfield, about Stephen, and James, and Franklin, and Roger, and says that I did not take exception to it. I did not answer it, and he repeats it again. I did not take exception to this figure of his. He has a right to be as playful as he pleases in throwing his arguments together, and I will not object; but I did take objection to his second Springfield speech, in which he stated that he intended his first speech as a charge of corruption or conspiracy against the Supreme Court of the United States, President Pierce, President Buchanan, and myself. That gave the offensive character to the charge. He then said that when he made it he did not know whether it was true or not; but inasmuch as Judge Douglas had not denied it, although he had replied to the other parts of his speech three times, he repeated it as a charge of conspiracy against me, thus charging me with moral turpitude. When he put it in that form, I did say that, inasmuch as he repeated the charge simply because I had not denied it, I would deprive him of the opportunity of ever repeating it again, by declaring that it was, in all its bearings, an infamous lie. He says he will repeat it until I answer his folly and nonsense about Stephen, and Franklin, and Roger, and Bob, and James.

He studied that out, prepared that one sentence with the greatest care, committed it to memory, and put it in his first Springfield speech; and now he carries that speech around, and reads that sentence to show how pretty it is. His vanity is wounded because I will not go into that beautiful figure of his about the building of a house. All I have to say is, that I am not green enough to let him make a charge which he acknowledges he does not know to be true, and then take up my time in answering it, when I know it to be false, and nobody else knows it to be true.

I have not brought a charge of moral turpitude against him. When he, or any other man, brings one against me, instead of disproving it, I will say that it is a lie, and let him prove it if he can.

I have lived twenty-five years in Illinois, I have served you with all the fidelity and ability which I possess, and Mr. Lincoln is at liberty to attack my public action, my votes, and my conduct; but when he dares to attack my moral integrity by a charge of conspiracy between myself, Chief Justice Taney and the Supreme Court, and two Presidents of the United States, I will repel it.

Mr. Lincoln has not character enough for integrity and truth, merely on his own *ipse dixit*, to arraign President Buchanan, President Pierce, and nine Judges of the Supreme Court, not one of whom would be complimented by being put on an equality with him. There is an unpardonable presumption in a man putting himself up before thousands of people, and pretending that his *ipse dixit*, without proof, without fact, and without truth, is enough to bring down and destroy the purest and best of living men.

Fellow-citizens, my time is fast expiring; I must pass on. Mr. Lincoln wants to know why I voted against Mr. Chase's amendment to the Nebraska Bill. I will tell him. In the first place, the bill already conferred all the power which Congress had, by giving the people the whole power over the subject. Chase offered a proviso that they might abolish slavery, which by implication would convey the idea that they could prohibit by not introducing that institution. General Cass asked him to modify his amendment so as to provide that the people might either prohibit or introduce slavery, and thus make it fair and equal. Chase refused to so modify his proviso, and then General Cass and all the rest of us voted it down. Those facts appeal on the journals and debates of Congress, where Mr. Lincoln found the charge; and if he had told the whole truth, there would have been no necessity for me to occupy your time in explaining the matter.

Mr. Lincoln wants to know why the word "State," as well as "Territory," was put into the Nebraska Bill. I will tell him. It was put there to meet just such false arguments as he has been adducing. That first, not only the people of the Territories should do as they pleased, but that when they come to be admitted as States, they should come into the Union with or without slavery, as the people determined. I meant to knock in the head this Abolition doctrine of Mr. Lincoln's, that there shall be no more slave States, even if the people want them. And it does not do for him to say, or for any other Black Republican to say, that there is nobody in favor of the doctrine of no more slave States, and that nobody wants to interfere with the right of the people to do as they please. What was the origin of the Missouri difficulty and the Missouri Compromise? The people of Missouri formed a constitution as a slave State, and asked admission into the Union; but the Free-soil party of the North, being in a majority, refused to admit her because she had slavery as one of her institutions. Hence this first slavery agitation arose upon a State, and not upon a Territory; and yet Mr. Lincoln does not know why the word "State" was placed in the Kansas-Nebraska Bill. The whole Abolition agitation arose on that doctrine of prohibiting a State from coming in with slavery or not, as it pleased, and that same doctrine is here in this Republican platform of 1854; it has never been repealed; and every Black Republican stands pledged by that platform never to vote for any man who is not in favor of it. Yet Mr. Lincoln does not know that there is a man in the world who is in favor of preventing a State from coming in as it pleases, notwithstanding. The Springfield platform says that they, the Republican party, will not allow a State to come in under such circumstances. He is an ignorant man.

Now, you see that upon these very points I am as far from bringing Mr. Lincoln up to the line as I ever was before. He does not want to avow his principles.

I do want to avow mine, as clear as sunlight in midday. Democracy is founded upon the eternal principle of right. The plainer these principles are avowed before the people, the stronger will be the support which they will receive. I only wish I had the power to make them so clear that they would shine in the heavens for every man, woman, and child to read. The first of those principles that I would proclaim would be in opposition to Mr. Lincoln's doctrine of uniformity between the different States, and I would declare instead the sovereign right of each State to decide the slavery question as well as all other domestic questions for themselves, without interference from any other State or power whatsoever.

When that principle is recognized, you will have peace and harmony and fraternal feeling between all the States of this Union; until you do recognize that doctrine, there will be sectional warfare agitating and distracting the country. What does Mr. Lincoln propose? He says that the Union cannot exist divided into free and slave States. If it cannot endure thus divided, then he must strive to make them all free or all slave, which will inevitably bring about a dissolution of the Union.

Gentlemen, I am told that my time is out, and I am obliged to stop.

# Second Joint Debate, at Freeport

*August 27, 1858*

### Mr. Lincoln's Opening Speech

Ladies and Gentlemen: On Saturday last, Judge Douglas and myself first met in public discussion. He spoke one hour, I an hour and a half, and he replied for half an hour. The order is now reversed. I am to speak an hour, he an hour and a half, and then I am to reply for half an hour. I propose to devote myself during the first hour to the scope of what was brought within the range of his half-hour speech at Ottawa. Of course there was brought within the scope in that half-hour's speech something of his own opening speech. In the course of that opening argument Judge Douglas proposed to me seven distinct interrogatories. In my speech of an hour and a half, I attended to some other parts of his speech, and incidentally, as I thought, intimated to him that I would answer the rest of his interrogatories on condition only that he should agree to answer as many for me. He made no intimation at the time of the proposition, nor did he in his reply allude at all to that suggestion of mine. I do him no injustice in saying that he occupied at least half of his reply in dealing with me as though I had *refused* to answer his interrogatories. I now propose that I will answer any of the interrogatories, upon condition that he will answer questions from me not exceeding the same number. I give him an opportunity to respond. The Judge remains silent. I now say that I will answer his interrogatories, whether he answers mine or not; and that after I have done so, I shall propound mine to him.

I have supposed myself, since the organization of the Republican party at Bloomington, in May, 1856, bound as a party man by the platforms of the party, then and since. If in any interrogatories which I shall answer I go beyond the scope of what is within these platforms, it will be perceived that no one is responsible but myself.

Having said thus much, I will take up the Judge's interrogatories as I find them printed in the Chicago *Times*, and answer them *seriatim*. In order that there may be no mistake about it, I have copied the interrogatories in writing, and also my answers to them. The first one of these interrogatories is in these words:

*Question* 1.—"I desire to know whether Lincoln to-day stands, as he did in 1854, in favor of the unconditional repeal of the Fugitive Slave law?"

*Answer.*—I do not now, nor ever did, stand in favor of the unconditional repeal of the Fugitive Slave law.

*Q.* 2. "I desire him to answer whether he stands pledged to-day, as he did in 1854, against the admission of any more slave States into the Union, even if the people want them?"

*A.* I do not now, nor ever did, stand pledged against the admission of any more slave States into the Union.

*Q.* 3. "I want to know whether he stands pledged against the admission of a new State into the Union with such a constitution as the people of that State may see fit to make?"

*A.* 1 do not stand pledged against the admission of a new State into the Union, with such a constitution as the people of that State may see fit to make.

*Q.* 4. "I want to know whether he stands to-day pledged to the abolition of slavery in the District of Columbia?"

*A.* I do not stand to-day pledged to the abolition of slavery in the District of Columbia.

*Q.* 5. "I desire him to answer whether he stands pledged to the prohibition of the slave-trade between the different States?"

*A.* I do not stand pledged to the prohibition of the slave-trade between the different States.

*Q.* 6. "I desire to know whether he stands pledged to prohibit slavery in all the Territories of the United States, north as well as south of the Missouri Compromise line?"

*A.* I am impliedly, if not expressly, pledged to a belief in the *right* and *duty* of Congress to prohibit slavery in all the United States Territories.

*Q.* 7. "I desire him to answer whether he is opposed to the acquisition of any new territory unless slavery is first prohibited therein?"

*A.* I am not generally opposed to honest acquisition of territory; and, in any given case, I would or would not oppose such acquisition, accordingly as I might think such acquisition would or would not aggravate the slavery question among ourselves.

Now, my friends, it will be perceived, upon an examination of these questions and answers, that so far I have only answered that I was not *pledged* to this, that, or the other. The Judge has not framed his interrogatories to ask me anything more than this, and I have answered in strict accordance with the interrogatories, and have answered truly, that I am not *pledged* at all upon any of the points to which I have answered. But I am not disposed to hang upon the exact form of his interrogatory. I am rather disposed to take up at least some of these questions, and state what I really think upon them.

As to the first one, in regard to the Fugitive Slave law, I have never hesitated to say, and I do not now hesitate to say, that I think, under the Constitution of the United States, the people of the Southern States are entitled to a Congressional Fugitive Slave law. Having said that, I have had nothing to say in regard to the existing Fugitive Slave law, further than that I think it should have been framed so as to be free from some of the objections that pertain to it, without lessening its efficiency. And inasmuch as we are not now in an agitation in regard to an alteration or modification of that law, I would not be the man to introduce it as a new subject of agitation upon the general question of slavery.

In regard to the other question, of whether I am pledged to the admission of any more slave States into the Union, I state to you very frankly that I would be exceedingly sorry ever to be put in a position of having to pass upon that question. I should be exceedingly glad to know that there would never be another slave State admitted into the Union; but I must add that if slavery shall be kept out of the Territories during the territorial existence of any one given Territory, and then the people shall, having a fair chance and a clear field, when they come to adopt the constitution, do such an extraordinary thing as to adopt a slave constitution, uninfluenced by the actual presence of the institution among them, I see no alternative, if we own the country, but to admit them into the Union.

The third interrogatory is answered by the answer to the second, it being, as I conceive, the same as the second.

The fourth one is in regard to the abolition of slavery in the District of Columbia. In relation to that, I have my mind very distinctly made up. I should be exceedingly glad to see slavery abolished in the District of Columbia. I believe that Congress possesses the constitutional power to abolish it. Yet as a member of Congress, I should not, with my present views, be in favor of *endeavoring* to abolish slavery in the District of Columbia, unless it would be upon these conditions: *First,* that the abolition should be gradual; *second,* that it should be on a vote of the majority of qualified voters in the District; and *third,* that compensation should be made to unwilling owners. With these three conditions, I confess I would be exceedingly glad to see Congress abolish slavery in the District of Columbia, and, in the language of Henry Clay, "sweep from our capital that foul blot upon our nation."

In regard to the fifth interrogatory, I must say here that, as to the question of the abolition of the slave-trade between the different States, I can truly answer, as I have, that I am *pledged* to nothing about it. It is a subject to which I have not given that mature consideration that would make me feel authorized to state a position so as to hold myself entirely bound by it. In other words, that question has never been prominently enough before me to induce me to investigate whether we really have the constitutional power to do it. I could investigate it if I had sufficient time to bring myself to a conclusion upon that subject; but I have not done so, and I say so frankly to you here, and to Judge Douglas. I must say, however, that if I should be of opinion that Congress does possess the constitutional power to abolish the slave-trade among the different States, I should still not be in favor of the exercise of that power, unless upon some conservative principle as I conceive it, akin to what I have said in relation to the abolition of slavery in the District of Columbia.

My answer as to whether I desire that slavery should be prohibited in all the Territories of the United States is full and explicit within itself, and cannot be made clearer by any comments of mine. So I suppose in regard to the question whether I am opposed to the acquisition of any more territory unless slavery is first prohibited therein, my answer is such that I could add nothing by way of illustration, or making myself better understood, than the answer which I have placed in writing.

Now in all this the Judge has me, and he has me on the record. I suppose he had flattered himself that I was really entertaining one set of opinions for one place, and another set for another place; that I was afraid to say at one place what I uttered at another. What I am saying here I suppose I say to a vast audience as strongly tending to Abolitionism as any audience in the State of Illinois, and I believe I am saying that which, if it would be offensive to any persons and render them enemies to myself, would be offensive to persons in this audience.

I now proceed to propound to the Judge the interrogatories, so far as I have framed them. I will bring forward a new installment when I get them ready. I will bring them forward now only reaching to number four.

The first one is:

*Question* 1.—If the people of Kansas shall, by means entirely unobjectionable in all other respects, adopt a State constitution, and ask admission into the Union under it, *before* they have the requisite number of inhabitants according to the English bill,—some ninety-three thousand,—will you vote to admit them?

*Q.* 2. Can the people of a United States Territory, in any lawful way, against the wish of any citizen of the United States, exclude slavery from its limits prior to the formation of a State constitution?

*Q.* 3. If the Supreme Court of the United States shall decide that States cannot exclude slavery from their limits, are you in favor of acquiescing in, adopting, and following such decision as a rule of political action?

*Q.* 4. Are you in favor of acquiring additional territory, in disregard of how such acquisition may affect the nation on the slavery question?

As introductory to these interrogatories which Judge Douglas propounded to me at Ottawa, he read a set of resolutions which he said Judge Trumbull and myself had participated in adopting, in the first Republican State Convention, held at Springfield in October, 1854. He insisted that I and Judge Trumbull, and perhaps the entire Republican party, were responsible for the doctrines contained in the set of resolutions which he read, and I understand that it was from that set of resolutions that he deduced the interrogatories which he propounded to me, using these resolutions as a sort of authority for propounding those questions to me. Now, I say here to-day that I do not answer his interrogatories because of their springing at all from that set of resolutions which he read. I answered them because Judge Douglas thought fit to ask them. I do not now, nor ever did, recognize any responsibility upon myself in that set of resolutions. When I replied to him on that occasion, I assured him that I never had anything to do with them. I repeat here to-day that I never in any possible form had anything to do with that set of resolutions. It turns out, I believe, that those resolutions were never passed in any convention held in Springfield. It turns out that they were never passed at any convention or any public meeting that I had any part in. I believe it turns out, in addition to all this, that there was not, in the fall of 1854, any convention holding a session in Springfield, calling itself a Republican State Convention; yet it is true there was a convention, or assemblage of men calling themselves a convention, at Springfield, that did pass *some* resolutions. But so little did I really know of the proceedings of that convention, or what set of resolutions they had passed, though having a general knowledge that there had been such an assemblage of men there, that when Judge Douglas read the resolutions, I really did not know but they had been the resolutions passed then and there. I did not question that they were the resolutions adopted. For I could not bring myself to suppose that Judge Douglas could say what he did upon this subject without *knowing* that it was true. I contented myself, on that occasion, with denying, as I truly could, all connection with them, not denying or affirming whether they were passed at Springfield. Now, it turns out that he had got hold of some resolutions passed at some convention or public meeting in Kane County I wish to say here, that I don't conceive that in any fair and just mind this discovery relieves me at all. I had just as much to do with the convention in Kane County as that at Springfield. I am as much responsible for the resolutions at Kane County as those at Springfield,—the amount of the responsibility being exactly nothing in either case; no more than there would be in regard to a set of resolutions passed in the moon.

I allude to this extraordinary matter in this canvass for some further purpose than anything yet advanced. Judge Douglas did not make his statement upon that occasion as matters that he believed to be true, but he stated them roundly as *being true*, in such form as to pledge his veracity for their truth. When the whole matter turns out as it does, and when we consider who Judge Douglas is,—that he is a distinguished Senator of the United States; that he has served nearly twelve years as such; that his character is not at all limited as an ordinary Senator of the United States, but that his name has become of world-wide renown,—it is *most extraordinary* that he should so far forget all the suggestions of justice to an adversary, or of prudence to himself, as to venture upon the assertion of that which the slightest investigation would have shown him to be wholly false. I can only account for his having done so upon the supposition that that evil genius which has attended him through his life, giving to him an apparent astonishing prosperity, such as to lead very many good men to doubt there being any advantage in virtue over vice,—I say I can only account for it on the supposition that that evil genius has as last made up its mind to forsake him.

And I may add that another extraordinary feature of the Judge's conduct in this canvass—made more extraordinary by this incident—is, that he is in the habit, in almost all the speeches he makes, of charging falsehood upon his adversaries, myself and others. I now ask whether he is able to find in anything that Judge Trumbull, for instance, has said, or in anything that I have said, a justification at all compared with what we have, in this instance, for that sort of vulgarity.

I have been in the habit of charging as a matter of belief on my part that, in the introduction of the Nebraska Bill into Congress, there was a conspiracy to make slavery perpetual and national. I have arranged from time to time the evidence which establishes and proves the truth of this charge. I recurred to this charge at Ottawa. I shall not now have time to dwell upon it at very great length; but inasmuch as Judge Douglas, in his reply of half an hour, made some points upon me in relation to it, I propose noticing a few of them.

The Judge insists that, in the first speech I made, in which I very distinctly made that charge, he thought for a good while I was in fun! that I was playful; that I was not sincere about it; and that he only grew angry and somewhat excited when he found that I insisted upon it as a matter of earnestness. He says he characterized it as a falsehood so far as I implicated his *moral character* in that transaction. Well, I did not know, till he presented that view, that I had implicated his moral character. He is very much in the habit, when he argues me up into a position I never thought of occupying, of very cosily saying he has no doubt Lincoln is "conscientious" in saying so. He should remember that I did not know but what *he* was ALTOGETHER "CONSCIENTIOUS" in that matter. I can conceive it possible for men to conspire to do a good thing, and I really find nothing in Judge Douglas's course of arguments that is contrary to or inconsistent with his belief of a conspiracy to nationalize and spread slavery as being a good and blessed thing; and so I hope he will understand that I do not at all question but that in all this matter he is entirely "conscientious."

But to draw your attention to one of the points I made in this case, beginning at the beginning: When the Nebraska Bill was introduced, or a short time afterward, by an amendment, I believe, it was provided that it must be considered "the true intent and meaning of this Act not to legislate slavery into any State or Territory, or to exclude it therefrom, but to leave the people thereof perfectly free to form and regulate their own domestic institutions in their own way, subject only to the Constitution of the United States." I have called his attention to the fact that when he and some others began arguing that they were giving an increased degree of liberty to the people in the Territories over and above what they formerly had on the question of slavery, a question was raised whether the law was enacted to give such unconditional liberty to the people; and to test the sincerity of this mode of argument, Mr. Chase, of Ohio, introduced an amendment, in which he made the law—if the amendment were adopted—expressly declare that the people of the Territory should have the power to exclude slavery if they saw fit. I have asked attention also to the fact that Judge Douglas and those who acted with him voted that amendment down, notwithstanding it expressed exactly the thing they said was the true intent and meaning of the law. I have called attention to the fact that in subsequent times a decision of the Supreme Court has been made, in which it has been declared that a Territorial Legislature has no constitutional right to exclude slavery. And I have argued and said that for men who did intend that the people of the Territory should have the right to exclude slavery absolutely and unconditionally, the voting down of Chase's amendment is wholly inexplicable. It is a puzzle, a riddle. But I have said, that with men who did look forward to such a decision, or who had it in contemplation that such a decision of the Supreme Court would or might be made, the voting down of that amendment would be perfectly rational and intelligible. It would keep Congress from coming in collision with the decision when it was made. Anybody can conceive that if there was an intention or expectation that such a decision was to follow, it would not be a very desirable party attitude to get into for the Supreme

Court—all or nearly all its members belonging to the same party—to decide one way, when the party in Congress had decided the other way. Hence it would be very rational for men expecting such a decision to keep the niche in that law clear for it. After pointing this out, I tell Judge Douglas that it looks to me as though here was the reason why Chase's amendment was voted down. I tell him that, as he did it, and knows why he did it, if it was done for a reason different from this, *he knows what that reason was and can tell us what it was.* I tell him, also, it will be vastly more satisfactory to the country for him to give some other plausible, intelligible reason *why* it was voted down than to stand upon his dignity and call people liars. Well, on Saturday he did make his answer; and what do you think it was? He says if I had only taken upon myself to tell the whole truth about that amendment of Chase's, no explanation would have been necessary on his part—or words to that effect. Now, I say here that I am quite unconscious of having suppressed anything material to the case, and I am very frank to admit if there is any sound reason other than that which appeared to me material, it is quite fair for him to present it. What reason does he propose? That when Chase came forward with his amendment expressly authorizing the people to exclude slavery from the limits of every Territory, General Cass proposed to Chase, if he (Chase) would add to his amendment that the people should have the power to *introduce* or exclude, they would let it go. This is substantially all of his reply. And because Chase would not do that, they voted his amendment down. Well, it turns out, I believe, upon examination, that General Cass took some part in the little running debate upon that amendment, and then ran away *and did not vote on it at all.* Is not that the fact? So confident, as I think, was General Cass that there was a snake somewhere about, he chose to run away from the whole thing. This is an inference I draw from the fact that, though he took part in the debate, his name does not appear in the ayes and noes. But does Judge Douglas's reply amount to a satisfactory answer? [Cries of "Yes," "Yes," and "No," "No."] There is some little difference of opinion here. But I ask attention to a few more views bearing on the question of whether it amounts to a satisfactory answer. The men who were determined that that amendment should not get into the bill, and spoil the place where the Dred Scott decision was to come in, sought an excuse to get rid of it somewhere. One of these ways—one of these excuses—was to ask Chase to add to his proposed amendment a provision that the people might *introduce* slavery if they wanted to. They very well knew Chase would do no such thing, that Mr. Chase was one of the men differing from them on the broad principle of his insisting that freedom was *better* than slavery,—a man who would not consent to enact a law, penned with his own hand, by which he was made to recognize slavery on the one hand,

and liberty on the other, as *precisely equal*; and when they insisted on his doing this, they very well knew they insisted on that which he would not for a moment think of doing, and that they were only bluffing him. I believe (I have not, since he made his answer, had a chance to examine the journals or *Congressional Globe* and therefore speak from memory)—I believe the state of the bill at that time, according to parliamentary rules, was such that no member could propose an additional amendment to Chase's amendment. I rather think this is the truth,— the Judge shakes his head. Very well. I would like to know, then, *if they wanted Chase's amendment fixed over, why somebody else could not have offered to do it?* If they wanted it amended, why did they not offer the amendment? Why did they not *put it in themselves?* But to put it on the other ground: suppose that there was such an amendment offered, and Chase's was an amendment to an amendment; until one is disposed of by parliamentary law, you cannot pile another on. Then all these gentlemen had to do was to vote Chase's on, and then, in the amended form in which the whole stood, add their own amendment to it, if they wanted to put it in that shape. This was all they were obliged to do, and the ayes and noes show that there were thirty-six who voted it down, against ten who voted in favor of it. The thirty-six held entire sway and control. They could in some form or other have put that bill in the exact shape they wanted. If there was a rule preventing their amending it at the time, they could pass that, and then, Chase's amendment being merged, put it in the shape they wanted. They did not choose to do so, but they went into a quibble with Chase to get him to add what they knew he would not add, and because he would not, they stand upon the flimsy pretext for voting down what they argued was the meaning and intent of their own bill. They left room thereby for this Dred Scott decision, which goes very far to make slavery national throughout the United States.

I pass one or two points I have, because my time will very soon expire; but I must be allowed to say that Judge Douglas recurs again, as he did upon one or two other occasions, to the enormity of Lincoln,—an insignificant individual like Lincoln,—upon his *ipse dixit* charging a conspiracy upon a large number of members of Congress, the Supreme Court, and two Presidents, to nationalize slavery. I want to say that, in the first place, I have made no charge of this sort upon my *ipse dixit*. I have only arrayed the evidence tending to prove it, and pre- sented it to the understanding of others, saying what I think it proves, but giving you the means of judging whether it proves it or not. This is precisely what I have done. I have not placed it upon my *ipse dixit* at all. On this occasion, I wish to recall his attention to a piece of evidence which I brought forward at Ottawa on Saturday, showing that he had made substantially the same charge against substantially the *same persons*, excluding his dear self from the category. I ask him to give some attention to the evidence which I brought forward that he himself had discovered a "fatal blow being struck" against the right of the people to exclude slavery from their limits, which fatal blow he assumed as in evidence in an article in the Washington *Union*, published "by authority." I ask by whose authority? He discovers a similar or identical provision in the Lecompton Constitution. Made by whom? The framers of that Constitution. Advocated by whom? By all the members of the party in the nation, who advocated the introduction of Kansas into the Union under the Lecompton Constitution.

I have asked his attention to the evidence that he arrayed to prove that such a fatal blow was being struck, and to the facts which he brought forward in support of that charge,—being identical with the one which he thinks so villainous in me. He pointed it, not at a newspaper editor merely, but at the President and his Cabinet and the members of Congress advocating the Lecompton Constitution and those framing that instrument. I must again be permitted to remind him that although my *ipse dixit* may not be as great as his, yet it somewhat reduces the force of his calling my attention to the *enormity* of my making a like charge against him.

Go on. Judge Douglas.

## MR. DOUGLAS'S REPLY

LADIES AND GENTLEMEN: The silence with which you have listened to Mr. Lincoln during his hour is creditable to this vast audience, composed of men of various political parties. Nothing is more honorable to any large mass of people assembled for the purpose of a fair discussion than that kind and respectful attention that is yielded, not only to your political friends, but to those who are opposed to you in politics.

I am glad that at last I have brought Mr. Lincoln to the conclusion that he had better define his position on certain political questions to which I called his attention at Ottawa. He there showed no disposition, no inclination, to answer them. I did not present idle questions for him to answer, merely for my gratification. I laid the foundation for those interrogatories by showing that they constituted the platform of the party whose nominee he is for the Senate. I did not presume that I had the right to catechise him as I saw proper, unless I showed that his party, or a majority of it, stood upon the platform and were in favor of the propositions upon which my questions were based. I desired simply to know, inasmuch as he had been nominated as the first, last, and only choice of his party, whether he concurred in the platform which that party had adopted for its government. In a

few minutes I will proceed to review the answers which he has given to these interrogatories; but, in order to relieve his anxiety, I will first respond to these which he
has presented to me. Mark you, he has not presented interrogatories which have
ever received the sanction of the party with which I am acting, and hence he has
no other foundation for them than his own curiosity.

First, he desires to know if the people of Kansas shall form a constitution by
means entirely proper and unobjectionable, and ask admission into the Union
as a State, before they have the requisite population for a member of Congress,
whether I will vote for that admission. Well, now, I regret exceedingly that he
did not answer that interrogatory himself before he put it to me, in order that we
might understand, and not be left to infer, on which side he is. Mr. Trumbull,
during the last session of Congress, voted from the beginning to the end against
the admission of Oregon, although a free State, because she had not the requisite
population for a member of Congress. Mr. Trumbull would not consent, under
any circumstances, to let a State, free or slave, come into the Union until it had
the requisite population. As Mr. Trumbull is in the held, fighting for Mr. Lincoln,
I would like to have Mr. Lincoln answer his own question, and tell me whether he
is fighting Trumbull on that issue or not. But I will answer his question. In reference to Kansas, it is my opinion that as she has population enough to constitute
a slave State, she has people enough for a free State. I will not make Kansas an
exceptional case to the other States of the Union. I hold it to be a sound rule, of
universal application, to require a Territory to contain the requisite population for
a member of Congress before it is admitted as a State into the Union. I made that
proposition in the Senate in 1856, and I renewed it during the last session, in a
bill providing that no Territory of the United States should form a constitution
and apply for admission until it had the requisite population. On another occasion I proposed that neither Kansas nor any other Territory should be admitted
until it had the requisite population. Congress did not adopt any of my propositions containing this general rule, but did make an exception of Kansas. I will
stand by that exception. Either Kansas must come in as a free State, with whatever
population she may have, or the rule must be applied to all the other Territories
alike. I therefore answer at once, that, it having been decided that Kansas has
people enough for a slave State, I hold that she has enough for a free State. I hope
Mr. Lincoln is satisfied with my answer; and now I would like to get his answer
to his own interrogatory,—whether or not he will vote to admit Kansas before
she has the requisite population. I want to know whether he will vote to admit
Oregon before that Territory has the requisite population. Mr. Trumbull will not,
and the same reason that commits Mr. Trumbull against the admission of Oregon

commits him against Kansas, even if she should apply for admission as a free State. If there is any sincerity, any truth, in the argument of Mr. Trumbull in the Senate, against the admission of Oregon because she had not 93,420 people, although the population was larger than that of Kansas, he stands pledged against the admission of both Oregon and Kansas until they have 93,420 inhabitants. I would like Mr. Lincoln to answer this question. I would like him to take his own medicine. If he differs with Mr. Trumbull, let him answer his argument against the admission of Oregon, instead of poking questions at me.

The next question propounded to me by Mr. Lincoln is, Can the people of a Territory in any lawful way, against the wishes of any citizen of the United States, exclude slavery from their limits prior to the formation of a State constitution? I answer emphatically, as Mr. Lincoln has heard me answer a hundred times from every stump in Illinois, that in my opinion the people of a Territory can, by lawful means, exclude slavery from their limits prior to the formation of a State constitution. Mr. Lincoln knew that I had answered that question over and over again. He heard me argue the Nebraska Bill on that principle all over the State in 1854, in 1855, and in 1856, and he has no excuse for pretending to be in doubt as to my position on that question. It matters not what way the Supreme Court may hereafter decide as to the abstract question whether slavery may or may not go into a Territory under the Constitution, the people have the lawful means to introduce it or exclude it as they please, for the reason that slavery cannot exist a day or an hour anywhere, unless it is supported by local police regulations. Those police regulations can only be established by the local legislature; and if the people are opposed to slavery, they will elect representatives to that body who will by unfriendly legislation effectually prevent the introduction of it into their midst. If, on the contrary, they are for it, their legislation will favor its extension. Hence, no matter what the decision of the Supreme Court may be on that abstract question, still the right of the people to make a slave Territory or a free Territory is perfect and complete under the Nebraska Bill. I hope Mr. Lincoln deems my answer satisfactory on that point.

In this connection, I will notice the charge which he has introduced in relation to Mr. Chase's amendment. I thought that I had chased that amendment out of Mr. Lincoln's brain at Ottawa; but it seems that it still haunts his imagination, and he is not yet satisfied. I had supposed that he would be ashamed to press that question further. He is a lawyer, and has been a member of Congress, and has occupied his time and amused you by telling you about parliamentary proceedings. He ought to have known better than to try to palm off his miserable impositions upon this intelligent audience. The Nebraska Bill provided that the legislative power and authority of the said Territory should extend to all rightful subjects of legislation consistent with the organic act and the Constitution of the United States. I did not make any exception as to slavery, but gave all the power that it was possible for Congress to give, without violating the Constitution, to the Territorial Legislature, with no exception or limitation on the subject of slavery at all. The language of that bill which I have quoted gave the full power and the full authority over the subject of slavery, affirmatively and negatively, to introduce it or exclude it, so far as the Constitution of the United States would permit. What more could Mr. Chase give by his amendment? Nothing. He offered his amendment for the identical purpose for which Mr. Lincoln is using it,—to enable demagogues in the country to try and deceive the people.

His amendment was to this effect: it provided that the Legislature should have the power to exclude slavery; and General Cass suggested, "Why not give the power to introduce as well as exclude?" The answer was, "They have the power already in the bill to do both." Chase was afraid his amendment would be adopted if he put the alternative proposition, and so made it fair both ways, but would not yield. He offered it for the purpose of having it rejected. He offered it, as he has himself avowed over and over again, simply to make capital out of it for the stump. He expected that it would be capital for small politicians in the country, and that they would make an effort to deceive the people with it; and he was not mistaken, for Lincoln is carrying out the plan admirably. Lincoln knows that the Nebraska Bill, without Chase's amendment, gave all the power which the Constitution would permit. Could Congress confer any more? Could Congress go beyond the Constitution of the country? We gave all a full grant, with no exception in regard to slavery one way or the other. We left that question as we left all others, to be decided by the people for themselves, just as they please. I will not occupy my time on this question. I have argued it before, all over Illinois. I have argued it in this beautiful city of Freeport; I have argued it in the North, the South, the East, and the West, avowing the same sentiments and the same principles. I have not been afraid to avow my sentiments up here for fear I would be trotted down into Egypt.

The third question which Mr. Lincoln presented is, if the Supreme Court of the United States shall decide that a State of this Union cannot exclude slavery from its own limits, will I submit to it? I am amazed that Lincoln should ask such a question. ["A schoolboy knows better."] Yes, a schoolboy does know better. Mr. Lincoln's object is to cast an imputation upon the Supreme Court. He knows that there never was but one man in America, claiming any degree of intelligence or decency, who ever for a moment pretended such a thing. It is true that the

Washington *Union*, in an article published on the 17th of last December, did put forth that doctrine, and I denounced the article on the floor of the Senate, in a speech which Mr. Lincoln now pretends was against the President. The *Union* had claimed that slavery had a right to go into the free States, and that any provisions in the constitution or laws of the free States to the contrary were null and void. I denounced it in the Senate, as I said before, and I was the first man who did. Lincoln's friends, Trumbull, and Seward, and Hale, and Wilson, and the whole Black Republican side of the Senate, were silent. They left it to me to denounce it. And what was the reply made to me on that occasion? Mr. Toombs, of Georgia, got up and undertook to lecture me on the ground that I ought not to have deemed the article worthy of notice, and ought not to have replied to it; that there was not one man, woman, or child south of the Potomac, in any slave State, who did not repudiate any such pretension. Mr. Lincoln knows that that reply was made on the spot, and yet now he asks this question. He might as well ask me, suppose Mr. Lincoln should steal a horse, would I sanction it; and it would be as genteel in me to ask him, in the event he stole a horse, what ought to be done with him. He casts an imputation upon the Supreme Court of the United States, by supposing that they would violate the Constitution of the United States. I tell him that such a thing is not possible. It would be an act of moral treason that no man on the bench could ever descend to. Mr. Lincoln himself would never in his partisan feelings so far forget what was right as to be guilty of such an act.

The fourth question of Mr. Lincoln is, Are you in favor of acquiring additional territory, in disregard as to how such acquisition may affect the Union on the slavery question? This question is very ingeniously and cunningly put.

The Black Republican creed lays it down expressly that under no circumstances shall we acquire any more territory, unless slavery is first prohibited in the country. I ask Mr. Lincoln whether he is in favor of that proposition. Are you [addressing Mr. Lincoln] opposed to the acquisition of any more territory, under any circumstances, unless slavery is prohibited in it? That he does not like to answer. When I ask him whether he stands up to that article in the platform of his party, he turns, Yankee-fashion, and without answering it, asks me whether I am in favor of acquiring territory without regard to how it may affect the Union on the slavery question. I answer that whenever it becomes necessary, in our growth and progress, to acquire more territory, that I am in favor of it, without reference to the question of slavery; and when we have acquired it, I will leave the people free to do as they please, either to make it slave or free territory, as they prefer. It is idle to tell me or you that we have territory enough. Our fathers supposed that we had enough when our territory extended to the Mississippi River; but a few years' growth and expansion satisfied them that we needed more, and the Louisiana territory, from the west bank of the Mississippi to the British possessions, was acquired. Then we acquired Oregon, then California and New Mexico. We have enough now for the present; but this is a young and growing nation. It swarms as often as a hive of bees; and as new swarms are turned out each year, there must be hives in which they can gather and make their honey. In less than fifteen years, if the same progress that has distinguished this country for the last fifteen years continues, every foot of vacant land between this and the Pacific Ocean, owned by the United States, will be occupied. Will you not continue to increase at the end of fifteen years as well as now? I tell you, increase, and multiply, and expand, is the law of this nation's existence. You cannot limit this great Republic by mere boundary lines, saying, "Thus far shalt thou go, and no farther." Any one of you gentlemen might as well say to a son twelve years old that he is big enough, and must not grow any larger; and in order to prevent his growth, put a hoop around him to keep him to his present size. What would be the result? Either the hoop must burst and be rent asunder, or the child must die. So it would be with this great nation. With our natural increase, growing with a rapidity unknown in any part of the globe, with the tide of emigration that is fleeing from despotism in the Old World to seek refuge in our own, there is a constant torrent pouring into this country that requires more land, more territory upon which to settle; and just as fast as our interests and our destiny require additional territory in the North, in the South, or on the islands of the ocean, I am for it; and when we acquire it, will leave the people, according to the Nebraska Bill, free to do as they please on the subject of slavery and every other question.

I trust now that Mr. Lincoln will deem himself answered on his four points. He racked his brain so much in devising these four questions that he exhausted himself, and had not strength enough to invent the others. As soon as he is able to hold a council with his advisers, Lovejoy, Farnsworth, and Fred Douglass, he will frame and propound others. ["Good, good."] You Black Republicans who say "good" I have no doubt think that they are all good men. I have reason to recollect that some people in this country think that Fred Douglass is a very good man. The last time I came here to make a speech, while talking from the stand to you, people of Freeport, as I am doing to-day, I saw a carriage—and a magnificent one it was—drive up and take a position on the outside of the crowd; a beautiful young lady was sitting on the box-seat, whilst Fred Douglass and her mother reclined inside, and the owner of the carriage acted as driver. I saw this in your own town. ["What of it?"] All I have to say of it is this, that if you. Black Republicans, think that the negro ought to be on a social equality with your wives and daughters, and ride in a carriage with your wife, whilst you drive the team, you have perfect right to do so. I am told that one of Fred Douglass's kinsmen, another rich black negro, is now travelling in this part of the State, making speeches for his friend Lincoln as the champion of black men. ["What have you to say against it?"] All I have to say on that subject is, that those of you who believe that the negro is your equal and ought to be on an equality with you socially, politically, and legally, have a right to entertain those opinions, and of course will vote for Mr. Lincoln.

I have a word to say on Mr. Lincoln's answers to the interrogatories contained in my speech at Ottawa, and which he has pretended to reply to here to-day. Mr. Lincoln makes a great parade of the fact that I quoted a platform as having been adopted by the Black Republican party at Springfield in 1854, which, it turns out, was adopted at another place. Mr. Lincoln loses sight of the thing itself in his ecstasies over the mistake I made in stating the place where it was done. He thinks that that platform was not adopted on the right "spot."

When I put the direct questions to Mr. Lincoln to ascertain whether he now stands pledged to that creed,—to the unconditional repeal of the Fugitive Slave law, a refusal to admit any more slave States into the Union, even if the people want them, a determination to apply the Wilmot Proviso, not only to all the territory we now have, but all that we may hereafter acquire,—he refused to answer; and his followers say, in excuse, that the resolutions upon which I based my interrogatories were not adopted at the "*right spot.*" Lincoln and his political friends are great on "*spots.*" In Congress, as a representative of this State, he declared the Mexican war to be unjust and infamous, and would not support it, or acknowledge his own country to be right in the contest, because he said that American blood was not shed on American soil in the "*right spot.*" And now he cannot answer the questions I put to him at Ottawa because the resolutions I read were not adopted at the "*right spot.*" It may be possible that I was led into an error as to the *spot* on which the resolutions I then read were proclaimed, but I was not, and am not, in error as to the fact of their forming the basis of the creed of the Republican party when that party was first organized. I will state to you the evidence I had, and upon which I relied for my statement that the resolutions in question were adopted at Springfield on the 5th of October, 1854. Although I was aware that such resolutions had been passed in this district, and nearly all the Northern Congressional districts and county conventions, I had not noticed whether or not they had been adopted by any State convention. In 1856, a debate arose in Congress between Major Thomas L. Harris, of the Springfield District, and Mr. Norton, of the Joliet District, on political matters connected with our State, in the course of which Major Harris quoted those resolutions as having been passed by the first Republican State Convention that ever assembled in Illinois. I knew that Major Harris was remarkable for his accuracy, that he was a very conscientious and sincere man, and I also noticed that Norton did not question the accuracy of this statement. I therefore took it for granted that it was so; and the other day when I concluded to use the resolutions at Ottawa I wrote to Charles H. Lanphier, editor of the *State Register*, at Springfield, calling his attention to them, telling him that I had been informed that Major Harris was lying sick at Springfield, and desiring him to call upon him and ascertain all the facts concerning the resolutions, the time and the place where they were adopted. In reply, Mr. Lanphier sent me two copies of his paper, which I have here. The first is a copy of the *State Register*, published at Springfield, Mr. Lincoln's own town, on the 16th of October, 1854, only eleven days after the adjournment of the Convention, from which I desire to read the following:

> During the late discussions in this city, Lincoln made a speech, to which Judge Douglas replied. In Lincoln's speech he took the broad ground that, according to the Declaration of Independence, the whites and blacks are equal. From this he drew the conclusion, which he several times repeated, that the white man had no right to pass laws for the government of the black man without the nigger's consent. This speech of Lincoln's was heard and applauded by all the Abolitionists assembled in Springfield. So soon as Mr. Lincoln was done speaking, Mr. Codding arose, and requested all the delegates to the Black Republican Convention to withdraw into the Senate chamber. They did so; and after long deliberation, they laid down the following Abolition platform as the platform on which they stood. We call the particular attention of all our readers to it.

Then follows the identical platform, word for word, which I read at Ottawa. Now, that was published in Mr. Lincoln's own town, eleven days after the Convention was held, and it has remained on record up to this day never contradicted.

When I quoted the resolutions at Ottawa and questioned Mr. Lincoln in relation to them, he said that his name was on the committee that reported them, but he did not serve, nor did he think he served, because he was, or thought he was, in Tazewell County at the time the Convention was in session. He did not deny that the resolutions were passed by the Springfield Convention. He did not know better, and evidently thought that they were; but afterward his friends declared that they had discovered that they varied in some respects from the resolutions passed by that Convention. I have shown you that I had good evidence for believing that the resolutions had been passed at Springfield. Mr. Lincoln ought to have known better; but not a word is said about his ignorance on the subject, whilst I, notwithstanding the circumstances, am accused of forgery.

Now, I will show you that if I have made a mistake as to the place where these resolutions were adopted,—and when I get down to Springfield I will investigate the matter, and see whether or not I have,—that the principles they enunciate were adopted as the Black Republican platform ["white, white"], in the various counties and Congressional districts throughout the north end of the State in 1854. This platform was adopted in nearly every county that gave a Black Republican majority for the Legislature in that year, and here is a man [pointing to Mr. Denio, who sat on the stand near Deacon Bross] who knows as well as any living man that it was the creed of the Black Republican party at that time. I would be willing to call Denio as a witness, or any other honest man belonging to that party. I will now read the resolutions adopted at the Rockford Convention on the 30th of August, 1854, which nominated Washburne for Congress. You elected him on the following platform:

> *Resolved,* That the continued and increasing aggressions of slavery in our country are destructive of the best rights of a free people, and that such aggressions cannot be successfully resisted without the united political action of all good men.
>
> *Resolved,* That the citizens of the United States hold in their hands a peaceful, constitutional, and efficient remedy against the encroachments of the slave power,—the ballot box; and if that remedy is boldly and wisely applied, the principles of liberty and eternal justice will be established.
>
> *Resolved,* That we accept this issue forced upon us by the slave power, and, in defence of freedom, will co-operate and be known as Republicans, pledged to the accomplishment of the following purposes:
>
> To bring the Administration of the Government back to the control of first principles; to restore Kansas and Nebraska to the position of Free Territories; to repeal and entirely abrogate the Fugitive Slave law; to restrict slavery to those States in which it exists; to prohibit the admission of any more slave States into the Union; to exclude slavery from all the Territories over which the General Government has exclusive jurisdiction; and

to resist the acquisition of any more Territories, unless the introduction of slavery therein forever shall have been prohibited.

*Resolved,* That in furtherance of these principles we will use such constitutional and lawful means as shall seem best adapted to their accomplishment, and that we will support no man for office under the General or State Government who is not positively committed to the support of these principles, and whose personal character and conduct is not a guarantee that he is reliable, and shall abjure all party allegiance and ties.

*Resolved,* That we cordially invite persons of all former political parties whatever, in favor of the object expressed in the above resolutions, to unite with us in carrying them into effect.

Well, you think that is a very good platform, do you not? If you do, if you approve it now, and think it is all right, you will not join with those men who say I libel you by calling these your principles, will you? Now, Mr. Lincoln complains; Mr. Lincoln charges that I did you and him injustice by saying that this was the platform of your party. I am told that Washburne made a speech in Galena last night, in which he abused me awfully for bringing to light this platform, on which he was elected to Congress. He thought that you had forgotten it, as he, and Mr. Lincoln desires too. He did not deny but that you had adopted it, and that he had subscribed to and was pledged by it, but he did not think it was fair to call it up and remind the people that it was their platform.

But I am glad to find that you are more honest in your Abolitionism than your leaders, by avowing that it is your platform, and right in your opinion.

In the adoption of that platform, you not only declared that you would resist the admission of any more slave States, and work for the repeal of the Fugitive Slave law, but you pledged yourselves not to vote for any man for State or Federal offices who was not committed to these principles. You were thus committed. Similar resolutions to those were adopted in your county convention here, and now, with your admissions that they are your platform and embody your sentiments now as they did then, what do you think of Mr. Lincoln, your candidate for the United States Senate, who is attempting to dodge the responsibility of this platform, because it was not adopted in the right spot. I thought that it was adopted in Springfield; but it turns out it was not, that it was adopted at Rockford, and in the various counties which comprise this Congressional district. When I get into the next district I will show that the same platform was adopted there, and so on through the State, until I nail the responsibility of it upon the Black Republican party throughout the State.

A VOICE: "Couldn't you modify, and call it brown?"

MR. DOUGLAS: Not a bit. I thought that you were becoming a little brown when your members in Congress voted for the Crittenden-Montgomery bill; but since you have backed out from that position and gone back to Abolitionism you are black, and not brown.

Gentlemen, I have shown you what your platform was in 1854. You still adhere to it. The same platform was adopted by nearly all the counties where the Black Republican party had a majority in 1854. I wish now to call your attention to the action of your representatives in the Legislature when they assembled together at Springfield. In the first place, you must remember that this was the organization of a new party. It is so declared in the resolutions themselves, which say that you are going to dissolve all old party ties and call the new party Republican. The old Whig party was to have its throat cut from ear to ear, and the Democratic party was to be annihilated and blotted out of existence, whilst in lieu of these parties the Black Republican party was to be organized on this Abolition platform. You know who the chief leaders were in breaking up and destroying these two great parties. Lincoln on the one hand, and Trumbull on the other, being disappointed politicians, and having retired or been driven to obscurity by an outraged constituency because of their political sins, formed a scheme to Abolitionize the two parties, and lead the old-line Whigs and old-line Democrats captive, bound hand and foot, into the Abolition camp. Giddings, Chase, Fred Douglass, and Lovejoy were here to christen them whenever they were brought in. Lincoln went to work to dissolve the old-line Whig party. Clay was dead; and although the sod was not yet green on his grave, this man undertook to bring into disrepute those great Compromise measures of 1850, with which Clay and Webster were identified. Up to 1854 the old Whig party and the Democratic party had stood on a common platform so far as this slavery question was concerned. You Whigs and we Democrats differed about the bank, the tariff, distribution, the specie circular, and the sub-treasury, but we agreed on this slavery question, and the true mode of preserving the peace and harmony of the Union. The Compromise measures of 1850 were introduced by Clay, were defended by Webster, and supported by Cass, and were approved by Fillmore, and sanctioned by the national men of both parties. They constituted a common plank upon which both Whigs and Democrats stood. In 1852 the Whig party, in its last National Convention at Baltimore, indorsed and approved these measures of Clay, and so did the National Convention of the Democratic party held that same year. Thus the old-line Whigs and the old-line Democrats stood pledged to the great principle of self-government, which guarantees to the people of each Territory the right to decide the slavery question for themselves. In 1854,

after the death of Clay and Webster, Mr. Lincoln, on the part of the Whigs, under-
took to Abolitionize the Whig party, by dissolving it, transferring the members
into the Abolition camp, and making them train under Giddings, Fred Douglass,
Lovejoy, Chase, Farnsworth, and other Abolition leaders. Trumbull undertook to
dissolve the Democratic party by taking old Democrats into the Abolition camp.
Mr. Lincoln was aided in his efforts by many leading Whigs throughout the
State, your member of Congress, Mr. Washburne, being one of the most active.
Trumbull was aided by many renegades from the Democratic party, among whom
were John Wentworth, Tom Turner, and others, with whom you are familiar.

[MR. TURNER, who was one of the moderators, here interposed, and said that
he had drawn the resolutions which Senator Douglas had read.]

MR. DOUGLAS: Yes, and Turner says that he drew these resolutions. ["Hurrah
for Turner," "Hurrah for Douglas."] That is right; give Turner cheers for drawing the resolutions if you approve them. If he drew those resolutions, he will not
deny that they are the creed of the Black Republican party.

MR. TURNER: They are our creed exactly.

MR. DOUGLAS: And yet Lincoln denies that he stands on them. Mr. Turner
says that the creed of the Black Republican party is the admission of no more
slave States, and yet Mr. Lincoln declares that he would not like to be placed
in a position where he would have to vote for them. All I have to say to friend
Lincoln is, that I do not think there is much danger of his being placed in such an
embarrassing position as to be obliged to vote on the admission of any more slave
States. I propose, out of mere kindness, to relieve him from any such necessity.

When the bargain between Lincoln and Trumbull was completed for
Abolitionizing the Whig and Democratic parties, they "spread" over the State,
Lincoln still pretending to be an old-line Whig, in order to "rope in" the Whigs,
and Trumbull pretending to be as good a Democrat as he ever was, in order to
coax the Democrats over into the Abolition ranks. They played the part that
"decoy ducks" play down on the Potomac River. In that part of the country
they make artificial ducks, and put them on the water in places where the wild
ducks are to be found, for the purpose of decoying them. Well, Lincoln and
Trumbull played the part of these "decoy ducks," and deceived enough old-line
Whigs and old-line Democrats to elect a Black Republican Legislature. When
that Legislature met, the first thing it did was to elect as Speaker of the House the
very man who is now boasting that he wrote the Abolition platform on which
Lincoln will not stand. I want to know of Mr. Turner whether or not, when he
was elected, he was a good embodiment of Republican principles?

MR. TURNER: I hope I was then, and am now.

MR. DOUGLAS: He swears that he hopes he was then, and is now. He wrote that Black Republican platform, and is satisfied with it now. I admire and acknowledge Turner's honesty. Every man of you knows that what he says about these resolutions being the platform of the Black Republican party is true, and you also know that each one of these men who are shuffling and trying to deny it are only trying to cheat the people out of their votes for the purpose of deceiving them still more after the election. I propose to trace this thing a little further, in order that you can see what additional evidence there is to fasten this revolutionary platform upon the Black Republican party. When the Legislature assembled, there was a United States Senator to elect in the place of General Shields, and before they proceeded to ballot. Love joy insisted on laying down certain principles by which to govern the party. It has been published to the world and satisfactorily proven that there was, at the time the alliance was made between Trumbull and Lincoln to Abolitionize the two parties, an agreement that Lincoln should take Shields's place in the United States Senate, and Trumbull should have mine so soon as they could conveniently get rid of me. When Lincoln was beaten for Shields's place, in a manner I will refer to in a few minutes, he felt very sore and restive; his friends grumbled, and some of them came out and charged that the most infamous treachery had been practiced against him; that the bargain was that Lincoln was to have had Shields's place, and Trumbull was to have waited for mine, but that Trumbull, having the control of a few Abolitionized Democrats, he prevented them from voting for Lincoln, thus keeping him within a few votes of an election until he succeeded in forcing the party to drop him and elect Trumbull. Well, Trumbull having cheated Lincoln, his friends made a fuss, and in order to keep them and Lincoln quiet, the party were obliged to come forward, in advance, at the last State election, and make a pledge that they would go for Lincoln and nobody else. Lincoln could not be silenced in any other way.

Now, there are a great many Black Republicans of you who do not know this thing was done. ["White, white," and great clamor.] I wish to remind you that while Mr. Lincoln was speaking there was not a Democrat vulgar and blackguard enough to interrupt him. But I know that the shoe is pinching you. I am clinching Lincoln now, and you are scared to death for the result. I have seen this thing before. I have seen men make appointments for joint discussions, and the moment their man has been heard, try to interrupt and prevent a fair hearing of the other side. I have seen your mobs before, and defy your wrath. [Tremendous applause.] My friends, do not cheer, for I need my whole time. The object of the opposition is to occupy my attention in order to prevent me from giving the whole evidence and nailing this double dealing on the Black Republican party. As I have before said, Lovejoy demanded a declaration of principles on the part of the Black Republicans of the Legislature before going into an election for United States Senator. He offered the following preamble and resolutions which I hold in my hand:

> WHEREAS, Human slavery is a violation of the principles of natural and revealed rights; and whereas the fathers of the Revolution, fully imbued with the spirit of these principles, declared freedom to be the inalienable birthright of all men; and whereas the preamble to the Constitution of the United States avers that that instrument was ordained to establish justice, and secure the blessings of liberty to ourselves and our posterity; and whereas, in furtherance of the above principles, slavery was forever prohibited in the old Northwest Territory, and more recently in all that Territory lying west and north of the State of Missouri, by the act of the Federal Government; and whereas the repeal of the prohibition last referred to was contrary to the wishes of the people of Illinois, a violation of an implied compact long deemed sacred by the citizens of the United States, and a wide departure from the uniform action of the General Government in relation to the extension of slavery; therefore,
>
> *Resolved, by the House of Representatives, the Senate concurring therein,* That our Senators in Congress be instructed, and our Representatives requested, to introduce, if not otherwise introduced, and to vote for a bill to restore such prohibition to the aforesaid Territories, and also to extend a similar prohibition to all territory which now belongs to the United States, or which may hereafter come under their jurisdiction.
>
> *Resolved,* That our Senators in Congress be instructed, and our Representatives requested, to vote against the admission of any State into the Union, the Constitution of which does not prohibit slavery, whether the territory out of which such State may have been formed shall have been acquired by conquest, treaty, purchase, or from original territory of the United States.
>
> *Resolved,* That our Senators in Congress be instructed, and our Representatives requested, to introduce and vote for a bill to repeal an Act entitled "An Act respecting fugitives from justice and persons escaping from the service of their masters"; and, failing in that, for such a modification of it as shall secure the

right of *habeas corpus* and trial by jury before the regularly constituted authorities of the State, to all persons claimed as owing
service or labor.

Those resolutions were introduced by Mr. Lovejoy immediately preceding
the election of Senator. They declared, first, that the Wilmot Proviso must be
applied to all territory north of 36 deg., 30 min. Secondly, that it must be applied
to all territory south of 36 deg., 30 min. Thirdly, that it must be applied to all
the territory now owned by the United States; and finally, that it must be applied
to all territory hereafter to be acquired by the United States. The next resolution
declares that no more slave States shall be admitted into this Union under any
circumstances whatever, no matter whether they are formed out of territory now
owned by us or that we may hereafter acquire, by treaty, by Congress, or in any
manner whatever. The next resolution demands the unconditional repeal of the
Fugitive Slave law, although its unconditional repeal would leave no provision
for carrying out that clause of the Constitution of the United States which guarantees the surrender of fugitives. If they could not get an unconditional repeal,
they demanded that that law should be so modified as to make it as nearly useless
as possible. Now, I want to show you who voted for these resolutions. When the
vote was taken on the first resolution it was decided in the affirmative,—yeas 41,
nays 32. You will find that this is a strict party vote, between the Democrats on
the one hand and the Black Republicans on the other. [Cries of "White, white,"
and clamor.] I know your name, and always call things by their right name. The
point I wish to call your attention to is this: that these resolutions were adopted
on the 7th day of February, and that on the 8th they went into an election for a
United States Senator, and that day every man who voted for these resolutions,
with but two exceptions, voted for Lincoln for the United States Senate. ["Give
us their names."] I will read the names over to you if you want them, but I believe
your object is to occupy my time.

On the next resolution the vote stood—yeas 33, nays 40; and on the third
resolution—yeas 35, nays 47. I wish to impress it upon you that every man who
voted for those resolutions, with but two exceptions, voted on the next day for
Lincoln for United States Senator. Bear in mind that the members who thus
voted for Lincoln were elected to the Legislature pledged to vote for no man for
office under the State or Federal Government who was not committed to this
Black Republican platform. They were all so pledged. Mr. Turner, who stands
by me, and who then represented you, and who says that he wrote those resolutions, voted for Lincoln, when he was pledged not to do so unless Lincoln was in

favor of those resolutions. I now ask Mr. Turner [turning to Mr. Turner], did you violate your pledge in voting for Mr. Lincoln, or did he commit himself to your platform before you cast your vote for him?

I could go through the whole list of names here, and show you that all the Black Republicans in the Legislature, who voted for Mr. Lincoln, had voted on the day previous for these resolutions. For instance, here are the names of Sargent and Little, of Jo Daviess and Carroll, Thomas J. Turner of Stephenson, Lawrence of Boone and McHenry, Swan of Lake, Pinckney of Ogle County, and Lyman of Winnebago. Thus you see every member from your Congressional district voted for Mr. Lincoln, and they were pledged not to vote for him unless he was committed to the doctrine of no more slave States, the prohibition of slavery in the Territories, and the repeal of the Fugitive Slave law. Mr. Lincoln tells you to-day that he is not pledged to any such doctrine. Either Mr. Lincoln was then committed to those propositions, or Mr. Turner violated his pledges to you when he voted for him. Either Lincoln was pledged to each one of those propositions, or else every Black Republican Representative from this Congressional district violated his pledge of honor to his constituents by voting for him. I ask you which horn of the dilemma will you take? Will you hold Lincoln up to the platform of his party or will you accuse every Representative you had in the Legislature of violating his pledge of honor to his constituents? There is no escape for you. Either Mr. Lincoln was committed to those propositions or your members violated their faith. Take either horn of the dilemma you choose. There is no dodging the question; I want Lincoln's answer. He says he was not pledged to repeal the Fugitive Slave law, that he does not quite like to do it; he will not introduce a law to repeal it, but thinks there ought to be some law; he does not tell what it ought to be; upon the whole, he is altogether undecided, and don't know what to think or do. That is the substance of his answer upon the repeal of the Fugitive Slave law. I put the question to him distinctly, whether he indorsed that part of the Black Republican platform which calls for the entire abrogation and repeal of the Fugitive Slave law. He answers, No! that he does not indorse that; but he does not tell what he is for, or what he will vote for. His answer is, in fact, no answer at all. Why cannot he speak out, and say what he is for, and what he will do?

In regard to there being no more slave States, he is not pledged to that. He would not like, he says, to be put in a position where he would have to vote one way or another upon that question. I pray you, do not put him in a position that would embarrass him so much. Gentlemen, if he goes to the Senate, he may be put in that position, and then which way will he vote?

A voice: "How will you vote?"

MR. DOUGLAS: I will vote for the admission of just such a State as by the form of their constitution the people show they want; if they want slavery, they shall have it; if they prohibit slavery, it shall be prohibited. They can form their institutions to please themselves, subject only to the Constitution; and I, for one, stand ready to receive them into the Union. Why cannot your Black Republican candidates talk out as plain as that when they are questioned?

I do not want to cheat any man out of his vote. No man is deceived in regard to my principles if I have the power to express myself in terms explicit enough to convey my ideas.

Mr. Lincoln made a speech when he was nominated for the United States Senate which covers all these Abolition platforms. He there lays down a proposition so broad in its Abolitionism as to cover the whole ground.

> In my opinion it [the slavery agitation] will not cease until a crisis shall have been reached and passed. "A house divided against itself cannot stand." I believe this government cannot endure permanently half slave and half free. I do not expect the house to fall, but I do expect it will cease to be divided. It will become all one thing or all the other. Either the opponents of slavery will arrest the further spread of it, and place it where the public mind shall rest in the belief that it is in the course of ultimate extinction, or its advocates will push it forward till it shall become alike lawful in all the States,—old as well as new, North as well as South.

There you find that Mr. Lincoln lays down the doctrine that this Union cannot endure divided as our fathers made it, with free and slave States. He says they must all become one thing, or all the other; that they must all be free or all slave, or else the Union cannot continue to exist; it being his opinion that to admit any more slave States, to continue to divide the Union into free and slave States, will dissolve it. I want to know of Mr. Lincoln whether he will vote for the admission of another slave State.

He tells you the Union cannot exist unless the States are all free or all slave; he tells you that he is opposed to making them all slave, and hence he is for making them all free, in order that the Union may exist; and yet he will not say that he will not vote against another slave State, knowing that the Union must be dissolved if he votes for it. I ask you if that is fair dealing? The true intent and inevitable conclusion to be drawn from his first Springfield speech is, that he is opposed to the admission of any more slave States under any circumstances. If he is so opposed, why not say so? If he believes this Union cannot endure divided into free and slave States, that they must all become free in order to save the Union, he is bound as an honest man to vote against any more slave States. If he believes it, he is bound to do it. Show me that it is my duty, in order to save the Union, to do a particular act, and I will do it if the Constitution does not prohibit it. I am not for the dissolution of the Union under any circumstances. I will pursue no course of conduct that will give just cause for the dissolution of the Union. The hope of the friends of freedom throughout the world rests upon the perpetuity of this Union. The downtrodden and oppressed people who are suffering under European despotism all look with hope and anxiety to the American Union as the only resting place and permanent home of freedom and self-government.

Mr. Lincoln says that he believes that this Union cannot continue to endure with slave States in it, and yet he will not tell you distinctly whether he will vote for or against the admission of any more slave States, but says he would not like to be put to the test. I do not think he will be put to the test. I do not think that the people of Illinois desire a man to represent them who would not like to be put to the test on the performance of a high constitutional duty. I will retire in shame from the Senate of the United States when I am not willing to be put to the test in the performance of my duty. I have been put to severe tests. I have stood by my principles in fair weather and in foul, in the sunshine and in the rain. I have defended the great principle of self-government here among you when Northern sentiment ran in a torrent against me, and I have defended that same great principle when Southern sentiment came down like an avalanche upon me. I was not afraid of any test they put to me. I knew I was right; I knew my principles were sound; I knew that the people would see in the end that I had done right, and I knew that the God of heaven would smile upon me if I was faithful in the performance of my duty.

Mr. Lincoln makes a charge of corruption against the Supreme Court of the United States, and two presidents of the United States, and attempts to bolster it up by saying that I did the same against the Washington *Union*. Suppose I did make that charge of corruption against the Washington *Union*, when it was true, does that justify him in making a false charge against me and others? That is the question I would put. He says that at the time the Nebraska Bill was introduced, and before it was passed, there was a conspiracy between the judges of the Supreme Court, President Pierce, President Buchanan, and myself, by that bill and the decision of the court to break down the barrier and establish slavery all over the Union. Does he not know that that charge is historically false as against President Buchanan? He knows that Mr. Buchanan was at that time in England, representing this country with distinguished ability at the Court of St. James, that he was there for a long time before and did not return for a year or more after. He knows that to be true, and that fact proves his charge to be false as against Mr. Buchanan. Then, again, I wish to call his attention to the fact that at the time the Nebraska Bill was passed the Dred Scott case was not before the Supreme Court at all; it was not upon the docket of the Supreme Court; it had not been brought there; and the judges in all probability knew nothing of it. Thus the history of the country proves the charge to be false as against them. As to President Pierce, his high character as a man of integrity and honor is enough to vindicate him from such a charge; and as to myself, I pronounce the charge an infamous lie, whenever and wherever made and by whomsoever made. I am willing that Mr. Lincoln should go and rake up every public act of mine, every measure I have introduced, report I have made, speech delivered, and criticise them; but when he charges upon me a corrupt conspiracy for the purpose of perverting the institutions of the country, I brand it as it deserves. I say the history of the country proves it to be false, and that it could not have been possible at the time. But now he tries to protect himself in this charge, because I made a charge against the Washington *Union*. My speech in the Senate against the Washington *Union* was made because it advocated a revolutionary doctrine, by declaring that the free States had not the right to prohibit slavery within their own limits. Because I made that charge against the Washington *Union,* Mr. Lincoln says it was a charge against Mr. Buchanan. Suppose it was: is Mr. Lincoln the peculiar defender of Mr. Buchanan? Is he so interested in the Federal Administration, and so bound to it, that he must jump to the rescue and defend it from every attack that I may make against it? I understand the whole thing. The Washington *Union*, under that most corrupt of all men, Cornelius Wendell, is advocating Mr. Lincoln's claim to the Senate. Wendell was the printer of the last Black Republican House of Representatives; he was a candidate before the present Democratic House, but was ignominiously kicked out; and then he took the money which he had made out of the public printing by means of the Black Republicans, bought the Washington *Union*, and is now publishing it in the name of the Democratic party, and advocating Mr. Lincoln's election to the Senate. Mr. Lincoln therefore considers an attack upon Wendell and his corrupt gang as a personal attack upon him. This only proves what I have charged,—that there is an alliance between Lincoln and his supporters and the Federal office-holders of this State, and the Presidential aspirants out of it, to break me down at home.

Mr. Lincoln feels bound to come in to the rescue of the Washington *Union.* In that speech which I delivered in answer to the Washington *Union,* I made it distinctly against the *Union,* and against the *Union* alone. I did not choose to go beyond that. If I have reason to attack the President's conduct, I will do it in language that will not be misunderstood. When I differed with the President, I spoke out so that you all heard me. That question passed away; it resulted in the triumph of my principle, by allowing the people to do as they please; and there is an end of the controversy, whenever the great principle of self-government,—the right of the people to make their own Constitution, and come into the Union with slavery or without it, as they see proper,—shall again arise, you will find me standing firm in defence of that principle, and fighting whoever fights it. If Mr. Buchanan stands, as I doubt not he will, by the recommendation contained in his message, that hereafter all State constitutions ought to be submitted to the people before the admission of the State into the Union, he will find me standing by him firmly, shoulder to shoulder, in carrying it out. I know Mr. Lincoln's object: he wants to divide the Democratic party, in order that he may defeat me and get to the Senate.

[MR. DOUGLAS's time here expired, and he stopped on the moment.]

## MR. LINCOLN'S REJOINDER

MY FRIENDS: It will readily occur to you that I cannot, in half an hour, notice all the things that so able a man as Judge Douglas can say in an hour and a half; and I hope, therefore, if there be anything that he has said upon which you would like to hear something from me, but which I omit to comment upon, you will bear in mind that it would be expecting an impossibility for me to go over his whole ground. I can but take up some of the points that he has dwelt upon, and employ my half-hour specially on them.

The first thing I have to say to you is a word in regard to Judge Douglas's declaration about the "vulgarity and blackguardism" in the audience,—that no such thing, as he says, was shown by any Democrat while I was speaking. Now, I only wish, by way of reply on this subject, to say that while I was speaking, *I* used no "vulgarity or blackguardism" toward any Democrat.

Now, my friends, I come to all this long portion of the Judge's speech,—perhaps half of it,—which he has devoted to the various resolutions and platforms that have been adopted in the different counties in the different Congressional districts, and in the Illinois Legislature, which he supposes are at variance with the positions I have assumed before you to-day. It is true that many of these resolutions are at variance with the positions I have here assumed. All I have to ask is that we talk reasonably and rationally about it. I happen to know, the Judge's opinion to the contrary notwithstanding, that I have never tried to conceal my opinions, nor tried to deceive any one in reference to them. He may go and examine all the members who voted for me for United States Senator in 1855, after the election of 1854. They were pledged to certain things here at home, and were determined to have pledges from me; and if he will find any of these persons who will tell him anything inconsistent with what I say now, I will resign, or rather retire from the race, and give him no more trouble. The plain truth is this: At the introduction of the Nebraska policy, we believed there was a new era being introduced in the history of the Republic, which tended to the spread and perpetuation of slavery. But in our opposition to that measure we did not agree with one another in everything. The people in the north end of the State were for stronger measures of opposition than we of the central and southern portions of the State, but we were all opposed to the Nebraska doctrine. We had that one feeling and that one sentiment in common. You at the north end met in your conventions and passed your resolutions. We in the middle of the State and farther south did not hold such conventions and pass the same resolutions, although we had in general a common view and a common sentiment. So that these meetings which the Judge has alluded to, and the resolutions he has read from, were local, and did not spread over the whole State. We at last met together in 1856, from all parts of the State, and we agreed upon a common platform. You, who held more extreme notions, either yielded those notions, or, if not wholly yielding them, agreed to yield them practically, for the sake of embodying the opposition to the measures which the opposite party were pushing forward at that time. We met you then, and if there was anything yielded, it was for practical purposes. We agreed then upon a platform for the party throughout the entire State of Illinois, and now we are all bound, as a party, *to that platform*. And I say here to you, if any one expects of me—in case of my election—that I will do anything not signified by our Republican platform and my answers here to-day, I tell you very frankly that person will be deceived. I do not ask for the vote of any one who supposes that I have secret purposes or pledges that I dare not speak out. Cannot the Judge be satisfied? If he fears, in the unfortunate case of my election, that my going to Washington will enable me to advocate sentiments contrary to those which I expressed when you voted for and elected me, I assure him that his fears are wholly needless and groundless. Is the Judge really afraid of any such thing? I'll tell you what he is afraid of. *He is afraid we'll all pull together.* This is what alarms him more than anything else. For my part, I do hope that all of us, entertaining a common sentiment in opposition to what appears to us a design to nationalize and perpetuate slavery, will waive minor differences on questions which either belong to the dead past or the distant future, and all pull together in this struggle. What are your sentiments? If it be true that on the ground which I occupy—ground which I occupy as frankly and boldly as Judge Douglas does his,—my views, though partly coinciding with yours, are not as perfectly in accordance with your feelings as his are, I do say to you in all candor, go for him, and not for me. I hope to deal in all things fairly with Judge Douglas, and with the people of the State, in this contest. And if I should never be elected to any office, I trust I may go down with no stain of falsehood upon my reputation, notwithstanding the hard opinions Judge Douglas chooses to entertain of me.

The Judge has again addressed himself to the Abolition tendencies of a speech of mine made at Springfield in June last. I have so often tried to answer what he is always saying on that melancholy theme that I almost turn with disgust from the discussion,—from the repetition of an answer to it. I trust that nearly all of this intelligent audience have read that speech. If you have, I may venture to leave it to you to inspect it closely, and see whether it contains any of those "bugaboos" which frighten Judge Douglas.

The Judge complains that I did not fully answer his questions. If I have the sense to comprehend and answer those questions, I have done so fairly. If it can be pointed out to me how I can more fully and fairly answer him, I aver I have not the sense to see how it is to be done. He says I do not declare I would in any event vote for the admission of a slave State into the Union. If I have been fairly reported, he will see that I did give an explicit answer to his interrogatories; I did not merely say that I would dislike to be put to the test, but I said clearly, if I were put to the test, and a Territory from which slavery had been excluded should present herself with a State constitution sanctioning slavery,—a most extraordinary thing, and wholly unlikely to happen,—I did not see how I could avoid voting for her admission. But he refuses to understand that I said so, and he wants this audience to understand that I did not say so. Yet it will be so reported in the printed speech that he cannot help seeing it.

He says if I should vote for the admission of a slave State I would be voting for a dissolution of the Union, because I hold that the Union cannot permanently exist half slave and half free. I repeat that I do not believe this government *can* endure permanently half slave and half free; yet I do not admit, nor does it at all follow, that the admission of a single slave State will permanently fix the character and establish this as a universal slave nation. The Judge is very happy indeed at working up these quibbles. Before leaving the subject of answering questions, I aver as my confident belief, when you come to see our speeches in print, that you will find every question which he has asked me more fairly and boldly and fully answered than he has answered those which I put to him. Is not that so? The two speeches may be placed side by side, and I will venture to leave it to impartial judges whether his questions have not been more directly and circumstantially answered than mine.

Judge Douglas says he made a charge upon the editor of the Washington *Union, alone,* of entertaining a purpose to rob the States of their power to exclude slavery from their limits. I undertake to say, and I make the direct issue, that he did *not* make his charge against the editor of the *Union* alone. I will undertake to prove by the record here that he made that charge against more and higher dignitaries than the editor of the Washington *Union.* I am quite aware that he was shirking and dodging around the form in which I put it, but I can make it manifest that he levelled his "fatal blow" against more persons than this Washington editor. Will he dodge it now by alleging that I am trying to defend Mr. Buchanan against the charge? Not at all. Am I not making the same charge myself? I am trying to show that you, Judge Douglas, are a witness on my side. I am not defending Buchanan, and I will tell Judge Douglas that in my opinion, when he made that charge, he had an eye farther north than he has to-day. He was then fighting against people who called *him* a Black Republican and an Abolitionist. It is mixed all through his speech, and it is tolerably manifest that his eye was a great deal farther north than it is to-day. The Judge says that though he made this charge, Toombs got up and declared there was not a man in the United States, except the editor of the *Union,* who was in favor of the doctrines put forth in that article. And thereupon I understand that the Judge withdrew the charge. Although he had taken extracts from the newspaper, and then from the Lecompton Constitution, to show the existence of a conspiracy to bring about a "fatal blow," by which the States were to be deprived of the right of excluding slavery, it all went to pot as soon as Toombs got up and told him it was not true. It reminds me of the story that John Phoenix, the California railroad surveyor, tells. He says they started out from the Plaza to the Mission of Dolores. They had two ways of determining distances. One was by a chain and pins taken over the ground. The other was by a "go-it-meter,"—an invention of his own,—a three-legged instrument, with which he computed a series of triangles between the points. At night he turned to the chain-man to ascertain what distance they had come, and found that by some mistake he had merely dragged the chain over the ground without keeping any record. By the "go-it-ometer," he found he had made ten miles. Being skeptical about this, he asked a drayman who was passing how far it was to the Plaza. The drayman replied it was just half a mile; and the surveyor put it down in his book,—just as Judge Douglas says, after he had made his calculations and computations, he took Toombs's statement. I have no doubt that after Judge Douglas had made his charge, he was as easily satisfied about its truth as the surveyor was of the drayman's statement of the distance to the Plaza.

Yet it is a fact that the man who put forth all that matter which Douglas deemed a "fatal blow" at State sovereignty was elected by the Democrats as public printer.

Now, gentlemen, you may take Judge Douglas's speech of March 22, 1858, beginning about the middle of page 21, and reading to the bottom of page 24, and you will find the evidence on which I say that he did not make his charge against the editor of the *Union* alone. I cannot stop to read it, but I will give it to the reporters. Judge Douglas said:

> Mr. President, you here find several distinct propositions advanced boldly by the Washington *Union* editorially, and apparently *authoritatively*, and every man who questions any of them is denounced as an Abolitionist, a Free-soiler, a fanatic. The propositions are, first, that the primary object of all government at its original institution is the protection of persons and property; second, that the Constitution of the United States declares that the citizens of each State shall be entitled to all the privileges and immunities of citizens in the several States; and that, therefore, thirdly, all State laws, whether organic or otherwise, which prohibit the citizens of one State from settling in another with their slave property, and especially declaring it forfeited, are direct violations of the original intention of the Government and Constitution of the United States; and, fourth, that the emancipation of the slaves of the Northern States was a gross outrage on the rights of property, inasmuch as it was involuntarily done on the part of the owner.
>
> Remember that this article was published in the *Union* on the 17th of November, and on the 18th appeared the first article giving the adhesion of the *Union* to the Lecompton Constitution. It was in these words:
>
> "KANSAS AND HER CONSTITUTION.—The vexed question is settled. The problem is solved. The dead point of danger is passed. All serious trouble to Kansas affairs is over and gone—"
>
> And a column, nearly, of the same sort. Then, when you come to look into the Lecompton Constitution, you find the same doctrine incorporated in it which was put forth editorially in the *Union*. What is it?
>
> "ARTICLE 7, *Section* 1. The right of property is before and higher than any constitutional sanction; and the right of the

owner of a slave to such slave and its increase is the same and as invariable as the right of the owner of any property whatever."

Then in the schedule is a provision that the Constitution may be amended after 1864 by a two-thirds vote.

"But no alteration shall be made to affect the right of property in the ownership of slaves."

It will be seen by these clauses in the Lecompton Constitution that they are identical in spirit with this *authoritative* article in the Washington *Union* of the day previous to its indorsement of this Constitution.

When I saw that article in the *Union* of the 17th of November, followed by the glorification of the Lecompton Constitution on the 18th of November, and this clause in the Constitution asserting the doctrine that a State has no right to prohibit slavery within its limits, I saw that there was a *fatal blow* being struck at the sovereignty of the States of this Union.

Here he says, "Mr. President, you here find several distinct propositions advanced boldly, and apparently *authoritatively.*" By whose authority, Judge Douglas? Again, he says in another place, "It will be seen by these clauses in the Lecompton Constitution that they are identical in spirit with this *authoritative* article." *By whose authority?* Who do you mean to say authorized the publication of these articles? He knows that the Washington *Union* is considered the organ of the Administration. *I* demand of Judge Douglas *by whose authority* he meant to say those articles were published, if not by the authority of the President of the United States and his Cabinet? I defy him to show whom he referred to, if not to these high functionaries in the Federal Government. More than this, he says the articles in that paper and the provisions of the Lecompton Constitution are "identical," and, being identical, he argues that the authors are co-operating and conspiring together. He does not use the word "conspiring," but what other construction can you put upon it? He winds up with this:

When I saw that article in the *Union* of the 17th of November, followed by the glorification of the Lecompton Constitution on the 18th of November, and this clause in the Constitution asserting the doctrine that a State has no right to prohibit slavery within its limits, I saw that there was a *fatal blow* being struck at the sovereignty of the States of the Union.

I ask him if all this fuss was made over the editor of this newspaper. It would be a terribly "*fatal blow*" indeed which a single man could strike, when no President, no Cabinet officer, no member of Congress, was giving strength and efficiency to the movement. Out of respect to Judge Douglas's good sense I must believe he didn't manufacture his idea of the "fatal" character of that blow out of such a miserable scapegrace as he represents that editor to be. But the Judge's eye is farther south now. Then, it was very peculiarly and decidedly north. His hope rested on the idea of visiting the great "Black Republican" party, and making it the tail of his new kite. He knows he was then expecting from day to day to turn Republican, and place himself at the head of our organization. He has found that these despised "Black Republicans" estimate him by a standard which he has taught them none too well. Hence he is crawling back into his old camp, and you will find him eventually installed in full fellowship among those whom he was then battling, and with whom he now pretends to be at such fearful variance. [Loud applause, and cries of "Go on, go on."] I cannot, gentlemen; my time has expired.

# Third Joint Debate, at Jonesboro

*September 15, 1858*

LADIES AND GENTLEMEN: I appear before you to-day in pursuance of a previous notice, and have made arrangements with Mr. Lincoln to divide time, and discuss with him the leading political topics that now agitate the country.

Prior to 1854 this country was divided into two great political parties known as Whig and Democratic. These parties differed from each other on certain questions which were then deemed to be important to the best interests of the Republic. Whigs and Democrats differed about a bank, the tariff, distribution, the specie circular and the sub-treasury. On those issues we went before the country and discussed the principles, objects, and measures of the two great parties. Each of the parties could proclaim its principles in Louisiana as well as in Massachusetts, in Kentucky as well as in Illinois. Since that period, a great revolution has taken place in the formation of parties, by which they now seem to be divided by a geographical line, a large party in the North being arrayed under the Abolition or Republican banner, in hostility to the Southern States, Southern people, and Southern institutions. It becomes important for us to inquire how this transformation of parties has occurred, made from those of national principles to geographical factions. You remember that in 1850 this country was agitated from its centre to its circumference about this slavery question. It became necessary for the leaders of the great Whig party and the leaders of the great Democratic party to postpone, for the time being, their particular disputes, and unite first to save the Union before they should quarrel as to the mode in which it was to he governed. During the Congress of 1849–'50, Henry Clay was the leader of the Union men, supported by Cass and Webster, and the leaders of the Democracy and the leaders of the Whigs, in opposition to Northern Abolitionists or Southern Disunionists. That great contest of 1850 resulted in the establishment of the Compromise measures of that year, which measures rested on the great principles that the people of each State and each Territory of this Union ought to be permitted to regulate their own domestic institutions in their own way, subject to no other limitation than that which the Federal Constitution imposes.

I now wish to ask you whether that principle was right or wrong which guaranteed to every State and every community the right to form and regulate their domestic institutions to suit themselves. These measures were adopted, as I have previously said, by the joint action of the Union Whigs and Union Democrats in opposition to Northern Abolitionists and Southern Disunionists. In 1858, when the Whig party assembled, at Baltimore, in National Convention for the last time, they adopted the principle of the Compromise measures of 1850 as their rule of party action in the future. One month thereafter the Democrats assembled at the same place to nominate a candidate for the presidency, and declared the same great principle as the rule of action by which the Democracy would be governed. The Presidential election of 1852 was fought on that basis. It is true that the Whigs claimed special merit for the adoption of those measures, because they asserted that their great Clay originated them, their godlike Webster defended them, and their Fillmore signed the bill making them the law of the land; but, on the other hand, the Democrats claimed special credit for the Democracy, upon the ground that we gave twice as many votes in both Houses of Congress for the passage of these measures as the Whig party.

Thus you see that in the Presidential election of 1852 the Whigs were pledged by their platform and their candidate to the principle of the Compromise measures of 1850, and the Democracy were likewise pledged by our principles, our platform, and our candidate to the same line of policy, to preserve peace and quiet between the different sections of this Union. Since that period the Whig party has been transformed into a sectional party, under the name of the Republican party, whilst the Democratic party continues the same national party it was at that day. All sectional men, all men of Abolition sentiments and principles, no matter whether they were old Abolitionists or had been Whigs or Democrats, rally under the sectional Republican banner, and consequently all national men, all Union-loving men, whether Whigs, Democrats, or by whatever name they have been known, ought to rally under the Stars and Stripes in defence of the Constitution as our fathers made it, and of the Union as it has existed under the Constitution.

How has this departure from the faith of the Democracy and the faith of the Whig party been accomplished? In 1854, certain restless, ambitious, and disappointed politicians throughout the land took advantage of the temporary excitement created by the Nebraska Bill to try and dissolve the old Whig party and the old Democratic party, to Abolitionize their members, and lead them, bound hand and foot, captives into the Abolition camp. In the State of New York a convention was held by some of these men, and a platform adopted, every plank of which was as black as night, each one relating to the negro, and not one referring to the interests of the white man. That example was followed throughout the Northern States, the effort being made to combine all the free States in hostile array against the slave States. The men who thus thought that they could build up a great sectional party, and through its organization control the political destinies of this country, based all their hopes on the single fact that the North was the stronger division of the nation, and hence, if the North could be combined against the South, a sure victory awaited their efforts. I am doing no more than justice to the truth of history when I say that in this State, Abraham Lincoln, on behalf of the Whigs, and Lyman Trumbull, on behalf of the Democrats, were the leaders who undertook to perform this grand scheme of Abolitionizing the two parties to which they belonged. They had a private arrangement as to what should be the political destiny of each of the contracting parties before they went into the operation. The arrangement was that Mr. Lincoln was to take the old-line Whigs with him, claiming that he was still as good a Whig as ever, over to the Abolitionists, and Mr. Trumbull was to run for Congress in the Belleville District, and, claiming to be a good Democrat, coax the old Democrats into the Abolition camp; and when, by the joint efforts of the Abolitionized Whigs, the Abolitionized Democrats, and the old-line Abolition and Free-soil party of this State, they should secure a majority in the Legislature, Lincoln was then to be made United States Senator in Shields's place, Trumbull remaining in Congress until I should be accommodating enough to die or resign, and give him a chance to follow Lincoln. That was a very nice little bargain so far as Lincoln and Trumbull were concerned, if it had been carried out in good faith and friend Lincoln had attained to senatorial dignity according to the contract. They went into the contest in every part of the State, calling upon all disappointed politicians to join in the crusade against the Democracy, and appealed to the prevailing sentiments and prejudices in all the northern counties of the State. In three Congressional districts in the north end of the State they adopted, as the platform of this new party thus formed by Lincoln and Trumbull in connection with the Abolitionists, all of those principles which aimed at a warfare on the part of the North against the South. They declared in that platform that the Wilmot Proviso was to be applied to all the Territories of the United States, north as well as south of 36 deg. 30 min., and not only to all the territory we then had, but all that we might hereafter acquire; that hereafter no more slave States should be admitted into this Union, even if the people of such State desired slavery; that the Fugitive Slave law should be absolutely and unconditionally repealed; that slavery should be abolished in the District of Columbia; that the slave trade should be abolished between the different States; and, in fact, every article in their creed related to this slavery question, and pointed to a Northern geographical party in hostility to the

Southern States of this Union. Such were their principles in northern Illinois. A little farther south they became bleached, and grew paler just in proportion as public sentiment moderated and changed in this direction. They were Republicans or Abolitionists in the north, anti-Nebraska men down about Springfield, and in this neighborhood they contented themselves with talking about the inexpediency of the repeal of the Missouri Compromise. In the extreme northern counties they brought out men to canvass the State whose complexion suited their political creed; and hence Fred Douglass, the negro, was to be found there, following General Cass, and attempting to speak on behalf of Lincoln, Trumbull, and Abolitionism, against that illustrious senator. Why, they brought Fred Douglass to Freeport, when I was addressing a meeting there, in a carriage driven by the white owner, the negro sitting inside with the white lady and her daughter. When I got through canvassing the northern counties that year, and progressed as far south as Springfield, I was met and opposed in discussion by Lincoln, Lovejoy, Trumbull, and Sidney Breese, who were on one side. Father Giddings, the high-priest of Abolitionism, had just been there, and Chase came about the time I left. ["Why didn't you shoot him?"] I did take a running shot at them; but as I was single-handed against the white, black, and mixed drove, I had to use a shotgun and fire into the crowd, instead of taking them off singly with a rifle. Trumbull had for his lieutenants, in aiding him to Abolitionize the Democracy, such men as John Wentworth of Chicago, Governor Reynolds of Belleville, Sidney Breese of Carlisle, and John Dougherty of Union, each of whom modified his opinions to suit the locality he was in. Dougherty, for instance, would not go much further than to talk about the inexpediency of the Nebraska Bill, whilst his allies at Chicago advocated negro citizenship and negro equality, putting the white man and the negro on the same basis under the law. Now, these men, four years ago, were engaged in a conspiracy to break down the Democracy; to-day they are again acting together for the same purpose! They do not hoist the same flag, they do not own the same principles or profess the same faith, but conceal their union for the sake of policy. In the northern counties, you find that all the conventions are called in the name of the Black Republican party; at Springfield, they dare not call a Republican convention, but invite all the enemies of the Democracy to unite; and when they get down into Egypt, Trumbull issues notices calling upon the "*Free Democracy*" to assemble and hear him speak. I have one of the handbills calling a Trumbull meeting at Waterloo the other day, which I received there, which is in the following language:

A meeting of the Free Democracy will take place in Waterloo, on Monday, Sept. 13th inst., whereat Hon. Lyman Trumbull,

Hon. John Baker and others will address the people upon the different political topics of the day. Members of all parties are cordially invited to be present, and hear and determine for themselves.

THE MONROE FREE DEMOCRACY

What is that name of "Free Democrats" put forth for, unless to deceive the people, and make them believe that Trumbull and his followers are not the same party as that which raises the black flag of Abolitionism in the northern part of this State and makes war upon the Democratic party throughout the State? When I put that question to them at Waterloo on Saturday last, one of them rose and stated that they had changed their name for political effect, in order to get votes. There was a candid admission. Their object in changing their party organization and principles in different localities was avowed to be an attempt to cheat and deceive some portion of the people until after the election. Why cannot a political party that is conscious of the rectitude of its purposes and the soundness of its principles declare them everywhere alike? I would disdain to hold any political principles that I could not avow in the same terms in Kentucky that I declared in Illinois, in Charleston as well as in Chicago, in New Orleans as well as in New York. So long as we live under a Constitution common to all the States, our political faith ought to be as broad, as liberal, and just as that Constitution itself, and should be proclaimed alike in every portion of the Union.

But it is apparent that our opponents find it necessary, for partisan effect, to change their colors in different counties in order to catch the popular breeze, and hope with these discordant materials combined together to secure a majority in the Legislature for the purpose of putting down the Democratic party. This combination did succeed in 1854 so far as to elect a majority of their confederates to the Legislature, and the first important act which they performed was to elect a Senator in the place of the eminent and gallant Senator Shields. His term expired in the United States Senate at that time, and he had to be crushed by the Abolition coalition for the simple reason that he would not join in their conspiracy to wage war against one half of the Union. That was the only objection to General Shields. He had served the people of his State with ability in the Legislature, he had served you with fidelity and ability as Auditor, he had performed his duties to the satisfaction of the whole country at the head of the Land Department at Washington, he had covered the State and the Union with immortal glory on the bloody fields of Mexico in defence of the honor of our flag, and yet he had to be stricken down by this unholy combination. And for what cause? Merely because he would not join a combination of one half of the States to make war upon the other half, after having poured out his heart's blood for all the States of the Union. Trumbull was put in his place by Abolitionism. How did Trumbull get there? Before the Abolitionists would consent to go into an election for United States Senator they required all the members of this new combination to show their hands upon this question of Abolitionism. Lovejoy, one of their high-priests, brought in resolutions defining the Abolition creed, and required them to commit themselves on it by their votes,—yea or nay. In that creed, as laid down by Lovejoy, they declared, first, that the Wilmot Proviso must be put on all the Territories of the United States, north as well as south of 36 deg. 30 min., and that no more territory should ever be acquired unless slavery was at first prohibited therein; second, that no more States should ever be received into the Union unless slavery was first prohibited, by constitutional provision, in such States; third, that the Fugitive Slave law must be immediately repealed, or, failing in that, then such amendments were to be made to it as would render it useless and inefficient for the objects for which it was passed, etc. The next day after these resolutions were offered they were voted upon, part of them carried, and the others defeated, the same men who voted for them, with only two exceptions, voting soon after for Abraham Lincoln as their candidate for the United States Senate. He came within one or two votes of being elected, but he could not quite get the number required, for the simple reason that his friend Trumbull, who was a party to the bargain by which Lincoln was to take Shields's place, controlled a few Abolitionized Democrats in the Legislature, and would not allow them all to vote for him, thus wronging Lincoln by permitting him on each ballot to be almost elected, but not quite, until he forced them to drop Lincoln and elect him (Trumbull), in order to unite the party. Thus you find that although the Legislature was carried that year by the bargain between Trumbull, Lincoln, and the Abolitionists, and the union of these discordant elements in one harmonious party, yet Trumbull violated his pledge, and played a Yankee trick on Lincoln when they came to divide the spoils. Perhaps you would like a little evidence on this point. If you would, I will call Colonel James H. Matheny, of Springfield, to the stand, Mr. Lincoln's especial confidential friend for the last twenty years, and see what he will say upon the subject of this bargain. Matheny is now the Black Republican, or Abolition, candidate for Congress in the Springfield District against the gallant Colonel Harris, and is making speeches all over that part of the State against me and in favor of Lincoln, in concert with Trumbull. He ought to be a good witness, and I will read an extract from a speech which he made in 1856, when he was mad because his friend Lincoln had been cheated.

It is one of numerous speeches of the same tenor that were made about that time, exposing this bargain between Lincoln, Trumbull, and the Abolitionists. Matheny then said:

> The Whigs, Abolitionists, Know-Nothings, and renegade Democrats made a solemn compact for the purpose of carrying this State against the Democracy, on this plan: 1st. That they would all combine and elect Mr. Trumbull to Congress, and thereby carry his district for the Legislature, in order to throw all the strength that could be obtained into that body against the Democrats. 2d. That when the Legislature should meet, the officers of that body, such as Speaker, clerks, door-keepers, etc., would be given to the Abolitionists; and 3d. That the Whigs were to have the United States Senator. That, accordingly, in good faith, Trumbull was elected to Congress, and his district carried for the Legislature, and, when it convened, the Abolitionists got all the officers of that body; and, thus far, the "bond" was fairly executed. The Whigs, on their part, demanded the election of Abraham Lincoln to the United States Senate, that the bond might be fulfilled, the other parties to the contract having already secured to themselves all that was called for. But, in the most perfidious manner, they refused to elect Mr. Lincoln, and the mean, low-lived, sneaking Trumbull succeeded, by pledging all that was required by any party, in thrusting Lincoln aside, and foisting himself, an excrescence from the rotten bowels of the Democracy, into the United States Senate: and thus it has ever been, that an *honest* man makes a bad bargain when he conspires or contracts with rogues.

Matheny thought that his friend Lincoln made a bad bargain when he conspired and contracted with such rogues as Trumbull and his Abolition associates in that campaign. Lincoln was shoved off the track, and he and his friends all at once began to mope, became sour and mad, and disposed to tell, but dare not; and thus they stood for a long time, until the Abolitionists coaxed and flattered him back by their assurances that he should certainly be a Senator in Douglas's place. In that way the Abolitionists have been enabled to hold Lincoln to the alliance up to this time, and now they have brought him into a fight against me, and he is to see if he is again to be cheated by them. Lincoln, this time, though, required more of them than a promise, and holds their bond, if not security, that Lovejoy shall not cheat him as Trumbull did.

When the Republican Convention assembled at Springfield, in June last, for the purpose of nominating State officers only, the Abolitionists could not get Lincoln and his friends into it until they would pledge themselves that Lincoln should be their candidate for the Senate; and you will find, in proof of this, that that Convention passed a resolution unanimously declaring that Abraham Line ln was the "first, last, and only choice" of the Republicans for United States Senator. He was not willing to have it understood that he was merely their first choice, or their last choice, but their *only* choice. The Black Republican party had nobody else. Browning was nowhere; Governor Bissell was of no account; Archie Williams was not to be taken into consideration; John Wentworth was not worth mentioning; John M. Palmer was degraded; and their party presented the extraordinary spectacle of having but one,—the first, the last, and only— choice for the Senate. Suppose that Lincoln should die, what a horrible condition the Republican party would be in! They would have nobody left. They have no other choice, and it was necessary for them to put themselves before the world in this ludicrous, ridiculous attitude of having no other choice, in order to quiet Lincoln's suspicions, and assure him that he was not to be cheated by Lovejoy, and the trickery by which Trumbull outgeneralled him. Well, gentlemen, I think they will have a nice time of it before they get through. I do not intend to give them any chance to cheat Lincoln at all this time. I intend to relieve him of all anxiety upon that subject, and spare them the mortification of more exposures of contracts violated, and the pledged honor of rogues forfeited.

But I wish to invite your attention to the chief points at issue between Mr. Lincoln and myself in this discussion. Mr. Lincoln, knowing that he was to be the candidate of his party, on account of the arrangement of which I have already spoken, knowing that he was to receive the nomination of the Convention for the United States Senate, had his speech, accepting that nomination, all written and committed to memory ready to be delivered the moment the nomination was announced. Accordingly, when it was made, he was in readiness, and delivered his speech, a portion of which I will read in order that I may state his political principles fairly, by repeating them in his own language:

> We are now far into the fifth year since a policy was insti-
> tuted for the avowed object, and with the confident promise, of
> putting an end to slavery agitation; under the operation of that
> policy, that agitation has not only not ceased, but has constantly

augmented. I believe it will not cease until a crisis shall have been reached and passed. "A house divided against itself cannot stand." I believe this government cannot endure permanently, half slave and half free. I do not expect the Union to be dissolved, I do not expect the house to fall; but I do expect it will cease to be divided. It will become all one thing or all the other. Either the opponents of slavery will arrest the spread of it, and place it where the public mind shall rest in the belief that it is in the course of ultimate extinction, or its advocates will push it forward until it shall become alike lawful in all the States, North as well as South.

There you have Mr. Lincoln's first and main proposition, upon which he bases his claims, stated in his own language. He tells you that this Republic cannot endure permanently divided into slave and free States, as our fathers made it. He says that they must all become free or all become slave, that they must all be one thing or all be the other, or this government cannot last. Why can it not last, if we will execute the government in the same spirit and upon the same principles upon which it is founded? Lincoln, by his proposition, says to the South: "If you desire to maintain your institutions as they are now, you must not be satisfied with minding your own business, but you must invade Illinois and all the other Northern States, establish slavery in them, and make it universal"; and in the same language he says to the North: "You must not be content with regulating your own affairs and minding your own business, but if you desire to maintain your freedom, you must invade the Southern States, abolish slavery there and everywhere, in order to have the States all one thing or all the other." I say that this is the inevitable and irresistible result of Mr. Lincoln's argument, inviting a warfare between the North and the South, to be carried on with ruthless vengeance until the one section or the other shall be driven to the wall, and become the victim of the rapacity of the other. What good would follow such a system of warfare? Suppose the North should succeed in conquering the South, how much would she be the gainer? or suppose the South should conquer the North, could the Union be preserved in that way? Is this sectional warfare to be waged between the Northern States and Southern States until they all shall become uniform in their local and domestic institutions, merely because Mr. Lincoln says that a house divided against itself cannot stand, and pretends that this Scriptural quotation, this language of our Lord and Master, is applicable to the American Union and the American Constitution? Washington and his compeers, in the convention that framed the Constitution, made this government divided into free and slave States. It was composed then of thirteen sovereign and independent States, each having sovereign authority over its local and domestic institutions, and all bound together by the Federal Constitution. Mr. Lincoln likens that bond of the Federal Constitution, joining free and slave States together, to a house divided against itself, and says that it is contrary to the law of God, and cannot stand. When did he learn, and by what authority does he proclaim, that this Government is contrary to the law of God and cannot stand? It has stood thus divided into free and slave States from its organization up to this day. During that period we have increased from four millions to thirty millions of people; we have extended our territory from the Mississippi to the Pacific Ocean; we have acquired the Floridas and Texas, and other territory sufficient to double our geographical extent; we have increased in population, in wealth, and in power beyond any example on earth; we have risen from a weak and feeble power to become the terror and admiration of the civilized world; and all this has been done under a Constitution which Mr. Lincoln, in substance, says is in violation of the law of God, and under a Union divided into free and slave States, which Mr. Lincoln thinks, because of such division, cannot stand. Surely Mr. Lincoln is a wiser man than those who framed the Government. Washington did not believe, nor did his compatriots, that the local laws and domestic institutions that were well adapted to the Green Mountains of Vermont were suited to the rice plantations of South Carolina; they did not believe at that day that in a republic so broad and expanded as this, containing such a variety of climate, soil, and interest, that uniformity in the local laws and domestic institutions was either desirable or possible. They believed then, as our experience has proved to us now, that each locality, having different interests, a different climate, and different surroundings, required different local laws, local policy, and local institutions, adapted to the wants of that locality. Thus our government was formed on the principle of diversity in the local institutions and laws, and not on that of uniformity.

As my time flies, I can only glance at these points, and not present them as fully as I would wish, because I desire to bring all the points in controversy between the two parties before you, in order to have Mr. Lincoln's reply. He makes war on the decision of the Supreme Court in the case known as the Dred Scott case. I wish to say to you, fellow-citizens, that I have no war to make on that decision, or any other ever rendered by the Supreme Court. I am content to take that decision as it stands delivered by the highest judicial tribunal on earth,—a tribunal established by the Constitution of the United States for that purpose; and hence that decision becomes the law of the land, binding on you, on me, and on every other good citizen, whether we like it or not. Hence I do not choose to go into an argument to prove before this audience whether or not Chief Justice Taney understood the law better than Abraham Lincoln.

Mr. Lincoln objects to that decision, first and mainly, because it deprives the negro of the rights of citizenship. I am as much opposed to his reason for that objection as I am to the objection itself. I hold that a negro is not and never ought to be a citizen of the United States. I hold that this government was made on the white basis, by white men, for the benefit of white men and their posterity forever, and should be administered by white men and none others. I do not believe that the Almighty made the negro capable of self-government. I am aware that all the Abolition lecturers that you find travelling about through the country are in the habit of reading the Declaration of Independence to prove that all men were created equal, and endowed by their Creator with certain inalienable rights, among which are life, liberty, and the pursuit of happiness. Mr. Lincoln is very much in the habit of following in the track of Lovejoy in this particular, by reading that part of the Declaration of Independence to prove that the negro was endowed by the Almighty with the inalienable right of equality with white men. Now, I say to you, my fellow-citizens, that in my opinion the signers of the Declaration had no reference to the negro whatever when they declared all men to be created equal. They desired to express by that phrase white men, men of European birth and European descent, and had no reference either to the negro, the savage Indians, the Fejee, the Malay, or any other inferior and degraded race, when they spoke of the equality of men. One great evidence that such was their understanding is to be found in the fact that at that time every one of the thirteen colonies was a slaveholding colony, every signer of the Declaration represented a slaveholding constituency, and we know that not one of them emancipated his slaves, much less offered citizenship to them, when they signed the Declaration; and yet, if they intended to declare that the negro was the equal of the white man, and entitled by divine right to an equality with him, they were bound, as honest men, that day and hour to have put their negroes on an equality with themselves. Instead of doing so, with uplifted eyes to heaven they implored the divine blessing upon them, during the seven years' bloody war they had to fight to maintain that Declaration, never dreaming that they were violating divine law by still holding the negroes in bondage and depriving them of equality.

My friends, I am in favor of preserving this government as our fathers made it. It does not follow by any means that because a negro is not your equal or mine, that hence he must necessarily be a slave. On the contrary, it does follow that we ought to extend to the negro every right, every privilege, every immunity, which he is capable of enjoying, consistent with the good of society. When you ask me what these rights are, what their nature and extent is, I tell you that that is a question which each State of this Union must decide for itself. Illinois has already decided the question. We have decided that the negro must not be a slave within our limits; but we have also decided that the negro shall not be citizen within our limits; that he shall not vote, hold office, or exercise any political rights. I maintain that Illinois, as a sovereign State, has a right thus to fix her policy with reference to the relation between the white man and the negro; but while we had that right to decide the question for ourselves, we must recognize the same right in Kentucky and in every other State to make the same decision, or a different one. Having decided our own policy with reference to the black race, we must leave Kentucky and Missouri and every other State perfectly free to make just such a decision as they see proper on that question.

Kentucky has decided that question for herself. She has said that within her limits a negro shall not exercise any political rights, and she also said that a portion of the negroes under the laws of that State shall be slaves. She had as much right to adopt that as her policy as we had to adopt the contrary for our policy. New York has decided that in that State a negro may vote if he has $250 worth of property, and if he owns that much he may vote upon an equality with the white man. I, for one, am utterly opposed to negro suffrage anywhere and under any circumstances; yet, inasmuch as the Supreme Court have decided in the celebrated Dred Scott case that a State has a right to confer the privilege of voting upon free negroes, I am not going to make war upon New York because she has adopted a policy repugnant to my feelings. But New York must mind her own business, and keep her negro suffrage to herself, and not attempt to force it upon us.

In the State of Maine they have decided that a negro may vote and hold office on an equality with a white man. I had occasion to say to the senators from Maine, in a discussion, last session, that if they thought that the white people within the limits of their State were no better than negroes, I would not quarrel with them for it, but they must not say that my white constituents of Illinois were no better than negroes, or we would be sure to quarrel.

The Dred Scott decision covers the whole question, and declares that each State has the right to settle this question of suffrage for itself, and all questions as to the relations between the white man and the negro. Judge Taney expressly lays down the doctrine. I receive it as law, and I say that while those States are adopting regulations on that subject disgusting and abhorrent, according to my views, I will not make war on them if they will mind their own business and let us alone.

I now come back to the question, Why cannot this Union exist forever, divided into free and slave States, as our fathers made it? It can thus exist if each

State will carry out the principles upon which our institutions were founded; to wit, the right of each State to do as it pleases, without meddling with its neighbors. Just act upon that great principle, and this Union will not only live forever, but it will extend and expand until it covers the whole continent, and makes this confederacy one grand, ocean-bound Republic. We must bear in mind that we are yet a young nation, growing with a rapidity unequalled in the history of the world, that our natural increase is great, and that the emigration from the Old World is increasing, requiring us to expand and acquire new territory from time to time, in order to give our people land to live upon. If we live upon the principle of State rights and State sovereignty, each State regulating its own affairs and minding its own business, we can go on and extend indefinitely, just as fast and as far as we need the territory. The time may come, indeed has now come, when our interests would be advanced by the acquisition of the island of Cuba. When we get Cuba we must take it as we find it, leaving the people to decide the question of slavery for themselves, without interference on the part of the Federal Government or of any State of this Union. So, when it becomes necessary to acquire any portion of Mexico or Canada, or of this continent or the adjoining islands, we must take them as we find them, leaving the people free to do as they please,—to have slavery or not, as they choose. I never have inquired and never will inquire whether a new State applying for admission has slavery or not for one of her institutions. If the constitution that is presented be the act and deed of the people, and embodies their will, and they have the requisite population, I will admit them, with slavery or without it, just as that people shall determine. My objection to the Lecompton Constitution did not consist in the fact that it made Kansas a slave State. I would have been as much opposed to its admission under such a constitution as a free State as I was opposed to its admission under it as a slave State. I hold that that was a question which the people had a right to decide for themselves, and that no power on earth ought to have interfered with that decision. In my opinion, the Lecompton Constitution was not the act and deed of the people of Kansas, and did not embody their will; and the recent election in that Territory, at which it was voted down by nearly ten to one, shows conclusively that I was right in saying, when the Constitution was presented, that it was not the act and deed of the people, and did not embody their will.

If we wish to preserve our institutions in their purity, and transmit them unimpaired to our latest posterity, we must preserve with religious good faith that great principle of self-government which guarantees to each and every State, old and new, the right to make just such constitutions as they desire, and come into the Union with their own constitution, and not one palmed upon them.

Whenever you sanction the doctrine that Congress may crowd a constitution down the throats of an unwilling people, against their consent, you will subvert the great fundamental principle upon which all our free institutions rest. In the future I have no fear that the attempt will ever be made. President Buchanan declared in his annual message that hereafter the rule adopted in the Minnesota case, requiring a constitution to be submitted to the people, should be followed in all future cases; and if he stands by that recommendation, there will be no division in the Democratic party on that principle in the future. Hence, the great mission of the Democracy is to unite the fraternal feeling of the whole country, restore peace and quiet, by teaching each State to mind its own business, and regulate its own domestic affairs, and all to unite in carrying out the constitution as our fathers made it, and thus to preserve the Union and render it perpetual in all time to come. Why should we not act as our fathers who made the government? There was no sectional strife in Washington's army. They were all brethren of a common confederacy; they fought under a common flag that they might bestow upon their posterity a common destiny; and to this end they poured out their blood in common streams, and shared, in some instances, a common grave.

## Mr. Lincoln's Reply

LADIES AND GENTLEMEN: There is very much in the principles that Judge Douglas has here enunciated that I most cordially approve, and over which I shall have no controversy with him. In so far as he has insisted that all the States have the right to do exactly as they please about all their domestic relations, including that of slavery, I agree entirely with him. He places me wrong in spite of all I can tell him, though I repeat it again and again, insisting that I have no difference with him upon this subject. I have made a great many speeches, some of which have been printed, and it will be utterly impossible for him to find anything that I have ever put in print contrary to what I now say upon this subject. I hold myself under constitutional obligations to allow the people in all the States, without interference, direct or indirect, to do exactly as they please; and I deny that I have any inclination to interfere with them, even if there were no such constitutional obligation. I can only say again that I am placed improperly—altogether improperly, in spite of all I can say—when it is insisted that I entertain any other view or purposes in regard to that matter.

While I am upon this subject, I will make some answers briefly to certain propositions that Judge Douglas has put. He says, "Why can't this Union endure permanently half slave and half free?" I have said that I supposed it could not, and I will try, before this new audience, to give briefly some of the reasons for entertaining that opinion. Another form of his question is, "Why can't we let it stand as our fathers placed it?" That is the exact difficulty between us. I say that Judge Douglas and his friends have changed it from the position in which our fathers originally placed it. I say, in the way our father's originally left the slavery question, the institution was in the course of ultimate extinction, and the public mind rested in the belief that it *was* in the course of ultimate extinction. I say when this government was first established it was the policy of its founders to prohibit the spread of slavery into the new Territories of the United States, where it had not existed. But Judge Douglas and his friends have broken up that policy, and placed it upon a new basis, by which it is to become national and perpetual. All I have asked or desired anywhere is that it should be placed back again upon the basis that the fathers of our government originally placed it upon. I have no doubt that it *would* become extinct, for all time to come, if we but readopted the policy of the fathers, by restricting it to the limits it has already covered,—restricting it from the new Territories.

I do not wish to dwell at great length on this branch of the subject at this time, but allow me to repeat one thing that I have stated before. Brooks—the man who assaulted Senator Sumner on the floor of the Senate, and who was complimented with dinners, and silver pitchers, and gold-headed canes, and a good many other things for that feat—in one of his speeches declared that when this government was originally established, nobody expected that the institution of slavery would last until this day. That was but the opinion of one man, but it was such an opinion as we can never get from Judge Douglas or anybody in favor of slavery, in the North, at all. You *can* sometimes get it from a Southern man. He said at the same time that the framers of our government did not have the knowledge that experience has taught us; that experience and the invention of the cotton-gin have taught us that the perpetuation of slavery is a necessity. He insisted, therefore, upon its being changed from the basis upon which the fathers of the government left it to the basis of its perpetuation and nationalization.

I insist that this is the difference between Judge Douglas and myself,—that Judge Douglas is helping that change along. I insist upon this government being placed where our fathers originally placed it.

I remember Judge Douglas once said that he saw the evidences on the statute books of Congress of a policy in the origin of government to divide slavery and freedom by a geographical line; that he saw an indisposition to maintain that policy, and therefore he set about studying up a way to settle the institution on the right basis,—the basis which he thought it ought to have been placed upon at first; and in that speech he confesses that he seeks to place it, not upon the basis that the fathers placed it upon, but upon one gotten up on "original principles." When he asks me why we cannot get along with it in the attitude where our fathers placed it, he had better clear up the evidences that he has himself changed it from that basis, that he has himself been chiefly instrumental in changing the policy of the fathers. Any one who will read his speech of the 22d of last March will see that he there makes an open confession, showing that he set about fixing the institution upon an altogether different set of principles. I think I have fully answered him when he asks me why we cannot let it alone upon the basis where our fathers left it, by showing that he has himself changed the whole policy of the government in that regard.

Now, fellow-citizens, in regard to this matter about a contract that was made between Judge Trumbull and myself, and all that long portion of Judge Douglas's speech on this subject,—I wish simply to say what I have said to him before, that he cannot know whether it is true or not, and I *do know* that there is not a word of truth in it. And I have told him so before. I don't want any harsh language indulged in, but I do not know how to deal with this persistent insisting on a story that I know to be utterly without truth. It used to be a fashion amongst men that when a charge was made, some sort of proof was brought forward to establish it, and if no proof was found to exist, the charge was dropped. I don't know how to meet this kind of an argument. I don't want to have a fight with Judge Douglas, and I have no way of making an argument up into the consistency of a corn-cob and stopping his mouth with it. All I can do is, good-humoredly to say that, from the beginning to the end of all that story about a bargain between Judge Trumbull and myself, *there is not a word of truth in it.* I can only ask him to show some sort of evidence of the truth of his story. He brings forward here and reads from what he contends is a speech by James H. Matheny, charging such a bargain between Trumbull and myself. My own opinion is that Matheny did do some such immoral thing as to tell a story that he knew nothing about. I believe he did. I contradicted it instantly, and it has been contradicted by Judge Trumbull, while nobody has produced any proof, because there is none. Now, whether the speech which the Judge brings forward here is really the one Matheny made, I do not know, and I hope the Judge will pardon me for doubting the genuineness of this document, since his production of those Springfield resolutions at Ottawa. I do not wish to dwell at any great length upon this matter. I can say nothing when a long story like this is told, except it is not true, and demand that he who insists upon it shall produce some proof. That is all any man can do, and I leave it in that way, for I know of no other way of dealing with it.

The Judge has gone over a long account of the old Whig and Democratic parties, and it connects itself with this charge against Trumbull and myself. He says that they agreed upon a compromise in regard to the slavery question in 1850; that in a National Democratic Convention resolutions were passed to abide by that compromise as a finality upon the slavery question. He also says that the Whig party in National Convention agreed to abide by and regard as a finality the Compromise of 1850. I understand the Judge to be altogether right about that; I understand that part of the history of the country as stated by him to be correct. I recollect that I, as a member of that party, acquiesced in that compromise. I recollect in the Presidential election which followed, when we had General Scott up for the presidency, Judge Douglas was around berating us Whigs as Abolitionists, precisely as he does to-day,—not a bit of difference. I have often heard him. We could do nothing when the old Whig party was alive that was not Abolitionism, but it has got an extremely good name since it has passed away.

When that Compromise was made it did not repeal the old Missouri Compromise. It left a region of United States territory half as large as the present territory of the United States, north of the line of 36 degrees 30 minutes, in which slavery was prohibited by Act of Congress. This Compromise did not repeal that one. It did not affect or propose to repeal it. But at last it became Judge Douglas's duty, as he thought (and I find no fault with him), as Chairman of the Committee on Territories, to bring in a bill for the organization of a territorial government,—first of one, then of two Territories north of that line. When he did so, it ended in his inserting a provision substantially repealing the Missouri Compromise. That was because the Compromise of 1850 *had not* repealed it. And now I ask why he could not have let that Compromise alone? We were quiet from the agitation of the slavery question. We were making no fuss about it. All had acquiesced in the Compromise measures of 1850. We never had been seriously disturbed by any Abolition agitation before that period. When he came to form governments for the Territories north of the line of 36 degrees 30 minutes, why could he not have let that matter stand as it was standing? Was it necessary to the organization of a Territory? Not at all. Iowa lay north of the line, and had been organized as a Territory and come into the Union as a State without disturbing that Compromise. There was no sort of necessity for destroying it to organize these Territories. But, gentlemen, it would take up all my time to meet all the little quibbling arguments of Judge Douglas to show that the Missouri Compromise was repealed by the Compromise of 1850. My own opinion is, that a careful investigation of all the arguments to sustain the position that that Compromise was virtually repealed by the Compromise of 1850 would show that they are the merest fallacies. I have the report that Judge Douglas first brought into Congress at the time of the introduction of the Nebraska Bill, which in its original form *did not* repeal the Missouri

Compromise, and he there expressly stated that he had forborne to do so *because it had not been done by the Compromise of 1850*. I close this part of the discussion on my part by asking him the question again, "Why, when we had peace under the Missouri Compromise, could you not have let it alone?"

In complaining of what I said in my speech at Springfield, in which he says I accepted my nomination for the senatorship (where, by the way, he is at fault, for if he will examine it, he will find no acceptance in it), he again quotes that portion in which I said that "a house divided against itself cannot stand." Let me say a word in regard to that matter.

He tries to persuade us that there must be a variety in the different institutions of the States of the Union; that that variety necessarily proceeds from the variety of soil, climate, of the face of the country, and the difference in the natural features of the States. I agree to all that. Have these very matters ever produced any difficulty amongst us? Not at all. Have we ever had any quarrel over the fact that they have laws in Louisiana designed to regulate the commerce that springs from the production of sugar? Or because we have a different class relative to the production of flour in this State? Have they produced any differences? Not at all. They are the very cements of this Union. They don't make the house a house divided against itself. They are the props that hold up the house and sustain the Union.

But has it been so with this element of slavery? Have we not always had quarrels and difficulties over it? And when will we cease to have quarrels over it? Like causes produce like effects. It is worth while to observe that we have generally had comparative peace upon the slavery question, and that there has been no cause for alarm until it was excited by the effort to spread it into new territory. Whenever it has been limited to its present bounds, and there has been no effort to spread it, there has been peace. All the trouble and convulsion has proceeded from efforts to spread it over more territory. It was thus at the date of the Missouri Compromise. It was so again with the annexation of Texas; so with the territory acquired by the Mexican war; and it is so now. Whenever there has been an effort to spread it, there has been agitation and resistance. Now, I appeal to this audience (very few of whom are my political friends), as national men, whether we have reason to expect that the agitation in regard to this subject will cease while the causes that tend to reproduce agitation are actively at work? Will not the same cause that produced agitation in 1820, when the Missouri Compromise was formed, that which produced the agitation upon the annexation of Texas, and at other times, work out the same results always? Do you think that the nature of man will be changed, that the same causes that produced agitation at one time will not have the same effect at another?

This has been the result so far as my observation of the slavery question and my reading in history extends. What right have we then to hope that the trouble will cease,—that the agitation will come to an end,—until it shall either be placed back where it originally stood, and where the fathers originally placed it, or, on the other hand, until it shall entirely master all opposition? This is the view I entertain, and this is the reason why I entertained it, as Judge Douglas has read from my Springfield speech.

Now, my friends, there is one other thing that I feel myself under some sort of obligation to mention. Judge Douglas has here to-day—in a very rambling way, I was about saying—spoken of the platforms for which he seeks to hold me responsible. He says, "Why can't you come out and make an open avowal of principles in all places alike?" and he reads from an advertisement that he says was used to notify the people of a speech to be made by Judge Trumbull at Waterloo. In commenting on it he desires to know whether we cannot speak frankly and manfully, as he and his friends do. How, I ask, do his friends speak out their own sentiments? A Convention of his party in this State met on the 21st of April at Springfield, and passed a set of resolutions which they proclaim to the country as their platform. This does constitute their platform, and it is because Judge Douglas claims it is his platform—that these are his principles and purposes—that he has a right to declare he speaks his sentiments "frankly and manfully." On the 9th of June Colonel John Dougherty, Governor Reynolds, and others, calling themselves National Democrats, met in Springfield and adopted a set of resolutions which are as easily understood, as plain and as definite in stating to the country and to the world what they believed in and would stand upon, as Judge Douglas's platform. Now, what is the reason that Judge Douglas is not willing that Colonel Dougherty and Governor Reynolds should stand upon their own written and printed platform as well as he upon his? Why must he look farther than their platform when he claims himself to stand by his platform?

Again, in reference to our platform: On the 16th of June the Republicans had their Convention and published their platform, which is as clear and distinct as Judge Douglas's. In it they spoke their principles as plainly and as definitely to the world. What is the reason that Judge Douglas is not willing I should stand upon that platform? Why must he go around hunting for some one who is supporting me or has supported me at some time in his life, and who has said something at some time contrary to that platform? Does the Judge regard that rule as a good one? If it turn out that the rule is a good one for me—that I am responsible for any and every opinion that any man has expressed who is my friend,—then it is a good rule for him. I ask, is it not as good a rule for him as it is for me? In my opinion, it is not a good rule for either of us. Do you think differently, Judge?

MR. DOUGLAS: I do not.

MR. LINCOLN: Judge Douglas says he does not think differently. I am glad of it. Then can he tell me why he is looking up resolutions of five or six years ago, and insisting that they were my platform, notwithstanding my protest that they are not, and never were my platform, and my pointing out the platform of the State Convention which he delights to say nominated me for the Senate? I cannot see what he means by parading these resolutions, if it is not to hold me responsible for them in some way. If he says to me here that he does not hold the rule to be good, one way or the other, I do not comprehend how he could answer me more fully if he answered me at greater length. I will therefore put in as my answer to the resolutions that he has hunted up against me, what I, as a lawyer, would call a good plea to a bad declaration. I understand that it is a maxim of law that a poor plea may be a good plea to a bad declaration. I think that the opinions the Judge brings from those who support me, yet differ from me, is a bad declaration against me; but if I can bring the same things against him, I am putting in a good plea to that kind of declaration, and now I propose to try it.

At Freeport, Judge Douglas occupied a large part of his time in producing resolutions and documents of various sorts, as I understood, to make me somehow responsible for them; and I propose now doing a little of the same sort of thing for him. In 1850 a very clever gentleman by the name of Thompson Campbell, a personal friend of Judge Douglas and myself, a political friend of Judge Douglas and opponent of mine, was a candidate for Congress in the Galena District. He was interrogated as to his views on this same slavery question. I have here before me the interrogatories, and Campbell's answers to them. I will read them:

### INTERROGATORIES

1st. Will you, if elected, vote for and cordially support a bill prohibiting slavery in the Territories of the United States?

2d. Will you vote for and support a bill abolishing slavery in the District of Columbia?

3d. Will you oppose the admission of any slave States which may be formed out of Texas or the Territories?

4th. Will you vote for and advocate the repeal of the Fugitive Slave law passed at the recent session of Congress?

5th. Will you advocate and vote for the election of a Speaker of the House of Representatives who shall be willing to organize the committees of that House so as to give the Free States their just influence in the business of legislation?

6th. What are your views, not only as to the constitutional right of Congress to prohibit the slave-trade between the States, but also as to the expediency of exercising that right immediately?

### CAMPBELL'S REPLY

To the first and second interrogatories, I answer unequivocally in the affirmative.

To the third interrogatory I reply, that I am opposed to the admission of any more Slave States into the Union, that may be formed out of Texas or any other Territory.

To the fourth and fifth interrogatories I unhesitatingly answer in the affirmative.

To the sixth interrogatory I reply, that so long as the slave States continue to treat slaves as articles of commerce, the Constitution confers power on Congress to pass laws regulating that peculiar COMMERCE, and that the protection of Human Rights imperatively demands the interposition of every constitutional means to prevent this most inhuman and iniquitous traffic.

T. CAMPBELL

I want to say here that Thompson Campbell was elected to Congress on that platform, as the Democratic candidate in the Galena District, against Martin P. Sweet.

JUDGE DOUGLAS: Give me the date of the letter.

MR. LINCOLN: The time Campbell ran was in 1850. I have not the exact date here. It was some time in 1850 that these interrogatories were put and the answer given. Campbell was elected to Congress, and served out his term. I think a second election came up before he served out his term, and he was not re-elected. Whether defeated or not nominated, I do not know. [Mr. Campbell was nominated for re-election by the Democratic party, by acclamation.] At the end of his term his very good friend Judge Douglas got him a high office from President Pierce, and sent him off to California. Is not that the fact? Just at the end of his term in Congress it appears that our mutual friend Judge Douglas got our mutual friend Campbell a good office, and sent him to California upon it. And not only so, but on the 27th of last month, when Judge Douglas and myself spoke at Freeport in joint discussion, there was his same friend Campbell, come all the way from California, to help the Judge beat me; and there was poor Martin P. Sweet standing on the platform, trying to help poor me to be elected. That is true of one of Judge Douglas's friends.

So again, in that same race of 1850, there was a Congressional Convention assembled at Joliet, and it nominated R. S. Molony for Congress, and unanimously adopted the following resolution:

> *Resolved,* That we are uncompromisingly opposed to the extension of slavery; and while we would not make such opposition a ground of interference with the interests of the States where it exists, yet we moderately but firmly insist that it is the duty of Congress to oppose its extension into Territory now free, by all means compatible with the obligations of the Constitution, and with good faith to our sister States; that these principles were recognized by the Ordinance of 1787, which received the sanction of Thomas Jefferson, who is acknowledged by all to be the great oracle and expounder of our faith.

Subsequently the same interrogatories were propounded to Dr. Molony which had been addressed to Campbell as above, with the exception of the 6th, respecting the interstate slave trade, to which Dr. Molony, the Democratic nominee for Congress, replied as follows:

> I received the written interrogatories this day, and, as you will see by the La Salle *Democrat* and Ottawa *Free Trader,* I took at Peru on the 5th, and at Ottawa on the 7th, the affirmative side of interrogatories 1st and 2d; and in relation to the admission of any more slave States from Free Territory, my position taken at these meetings, as correctly reported in said papers, was *emphatically* and *distinctly* opposed to it. In relation to the admission of any more slave States from Texas, whether I shall go against it or not will depend upon the opinion that I may hereafter form of the true meaning and nature of the resolutions of annexation. If, by said resolutions, the honor and good faith of the nation is pledged to admit more slave States from Texas when she (Texas) may apply for the admission of such State, then I should, if in

Congress, vote for their admission. But if not so PLEDGED and bound by sacred contract, then a bill for the admission of more slave States from Texas would *never* receive my vote.

To your fourth interrogatory I answer *most decidedly* in the affirmative, and for reasons set forth in my reported remarks at Ottawa last Monday.

To your fifth interrogatory I also reply in the affirmative *most cordially*, and that I will use my utmost exertions to secure the nomination and election of a man who will accomplish the objects of said interrogatories. I most cordially approve of the resolutions adopted at the Union meeting held at Princeton on the 27th September ult.

Yours, etc., R. S. MOLONY

All I have to say in regard to Dr. Molony is that he was the regularly nominated Democratic candidate for Congress in his district; was elected at that time; at the end of his term was appointed to a land-office at Danville. (I never heard anything of Judge Douglas's instrumentality in this.) He held this office a considerable time, and when we were at Freeport the other day there were handbills scattered about notifying the public that after our debate was over R. S. Molony would make a Democratic speech in favor of Judge Douglas. That is all I know of my own personal knowledge. It is added here to this resolution, and truly I believe, that—

Among those who participated in the Joliet Convention, and who supported its nominee, with his platform as laid down in the resolution of the Convention and in his reply as above given, we call at random the following names, all of which are recognized at this day as leading Democrats:

Cook County,—E. B. Williams, Charles McDonell, Arno Voss, Thomas Hoyne, Isaac Cook.

I reckon we ought to except Cook.

F. C. Sherman.
Will,—Joel A. Matteson, S. W. Bowen.
Kane,—B. F. Hall, G. W. Renwick, A. M. Herrington, Elijah Wilcox.
McHenry,—W. M. Jackson, Enos W. Smith, Neil Donnelly.
La Salle,—John Hise, William Reddick.

William Reddick! another one of Judge Douglas's friends that stood on the stand with him at Ottawa, at the time the Judge says my knees trembled so that I had to be carried away. The names are all here:

Du Page,—Nathan Allen.
De Kalb,—Z. B. Mayo.

Here is another set of resolutions which I think are apposite to the matter in hand.

On the 28th of February of the same year a Democratic District Convention was held at Naperville to nominate a candidate for Circuit Judge. Among the delegates were Bowen and Kelly of Will; Captain Naper, H. H. Cody, Nathan Allen, of Du Page; W. M. Jackson, J. M. Strode, P. W. Platt, and Enos W. Smith of McHenry; J. Horsman and others of Winnebago. Colonel Strode presided over the Convention. The following resolutions were unanimously adopted,— the first on motion of P. W. Platt, the second on motion of William M. Jackson:

> *Resolved,* That this Convention is in favor of the Wilmot Proviso, both in *Principle* and *Practice,* and that we know of no good reason why any *person* should oppose the largest latitude in *Free Soil, Free Territory* and *Free Speech.*
>
> *Resolved,* That in the opinion of this Convention, the time has arrived when *all men should be free,* whites as well as others.

JUDGE DOUGLAS: What is the date of those resolutions?

MR. LINCOLN: I understand it was in 1850, but I do not *know* it. I do not state a thing and say I know it, when I do not. But I have the highest belief that this is so. I know of no way to arrive at the conclusion that there is an error in it. I mean to put a case no stronger than the truth will allow. But what I was going to comment upon is an extract from a newspaper in De Kalb County; and it strikes me as being rather singular, I confess, under the circumstances. There is a Judge Mayo in that county, who is a candidate for the Legislature, for the purpose, if he secures his election, of helping to re-elect Judge Douglas. He is the editor of a newspaper [De Kalb County *Sentinel*], and in that paper I find the extract I am going to read. It is part of an editorial article in which he was electioneering as fiercely as he could for Judge Douglas and against me. It was a curious thing, I think, to be in such a paper. I will agree to that, and the Judge may make the most of it:

Our education has been such that we have been rather *in favor of the equality of the blacks; that is, that they should enjoy all the privileges of the whites where they reside.* We are aware that this is not a very popular doctrine. We have had many a confab with some who are now strong "Republicans," we taking the broad ground of equality, and they the opposite ground.

We were brought up in a State where blacks were voters, and we do not know of any inconvenience resulting from it, though perhaps it would not work as well where the blacks are more numerous. We have no doubt of the right of the whites to guard against such an evil, if it is one. Our opinion is that it would be best for all concerned to have the colored population in a State by themselves [in this I agree with him]; but if within the jurisdiction of the United States, *we say by all means they should have the right to have their Senators and Representatives in Congress, and to vote for President.* With us "worth makes the man, and want of it the fellow." We have seen many a "nigger" that we thought more of than some white men.

That is one of Judge Douglas's friends. Now, I do not want to leave myself in an attitude where I can be misrepresented, so I will say I do not think the Judge is responsible for this article; but he is quite as responsible for it as I would be if one of my friends had said it. I think that is fair enough.

I have here also a set of resolutions passed by a Democratic State Convention in Judge Douglas's own good State of Vermont, that I think ought to be good for him too:

> *Resolved,* That liberty is a right inherent and inalienable in man, and that herein *all men are equal.*
>
> *Resolved,* That we claim no authority in the Federal Government to abolish slavery in the several States, but we do claim for it Constitutional power perpetually to prohibit the introduction of slavery into territory now free, and abolish it wherever, under the jurisdiction of Congress, it exists.
>
> *Resolved,* That this power ought immediately to be exercised in prohibiting the introduction and existence of slavery in New Mexico and California, in abolishing slavery and the slave-trade in the District of Columbia, on the high seas, and wherever else, under the Constitution, it can be reached.

*Resolved,* That no more Slave States should be admitted into the Federal Union.

*Resolved,* That the Government ought to return to its ancient policy, not to extend, nationalize, or encourage, but to limit, localize, and discourage slavery.

At Freeport I answered several interrogatories that had been propounded to me by Judge Douglas at the Ottawa meeting. The Judge has not yet seen fit to find any fault with the position that I took in regard to those seven interrogatories, which were certainly broad enough, in all conscience, to cover the entire ground. In my answers, which have been printed, and all have had the opportunity of seeing, I take the ground that those who elect me must expect that I will do nothing which will not be in accordance with those answers. I have some right to assert that Judge Douglas has no fault to find with them. But he chooses to still try to thrust me upon different ground, without paying any attention to my answers, the obtaining of which from me cost him so much trouble and concern. At the same time I propounded four interrogatories to him, claiming it as a right that he should answer as many interrogatories for me as I did for him, and I would reserve myself for a future instalment when I got them ready. The Judge, in answering me upon that occasion, put in what I suppose he intends as answers to all four of my interrogatories. The first one of these interrogatories I have before me, and it is in these words:

> *Question* 1.—If the people of Kansas shall, by means entirely unobjectionable in all other respects, adopt a State constitution, and ask admission into the Union under it, *before* they have the requisite number of inhabitants according to the English bill,— some ninety-three thousand,—will you vote to admit them?

As I read the Judge's answer in the newspaper, and as I remember it as pronounced at the time, he does not give any answer which is equivalent to yes or no,—I will or I won't. He answers at very considerable length, rather quarrelling with me for asking the question, and insisting that Judge Trumbull had done something that I ought to say something about, and finally getting out such statements as induce me to infer that he means to be understood he will, in that supposed case, vote for the admission of Kansas. I only bring this forward now for the purpose of saying that if he chooses to put a different construction upon his answer, he may do it. But if he does not, I shall from this time forward assume that he will vote for the admission of Kansas in disregard of the English bill. He has the right to remove any misunderstanding I may have. I only mention it now, that I may hereafter assume this to be the true construction of his answer, if he does not now choose to correct me.

The second interrogatory that I propounded to him was this:

> *Question 2.*—Can the people of a United States Territory, in any lawful way, against the wish of any citizen of the United States, exclude slavery from its limits prior to the formation of a State Constitution?

To this Judge Douglas answered that they can lawfully exclude slavery from the Territory prior to the formation of a constitution. He goes on to tell us how it can be done. As I understand him, he holds that it can be done by the Territorial Legislature refusing to make any enactments for the protection of slavery in the Territory, and especially by adopting unfriendly legislation to it. For the sake of clearness, I state it again: that they can exclude slavery from the Territory, 1st, by withholding what he assumes to be an indispensable assistance to it in the way of legislation; and, 2d, by unfriendly legislation. If I rightly understand him, I wish to ask your attention for a while to his position.

In the first place, the Supreme Court of the United States has decided that any Congressional prohibition of slavery in the Territories is unconstitutional; that they have reached this proposition as a conclusion from their former proposition, that the Constitution of the United States expressly recognizes property in slaves, and from that other Constitutional provision, that no person shall be deprived of property without due process of law. Hence they reach the conclusion that as the Constitution of the United States expressly recognizes property in slaves, and prohibits any person from being deprived of property without due process of law, to pass an Act of Congress by which a man who owned a slave on one side of a line would be deprived of him if he took him on the other side, is depriving him of that property without due process of law. That I understand to be the decision of the Supreme Court. I understand also that Judge Douglas adheres most firmly to that decision; and the difficulty is, how is it possible for any power to exclude slavery from the Territory, unless in violation of that decision? That is the difficulty.

In the Senate of the United States, in 1850, Judge Trumbull, in a speech substantially, if not directly, put the same interrogatory to Judge Douglas, as to whether the people of a Territory had the lawful power to exclude slavery prior to the formation of a constitution. Judge Douglas then answered at considerable length, and his answer will be found in the *Congressional Globe*, under date of June 9th, 1856. The Judge said that whether the people could exclude slavery prior to the formation of a constitution or not *was a question to be decided by the Supreme Court*. He put that proposition, as will be seen by the *Congressional Globe*, in a variety of forms, all running to the same thing in substance,—that it was a question for the Supreme Court. I maintain that when he says, after the Supreme Court have decided the question, that the people may yet exclude slavery by any means whatever, he does virtually say that it is *not* a question for the Supreme Court. He shifts his ground. I appeal to you whether he did not say it was a question for the Supreme Court? Has not the Supreme Court decided that question? When he now says the people *may* exclude slavery, does he not make it a question for the people? Does he not virtually shift his ground and say that it is *not* a question for the court, but for the people? This is a very simple proposition,—a very plain and naked one. It seems to me that there is no difficulty in deciding it. In a variety of ways he said that it was a question for the Supreme Court. He did not stop then to tell us that, whatever the Supreme Court decides, the people can by withholding necessary "police regulations" keep slavery out. He did not make any such answer. I submit to you now whether the new state of the case has not induced the Judge to sheer away from his original ground. Would not this be the impression of every fair-minded man?

I hold that the proposition that slavery cannot enter a new country without police regulations is historically false. It is not true at all. I hold that the history of this country shows that the institution of slavery was originally planted upon this continent *without* these "police regulations," which the Judge now thinks necessary for the actual establishment of it. Not only so, but is there not another fact: how came this Dred Scott decision to be made? It was made upon the case of a negro being taken and actually held in slavery in Minnesota Territory, claiming his freedom because the Act of Congress prohibited his being so held there. *Will the Judge pretend that Dred Scott was not held there without police regulations?* There is at least one matter of record as to his having been held in slavery in the Territory, not only without police regulations, but in the teeth of Congressional legislation supposed to be valid at the time. This shows that there is vigor enough in slavery to plant itself in a new country even against unfriendly legislation. It takes not only law, but the *enforcement* of law to keep it out. That is the history of this country upon the subject.

I wish to ask one other question. It being understood that the Constitution of the United States guarantees property in slaves in the Territories, if there is any infringement of the right of that property, would not the United States courts, organized for the government of the Territory, apply such remedy as might be necessary in that case? It is a maxim held by the courts that there is no wrong without its remedy; and the courts have a remedy for whatever is acknowledged and treated as a wrong.

Again: I will ask you, my friends, if you were elected members of the Legislature, what would be the first thing you would have to do before entering upon your duties? *Swear to support the Constitution of the United States.* Suppose you believe, as Judge Douglas does, that the Constitution of the United States guarantees to your neighbor the right to hold slaves in that Territory; that they are his property: how can you clear your oaths unless you give him such legislation as is necessary to enable him to enjoy that property? What do you understand by supporting the Constitution of a State, or of the United States? Is it not to give such constitutional helps to the rights established by that Constitution as may be practically needed? Can you, if you swear to support the Constitution, and believe that the Constitution establishes a right, clear your oath, without giving it support? Do you support the Constitution if, knowing or believing there is a right established under it which needs specific legislation, you withhold that legislation? Do you not violate and disregard your oath? I can conceive of nothing plainer in the world. There can be nothing in the words "support the Constitution," if you may run counter to it by refusing support to any right established under the Constitution. And what I say here will hold with still more force against the Judge's doctrine of "unfriendly legislation." How could you, having sworn to support the Constitution, and believing it guaranteed the right to hold slaves in the Territories, assist in legislation *intended to defeat that right?* That would be violating your own view of the Constitution. Not only so, but if you were to do so, how long would it take the courts to hold your votes unconstitutional and void? Not a moment.

Lastly, I would ask: Is not Congress itself under obligation to give legislative support to any right that is established under the United States Constitution? I repeat the question: Is not Congress itself bound to give legislative support to any right that is established in the United States Constitution? A member of Congress swears to support the Constitution of the United States: and if he sees a right established by that Constitution which needs specific legislative protection, can he clear his oath without giving that protection? Let me ask you why many of us who are opposed to slavery upon principle give our acquiescence to a Fugitive Slave law? Why do we hold ourselves under obligations to pass such a law, and abide by it when it is passed? Because the Constitution makes provision that the owners of slaves shall have the right to reclaim them. It gives the right to reclaim slaves; and that right is, as Judge Douglas says, a barren right, unless there is legislation that will enforce it.

The mere declaration, "No person held to service or labor in one State under the laws thereof, escaping into another, shall in consequence of any law or regulation therein be discharged from such service or labor, but shall be delivered up on claim of the party to whom such service or labor may be due," is powerless without specific legislation to enforce it. Now, on what ground would a member of Congress, who is opposed to slavery in the abstract, vote for a Fugitive law, as I would deem it my duty to do? Because there is a constitutional right which needs legislation to enforce it. And although it is distasteful to me, I have sworn to support the Constitution; and having so sworn, I cannot conceive that I do support it if I withhold from that right any necessary legislation to make it practical. And if that is true in regard to a Fugitive Slave law, is the right to have fugitive slaves reclaimed any better fixed in the Constitution than the right to hold slaves in the Territories? For this decision is a just exposition of the Constitution, as Judge Douglas thinks. Is the one right any better than the other? Is there any man who, while a member of Congress, would give support to the one any more than the other? If I wished to refuse to give legislative support to slave property in the Territories, if a member of Congress, I could not do it, holding the view that the Constitution establishes that right. If I did it at all, it would be because I deny that this decision properly construes the Constitution. But if I acknowledge, with Judge Douglas, that this decision properly construes the Constitution, I cannot conceive that I would be less than a perjured man if I should refuse in Congress to give such protection to that property as in its nature it needed.

At the end of what I have said here I propose to give the Judge my fifth interrogatory, which he may take and answer at his leisure. My fifth interrogatory is this:

If the slaveholding citizens of a United States Territory should need and demand Congressional legislation for the protection of their slave property in such Territory, would you, as a member of Congress, vote for or against such legislation?

JUDGE DOUGLAS: Will you repeat that? I want to answer that question.

MR. LINCOLN: If the slaveholding citizens of a United States Territory should need and demand Congressional legislation for the protection of their slave property in such Territory, would you, as a member of Congress, vote for or against such legislation?

I am aware that in some of the speeches Judge Douglas has made, he has spoken as if he did not know or think that the Supreme Court had decided that a Territorial Legislature cannot exclude slavery. Precisely what the Judge would say upon the subject—whether he would say definitely that he does not understand they have so decided, or whether he would say he does understand that the court have so decided,—I do not know; but I know that in his speech at Springfield he spoke of it as a thing they had not decided yet; and in his answer to me at Freeport, he spoke of it, so far, again, as I can comprehend it, as a thing that had not yet been decided. Now, I hold that if the Judge does entertain that view, I think that he is not mistaken in so far as it can be said that the court has not decided anything save the mere question of jurisdiction. I know the legal arguments that can be made,—that after a court has decided that it cannot take jurisdiction in a case, it then has decided all that is before it, and that is the end of it. A plausible argument can be made in favor of that proposition; but I know that Judge Douglas has said in one of his speeches that the court went forward, *like honest men as they were,* and decided all the points in the case. If any points are really extra-judicially decided, because not necessarily before them, then this one as to the power of the Territorial Legislature, to exclude slavery is one of them, as also the one that the Missouri Compromise was null and void. They are both extra-judicial, or neither is, according as the court held that they had no jurisdiction in the case between the parties, because of want of capacity of one party to maintain a suit in that court. I want, if I have sufficient time, to show that the court did *pass its opinion*; but that is the only thing actually done in the case. If they did not decide, they showed what they were ready to decide whenever the matter was before them. What is that opinion? After having argued that Congress had no power to pass a law excluding slavery from a United States Territory, they then used language to this effect: That inasmuch as Congress itself could not exercise such a power, it followed as a matter of course that it could not authorize a Territorial government to exercise it; for the Territorial Legislature can do no more than Congress could do. Thus it expressed its opinion emphatically against the power of a Territorial Legislature to exclude slavery, leaving us in just as little doubt on that point as upon any other point they really decided.

Now, my fellow-citizens, I will detain you only a little while longer; my time is nearly out. I find a report of a speech made by Judge Douglas at Joliet, since we last met at Freeport,—published, I believe, in the *Missouri Republican,*—on the 9th of this month, in which Judge Douglas says:

> You know at Ottawa I read this platform, and asked him if he concurred in each and all of the principles set forth in it. He would not answer these questions. At last I said frankly, I wish you to answer them, because when I get them up here where the color of your principles are a little darker than in Egypt, I

intend to trot you down to Jonesboro. The very notice that I
was going to take him down to Egypt made him tremble in his
knees so that he had to be carried from the platform. He laid up
seven days, and in the meantime held a consultation with his
political physicians; they had Lovejoy and Farnsworth and all
the leaders of the Abolition party, they consulted it all over, and
at last Lincoln came to the conclusion that he would answer, so
he came up to Freeport last Friday.

Now, that statement altogether furnishes a subject for philosophical contemplation. I have been treating it in that way, and I have really come to the conclusion that I can explain it in no other way than by believing the Judge is crazy. If
he was in his right mind I cannot conceive how he would have risked disgusting
the four or five thousand of his own friends who stood there and knew, as to my
having been carried from the platform, that there was not a word of truth in it.

JUDGE DOUGLAS: Didn't they carry you off?

MR. LINCOLN: There! that question illustrates the character of this man
Douglas exactly. He smiles now, and says, "Didn't they carry you off?" but he
said then *"he had to be carried off"*; and he said it to convince the country that he
had so completely broken me down by his speech that I had to be carried away.
Now he seeks to dodge it, and asks, "Didn't they carry you off?" Yes, they did.
*"But, Judge Douglas, why didn't you tell the truth?"* I would like to know why you
didn't tell the truth about it. And then again "He laid up seven days." He put this
in print for the people of the country to read as a serious document. I think if he
had been in his sober senses he would not have risked that barefacedness in the
presence of thousands of his own friends who knew that I made speeches within
six of the seven days at Henry, Marshall County, Augusta, Hancock County, and
Macomb, McDonough County, including all the necessary travel to meet him
again at Freeport at the end of the six days. Now I say there is no charitable way
to look at that statement, except to conclude that he is actually crazy. There is
another thing in that statement that alarmed me very greatly as he states it, that
he was going to "trot me down to Egypt." Thereby he would have you infer that
I would not come to Egypt unless he forced me—that I could not be got here
unless he, giant-like, had hauled me down here. That statement he makes, too,
in the teeth of the knowledge that I had made the stipulation to come down here
*and that he himself had been very reluctant to enter into the stipulation.* More than
all this: Judge Douglas, when he made that statement, must have been crazy and
wholly out of his sober senses, or else he would have known that when he got me

down here, that promise—that windy promise—of his powers to annihilate me, wouldn't amount to anything. Now, how little do I look like being carried away trembling? Let the Judge go on; and after he is done with his half-hour, I want you all, if I can't go home myself, to let me stay and rot here; and if anything happens to the Judge, if I cannot carry him to the hotel and put him to bed, let me stay here and rot. I say, then, here is something *extraordinary* in this statement. I ask you if you know any other living man who would make such a statement? I will ask my friend Casey, over there, if he would do such a thing? Would he send that out and have his men take it as the truth? Did the Judge talk of trotting me down to Egypt to scare me to death? Why, I know this people better than he does. I was raised just a little east of here. I am a part of this people. But the Judge was raised farther north, and perhaps he has some horrid idea of what this people might be induced to do. But really I have talked about this matter perhaps longer than I ought, for it is no great thing; and yet the smallest are often the most difficult things to deal with. The Judge has set about seriously trying to make the impression that when we meet at different places I am literally in his clutches—that I am a poor, helpless, decrepit mouse, and that I can do nothing at all. This is one of the ways he has taken to create that impression. I don't know any other way to meet it except this. I don't want to quarrel with him—to call him a liar; but when I come square up to him I don't know what else to call him if I must tell the truth out. I want to be at peace, and reserve all my fighting powers for necessary occasions. My time now is very nearly out, and I give up the trifle that is left to the Judge, to let him set my knees trembling again, if he can.

## Mr. Douglas's Rejoinder

My Friends: While I am very grateful to you for the enthusiasm which you show for me, I will say in all candor that your quietness will be much more agreeable than your applause, inasmuch as you deprive me of some part of my time whenever you cheer.

I will commence where Mr. Lincoln left off, and make a remark upon this serious complaint of his about my speech at Joliet. I did say there in a playful manner that when I put these questions to Mr. Lincoln at Ottawa he failed to answer, and that he trembled and had to be carried off the stand and required seven days to get up his reply. That he did not walk off from that stand he will not deny. That when the crowd went away from the stand with me, a few persons carried him home on their shoulders and laid him down, he will admit. I wish to say to you that whenever I degrade my friends and myself by allowing them to carry me on their backs along through the public streets, when I am able to walk, I am willing to be deemed crazy. I did not say whether I beat him or he beat me in the argument. It is true I put these questions to him, and I put them not as mere idle questions, but showed that I based them upon the creed of the Black Republican party as declared by their conventions in that portion of the State which he depends upon to elect him, and desired to know whether he indorsed that creed. He would not answer. When I reminded him that I intended bringing him into Egypt and renewing my questions if he refused to answer, he then consulted and did get up his answers one week after,—answers which I may refer to in a few minutes and show you how equivocal they are. My object was to make him avow whether or not he stood by the platform of his party; the resolutions I then read and upon which I based my questions had been adopted by his party in the Galena Congressional District and the Chicago and Bloomington Congressional Districts, composing a large majority of the counties in this State that give Republican or Abolition majorities. Mr. Lincoln cannot and will not deny that the doctrines laid down in these resolutions were in substance put forth in Lovejoy's resolutions, which were voted for by a majority of his party, some of them, if not all, receiving the support of every man of his party. Hence I laid a foundation for my questions to him before I asked him whether that was or was not the platform of his party. He says that he answered my questions. One of them was whether he would vote to admit any more slave States into the Union. The creed of the Republican party as set forth in the resolutions of their various conventions was that they would under no circumstances vote to admit another slave State. It was put forth in the Lovejoy resolutions in the Legislature; it was put forth and passed in a majority of all the counties of this State which give Abolition or Republican majorities, or elect members to the Legislature of that school of politics. I had a right to know whether he would vote for or against the admission of another slave State in the event the people wanted it. He first answered that he was not pledged on the subject and then said:

> In regard to the other question, of whether I am pledged to
> the admission of any more slave States into the Union, I state
> to you very frankly that I would be exceedingly sorry ever to be
> put in the position of having to pass on that question. I should
> be exceedingly glad to know that there would never be another
> slave State admitted into the Union; but I must add that if slav-
> ery shall be kept out of the Territories during the Territorial
> existence of any one given Territory, and then the people, hav-
> ing a fair chance and clean field, when they come to adopt a

constitution, do such an extraordinary thing as adopt a slave constitution, uninfluenced by the actual presence of the institution among them, I see no alternative, if we own the country, but to admit them into the Union.

Now analyze that answer. In the first place, he says he would be exceedingly sorry to be put in a position where he would have to vote on the question of the admission of a slave State. Why is he a candidate for the Senate if he would be sorry to be put in that position? I trust the people of Illinois will not put him in a position which he would be so sorry to occupy. The next position he takes is that he would be glad to know that there would never be another slave State, yet, in certain contingencies, he might have to vote for one. What is that contingency? If Congress keeps slavery out by law while it is a Territory, and then the people should have a fair chance and should adopt slavery, uninfluenced by the presence of the institution, he supposed he would have to admit the State. Suppose Congress should not keep slavery out during their Territorial existence, then how would he vote when the people applied for admission into the Union with a slave constitution? That he does not answer; and that is the condition of every Territory we have now got. Slavery is not kept out of Kansas by Act of Congress; and when I put the question to Mr. Lincoln, whether he will vote for the admission with or without slavery, as her people may desire, he will not answer, and you have not an answer from him. In Nebraska, slavery is not prohibited by Act of Congress, but the people are allowed, under the Nebraska Bill, to do as they please on the subject; and when I ask him whether he will vote to admit Nebraska with a slave constitution if her people desire it, he will not answer. So with New Mexico, Washington Territory, Arizona, and the four new States to be admitted from Texas. You cannot get an answer from him to these questions. His answer only applies to a given case, to a condition,—things which he knows do not exist in any one Territory in the Union. He tries to give you to understand that he would allow the people to do as they please, and yet he dodges the question as to every Territory in the Union. I now ask why cannot Mr. Lincoln answer to each of these Territories? He has not done it, and he will not do it. The Abolitionists up north understand that this answer is made with a view of not committing himself on any one Territory now in existence. It is so understood there, and you cannot expect an answer from him on a case that applies to any one Territory, or applies to the new States which by compact we are pledged to admit out of Texas, when they have the requisite population and desire admission. I submit to you whether he has made a frank answer, so that you can tell how he would vote in any one of these cases. "He would be sorry to be put in the position." Why would he be sorry to be put in this position if his duty required him to give the vote? If the people of a Territory ought to be permitted to come into the Union as a State, with slavery or without it, as they pleased, why not give the vote admitting them cheerfully? If in his opinion they ought not to come in with slavery, even if they wanted to, why not say that he would cheerfully vote against their admission? His intimation is that conscience would not let him vote "No," and he would be sorry to do that which his conscience would compel him to do as an honest man.

In regard to the contract, or bargain, between Trumbull, the Abolitionists, and him, which he denies, I wish to say that the charge can be proved by notorious historical facts. Trumbull, Lovejoy, Giddings, Fred Douglass, Hale and Banks were travelling the State at that time making speeches on the same side and in the same cause with him. He contents himself with the simple denial that any such thing occurred. Does he deny that he, and Trumbull, and Breese, and Giddings, and Chase, and Fred Douglass, and Lovejoy, and all those Abolitionists and deserters from the Democratic party did make speeches all over this State in the same common cause? Does he deny that Jim Matheny was then, and is now, his confidential friend, and does he deny that Matheny made the charge of the bargain and fraud in his own language, as I have read it from his printed speech? Matheny spoke of his own personal knowledge of that bargain existing between Lincoln, Trumbull, and the Abolitionists. He still remains Lincoln's confidential friend, and is now a candidate for Congress, and is canvassing the Springfield District for Lincoln. I assert that I can prove the charge to be true in detail if I can ever get it where I can summon and compel the attendance of witnesses. I have the statement of another man to the same effect as that made by Matheny, which I am not permitted to use yet; but Jim Matheny is a good witness on that point, and the history of the country is conclusive upon it. That Lincoln up to that time had been a Whig, and then undertook to Abolitionize the Whigs and bring them into the Abolition camp, is beyond denial; that Trumbull up to that time had been a Democrat, and deserted, and undertook to Abolitionize the Democracy, and take them into the Abolition camp, is beyond denial; that they are both now active, leading, distinguished members of this Abolition Republican party, in full communion, is a fact that cannot be questioned or denied.

But Lincoln is not willing to be responsible for the creed of his party. He complains because I hold him responsible; and in order to avoid the issue, he attempts to show that individuals in the Democratic party, many years ago, expressed Abolition sentiments. It is true that Tom Campbell, when a candidate for Congress in 1850, published the letter which Lincoln read. When I asked Lincoln for the date of that letter, he could not give it. The date of the letter has been suppressed by other speakers who have used it, though I take it for granted that Lincoln did not know the date. If he will take the trouble to examine, he will find that the letter was published only two days before the election, and was never seen until after it, except in one county. Tom Campbell would have been beat to death by the Democratic party if that letter had been made public in his district. As to Molony, it is true he uttered sentiments of the kind referred to by Mr. Lincoln, and the best Democrats would not vote for him for that reason. I returned from Washington after the passage of the Compromise measures in 1850, and when I found Molony running under Wentworth's tutelage and on his platform, I denounced him, and declared that he was no Democrat. In my speech at Chicago, just before the election that year, I went before the infuriated people of that city and vindicated the Compromise measures of 1850. Remember the city council had passed resolutions nullifying Acts of Congress and instructing the police to withhold their assistance from the execution of the laws; and as I was the only man in the city of Chicago who was responsible for the passage of the Compromise measures, I went before the crowd, justified each and every one of those measures; and let it be said, to the eternal honor of the people of Chicago, that when they were convinced by my exposition of those measures that they were right, and they had done wrong in opposing them, they repealed their nullifying resolutions, and declared that they would acquiesce in and support the laws of the land. These facts are well known, and Mr. Lincoln can only get up individual instances, dating back to 1849–'50, which are contradicted by the whole tenor of the Democratic creed.

But Mr. Lincoln does not want to be held responsible for the Black Republican doctrine of no more slave States. Farnsworth is the candidate of his party to-day in the Chicago District, and he made a speech in the last Congress in which he called upon God to palsy his right arm if he ever voted for the admission of another slave State, whether the people wanted it or not. Lovejoy is making speeches all over the State for Lincoln now, and taking ground against any more slave States. Washburne, the Black Republican candidate for Congress in the Galena District, is making speeches in favor of this same Abolition platform, declaring no more slave States. Why are men running for Congress in the northern districts, and taking that Abolition platform for their guide, when Mr. Lincoln does not want to be held to it down here in Egypt and in the centre of the State, and objects to it so as to get votes here? Let me tell Mr. Lincoln that his party in the northern part of the State hold to that Abolition platform, and that if they do not in the south and in the centre, they present the extraordinary spectacle of a "house divided against itself," and hence "cannot stand." I now bring down upon him the vengeance of his own Scriptural quotation, and give it a more appropriate application than he did, when I say to him that his party, Abolition in one end of the State, and opposed to it in the other, is a house divided against itself, and cannot stand, and ought not to stand, for it attempts to cheat the American people out of their votes by disguising its sentiments.

Mr. Lincoln attempts to cover up and get over his Abolitionism by telling you that he was raised a little east of you, beyond the Wabash in Indiana, and he thinks that makes a mighty sound and good man of him on all these questions. I do not know that the place where a man is born or raised has much to do with his political principles. The worst Abolitionists I have ever known in Illinois have been men who have sold their slaves in Alabama and Kentucky, and have come here and turned Abolitionists whilst spending the money got for the negroes they sold; and I do not know that an Abolitionist from Indiana or Kentucky ought to have any more credit because he was born and raised among slaveholders. I do not know that a native of Kentucky is more excusable because, raised among slaves, his father and mother having owned slaves, he comes to Illinois, turns Abolitionist, and slanders the graves of his father and mother, and breathes curses upon the institutions under which he was born, and his father and mother bred. True, I was not born out west here. I was born away down in Yankee land, I was born in a valley in Vermont, with the high mountains around me. I love the old green mountains and valleys of Vermont, where I was born, and where I played in my childhood. I went up to visit them some seven or eight years ago, for the first time for twenty odd years. When I got there they treated me very kindly. They invited me to the Commencement of their college, placed me on the seats with their distinguished guests, and conferred upon me the degree of LL.D., in Latin (Doctor of Laws),— the same as they did Old Hickory, at Cambridge, many years ago; and I give you my word and honor I understood just as much of the Latin as he did. When they got through conferring the honorary degree they called upon me for a speech; and I got up, with my heart full and swelling with gratitude for their kindness, and I said to them: "My friends, Vermont is the most glorious spot on the face of this globe for a man to be born in, *provided* he emigrates when he is very young."

I emigrated when I was very young. I came out here when I was a boy, and I found my mind liberalized, and my opinions enlarged, when I got on these broad prairies, with only the heavens to bound my vision, instead of having them circumscribed by the little narrow ridges that surrounded the valley where I was born. But I discard all flings of the land where a man was born; I wish to be judged by my principles, by those great public measures and constitutional principles upon which the peace, the happiness and the perpetuity of this Republic now rest.

Mr. Lincoln has framed another question, propounded it to me, and desired my answer. As I have said before, I did not put a question to him that I did not first lay a foundation for by showing that it was a part of the platform of the party whose votes he is now seeking, adopted in a majority of the counties where he now hopes to get a majority, and supported by the candidates of his party now running in those counties. But I will answer his question. It is as follows: "If the slaveholding citizens of a United States Territory should need and demand Congressional legislation for the protection of their slave property in such Territory, would you, as a member of Congress, vote for or against such legislation?" I answer him that it is a fundamental article in the Democratic creed that there should be non-interference and non-intervention by Congress with slavery in the States or Territories. Mr. Lincoln could have found an answer to his question in the Cincinnati platform, if he had desired it. The Democratic party have always stood by that great principle of non-interference and non-intervention by Congress with slavery in the States and Territories alike, and I stand on that platform now.

Now, I desire to call your attention to the fact that Lincoln did not define his own position in his own question. How does he stand on that question? He put the question to me at Freeport whether or not I would vote to admit Kansas into the Union before she had 93,420 inhabitants. I answered him at once that, it having been decided that Kansas had now population enough for a slave State, she had population enough for a free State.

I answered the question unequivocally; and then I asked him whether he would vote for or against the admission of Kansas before she had 93,420 inhabitants and he would not answer me. To-day he has called attention to the fact that in his opinion my answer on that question was not quite plain enough, and yet he has not answered it himself. He now puts a question in relation to Congressional interference in the Territories to me. I answer him direct, and yet he has not answered the question himself. I ask you whether a man has any right in common decency to put questions in these public discussions to his opponent which he will not answer himself when they are pressed home to him. I have asked him three times whether he would vote to admit Kansas whenever the people applied with a constitution of their own making and their own adoption under circumstances that were fair, just, and unexceptionable; but I cannot get an answer from him. Nor will he answer the question which he put to me, and which I have just answered, in relation to Congressional interference in the Territories by making a slave code there.

It is true that he goes on to answer the question by arguing that under the decision of the Supreme Court it is the duty of a man to vote for a slave code in the Territories. He says that it is his duty, under the decision that the court has made; and if he believes in that decision he would be a perjured man if he did not give the vote. I want to know whether he is not bound to a decision which is contrary to his opinions just as much as to one in accordance with his opinions. If the decision of the Supreme Court, the tribunal created by the Constitution to decide the question, is final and binding, is he not bound by it just as strongly as if he was for it instead of against it originally? Is every man in this land allowed to resist decisions he does not like, and only support those that meet his approval? What are important courts worth, unless their decisions are binding on all good citizens? It is the fundamental principle of the judiciary that its decisions are final. It is created for that purpose; so that when you cannot agree among yourselves on a disputed point, you appeal to the judicial tribunal, which steps in and decides for you; and that decision is then binding on every good citizen. It is the law of the land just as much with Mr. Lincoln against it as for it. And yet he says if that decision is binding he is a perjured man if he does not vote for a slave code in the different Territories of this Union. Well, if you [turning to Mr. Lincoln] are not going to resist the decision, if you obey it and do not intend to array mob law against the constituted authorities, then, according to your own statement, you will be a perjured man if you do not vote to establish slavery in these Territories. My doctrine is that, even taking Mr. Lincoln's view, that the decision recognizes the right of a man to carry his slaves into the Territories of the United States if he pleases, yet after he gets there he needs affirmative law to make that right of any value. The same doctrine not only applies to slave property, but all other kinds of property. Chief Justice Taney places it upon the ground that slave property is on an equal footing with other property. Suppose one of your merchants should move to Kansas and open a liquor store: he has a right to take groceries and liquors there; but the mode of selling them, and the circumstances under which they shall be sold, and all the remedies, must be prescribed by local legislation; and if that is unfriendly, it will drive him out just as effectually as if there was a constitutional provision against the sale of liquor. So the absence of local legisla-tion to encourage and support slave property in a Territory excludes it practically just as effectually as if there was a positive constitutional provision against it. Hence I assert that under the Dred Scott decision you cannot maintain slavery a day in a Territory where there is an unwilling people and unfriendly legislation. If the people are opposed to it, our right is a barren, worthless, useless right; and if they are for it, they will support and encourage it. We come right back, therefore, to the practical question,—if the people of a Territory want slavery, they will have it; and if they do not want it, you cannot force it on them. And this is the practi-cal question, the great principle, upon which our institutions rest. I am willing to take the decision of the Supreme Court as it was pronounced by that august tribunal, without stopping to inquire whether I would have decided that way or not. I have had many a decision made against me on questions of law which I did not like, but I was bound by them just as much as if I had had a hand in making them and approved them. Did you ever see a lawyer or a client lose his case that he approved the decision of the court? They always think the decision unjust when it is given against them. In a government of laws, like ours, we must sustain the Constitution as our fathers made it, and maintain the rights of the States as they are guaranteed under the Constitution; and then we will have peace and harmony between the different States and sections of this glorious Union.

# Fourth Joint Debate, at Charleston

*September 18, 1858*

### Mr. Lincoln's Opening Speech

Ladies and Gentlemen: It will be very difficult for an audience so large as this to hear distinctly what a speaker says, and consequently it is important that as profound silence be preserved as possible.

While I was at the hotel to-day, an elderly gentleman called upon me to know whether I was really in favor of producing a perfect equality between the negroes and white people. While I had not proposed to myself on this occasion to say much on that subject, yet as the question was asked me I thought I would occupy perhaps five minutes in saying something in regard to it. I will say, then, that I am not, nor ever have been, in favor of bringing about in any way the social and political equality of the white and black races; that I am not, nor ever have been, in favor of making voters or jurors of negroes, nor of qualifying them to hold office, nor to intermarry with white people; and I will say, in addition to this, that there is a physical difference between the white and black races which I believe will forever forbid the two races living together on terms of social and political equality. And inasmuch as they cannot so live, while they do remain together there must be the position of superior and inferior, and I as much as any other man am in favor of having the superior position assigned to the white race. I say upon this occasion I do not perceive that because the white man is to have the superior position the negro should be denied everything. I do not understand that because I do not want a negro woman for a slave I must necessarily want her for a wife. My understanding is that I can just let her alone. I am now in my fiftieth year, and I certainly never have had a black woman for either a slave or a wife. So it seems to me quite possible for us to get along without making either slaves or wives of negroes. I will add to this that I have never seen, to my knowledge, a man, woman, or child who was in favor of producing a perfect equality, social and political, between negroes and white men. I recollect of but one distinguished instance that I ever heard of so frequently as to be entirely satisfied of its correctness, and that is the case of Judge Douglas's old friend Colonel Richard M. Johnson. I will also add to the remarks I have made (for I am not going to enter at large upon this subject), that I have never had the least apprehension that I or my friends would marry negroes if there was no law to keep them from it; but as Judge Douglas and his friends seem to be in great apprehension that they might, if there were no law to keep them from it, I give him the most solemn pledge that I will to the very last stand by the law of this State which forbids the marrying of white people with negroes. I will add one further word, which is this: that I do not understand that there is any place where an alteration of the social and political relations of the negro and the white man can be made, except in the State Legislature,—not in the Congress of the United States; and as I do not really apprehend the approach of any such thing myself, and as Judge Douglas seems to be in constant horror that some such danger is rapidly approaching, I propose as the best means to prevent it that the Judge be kept at home, and placed in the State Legislature to fight the measure. I do not propose dwelling longer at this time on this subject.

When Judge Trumbull, our other Senator in Congress, returned to Illinois in the month of August, he made a speech at Chicago, in which he made what may be called a *charge* against Judge Douglas, which I understand proved to be very offensive to him. The Judge was at that time out upon one of his speaking tours through the country, and when the news of it reached him, as I am informed, he denounced Judge Trumbull in rather harsh terms for having said what he did in regard to that matter. I was travelling at that time, and speaking at the same places with Judge Douglas on subsequent days, and when I heard of what Judge Trumbull had said of Douglas, and what Douglas had said back again, I felt that I was in a position where I could not remain entirely silent in regard to the matter. Consequently, upon two or three occasions I alluded to it, and alluded to it in no other wise than to say that in regard to the charge brought by Trumbull against Douglas, I *personally* knew nothing, and sought to say nothing about it; that I did personally know Judge Trumbull; that I believed him to be a man of veracity; that I believed him to be a man of capacity sufficient to know very well whether an assertion he was making, as a conclusion drawn from a set of facts, was true or false; and as a conclusion of my own from that, I stated it as my belief if Trumbull should ever be called upon, he would prove everything he had said. I said this upon two or three occasions. Upon a subsequent occasion, Judge Trumbull spoke again before an audience at Alton, and upon that occasion not only repeated his charge against Douglas, but arrayed the evidence he relied upon to substantiate it. This speech was published at length; and subsequently at Jacksonville Judge Douglas alluded to the matter. In the course of his speech, and near the close of it, he stated in regard to myself what I will now read: "Judge Douglas proceeded to remark that he should not hereafter occupy his time in refuting such charges made by Trumbull, but that, Lincoln having indorsed the character of Trumbull for veracity, he should hold him (Lincoln) responsible for the slanders." I have done simply what I have told you, to subject me to this invitation to notice the charge. I now wish to say that it had not originally been my purpose to discuss that matter at all. But inasmuch as it seems to be the wish of Judge Douglas to hold me responsible for it, then for once in my life I will play General Jackson, and to the just extent I take the responsibility.

I wish to say at the beginning that I will hand to the reporters that portion of Judge Trumbull's Alton speech which was devoted to this matter, and also that portion of Judge Douglas's speech made at Jacksonville in answer to it. I shall thereby furnish the readers of this debate with the complete discussion between Trumbull and Douglas. I cannot now read them, for the reason that it would take half of my first hour to do so. I can only make some comments upon them. Trumbull's charge is in the following words: "Now, the charge is, that there was a plot entered into to have a constitution formed for Kansas, and put in force, without giving the people an opportunity to vote upon it, and that Mr. Douglas was in the plot." I will state, without quoting further, for all will have an opportunity of reading it hereafter, that Judge Trumbull brings forward what he regards as sufficient evidence to substantiate this charge.*

It will be perceived Judge Trumbull shows that Senator Bigler, upon the floor of the Senate, had declared there had been a conference among the senators, in which conference it was determined to have an enabling act passed for the people of Kansas to form a constitution under, and in this conference it was agreed among them that it was best not to have a provision for submitting the constitution to a vote of the people after it should be formed. He then brings forward to show, and showing, as he deemed, that Judge Douglas reported the bill back to the Senate with that clause stricken out. He then shows that there was a new clause inserted into the bill, which would in its nature *prevent* a reference of the constitution back for a vote of the people,—if, indeed, upon a mere silence in the law, it could be assumed that they had the right to vote upon it. These are the general statements that he has made.

I propose to examine the points in Judge Douglas's speech in which he attempts to answer that speech of Judge Trumbull's. When you come to examine Judge Douglas's speech, you will find that the first point he makes is: "Suppose it were true that there was such a change in the bill, and that I struck it out,—is that a proof of a plot to force a constitution upon them against their will?" His

---

*See Trumbull's speech at the close of this debate.

striking out such a provision, if there was such a one in the bill, he argues, does not establish the proof that it was stricken out for the purpose of robbing the people of that right. I would say, in the first place, that that would be a *most manifest* reason for it. It is true, as Judge Douglas states, that many Territorial bills have passed without having such a provision in them. I believe it is true, though I am not certain, that in some instances constitutions framed under such bills have been submitted to a vote of the people with the law silent upon the subject; but it does not appear that they once had their enabling acts framed with an express provision *for* submitting the constitution to be framed to a vote of the people, and then that they were stricken out when Congress did not mean to alter the effect of the law. That there have been bills which never had the provision in, I do not question; but when was that provision taken out of one that it was in? More especially does this evidence tend to prove the proposition that Trumbull advanced, when we remember that the provision was stricken out of the bill almost simultaneously with the time that Bigler says there was a conference among certain senators, and in which it was agreed that a bill should be passed leaving that out. Judge Douglas, in answering Trumbull, omits to attend to the testimony of Bigler, that there was a meeting in which it was agreed they should so frame the bill that there should be no submission of the constitution to a vote of the people. The Judge does not notice this part of it. If you take this as one piece of evidence, and then ascertain that simultaneously Judge Douglas struck out a provision that did require it to be submitted, and put the two together, I think it will make a pretty fair show of proof that Judge Douglas did, as Trumbull says, enter into a plot to put in force a constitution for Kansas, without giving the people any opportunity of voting upon it.

But I must hurry on. The next proposition that Judge Douglas puts is this: "But upon examination it turns out that the Toombs bill never did contain a clause requiring the constitution to be submitted." This is a mere question of fact, and can be determined by evidence. I only want to ask this question: Why did not Judge Douglas say that these words were not stricken out of the Toombs bill, or this bill from which it is alleged the provision was stricken out,—a bill which goes by the name of Toombs, because he originally brought it forward? I ask why, if the Judge wanted to make a direct issue with Trumbull, did he not take the exact proposition Trumbull made in his speech, and say it was not stricken out? Trumbull has given the exact words that he says were in the Toombs bill, and he alleges that when the bill came back, they were stricken out. Judge Douglas does not say that the words which Trumbull says were stricken out were not so stricken out, but he says there was no provision in the Toombs bill to submit the constitution to a vote of the people. We see at once that he is merely making an issue upon the meaning of the words. He has not undertaken to say that Trumbull tells a lie about these words being stricken out, but he is really, when pushed up to it, only taking an issue upon the meaning of the words. Now, then, if there be any issue upon the meaning of the words, or if there be upon the question of fact as to whether these words were stricken out, I have before me what I suppose to be a genuine copy of the Toomb's bill, in which it can be shown that the words Trumbull says were in it were, in fact, originally there. If there be any dispute upon the fact, I have got the documents here to show they were there. If there be any controversy upon the sense of the words,—whether these words which were stricken out really constituted a provision for submitting the matter to a vote of the people,—as that is a matter of argument, I think I may as well use Trumbull's own argument. He says that the proposition is in these words:

> That the following propositions be and the same are hereby offered to the said Convention of the people of Kansas when formed, for their free acceptance or rejection; which, if accepted by the Convention *and ratified by the people at the election for the adoption of the constitution,* shall be obligatory upon the United States and the said State of Kansas.

Now, Trumbull alleges that these last words were stricken out of the bill when it came back, and he says this was a provision for submitting the constitution to a vote of the people; and his argument is this: "Would it have been possible to ratify the land propositions at the election for the adoption of the constitution, unless such an election was to be held?" This is Trumbull's argument. Now, Judge Douglas does not meet the charge at all, but he stands up and says there was no such proposition in that bill for submitting the constitution to be framed to a vote of the people. Trumbull admits that the language is not a direct provision for submitting it, but it is a provision necessarily implied from another provision. He asks you how it is possible to ratify the land proposition at the election for the adoption of the constitution, if there was no election to be held for the adoption of the constitution. And he goes on to show that it is not any less a law because the provision is put in that indirect shape than it would be if it were put directly. But I presume I have said enough to draw attention to this point, and I pass it by also.

Another one of the points that Judge Douglas makes upon Trumbull, and at very great length, is, that Trumbull, while the bill was pending, said in a speech in the Senate that he supposed the constitution to be made would have to be submitted to the people. He asks, if Trumbull thought so then, what ground is there for anybody thinking otherwise now? Fellow-citizens, this much may be said in reply: That bill had been in the hands of a party to which Trumbull did not belong. It had been in the hands of the committee at the head of which Judge Douglas stood. Trumbull perhaps had a printed copy of the original Toombs bill. I have not the evidence on that point except a sort of inference I draw from the general course of business there. What alterations, or what provisions in the way of altering, were going on in committee, Trumbull had no means of knowing, until the altered bill was reported back. Soon afterwards, when it was reported back, there was a discussion over it, and perhaps Trumbull in reading it hastily in the altered form did not perceive all the bearings of the alterations. He was hastily borne into the debate, and it does not follow that because there was something in it Trumbull did not perceive, that something did not exist. More than this, is it true that what Trumbull did can have any effect on what Douglas did? Suppose Trumbull had been in the plot with these other men, would that let Douglas out of it? Would it exonerate Douglas that Turnbull didn't then perceive he was in the plot? He also asks the question: Why didn't Trumbull propose to amend the bill, if he thought it needed any amendment? Why, I believe that everything Judge Trumbull had proposed, particularly in connection with this question of Kansas and Nebraska, since he had been on the floor of the Senate, had been promptly voted down by Judge Douglas and his friends. He had no promise that an amendment offered by him to anything on this subject would receive the slightest consideration. Judge Trumbull did bring to the notice of the Senate at that time the fact that there was no provision for submitting the constitution about to be made for the people of Kansas to a vote of the people. I believe I may venture to say that Judge Douglas made some reply to this speech of Judge Trumbull's, *but he never noticed that part of it at all.* And so the thing passed by. I think, then, the fact that Judge Trumbull offered no amendment does not throw much blame upon him; and if it did, it does not reach the question of fact *as to what Judge Douglas was doing.* I repeat, that if Trumbull had himself been in the plot, it would not at all relieve the others who were in it from blame. If I should be indicted for murder, and upon the trial it should be discovered that I had been implicated in that murder, but that the prosecuting witness was guilty too, that would not at all touch the question of my crime. It would be no relief to my neck that they discovered this other man who charged the crime upon me to be guilty too.

Another one of the points Judge Douglas makes upon Judge Trumbull is, that when he spoke in Chicago he made his charge to rest upon the fact that the bill had the provision in it for submitting the constitution to a vote of the people when it went into his (Judge Douglas's) hands, that it was missing when he reported it to the Senate, and that in a public speech he had subsequently said the alterations in the bill were made while it was in committee, and that they were made in consultation between him (Judge Douglas) and Toombs. And Judge Douglas goes on to comment upon the fact of Trumbull's adducing in his Alton speech the proposition that the bill not only came back with that proposition stricken out, but with another clause and another provision in it, saying that "until the complete execution of this Act there shall be no election in said Territory,"—which, Trumbull argued, was not only taking the provision for submitting to a vote of the people out of the bill, but was adding an affirmative one, in that it prevented the people from exercising the right under a bill that was merely silent on the question. Now, in regard to what he says, that Trumbull shifts the issue, that he shifts his ground,—and I believe he uses the term that, "it being proven false, he has changed ground,"—I call upon all of you, when you come to examine that portion of Trumbull's speech (for it will make a part of mine), to examine whether Trumbull has shifted his ground or not. I say he did not shift his ground, but that he brought forward his original charge and the evidence to sustain it yet more fully, but precisely as he originally made it. Then, in addition thereto, he brought in a new piece of evidence. He shifted no ground. He brought no new piece of evidence inconsistent with his former testimony; but he brought a new piece, tending, as he thought, and as I think, to prove his proposition. To illustrate: A man brings an accusation against another, and on trial the man making the charge introduces A and B to prove the accusation. At a second trial he introduces the same witnesses, who tell the same story as before, and a third witness, who tells the same thing, and in addition gives further testimony corroborative of the charge. So with Trumbull. There was no shifting of ground, nor inconsistency of testimony between the new piece of evidence and what he originally introduced.

But Judge Douglas says that he himself moved to strike out that last provision of the bill, and that on his motion it was stricken out and a substitute inserted. That I presume is the truth. I presume it is true that that last proposition was stricken out by Judge Douglas. Trumbull has not said it was not; Trumbull has himself said that it was so stricken out. He says: "I am now speaking of the bill as Judge Douglas reported it back. It was amended somewhat in the Senate before it passed, but I am speaking of it as he brought it back." Now, when Judge Douglas parades the fact that the provision was stricken out of the bill when it came back, he asserts nothing contrary to what Trumbull alleges. Trumbull has only said that he originally put it in,—not that he did not strike it out. Trumbull says it was not in the bill when it went to the committee. When it came back it was in, and Judge Douglas said the alterations were made by him in consultation with Toombs. Trumbull alleges, therefore, as his conclusion, that Judge Douglas put it in. Then, if Douglas wants to contradict Trumbull and call him a liar, let him say he did not put it in, and not that he didn't take it out again. It is said that a bear is sometimes hard enough pushed to drop a cub; and so I presume it was in this case, I presume the truth is that Douglas put it in, and afterward took it out. That, I take it, is the truth about it. Judge Trumbull says one thing, Douglas says another thing, and the two don't contradict one another at all. The question is, what did he put it in for? In the first place, what did he take the other provision out of the bill for,—the provision which Trumbull argued was necessary for submitting the constitution to a vote of the people? What did he take that out for; and, having taken it out, what did he put this in for? I say that in the run of things it is not unlikely forces conspire to render it vastly expedient for Judge Douglas to take that latter clause out again. The question that Trumbull has made is that Judge Douglas put it in; and he don't meet Trumbull at all unless he denies that.

In the clause of Judge Douglas's speech upon this subject he uses this language toward Judge Trumbull. He says: "He forges his evidence from beginning to end; and by falsifying the record, he endeavors to bolster up his false charge." Well, that is a pretty serious statement—Trumbull forges his evidence from beginning to end. Now, upon my own authority I say that it is not true. What is a forgery? Consider the evidence that Trumbull has brought forward. When you come to read the speech, as you will be able to, examine whether the evidence is a forgery from beginning to end. He had the bill or document in his hand like that [holding up a paper]. He says that is a copy of the Toombs bill,—the amendment offered by Toombs. He says that is a copy of the bill as it was introduced and went into Judge Douglas's hands. Now, does Judge Douglas say that is a forgery? That is one thing Trumbull brought forward. Judge Douglas says he forged it from beginning to end! That is the "beginning," we will say. Does Douglas say that is a forgery? Let him say it to-day, and we will have a subsequent examination upon this subject. Trumbull then holds up another document like this, and says that is an exact copy of the bill as it came back in the amended form out of Judge Douglas's hands. Does Judge Douglas say that is a forgery? Does he say it in his general sweeping charge? Does he say so now? If he does not, then take this Toombs bill and the bill in the amended form, and it only needs to compare them to see that the provision is in the one and not in the other; it leaves the inference inevitable that it was taken out.

But, while I am dealing with this question, let us see what Trumbull's other evidence is. One other piece of evidence I will read. Trumbull says there are in this original Toombs bill these words:

That the following propositions be and the same are hereby offered to the said Convention of the people of Kansas, when formed, for their free acceptance or rejection; which, if accepted by the Convention and ratified by the people at the election for the adoption of the constitution, shall be obligatory upon the United States and the said State of Kansas.

Now, if it is said that this is a forgery, we will open the paper here and see whether it is or not. Again, Trumbull says, as he goes along, that Mr. Bigler made the following statement in his place in the Senate, December 9, 1857:

I was present when that subject was discussed by senators before the bill was introduced, and the question was raised and discussed, whether the constitution, when formed, should be submitted to a vote of the people. It was held by those most intelligent on the subject that, in view of all the difficulties surrounding that Territory, the danger of any experiment at that time of a popular vote, it would be better there should be no such provision in the Toombs bill; and it was my understanding, in all the intercourse I had, that the Convention would make a constitution, and send it here, without submitting it to the popular vote.

Then Trumbull follows on:

In speaking of this meeting again on the 21st December, 1857 [*Congressional Globe,* same vol., page 113], Senator Bigler said:

"Nothing was further from my mind than to allude to any social or confidential interview. The meeting was not of that character. Indeed, it was semi-official, and called to promote the public good. My recollection was clear that I left the conference under the impression that it had been deemed best to adopt measures to admit Kansas as a State through the agency of one popular election, and that for delegates to this Convention. This impression was stronger because I thought the spirit of the bill infringed upon the doctrine of non-intervention, to which I had great aversion; but with the hope of accomplishing a great good, and as no movement had been made in that direction in the Territory, I waived this objection, and concluded to support the measure. I have a few items of testimony as to the correctness of these impressions, and with their submission I shall be content. I have before me the bill reported by the senator from Illinois on the 7th of March, 1856, providing for the admission of Kansas as a State, the third section of which reads as follows:

"'That the following propositions be, and the same are hereby offered to the said Convention of the people of Kansas, when formed, for their free acceptance or rejection; which, if accepted by the Convention and ratified by the people at the election for the adoption of the constitution, shall be obligatory upon the United States and the said State of Kansas.'

"The bill read in his place by the senator from Georgia on the 25th of June, and referred to the Committee on Territories, contained the same section word for word. Both these bills were under consideration at the conference referred to; but, sir, when the senator from Illinois reported the Toombs bill to the Senate with amendments, the next morning, it did not contain that portion of the third section which indicated to the Convention that the constitution should be approved by the people. The words 'and ratified by the people at the election for the adoption of the constitution' had been stricken out."

Now, these things Trumbull says were stated by Bigler upon the floor of the Senate on certain days, and that they are recorded in the *Congressional Globe* on certain pages. Does Judge Douglas say this is a forgery? Does he say there is no such thing in the *Congressional Globe*? What does he mean when he says Judge Trumbull forges his evidence from beginning to end? So again he says in another place that Judge Douglas, in his speech, December 9, 1857 (*Congressional Globe*, part I, page 15), stated:

That during the last session of Congress, I [Mr. Douglas] reported a bill from the Committee on Territories, to authorize the people of Kansas to assemble and form a constitution for themselves. Subsequently the senator from Georgia [Mr. Toombs] brought forward a substitute for my bill, which, *after having been modified by him and myself in consultation*, was passed by the Senate.

Now, Trumbull says this is a quotation from a speech of Douglas, and is recorded in the *Congressional Globe*. Is *it* a forgery? Is it there or not? It may not be there, but I want the Judge to take these pieces of evidence, and distinctly say they are forgeries if he dare do it.

A VOICE: "He will."

MR. LINCOLN: Well, sir, you had better not commit him. He gives other quotations,—another from Judge Douglas. He says:

> I will ask the senator to show me an intimation, from any one member of the Senate, in the whole debate on the Toombs bill, and in the Union, from any quarter, that the constitution was not to be submitted to the people. I will venture to say that on all sides of the chamber it was so understood at the time. If the opponents of the bill had understood it was not, they would have made the point on it; and if they had made it, we should certainly have yielded to it, and put in the clause. That is a discovery made since the President found out that it was not safe to take it for granted that that would be done, which ought in fairness to have been done.

Judge Trumbull says Douglas made that speech, and it is recorded. Does Judge Douglas say it is a forgery, and was not true? Trumbull says somewhere, and I propose to skip it, but it will be found by any one who will read this debate, that he did distinctly bring it to the notice of those who were engineering the bill, that it lacked that provision; and then he goes on to give another quotation from Judge Douglas, where Judge Trumbull uses this language:

> Judge Douglas, however, on the same day and in the same debate, probably recollecting or being reminded of the fact that I had objected to the Toombs bill when pending that it did not provide for a submission of the constitution to the people, made another statement, which is to be found in the same volume of the *Globe*, page 22, in which he says:
>
> "That the bill was silent on this subject was true, and my attention was called to that about the time it was passed; and I took the fair construction to be, that powers not delegated were reserved, and that of course the constitution would be submitted to the people."

Whether this statement is consistent with the statement just before made, that had the point been made it would have been yielded to, or that it was a new discovery, you will determine.

So I say. I do not know whether Judge Douglas will dispute this, and yet maintain his position that Trumbull's evidence "was forged from beginning to end." I will remark that I have not got these *Congressional Globes* with me. They are large books, and difficult to carry about, and if Judge Douglas shall say that on these points where Trumbull has quoted from them there are no such passages there, I shall not be able to prove they are there upon this occasion, but I will have another chance. Whenever he points out the forgery and says, "I declare that this particular thing which Trumbull has uttered is not to be found where he says it is," then my attention will be drawn to that, and I will arm myself for the contest,—stating now that I have not the slightest doubt on earth that I will find every quotation just where Trumbull says it is. Then the question is, How can Douglas call that a forgery? How can he make out that it is a forgery? What is a forgery? It is the bringing forward something in writing or in print purporting to be of certain effect when it is altogether untrue. If you come forward with my note for one hundred dollars when I have never given such a note, there is a forgery. If you come forward with a letter purporting to be written by me which I never wrote, there is another forgery. If you produce anything in writing or in print saying it is so and so, the document not being genuine, a forgery has been committed. How do you make this a forgery when every piece of the evidence is genuine? If Judge Douglas does say these documents and quotations are false and forged, he has a full right to do so; but until he does it specifically, we don't know how to get at him. If he does say they are false and forged, I will then look further into it, and I presume I can procure the certificates of the proper officers that they are genuine copies. I have no doubt each of these extracts will be found exactly where Trumbull says it is. Then I leave it to you if Judge Douglas, in making his sweeping charge that Judge Trumbull's evidence is forged from beginning to end, at all meets the case,—if that is the way to get at the facts. I repeat again, if he will point out which one is a forgery, I will carefully examine it, and if it proves that any one of them is really a forgery, it will not be me who will hold to it any longer. I have always wanted to deal with everyone I meet candidly and honestly. If I have made any assertion not warranted by facts, and it is pointed out to me, I will withdraw it cheerfully. But I do not choose to see Judge Trumbull calumniated, and the evidence he has brought forward branded in general terms "a forgery from beginning to end." This is not the legal way of meeting a charge, and

I submit to all intelligent persons, both friends of Judge Douglas and of myself, whether it is.

The point upon Judge Douglas is this: The bill that went into his hands had the provision in it for a submission of the constitution to the people; and I say its language amounts to an express provision for a submission, and that he took the provision out. He says it was known that the bill was silent in this particular; *but I say, Judge Douglas, it was not silent when you got it.* It was vocal with the declaration, when you got it, for a submission of the constitution to the people. And now, my direct question to Judge Douglas is, to answer why, if he deemed the bill silent on this point, he found it necessary to strike out those particular harmless words. If he had found the bill silent and without this provision, he might say what he does now. If he supposes it was implied that the constitution would be submitted to a vote of the people, how could these two lines so encumber the statute as to make it necessary to strike them out? How could he infer that a submission was still implied, after its express provision had been stricken from the bill? I find the bill vocal with the provision, while he silenced it. He took it out, and although he took out the other provision preventing a submission to a vote of the people, I ask, *Why did you first put it in?* I ask him whether he took the original provision out, which Trumbull alleges was in the bill. If he admits that he did take it, *I ask him what he did it for.* It looks to us as if he had altered the bill. If it looks differently to him,—if he has a different reason for his action from the one we assign him—he can tell it. I insist upon knowing why he made the bill silent upon that point when it was vocal before he put his hands upon it.

I was told, before my last paragraph, that my time was within three minutes of being out. I presume it is expired now; I therefore close.

## Mr. Douglas's Reply

Ladies and Gentlemen: I had supposed that we assembled here to-day for the purpose of a joint discussion between Mr. Lincoln and myself upon the political questions that now agitate the whole country. The rule of such discussions is, that the opening speaker shall touch upon all the points he intends to discuss, in order that his opponent, in reply, shall have the opportunity of answering them. Let me ask you what questions of public policy, relating to the welfare of this State or the Union, has Mr. Lincoln discussed before you? Mr. Lincoln simply contented himself at the outset by saying that he was not in favor of social and political equality between the white man and the negro, and did not desire the law so changed as to make the latter voters or eligible to office. I am glad that I have at last succeeded in getting an answer out of him upon this question of negro citizenship and eligibility to office, for I have been trying to bring him to the point on it ever since this canvass commenced.

I will now call your attention to the question which Mr. Lincoln has occupied his entire time in discussing. He spent his whole hour in retailing a charge made by Senator Trumbull against me. The circumstances out of which that charge was manufactured occurred prior to the last Presidential election, over two years ago. If the charge was true, why did not Trumbull make it in 1856, when I was discussing the questions of that day all over this State with Lincoln and him, and when it was pertinent to the then issue? He was then as silent as the grave on the subject. If that charge was true, the time to have brought it forward was the canvass of 1856, the year when the Toombs bill passed the Senate. When the facts were fresh in the public mind, when the Kansas question was the paramount question of the day, and when such a charge would have had a material bearing on the election, why did he and Lincoln remain silent then, knowing that such a charge could be made and proven if true? Were they not false to you and false to the country in going through that entire campaign concealing their knowledge of this enormous conspiracy which, Mr. Trumbull says, he then knew and would not tell? Mr. Lincoln intimates, in his speech, a good reason why Mr. Trumbull would not tell, for he says that it might be true, as I proved that it was at Jacksonville, that Trumbull was also in the plot, yet that the fact of Trumbull's being in the plot would not in any way relieve me. He illustrates this argument by supposing himself on trial for murder, and says that it would be no extenuating circumstance if, on his trial another man was found to be a party to his crime. Well, if Trumbull was in the plot, and concealed it in order to escape the odium which would have fallen upon himself, I ask you whether you can believe him now when he turns State's evidence, and avows his own infamy in order to implicate me. I am amazed that Mr. Lincoln should now come forward and indorse that charge, occupying his whole hour in reading Mr. Trumbull's speech in support of it. Why, I ask, does not Mr. Lincoln make a speech of his own instead of taking up his time reading Trumbull's speech at Alton? I supposed that Mr. Lincoln was capable of making a public speech on his own account, or I should not have accepted the banter from him for a joint discussion. ["How about the charges?"] Do not trouble yourselves. I am going to make my speech in my own way, and I trust, as the Democrats listened patiently and respectfully to Mr. Lincoln, that his friends will not interrupt me when I am answering him. When Mr. Trumbull returned from the East, the first thing he did when he landed in Chicago was to make a speech wholly devoted to assaults upon my public character and public action. Up to that time I had never alluded to his course in Congress, or to him directly or indirectly, and hence his assaults upon me were entirely without provocation and without excuse. Since then he has been travelling from one end of the State to the other, repeating his vile charge. I propose now to read it in his own language:

> Now, fellow-citizens, I make the distinct charge that there was a preconcerted arrangement and plot entered into by the very men who now claim credit for opposing a constitution formed and put in force without giving the people any opportunity to pass upon it. This, my friends, is a serious charge, but I charge it to-night that the very men who traverse the country under banners proclaiming popular sovereignty, by design concocted a bill on purpose to force a constitution upon that people.

In answer to some one in the crowd who asked him a question, Trumbull said:

> And you want to satisfy yourself that he was in the plot to force a constitution upon that people? I will satisfy you. I will cram the truth down any honest man's throat until he cannot deny it. And to the man who does deny it, I will cram the lie down his throat till he shall cry "Enough!"
>
> It is preposterous; it is the most damnable effrontery that man ever put on, to conceal a scheme to defraud and cheat the people out of their rights, and then claim credit for it.

That is the polite language Senator Trumbull applied to me, his colleague, when I was two hundred miles off. Why did he not speak out as boldly in the Senate of the United States, and cram the lie down my throat when I denied the charge, first made by Bigler, and made him take it back? You all recollect how Bigler assaulted me when I was engaged in a hand-to-hand fight, resisting a scheme to force a constitution on the people of Kansas against their will. He then attacked me with this charge; but I proved its utter falsity, nailed the slander to the counter, and made him take the back track. There is not an honest man in America who read that debate who will pretend that the charge is true. Trumbull was then present in the Senate, face to face with me; and why did he not then rise and repeat the charge, and say he would cram the lie down my throat? I tell you that Trumbull then knew it was a lie. He knew that Toombs denied that there ever was a clause in the bill he brought forward calling for and requiring a submission of the Kansas Constitution to the people. I will tell you what the facts of the case were: I introduced a bill to authorize the people of Kansas to form a constitution, and come into the Union as a State whenever they should have the requisite population for a member of Congress, and Mr. Toombs proposed a substitute, authorizing the people of Kansas, with their then population of only 25,000, to form a constitution, and come in at once. The question at issue was, whether we would admit Kansas with a population of 25,000 or make her wait until she had the ratio entitling her to a representative in Congress, which was 93,420. That was the point of dispute in the Committee on Territories, to which both my bill and Mr. Toombs's substitute had been referred. I was overruled by a majority of the committee, my proposition rejected, and Mr. Toombs's proposition to admit Kansas then, with her population of 25,000, adopted. Accordingly a bill to carry out his idea of immediate admission was reported as a substitute for mine; the only points at issue being, as I have already said, the question of population, and the adoption of safeguards against frauds at the election. Trumbull knew this,—the whole Senate knew it,—and hence he was silent at that time. He waited until I became engaged in this canvass, and finding that I was showing up Lincoln's Abolitionism and negro equality doctrines, that I was driving Lincoln to the wall, and white men would not support his rank Abolitionism, he came back from the East and trumped up a system of charges against me, hoping that I would be compelled to occupy my entire time in defending myself, so that I would not be able to show up the enormity of the principles of the Abolitionists. Now, the only reason, and the true reason, why Mr. Lincoln has occupied the whole of his first hour in this issue between Trumbull and myself, is, to conceal from this vast audience the real questions which divide the two great parties.

I am not going to allow them to waste much of my time with these personal matters. I have lived in this State twenty-five years, most of that time have been in public life, and my record is open to you all. If that record is not enough to vindicate me from these petty, malicious assaults, I despise ever to be elected to office by slandering my opponents and traducing other men. Mr. Lincoln asks you to elect him to the United States Senate to-day solely because he and Trumbull can slander me. Has he given any other reason? Has he avowed what he was desirous to do in Congress on any one question? He desires to ride into office not upon his own merits, not upon the merits and soundness of his principles, but upon his success in fastening a stale old slander upon me.

I wish you to bear in mind that up to the time of the introduction of the Toombs bill, and after its introduction, there had never been an Act of Congress for the admission of a new State which contained a clause requiring its constitution to be submitted to the people. The general rule made the law silent on the subject, taking it for granted that the people would demand and compel a popular vote on the ratification of their constitution. Such was the general rule under Washington, Jefferson, Madison, Jackson, and Polk, under the Whig Presidents and the Democratic Presidents, from the beginning of the government down, and nobody dreamed that an effort would ever be made to abuse the power thus confided to the people of a Territory. For this reason our attention was not called to the fact of whether there was or was not a clause in the Toombs bill compelling submission, but it was taken for granted that the constitution would be submitted to the people whether the law compelled it or not.

Now, I will read from the report by me as chairman of the Committee on Territories at the time I reported back the Toombs substitute to the Senate. It contained several things which I had voted against in committee, but had been overruled by a majority of the members, and it was my duty as chairman of the Committee to report the bill back as it was agreed upon by them. The main point upon which I had been overruled was the question of population. In my report accompanying the Toombs bill, I said:

> In the opinion of your Committee, whenever a constitution shall be formed in any Territory, preparatory to its admission into the Union as a State, justice, the genius of our institutions, the whole theory of our republican system, imperatively demand that the voice of the people shall be fairly expressed, and their will embodied in that fundamental law, without fraud, or violence, or intimidation, or any other improper or unlawful influence, and subject to no other restrictions than those imposed by the Constitution of the United States.

There you find that we took it for granted that the constitution was to be submitted to the people, whether the bill was silent on the subject or not. Suppose I had reported it so, following the example of Washington, Adams, Jefferson, Madison, Monroe, Adams, Jackson, Van Buren, Harrison, Tyler, Polk, Taylor, Fillmore, and Pierce, would that fact have been evidence of a conspiracy to force a constitution upon the whole people of Kansas against their will? If the charge which Mr. Lincoln makes be true against me, it is true against Zachary Taylor, Millard Fillmore, and every Whig President, as well as every Democratic President, and against Henry Clay, who, in the Senate or House, for forty years advocated bills similar to the one I reported, no one of them containing a clause compelling the submission of the constitution to the people. Are Mr. Lincoln and Mr. Trumbull prepared to charge upon all those eminent men, from the beginning of the government down to the present day, that the absence of a provision compelling submission, in the various bills passed by them, authorizing the people of Territories to form State constitutions, is evidence of a corrupt design on their part to force a constitution upon an unwilling people?

I ask you to reflect on these things, for I tell you that there is a conspiracy to carry this election for the Black Republicans by slander, and not by fair means. Mr. Lincoln's speech this day is conclusive evidence of the fact. He has devoted his entire time to an issue between Mr. Trumbull and myself, and has not uttered a word about the politics of the day. Are you going to elect Mr. Trumbull's colleague upon an issue between Mr. Trumbull and me? I thought I was running against Abraham Lincoln, that he claimed to be my opponent, had challenged me to a discussion of the public questions of the day with him, and was discussing these questions with me; but it turns out that his only hope is to ride into office on Trumbull's back, who will carry him by falsehood.

Permit me to pursue this subject a little further. An examination of the record proves that Trumbull's charge—that the Toombs bill originally contained a clause requiring the constitution to be submitted to the people—*is false*. The printed copy of the bill which Mr. Lincoln held up before you, and which he pretends contains such a clause, merely contains a clause requiring a submission of the land grant, and *there is no clause in it requiring a submission of the constitution*. Mr. Lincoln cannot find such a clause in it. My report shows that we took it for granted that the people would require a submission of the constitution, and secure it for themselves. There never was a clause in the Toombs bill requiring the constitution to be submitted; Trumbull knew it at the time, and his speech made on the night of its passage discloses the fact that he knew it was silent on the subject. Lincoln pretends, and tells you, that Trumbull has not changed his evidence in support of his charge since he made his speech in Chicago. Let us see. The Chicago *Times* took up Trumbull's Chicago speech, compared it with the official records of Congress, and proved that speech to be false in its charge that the original Toombs bill required a submission of the constitution to the people. Trumbull then saw that he was caught, and his falsehood exposed, and he went to Alton, and, under the very walls of the penitentiary, made a new speech, in which he predicated his assault upon me in the allegation that I had caused to be voted into the Toombs bill a clause which prohibited the Convention from submitting the constitution to the people, and quoted what he pretended was the clause.

Now, has not Mr. Trumbull entirely changed the evidence on which he bases his charge? The clause which he quoted in his Alton speech (which he has published and circulated broadcast over the State) as having been put into the Toombs bill by me, is in the following words: "And until the complete execution of this Act, no other election shall be held in said Territory."

Trumbull says that the object of that amendment was to prevent the Convention from submitting the constitution to a vote of the people.

Now, I will show you that when Trumbull made that statement at Alton he knew it to be untrue. I read from Trumbull's speech in the Senate on the Toombs bill on the night of its passage. He then said:

> There is nothing said in this bill, so far as I have discovered, about submitting the constitution, which is to be formed, to the people for their sanction or rejection. Perhaps the Convention will have the right to submit it, if it should think proper, but it is certainly not compelled to do so, according to the provisions of the bill.

Thus you see that Trumbull, when the bill was on its passage in the Senate, said that it was silent on the subject of submission, and that there was nothing in the bill one way or the other on it. In his Alton speech he says there was a clause in the bill preventing its submission to the people, and that I had it voted in as an amendment. Thus I convict him of falsehood and slander by quoting from him, on the passage of the Toombs bill in the Senate of the United States, his own speech, made on the night of July 2, 1856, and reported in the *Congressional Globe* for the first session of the thirty-fourth Congress, vol. 33. What will you think of a man who makes a false charge, and falsifies the records to prove it? I will now show you that the clause which Trumbull says was put in the bill on my motion was never put in at all by me, but was stricken out on my motion, and another substituted in its place. I call your attention to the same volume of the *Congressional Globe* to which I have already referred, page 795, where you will find the following report of the proceedings of the Senate:

> Mr. Douglas: I have an amendment to offer from the Committee on Territories. On page 8, section 11, strike out the words "until the complete execution of this Act, no other election shall be held in said Territory," and insert the amendment which I hold in my hand.

You see from this that I moved to strike out the very words that Trumbull says I put in. The Committee on Territories overruled me in committee, and put the clause in; but as soon as I got the bill back into the Senate, I moved to strike it out, and put another clause in its place. On the same page you will find that my amendment was agreed to *unanimously*. I then offered another amendment, recognizing the right of the people of Kansas, under the Toombs bill, to order just such elections as they saw proper. You can find it on page 796 of the same volume. I will read it:

> MR. DOUGLAS: I have another amendment to offer from the Committee, to follow the amendment which has been adopted. The bill reads now: "And until the complete execution of this Act, no other election shall be held in said Territory." It has been suggested that it should be modified in this way, "And to avoid conflict in the complete execution of this Act, all other elections in said Territory are hereby postponed until such time as said Convention shall appoint," so that they can appoint the day in the event that there should be a failure to come into the Union.

The amendment was *unanimously* agreed to,—clearly and distinctly recognizing the right of the convention to order just as many elections as they saw proper in the execution of the act. Trumbull concealed in his Alton speech the fact that the clause he quoted had been stricken out in my motion, and the other fact that this other clause was put in the bill on my motion, and made the false charge that I incorporated into the bill a clause preventing submission, in the face of the fact, that, on my motion, the bill was so amended before it passed as to recognize in express words the right and duty of submission.

On this record that I have produced before you, I repeat my charge that Trumbull did falsify the public records of the country, in order to make his charge against me, and I tell Mr. Abraham Lincoln that if he will examine these records, he will then know that what I state is true. Mr. Lincoln has this day indorsed Mr. Trumbull's veracity after he had my word for it that that veracity was proved to be violated and forfeited by the public records. It will not do for Mr. Lincoln, in parading his calumnies against me, to put Mr. Trumbull between him and the odium and responsibility which justly attaches to such calumnies. I tell him that I am as ready to prosecute the indorser as the maker of a forged note. I regret the necessity of occupying my time with these petty personal matters. It is unbecoming the dignity of a canvass for an office of the character for which we are candidates. When I commenced the canvass at Chicago, I spoke of Mr. Lincoln in terms of kindness as an old friend; I said that he was a good citizen, of unblemished character, against whom I had nothing to say. I repeated these complimentary remarks about him in my successive speeches, until he became the indorser for these and other slanders against me. If there is anything personally disagreeable, uncourteous, or disreputable in these personalities, the sole responsibility rests on Mr. Lincoln, Mr. Trumbull, and their backers.

I will show you another charge made by Mr. Lincoln against me, as an offset to his declaration of willingness to take back anything that is incorrect, and to correct any false statement he may have made. He has several times charged that the Supreme Court, President Pierce, President Buchanan, and myself, at the time I introduced the Nebraska Bill in January, 1854, at Washington, entered into a conspiracy to establish slavery all over this country. I branded this charge as a falsehood, and then he repeated it, asked me to analyze its truth and answer it. I told him: "Mr. Lincoln, I know what you are after—you want to occupy my time in personal matters, to prevent me from showing up the revolutionary principles which the Abolition party—whose candidate you are—have proclaimed to the world." But he asked me to analyze his proof, and I did so. I called his attention to the fact that at the time the Nebraska Bill was introduced, there was no such case as the Dred Scott case pending in the Supreme Court, nor was it brought there for years afterwards, and hence that it was impossible there could have been any conspiracy between the judges of the Supreme Court and the other parties involved. I proved by the record that the charge was false, and what did he answer? Did he take it back like an honest man and say that he had been mistaken? No; he repeated the charge, and said that, although there was no such case pending that year, there was an understanding between the Democratic owners of Dred Scott and the judges of the Supreme Court and other parties involved, that the case should be brought up. I then demanded to know who these Democratic owners of Dred Scott were. He could not or would not tell; he did not know. In truth, there were no Democratic owners of Dred Scott on the face of the land. Dred Scott was owned at that time by the Rev. Dr. Chaffee, an Abolition member of Congress from Springfield, Massachusetts, and his wife; and Mr. Lincoln ought to have known that Dred Scott was so owned, for the reason that as soon as the decision was announced by the court Dr. Chaffee and his wife executed a deed emancipating him, and put that deed on record. It was a matter of public record, therefore, that at the time the case was taken to the Supreme Court Dred Scott was owned by an Abolition member of Congress, a friend of Lincoln's and a lead-ing man of his party, while the defence was conducted by Abolition lawyers,—

and thus the Abolitionists managed both sides of the case. I have exposed these facts to Mr. Lincoln, and yet he will not withdraw his charge of conspiracy. I now submit to you whether you can place any confidence in a man who continues to make a charge when its utter falsity is proven by the public records. I will state another fact to show how utterly reckless and unscrupulous this charge against the Supreme Court, President Pierce, President Buchanan, and myself is. Lincoln says that President Buchanan was in the conspiracy at Washington in the winter of 1854, when the Nebraska Bill was introduced. The history of this country shows that James Buchanan was at that time representing this country at the Court of St. James, Great Britain, with distinguished ability and usefulness, that he had not been in the United States for nearly a year previous, and that he did not return until about three years after. Yet Mr. Lincoln keeps repeating this charge of conspiracy against Mr. Buchanan when the public records prove it to be untrue. Having proved it to be false as far as the Supreme Court and President Buchanan are concerned, I drop it, leaving the public to say whether I, by myself, without their concurrence, could have gone into a conspiracy with them. My friends, you see that the object clearly is to conduct the canvass on personal matters, and hunt me down with charges that are proven to be false by the public records of the country. I am willing to throw open my whole public and private life to the inspection of any man or all men who desire to investigate it. Having resided among you twenty-five years, during nearly the whole of which time a public man, exposed to more assaults, perhaps more abuse, than any man living of my age, or who ever did live, and having survived it all and still commanded your confidence, I am willing to trust to your knowledge of me and my public conduct without making any more defence against these assaults.

Fellow-citizens, I came here for the purpose of discussing the leading political topics which now agitate the country. I have no charges to make against Mr. Lincoln, none against Mr. Trumbull, and none against any man who is a candidate, except in repelling their assaults upon me. If Mr. Lincoln is a man of bad character, I leave you to find it out; if his votes in the past are not satisfactory, I leave others to ascertain the fact; if his course on the Mexican war was not in accordance with your notions of patriotism and fidelity to our own country as against a public enemy, I leave you to ascertain the fact. I have no assaults to make upon him, except to trace his course on the questions that now divide the country and engross so much of the people's attention.

You know that prior to 1854 this country was divided into two great political parties, one the Whig, the other the Democratic. I, as a Democrat for twenty years prior to that time, had been in public discussions in this State as an advocate of Democratic principles, and I can appeal with confidence to every old-line Whig within the hearing of my voice to bear testimony that during all that period I fought you Whigs like a man on every question that separated the two parties. I had the highest respect for Henry Clay as a gallant party leader, as an eminent statesman, and as one of the bright ornaments of this country; but I conscientiously believed that the Democratic party was right on the questions which separated the Democrats from the Whigs. The man does not live who can say that I ever personally assailed Henry Clay or Daniel Webster, or any one of the leaders of that great party, whilst I combated with all my energy the measures they advocated. What did we differ about in those days? Did Whigs and Democrats differ about this slavery question? On the contrary, did we not, in 1850, unite to a man in favor of that system of Compromise measures which Mr. Clay introduced, Webster defended, Cass supported, and Fillmore approved and made the law of the land by his signature? While we agreed on those Compromise measures, we differed about a bank, the tariff, distribution, the specie circular, the sub-treasury, and other questions of that description. Now, let me ask you which one of those questions on which Whigs and Democrats then differed now remains to divide the two great parties? Every one of those questions which divided Whigs and Democrats has passed away, the country has outgrown them, they have passed into history. Hence it is immaterial whether you were right or I was right on the bank, the sub-treasury, and other questions, because they no longer continue living issues. What, then, has taken the place of those questions about which we once differed? The slavery question has now become the leading and controlling issue; that question on which you and I agreed, on which the Whigs and Democrats united, has now become the leading issue between the national Democracy on the one side and the Republican, or Abolition, party on the other.

Just recollect for a moment the memorable contest of 1850, when this country was agitated from its centre to its circumference by the slavery agitation. All eyes in this nation were then turned to the three great lights that survived the days of the Revolution. They looked to Clay, then in retirement at Ashland, and to Webster and Cass, in the United States Senate. Clay had retired to Ashland, having, as he supposed, performed his mission on earth, and was preparing himself for a better sphere of existence in another world. In that retirement he heard the discordant, harsh, and grating sounds of sectional strife and disunion, and he aroused and came forth and resumed his seat in the Senate, that great theatre of his great deeds. From the moment that Clay arrived among us he became the leader of all the Union men, whether Whigs or Democrats. For nine months we each assembled, each day, in the council-chamber, Clay in the chair, with Cass upon his right hand, and Webster upon his left, and the Democrats and Whigs gathered around, forgetting differences, and only animated by one common, patriotic sentiment, to devise means and measures by which we could defeat the mad and revolutionary scheme of the Northern Abolitionists and Southern Disunionists. We did devise those means, Clay brought them forward, Cass advocated them, the Union Democrats and Union Whigs voted for them, Fillmore signed them, and they gave peace and quiet to the country. Those Compromise measures of 1850 were founded upon the great fundamental principle that the people of each State and each Territory ought to be left free to form and regulate their own domestic institutions in their own way, subject only to the Federal Constitution. I will ask every old-line Democrat and every old-line Whig within the hearing of my voice if I have not truly stated the issues as they then presented themselves to the country. You recollect that the Abolitionists raised a howl of indignation, and cried for vengeance and the destruction of Democrats and Whigs both, who supported those Compromise measures of 1850. When I returned home to Chicago, I found the citizens inflamed and infuriated against the authors of those great measures. Being the only man in that city who was held responsible for affirmative votes on all those measures, I came forward and addressed the assembled inhabitants, defended each and every one of Clay's Compromise measures as they passed the Senate and the House and were approved by President Fillmore. Previous to that time, the city council had passed resolutions nullifying the Act of Congress, and instructing the police to withhold all assistance from its execution; but the people of Chicago listened to my defence, and, like candid, frank, conscientious men, when they became convinced that they had done an injustice to Clay, Webster, Cass, and all of us who had supported those measures, they repealed their nullifying resolutions, and declared that the laws should be executed and the supremacy of the Constitution maintained. Let it always be recorded in history to the immortal honor of the people of Chicago that they returned to their duty when they found that they were wrong, and did justice to those whom they had blamed and abused unjustly. When the Legislature of this State assembled that year, they proceeded to pass resolutions approving the Compromise measures of 1850. When the Whig party assembled in 1852 at Baltimore in National Convention for the last time, to nominate Scott for the presidency, they adopted as a part of their platform the Compromise measures of 1850, as the cardinal plank upon which every Whig would stand, and by which he would regulate his future conduct. When the Democratic party assembled at the same place one month after, to nominate General Pierce, we adopted the same platform so far as those Compromise measures were concerned, agreeing that we would stand by those glorious measures as a cardinal article in the Democratic faith. Thus you see that in 1852 all the old Whigs and all the old Democrats stood on a common plank so far as this slavery question was concerned, differing on other questions.

Now, let me ask, how is it that since that time so many of you Whigs have wandered from the true path marked out by Clay, and carried out broad and wide by the great Webster? How is it that so many old-line Democrats have abandoned the old faith of their party, and joined with Abolitionism and Free-soilism to over-turn the platform of the old Democrats, and the platform of the old Whigs? You cannot deny that since 1854 there has been a great revolution on this one question. How has it been brought about? I answer, that no sooner was the sod grown green over the grave of the immortal Clay, no sooner was the rose planted on the tomb of the godlike Webster, than many of the leaders of the Whig party, such as Seward of New York, and his followers, led off and attempted to Abolitionize the Whig party, and transfer all your old Whigs, bound hand and foot, into the Abolition camp. Seizing hold of the temporary excitement produced in this country by the introduction of the Nebraska Bill, the disappointed politicians in the Democratic party united with the disappointed politicians in the Whig party, and endeav-ored to form a new party, composed of all the Abolitionists, or Abolitionized Democrats and Abolitionized Whigs, banded together in an Abolition platform.

And who led that crusade against national principles in this State? I answer, Abraham Lincoln on behalf of the Whigs, and Lyman Trumbull on behalf of the Democrats, formed a scheme by which they would Abolitionize the two great par-ties in this State, on condition that Lincoln should be sent to the United States Senate in place of General Shields, and that Trumbull should go to Congress from the Belleville District until I would be accommodating enough either to die or resign for his benefit, and then he was to go to the Senate in my place. You all remember that during the year 1854 these two worthy gentlemen, Mr. Lincoln and Mr. Trumbull, one an old-line Whig and the other an old-line Democrat, were hunting in partnership to elect a Legislature against the Democratic party. I canvassed the State that year from the time I returned home until the election came off, and spoke in every county that I could reach during that period. In the northern part of the State I found Lincoln's ally in the person of Fred Douglass, the negro, preaching Abolition doctrines, while Lincoln was discussing the same principles down here, and Trumbull, a little farther down, was advocating the elec-tion of members to the Legislature who would act in concert with Lincoln's and Fred Douglass's friends. I witnessed an effort made at Chicago by Lincoln's then associates, and now supporters, to put Fred Douglass, the negro, on the stand, at a Democratic meeting, to reply to the illustrious General Cass when he was addressing the people there. They had the same negro hunting me down, and they now have a negro traversing the northern counties of the State and speaking in behalf of Lincoln. Lincoln knows that when we were at Freeport in joint discussion there was a distinguished colored friend of his there then who was on the stump for him, and who made a speech there the night before we spoke, and another the night after, a short distance from Freeport, in favor of Lincoln; and in order to show how much interest the colored brethren felt in the success of their brother Abe, I have with me here, and would read it if it would not occupy too much of my time, a speech made by Fred Douglass in Poughkeepsie, N.Y., a short time since, to a large convention in which he conjures all the friends of negro equality and negro citizenship to rally as one man around Abraham Lincoln, the perfect embodiment of their principles, and by all means to defeat Stephen A. Douglas. Thus you find that this Republican party in the northern part of the State had colored gentlemen for their advocates in 1854, in company with Lincoln and Trumbull, as they have now. When, in October, 1854, I went down to Springfield to attend the State Fair, I found the leaders of this party all assembled together under the title of an anti-Nebraska meeting. It was Black Republicans up north and anti-Nebraska at Springfield. I found Lovejoy, a high-priest of Abolitionism, and Lincoln, one of the leaders who was towing the old-line Whigs into the Abolition camp, and Trumbull, Sidney Breese, and Governor Reynolds, all making speeches against the Democratic party and myself, at the same place and in the same cause. The same men who are now fighting the Democratic party and the regular Democratic nominees in this State were fighting us then. They did not then acknowledge that they had become Abolitionists, and many of them deny it now. Breese, Dougherty, and Reynolds were then fighting the Democracy under the title of anti-Nebraska men, and now they are fighting the Democracy under the pretence that they are *Simon pure* Democrats, saying that they are authorized to have every office-holder in Illinois beheaded who prefers the election of Douglas to that of Lincoln or the success of the Democratic ticket in preference to the Abolition ticket for members of Congress, State officers, members of the Legislature, or any office in the State. They canvassed the State against us in 1854, as they are doing now, owning different names and different principles in different localities, but having a common object in view, viz.: the defeat of all men holding national principles in opposition to this sectional Abolition party. They carried the Legislature in 1854, and when it assembled in Springfield they proceeded to elect a United States Senator, all voting for Lincoln, with one or two exceptions, which exceptions prevented them from quite electing him. And why should they not elect him? Had not Trumbull agreed that Lincoln should have Shields's place? Had not the Abolitionists agreed to it? Was it not the solemn compact, the condition on which Lincoln agreed to Abolitionize the old Whigs, that he should be Senator? Still, Trumbull, having control of a few Abolitionized Democrats, would not allow them all to vote for Lincoln on any one ballot, and thus kept him for some time within one or two votes of an election, until he worried out Lincoln's friends, and compelled them to drop him and elect Trumbull, in violation of the bargain. I desire to read you a piece of testimony in confirmation of the notoriously public facts which I have stated to you. Colonel James H. Matheny, of Springfield, is, and for twenty years has been, the confidential personal and political friend and manager of Mr. Lincoln. Matheny is this very day the candidate of the Republican or Abolition party for Congress against the gallant Major Thos. L. Harris, in the Springfield District, and is making speeches for Lincoln and against me. I will read you the testimony of Matheny about this bargain between Lincoln and Trumbull when they undertook to Abolitionize Whigs and Democrats only four years ago. Matheny, being mad at Trumbull for having played a Yankee trick on Lincoln, exposed the bargain in a public speech two years ago, and I will read the published report of that speech, the correctness of which Mr. Lincoln will not deny:

> The Whigs, Abolitionists, Know-Nothings, and renegade Democrats made a solemn compact for the purpose of carrying this State against the Democracy, on this plan: 1st, that they would all combine and elect Mr. Trumbull to Congress, and thereby carry his district for the Legislature, in order to throw all the strength that could be obtained into that body against the Democrats; 2d, that when the Legislature should meet, the officers of that body, such as Speaker, clerks, door-keepers, etc. would be given to the Abolitionists; and, 3d, that the Whigs were to have the United States Senator. That accordingly, in good faith, Trumbull was elected to Congress, and his district carried for the Legislature; and when it convened, the Abolitionists got all the officers of that body, and thus far the "bond" was fairly executed. The Whigs, on their part, demanded the election of Abraham Lincoln to the United States Senate, that the bond might be fulfilled, the other parties to the contract having already secured to themselves all that was called for. But, in the most perfidious manner, they refused to elect Mr. Lincoln; and the mean, low-lived, sneaking Trumbull succeeded, by pleading all that was required by any party, in thrusting Lincoln aside,

and foisting himself, an excrescence from the rotten bowels of the Democracy, into the United States Senate; and thus it has ever been, that an *honest* man makes a bad bargain when he conspires or contracts with rogues.

Lincoln's confidential friend Matheny thought that Lincoln made a bad bargain when he conspired with such rogues as Trumbull and the Abolitionists. I would like to know whether Lincoln had as high opinion of Trumbull's veracity when the latter agreed to support him for the Senate and then cheated him as he does now, when Trumbull comes forward and makes charges against me. You could not then prove Trumbull an honest man either by Lincoln, by Matheny, or by any of Lincoln's friends. They charged everywhere that Trumbull had cheated them out of the bargain, and Lincoln found sure enough that it was a *bad bargain* to contract and conspire with rogues.

And now I will explain to you what has been a mystery all over the State and Union—the reason why Lincoln was nominated for the United States Senate by the Black Republican Convention. You know it has never been usual for any party or any convention to nominate a candidate for United States Senator. Probably this was the first time that such a thing was ever done. The Black Republican Convention had not been called for that purpose, but to nominate a State ticket, and every man was surprised and many disgusted when Lincoln was nominated. Archie Williams thought he was entitled to it, Browning knew that he deserved it, Wentworth was certain that he would get it. Peck had hopes, Judd felt sure that he was the man, and Palmer had claims and had made arrangements to secure it; but to their utter amazement, Lincoln was nominated by the Convention, and not only that, but he received the nomination unanimously, by a resolution declaring that Abraham Lincoln was "the first, last, and only choice" of the Republican party. How did this occur? Why, because they could not get Lincoln's friends to make another bargain with "rogues," unless the whole party would come up as one man and pledge their honor that they would stand by Lincoln first, last, and all the time, and that he should not be cheated by Lovejoy this time, as he was by Trumbull before. Thus, by passing this resolution, the Abolitionists are all for him. Lovejoy and Farnsworth are canvassing for him, Giddings is ready to come here in his behalf, and the negro speakers are already on the stump for him, and he is sure not to be cheated this time. He would not go into the arrangement until he got their bond for it, and Trumbull is compelled now to take the stump, get up false charges against me, and travel all over the State to try and elect Lincoln, in order to keep Lincoln's friends quiet about the bargain in which Trumbull cheated them four years ago. You see, now, why it is that Lincoln and Trumbull are so mighty fond of each other. They have entered into a conspiracy to break me down by these assaults upon my public character, in order to draw my attention from a fair exposure of the mode in which they attempted to Abolitionize the old Whig and the old Democratic parties and lead them captive into the Abolition camp. Do you not all remember that Lincoln went around here four years ago making speeches to you, and telling that you should all go for the Abolition ticket, and swearing that he was as good a Whig as he ever was? and that Trumbull went all over the State making pledges to the old Democrats, and trying to coax them into the Abolition camp, swearing by his Maker, with the uplifted hand, that he was still a Democrat, always intended to be, and that never would he desert the Democratic party? He got your votes to elect an Abolition Legislature, which passed Abolition resolutions, attempted to pass Abolition laws, and sustained Abolitionists for office, State and National. Now the same game is attempted to be played over again. Then Lincoln and Trumbull made captives of the old Whigs and old Democrats and carried them into the Abolition camp, where Father Giddings, the high-priest of Abolitionism, received and christened them in the dark cause just as fast as they were brought in. Giddings found the converts so numerous that he had to have assistance, and he sent for John P. Hale, N. P. Banks, Chase, and other Abolitionists, and they came on, and with Lovejoy and Fred Douglass, the negro, helped to baptize these new converts as Lincoln, Trumbull, Breese, Reynolds, and Dougherty could capture them and bring them within the Abolition clutch. Gentlemen, they are now around, making the same kind of speeches. Trumbull was down in Monroe County the other day, assailing me, and making a speech in favor of Lincoln; and I will show you under what notice his meeting was called. You see these people are Black Republicans or Abolitionists up north, while at Springfield to-day they dare not call their Convention "Republican," but are obliged to say "a Convention of all men opposed to the Democratic party"; and in Monroe County and lower Egypt Trumbull advertises their meetings as follows:

A meeting of the Free Democracy will take place at Waterloo on Monday, September 21st inst., whereat Hon. Lyman Trumbull, Hon. John Baker, and others will address the people upon the different political topics of the day. Members of all parties are cordially invited to be present, and hear and determine for themselves.

THE FREE DEMOCRACY
*September 9, 1858*

Did you ever before hear of this new party, called the "Free Democracy"?

What object have these Black Republicans in changing their name in every county? They have one name in the north, another in the centre, and another in the south. When I used to practise law before my distinguished judicial friend whom I recognize in the crowd before me, if a man was charged with horse-stealing, and the proof showed that he went by one name in Stephenson County, another in Sangamon, a third in Monroe, and a fourth in Randolph, we thought that the fact of his changing his name so often to avoid detection was pretty strong evidence of his guilt. I would like to know why it is that this great Free-soil Abolition party is not willing to avow the same name in all parts of the State? If this party believes that its course is just, why does it not avow the same principles in the North and in the South, in the East and in the West, wherever the American flag waves over American soil?

A VOICE: "The party does not call itself Black Republican in the North."

MR. DOUGLAS: Sir, if you will get a copy of the paper published at Waukegan, fifty miles from Chicago, which advocates the election of Mr. Lincoln, and has his name flying at its mast-head, you will find that it declares that "this paper is devoted to the cause" of *Black Republicanism*. I had a copy of it, and intended to bring it down here into Egypt to let you see what name the party rallied under up in the northern part of the State, and to convince you that their principles are as different in the two sections of the State as is their name. I am sorry that I have mislaid it and have not got it here. Their principles in the north are jet-black, in the centre they are in color a decent mulatto, and in lower Egypt they are almost white. Why, I admired many of the white sentiments contained in Lincoln's speech at Jonesboro, and could not help but contrast them with the speeches of the same distinguished orator made in the northern part of the State. Down here he denies that the Black Republican party is opposed to the admission of any more slave States, under any circumstances, and says that they are willing to allow the people of each State, when it wants to come into the Union, to do just as it pleases on the question of slavery. In the north, you find Lovejoy, their candidate for Congress in the Bloomington District, Farnsworth, their candidate in the Chicago District, and Washburne, their candidate in the Galena District, all declaring that never will they consent, under any circumstances, to admit another slave State, even if the people want it. Thus, while they avow one set of principles up there, they avow another and entirely different set down here. And here let me recall to Mr. Lincoln the Scriptural quotation which he has applied to the Federal Government, that a house divided against itself cannot stand, and ask him how does he expect this Abolition party to stand when in one half of the State it advocates a set of principles which it has repudiated in the other half.

I am told that I have but eight minutes more. I would like to talk to you an hour and a half longer, but I will make the best use I can of the remaining eight minutes. Mr. Lincoln said in his first remarks that he was not in favor of the social and political equality of the negro with the white man. Everywhere up north he has declared that he was not in favor of the social and political equality of the negro, but he would not say whether or not he was opposed to negroes voting and negro citizenship. I want to know whether he is for or against negro citizenship. He declared his utter opposition to the Dred Scott decision, and advanced as a reason that the court had decided that it was not possible for a negro to be a citizen under the Constitution of the United States. If he is opposed to the Dred Scott decision for that reason, he must be in favor of conferring the right and privilege of citizenship upon the negro. I have been trying to get an answer from him on that point, but have never yet obtained one, and I will show you why. In every speech he made in the north he quoted the Declaration of Independence to prove that all men were created equal, and insisted that the phrase "all men" included the negro as well as the white man, and that the equality rested upon divine law. Here is what he said on that point:

> I should like to know if, taking this old Declaration of Independence, which declares that all men are equal upon principle, and making exceptions to it, where will it stop? If one man says it does not mean a negro, why may not another say it does not mean some other man? If that Declaration is not the truth, let us get the statute book in which we find it and tear it out.

Lincoln maintains there that the Declaration of Independence asserts that the negro is equal to the white man, and that under divine law; and if he believes so it was rational for him to advocate negro citizenship, which when allowed puts the negro on an equality under the law. I say to you in all frankness, gentlemen, that in my opinion a negro is not a citizen, cannot be, and ought not to be under the Constitution of the United States. I will not even qualify my opinion to meet the declaration of one of the judges of the Supreme Court in the Dred Scott case, that "a negro descended from African parents, who was imported into this country as a slave, is not a citizen, and cannot be." I say that this government was established on the white basis. It was made by white men for the benefit of white men and their posterity forever, and never should be administered by any except white men. I declare that a negro ought not to be a citizen, whether his parents were imported into this country as slaves or not, or whether or not he was born here. It does not depend upon the place a negro's parents were born, or whether they were slaves or not, but upon the fact that he is a negro, belonging to a race incapable of self-government, and for that reason ought not to be on an equality with white men.

My friends, I am sorry that I have not time to pursue this argument further, as I might have done but for the fact that Mr. Lincoln compelled me to occupy a portion of my time in repelling those gross slanders and falsehoods that Trumbull has invented against me and put in circulation. In conclusion, let me ask you why should this government be divided by a geographical line—arraying all men North in one great hostile party against all men South? Mr. Lincoln tells you in his speech at Springfield that a house divided against itself cannot stand; that this government divided into free and slave States cannot endure permanently; that they must either be all free or all slave; all one thing or all the other. Why cannot this government endure divided into free and slave States, as our fathers made it? When this government was established by Washington, Jefferson, Madison, Jay, Hamilton, Franklin, and the other sages and patriots of that day, it was composed of free States and slave States, bound together by one common Constitution. We have existed and prospered from that day to this thus divided, and have increased with a rapidity never before equalled, in wealth, the extension of territory, and all the elements of power and greatness, until we have become the first nation on the face of the globe. Why can we not thus continue to prosper? We can if we will live up to and execute the government upon those principles upon which our fathers established it. During the whole period of our existence Divine Providence has smiled upon us, and showered upon our nation richer and more abundant blessings than have ever been conferred upon any other.

## MR. LINCOLN'S REJOINDER

FELLOW-CITIZENS: It follows as a matter of course that a half-hour answer to a speech of an hour and a half can be but a very hurried one. I shall only be able to touch upon a few of the points suggested by Judge Douglas, and give them a brief attention, while I shall have to totally omit others for the want of time.

Judge Douglas has said to you that he has not been able to get from me an answer to the question whether I am in favor of negro citizenship. So far as I know the Judge never asked me the question before. He shall have no occasion to ever ask it again, for I tell him very frankly that I am not in favor of negro citizenship. This furnishes me an occasion for saying a few words upon the subject. I mentioned in a certain speech of mine, which has been printed, that the Supreme Court had decided that a negro could not possibly be made a citizen; and without saying what was my ground of complaint in regard to that, or whether I had any ground of complaint, Judge Douglas has from that thing manufactured nearly everything that he ever says about my disposition to produce an equality between the negroes and the white people. If any one will read my speech, he will find I mentioned that as one of the points decided in the course of the Supreme Court opinions, but I did not state what objection I had to it. But Judge Douglas tells the people what my objection was when I did not tell them myself. Now, my opinion is that the different States have the power to make a negro a citizen under the Constitution of the United States if they choose. The Dred Scott decision decides that they have not that power. If the State of Illinois had that power, I should be opposed to the exercise of it. That is all I have to say about it.

Judge Douglas has told me that he heard my speeches north and my speeches south; that he had heard me at Ottawa and at Freeport in the north and recently at Jonesboro in the south, and there was a very different cast of sentiment in the speeches made at the different points. I will not charge upon Judge Douglas that he wilfully misrepresents me, but I call upon every fair-minded man to take these speeches and read them, *and I dare him to point out any difference between my speeches north and south.* While I am here perhaps I ought to say a word, if I have the time, in regard to the latter portion of the Judge's speech, which was a sort of declamation in reference to my having said I entertained the belief that this government would not endure half slave and half free. I have said so, and I did not say it without what seemed to me to be good reasons. It perhaps would require more time than I have now to set forth these reasons in detail; but let me ask you a few questions. Have we ever had any peace on this slavery question? When are we to have peace upon it, if it is kept in the position it now occupies? How are we ever to have peace upon it? That is an important question. To be sure, if we will all stop, and allow Judge Douglas and his friends to march on in their present career until they plant the institution all over the nation, here and wherever else our flag waves, and we acquiesce in it, there will be peace. But let me ask Judge Douglas how he is going to get the people to do that? They have been wrangling over this question for at least forty years. This was the cause of the agitation resulting in the Missouri Compromise; this produced the troubles at the annexation of Texas, in the acquisition of the territory acquired in the Mexican War. Again, this was the trouble which was quieted by the Compromise of 1850, when it was settled *"forever"* as both the great political parties declared in their National Conventions. That "forever" turned out to be just four years, *when Judge Douglas himself reopened it.* When is it likely to come to an end? He introduced the Nebraska Bill in 1854 to put *another end* to the slavery agitation. He promised that it would finish it all up immediately, and he has never made a speech since, until he got into a quarrel with the President about the Lecompton Constitution, in which he has not declared that we are *just at the end* of the slavery agitation. But in one speech, I think last winter, he did say that he didn't quite see when the end of the slavery agitation would come. Now he tells us again that it is all over and the people of Kansas have voted down the Lecompton Constitution. How is it over? That was only one of the attempts at putting an end to the slavery agitation—one of these "final settle-ments." Is Kansas in the Union? Has she formed a constitution that she is likely to come in under? Is not the slavery agitation still an open question in that Territory? Has the voting down of that constitution put an end to all the trouble? Is that more likely to settle it than every one of these previous attempts to settle the slavery agita-tion? Now, at this day in the history of the world we can no more foretell where the end of this slavery agitation will be than we can see the end of the world itself. The Nebraska-Kansas Bill was introduced four years and a half ago, and if the agitation is ever to come to an end we may say we are four years and a half nearer the end. So, too, we can say we are four years and a half nearer the end of the world, and we can just as clearly see the end of the world as we can see the end of this agitation. The Kansas settlement did not conclude it. If Kansas should sink to-day, and leave a great vacant space in the earth's surface, this vexed question would still be among us. I say, then, there is no way of putting an end to the slavery agitation amongst us but to put it back upon the basis where our fathers placed it; no way but to keep it out of our new Territories,—to restrict it forever to the old States where it now exists. Then the public mind *will* rest in the belief that it is in the course of ultimate extinction. That is one way of putting an end to the slavery agitation.

The other way is for us to surrender and let Judge Douglas and his friends have their way and plant slavery over all the States; cease speaking of it as in any way a wrong; regard slavery as one of the common matters of property, and speak of negroes as we do of our horses and cattle. But while it drives on in its state of progress as it is now driving, and as it has driven for the last five years, I have ventured the opinion, and I say to-day, that we will have no end to the slavery agitation until it takes one turn or the other. I do not mean that when it takes a turn toward ultimate extinction it will be in a day, nor in a year, nor in two years. I do not suppose that in the most peaceful way ultimate extinction would occur in less than a hundred years at least; but that it will occur in the best way for both races, in God's own good time, I have no doubt. But, my friends, I have used up more of my time than I intended on this point.

Now, in regard to this matter about Trumbull and myself having made a bargain to sell out the entire Whig and Democratic parties in 1854: Judge Douglas brings forward no evidence to sustain his charge, except the speech Matheny is said to have made in 1856, in which he told a cock-and-bull story of that sort, upon the same moral principles that Judge Douglas tells it here to-day. This is the simple truth. I do not care greatly for the story, but this is the truth of it: and I have twice told Judge Douglas to his face that from beginning to end there is not one word of truth in it. I have called upon him for the proof, and he does not at all meet me as Trumbull met him upon that of which we were just talking, by producing the record. He didn't bring the record because there was no record for him to bring. When he asks if I am ready to indorse Trumbull's veracity after he has broken a bargain with me, I reply that if Trumbull *had* broken a bargain with me I would not be likely to indorse his veracity; but I am ready to indorse his veracity; because *neither in that thing, nor in any other, in all the years that I have known Lyman Trumbull, have I known him to fail of his word or tell a falsehood large or small.* It is for that reason that I indorse Lyman Trumbull.

Mr. James Brown (*Douglas postmaster*): What does Ford's History say about him?

Mr. Lincoln: Some gentleman asks me what Ford's History says about him. My own recollection is that Ford speaks of Trumbull in very disrespectful terms in several portions of his book, *and that he talks a great deal worse of Judge Douglas.* I refer you, sir, to the History for examination.

Judge Douglas complains at considerable length about a disposition on the part of Trumbull and myself to attack him personally. I want to attend to that suggestion a moment. I don't want to be unjustly accused of dealing illiberally or unfairly with an adversary, either in court or in a political canvass or anywhere else. I would despise myself if I supposed myself ready to deal less liberally with an adversary than I was willing to be treated myself. Judge Douglas in a general way, without putting it in a direct shape, revives the old charge against me in reference to the Mexican War. He does not take the responsibility of putting it in a very definite form, but makes a general reference to it. That charge is more than ten years old. He complains of Trumbull and myself because he says we bring charges against him one or two years old. He knows, too, that in regard to the Mexican War story the more respectable papers of his own party throughout the State have been compelled to take it back and acknowledge that it was a lie.

[Here Mr. Lincoln turned to the crowd on the platform, and, selecting Hon. Orlando B. Ficklin, led him forward and said:]

I do not mean to do anything with Mr. Ficklin except to present his face and tell you that *he personally knows it to be a lie!* He was a member of Congress at the only time I was in Congress, and [Ficklin] knows that whenever there was an attempt to procure a vote of mine which would indorse the origin and justice of the war, I refused to give such indorsement and voted against it; but I never voted against the supplies for the army, and he knows, as well as Judge Douglas, that whenever a dollar was asked by way of compensation or otherwise for the benefit of the soldiers *I gave all the votes that Ficklin or Douglas did, and perhaps more.*

MR. FICKLIN: My friends, I wish to say this in reference to the matter: Mr. Lincoln and myself are just as good personal friends as Judge Douglas and myself. In reference to this Mexican War, my recollection is that when Ashmun's resolution [amendment] was offered by Mr. Ashmun of Massachusetts, in which he declared that the Mexican War was unnecessary and unconstitutionally commenced by the President—my recollection is that Mr. Lincoln voted for that resolution.

MR. LINCOLN: That is the truth. Now, you all remember that was a resolution censuring the President for the manner in which the war was *begun.* You know they have charged that I voted against the supplies, by which I starved the soldiers who were out fighting the battles of their country. I say that Ficklin knows it is false. When that charge was brought forward by the Chicago *Times,* the Springfield *Register* [Douglas's organ] reminded the *Times* that the charge really applied to John Henry; and I do know that John Henry *is now making speeches and fiercely battling for Judge Douglas.* If the Judge now says that he offers this as a sort of setoff to what I said to-day in reference to Trumbull's charge, then I remind him that he made this charge before I said a word about Trumbull's. He brought this forward at Ottawa, the first time we met face to face; and in the opening speech that Judge Douglas made he attacked me in regard to a matter ten years old. Isn't he a pretty man to be whining about people making charges against him only *two* years old!

The Judge thinks it is altogether wrong that I should have dwelt upon this charge of Trumbull's at all. I gave the apology for doing so in my opening speech. Perhaps it didn't fix your attention. I said that when Judge Douglas was speaking at places where I spoke on the succeeding day he used very harsh language about this charge. Two or three times afterward I said I had confidence in Judge Trumbull's veracity and intelligence; and my own opinion was, from what I knew of the character of Judge Trumbull, that he would vindicate his position and prove whatever he had stated to be true. This I repeated two or three times; and then I dropped it, without saying anything more on the subject for weeks—perhaps a month. I passed it by without noticing it at all till I found, at Jacksonville, Judge Douglas in the plenitude of his power is not willing to answer Trumbull and let me alone, but he comes out there and uses this language: "He should not hereafter occupy his time in refuting such charges made by Trumbull but that, Lincoln having indorsed the character of Trumbull for veracity, he should hold him [Lincoln] responsible for the slanders." What was Lincoln to do? Did he not do right, when he had the fit opportunity of meeting Judge Douglas here, to tell him he was ready for the responsibility? I ask a candid audience whether in doing thus Judge Douglas was not the assailant rather than I? Here I meet him face to face, and say I am ready to take the responsibility, so far as it rests on me.

Having done so I ask the attention of this audience to the question whether I have succeeded in sustaining the charge, and whether Judge Douglas has at all succeeded in rebutting it? You all heard me call upon him to say *which of these pieces of evidence was a forgery.* Does he say that what I present here as a copy of the original Toombs bill is a forgery? Does he say that what I present as a copy of the bill reported by himself is a forgery, or what is presented as a transcript from the *Globe* of the quotations from Bigler's speech is a forgery? Does he say the quotations from his own speech are forgeries? Does he say this transcript from Trumbull's speech is a forgery? ["He didn't deny one of them."] *I would then like to know how it comes about that when each piece of a story is true the whole story turns out false.* I take it these people have some sense; they see plainly that Judge Douglas is playing cuttle-fish—a small species of fish that has no mode of defending itself when pursued except by throwing out a black fluid, which makes the water so dark the enemy cannot see it, and thus it escapes. Ain't the Judge playing the cuttle-fish?

Now, I would ask very special attention to the consideration of Judge Douglas's speech at Jacksonville; and when you shall read his speech of to-day, I ask you to watch closely and see which of these pieces of testimony, every one of which he says is a forgery, he has shown to be such. *Not one of them has he shown to be a forgery.* Then I ask the original question, if each of the pieces of testimony is true, *how is it possible that the whole is a falsehood?*

In regard to Trumbull's charge that he [Douglas] inserted a provision into the bill to prevent the constitution being submitted to the people, what was his answer? He comes here and reads from the *Congressional Globe* to show that on his motion that provision was struck out of the bill. Why, Trumbull has not said it was not stricken out, but Trumbull says he [Douglas] put it in; and it is no answer to the charge to say he afterwards took it out. Both are perhaps true. It was in regard to that thing precisely that I told him he had dropped the cub. Trumbull shows you that by his introducing the bill it was his cub. It is no answer to that assertion to call Trumbull a liar merely because he did not specially say that Douglas struck it out. Suppose that were the case, does it answer Trumbull? I assert that you [pointing to an individual] are here to-day, and you undertake to prove me a liar by showing that you were in Mattoon yesterday. I say that you took your hat off your head, and you prove me a liar by putting it on your head. That is the whole force of Douglas's argument.

Now, I want to come back to my original question. Trumbull says that Judge Douglas had a bill with a provision in it for submitting a constitution to be made to a vote of the people of Kansas. Does Judge Douglas deny that fact? Does he deny that the provision which Trumbull reads was put in that bill? Then Trumbull says he struck it out. Does he dare to deny that? He does not, and I have the right to repeat the question,—*Why Judge Douglas took it out?* Bigler has said there was a combination of certain senators, among whom he did not include Judge Douglas, by which it was agreed that the Kansas Bill should have a clause in it not to have the constitution formed under it submitted to a vote of the people. He did not say that Douglas was among them, but we prove by another source that about the same time Douglas comes into the Senate *with that provision stricken out of the bill.* Although Bigler cannot say they were all working in concert, yet it looks very much as if the thing was agreed upon and done with a mutual understanding after the conference; and while we do not know that it was absolutely so, yet it looks so probable that we have a right to call upon the man who knows the true reason why it was done *to tell what the true reason was.* When he will not tell what the true reason was, he stands in the attitude of an accused thief who has stolen goods in his possession, and when called to account refuses to tell where he got them. Not only is this the evidence, but when he comes in with the bill having the provision stricken out, he tells us in a speech, not then but since, that these alterations and modifications in the bill *had been made by* HIM, *in consultation with Toombs, the originator of the bill.* He tells us the same to-day. He says there were certain modifications made in the bill in committee that he did not vote for. I ask you to remember, while certain amendments were made which he disapproved of, but which a majority of the committee voted in, he has himself told us that in this particular *the alterations and modifications were made by him, upon consultation with Toombs.* We have his own word that these alterations were made *by him,* and not by the committee. Now, I ask, what is the reason Judge Douglas is so chary about coming to the exact question? What is the reason he will not tell you anything about HOW it was made, BY WHOM it was made, or that he remembers it being made at all? Why does he stand playing upon the meaning of words and quibbling around the edges of the evidence? If he can explain all this, but leaves it unexplained, I have the right to infer that

Judge Douglas understood it was the purpose of his party, in engineering that bill through, to make a constitution, and have Kansas come into the Union with that constitution, *without its being submitted to a vote of the people*. If he will explain his action on this question, by giving a *better reason* for the facts that happened than he has done, it will be satisfactory. But until he does that—until he gives a better or more plausible reason than he has offered against the evidence in the case—*I suggest to him it will not avail him at all that he swells himself up, takes on dignity, and calls people liars*. Why, sir, there is not a word in Trumbull's speech that depends on Trumbull's veracity at all. He has only arrayed the evidence and told you what follows as a matter of reasoning. There is not a statement in the whole speech that depends on Trumbull's word. If you have ever studied geometry, you remember that by a course of reasoning Euclid proves that all the angles in a triangle are equal to two right angles. Euclid has shown you how to work it out. Now, if you undertake to disprove that proposition, and to show that it is erroneous, would you prove it to be false by calling Euclid a liar? They tell me that my time is out, and therefore I close.

### EXTRACT FROM MR. TRUMBULL'S SPEECH MADE AT ALTON, REFERRED TO BY MR. LINCOLN IN HIS OPENING AT CHARLESTON

I come now to another extract from a speech of Mr. Douglas, made at Beardstown, and reported in the *Missouri Republican*. This extract has reference to a statement made by me at Chicago, wherein I charged that an agreement had been entered into by the very persons now claiming credit for opposing a constitution not submitted to the people, to have a constitution formed and put in force without giving the people of Kansas an opportunity to pass upon it. Without meeting this charge, which I substantiated by a reference to the record, my colleague is reported to have said:

> For when this charge was made once in a much milder form, in the Senate of the United States, I did brand it as I he m the presence of Mr. Trumbull, and Mr. Trumbull sat and heard it thus branded, without daring to say it was true. I tell you he knew it to be false when he uttered it at Chicago; and yet he says he is going to cram the lie down his throat until he should cry Enough. The miserable, craven-hearted wretch! He would rather have both ears cut off than to use that language in my presence, where I could call him to account. I see the object is to draw me into a personal controversy, with the hope thereby of concealing

> from the public the enormity of the principles to which they are committed. I shall not allow much of my time in this canvass to be occupied by these personal assaults: I have none to make on Mr. Lincoln; I have none to make on Mr. Trumbull; I have none to make on any other political opponent. If I cannot stand on my own public record, on my own private and public character as history will record it, I will not attempt to rise by traducing the character of other men. I will not make a blackguard of myself by imitating the course they have pursued against me. I have no charges to make against them.

This is a singular statement, taken altogether. After indulging in language which would disgrace a loafer in the filthiest purlieus of a fish market, he winds up by saying that he will not make a blackguard of himself, that he has no charges to make against me. So I suppose he considers that to say of another that he knew a thing to be false when he uttered it, that he was a "miserable, craven-hearted wretch," does not amount to a personal assault, and does not make a man a blackguard. A discriminating public will judge of that for themselves; but as he says he has "no charges to make on Mr. Trumbull," I suppose politeness requires I should believe him. At the risk of again offending this mighty man of war, and losing something more than my ears, I shall have the audacity to again read the record upon him, and prove and pin upon him, so that he cannot escape it, the truth of every word I uttered at Chicago. You, fellow-citizens, are the judges to determine whether I do this. My colleague says he is willing to stand on his public record. By that shall he be tried; and if he had been able to discriminate between the exposure of a public act by the record, and a personal attack upon the individual, he would have discovered that there was nothing personal in my Chicago remarks, unless the condemnation of himself by his own public record is personal; and then you must judge who is most to blame for the torture his public record inflicts upon him—he for making, or I for reading it after it was made. As an individual, I care very little about Judge Douglas one way or the other. It is his public acts with which I have to do, and if they condemn, disgrace, and consign him to oblivion, he has only himself, not me, to blame.

Now, the charge is that there was a plot entered into to have a constitution formed for Kansas, and put in force, without giving the people an opportunity to pass upon it, and that Mr. Douglas was in the plot. That is as susceptible of proof by the record as is the fact that the State of Minnesota was admitted into the Union at the last session of Congress.

On the 25th of June, 1856, a bill was pending in the United States Senate to authorize the people of Kansas to form a constitution and come into the Union. On that day Mr. Toombs offered an amendment which he intended to propose to the bill, which was ordered to be printed, and, with the original bill and other amendments, recommended to the Committee on Territories, of which Mr. Douglas was chairman. This amendment of Mr. Toombs, printed by order of the Senate, and a copy of which I have here present, provided for the appointment of commissioners who were to take a census of Kansas, divide the Territory into election districts, and superintend the election of delegates to form a constitution, and contains a clause in the 18th section which I will read to you, requiring the constitution which should be formed to be submitted to the people for adoption. It reads as follows:

> That the following propositions be and the same are hereby offered to the said Convention of the people of Kansas, when formed, for their free acceptance or rejection, which, if accepted by the Convention, and ratified by the people at the election for the adoption of the constitution, shall be obligatory on the United States, and upon the said State of Kansas, etc.

It has been contended by some of the newspaper press that this section did not require the constitution which should be formed to be submitted to the people for approval, and that it was only the land propositions which were to be submitted. You will observe the language is that the propositions are to be "ratified by the people at the election for the adoption of the constitution." Would it have been possible to ratify the land propositions "at the election for the adoption of the constitution," unless such an election was to be held?

When one thing is required by a contract or law to be done, the doing of which is made dependent upon and cannot be performed without the doing of some other thing, is not that other thing just as much required by the contract or law as the first? It matters not in what part of the act, nor in what phraseology, the intention of the Legislature is expressed, so you can clearly ascertain what it is; and whenever that intention is ascertained from an examination of the language used, such intention is part of and a requirement of the law. Can any candid, fair-minded man read the section I have quoted, and say that the intention to have the constitution which should be formed submitted to the people for their adoption, is not clearly expressed? In my judgment, there can be no controversy among honest men upon a proposition so plain as this. Mr. Douglas has never pretended to deny, so far as I am aware, that the Toombs amendment, as originally introduced, did require a submission of the constitution to the people. This amendment of Mr. Toombs's was referred to the committee of which Mr. Douglas was chairman, and reported back by him on the 30th of June, with the words "and ratified by the people at the election for the adoption of the constitution" stricken out. I have here a copy of the bill as reported back by Mr. Douglas, to substantiate the statement I make. Various other alterations were also made in the bill, to which I shall presently have occasion to call attention. There was no other clause in the original Toombs bill requiring a submission of the constitution to the people than the one I have read, and there was no clause whatever, after that was struck out, in the bill, as reported back by Judge Douglas, requiring a submission. I will now introduce a witness whose testimony cannot be impeached, he acknowledging himself to have been one of the conspirators and privy to the fact about which he testifies.

Senator Bigler, alluding to the Toombs bill, as it was called, and which, after sundry amendments, passed the Senate, and to the propriety of submitting the constitution which should be formed to a vote of the people, made the following statement in his place in the Senate, December 9th, 1857. I read from part 1, *Congressional Globe* of last session, paragraph 21:

> I was present when that subject was discussed by senators, before the bill was introduced, and the question was raised and discussed whether the constitution, when formed, should be submitted to a vote of the people. It was held by the most intelligent on the subject that in view of all the difficulties surrounding that Territory, the danger of any experiment at that time of a popular vote, it would be better that there should be no such provision in the Toombs bill; and it was my understanding, in all the intercourse I had, that that convention would make a constitution and send it here, without submitting it to the popular vote.

In speaking of this meeting again on the 21st December, 1857 (*Congressional Globe,* same volume, page 113), Senator Bigler said:

> Nothing was farther from my mind than to allude to any social or confidential interview. The meeting was not of that character. Indeed, it was semi-official, and called to promote the

public good. My recollection was clear that I left the conference under the impression that it had been deemed best to adopt
measures to admit Kansas as a State through the agency of one
popular election, and that for delegates to the Convention. This
impression was the stronger, because I thought the spirit of the
bill infringed upon the doctrine of non-intervention, to which
I had great aversion; but with the hope of accomplishing great
good, and as no movement had been made in that direction in
the Territory, I waived this objection, and concluded to support
the measure. I have a few items of testimony, as to the correctness of these impressions, and with their submission I shall be
content. I have before me the bill reported by the Senator from
Illinois, on the 7th of March, 1856, providing for the admission
of Kansas as a State, the third section of which reads as follows:

"That the following propositions be, and the same are
hereby offered to the said Convention of the people of Kansas,
when formed, for their free acceptance or rejection; which, if
accepted by the Convention and ratified by the people at the
election for the adoption of the constitution, shall be obligatory
upon the United States and upon the said State of Kansas."

The bill read in place by the Senator from Georgia, on the
25th of June, and referred to the Committee on Territories,
contained the same section, word for word. Both these bills
were under consideration at the conference referred to; but, sir,
when the Senator from Illinois reported the Toombs bill to the
Senate, with amendments, the next morning, it did not contain that portion of the third section which indicated to the
Convention that the constitution should be approved by the
people. The words "and ratified by the people at the election for
the adoption of the constitution" had been stricken out.

I am not now seeking to prove that Douglas was in the plot to force a constitution upon Kansas without allowing the people to vote directly upon it. I shall
attend to that branch of the subject by and by. My object now is to prove the
existence of the plot, what the design was, and I ask if I have not already done so.
Here are the facts:

The introduction of a bill on the 7th of March, 1856, providing for the calling of a convention in Kansas to form a State constitution, and providing that the

constitution should be submitted to the people for adoption; an amendment to this bill, proposed by Mr. Toombs, containing the same requirement; a reference of these various bills to the Committee on Territories; a consultation of senators to determine whether it was advisable to have the constitution submitted for ratification; the determination that it was not advisable; and a report of the bill back to the Senate next morning, with the clause providing for the submission stricken out. Could evidence be more complete to establish the first part of the charge I have made of a plot having been entered into by somebody, to have a constitution adopted without submitting it to the people?

Now for the other part of the charge, that Judge Douglas was in this plot, whether knowingly or ignorantly is not material to my purpose. The charge is that he was an instrument co-operating in the project to have a constitution formed and put into operation, without affording the people an opportunity to pass upon it. The first evidence to sustain the charge is the fact that he reported back the Toombs amendment with the clause providing for the submission stricken out,—this in connection with his speech in the Senate on the 9th of December, 1857 (*Congressional Globe*, part 1, page 14), wherein he stated:

> That during the last Congress I [Mr. Douglas] reported a
> bill from the Committee on Territories, to authorize the people
> of Kansas to assemble and form a constitution for themselves.
> Subsequently the Senator from Georgia (Mr. Toombs) brought
> forward a substitute for my bill, which, after having been modi-
> fied by him and myself in consultation, was passed by the Senate.

This of itself ought to be sufficient to show that my colleague was an instrument in the plot to have a constitution put in force without submitting it to the people, and to forever close his mouth from attempting to deny. No man can reconcile his acts and former declarations with his present denial, and the only charitable conclusion would be that he was being used by others without knowing it. Whether he is entitled to the benefit of even this excuse, you must judge on a candid hearing of the facts I shall present. When the charge was first made in the United States Senate, by Mr. Bigler, that my colleague had voted for an Enabling Act which put a government in operation without submitting the constitution to the people, my colleague (*Congressional Globe,* last session, part 1, page 24) stated:

> I will ask the Senator to show me an intimation from any
> one member of the Senate, in the whole debate on the Toombs

bill, and in the Union from any quarter, that the constitution was not be to submitted to the people. I will venture to say that on all sides of the chamber it was so understood at the time. If the opponents of the bill had understood it was not, they would have made the point on it; and if they had made it, we should certainly have yielded to it, and put in the clause. That is a discovery made since the President found out that it was not safe to take it for granted that that would be done which ought in fairness to have been done.

I knew at the time this statement was made that I had urged the very objection to the Toombs bill two years before, that it did not provide for the submission of the constitution. You will find my remarks, made on the 2nd of July, 1856, in the appendix to the *Congressional Globe* of that year, page 179, urging this very objection. Do you ask why I did not expose him at the time? I will tell you: Mr. Douglas was then doing good service against the Lecompton iniquity. The Republicans were then engaged in a hand-to-hand fight with the National Democracy to prevent the bringing of Kansas into the Union as a slave State against the wishes of its inhabitants, and of course I was unwilling to turn our guns from the common enemy to strike down an ally. Judge Douglas, however, on the same day, and in the same debate, probably recollecting, or being reminded of, the fact that I had objected to the Toombs bill when pending, that it did not provide for the submission of the constitution to the people, made another statement, which is to be found in the same volume of the *Congressional Globe*, page 22, in which he says:

> That the bill was silent on the subject is true, and my attention was called to that about the time it was passed; and I took the fair construction to be, that powers not delegated were reserved, and that of course the constitution would be submitted to the people.

Whether this statement is consistent with the statement just before made, that had the point been made it would have been yielded to, or that it was a new discovery, you will determine; for if the public records do not convict and condemn him, he may go uncondemned, so far as I am concerned. I make no use here of the testimony of Senator Bigler to show that Judge Douglas must have been privy to the consultation held at his house, when it was determined not to submit the constitution to the people, because Judge Douglas denies it, and I wish to use his own acts and declarations, which are abundantly sufficient for my purpose.

I come to a piece of testimony which disposes of all these various pretences which have been set up for striking out of the original Toombs proposition the clause requiring a submission of the constitution to the people, and shows that it was not done either by accident, by inadvertence, or because it was believed that, the bill being silent on the subject, the constitution would necessarily be submitted to the people for approval. What will you think, after listening to the facts already presented, to show that there was a design with those who concocted the Toombs bill, as amended, not to submit the constitution to the people, if I now bring before you the amended bill as Judge Douglas reported it back, and show the clause of the original bill requiring submission was not only struck out, but that other clauses were inserted in the bill, putting it absolutely out of the power of the Convention to submit the constitution to the people for approval, had they desired to do so? If I can produce such evidence as that, will you not all agree that it clinches and establishes forever all I charged at Chicago, and more too?

I propose now to furnish that evidence. It will be remembered that Mr. Toombs's bill provided for holding an election for delegates to form a constitution under the supervision of commissioners to be appointed by the President; and in the bill as reported back by Judge Douglas, these words, *not to be found in the original bill*, are inserted at the close of the 11th section, viz.:

> And until the complete execution of this Act, no other election shall be held in said Territory.

This clause put it out of the power of the Convention to refer to the people for adoption; it absolutely prohibited the holding of any other election than that for the election of delegates, till that act was completely executed, which would not have been until Kansas was admitted as a State, or at all events till her constitution was fully prepared and ready for submission to Congress for admission. Other amendments reported by Judge Douglas to the original Toombs bill clearly show that the intention was to enable Kansas to become a State without any further action than simply a resolution of admission. The amendment reported by Mr. Douglas, that "until the next Congressional apportionment, the said State shall have one representative," clearly shows this, no such provision being contained in the original Toombs bill. For what other earthly purpose could the clause to prevent any other election in Kansas, except that of delegates, till it was admitted as a State, have been inserted, except to prevent a submission of the constitution, when formed, to the people?

The Toombs bill did not pass in the exact shape in which Judge Douglas reported it. Several amendments were made to it in the Senate. I am now dealing with the action of Judge Douglas as connected with that bill, and speak of the bill as he recommended it. The facts I have stated in regard to this matter appear upon the records, which I have here present to show to any man who wishes to look at them. They establish beyond the power of controversy all the charges I have made, and show that Judge Douglas was made use of as an instrument by others, or else knowingly was a party to the scheme, to have a government put in force over the people of Kansas without giving them an opportunity to pass upon it. That others high in position in the so-called Democratic party were parties to such a scheme is confessed by Governor Bigler; and the only reason why the scheme was not carried, and Kansas long ago forced into the Union as a slave State, is the fact, that the Republicans were sufficiently strong in the House of Representatives to defeat the measure.

### EXTRACT FROM MR. DOUGLAS'S SPEECH MADE AT JACKSONVILLE, AND REFERRED TO BY MR. LINCOLN IN HIS OPENING AT CHARLESTON

I have been reminded by a friend behind me that there is another topic upon which there has been a desire expressed that I should speak. I am told that Mr. Lyman Trumbull, who has the good fortune to hold a seat in the United States Senate, in violation of the bargain between him and Lincoln, was here the other day and occupied his time in making certain charges against me, involving, if they be true, moral turpitude. I am also informed that the charges he made here were substantially the same as those made by him in the city of Chicago, which were printed in the newspapers of that city. I now propose to answer those charges and to annihilate every pretext that an honest man has ever had for repeating them.

In order that I may meet these charges fairly, I will read them, as made by Mr. Trumbull, in his Chicago speech, in his own language. He says:

> Now, fellow-citizens, I make the distinct charge that there was a preconcerted arrangement and plot entered into by the very men who now claim credit for opposing a constitution not submitted to the people, to have a constitution formed and put in force without giving the people an opportunity to pass upon it. This, my friends, is a serious charge, but I charge it to-night that the very men who traverse the country under

banners proclaiming popular sovereignty, by design concocted a bill on purpose to force a constitution upon that people.

Again, speaking to some one in the crowd, he says:

> And you want to satisfy yourself that he was in the plot to force a constitution upon that people? I will satisfy you. I will cram the truth down any honest man's throat until he cannot deny it, and to the man who does deny it I will cram the lie down his throat till he shall cry, "Enough!" It is preposterous; it is the most damnable effrontery that man ever put on to conceal a scheme to defraud and cheat the people out of their rights, and then claim credit for it.

That is polite and decent language for a Senator of the United States. Remember that that language was used without any provocation whatever from me. I had not alluded to him in any manner in any speech that I had made, hence without provocation. As soon as he sets his foot within the State, he makes the direct charge that I was a party to a plot to force a constitution upon the people of Kansas against their will, and, knowing that it would be denied, he talks about cramming the lie down the throat of any man who shall deny it, until he cries, "Enough!"

Why did he take it for granted that it would be denied, unless he knew it to be false? Why did he deem it necessary to make a threat in advance that he would "cram the lie" down the throat of any man that should deny it? I have no doubt that the entire Abolition party consider it very polite for Mr. Trumbull to go round uttering calumnies of that kind, bullying, and talking of cramming lies down men's throats; but if I deny any of his lies by calling him a liar, they are shocked at the indecency of the language; hence, to-day, instead of calling him a liar, I intend to prove that he is one.

I wish, in the first place, to refer to the evidence adduced by Trumbull, at Chicago, to sustain his charge. He there declared that Mr. Toombs, of Georgia, introduced a bill into Congress authorizing the people of Kansas to form a constitution and come into the Union, that when introduced it contained a clause requiring the constitution to be submitted to the people, and that I struck out the words of that clause.

Suppose it were true that there was such a clause in the bill, and that I struck it out, is that proof of a plot to force a constitution upon a people against their will?

Bear in mind that from the days of George Washington to the Administration of Franklin Pierce, there had never been passed by Congress a bill requiring the submission of a constitution to the people. If Trumbull's charge, that I struck out that clause, were true, it would only prove that I had reported the bill in the exact shape of every bill of like character that passed under Washington, Jefferson, Madison, Monroe, Jackson, or any other President, to the time of the then present Administration. I ask you, would that be evidence of a design to force a constitution on a people against their will? If it were so, it would be evidence against Washington, Jefferson, Madison, Jackson, Van Buren, and every other President.

But, upon examination, it turns out that the Toombs bill never did contain a clause requiring the constitution to be submitted. Hence no such clause was ever stricken out, by me or anybody else. It is true, however, that the Toombs bill and its authors all took it for granted that the constitution would be submitted. There had never been, in the history of this government, any attempt made to force a constitution upon an unwilling people, and nobody dreamed that any such attempt would be made, or deemed it necessary to provide for such a contingency. If such a clause was necessary in Mr. Trumbull's opinion, why did he not offer an amendment to that effect?

In order to give more pertinency to that question, I will read an extract from Trumbull's speech in the Senate, on the Toombs bill, made on the 2nd of July, 1856. He said:

> We are asked to amend this bill and make it perfect, and a liberal spirit seems to be manifested on the part of some senators to have a fair bill. It is difficult, I admit, to frame a bill that will give satisfaction to all, but to approach it, or come near it, I think two things must be done.

The first, then, he goes on to say, was the application of the Wilmot Proviso to the Territories, and the second the repeal of all the laws passed by the Territorial Legislature. He did not then say that it was necessary to put in a clause requiring the submission of the constitution. Why, if he thought such a provision necessary, did he not introduce it? He says in his speech that he was invited to offer amendments. Why did he not do so? He cannot pretend that he had no chance to do this, for he did offer some amendments, but none requiring submission.

I now proceed to show that Mr. Trumbull knew at the time that the bill was silent as to the subject of submission, and also that he, and everybody else, took it for granted that the constitution would be submitted. Now for the evidence.

In his second speech he says: "The bill in many of its features meets my approbation." So he did not think it so very bad.

Further on he says:

> In regard to the measure introduced by the Senator from
> Georgia [Mr. Toombs], and recommended by the committee, I
> regard it, in many respects, as a most excellent bill; but we must
> look at it in the light of surrounding circumstances. In the con-
> dition of things now existing in the country, I do not consider it
> as a safe measure, nor one which will give peace; and I will give
> my reasons. First, it affords no immediate relief. It provides for
> taking a census of the voters in the Territory for an election in
> November, and the assembling of a convention in December,
> to form, if it thinks proper, a constitution for Kansas, prepara-
> tory to its admission into the Union as a State. It is not until
> December that the Convention is to meet. It would take some
> time to form a constitution. *I suppose that constitution would
> have to be ratified by the people before it becomes valid.*

He there expressly declared that he supposed, under the bill, the constitution
would have to be submitted to the people before it became valid. He went on
to say:

> No provision is made in this bill for such a ratification. This
> is objectionable to my mind. I do not think the people should
> be bound by a constitution without passing upon it directly,
> themselves.

Why did he not offer an amendment providing for such a submission, if he
thought it necessary? Notwithstanding the absence of such a clause he took it
for granted that the constitution would have to be ratified by the people, under
the bill.

In another part of the same speech, he says:

> There is nothing said in this bill, so far as I have discovered,
> about submitting the constitution which is to be framed to the
> people, for their sanction or rejection. Perhaps the Convention
> would have the right to submit it, if it should think proper; but

it is certainly not compelled to do so, according to the provisions of the bill. If it is to be submitted to the people, it will take time, and it will not be until some time next year that this new constitution, affirmed and ratified by the people, would be submitted here to Congress for its acceptance; and what is to be the condition of that people in the meantime?

You see that his argument then was that the Toombs bill would not get Kansas into the Union quick enough, and was objectionable on that account. He had no fears about this submission, or why did he not introduce an amendment to meet the case?

A VOICE: Why did n't you? You were chairman of the committee.

MR. DOUGLAS: I will answer that question for you.

In the first place, no provision had ever before been put in any similar act passed by Congress. I did not suppose that there was an honest man who would pretend that the omission of such a clause furnished evidence of a conspiracy or attempt to impose on the people. It could not be expected that such of us as did not think that omission was evidence of such a scheme would offer such an amendment; but if Trumbull then believed what he now says, why did he not offer the amendment, and try to prevent it, when he was, as he says, invited to do so?

In this connection I will tell you what the main point of discussion was: There was a bill pending to admit Kansas whenever she should have a population of 93,420, that being the ratio required for a member of Congress. Under that bill Kansas could not have become a State for some years, because she could not have had the requisite population. Mr. Toombs took it into his head to bring in a bill to admit Kansas then, with only twenty-five or thirty thousand people, and the question was whether we would allow Kansas to come in under this bill, or keep her out under mine until she had 93,420 people. The committee considered that question, and overruled me, by deciding in favor of the immediate admission of Kansas, and I reported accordingly. I hold in my hand a copy of the report which I made at that time. I will read from it:

> The point upon which your committee have entertained the most serious and grave doubts in regard to the propriety of indorsing the proposition relates to the fact that, in the absence of any census of the inhabitants, there is reason to apprehend that the Territory does not contain sufficient population to

entitle them to demand admission under the treaty with France, if we take the ratio of representation for a member of Congress as the rule.

Thus you see that in the written report accompanying the bill, I said that the great difficulty with the committee was the question of population. In the same report I happened to refer to the question of submission. Now, listen to what I said about that:

> In the opinion of your committee, whenever a consitution shall be formed in any Territory, preparatory to its admission into the Union as a State, justice, the genius of our institutions, the whole theory of our republican system, imperatively demand that the voice of the people shall be fairly expressed, and their will embodied in that fundamental law, without fraud, or violence, or intimidation, or any other improper or unlawful influence, and subject to no other restrictions than those imposed by the Constitution of the United States.

I read this from the report I made at the time, on the Toombs bill. I will read yet another passage from the same report; after setting out the features of the Toombs bill, I contrast it with the proposition of Senator Seward, saying:

> The revised proposition of the Senator from Georgia refers all matters in dispute to the decision of the present population, with guarantees of fairness and safeguards against frauds and violence to which no reasonable man can find just grounds of exception; while the Senator from New York, if his proposition is designed to recognize and impart vitality to the Topeka Constitution, proposes to disfranchise, not only all the emigrants who have arrived in the Territory this year, but all the law-abiding men who refused to join in the act of open rebellion against the constituted authorities of the Territory last year, by making the unauthorized and unlawful action of a political party the fundamental law of the whole people.

Then, again, I repeat that under that bill the question is to be referred to the present population to decide for or against coming into the Union under the constitution they may adopt.

Mr. Trumbull, when at Chicago, rested his charge upon the allegation that the clause requiring submission was originally in the bill, and was stricken out by me. When that falsehood was exposed by a publication of the record, he went to Alton and made another speech, repeating the charge and referring to other and different evidence to sustain it. He saw that he was caught in his first falsehood, so he changed the issue, and instead of resting upon the allegation of striking out, he made it rest upon the declaration that I had introduced a clause into the bill prohibiting the people from voting upon the constitution. I am told that he made the same charge here that he made at Alton, that I had actually introduced and incorporated into the bill a clause which prohibited the people from voting upon their constitution. I hold his Alton speech in my hand, and will read the amendment which he alleges that I offered. It is in these words:

> And until the complete execution of this Act, no other election shall be held in said Territory.

Trumbull says the object of that amendment was to prevent the Convention from submitting the constitution to a vote of the people. I will read what he said at Alton on that subject:

> This clause put it out of the power of the Convention, had it been so disposed, to submit the constitution to the people for adoption; for it absolutely prohibited the holding of any other election than that for the election of delegates, till that Act was completely executed, which would not have been till Kansas was admitted as a State, or, at all events, till her constitution was fully prepared and ready for submission to Congress for admission.

Now, do you suppose that Mr. Trumbull supposed that that clause prohibited the Convention from submitting the constitution to the people, when, in his speech in the Senate, he declared that the Convention had a right to submit it? In his Alton speech, as will be seen by the extract which I have read, he declared the clause put it out of the power of the Convention to submit the constitution, and in his speech in the Senate he said:

> There is *nothing said in this bill*, so far as I have discovered, about submitting the constitution which is to be formed to the people, for their sanction or rejection. Perhaps the Convention

would have the right to submit it, if it should think proper, but
it is certainly not compelled to do so according to the provisions
of the bill.

Thus you see that, in Congress, he declared the bill to be silent on the subject, and a few days since, at Alton, he made a speech and said that there was a
provision in the bill prohibiting submission.

I have two answers to make to that. In the first place, the amendment which
he quotes as depriving the people of an opportunity to vote upon the constitution *was stricken out on my motion,*—absolutely stricken out, and not voted on
at all! In the second place, in lieu of it, a provision was voted in, authorizing the
Convention to order an election whenever it pleased. I will read. After Trumbull
had made his speech in the Senate, declaring that the constitution would probably be submitted to the people, although the bill was silent upon that subject,
I made a few remarks, and offered two amendments, which you may find in
the Appendix to the *Congressional Globe,* volume thirty-three, first session of the
Thirty-fourth Congress, page 795. I quote:

> MR. DOUGLAS: I have an amendment to offer from the
> Committee on Territories. On page 8, section 11, *strike out the
> words* "until the complete execution of this act no other elec-
> tion shall be held in said Territory," and insert the amendment
> which I hold in my hand.

The amendment was as follows:

> That all persons who shall possess the other qualifica-
> tions prescribed for voters under this Act, and who shall have
> been *bona fide* inhabitants of said Territory since its organi-
> zation, and who shall have absented themselves therefrom in
> consequence of the disturbances therein, and who shall return
> before the first day of October next, and become *bona fide*
> inhabitants of the Territory, with the intent of making it their
> permanent home, and shall present satisfactory evidence of these
> facts to the Board of Commissioners, shall be entitled to vote at
> said election, and shall have their names placed on said corrected
> list of voters for that purpose.

That amendment was adopted unanimously. After its adoption, the record shows the following:

> MR. DOUGLAS: I have another amendment to offer from the Committee, to follow the one which has been adopted. The bill reads now, "And until the complete execution of this Act, no other election shall be held in said Territory." It has been suggested that it should be modified in this way, "And to avoid all conflict in the complete execution of this Act, all other elections in said Territory are hereby postponed until such time as said Convention shall appoint," so that they can appoint the day in the event that there should be a failure to come into the Union.

This amendment was also agreed to, without dissent.

Thus you see that the amendment quoted by Trumbull at Alton as evidence against me, instead of being put into the bill by me, was stricken out on my motion, and never became a part thereof at all. You also see that the substituted clause expressly authorized the Convention to appoint such day of election as it should deem proper.

Mr. Trumbull when he made that speech knew these facts. He forged his evidence from beginning to end, and by falsifying the record he endeavors to bolster up his false charge. I ask you what you think of Trumbull thus going around the country, falsifying and garbling the public records. I ask you whether you will sustain a man who will descend to the infamy of such conduct.

MR. DOUGLAS proceeded to remark that he should not hereafter occupy his time in refuting such charges made by Trumbull, but that, Lincoln having indorsed the character of Trumbull for veracity, he should hold him [Lincoln] responsible for the slanders.

# Fifth Joint Debate, at Galesburgh

*October 7, 1858*

### MR. DOUGLAS'S OPENING SPEECH

LADIES AND GENTLEMEN: Four years ago I appeared before the people of Knox County for the purpose of defending my political action upon the Compromise measures of 1850 and the passage of the Kansas-Nebraska Bill. Those of you before me who were present then will remember that I vindicated myself for supporting those two measures by the fact that they rested upon the great fundamental principle that the people of each State and each Territory of this Union have the right, and ought to be permitted to exercise the right, of regulating their own domestic concerns in their own way, subject to no other limitation or restriction than that which the Constitution of the United States imposes upon them. I then called upon the people of Illinois to decide whether that principle of self-government was right or wrong. If it was and is right, then the Compromise measures of 1850 were right, and consequently, the Kansas and Nebraska Bill, based upon the same principle, must necessarily have been right.

The Kansas and Nebraska Bill declared, in so many words, that it was the true intent and meaning of the act not to legislate slavery into any State or Territory, nor to exclude it therefrom, but to leave the people thereof perfectly free to form and regulate their domestic institutions in their own way, subject only to the Constitution of the United States. For the last four years I have devoted all my energies, in private and public, to commend that principle to the American people. Whatever else may be said in condemnation or support of my political course I apprehend that no honest man will doubt the fidelity with which, under all circumstances, I have stood by it.

During the last year a question arose in the Congress of the United States whether or not that principle would be violated by the admission of Kansas into the Union under the Lecompton Constitution. In my opinion, the attempt to force Kansas in under that constitution was a gross violation of the principle enunciated in the Compromise measures of 1850, and Kansas and Nebraska Bill of 1854, and therefore I led off in the fight against the Lecompton Constitution, and conducted it until the effort to carry that constitution through Congress was abandoned. And I can appeal to all men, friends and foes, Democrats and Republicans, Northern men and Southern men, that during the whole of that fight I carried the banner of popular sovereignty aloft, and never allowed it to trail in the dust, or lowered my flag until victory perched upon our arms. When the Lecompton Constitution was defeated, the question arose in the minds of those who had advocated it what they should next resort to in order to carry out their views. They devised a measure known as the English bill, and granted a general amnesty and political pardon to all men who had fought against the Lecompton Constitution, provided they would support that bill. I for one did not choose to accept the pardon, or to avail myself of the amnesty granted on that condition. The fact that the supporters of Lecompton were willing to forgive all differences of opinion at that time in the event those who opposed it favored the English bill, was an admission they did not think that opposition to Lecompton impaired a man's standing in the Democratic party. Now, the question arises, what was that English bill which certain men are now attempting to make a test of political orthodoxy in this country? It provided, in substance, that the Lecompton Constitution should be sent back to the people of Kansas for their adoption or rejection, at an election which was held in August last, and in case they refused admission under it, that Kansas should be kept out of the Union until she had 93,420 inhabitants. I was in favor of sending the constitution back in order to enable the people to say whether or not it was their act and deed, and embodied their will; but the other proposition, that if they refused to come into the Union under it they should be kept out until they had double or treble the population they then had, I never would sanction by my vote. The reason why I could not sanction it is to be found in the fact that by the English bill, if the people of Kansas had only agreed to become a slaveholding State under the Lecompton Constitution, they could have done so with 35,000 people, but if they insisted on being a free State, as they had a right to do, then they were to be punished by being kept out of the Union until they had nearly three times that population. I then said in my place in the Senate, as I now say to you, that whenever Kansas has population enough for a slave State she has population enough for a free State. I have never yet given a vote, and I never intend to record one, making an odious and unjust distinction between the different States of this Union. I hold it to be a fundamental principle in our republican form of government that all the States of this Union, old and new, free and slave, stand on an exact equality. Equality among the different States is a cardinal principle on which all our institutions rest. Wherever, therefore, you make a discrimination, saving to a slave State that it shall be admitted with 35,000 inhabitants, and a free State that it shall not be admitted until it has 93,000 or 100,000 inhabitants, you are throwing the whole weight of the Federal Government into the scale in favor of one class of States against the other. Nor would I, on the other hand, any sooner sanction the doctrine that a free State could be admitted into the Union with 35,000 people, while a slave State was kept out until it had 93,000. I have always declared in the Senate my willingness, and I am willing now to adopt the rule, that no Territory shall ever become a State until it has the requisite population for a member of Congress, according to the then existing ratio. But while I have always been, and am now, willing to adopt that general rule, I was not willing and would not consent to make an exception of Kansas, as a punishment for her obstinacy in demanding the right to do as she pleased in the formation of her constitution. It is proper that I should remark here, that my opposition to the Lecompton Constitution did not rest upon the peculiar position taken by Kansas on the subject of slavery. I held then, and hold now, that if the people of Kansas want a slave State, it is their right to make one, and be received into the Union under it; if, on the contrary, they want a free State, it is their right to have it, and no man should ever oppose their admission because they ask it under the one or the other. I hold to that great principle of self-government which asserts the right of every people to decide for themselves the nature and character of the domestic institutions and fundamental law under which they are to live.

The effort has been and is now being made in this State by certain postmasters and other Federal office-holders to make a test of faith on the support of the English bill. These men are now making speeches all over the State against me and in favor of Lincoln, either directly or indirectly, because I would not sanction a discrimination between slave and free States by voting for the English bill. But while that bill is made a test in Illinois for the purpose of breaking up the Democratic organization in this State, how is it in the other States? Go to Indiana, and there you find English himself, the author of the English bill, who is a candidate for re-election to Congress, has been forced by public opinion to abandon his own darling project, and to give a promise that he will vote for the admission of Kansas at once, whenever she forms a constitution in pursuance of law and ratifies it by a majority vote of her people. Not only is this the case with English himself, but I am informed that every Democratic candidate for Congress in Indiana takes the same ground. Pass to Ohio, and there you find that Groesbeck, and Pendleton, and Cox, and all the other anti-Lecompton men who stood shoulder to shoulder with me against the Lecompton Constitution, but voted for the English bill, now repudiate it and take the same ground that I do on that question. So it is with the Joneses and others of Pennsylvania, and so it is with every other

Lecompton Democrat in the free States. They now abandon even the English bill, and come back to the true platform which I proclaimed at the time in the Senate, and upon which the Democracy of Illinois now stand. And yet, notwithstanding the fact that every Lecompton and anti-Lecompton Democrat in the free States has abandoned the English bill, you are told that it is to be made a test upon me, while the power and patronage of the Government are all exerted to elect men to Congress in the other States who occupy the same position with reference to it that I do. It seems that my political offence consists in the fact that I first did not vote for the English bill, and thus pledge myself to keep Kansas out of the Union until she has a population of 93,420, and then return home, violate that pledge, repudiate the bill, and take the opposite ground. If I had done this, perhaps the Administration would now be advocating my re-election, as it is that of the others who have pursued this course. I did not choose to give that pledge, for the reason that I did not intend to carry out that principle. I never will consent, for the sake of conciliating the frowns of power, to pledge myself to do that which I do not intend to perform. I now submit the question to you, as my constituency, whether I was not right, first, in resisting the adopting of the Lecompton Constitution, and, secondly, in resisting the English bill. I repeat that I opposed the Lecompton Constitution because it was not the act and deed on the people of Kansas, and did not embody their will. I denied the right of any power on earth, under our system of government, to force a constitution on an unwilling people. There was a time when some men could pretend to believe that the Lecompton Constitution embodied the will of the people of Kansas; but that time has passed. The question was referred to the people of Kansas under the English bill last August, and then, at a fair election, they rejected the Lecompton Constitution by a vote of from eight to ten against it to one in its favor. Since it has been voted down by so overwhelming a majority, no man can pretend that it was the act and deed of that people. I submit the question to you whether or not, if it had not been for me, that constitution would have been crammed down the throats of the people of Kansas against their consent. While at least ninety-nine out of every hundred people here present agree that I was right in defeating that project, yet my enemies use the fact that I did defeat it, by doing right, to break me down and put another man in the United States Senate in my place. The very men who acknowledge that I was right in defeating Lecompton now form an alliance with Federal office-holders, professed Lecompton men, to defeat me, because I did right. My political opponent, Mr. Lincoln, has no hope on earth, and has never dreamed that he had a chance of success, were it not for the aid that he is receiving from Federal office-holders, who are using their influence and the patronage of the government against me in revenge for my having defeated the Lecompton Constitution. What do you Republicans think of a political organization that will try to make an unholy and unnatural combination with its professed foes to beat a man merely because he has done right? You know such is the fact with regard to your own party. You know that the axe of decapitation is suspended over every man in office in Illinois, and the terror of proscription is threatened every Democrat by the present Administration, unless he supports the Republican ticket in preference to my Democratic associates and myself. I could find an instance in the postmaster of the city of Galesburgh, and in every other postmaster in this vicinity, all of whom have been stricken down simply because they discharged the duties of their offices honestly, and supported the regular Democratic ticket in this State in the right. The Republican party is availing itself of unworthy means in the present contest to carry the election, because its leaders know that if they let this chance slip they will never have another, and their hopes of making this a Republican State will be blasted forever.

Now, let me ask you whether the country has any interest in sustaining this organization, known as the Republican party. That party is unlike all other political organizations in this country. All other parties have been national in their character,—have avowed their principles alike in the slave and free States, in Kentucky as well as Illinois, in Louisiana as well as in Massachusetts. Such was the case with the old Whig party, and such was and is the case with the Democratic party. Whigs and Democrats could proclaim their principles boldly and fearlessly in the North and in the South, in the East and in the West, wherever the Constitution ruled, and the American flag waved over American soil.

But now you have a sectional organization, a party which appeals to the Northern section of the Union against the Southern, a party which appeals to Northern passion, Northern pride, Northern ambition, and Northern prejudices, against Southern people, the Southern States, and Southern institutions. The leaders of that party hope that they will be able to unite the Northern States in one great sectional party; and inasmuch as the North is the strongest section, that they will thus be enabled to outvote, conquer, govern and control the South. Hence you find that they now make speeches advocating principles and measures which cannot be defended in any slaveholding State of this Union. Is there a Republican residing in Galesburgh who can travel into Kentucky and carry his principles with him across the Ohio? What Republican from Massachusetts can visit the Old Dominion without leaving his principles behind him when he crosses Mason and Dixon's line? Permit me to say to you in perfect good humor, but in all sincerity, that no political creed is sound which cannot be proclaimed fearlessly in every

State of this Union where the Federal Constitution is the supreme law of the land. Not only is this Republican party unable to proclaim its principles alike in the North and South, in the free States and in the slave States, but it cannot even proclaim them in the same forms and give them the same strength and meaning in all parts of the same State. My friend Lincoln finds it extremely difficult to manage a debate in the centre part of the State, where there is a mixture of men from the North and the South. In the extreme northern part of Illinois he can proclaim as bold and radical Abolitionism as ever Giddings, Lovejoy, or Garrison enunciated; but when he gets down a little farther south he claims that he is an old-line Whig, a disciple of Henry Clay, and declares that he still adheres to the old-line Whig creed, and has nothing whatever to do with Abolitionism, or negro equality, or negro citizenship. I once before hinted this of Mr. Lincoln in a public speech, and at Charleston he defied me to show that there was any difference between his speeches in the North and in the South, and that they were not in strict harmony. I will now call your attention to two of them, and you can then say whether you would be apt to believe that the same man ever uttered both. In a speech in reply to me at Chicago in July last, Mr. Lincoln, in speaking of the equality of the negro with the white man, used the following language:

> I should like to know, if, taking this old Declaration of Independence, which declares that all men are equal upon principle, and making exceptions to it, where will it stop? If one man says it does not mean a negro, which may not another man say it does not mean another man? If the Declaration is not the truth, let us get the statute book in which we find it, and tear it out. Who is so bold as to do it? If it is not true, let us tear it out.

You find that Mr. Lincoln there proposed that if the doctrine of the Declaration of Independence, declaring all men to be born equal, did not include the negro and put him on an equality with the white man, that we should take the statute book and tear it out. He there took the ground that the negro race is included in the Declaration of Independence as the equal of the white race, and that there could be no such thing as a distinction in the races, making one superior and the other inferior. I read now from the same speech:

> My friends [he says], I have detained you about as long as I desire to do, and I have only to say, let us discard all this quibbling about this man and the other man, this race and that

race and the other race being inferior, and therefore they must be placed in an inferior position, discarding our standard that we have left us. Let us discard all these things, and unite as one people throughout this land, until we shall once more stand up declaring that all men are created equal.

["That's right," etc.]

Yes, I have no doubt that you think it is right; but the Lincoln men down in Coles, Tazewell, and Sangamon counties *do not* think it is right. In the conclusion of the same speech, talking to the Chicago Abolitionists, he said: "I leave you, hoping that the lamp of liberty will burn in your bosoms until there shall no longer be a doubt that all men are created free and equal." ["Good, good."] Well, you say "Good" to that, and you are going to vote for Lincoln because he holds that doctrine. I will not blame you for supporting him on that ground, but I will show you, in immediate contrast with that doctrine, what Mr. Lincoln said down in Egypt in order to get votes in that locality, where they do not hold to such a doctrine. In a joint discussion between Mr. Lincoln and myself, at Charleston, I think, on the 18th of last month, Mr. Lincoln, referring to this subject, used the following language:

> I will say then, that I am not, nor never have been, in favor of bringing about in any way the social and political equality of the white and black races; that I am not, nor ever have been, in favor of making voters of the free negroes, or jurors, or qualifying them to hold office, or having them to marry with white people. I will say, in addition, that there is a physical difference between the white and black races which, I suppose, will forever forbid the two races living together upon terms of social and political equality; and inasmuch as they cannot so live, that while they do remain together there must be the position of superior and inferior, that I as much as any other man am in favor of the superior position being assigned to the white man.

["Good for Lincoln."]

Fellow-citizens, here you find men hurrahing for Lincoln, and saying that he did right, when in one part of the State he stood up for negro equality, and in another part, for political effect, discarded the doctrine, and declared that there always must be a superior and inferior race. Abolitionists up North are expected and required to vote for Lincoln because he goes for the equality of the races, holding that by the Declaration of Independence the white man and the negro were created equal, and endowed by the divine law with that equality, and down South he tells the old Whigs, the Kentuckians, Virginians, and Tennesseeans, that there is a physical difference in the races, making one superior and the other inferior, and that he is in favor of maintaining the superiority of the white race over the negro. Now, how can you reconcile those two positions of Mr. Lincoln? He is to be voted for in the South as a pro-slavery man, and he is to be voted for in the North as an Abolitionist. Up here he thinks it is all nonsense to talk about a difference between the races, and says that we must "discard all quibbling about this race and that race and the other race being inferior, and therefore they must be placed in an inferior position." Down South he makes this "quibble" about this race and that race and the other race being inferior as the creed of his party, and declares that the negro can never be elevated to the position of the white man. You find that his political meetings are called by different names in different counties in the State. Here they are called Republican meetings; but in old Tazewell, where Lincoln made a speech last Tuesday, he did not address a *Republican* meeting, but "a grand rally of the *Lincoln men*." There are very few Republicans there, because Tazewell County is filled with old Virginians and Kentuckians, all of whom are Whigs or Democrats; and if Mr. Lincoln had called an Abolition or Republican meeting there, he would not get many votes. Go down into Egypt, and you will find that he and his party are operating under an alias there, which his friend Trumbull has given them, in order that they may cheat the people. When I was down in Monroe County a few weeks ago, addressing the people, I saw handbills posted announcing that Mr. Trumbull was going to speak in behalf of Lincoln; and what do you think the name of his party was there? Why, the "*Free Democracy*." Mr. Trumbull and Mr. Jehu Baker were announced to address the Free Democracy of Monroe County, and the bill was signed, "Many Free Democrats." The reason that Lincoln and his party adopted the name of "Free Democracy" down there was because Monroe County has always been an old-fashioned Democratic county, and hence it was necessary to make the people believe that they were Democrats, sympathized with them, and were fighting for Lincoln as Democrats. Come up to Springfield, where Lincoln now lives, and always has lived, and you find that the Convention of his party which assembled to nominate candidates for Legislature, who are expected to vote for him if elected, dare not adopt the name of Republican, but assembled under the title of "all opposed to the Democracy." Thus you find that Mr. Lincoln's creed cannot travel through even one half of the counties of this State, but that it changes its hues and becomes lighter and lighter as it travels from the extreme north, until it is nearly white when it reaches the extreme south end of the State.

I ask you, my friends, why cannot Republicans avow their principles alike everywhere? I would despise myself if I thought that I was procuring your votes by concealing my opinions, and by avowing one set of principles in one part of the State, and a different set in another part. If I do not truly and honorably represent your feelings and principles, then I ought not to be your Senator; and I will never conceal my opinions, or modify or change them a hair's breadth, in order to get votes. I tell you that this Chicago doctrine of Lincoln's—declaring that the negro and the white man are made equal by the Declaration of Independence and by Divine Providence—is a monstrous heresy. The signers of the Declaration of Independence never dreamed of the negro when they were writing that document. They referred to white men, to men of European birth, and European descent, when they declared the equality of all men. I see a gentleman there in the crowd shaking his head. Let me remind him that when Thomas Jefferson wrote that document, he was the owner, and so continued until his death, of a large number of slaves. Did he intend to say in that Declaration that his negro slaves, which he held and treated as property, were created his equals by divine law, and that he was violating the law of God every day of his life by holding them as slaves? It must be borne in mind that when that Declaration was put forth, every one of the thirteen Colonies were slaveholding Colonies, and every man who signed that instrument represented a slaveholding constituency. Recollect, also, that no one of them emancipated his slaves, much less put them on an equality with himself, after he signed the Declaration. On the contrary, they all continued to hold their negroes as slaves during the Revolutionary War. Now, do you believe—are you willing to have it said—that every man who signed the Declaration of Independence declared the negro his equal, and then was hypocrite enough to continue to hold him as a slave, in violation of what he believed to be the divine law? And yet when you say that the Declaration of Independence includes the negro, you charge the signers of it with hypocrisy.

I say to you, frankly, that in my opinion this government was made by our fathers on the white basis. It was made by white men for the benefit of white men and their posterity forever, and was intended to be administered by white men in all time to come. But while I hold that under our Constitution and political system the negro is not a citizen, cannot be a citizen, and ought not to be a citizen, it does not follow by any means that he should be a slave. On the contrary, it does follow that the negro, as an inferior race, ought to possess every right, every privilege, every immunity, which he can safely exercise, consistent with the safety of the society in which he lives. Humanity requires, and Christianity commands, that you shall extend to every inferior being, and every dependent being, all the privileges, immunities, and advantages which can be granted to them, consistent with the safety of society. If you ask me the nature and extent of these privileges, I answer that that is a question which the people of each State must decide for themselves. Illinois has decided that question for herself. We have said that in this State the negro shall not be a slave, nor shall he be a citizen. Kentucky holds a different doctrine. New York holds one different from either, and Maine one different from all. Virginia, in her policy on this question, differs in many respects from the others, and so on, until there are hardly two States whose policy is exactly alike in regard to the relation of the white man and the negro. Nor can you reconcile them and make them alike. Each State must do as it pleases. Illinois had as much right to adopt the policy which we have on that subject as Kentucky had to adopt a different policy. The great principle of this government is, that each State has the right to do as it pleases on all these questions, and no other State or power on earth has the right to interfere with us, or complain of us merely because our system differs from theirs. In the Compromise measures of 1850, Mr. Clay declared that this great principle ought to exist in the Territories as well as in the States, and I reasserted his doctrine in the Kansas and Nebraska Bill of 1854.

But Mr. Lincoln cannot be made to understand, and those who are determined to vote for him, no matter whether he is a pro-slavery man in the South and a negro equality advocate in the North, cannot be made to understand how it is that in a Territory the people can do as they please on the slavery question under the Dred Scott decision. Let us see whether I cannot explain it to the satisfaction of all impartial men. Chief Justice Taney has said, in his opinion in the Dred Scott case, that a negro slave, being property, stands on an equal footing with other property, and that the owner may carry them into United States territory the same as he does other property. Suppose any two of you, neighbors, should conclude to go to Kansas, one carrying $100,000 worth of negro slaves, and the other $100,000 worth of mixed merchandise, including quantities of liquors. You both agree that under that decision you may carry your property to Kansas; but when you get it there, the merchant who is possessed of the liquors is met by the Maine liquor law, which prohibits the sale or use of his property, and the owner of the slaves is met by equally unfriendly legislation, which makes his property worthless after he gets it there. What is the right to carry your property into the Territory worth to either, when unfriendly legislation in the Territory renders it worthless after you get it there? The slaveholder when he gets his slaves there finds that there is no local law to protect him in holding them, no slave code, no police regulation maintaining and supporting him in his right, and he discovers at once that the absence of such friendly legislation excludes his property from the Territory just as irresistibly as if there was a positive constitutional prohibition excluding it. Thus you find it is with any kind of property in a Territory: it depends for its protection on the local and municipal law. If the people of a Territory want slavery, they make friendly legislation to introduce it; but if they do not want it, they withhold all protection from it, and then it cannot exist there. Such was the view taken on the subject by different Southern men when the Nebraska Bill passed. See the speech of Mr. Orr, of South Carolina, the present Speaker of the House of Representatives of Congress, made at that time; and there you will find this whole doctrine argued out at full length. Read the speeches of other Southern Congressmen, Senators and Representatives, made in 1854, and you will find that they took the same view of the subject as Mr. Orr,—that slavery could never be forced on a people who did not want it. I hold that in this country there is no power on the face of the globe that can force any institution on an unwilling people. The great fundamental principle of our government is that the people of each State and each Territory shall be left perfectly free to decide for themselves what shall be the nature and character of their institutions. When this government was made, it was based on that principle. At the time of its formation there were twelve slaveholding States and one free State in this Union. Suppose this doctrine of Mr. Lincoln and the Republicans, of uniformity of laws of all the States on the subject of slavery, had prevailed; suppose Mr. Lincoln himself had been a member of the Convention which framed the Constitution, and that he had risen in that august body, and, addressing the father of his country, had said as he did at Springfield: "A house divided against itself cannot stand. I believe this government cannot endure permanently, half slave and half free. I do not expect the Union to be dissolved, I do not expect the house to fall, but I do expect it will cease to be divided. It will become all one thing or all the other." What do you think would have been the result? Suppose he had made that Convention believe that doctrine, and they had acted upon it, what do you think would have been the result? Do you believe that the one free State would have outvoted the twelve slaveholding States, and thus abolish slavery? On the contrary, would not the twelve slaveholding States have outvoted the one free State, and under his doctrine have fastened slavery by an irrevocable constitutional provision upon every inch of the American Republic? Thus you see that the doctrine he now advocates, if proclaimed at the beginning of the government, would have established slavery everywhere throughout the American continent; and are you willing, now that we have the majority section, to exercise a power which we never would have submitted to when we were in the minority? If the Southern States had attempted to control our institutions, and make the States all slave, when they had the power, I ask would you have submitted to it? If you would not, are you willing, now that we have become the strongest, under that great principle of self-government that allows each State to do as it pleases, to attempt to control the Southern institutions? Then, my friends, I say to you that there is but one path of peace in this Republic, and that is to administer this government as our fathers made it, divided into free and slave States, allowing each State to decide for itself whether it wants slavery or not. If Illinois will settle the slavery question for herself, and mind her own business and let her neighbors alone, we will be at peace with Kentucky and every other Southern State. If every other State in the Union will do the same, there will be peace between the North and the South, and in the whole Union.

### Mr. Lincoln's Reply

My Fellow-Citizens: A very large portion of the speech which Judge Douglas has addressed to you has previously been delivered and put in print. I do not mean that for a hit upon the Judge at all. If I had not been interrupted, I was going to say that such an answer as I was able to make to a very large portion of it had already been more than once made and published. There has been an opportunity afforded to the public to see our respective views upon the topics discussed in a large portion of the speech which he has just delivered. I make these remarks for the purpose of excusing myself for not passing over the entire ground that the Judge has traversed. I however desire to take up some of the points that he has attended to, and ask your attention to them, and I shall follow him backwards upon some notes which I have taken, reversing the order, by beginning where he concluded.

The Judge has alluded to the Declaration of Independence, and insisted that negroes are not included in that Declaration; and that it is a slander upon the framers of that instrument to suppose that negroes were meant therein; and he asks you: Is it possible to believe that Mr. Jefferson, who penned the immortal paper, could have supposed himself applying the language of that instrument to the negro race, and yet held a portion of that race in slavery? Would he not at once have freed them? I only have to remark upon this part of the Judge's speech (and that, too, very briefly, for I shall not detain myself, or you, upon that point for any great length of time), that I believe the entire records of the world, from the date of the Declaration of Independence up to within three years ago, may be searched in vain for one single affirmation, from one single man, that the negro was not included in the Declaration of Independence; I think I may defy Judge Douglas to show that he ever said so, that Washington ever said so, that any President ever said so, that any member of Congress ever said so, or that any living man upon the whole earth ever said so, until the necessities of the present policy of the Democratic party, in regard to slavery, had to invent that affirmation. And I will remind Judge Douglas and this audience that while Mr. Jefferson was the owner of slaves, as undoubtedly he was, in speaking upon this very subject he used the strong language that "he trembled for his country when he remembered that God was just"; and I will offer the highest premium in my power to Judge Douglas if he will show that he, in all his life, ever uttered a sentiment at all akin to that of Jefferson.

The next thing to which I will ask your attention is the Judge's comments upon the fact, as he assumes it to be, that we cannot call our public meetings as Republican meetings; and he instances Tazewell County as one of the places where the friends of Lincoln have called a public meeting and have not dared to name it a Republican meeting. He instances Monroe County as another, where Judge Trumbull and Jehu Baker addressed the persons whom the Judge assumes to be the friends of Lincoln, calling them the "Free Democracy." I have the honor to inform Judge Douglas that he spoke in that very county of Tazewell last Saturday, and I was there on Tuesday last; and when he spoke there, he spoke under a call not venturing to use the word "Democrat." [Turning to Judge Douglas.] What think you of this?

So, again, there is another thing to which I would ask the Judge's attention upon this subject. In the contest of 1856 his party delighted to call themselves together as the "National Democracy"; but now, if there should be a notice put up anywhere for a meeting of the "National Democracy," Judge Douglas and his friends would not come. They would not suppose themselves invited. They would understand that it was a call for those hateful postmasters whom he talks about.

Now a few words in regard to these extracts from speeches of mine which Judge Douglas has read to you, and which he supposes are in very great contrast to each other. Those speeches have been before the public for a considerable time, and if they have any inconsistency in them, if there is any conflict in them, the public have been able to detect it. When the Judge says, in speaking on this subject, that I make speeches of one sort for the people of the northern end of the State, and of a different sort for the southern people, he assumes that I do not understand that my speeches will be put in print and read north and south. I knew all the while that the speech that I made at Chicago, and the one I made at Jonesboro and the one at Charleston, would all be put in print, and all the reading and intelligent men in the community would see them and know all about my opinions. And I have not supposed, and do not now suppose, that there is any conflict whatever between them. But the Judge will have it that if we do not confess that there is a sort of inequality between the white and black races which justifies us in making them slaves, we must then insist that there is a degree of equality that requires us to make them our wives. Now, I have all the while taken a broad distinction in regard to that matter; and that is all there is in these different speeches which he arrays here; and the entire reading of either of the speeches will show that that distinction was made. Perhaps by taking two parts of the same speech he could have got up as much of a conflict as the one he has found. I have all the while maintained that in so far as it should be insisted that there was an equality between the white and black races that should produce a perfect social and political equality, it was an impossibility. This you have seen in my printed speeches, and with it I have said that in their right to "life, liberty, and the pursuit of happiness," as proclaimed in that old Declaration, the inferior races are our equals. And these declarations I have constantly made in reference to the abstract moral question, to contemplate and consider when we are legislating about any new country which is not already cursed with the actual presence of the evil,— slavery. I have never manifested any impatience with the necessities that spring from the actual presence of black people amongst us, and the actual existence of slavery amongst us where it does already exist; but I have insisted that, in legislating for new countries where it does not exist there is no just rule other than that of moral and abstract right! With reference to those new countries, those maxims as to the right of a people to "life, liberty, and the pursuit of happiness" were the just rules to be constantly referred to. There is no misunderstanding this, except by men interested to misunderstand it. I take it that I have to address an intelligent and reading community, who will peruse what I say, weigh it, and then judge whether I advanced improper or unsound views, or whether I advanced hypocritical, and deceptive, and contrary views in different portions of the country. I believe myself to be guilty of no such thing as the latter, though, of course, I cannot claim that I am entirely free from all error in the opinions I advance.

The Judge has also detained us awhile in regard to the distinction between his party and our party. His he assumes to be a national party,—ours a sectional one. He does this in asking the question whether this country has any interest in the maintenance of the Republican party. He assumes that our party is altogether sectional, that the party to which he adheres is national; and the argument is, that no party can be a rightful party—can be based upon rightful principles— unless it can announce its principles everywhere. I presume that Judge Douglas could not go into Russia and announce the doctrine of our national Democracy; he could not denounce the doctrine of kings and emperors and monarchies in Russia; and it may be true of this country that in some places we may not be able to proclaim a doctrine as clearly true as the truth of democracy, because there is a section so directly opposed to it that they will not tolerate us in doing so. Is it the true test of the soundness of a doctrine that in some places people won't let you proclaim it? Is that the way to test the truth of any doctrine? Why, I understood that at one time the people of Chicago would not let Judge Douglas preach a certain favorite doctrine of his. I commend to his consideration the question whether he takes that as a test of the unsoundness of what he wanted to preach.

There is another thing to which I wish to ask attention for a little while on this occasion. What has always been the evidence brought forward to prove that the Republican party is a sectional party? The main one was that in the Southern portion of the Union the people did not let the Republicans proclaim their doctrines amongst them. That has been the main evidence brought forward,—that they had no supporters, or substantially none, in the slave States. The South have not taken hold of our principles as we announce them; nor does Judge Douglas now grapple with those principles. We have a Republican State Platform, laid down in Springfield in June last, stating our position all the way through the questions before the country. We are now far advanced in this canvass. Judge Douglas and I have made perhaps forty speeches apiece, and we have now for the fifth time met face to face in debate, and up to this day I have not found either Judge Douglas or any friend of his taking hold of the Republican platform, or laying his finger upon anything in it that is wrong. I ask you all to recollect that. Judge Douglas turns away from the platform of principles to the fact that he can find people somewhere who will not allow us to announce those principles. If he had great confidence that our principles were wrong, he would take hold of them and demonstrate them to be wrong. But he does not do so. The only evidence he has of their being wrong is in the fact that there are people who won't allow us to preach them. I ask again, is that the way to test the soundness of a doctrine?

I ask his attention also to the fact that by the rule of nationality he is himself fast becoming sectional. I ask his attention to the fact that his speeches would not go as current now south of the Ohio River as they have formerly gone there. I ask his attention to the fact that he felicitates himself to-day that all the Democrats of the free States are agreeing with him, while he omits to tell us that the Democrats of any slave State agree with him. If he has not thought of this, I commend to his consideration the evidence in his own declaration, on this day, of his becoming sectional too. I see it rapidly approaching. Whatever may be the result of this ephemeral contest between Judge Douglas and myself, I see the day rapidly approaching when his pill of sectionalism, which he has been thrusting down the throats of Republicans for years past, will be crowded down his own throat.

Now, in regard to what Judge Douglas said (in the beginning of his speech) about the Compromise of 1850 containing the principle of the Nebraska Bill, although I have often presented my views upon that subject, yet as I have not done so in this canvass, I will, if you please, detain you a little with them. I have always maintained, so far as I was able, that there was nothing of the principle of the Nebraska Bill in the Compromise of 1850 at all,—nothing whatever. Where can you find the principle of the Nebraska Bill in that Compromise? If anywhere, in the two pieces of the Compromise organizing the Territories of New Mexico and Utah. It was expressly provided in these two acts that when they came to be admitted into the Union they should be admitted with or without slavery, as they should choose, by their own constitutions. Nothing was said in either of those acts as to what was to be done in relation to slavery during the Territorial existence of those Territories, while Henry Clay constantly made the declaration (Judge Douglas recognizing him as a leader) that, in his opinion, the old Mexican laws would control that question during the Territorial existence, and that these old Mexican laws excluded slavery. How can that be used as a principle for declaring that during the Territorial existence as well as at the time of framing the constitution, the people, if you please, might have slaves if they wanted them? I am not discussing the question whether it is right or wrong; but how are the New Mexican and Utah laws patterns for the Nebraska Bill? I maintain that the organization of Utah and New Mexico *did not* establish a general principle at all. It had no feature of establishing a general principle. The acts to which I have referred were a part of a general system of Compromises. They did not lay down what was proposed as a regular policy for the Territories, only an agreement in this particular case to do in that way, because other things were done that were to be a compensation for it. They were allowed to come in in that shape, because in another way it was paid for,—considering that as a part of that system of measures called the Compromise of 1850, which finally included half-a-dozen acts. It included the admission of California as a free State, which was kept out of the Union for half a year because it had formed a free constitution. It included the settlement of the boundary of Texas, which had been undefined before, which was in itself a slavery question; for if you pushed the line farther west, you made Texas larger, and made more slave territory; while, if you drew the line toward the east, you narrowed the boundary and diminished the domain of slavery, and by so much increased free territory. It included the abolition of the slave trade in the District of Columbia. It included the passage of a new Fugitive Slave law. All these things were put together, and though passed in separate acts, were nevertheless, in legislation (as the speeches at the time will show), made to depend upon each other. Each got votes with the understanding that the other measures were to pass, and by this system of compromise, in that series of measures, those two bills—the New Mexico and Utah bills—were passed: and I say for that reason they could not be taken as models, framed upon their own intrinsic principle, for all future Territories. And I have the evidence of this in the fact that Judge Douglas, a year afterward, or more than a year afterward, perhaps, when he first introduced bills for the purpose of framing new Territories, did not attempt to follow these bills of New Mexico and Utah; and even when he introduced this Nebraska Bill, I think you will discover that he did not exactly follow them. But I do not wish to dwell at great length upon this branch of the discussion. My own opinion is, that a thorough investigation will show most plainly that the New Mexico and Utah bills were part of a system of compromise, and not designed as patterns for future Territorial legislation; and that this Nebraska Bill did not follow them as a pattern at all.

The Judge tells, in proceeding, that he is opposed to making any odious distinctions between free and slave States. I am altogether unaware that the Republicans are in favor of making any odious distinctions between the Free and slave States. But there is still a difference, I think, between Judge Douglas and the Republicans in this. I suppose that the real difference between Judge Douglas and his friends, and the Republicans on the contrary, is, that the Judge is not in favor of making any difference between slavery and liberty; that he is in favor of eradicating, of pressing out of view, the questions of preference in this country for free or slave institutions; and consequently every sentiment he utters discards the idea that there is any wrong in slavery. Everything that emanates from him or his coadjutors in their course of policy carefully excludes the thought that there is anything wrong in slavery. All their arguments, if you will consider them, will be seen to exclude the thought that there is anything whatever wrong in slavery. If you will take the Judge's speeches, and select the short and pointed sentences expressed by him,—as his declaration that he "don't care whether slavery is voted up or down," you will see at once that this is perfectly logical, if you do not admit that slavery is wrong. If you do admit that it is wrong, Judge Douglas cannot logically say he don't care whether a wrong is voted up or voted down. Judge Douglas declares that if any community wants slavery they have a right to have it. He can say that logically, if he says that there is no wrong in slavery; but if you admit that there is a wrong in it, he cannot logically say that anybody has a right to do wrong. He insists that upon the score of equality the owners of slaves and owners of property—of horses and every other sort of property—should be alike, and hold them alike in a new Territory. That is perfectly logical if the two species of property are alike and are equally founded in right. But if you admit that one of them is wrong, you cannot institute any equality between right and wrong. And from this difference of sentiment,—the belief on the part of one that the institution is wrong, and a policy springing from that belief which looks to the arrest of the enlargement of that wrong, and this other sentiment, that it is no wrong, and a policy sprung from that sentiment, which will tolerate no idea of preventing the wrong from growing larger, and looks to there never being an end to it through all the existence of things,—arises the real difference between Judge Douglas and his friends on the one hand and the Republicans on the other. Now, I confess myself as belonging to that class in the country who contemplate slavery as a moral, social, and political evil, having due regard for its actual existence amongst us and the difficulties of getting rid of it in any satisfactory way, and to all the constitutional obligations which have been thrown about it; but, nevertheless, desire a policy that looks to the prevention of it as a wrong, and looks hopefully to the time when as a wrong it may come to an end.

Judge Douglas has again, for, I believe, the fifth time, if not the seventh, in my presence, reiterated his charge of a conspiracy or combination between the National Democrats and Republicans. What evidence Judge Douglas has upon this subject I know not, inasmuch as he never favors us with any. I have said upon a former occasion, and I do not choose to suppress it now, that I have no objection to the division in the Judge's party. He got it up himself. It was all his and their work. He had, I think, a great deal more to do with the steps that led to the Lecompton Constitution than Mr. Buchanan had; though at last, when they reached it, they quarrelled over it, and their friends divided upon it. I am very free to confess to Judge Douglas that I have no objection to the division; but I defy the Judge to show any evidence that I have in any way promoted that division, unless he insists on being a witness himself in merely saying so. I can give all fair friends of Judge Douglas here to understand exactly the view that Republicans take in regard to that division. Don't you remember how two years ago the opponents of the Democratic party were divided between Fremont and Fillmore? I guess you do. Any Democrat who remembers that division will remember also that he was at the time very glad of it, and then he will be able to see all there is between the National Democrats and the Republicans. What we now think of the two divisions of Democrats, you then thought of the Fremont and Fillmore divisions. That is all there is of it.

But if the Judge continues to put forward the declaration that there is an unholy and unnatural alliance between the Republicans and the National Democrats, I now want to enter my protest against receiving him as an entirely competent witness upon that subject. I want to call to the Judge's attention an attack he made upon me in the first one of these debates, at Ottawa, on the 21st of August. In order to fix extreme Abolitionism upon me, Judge Douglas read a set of resolutions which he declared had been passed by a Republican State Convention, in October, 1854, at Springfield, Illinois, and he declared I had taken part in that Convention. It turned out that although a few men calling themselves an anti-Nebraska State Convention had sat at Springfield about that time, yet neither did I take any part in it, nor did it pass the resolutions or any such resolutions as Judge Douglas read. So apparent had it become that the resolutions which he read had not been passed at Springfield at all, nor by a State Convention in which I had taken part, that seven days afterward, at Freeport, Judge Douglas declared that he had been misled by Charles H. Lanphier, editor of the *State Register,* and Thomas L. Harris, member of Congress in that District, and he promised in that speech that when he went to Springfield he would investigate the matter. Since then Judge Douglas has been to Springfield, and I presume has made the investigation; but a month has passed since he has been there, and, so far as I know, he has made no report of the result of his investigation. I have waited as I think sufficient time for the report of that investigation, and I have some curiosity to see and hear it. A fraud, an absolute forgery was committed, and the perpetration of it was traced to the three,—Lanphier, Harris, and Douglas. Whether it can be narrowed in any way so as to exonerate any one of them, is what Judge Douglas's report would probably show.

It is true that the set of resolutions read by Judge Douglas were published in the Illinois *State Register* on the 16th of October, 1854, as being the resolutions of an anti-Nebraska Convention which had sat in that same month of October, at Springfield. But it is also true that the publication in the *Register* was a forgery then, and the question is still behind, which of the three, if not all of them, committed that forgery. The idea that it was done by mistake is absurd. The article in the Illinois *State Register* contains part of the real proceedings of that Springfield Convention showing that the writer of the article had the real proceedings before him, and purposely threw out the genuine resolutions passed by the Convention, and fraudulently substituted the others. Lanphier then, as now, was the editor of the *Register,* so that there seems to be but little room for his escape. But then it is to be borne in mind that Lanphier had less interest in the object of that forgery than either of the other two. The main object of that forgery at that time was to beat Yates and elect Harris to Congress, and that object was known to be exceedingly dear to Judge Douglas at that time. Harris and Douglas were both in Springfield when the Convention was in session, and although they both left before the fraud appeared in the *Register,* subsequent events show that they have both had their eyes fixed upon that Convention.

The fraud having been apparently successful upon the occasion, both Harris and Douglas have more than once since then been attempting to put it to new uses. As the fisherman's wife, whose drowned husband was brought home with his body full of eels, said when she was asked what was to be done with him, *"Take the eels out and set him again,"* so Harris and Douglas have shown a disposition to take the eels out of that stale fraud by which they gained Harris's election, and set the fraud again more than once. On the 9th of July, 1856, Douglas attempted a repetition of it upon Trumbull on the floor of the Senate of the United States, as will appear from the appendix of the *Congressional Globe* of that date.

On the 9th of August, Harris attempted it again upon Norton in the House of Representatives, as will appear by the same documents,—the appendix to the *Congressional Globe* of that date. On the 21st of August last, all three—Lanphier, Douglas, and Harris—reattempted it upon me at Ottawa. It has been clung to and played out again and again as an exceedingly high trump by this blessed trio. And now that it has been discovered publicly to be a fraud we find that Judge Douglas manifests no surprise at it at all. He makes no complaint of Lanphier, who must have known it to be a fraud from the beginning. He, Lanphier, and Harris are just as cosey now and just as active in the concoction of new schemes as they were before the general discovery of this fraud. Now, all this is very natural if they are all alike guilty in that fraud, and it is very unnatural if any one of them is innocent. Lanphier perhaps insists that the rule of honor among thieves does not quite require him to take all upon himself, and consequently my friend Judge Douglas finds it difficult to make a satisfactory report upon his investigation. But meanwhile the three are agreed that each is *"a most honorable man."*

Judge Douglas requires an indorsement of his truth and honor by a re-election to the United States Senate, and he makes and reports against me and against Judge Trumbull, day after day, charges which we know to be utterly untrue, without for a moment seeming to think that this one unexplained fraud, which he promised to investigate, will be the least drawback to his claim to belief. Harris ditto. He asks a re-election to the lower House of Congress without seeming to remember at all that he is involved in this dishonorable fraud! The Illinois *State Register*, edited by Lanphier, then, as now, the central organ of both Harris and Douglas, continues to din the public ear with this assertion, without seeming to suspect that these assertions are at all lacking in title to belief.

After all, the question still recurs upon us. How did that fraud originally get into the *State Register*? Lanphier then, as now, was the editor of that paper. Lanphier knows. Lanphier cannot be ignorant of how and by whom it was originally concocted. Can he be induced to tell, or, if he has told, can Judge Douglas be induced to tell how it originally was concocted? It may be true that Lanphier insists that the two men for whose benefit it was originally devised shall at least bear their share of it! How that is, I do not know, and while it remains unexplained I hope to be pardoned if I insist that the mere fact of Judge Douglas making charges against Trumbull and myself is not quite sufficient evidence to establish them!

While we were at Freeport, in one of these joint discussions, I answered certain interrogatories which Judge Douglas had propounded to me, and then in turn propounded some to him, which he in a sort of way answered. The third one of these interrogatories I have with me, and wish now to make some comments upon it. It was in these words: "If the Supreme Court of the United States shall decide that the States cannot exclude slavery from their limits, are you in favor of acquiescing in, adhering to, and following such decision as a rule of political action?"

To this interrogatory Judge Douglas made no answer in any just sense of the word. He contented himself with sneering at the thought that it was possible for the Supreme Court ever to make such a decision. He sneered at me for propounding the interrogatory. I had not propounded it without some reflection, and I wish now to address to this audience some remarks upon it.

In the second clause of the sixth article, I believe it is, of the Constitution of the United States, we find the following language:

> This Constitution and the laws of the United States which shall be made in pursuance thereof, and all treaties made, or which shall be made, under the authority of the United States, shall be the supreme law of the land; and the judges in every State shall be bound thereby, anything in the Constitution or laws of any State to the contrary notwithstanding.

The essence of the Dred Scott case is compressed into the sentence which I will now read: "Now, as we have already said in an earlier part of this opinion, upon a different point, the right of property in a slave is distinctly and expressly affirmed in the Constitution." I repeat it, *The right of property in a slave is distinctly and expressly affirmed in the Constitution*! What is it to be "*affirmed*" in the Constitution? Made firm in the Constitution,—so made that it cannot be separated from the Constitution without breaking the Constitution; durable as the Constitution, and part of the Constitution. Now, remembering the provision of the Constitution which I have read—affirming that that instrument is the supreme law of the land; that the judges of every State shall be bound by it, any law or constitution of any State to the contrary notwithstanding; that the right of property in a slave is affirmed in that Constitution, is made, formed into, and cannot be separated from it without breaking it; durable as the instrument; part of the instrument;—what follows as a short and even syllogistic argument from it? I think it follows, and I submit to the consideration of men capable of arguing whether, as I state it, in syllogistic form, the argument has any fault in it:

Nothing in the Constitution or laws of any State can destroy a right distinctly and expressly affirmed in the Constitution of the United States.

The right of property in a slave is distinctly and expressly affirmed in the Constitution of the United States.

Therefore, nothing in the Constitution or laws of any State can destroy the right of property in a slave.

I believe that no fault can be pointed out in that argument; assuming the truth of the premises, the conclusion, so far as I have capacity at all to understand it, follows inevitably. There is a fault in it as I think, but the fault is not in the reasoning; but the falsehood in fact is a fault of the premises. I believe that the right of property in a slave *is not* distinctly and expressly affirmed in the Constitution, and Judge Douglas thinks it *is*. I believe that the Supreme Court and the advocates of that decision may search in vain for the place in the Constitution where the right of property in a slave is distinctly and expressly affirmed. I say, therefore, that I think one of the premises is not true in fact. But it is true with Judge Douglas. It is true with the Supreme Court who pronounced it. They are stopped from denying it, and being stopped from denying it, the conclusion follows that, the Constitution of the United States being the supreme law, no constitution or law can interfere with it. It being affirmed in the decision that the right of property in a slave is distinctly and expressly affirmed in the Constitution, the conclusion inevitably follows that no State law or constitution can destroy that right. I then say to Judge Douglas and to all others that I think it will take a better answer than a sneer to show that those who have said that the right of property in a slave is distinctly and expressly affirmed in the Constitution, are not prepared to show that no constitution or law can destroy that right. I say I believe it will take a far better argument than a mere sneer to show to the minds of intelligent men that whoever has so said is not prepared, whenever public sentiment is so far advanced as to justify it, to say the other. This is but an opinion, and the opinion of one very humble man; but it is my opinion that the Dred Scott decision, as it is, never would have been made in its present form if the party that made it had not been sustained previously by the elections. My own opinion is, that the new Dred Scott decision, deciding against the right of the people of the States to exclude slavery, will never be made if that party is not sustained by the elections.

I believe, further, that it is just as sure to be made as to-morrow is to come, if that party shall be sustained. I have said, upon a former occasion, and I repeat it now, that the course of argument that Judge Douglas makes use of upon this subject (I charge not his motives in this), is preparing the public mind for that new Dred Scott decision. I have asked him again to point out to me the reasons for his first adherence to the Dred Scott decision as it is. I have turned his attention to the fact that General Jackson differed with him in regard to the political obligation of a Supreme Court decision. I have asked his attention to the fact that Jefferson differed with him in regard to the political obligation of a Supreme Court decision. Jefferson said that "Judges are as honest as other men, and not more so." And he said, substantially, that whenever a free people should give up in absolute submission to any department of government, retaining for themselves no appeal from it, their liberties were gone. I have asked his attention to the fact that the Cincinnati platform, upon which he says he stands, disregards a time-honored decision of the Supreme Court, in denying the power of Congress to establish a National Bank. I have asked his attention to the fact that he himself was one of the most active instruments at one time in breaking down the Supreme Court of the State of Illinois because it had made a decision distasteful to him,—a struggle ending in the remarkable circumstance of his sitting down as one of the new Judges who were to overslaugh that decision; getting his title of Judge in that very way.

So far in this controversy I can get no answer at all from Judge Douglas upon these subjects. Not one can I get from him, except that he swells himself up and says, "All of us who stand by the decision of the Supreme Court are the friends of the Constitution; all you fellows that dare question it in any way are the enemies of the Constitution." Now, in this very devoted adherence to this decision, in opposition to all the great political leaders whom he has recognized as leaders, in opposition to his former self and history, there is something very marked. And the manner in which he adheres to it,—not as being right upon the merits, as he conceives (because he did not discuss that at all), but as being absolutely obligatory upon every one simply because of the source from whence it comes, as that which no man can gainsay, whatever it may be,—this is another marked feature of his adherence to that decision. It marks it in this respect, that it commits him to the next decision, whenever it comes, as being as obligatory as this one, since he does not investigate it, and won't inquire whether this opinion is right or wrong. So he takes the next one without inquiring whether *it* is right or wrong. He teaches men this doctrine, and in so doing prepares the public mind to take the next decision when it comes, without any inquiry. In this I think I argue fairly (without questioning motives at all) that Judge Douglas is most ingeniously and powerfully preparing the public mind to take that decision when it comes; and not only so, but he is doing it in various other ways. In these general maxims about liberty, in his assertions that he "don't care whether slavery is voted up or voted down"; that "whoever wants slavery has a right to have it"; that "upon principles of equality it should be allowed to go everywhere"; that "there is no inconsistency between free and slave institutions"—in this he is also preparing (whether purposely or not) the way for making the institution of slavery national! I repeat again, for I wish no misunderstanding, that I do not charge that he means it so; but I call upon your minds to inquire, if you were going to get the best instrument you could, and then set it to work in the most ingenious way, to prepare the public mind for this movement, operating in the free States, where there is now an abhorrence of the institution of slavery, could you find an instrument so capable of doing it as Judge Douglas, or one employed in so apt a way to do it?

I have said once before, and I will repeat it now, that Mr. Clay, when he was once answering an objection to the Colonization Society, that it had a tendency to the ultimate emancipation of the slaves, said that:

> those who would repress all tendencies to liberty and ultimate emancipation must do more than put down the benevolent efforts of the Colonization Society: they must go back to the era of our liberty and independence, and muzzle the cannon that thunders its annual joyous return; they must blow out the moral lights around us; they must penetrate the human soul, and eradicate the light of reason and the love of liberty!

And I do think—I repeat, though I said it on a former occasion—that Judge Douglas and whoever, like him, teaches that the negro has no share, humble though it may be, in the Declaration of Independence, is going back to the era of our liberty and independence, and, so far as in him lies, muzzling the cannon that thunders its annual joyous return; that he is blowing out the moral lights around us, when he contends that whoever wants slaves has a right to hold them; that he is penetrating, so far as lies in his power, the human soul, and eradicating the light of reason and the love of liberty, when he is in every possible way preparing the public mind, by his vast influence, for making the institution of slavery perpetual and national.

There is, my friends, only one other point to which I will call your attention for the remaining time that I have left me, and perhaps I shall not occupy the entire time that I have, as that one point may not take me clear through it.

Among the interrogatories that Judge Douglas propounded to me at Freeport, there was one in about this language: "Are you opposed to the acquisition of any further territory to the United States, unless slavery shall first be prohibited therein?" I answered, as I thought, in this way: that I am not generally opposed to the acquisition of additional territory, and that I would support a proposition for the acquisition of additional territory according as my supporting it was or was not calculated to aggravate this slavery question amongst us. I then proposed to Judge Douglas another interrogatory, which was correlative to that: "Are you in favor of acquiring additional territory, in disregard of how it may affect us upon the slavery question?" Judge Douglas answered,—that is, in his own way he answered it. I believe that, although he took a good many words to answer it, it was a little more fully answered than any other. The substance of his answer was that this country would continue to expand; that it would need additional territory; that it was as absurd to suppose that we could continue upon our present territory, enlarging in population as we are, as it would be to hoop a boy twelve years of age, and expect him to grow to man's size without bursting the hoops. I believe it was something like, that. Consequently, he was in favor of the acquisition of further territory as fast as we might need it, in disregard of how it might affect the slavery question. I do not say this as giving his exact language, but he said so substantially; and he would leave the question of slavery, where the territory was acquired, to be settled by the people of the acquired territory. ["That's the doctrine."] May be it is; let us consider that for a while. This will probably, in the run of things, become one of the concrete manifestations of this slavery question. If Judge Douglas's policy upon this question succeeds, and gets fairly settled down, until all opposition is crushed out, the next thing will be a grab for the territory of poor Mexico, an invasion of the rich lands of South America, then the adjoining islands will follow, each one of which promises additional slave-fields. And this question is to be left to the people of those countries for settlement. When we get Mexico, I don't know whether the Judge will be in favor of the Mexican people that we get with it settling that question for themselves and all others; because we know the Judge has a great horror for mongrels, and I understand that the people of Mexico are most decidedly a race of mongrels. I understand that there is not more than one person there out of eight who is pure white, and I suppose from the Judge's previous declaration that when we get Mexico, or any considerable portion of it, that he will be in favor of these mongrels settling the question, which would bring him somewhat into collision with his horror of an inferior race.

It is to be remembered, though, that this power of acquiring additional territory is a power confided to the President and the Senate of the United States.

It is a power not under the control of the representatives of the people any further than they, the President and the Senate, can be considered the representatives of the people. Let me illustrate that by a case we have in our history. When we acquired the territory from Mexico in the Mexican War, the House of Representatives, composed of the immediate representatives of the people, all the time insisted that the territory thus to be acquired should be brought in upon condition that slavery should be forever prohibited therein, upon the terms and in the language that slavery had been prohibited from coming into this country. That was insisted upon constantly and never failed to call forth an assurance that any territory thus acquired should have that prohibition in it, so far as the House of Representatives was concerned. But at last the President and Senate acquired the territory without asking the House of Representatives anything about it, and took it without that prohibition. They have the power of acquiring territory without the immediate representatives of the people being called upon to say anything about it, and thus furnishing a very apt and powerful means of bringing new territory into the Union, and, when it is once brought into the country, involving us anew in this slavery agitation. It is therefore, as I think, a very important question for the consideration of the American people, whether the policy of bringing in additional territory, without considering at all how it will operate upon the safety of the Union in reference to this one great disturbing element in our national politics, shall be adopted as the policy of the country. You will bear in mind that it is to be acquired, according to the Judge's view, as fast as it is needed, and the indefinite part of this proposition is that we have only Judge Douglas and his class of men to decide how fast it is needed. We have no clear and certain way of determining or demonstrating how fast territory is needed by the necessities of the country. Whoever wants to go out filibustering, then, thinks that more territory is needed. Whoever wants wider slave-fields feels sure that some additional territory is needed as slave territory. Then it is as easy to show the necessity of additional slave-territory as it is to assert anything that is incapable of absolute demonstration. Whatever motive a man or a set of men may have for making annexation of property or territory, it is very easy to assert, but much less easy to disprove, that it is necessary for the wants of the country.

And now it only remains for me to say that I think it is a very grave question for the people of this Union to consider, whether, in view of the fact that this slavery question has been the only one that has ever endangered our Republican institutions, the only one that has ever threatened or menaced a dissolution of the Union, that has ever disturbed us in such a way as to make us fear for the perpetuity of our liberty,—in view of these facts, I think it is an exceedingly interesting and important question for this people to consider whether we shall engage in the policy of acquiring additional territory, discarding altogether from our consideration, while obtaining new territory, the question how it may affect us in regard to this, the only endangering element to our liberties and national greatness. The Judge's view has been expressed. I, in my answer to his question, have expressed mine. I think it will become an important and practical question. Our views are before the public. I am willing and anxious that they should consider them fully; that they should turn it about and consider the importance of the question, and arrive at a just conclusion as to whether it is or is not wise in the people of this Union, in the acquisition of new territory, to consider whether it will add to the disturbance that is existing amongst us—whether it will add to the one only danger that has ever threatened the perpetuity of the Union or our own liberties. I think it is extremely important that they shall decide, and rightly decide, that question before entering upon that policy.

And now, my friends, having said the little I wish to say upon this head, whether I have occupied the whole of the remnant of my time or not, I believe I could not enter upon any new topic so as to treat it fully, without transcending my time, which I would not for a moment think of doing. I give way to Judge Douglas.

### Mr. Douglas's Rejoinder

GENTLEMEN: The highest compliment you can pay me during the brief half-hour that I have to conclude is by observing a strict silence. I desire to be heard rather than to be applauded.

The first criticism that Mr. Lincoln makes on my speech was that it was in substance what I have said everywhere else in the State where I have addressed the people. I wish I could say the same of his speech. Why, the reason I complain of him is because he makes one speech north, and another south—because he has one set of sentiments for the Abolition counties, and another set for the counties opposed to Abolitionism. My point of complaint against him is that I cannot induce him to hold up the same standard, to carry the same flag, in all parts of the State. He does not pretend, and no other man will, that I have one set of principles for Galesburgh, and another for Charleston. He does not pretend that I hold to one doctrine in Chicago, and an opposite one in Jonesboro. I have proved that he has a different set of principles for each of these localities. All I asked of him was that he should deliver the speech that he has made here to-day in Coles County instead of in old Knox. It would have settled the question between us in that doubtful county. Here I understand him to reaffirm the doctrine of negro equality, and to assert that by the Declaration of Independence the negro is declared equal to the white man. He tells you to-day that the negro was included in the Declaration of Independence when it asserted that all men were created equal. ["We believe it."] Very well.

Mr. Lincoln asserts to-day, as he did at Chicago, that the negro was included in that clause of the Declaration of Independence which says that all men were created equal and endowed by the Creator with certain inalienable rights, among which are life, liberty, and the pursuit of happiness. If the negro was made his equal and mine, if that equality was established by divine law, and was the negro's inalienable right, how came he to say at Charleston to the Kentuckians residing in that section of our State that the negro was physically inferior to the white man, belonged to an inferior race, and he was for keeping him in that inferior condition. There he gave the people to understand that there was no moral question involved, because, the inferiority being established, it was only a question of degree, and not a question of right; here, to-day, instead of making it a question of degree, he makes it a moral question; says that it is a great crime to hold the negro in that inferior condition. ["He's right."] Is he right now, or was he right in Charleston? ["Both."] He is right, then, sir, in your estimation, not because he is consistent, but because he can trim his principles any way, in any section, so as to secure votes. All I desire of him is that he will declare the same principles in the south that he does in the north.

But did you notice how he answered my position that a man should hold the same doctrines throughout the length and breadth of this Republic? He said, "Would Judge Douglas go to Russia and proclaim the same principles he does here?" I would remind him that Russia is not under the American Constitution. If Russia was a part of the American Republic, under our Federal Constitution, and I was sworn to support the Constitution, I would maintain the same doctrine in Russia that I do in Illinois. The slaveholding States are governed by the same Federal Constitution as ourselves, and hence a man's principles, in order to be in harmony with the Constitution, must be the same in the South as they are in the North, the same in the free States as they are in the slave States. Whenever a man advocates one set of principles in one section, and another set in another section, his opinions are in violation of the spirit of the Constitution which he has sworn to support. When Mr. Lincoln went to Congress in 1847 and, laying his hand upon the Holy Evangelists, made a solemn vow, in the presence of high Heaven, that he would be faithful to the Constitution, what did he mean,—the Constitution as he expounds it in Galesburgh, or the Constitution as he expounds it in Charleston?

Mr. Lincoln has devoted considerable time to the circumstance that at Ottawa I read a series of resolutions as having been adopted at Springfield, in this State, on the 4th or 5th of October, 1854, which happened not to have been adopted there. He has used hard names; has dared to talk about fraud, about forgery, and has insinuated that there was a conspiracy between Mr. Lanphier, Mr. Harris, and myself to perpetrate a forgery. Now, bear in mind that he does not deny that these resolutions were adopted in a majority of all the Republican counties of this State in that year; he does not deny that they were declared to be the platform of this Republican party in the first Congressional District, in the second, in the third, and in many counties of the fourth, and that they thus became the platform of his party in a majority of the counties upon which he now relies for support; he does not deny the truthfulness of the resolutions, but takes exception to the *spot* on which they were adopted. He takes to himself great merit because he thinks they were not adopted on the right spot for me to use them against him, just as he was very severe in Congress upon the Government of his country when he thought that he had discovered that the Mexican War was not begun in the right *spot*, and was therefore unjust. He tries very hard to make out that there is something very extraordinary in the place where the thing was done, and not in the thing itself. I never believed before that Abraham Lincoln would be guilty of what he has done this day in regard to those resolutions. In the first place, the moment it was intimated to me that they had been adopted at Aurora and Rockford instead of Springfield, I did not wait for him to call my attention to the fact, but led off, and explained in my first meeting after the Ottawa debate what the mistake was, and how it had been made. I supposed that for an honest man, conscious of his own rectitude, that explanation would be sufficient. I did not wait for him, after the mistake was made, to call my attention to it, but frankly explained it at once as an honest man would. I also gave the authority on which I had stated that these resolutions were adopted by the Springfield Republican Convention; that I had seen them quoted by Major Harris in a debate in Congress, as having been adopted by the first Republican State Convention in Illinois, and that I had written to him and asked him for the authority as to the time and place of their adoption; that, Major Harris being extremely ill, Charles H. Lanphier had written to me, for him, that they were adopted at Springfield on the 5th of October, 1854, and had sent me a copy of the Springfield paper containing them. I read them from the newspaper just as Mr. Lincoln reads the proceedings of meetings held years ago from the newspapers. After giving that explanation, I did not think there was an honest man in the State of Illinois who doubted that I had been led into the error, if it was such, innocently, in the way I detailed; and I will now say that I do not now believe that there is an honest man on the face of the globe who will not regard with abhorrence and disgust Mr. Lincoln's insinuations of my complicity in that forgery, if it was a forgery. Does Mr. Lincoln wish to push these things to the point of personal difficulties here? I commenced this contest by treating him courteously and kindly; I always spoke of him in words of respect; and in return he has sought and is now seeking to divert public attention from the enormity of his revolutionary principles by impeaching men's sincerity and integrity, and inviting personal quarrels.

I desired to conduct this contest with him like a gentleman; but I spurn the insinuation of complicity and fraud made upon the simple circumstance of an editor of a newspaper having made a mistake as to the place where a thing was done, but not as to the thing itself. These resolutions were the platform of this Republican party of Mr. Lincoln's of that year. They were adopted in a majority of the Republican counties in the State; and when I asked him at Ottawa whether they formed the platform upon which he stood, he did not answer, and I could not get an answer out of him. He then thought, as I thought, that those resolutions were adopted at the Springfield Convention, but excused himself by saying that he was not there when they were adopted, but had gone to Tazewell court in order to avoid being present at the Convention. He saw them published as having been adopted at Springfield, and so did I, and he knew that if there was a mistake in regard to them, that I had nothing under heaven to do with it. Besides, you find that in all these northern counties where the Republican candidates are running pledged to him, that the conventions which nominated them adopted that identical platform. One cardinal point in that platform which he shrinks from is this: that there shall be no more slave States admitted into the Union, even if the people want them. Lovejoy stands pledged against the admission of any more slave States. ["Right, so do we."] So do you, you say. Farnsworth stands pledged against the admission of any more slave States. Washburne stands pledged the same way. The candidate for the Legislature who is running on Lincoln's ticket in Henderson and Warren stands committed by his vote in the Legislature to the same thing; and I am informed, but do not know of the fact, that your candidate here is also so pledged. ["Hurrah for him! Good!"] Now, you Republicans all hurrah for him, and for the doctrine of "no more slave States," and yet Lincoln tells you that his conscience will not permit him to sanction that doctrine, and complains because the resolutions I read at Ottawa made him, as a member of the party, responsible for sanctioning the doctrine of no more slave States. You are one way, you confess, and he is, or pretends to be, the other; and yet you are both governed by *principle* in supporting one another. If it be true, as I have shown it is, that the whole Republican party in the northern part of the State stands committed to the doctrine of no more slave States, and that this same doctrine is repudiated by the Republicans in the other part of the State,

I wonder whether Mr. Lincoln and his party do not present the case which he cited from the Scriptures, of a house divided against itself which cannot stand! I desire to know what are Mr. Lincoln's principles and the principles of his party. I hold, and the party with which I am identified hold, that the people of each State, old and new, have the right to decide the slavery question for themselves; and when I used the remark that I did not care whether slavery was voted up or down, I used it in the connection that I was for allowing Kansas to do just as she pleased on the slavery question. I said that I did not care whether they voted slavery up or down, because they had the right to do as they pleased on the question, and therefore my action would not be controlled by any such consideration. Why cannot Abraham Lincoln, and the party with which he acts, speak out their principles so that they may be understood? Why do they claim to be one thing in one part of the State, and another in the other part? Whenever I allude to the Abolition doctrines, which he considers a slander to be charged with being in favor of, you all indorse them, and hurrah for them, not knowing that your candidate is ashamed to acknowledge them.

I have a few words to say upon the Dred Scott decision, which has troubled the brain of Mr. Lincoln so much. He insists that that decision would carry slavery into the free States, notwithstanding that the decision says directly the opposite, and goes into a long argument to make you believe that I am in favor of, and would sanction, the doctrine that would allow slaves to be brought here and held as slaves contrary to our Constitution and laws. Mr. Lincoln knew better when he asserted this; he knew that one newspaper, and, so far as is within my knowledge, but one, ever asserted that doctrine, and that I was the first man in either House of Congress that read that article in debate, and denounced it on the floor of the Senate as revolutionary. When the Washington *Union,* on the 17th of last November, published an article to that effect, I branded it at once, and denounced it; and hence the *Union* has been pursuing me ever since. Mr. Toombs, of Georgia, replied to me, and said that there was not a man in any of the slave States south of the Potomac River that held any such doctrine. Mr. Lincoln knows that there is not a member of the Supreme Court who holds that doctrine; he knows that every one of them, as shown by their opinions, holds the reverse. Why this attempt, then, to bring the Supreme Court into disrepute among the people? It looks as if there was an effort being made to destroy public confidence in the highest judicial tribunal on earth. Suppose he succeeds in destroying public confidence in the court, so that the people will not respect its decisions, but will feel at liberty to disregard them and resist the laws of the land, what will he have gained? He will have changed the government from one of laws into that of a mob, in which the strong arm of violence will be substituted for the decisions of the courts of justice. He complains because I did not go into an argument reviewing Chief Justice Taney's opinion, and the other opinions of the different judges, to determine whether their reasoning is right or wrong on the questions of law. What use would that be? He wants to take an appeal from the Supreme Court to this meeting, to determine whether the questions of law were decided properly. He is going to appeal from the Supreme Court of the United States to every town meeting, in the hope that he can excite a prejudice against that court, and on the wave of that prejudice ride into the Senate of the United States, when he could not get there on his own principles or his own merits. Suppose he should succeed in getting into the Senate of the United States, what then will he have to do with the decision of the Supreme Court in the Dred Scott case? Can he reverse that decision when he gets there? Can he act upon it? Has the Senate any right to reverse it or revise it? He will not pretend that it has. Then why drag the matter into this contest, unless for the purpose of making a false issue, by which he can direct public attention from the real issue.

He has cited General Jackson in justification of the war he is making on the decision of the court. Mr. Lincoln misunderstands the history of the country if he believes there is any parallel in the two cases. It is true that the Supreme Court once decided that if a Bank of the United States was a necessary fiscal agent of the government, it was constitutional, and if not, that it was unconstitutional, and also, that whether or not it was necessary for that purpose was a political question for Congress, and not a judicial one for the courts to determine. Hence the court would not determine the bank unconstitutional. Jackson respected the decision, obeyed the law, executed it, and carried it into effect during its existence; but after the charter of the bank expired, and a proposition was made to create a new bank, General Jackson said, "It is unnecessary and improper, and therefore I am against it on constitutional grounds as well as those of expediency." Is Congress bound to pass every act that is constitutional? Why, there are a thousand things that are constitutional, but yet are inexpedient and unnecessary, and you surely would not vote for them merely because you had the right to? And because General Jackson would not do a thing which he had a right to do, but did not deem expedient or proper, Mr. Lincoln is going to justify himself in doing that which he has no right to do. I ask him whether he is not bound to respect and obey the decisions of the Supreme Court as well as I. The Constitution has created that court to decide all constitutional questions in the last resort; and when such decisions have been made, they become the law of the land, and you, and he, and myself, and every other good citizen, are bound by them. Yet he argues that I am bound by their decisions, and he is not. He says that their decisions are binding on Democrats, but not on Republicans. Are not Republicans bound by the laws of the land as well as Democrats? And when the court has fixed the construction of the Constitution on the validity of a given law, is not their decision binding upon Republicans as well as upon Democrats? Is it possible that you Republicans have the right to raise your mobs and oppose the laws of the land and the constituted authorities, and yet hold us Democrats bound to obey them? My time is within half a minute of expiring, and all I have to say is, that I stand by the laws of the land. I stand by the Constitution as our fathers made it, by the laws as they are enacted, and by the decisions of the court, upon all points within their jurisdiction, as they are pronounced by the highest tribunal on earth; and any man who resists these must resort to mob law and violence to overturn the government of laws.

# Sixth Joint Debate, at Quincy

## October 13, 1858

### Mr. Lincoln's Opening Speech

Ladies and Gentlemen: I have had no immediate conference with Judge Douglas, but I will venture to say that he and I will perfectly agree that your entire silence, both when I speak and when he speaks, will be most agreeable to us.

In the month of May, 1856, the elements in the State of Illinois which have since been consolidated into the Republican party assembled together in a State Convention at Bloomington. They adopted at that time what, in political language, is called a platform. In June of the same year the elements of the Republican party in the nation assembled together in a National Convention at Philadelphia. They adopted what is called the National Platform. In June, 1858,—the present year,—the Republicans of Illinois reassembled at Springfield, in State Convention, and adopted again their platform, as I suppose not differing in any essential particular from either of the former ones, but perhaps adding something in relation to the new developments of political progress in the country.

The Convention that assembled in June last did me the honor, if it be one, and I esteem it such, to nominate me as their candidate for the United States Senate. I have supposed that, in entering upon this canvass, I stood generally upon these platforms. We are now met together on the 13th of October of the same year, only four months from the adoption of the last platform, and I am unaware that in this canvass, from the beginning until to-day, any one of our adversaries has taken hold of our platforms, or laid his finger upon anything that he calls wrong in them.

In the very first one of these joint discussions between Senator Douglas and myself, Senator Douglas, without alluding at all to these platforms, or any one of them, of which I have spoken, attempted to hold me responsible for a set of resolutions passed long before the meeting of either one of these conventions of which I have spoken. And as a ground for holding me responsible for these resolutions, he assumed that they had been passed at a State Convention of the Republican party, and that I took part in that Convention. It was discovered afterward that this was erroneous, that the resolutions which he endeavored to hold me responsible for had not been passed by any State Convention anywhere, had not been passed at Springfield, where he supposed they had, or assumed that they had, and that they had been passed in no convention in which I had taken part. The Judge, nevertheless, was not willing to give up the point that he was endeavoring to make upon me, and he therefore thought to still hold me to the point that he was endeavoring to make, by showing that the resolutions that he read had been passed at a local convention in the northern part of the State, although it was not a local convention that embraced my residence at all, nor one that reached, as I suppose, nearer than one hundred and fifty or two hundred miles of where I was when it met, nor one in which I took any part at all. He also introduced other resolutions, passed at other meetings, and by combining the whole, although they were all antecedent to the two State Conventions and the one National Convention I have mentioned, still he insisted, and now insists, as I understand, that I am in some way responsible for them.

At Jonesboro, on our third meeting, I insisted to the Judge that I was in no way rightfully held responsible for the proceedings of this local meeting or convention, in which I had taken no part, and in which I was in no way embraced; but I insisted to him that if he thought I was responsible for every man or every set of men everywhere, who happen to be my friends, the rule ought to work both ways, and he ought to be responsible for the acts and resolutions of all men or sets of men who were or are now his supporters and friends, and gave him a pretty long string of resolutions, passed by men who are now his friends, and announcing doctrines for which he does not desire to be held responsible.

This still does not satisfy Judge Douglas. He still adheres to his proposition, that I am responsible for what some of my friends in different parts of the State have done, but that he is not responsible for what his have done. At least, so I understand him. But in addition to that, the Judge, at our meeting in Galesburgh, last week, undertakes to establish that I am guilty of a species of double dealing with the public; that I make speeches of a certain sort in the north, among the Abolitionists, which I would not make in the south, and that I make speeches of a certain sort in the south which I would not make in the north. I apprehend, in the course I have marked out for myself, that I shall not have to dwell at very great length upon this subject.

As this was done in the Judge's opening speech at Galesburgh, I had an opportunity, as I had the middle speech then, of saying something in answer to it. He brought forward a quotation or two from a speech of mine delivered at Chicago, and then, to contrast with it, he brought forward an extract from a speech of mine at Charleston, in which he insisted that I was greatly inconsistent, and insisted that his conclusion followed, that I was playing a double part, and speaking in one region one way, and in another region another way. I have not time now to dwell on this as long as I would like, and wish only now to requote that portion of my speech at Charleston which the Judge quoted, and then make some comments upon it. This he quotes from me as being delivered at Charleston, and I believe correctly:

> I will say, then, that I am not, nor ever have been, in favor of bringing about in any way the social and political equality of the white and black races; that I am not, nor ever have been, in favor of making voters or jurors of negroes, nor of qualifying them to hold office, nor to intermarry with white people; and I will say, in addition to this, that there is a physical difference between the white and black races which will forever forbid the two races living together on terms of social and political equality. And inasmuch as they cannot so live while they do remain together, there must be the position of superior and inferior. I am as much as any other man in favor of having the superior position assigned to the white race.

This, I believe, is the entire quotation from the Charleston speech, as Judge Douglas made it. His comments are as follows:

> Yes, here you find men who hurrah for Lincoln, and say he is right when he discards all distinction between races, or when he declares that he discards the doctrine that there is such a thing as a superior and inferior race; and Abolitionists are required and expected to vote for Mr. Lincoln because he goes for the equality of races, holding that in the Declaration of Independence the white man and negro were declared equal, and endowed by divine law with equality. And down South, with the old-line Whigs, with the Kentuckians, the Virginians, and the Tennesseeans, he tells you that there is a physical difference between the races, making the one superior, the other inferior, and he is in favor of maintaining the superiority of the white race over the negro.

Those are the Judges comments. Now, I wish to show you that a month, or only lacking three days of a month, before I made the speech at Charleston, which the Judge quotes from, he had himself heard me say substantially the same thing. It was in our first meeting, at Ottawa—and I will say a word about where it was, and the atmosphere it was in, after a while—but at our first meeting, at Ottawa, I read an extract from an old speech of mine, made nearly four years ago, not merely to show my sentiments, but to show that my sentiments were long entertained and openly expressed; in which extract I expressly declared that my own feelings would not admit a social and political equality between the white and black races, and that even if my own feelings would admit of it, I still knew that the public sentiment of the country would not, and that such a thing was an utter impossibility, or substantially that. That extract from my old speech the reporters by some sort of accident passed over, and it was not reported. I lay no blame upon anybody. I suppose they thought that I would hand it over to them, and dropped reporting while I was reading it, but afterward went away without getting it from me. At the end of that quotation from my old speech, which I read at Ottawa, I made the comments which were reported at that time, and which I will now read, and ask you to notice how very nearly they are the same as Judge Douglas says were delivered by me down in Egypt. After reading, I added these words:

> Now, gentlemen, I don't want to read at any great length; but this is the true complexion of all I have ever said in regard to the institution of slavery or the black race, and this is the whole of it: anything that argues me into his idea of perfect social and political equality with the negro, is but a specious and fantastical arrangement of words by which a man can prove a horse-chestnut to be a chestnut horse. I will say here, while upon this subject, that I have no purpose, directly or indirectly, to interfere with the institution in the States where it exists. I believe I have no right to do so. I have no inclination to do so. I have no purpose to introduce political and social equality between the white and black races. There is a physical difference between the two which, in my judgment, will probably forever forbid their living together on the footing of perfect equality; and inasmuch as it becomes a necessity that there must be a difference, I, as well as Judge Douglas, am in favor of the race to which I belong having the superior position. I have never said anything to the contrary, but I hold that, notwithstanding all this, there is no reason in the world why the negro is not entitled to all the rights enumerated in the Declaration of Independence,—the right of

life, liberty, and the pursuit of happiness. I hold that he is as much entitled to these as the white man. I agree with Judge Douglas that he is not my equal in many respects, certainly not in color, perhaps not in intellectual and moral endowments; but in the right to eat the bread, without the leave of anybody else, which his own hand earns, he is my equal and the equal of Judge Douglas, and the equal of every other man.

I have chiefly introduced this for the purpose of meeting the Judge's charge that the quotation he took from my Charleston speech was what I would say down South among the Kentuckians, the Virginians, etc., but would not say in the regions in which was supposed to be more of the Abolition element. I now make this comment: That speech from which I have now read the quotation, and which is there given correctly—perhaps too much so for good taste—was made away up North in the Abolition District of this State *par excellence*, in the Lovejoy District, in the personal presence of Lovejoy, for he was on the stand with us when I made it. It had been made and put in print in that region only three days less than a month before the speech made at Charleston, the like of which Judge Douglas thinks I would not make where there was any Abolition element. I only refer to this matter to say that I am altogether unconscious of having attempted any double-dealing anywhere; that upon one occasion I may say one thing, and leave other things unsaid, and *vice versa,* but that I have said anything on one occasion that is inconsistent with what I have said elsewhere, I deny,—at least I deny it so far as the intention is concerned. I find that I have devoted to this topic a larger portion of my time than I had intended. I wished to show, but I will pass it upon this occasion, that in the sentiment I have occasionally advanced upon the Declaration of Independence I am entirely borne out by the sentiments advanced by our old Whig leader, Henry Clay, and I have the book here to show it from; but because I have already occupied more time than I intended to do on that topic, I pass over it.

At Galesburgh, I tried to show that by the Dred Scott decision, pushed to its legitimate consequences, slavery would be established in all the States as well as in the Territories. I did this because, upon a former occasion, I had asked Judge Douglas whether, if the Supreme Court should make a decision declaring that the States had not the power to exclude slavery from their limits, he would adopt and follow that decision as a rule of political action; and because he had not directly answered that question, but had merely contented himself with sneering at it, I again introduced it, and tried to show that the conclusion that I stated followed inevitably and logically from the proposition already decided by the court. Judge Douglas had the privilege of replying to me at Galesburgh, and again he gave me no direct answer as to whether he would or would not sustain such a decision if made. I give him his third chance to say yes or no. He is not obliged to do either,— probably he will not do either; but I give him the third chance. I tried to show then that this result, this conclusion, inevitably followed from the point already decided by the court. The Judge, in his reply, again sneers at the thought of the court making any such decision, and in the course of his remarks upon this subject uses the language which I will now read. Speaking of me, the Judge says: "He goes on and insists that the Dred Scott decision would carry slavery into the free States, notwithstanding the decision itself says the contrary." And he adds: "Mr. Lincoln knows that there is no member of the Supreme Court that holds that doctrine. He knows that every one of them in their opinions held the reverse."

I especially introduce this subject again for the purpose of saying that I have the Dred Scott decision here, and I will thank Judge Douglas to lay his finger upon the place in the entire opinions of the court where any one of them "says the contrary." It is very hard to affirm a negative with entire confidence. I say, however, that I have examined that decision with a good deal of care, as a law-yer examines a decision, and, so far as I have been able to do so, the court has nowhere in its opinions said that the States have the power to exclude slavery, nor have they used other language saying substantially that. I also say, so far as I can find, not one of the concurring judges has said that the States can exclude slavery, nor said anything that was substantially that. The nearest approach that any one of them has made to it, so far as I can find, was by Judge Nelson, and the approach he made to it was exactly, in substance, the Nebraska Bill,—that the States had the exclusive power over the question of slavery, so far as they are not limited by the Constitution of the United States. I asked the question, therefore, if the non-concurring judges, McLean or Curtis, had asked to get an express declaration that the States could absolutely exclude slavery from their limits, what reason have we to believe that it would not have been voted down by the majority of the judges, just as Chase's amendment was voted down by Judge Douglas and his compeers when it was offered to the Nebraska Bill.

Also, at Galesburgh, I said something in regard to those Springfield resolu-tions that Judge Douglas had attempted to use upon me at Ottawa, and com-mented at some length upon the fact that they were, as presented, not genuine. Judge Douglas in his reply to me seemed to be somewhat exasperated. He said he would never have believed that Abraham Lincoln, as he kindly called me, would have attempted such a thing as I had attempted upon that occasion; and among other expressions which he used toward me, was that I dared to say forgery,— that I had *dared* to say forgery [turning to Judge Douglas]. Yes, Judge, I did dare to say forgery. But in this political canvass the Judge ought to remember that I was not the first who *dared* to say forgery. At Jacksonville, Judge Douglas made a speech in answer to something said by Judge Trumbull, and at the close of what he said upon that subject, he *dared* to say that Trumbull had forged his evidence. He said, too, that he should not concern himself with Trumbull any more, but thereafter he should hold Lincoln responsible for the slanders upon him. When I met him at Charleston after that, although I think that I should not have noticed the subject if he had not said he would hold me responsible for it, I spread out before him the statements of the evidence that Judge Trumbull had used, and I asked Judge Douglas, piece by piece, to put his finger upon one piece of all that evidence that he would say was a forgery! When I went through with each and every piece. Judge Douglas did not *dare* then to say that any piece of it was a forgery. So it seems that there are some things that Judge Douglas dares to do, and some that he dares not to do.

A VOICE: "It's the same thing with you."

MR. LINCOLN: Yes, sir, it's the same thing with me. I do dare to say forgery when it's true, and don't dare to say forgery when it's false. Now I will say here to this audience and to Judge Douglas I have not dared to say he committed a forgery, and I never shall until I know it; but I did dare to say—just to suggest to the Judge—that a forgery had been committed, which by his own showing had been traced to him and two of his friends. I dared to suggest to him that he had expressly promised in one of his public speeches to investigate that matter, and I dared to suggest to him that there was an implied promise that when he investigated it he would make known the result. I dared to suggest to the Judge that he could not expect to be quite clear of suspicion of that fraud, for since the time that promise was made he had been with those friends, and had not kept his promise in regard to the investigation and the report upon it. I am not a very daring man, but I dared that much, Judge, and I am not much scared about it yet. When the Judge says he wouldn't have believed of Abraham Lincoln that he would have made such an attempt as that he reminds me of the fact that he entered upon this canvass with the purpose to treat me courteously; that touched me somewhat. It sets me to thinking. I was aware, when it was first agreed that Judge Douglas and I were to have these seven joint discussions, that they were the successive acts of a drama, perhaps I should say, to be enacted, not merely in the face of audiences like this, but in the face of the nation, and to some extent, by my relation to him, and not from anything in myself, in the face of the world; and I am anxious that they should be conducted with dignity and in the good temper which would be befitting the vast audiences before which it was conducted. But when Judge Douglas got home from Washington and made his first speech in Chicago, the evening afterward I made some sort of a reply to it. His second speech was made at Bloomington, in which he commented upon my speech at Chicago and said that I had used language ingeniously contrived to conceal my intentions,—or words to that effect. Now, I understand that this is an imputation upon my veracity and my candor. I do not know what the Judge understood by it, but in our first discussion, at Ottawa, he led off by charging a bargain, somewhat corrupt in its character, upon Trumbull and myself,—that we had entered into a bargain, one of the terms of which was that Trumbull was to Abolitionize the old Democratic party, and I (Lincoln) was to Abolitionize the old Whig party; I pretending to be as good an old-line Whig as ever. Judge Douglas may not understand that he implicated my truthfulness and my honor when he said I was doing one thing and pretending another; and I misunderstood him if he thought he was treating me in a dignified way, as a man of honor and truth, as he now claims he was disposed to treat me. Even after that time, at Galesburgh, when he brings forward an extract from a speech made at Chicago and an extract from a speech made at Charleston, to prove that I was try-ing to play a double part,—that I was trying to cheat the public, and get votes upon one set of principles at one place, and upon another set of principles at another place,—I do not understand but what he impeaches my honor, my veracity, and my candor; and because *he* does this, I do not understand that I am bound, if I see a truthful ground for it, to keep my hands off of him. As soon as I learned that Judge Douglas was disposed to treat me in this way, I signified in one of my speeches that I should be driven to draw upon whatever of humble resources I might have,—to adopt a new course with him. I was not entirely sure that I should be able to hold my own with him, but I at least had the purpose made to do as well as I could upon him; and now I say that I will not be the first to cry "Hold." I think it originated with the Judge, and when he quits, I probably will. But I shall not ask any favors at all. He asks me, or he asks the audience, if I wish to push this matter to the point of personal difficulty. I tell him, no. He did not make a mistake, in one of his early speeches, when he called me an "amiable" man, though perhaps he did when he called me an "intelligent" man. It really hurts me very much to suppose that I have wronged anybody on earth. I again tell him, no! I very much prefer, when this canvass shall be over, however it may result, that we at least part without any bitter recollections of personal difficulties.

The Judge, in his concluding speech at Galesburgh, says that I was pushing this matter to a personal difficulty, to avoid the responsibility for the enormity of my principles. I say to the Judge and this audience, now, that I will again state our principles, as well as I hastily can, in all their enormity, and if the Judge hereafter chooses to confine himself to a war upon these principles, he will probably not find me departing from the same course.

We have in this nation this element of domestic slavery. It is a matter of absolute certainty that it is a disturbing element. It is the opinion of all the great men who have expressed an opinion upon it, that it is a dangerous element. We keep up a controversy in regard to it. That controversy necessarily springs from difference of opinion; and if we can learn exactly—can reduce to the lowest elements—what that difference of opinion is, we perhaps shall be better prepared for discussing the different systems of policy that we would propose in regard to that disturbing element. I suggest that the difference of opinion, reduced to its lowest of terms, is no other than the difference between the men who think slavery a wrong and those who do not think it wrong. The Republican party think it wrong; we think it is a moral, a social, and a political wrong. We think it as a wrong not confining itself merely to the persons or the States where it exists, but that it is a wrong in its tendency, to say the least, that extends itself to the existence of the whole nation. Because we think it wrong, we propose a course of policy that shall deal with it as a wrong. We deal with it as with any other wrong, in so far as we can prevent its growing any larger, and so deal with it that in the run of time there may be some promise of an end to it. We have a due regard to the actual presence of it amongst us, and the difficulties of getting rid of it in any satisfactory way, and all the constitutional obligations thrown about it. I suppose that in reference both to its actual existence in the nation, and to our constitutional obligations, we have no right at all to disturb it in the States where it exists, and we profess that we have no more inclination to disturb it than we have the right to do it. We go further than that: we don't propose to disturb it where, in one instance, we think the Constitution would permit us. We think the Constitution would permit us to disturb it in the District of Columbia. Still, we do not propose to do that, unless it should be in terms which I don't suppose the nation is very likely soon to agree to,—the terms of making the emancipation gradual, and compensating the unwilling owners. Where we suppose we have the constitutional right, we restrain ourselves in reference to the actual existence of the institution and the difficulties thrown about it. We also oppose it as an evil so far as it seeks to spread itself. We insist on the policy that shall restrict it to its present limits. We don't suppose that in doing this we violate anything due to the actual presence of the institution, or anything due to the constitutional guaranties thrown around it.

We oppose the Dred Scott decision in a certain way, upon which I ought perhaps to address you a few words. We do not propose that when Dred Scott has been decided to be a slave by the court, we, as a mob, will decide him to be free. We do not propose that, when any other one, or one thousand, shall be decided by that court to be slaves, we will in any violent way disturb the rights of property thus settled; but we nevertheless do oppose that decision as a political rule which shall be binding on the voter to vote for nobody who thinks it wrong, which shall be binding on the members of Congress or the President to favor no measure that does not actually concur with the principles of that decision. We do not propose to be bound by it as a political rule in that way, because we think it lays the foundation, not merely of enlarging and spreading out what we consider an evil, but it lays the foundation for spreading that evil into the States themselves. We propose so resisting it as to have it reversed if we can, and a new judicial rule established upon this subject.

I will add this: that if there be any man who does not believe that slavery is wrong in the three aspects which I have mentioned, or in any one of them, that man is misplaced, and ought to leave us; while on the other hand, if there be any man in the Republican party who is impatient over the necessity springing from its actual presence, and is impatient of the constitutional guaranties thrown around it, and would act in disregard of these, he too is misplaced, standing with us. He will find his place somewhere else; for we have a due regard, so far as we are capable of understanding them, for all these things. This, gentlemen, as well as I can give it, is a plain statement of our principles in all their enormity.

I will say now that there is a sentiment in the country contrary to me,—a sentiment which holds that slavery is not wrong, and therefore it goes for the policy that does not propose dealing with it as a wrong. That policy is the Democratic policy, and that sentiment is the Democratic sentiment. If there be a doubt in the mind of any one of this vast audience that this is really the central idea of the Democratic party in relation to this subject, I ask him to bear with me while I state a few things tending, as I think, to prove that proposition. In the first place, the leading man—I think I may do my friend Judge Douglas the honor of calling him such—advocating the present Democratic policy never himself says it is wrong. He has the high distinction, so far as I know, of never having said slavery is either right or wrong. Almost everybody else says one or the other, but the Judge never does. If there be a man in the Democratic party who thinks it is wrong, and yet clings to that party, I suggest to him, in the first place, that his leader don't talk as he does, for he never says that it is wrong. In the second place, I suggest to him that if he will examine the policy proposed to be carried forward, he will find that he carefully excludes the idea that there is anything wrong in it. If you will examine the arguments that are made on it, you will find that every one carefully excludes the idea that there is anything wrong in slavery. Perhaps that Democrat who says he is as much opposed to slavery as I am will tell me that I am wrong about this. I wish him to examine his own course in regard to this matter a moment, and then see if his opinion will not be changed a little. You say it is wrong; but don't you constantly object to anybody else saying so? Do you not constantly argue that this is not the right place to oppose it? You say it must not be opposed in the free States, because slavery is not here; it must not be opposed in the slave States, because it is there; it must not be opposed in politics, because that will make a fuss; it must not be opposed in the pulpit, because it is not religion. Then where is the place to oppose it? There is no suitable place to oppose it. There is no place in the country to oppose this evil overspreading the continent, which you say yourself is coming. Frank Blair and Gratz Brown tried to get up a system of gradual emancipation in Missouri, had an election in August, and got beat, and you, Mr. Democrat, threw up your hat, and hallooed "Hurrah for Democracy!" So I say, again, that in regard to the arguments that are made, when Judge Douglas says he "don't care whether slavery is voted up or voted down," whether he means that as an individual expression of sentiment, or only as a sort of statement of his views on national policy, it is alike true to say that he can thus argue logically if he don't see anything wrong in it; but he cannot say so logically if he admits that slavery is wrong. He cannot say that he would as soon see a wrong voted up as voted down. When Judge Douglas says that whoever or whatever community wants slaves, they have a right to have them, he is perfectly logical, if there is nothing wrong in the institution; but if you admit that it is wrong, he cannot logically say that anybody has a right to do wrong. When he says that slave property and horse and hog property are alike to be allowed to go into the Territories, upon the principles of equality, he is reasoning truly, if there is no difference between them as property; but if the one is property held rightfully, and the other is wrong, then there is no equality between the right and wrong; so that, turn it in any way you can, in all the arguments sustaining the Democratic policy, and in that policy itself, there is a careful, studied exclusion of the idea that there is anything wrong in slavery. Let us understand this. I am not, just here, trying to prove that we are right, and they are wrong. I have been stating where we and they stand, and trying to show what is the real difference between us; and I now say that whenever we can get the question distinctly stated, can get all these men who believe that slavery is in some of these respects wrong to stand and act with us in treating it as a wrong,—then, and not till then, I think we will in some way come to an end of this slavery agitation.

## MR. DOUGLAS'S REPLY

LADIES AND GENTLEMEN: Permit me to say that unless silence is observed it will be impossible for me to be heard by this immense crowd, and my friends can confer no higher favor upon me than by omitting all expressions of applause or approbation. I desire to be heard rather than to be applauded. I wish to address myself to your reason, your judgment, your sense of justice, and not to your passions.

I regret that Mr. Lincoln should have deemed it proper for him again to indulge in gross personalities and base insinuations in regard to the Springfield resolutions. It has imposed upon me the necessity of using some portion of my time for the purpose of calling your attention to the facts of the case, and it will then be for you to say what you think of a man who can predicate such a charge upon the circumstances as he has in this. I had seen the platform adopted by a Republican Congressional Convention held in Aurora, the Second Congressional District, in September, 1854, published as purporting to be the platform of the Republican party. That platform declared that the Republican party was pledged never to admit another slave State into the Union, and also that it was pledged to prohibit slavery in all the Territories of the United States, not only all that we then had, but all that we should thereafter acquire, and to repeal unconditionally the Fugitive Slave law, abolish slavery in the District of Columbia, and prohibit the slave-trade between the different States. These and other articles against slavery were contained in this platform, and unanimously adopted by the Republican Congressional Convention in that district. I had also seen that the Republican Congressional Conventions at Rockford, in the First District, and at Bloomington, in the Third, had adopted the same platform that year, nearly word for word, and had declared it to be the platform of the Republican party. I had noticed that Major Thomas L. Harris, a member of Congress from the Springfield District, had referred to that platform in a speech in Congress as having been adopted by the first Republican State Convention which assembled in Illinois. When I had occasion to use the fact in this canvass, I wrote to Major Harris to know on what day that Convention was held, and to ask him to send me its proceedings. He being sick, Charles H. Lanphier answered my letter by sending me the published proceedings of the Convention held at Springfield on the 5th of October, 1854, as they appeared in the report of the *State Register*. I read those resolutions from that newspaper the same as any of you would refer back and quote any fact from the files of a newspaper which had published it. Mr. Lincoln pretends that after I had so quoted those resolutions he discovered that they had never been adopted at Springfield. He does not deny their adoption by the Republican party at Aurora, at Bloomington, and at Rockford, and by nearly all the Republican County Conventions in northern Illinois where his party is in a majority, but merely because they were not adopted on the *"spot"* on which I said they were, he chooses to quibble about the place rather than meet and discuss the merits of the resolutions themselves. I stated when I quoted them that I did so from the *State Register*. I gave my authority. Lincoln believed at the time, as he has since admitted, that they had been adopted at Springfield, as published. Does he believe now that I did not tell the truth when I quoted those resolutions? He knows, in his heart, that I quoted them in good faith, believing at the time that they had been adopted at Springfield. I would consider myself an infamous wretch, if, under such circumstances, I could charge any man with being a party to a trick or a fraud. And I will tell him, too, that it will not do to charge a forgery on Charles H. Lanphier or Thomas L. Harris. No man an earth, who knows them, and knows Lincoln, would take his oath against their word. There are not two men in the State of Illinois who have higher characters for truth, for integrity, for moral character and for elevation of tone, as gentlemen, than Mr. Lanphier and Mr. Harris. Any man who attempts to make such charges as Mr. Lincoln has indulged in against them, only proclaims himself a slanderer.

I will now show you that I stated with entire fairness, as soon as it was made known to me, that there was a mistake about the spot where the resolutions had been adopted, although their truthfulness, as a declaration of the principles of the Republican party, had not and could not be questioned. I did not wait for Lincoln to point out the mistake, but the moment I discovered it, I made a speech, and published it to the world, correcting the error. I corrected it myself, as a gentleman and an honest man, and as I always feel proud to do when I have made a mistake. I wish Mr. Lincoln could show that he has acted with equal fairness and truthfulness when I have convinced him that he has been mistaken. I will give you an illustration to show you how he acts in a similar case: In a speech at Springfield, he charged Chief Justice Taney and his associates. President Pierce, President Buchanan, and myself, with having entered into a conspiracy at the time the Nebraska Bill was introduced, by which the Dred Scott decision was to be made by the Supreme Court, in order to carry slavery everywhere under the Constitution. I called his attention to the fact that at the time alluded to, to wit, the introduction of the Nebraska Bill, it was not possible that such a conspiracy could have been entered into, for the reason that the Dred Scott case had never been taken before the Supreme Court, and was not taken before it for a year after; and I asked him to take back that charge. Did he do it? I showed him that it was impossible that the charge could be true; I proved it by the record; and I then called upon him to retract his false charge. What was his answer? Instead of coming out like an honest man and doing so, he reiterated the charge, and said that if the case had not gone up to the Supreme Court from the courts of Missouri at the time he charged that the judges of the Supreme Court entered into the conspiracy, yet, that there was an understanding with the Democratic owners of Dred Scott that they would take it up. I have since asked him who the Democratic owners of Dred Scott were, but he could not tell, and why? Because there were no such Democratic owners in existence. Dred Scott at the time was owned by the Rev. Dr. Chaffee, an Abolition member of Congress, of Springfield, Massachusetts, in right of his wife. He was owned by one of Lincoln's friends, and not by Democrats at all; his case was conducted in court by Abolition lawyers, so that both the prosecution and the defence were in the hands of the Abolition political friends of Mr. Lincoln. Notwithstanding I thus proved by the record that his charge against the Supreme Court was false, instead of taking it back, he resorted to another false charge to sustain the infamy of it. He also charged President Buchanan with having been a party to the conspiracy. I directed his attention to the fact that the charge could not possibly be true, for the reason that at the time specified, Mr. Buchanan was not in America, but was three thousand miles off, representing the United States at the Court of St. James, and had been there for a year previous, and did not return until three years afterward. Yet I never could get Mr. Lincoln to take back his false charge, although I have called upon him over and over again. He refuses to do it, and either remains silent or resorts to other tricks to try and palm his slander off on the country. Therein you will find the difference between Mr. Lincoln and myself. When I make a mistake, as an honest man I correct it without being asked to do so; but when he makes a false charge, he sticks to it, and never corrects it. One word more in regard to these resolutions: I quoted them at Ottawa merely to ask Mr. Lincoln whether he stood on that platform. That was the purpose for which I quoted them. I did not think that I had a right to put idle questions to him, and I first laid a foundation for my questions by showing that the principles which I wished him either to affirm or deny had been adopted by some portion of his friends, at least, as their creed. Hence I read the resolutions and put the questions to him, and he then refused to answer them. Subsequently, one week afterward, he did answer a part of them, but the others he has not answered up to this day.

Now, let me call your attention for a moment to the answers which Mr. Lincoln made at Freeport to the questions which I propounded to him at Ottawa, based upon the platform adopted by a majority of the Abolition counties of the State, which now, as then, supported him. In answer to my question whether he indorsed the Black Republican principle of "no more slave States," he answered that he was not pledged against the admission of any more slave States, but that he would be very sorry if he should ever be placed in a position where he would have to vote on the question; that he would rejoice to know that no more slave States would be admitted into the Union.

> But [he added] if slavery shall be kept out of the Territories during the Territorial existence of any one given Territory, and then the people shall, having a fair chance and a clear field when they come to adopt the constitution, do such an extraordinary thing as to adopt a slave constitution, uninfluenced by the actual presence of the institution among them, I see no alternative, if we own the country, but to admit them into the Union.

The point I wish him to answer is this: Suppose Congress should not prohibit slavery in the Territory, and it applied for admission with a constitution recognizing slavery, then how would he vote? His answer at Freeport does not apply to any territory in America. I ask you [turning to Lincoln], will you vote to admit Kansas into the Union, with just such a constitution as her people want, with slavery or without, as they shall determine? He will not answer. I have put that question to him time and time again, and have not been able to get an answer out of him. I ask you again, Lincoln, will you vote to admit New Mexico, when she has the requisite population, with such a constitution as her people adopt, either recognizing slavery or not, as they shall determine? He will not answer. I put the same question to him in reference to Oregon and the new States to be carved out of Texas, in pursuance of the contract between Texas and the United States, and he will not answer. He will not answer these questions in reference to any Territory now in existence, but says that if Congress should prohibit slavery in a Territory, and when its people asked for admission as a State they should adopt slavery as one of their institutions, that he supposes he would have to let it come in. I submit to you whether that answer of his to my question does not justify me in saying that he has a fertile genius in devising language to conceal his thoughts. I ask you whether there is an intelligent man in America who does not believe that that answer was made for the purpose of concealing what he intended to do. He wished to make the old-line Whigs believe that he would stand by the Compromise measures of 1850, which declared that the States might come into the Union with slavery, or without, as they pleased, while Lovejoy and his Abolition allies up north explained to the Abolitionists that in taking this ground he preached good Abolition doctrine, because his proviso would not apply to any Territory in America, and therefore there was no chance of his being governed by it. It would have been quite easy for him to have said that he would let the people of a State do just as they pleased, if he desired to convey such an idea. Why did he not do it? He would not answer my question directly, because up north the Abolition creed declares that there shall be no more slave States, while down south, in Adams County, in Coles, and in Sangamon, he and his friends are afraid to advance that doctrine. Therefore, he gives an evasive and equivocal answer, to be construed one way in the south and another way in the north, which, when analyzed, it is apparent is not an answer at all with reference to any territory now in existence.

Mr. Lincoln complains that in my speech the other day at Galesburgh I read an extract from a speech delivered by him at Chicago, and then another from his speech at Charleston, and compared them, thus showing the people that he had one set of principles in one part of the State, and another in the other part. And how does he answer that charge? Why, he quotes from his Charleston speech as I quoted from it, and then quotes another extract from a speech which he made at another place, which he says is the same as the extract from his speech at Charleston; but he does not quote the extract from his Chicago speech, upon which I convicted him of double-dealing. I quoted from his Chicago speech to prove that he held one set of principles up north among the Abolitionists, and from his Charleston speech to prove that he held another set down at Charleston and in southern Illinois. In his answer to this charge, he ignores entirely his Chicago speech, and merely argues that he said the same thing which he said at Charleston at another place. If he did, it follows that he has twice, instead of once, held one creed in one part of the State, and a different creed in another part. Up at Chicago, in the opening of the campaign, he reviewed my reception speech, and undertook to answer my argument attacking his favorite doctrine of negro equality, I had shown that it was a falsification of the Declaration of Independence to pretend that that instrument applied to and included negroes in the clause declaring that all men were created equal. What was Lincoln's reply? I will read from his Chicago speech and the one which he did not quote, and dare not quote, in this part of the State. He said:

> I should like to know if, taking this old Declaration of Independence, which declares that all men are equal upon principle, and making exceptions to it, where will it stop? If one man says it does not mean a negro, why may not another man say it does not mean another man? If that declaration is not the truth, let us get the statute book in which we find it, and tear it out.

There you find that Mr. Lincoln told the Abolitionists of Chicago that if the Declaration of Independence did not declare that the negro was created by the Almighty the equal of the white man, that you ought to take that instrument and tear out the clause which says that all men were created equal. But let me call your attention to another part of the same speech. You know that in his Charleston speech, an extract from which he has read, he declared that the negro belongs to an inferior race, is physically inferior to the white man, and should always be kept in an inferior position. I will now read to you what he said at Chicago on that point. In concluding his speech at that place, he remarked:

> My friends, I have detained you about as long as I desire to do, and I have only to say, let us discard all this quibbling about this man and the other man, this race, and that race, and the other race being inferior, and therefore they must be placed in an inferior position, discarding our standard that we have left us. Let us discard all these things, and unite as one people throughout this land until we shall once more stand up declaring that all men are created equal.

Thus you see that when addressing the Chicago Abolitionists he declared that all distinctions of race must be discarded and blotted out, because the negro stood on an equal footing with the white man; that if one man said the Declaration of Independence did not mean a negro when it declared all men created equal, that another man would say that it did not mean another man; and hence we ought to discard all differences between the negro race and all other races, and declare them all created equal. Did old Giddings, when he came down among you four years ago, preach more radical Abolitionism than this? Did Lovejoy, or Lloyd Garrison, or Wendell Phillips, or Fred Douglass ever take higher Abolition grounds than that? Lincoln told you that I had charged him with getting up these personal attacks to conceal the enormity of his principles, and then commenced talking about something else, omitting to quote this part of his Chicago speech which contained the enormity of his principles to which I alluded. He knew that I alluded to his negro-equality doctrines when I spoke of the enormity of his principles, yet he did not find it convenient to answer on that point. Having shown you what he said in his Chicago speech in reference to negroes being created equal to white men, and about discarding all distinctions between the two races, I will again read to you what he said at Charleston:

I will say, then, that I am not nor ever have been in favor of bringing about in any way the social and political equality of the white and black races; that I am not nor ever have been in favor of making voters of the free negroes, or jurors, or qualifying them to hold office, or having them to marry with white people. I will say in addition, that there is a physical difference between the white and black races, which, I suppose, will forever forbid the two races living together upon terms of social and political equality, and inasmuch as they cannot so live, that while they do remain together there must be the position of superior and inferior, that I as much as any other man am in favor of the superior position being assigned to the white man.

A VOICE: "That's the doctrine."

MR. DOUGLAS: Yes, sir, that is good doctrine; but Mr. Lincoln is afraid to advocate it in the latitude of Chicago, where he hopes to get his votes. It is good doctrine in the anti-Abolition counties for him, and his Chicago speech is good doctrine in the Abolition counties. I assert, on the authority of these two speeches of Mr. Lincoln, that he holds one set of principles in the Abolition counties, and a different and contradictory set in the other counties. I do not question that he said at Ottawa what he quoted; but that only convicts him further, by proving that he has twice contradicted himself, instead of once. Let me ask him why he cannot avow his principles the same in the north as in the south,—the same in every county,—if he has a conviction that they are just? But I forgot,—he would not be a Republican if his principles would apply alike to every part of the country. The party to which he belongs is bounded and limited by geographical lines. With their principles, they cannot even cross the Mississippi River on your ferry-boats. They cannot cross over the Ohio into Kentucky. Lincoln himself cannot visit the land of his fathers, the scenes of his childhood, the graves of his ancestors, and carry his Abolition principles, as he declared them at Chicago, with him.

This Republican organization appeals to the North against the South; it appeals to Northern passion, Northern prejudice, and Northern ambition, against Southern people, Southern States, and Southern institutions, and its only hope of success is by that appeal. Mr. Lincoln goes on to justify himself in making a war upon slavery upon the ground that Frank Blair and Gratz Brown did not succeed in their warfare upon the institution in Missouri. Frank Blair was elected to Congress in 1856, from the State of Missouri, as a Buchanan Democrat, and he turned Fremonter after the people elected him, thus belonging to one party before election, and another afterward. What right then had he to expect, after having thus cheated his constituency, that they would support him at another election? Mr. Lincoln thinks it is his duty to preach a crusade in the free States against slavery, because it is a crime, as he believes, and ought to be extinguished, and because the people of the slave States will never abolish it. How is he going to abolish it? Down in the southern part of the State he takes the ground openly that he will not interfere with slavery where it exists, and says that he is not now and never was in favor of interfering with slavery where it exists in the States. Well, if he is not in favor of that, how does he expect to bring slavery in a course of ultimate extinction? How can he extinguish it in Kentucky, in Virginia, in all the slave States by his policy, if he will not pursue a policy which will interfere with it in the States where it exists? In his speech at Springfield before the Abolition, or Republican, Convention, he declared his hostility to any more slave States in this language:

> Under the operation of that policy the agitation has not only not ceased, but has constantly augmented. In my opinion, it will not cease until a crisis shall have been reached and passed. "A house divided against itself cannot stand." I believe this government cannot endure permanently half slave and half free. I do not expect the Union to be dissolved, I do not expect the house to fall; but I do expect it will cease to be divided. It will become all one thing, or all the other. Either the opponents of slavery will arrest the further spread of it, and place it where the public mind shall rest in the belief that it is in the course of ultimate extinction, or its advocates will push it forward until it shall become alike lawful in all the States,—old as well as new, North as well as South.

Mr. Lincoln there told his Abolition friends that this government could not endure permanently, divided into free and slave States as our fathers made it, and that it must become all free or all slave; otherwise, that the government could not exist. How then does Lincoln propose to save the Union, unless by compelling all the States to become free, so that the house shall not be divided against itself? He intends making them all free; he will preserve the Union in that way; and yet he is not going to interfere with slavery where it now exists. How is he going to bring it about? Why he will agitate, he will induce the North to agitate, until the South shall be worried out and forced to abolish slavery. Let us examine the policy by which that is to be done. He first tells you that he would prohibit slavery everywhere in the Territories. He would thus confine slavery within its present limits. When he thus gets it confined, and surrounded, so that it cannot spread, the natural laws of increase will go on until the negroes will be so plenty that they cannot live on the soil. He will hem them in until starvation seizes them, and by starving them to death he will put slavery in the course of ultimate extinction. If he is not going to interfere with slavery in the States, but intends to interfere and prohibit it in the Territories, and thus smother slavery out, it naturally follows that he can extinguish it only by extinguishing the negro race; for his policy would drive them to starvation. This is the humane and Christian remedy that he proposes for the great crime of slavery!

He tells you that I will not argue the question of whether slavery is right or wrong. I tell you why I will not do it. I hold that, under the Constitution of the United States, each State of this Union has a right to do as it pleases on the subject of slavery. In Illinois we have exercised that sovereign right by prohibiting slavery within our own limits. I approve of that line of policy. We have performed our whole duty in Illinois. We have gone as far as we have a right to go under the Constitution of our common country. It is none of our business whether slavery exists in Missouri or not. Missouri is a sovereign State of this Union, and has the same right to decide the slavery question for herself that Illinois has to decide it for herself. Hence I do not choose to occupy the time allotted to me in discussing a question that we have no right to act upon. I thought that you desired to hear us upon those questions coming within our constitutional power of action. Lincoln will not discuss these. What one question has he discussed that comes within the power or calls for the action or interference of an United States Senator? He is going to discuss the rightfulness of slavery when Congress cannot act upon it either way. He wishes to discuss the merits of the Dred Scott decision when, under the Constitution, a senator has no right to interfere with the decision of judicial tribunals. He wants your exclusive attention to two questions that he has no power to act upon; to two questions that he could not vote upon if he was in Congress; to two questions that are not practical,—in order to conceal from your attention other questions which he might be required to vote upon should he ever become a member of Congress. He tells you that he does not like the Dred Scott decision. Suppose he does not, how is he going to help himself? He says that he will reverse it. How will he reverse it? I know of but one mode of reversing judicial decisions, and that is by appealing from the inferior to the superior court. But I have never yet learned how or where an appeal could be taken from the Supreme Court of the United States! The Dred Scott decision was pronounced by the highest tribunal on earth. From that decision there is no appeal, this side of heaven. Yet, Mr. Lincoln says he is going to reverse that decision. By what tribunal will he reverse it? Will he appeal to a mob? Does he intend to appeal to violence, to Lynch law? Will he stir up strife and rebellion in the land, and overthrow the court by violence? He does not deign to tell you how he will reverse the Dred Scott decision, but keeps appealing each day from the Supreme Court of the United States to political meetings in the country. He wants me to argue with you the merits of each point of that decision before this political meeting. I say to you, with all due respect, that I choose to abide by the decisions of the Supreme Court as they are pronounced. It is not for me to inquire, after a decision is made, whether I like it in all the points or not. When I used to practise law with Lincoln, I never knew him to be beat in a case that he did not get mad at the judge, and talk about appealing; and when I got beat, I generally thought the court was wrong, but I never dreamed of going out of the courthouse and making a stump speech to the people against the judge, merely because I had found out that I did not know the law as well as he did. If the decision did not suit me, I appealed until I got to the Supreme Court; and then if that court, the highest tribunal in the world, decided against me, I was satisfied, because it is the duty of every law-abiding man to obey the constitutions, the laws, and the constituted authorities. He who attempts to stir up odium and rebellion in the country against the constituted authorities is stimulating the passions of men to resort to violence and to mobs instead of to the law. Hence, I tell you that I take the decisions of the Supreme Court as the law of the land, and I intend to obey them as such.

But Mr. Lincoln says that I will not answer his question as to what I would do in the event of the court making so ridiculous a decision as he imagines they would by deciding that the free State of Illinois could not prohibit slavery within her own limits. I told him at Freeport why I would not answer such a question. I told him that there was not a man possessing any brains in America, lawyer or not, who ever dreamed that such a thing could be done. I told him then, as I do now, that by all the principles set forth in the Dred Scott decision, it is impossible. I told him then, as I do now, that it is an insult to men's understanding, and a gross calumny on the court, to presume in advance that it was going to degrade itself so low as to make a decision known to be in direct violation of the Constitution.

A VOICE: "The same thing was said about the Dred Scott decision before it passed."

MR. DOUGLAS: Perhaps you think that the court did the same thing in reference to the Dred Scott decision: I have heard a man talk that way before. The
principles contained in the Dred Scott decision had been affirmed previously in
various other decisions. What court or judge ever held that a negro was a citizen?
The State courts had decided that question over and over again, and the Dred
Scott decision on that point only affirmed what every court in the land knew to
be the law.

But I will not be drawn off into an argument upon the merits of the Dred
Scott decision. It is enough for me to know that the Constitution of the United
States created the Supreme Court for the purpose of deciding all disputed questions touching the true construction of that instrument, and when such decisions
are pronounced, they are the law of the land, binding on every good citizen. Mr.
Lincoln has a very convenient mode of arguing upon the subject. He holds that
because he is a Republican that he is not bound by the decisions of the court, but
that I, being a Democrat, am so bound. It may be that Republicans do not hold
themselves bound by the laws of the land and the Constitution of the country as
expounded by the courts; it may be an article in the Republican creed that men
who do not like a decision have a right to rebel against it: but when Mr. Lincoln
preaches that doctrine, I think he will find some honest Republican—some law-
abiding man in that party—who will repudiate such a monstrous doctrine. The
decision in the Dred Scott case is binding on every American citizen alike; and
yet Mr. Lincoln argues that the Republicans are not bound by it because they are
opposed to it, whilst Democrats are bound by it, because we will not resist it. A
Democrat cannot resist the constituted authorities of this country; a Democrat
is a law-abiding man; a Democrat stands by the Constitution and the laws, and
relies upon liberty as protected by law, and not upon mob or political violence.

I have never yet been able to make Mr. Lincoln understand, nor can I make
any man who is determined to support him, right or wrong, understand how
it is that under the Dred Scott decision the people of a Territory, as well as a
State, can have slavery or not, just as they please. I believe that I can explain that
proposition to all constitution-loving, law-abiding men in a way that they cannot fail to understand it. Chief Justice Taney, in his opinion in the Dred Scott
case, said that, slaves being property, the owner of them has a right to take them
into a Territory the same as he would any other property; in other words, that
slave property, so far as the right to enter a Territory is concerned, stands on the
same footing with other property. Suppose we grant that proposition. Then any
man has a right to go to Kansas and take his property with him; but when he
gets there, he must rely upon the local law to protect his property, whatever it

may be. In order to illustrate this, imagine that three of you conclude to go to Kansas. One takes $10,000 worth of slaves, another $10,000 worth of liquors, and the third $10,000 worth of dry-goods. When the man who owns the dry-goods arrives out there and commences selling them, he finds that he is stopped and prohibited from selling until he gets a license, to pay for which will destroy all the profits he can make on his goods. When the man with the liquors gets there and tries to sell, he finds a Maine liquor law in force which prevents him. Now, of what use is his right to go there with his property unless he is protected in the enjoyment of that right after he gets there? The man who gets there with his slaves finds that there is no law to protect him when he arrives there. He has no remedy if his slaves run away to another country; there is no slave code or police regulations; and the absence of them excludes his slaves from the Territory just as effectually and as positively as a constitutional prohibition could.

Such was the understanding when the Kansas and Nebraska Bill was pending in Congress. Read the speech of Speaker Orr, of South Carolina, in the House of Representatives, in 1856, on the Kansas question, and you will find that he takes the ground that while the owner of a slave has a right to go into a Territory and carry his slaves with him, that he can not hold them one day or hour unless there is a slave code to protect him. He tells you that slavery would not exist a day in South Carolina, or any other State, unless there was a friendly people and friendly legislation. Read the speeches of that giant in intellect, Alexander H. Stephens, of Georgia, and you will find them to the same effect. Read the speeches of Sam Smith, of Tennessee, and of all Southern men, and you will find that they all understood this doctrine then as we understand it now. Mr. Lincoln cannot be made to understand it, however. Down at Jonesboro, he went on to argue that if it be the law that a man has a right to take his slaves into territory of the United States under the Constitution, that then a member of Congress was perjured if he did not vote for a slave code. I ask him whether the decision of the Supreme Court is not binding upon him as well as on me? If so, and he holds that he would be perjured if he did not vote for a slave code under it, I ask him whether, if elected to Congress, he will so vote. I have a right to his answer, and I will tell you why. He put that question to me down in Egypt, and did it with an air of triumph. This was about the form of it: In the event that a slaveholding citizen of one of the Territories should need and demand a slave code to protect his slaves, will you vote for it? I answered him that a fundamental article in the Democratic creed, as put forth in the Nebraska Bill and the Cincinnati platform, was non-intervention by Congress with slavery in the States and Territories, and hence that I would not vote in Congress for any code of laws either for or against slavery in any Territory. I will leave the people perfectly free to decide that question for themselves.

Mr. Lincoln and the Washington *Union* both think this a monstrous bad doctrine. Neither Mr. Lincoln nor the Washington *Union* like my Freeport speech on that subject. The *Union*, in a late number, has been reading me out of the Democratic party because I hold that the people of a Territory, like those of a State, have the right to have slavery or not, as they please. It has devoted three and a half columns to prove certain propositions, one of which I will read. It says:

> We propose to show that Judge Douglas's action in 1850 and 1854 was taken with especial reference to the announcement of doctrine and programme which was made at Freeport. The declaration at Freeport was that "in his opinion the people can, by lawful means, exclude slavery from a Territory before it comes in as a State"; and he declared that his competitor had "heard him argue the Nebraska Bill on that principle all over Illinois in 1854, 1855, and 1856, and had no excuse to pretend to have any doubt upon that subject."

The Washington *Union* there charges me with the monstrous crime of now proclaiming on the stump the same doctrine that I carried out in 1850, by supporting Clay's Compromise measures. The *Union* also charges that I am now proclaiming the same doctrine that I did in 1854 in support of the Kansas and Nebraska Bill. It is shocked that I should now stand where I stood in 1850, when I was supported by Clay, Webster, Cass, and the great men of that day, and where I stood in 1854 and in 1856, when Mr. Buchanan was elected President. It goes on to prove, and succeeds in proving, from my speeches in Congress on Clay's Compromise measures, that I held the same doctrines at that time that I do now, and then proves that by the Kansas and Nebraska Bill I advanced the same doctrine that I now advance. It remarks:

> So much for the course taken by Judge Douglas on the Compromises of 1850. The record shows, beyond the possibility of cavil or dispute, that he expressly intended in those bills to give the Territorial Legislatures power to exclude slavery. How stands his record in the memorable session of 1854, with reference to the Kansas-Nebraska Bill itself? We shall not overhaul

the votes that were given on that notable measure; our space will not afford it. We have his own words, however, delivered in his speech closing the great debate on that bill on the night of March 3, 1854, to show that *he meant* to do in 1854 precisely what *he had meant* to do in 1858. The Kansas-Nebraska Bill being upon its passage, he said:

It then quotes my remarks upon the passage of the bill as follows:

The principle which we propose to carry into effect by this bill is this: That Congress shall neither legislate slavery into any Territory or State, nor out of the same; but the people shall be left free to regulate their domestic concerns in their own way, subject only to the Constitution of the United States. In order to carry this principle into practical operation, it becomes necessary to remove whatever legal obstacles might be found in the way of its free exercise. It is only for the purpose of carrying out this great fundamental principle of self-government that the bill renders the eighth section of the Missouri Act inoperative and void.

Now, let me ask, will those senators who have arraigned me, or any one of them, have the assurance to rise in his place and declare that this great principle was never thought of or advocated as applicable to Territorial bills, in 1850; that, from that session until the present, nobody ever thought of incorporating this principle in all new Territorial organizations, etc., etc.? I will begin with the Compromises of 1850. Any senator who will take the trouble to examine our journals will find that on the 25th of March of that year I reported from the Committee on Territories two bills, including the following measures: the admission of California, a Territorial government for Utah, a Territorial government for New Mexico, and the adjustment of the Texas boundary. These bills proposed to leave the people of Utah and New Mexico free to decide the slavery question for themselves, *in the precise language of the Nebraska Bill* now under discussion. A few weeks afterward the committee of thirteen took those bills and put a wafer between them, and reported them back to the Senate as one bill, with some slight amendments. *One of these amendments was, that the Territorial Legislatures should not legislate upon the subject of African slavery. I objected to this provision,* upon the ground that it subverted the great principle of self-government, *upon which the bill had been originally framed by the Territorial Committee.* On the first trial the Senate refused to strike it out, but subsequently did so, upon full debate, in order to establish that principle as the rule of action in Territorial organizations.

The *Union* comments thus upon my speech on that occasion:

> Thus it is seen that, in framing the Nebraska-Kansas Bill, Judge Douglas framed it in the terms and upon the model of those of Utah and New Mexico, and that in the debate he took pains expressly to revive the recollection of the voting which had taken place upon amendments affecting the powers of the Territorial Legislatures over the subject of slavery in the bills of 1850, in order to give the same meaning, force, and effect to the Nebraska-Kansas Bill on this subject as had been given to those of Utah and New Mexico.

The *Union* proves the following propositions: First, that I sustained Clay's Compromise measures on the ground that they established the principle of self-government in the Territories. Secondly, that I brought in the Kansas and Nebraska Bill, founded upon the same principles as Clay's Compromise measures of 1850; and, thirdly, that my Freeport speech is in exact accordance with those principles. And what do you think is the imputation that the *Union* casts upon me for all this? It says that my Freeport speech is not Democratic, and that I was not a Democrat in 1854 or in 1850! Now is not that funny? Think that the author of the Kansas and Nebraska Bill was not a Democrat when he introduced it! The *Union* says I was not a sound Democrat in 1850, nor in 1854, nor in 1856, nor am I in 1858, because I have always taken and now occupy the ground that the people of a Territory, like those of a State, have the right to decide for themselves whether slavery shall or shall not exist in a Territory! I wish to cite, for the benefit of the Washington *Union* and the followers of that sheet, one authority on that point, and I hope the authority will be deemed satisfactory to that class of politicians. I will read from Mr. Buchanan's letter accepting the nomination of the Democratic Convention, for the Presidency. You know that Mr. Buchanan, after he was nominated, declared to the Keystone Club, in a public speech, that he was no longer James Buchanan but the embodiment of the Democratic platform. In his letter to the committee which informed him of his nomination, accepting it, he defined the meaning of the Kansas and Nebraska Bill and the Cincinnati platform in these words:

> The recent legislation of Congress respecting domestic slavery, derived as it has been from the original and pure fountain of legitimate political power, the will of the majority, promises ere long to allay the dangerous excitement. This legislation is founded upon principles as ancient as free government itself, and, in accordance with them, has simply declared that the people of a Territory, like those of a State, shall decide for themselves whether slavery shall or shall not exist within their limits.

Thus you see that James Buchanan accepted the nomination at Cincinnati on the condition that the people of a Territory, like those of a State, should be left to decide for themselves whether slavery should or should not exist within their limits. I sustained James Buchanan for the Presidency on that platform as adopted at Cincinnati, and expounded by himself. He was elected President on that platform, and now we are told by the Washington *Union* that no man is a true Democrat who stands on the platform on which Mr. Buchanan was nominated, and which he has explained and expounded himself. We are told that a man is not a Democrat who stands by Clay, Webster, and Cass, and the Compromise measures of 1850, and the Kansas and Nebraska Bill of 1854. Whether a man be a Democrat or not on that platform, I intend to stand there as long as I have life. I intend to cling firmly to that principle which declares the right of each State and each Territory to settle the question of slavery, and every other domestic question, for themselves. I hold that if they want a slave State they have a right under the Constitution of the United States to make it so, and if they want a free State, it is their right to have it. But the *Union*, in advocating the claims of Lincoln over me to the Senate, lays down two unpardonable heresies which it says I advocate. The first is the right of the people of a Territory, the same as a State, to decide for themselves the question whether slavery shall exist within their limits, in the language of Mr. Buchanan; and the second is, that a constitution shall be submitted to the people of a Territory for its adoption or rejection before their admission as a State under it. It so happens that Mr. Buchanan is pledged to both these heresies, for supporting which the

Washington *Union* has read me out of the Democratic church. In his annual message he said he trusted that the example of the Minnesota case would be followed in all future cases, requiring a submission of the constitution; and in his letter of acceptance, he said that the people of a Territory, the same as a State, had the right to decide for themselves whether slavery should exist within their limits. Thus you find that this little corrupt gang who control the *Union* and wish to elect Lincoln in preference to me,—because, as they say, of these two heresies which I support,—denounce President Buchanan when they denounce me, if he stands now by the principles on which he was elected. Will they pretend that he does not now stand by the principles on which he was elected? Do they hold that he has abandoned the Kansas-Nebraska Bill, the Cincinnati platform, and his own letter accepting his nomination, all of which declare the right of the people of a Territory, the same as a State, to decide the slavery question for themselves? I will not believe that he has betrayed or intends to betray the platform which elected him, but if he does I will not follow him. I will stand by that great principle no matter who may desert it. I intend to stand by it, for the purpose of preserving peace between the North and the South, the free and the slave States. If each State will only agree to mind its own business and let its neighbors alone, there will be peace forever between us.

We in Illinois tried slavery when a Territory, and found it was not good for us in this climate, and with our surroundings, and hence we abolished it. We then adopted a free State constitution, as we had a right to do. In this State we have declared that a negro shall not be a citizen, and we have also declared that he shall not be a slave. We had a right to adopt that policy. Missouri has just as good a right to adopt the other policy. I am now speaking of rights under the Constitution, and not of moral or religious rights. I do not discuss the morals of the people of Missouri, but let them settle that matter for themselves. I hold that the people of the slave-holding States are civilized men as well as ourselves, that they bear consciences as well as we, and that they are accountable to God and their posterity, and not to us. It is for them to decide, therefore, the moral and religious right of the slavery question for themselves, within their own limits. I assert that they had as much right under the Constitution to adopt the system of policy which they have as we had to adopt ours. So it is with every other State in this Union. Let each State stand firmly by that great constitutional right, let each State mind its own business and let its neighbors alone, and there will be no trouble on this question. If we will stand by that principle, then Mr. Lincoln will find that this Republic can exist forever divided into free and slave States, as our fathers made it and the people of each State have decided. Stand by that great principle, and we can go on as we have been, increasing in wealth, in population, in power, and in all the elements of greatness, until we shall be the admiration and terror of the world. We can go on and enlarge as our population increases and requires more room, until we make this continent one ocean-bound republic. Under that principle the United States can perform that great mission, that destiny, which Providence has marked out for us. Under that principle we can receive with entire safety that stream of intelligence which is constantly flowing from the Old World to the New, filling up our prairies, clearing our wildernesses, and building cities, towns, railroads, and other internal improvements, and thus make this the asylum of the oppressed of the whole earth. We have this great mission to perform, and it can only be performed by adhering faithfully to that principle of self-government on which our institutions were all established. I repeat that the principle is the right of each State, each Territory, to decide this slavery question for itself, to have slavery or not, as it chooses; and it does not become Mr. Lincoln, or anybody else, to tell the people of Kentucky that they have no consciences, that they are living in a state of iniquity, and that they are cherishing an institution to their bosoms in violation of the law of God. Better for him to adopt the doctrine of "Judge not, lest ye shall be judged." Let him perform his own duty at home, and he will have a better fate in the future. I think there are objects of charity enough in the free States to excite the sympathies and open the pockets of all the benevolence we have amongst us, without going abroad in search of negroes, of whose condition we know nothing. We have enough objects of charity at home, and it is our duty to take care of our own poor and our own suffering, before we go abroad to intermeddle with other people's business.

My friends, I am told that my time is within two minutes of expiring. I have omitted many topics that I would like to have discussed before you at length. There were many points touched by Mr. Lincoln that I have not been able to take up for the want of time. I have hurried over each subject that I have discussed as rapidly as possible, so as to omit but few; but one hour and a half is not time sufficient for a man to discuss at length one half of the great questions which are now dividing the public mind.

In conclusion, I desire to return to you my grateful acknowledgments for the kindness and the courtesy with which you have listened to me. It is something remarkable that in an audience as vast as this, composed of men of opposite politics and views, with their passions highly excited, there should be so much courtesy, kindness, and respect exhibited, not only toward one another, but toward the speakers; and I feel that it is due to you that I should thus express my gratitude for the kindness with which you have treated me.

### MR. LINCOLN'S REJOINDER

MY FRIENDS: Since Judge Douglas has said to you in his conclusion that he had not time in an hour and a half to answer all I had said in an hour, it follows of course that I will not be able to answer in half an hour all that he said in an hour and a half.

I wish to return to Judge Douglas my profound thanks for his public annunciation here to-day, to be put on record, that his system of policy in regard to the institution of slavery *contemplates that it shall last forever*. We are getting a little nearer the true issue of this controversy, and I am profoundly grateful for this one sentence. Judge Douglas asks you, Why cannot the institution of slavery, or rather, why cannot the nation, part slave and part free, continue as our fathers made it, *forever*? In the first place, I insist that our fathers *did not* make this nation half slave and half free, or part slave and part free. I insist that they found the institution of slavery existing here. They did not make it so but they left it so because they knew of no way to get rid of it at that time. When Judge Douglas undertakes to say that, as a matter of choice, the fathers of the government made this nation part slave and part free, *he assumes what is historically a falsehood*. More than that: when the fathers of the government cut off the source of slavery by the abolition of the slave-trade, and adopted a system of restricting it from the new Territories where it had not existed, I maintain that they placed it where they understood, and all sensible men understood, it was in the course of ultimate extinction; and when Judge Douglas asks me why it cannot continue as our fathers made it, I ask him why he and his friends could not let it remain as our fathers made it?

It is precisely all I ask of him in relation to the institution of slavery, that it shall be placed upon the basis that our fathers placed it upon. Mr. Brooks, of South Carolina, once said, and truly said, that when this government was established, no one expected the institution of slavery to last until this day, and that the men who formed this government were wiser and better than the men of these days; but the men of these days had experience which the fathers had not, and that experience had taught them the invention of the cotton-gin, and this had made the perpetuation of the institution of slavery a necessity in this country. Judge Douglas could not let it stand upon the basis which our fathers placed it, but removed it, and *put it upon the cotton-gin basis*. It is a question, therefore, for him and his friends to answer, why they could not let it remain where the fathers of the government originally placed it.

I hope nobody has understood me as trying to sustain the doctrine that we have a right to quarrel with Kentucky, or Virginia, or any of the slave States, about the institution of slavery,—thus giving the Judge an opportunity to be eloquent and valiant against us in fighting for their rights. I expressly declared in my opening speech that I had neither the inclination to exercise, nor the belief in the existence of, the right to interfere with the States of Kentucky or Virginia in doing as they pleased with slavery or any other existing institution. Then what becomes of all his eloquence in behalf of the rights of States, which are assailed by no living man?

But I have to hurry on, for I have but a half hour. The Judge has informed me, or informed this audience, that the Washington *Union* is laboring for my election to the United States Senate. This is news to me,—not very ungrateful news either. [Turning to Mr. W. H. Carlin, who was on the stand]—I hope that Carlin will be elected to the State Senate, and will vote for me. [Mr. Carlin shook his head.] Carlin don't fall in, I perceive, and I suppose he will not do much for me; but I am glad of all the support I can get, anywhere, if I can get it without practising any deception to obtain it. In respect to this large portion of Judge Douglas's speech in which he tries to show that in the controversy between himself and the Administration party he is in the right, I do not feel myself at all competent or inclined to answer him. I say to him, "Give it to them,—give it to them just all you can!" and, on the other hand, I say to Carlin, and Jake Davis, and to this man Wogley up here in Hancock, "Give it to Douglas,—just pour it into him!"

Now, in regard to this matter of the Dred Scott decision, I wish to say a word or two. After all, the Judge will not say whether, if a decision is made holding that the people of the *States* cannot exclude slavery, he will support it or not. He obstinately refuses to say what he will do in that case. The judges of the Supreme Court as obstinately refused to say what they would do on this subject. Before this I reminded him that at Galesburgh he said the judges had expressly declared the contrary, and you remember that in my opening speech I told him I had the book containing that decision here, and I would thank him to lay his finger on the place where any such thing was said. He has occupied his hour and a half, and he has not ventured to try to sustain his assertion. *He never will.* But he is desirous of knowing how we are going to reverse that Dred Scott decision. Judge Douglas ought to know how. Did not he and his political friends find a way to reverse the decision of that same court in favor of the constitutionality of the National Bank? Didn't they find a way to do it so effectually that they have reversed it as completely as any decision ever was reversed, so far as its practical operation is concerned? And let me ask you, didn't Judge Douglas find a way to reverse the decision of our Supreme Court when it decided that Carlin's father—old Governor Carlin had not the constitutional power to remove a Secretary of State? Did he not appeal to the "MOBS," as he calls them? Did he not make speeches in the lobby to show how villainous that decision was, and how it ought to be overthrown? Did he not succeed, too, in getting an act passed by the Legislature to have it overthrown? And didn't he himself sit down on that bench as one of the five added judges, who were to overslaugh the four old ones,—getting his name of "Judge" in that way, and no other? If there is a villainy in using disrespect or making opposition to Supreme Court decisions, I commend it to Judge Douglas's earnest consideration. I know of no man in the State of Illinois who ought to know so well about *how much* villainy it takes to oppose a decision of the Supreme Court as our honorable friend Stephen A. Douglas.

Judge Douglas also makes the declaration that I say the Democrats are bound by the Dred Scott decision, while the Republicans are not. In the sense in which he argues, I never said it; but I will tell you what I have said and what I do not hesitate to repeat to-day. I have said that as the Democrats believe that decision to be correct, and that the extension of slavery is affirmed in the National Constitution, they are bound to support it as such; and I will tell you here that General Jackson once said each man was bound to support the Constitution "as he understood it." Now, Judge Douglas understands the Constitution according to the Dred Scott decision, and he is bound to support it as he understands it. I understand it another way, and therefore I am bound to support it in the way in which I understand it. And as Judge Douglas believes that decision to be correct, I will remake that argument if I have time to do so. Let me talk to some gentleman down there among you who looks me in the face. We will say you are a member of the Territorial Legislature, and, like Judge Douglas, you believe that the right to take and hold slaves there is a constitutional right. The first thing you do is to *swear you will support the Constitution* and all rights guaranteed therein; that you will, whenever your neighbor needs your legislation to support his constitutional rights, not withhold that legislation. If you withhold that necessary legislation for the support of the Constitution and constitutional rights, do you not commit perjury? I ask every sensible man if that is not so? That is undoubtedly just so, say what you please. Now, that is precisely what Judge Douglas says, that this is a constitutional right. Does the Judge mean to say that the Territorial Legislature in legislating may, by withholding necessary laws, or by passing unfriendly laws, *nullify that constitutional right?* Does he mean to say that? Does he mean to ignore the proposition so long and well established in law, that what you cannot do directly, you cannot do indirectly? Does he mean that? The truth about the matter is this: Judge Douglas has sung paeans to his "Popular Sovereignty" doctrine until his Supreme Court, co-operating with him, has *squatted* his Squatter Sovereignty out. But he will keep up this species of humbuggery about Squatter Sovereignty. He has at last invented this sort of *do-nothing sovereignty,*—that the people may exclude slavery by a sort of "sovereignty" that is exercised by doing nothing at all. Is not that running his Popular Sovereignty down awfully? Has it not got down as thin as the homoeopathic soup that was made by boiling the shadow of a pigeon that had starved to death? But at last, when it is brought to the test of close reasoning, there is not even that thin decoction of it left. It is a presumption impossible in the domain of thought. It is precisely no other than the putting of that most unphilosophical proposition, that two bodies can occupy the same space at the same time. The Dred Scott decision covers the whole ground, and while it occupies it, there is no room even for the shadow of a starved pigeon to occupy the same ground.

Judge Douglas, in reply to what I have said about having upon a previous occasion made the speech at Ottawa as the one he took an extract from at Charleston, says it only shows that I practised the deception twice. Now, my friends, are any of you obtuse enough to swallow that? Judge Douglas had said I had made a speech at Charleston that I would not make up north, and I turned around and answered him by showing I *had* made that same speech up north,—had made it at Ottawa; made it in his hearing; made it in *the* Abolition District,—in Lovejoy's District,—in the personal presence of Lovejoy himself,—in the same atmosphere exactly in which I had made my Chicago speech, of which he complains so much.

Now, in relation to my not having said anything about the quotation from the Chicago speech: he thinks that is a terrible subject for me to handle. Why, gentlemen, I can show you that the substance of the Chicago speech I delivered two years ago in "Egypt," as he calls it. It was down at Springfield. That speech is here in this book, and I could turn to it and read it to you but for the lack of time. I have not now the time to read it. ["Read it, read it."] No, gentlemen, I am obliged to use discretion in disposing most advantageously of my brief time. The Judge has taken great exception to my adopting the heretical statement in the Declaration of Independence, that "all men are created equal," and he has a great deal to say about negro equality. I want to say that in sometimes alluding to the Declaration of Independence, I have only uttered the sentiments that Henry Clay used to hold. Allow me to occupy your time a moment with what he said. Mr. Clay was at one time called upon in Indiana, and in a way that I suppose was very insulting, to liberate his slaves; and he made a written reply to that application, and one portion of it is in these words:

What is the *foundation* of this appeal to me in Indiana to liberate the slaves under my care in Kentucky? It is a general declaration in the act announcing to the world the independence of the thirteen American colonies, that *"men are created equal."* Now, as an abstract principle, *there is no doubt of the truth of that declaration*, and it is desirable in the *original construction* of society, and in organized societies, to keep it in view as a great fundamental principle.

When I sometimes, in relation to the organization of new societies in new countries, where the soil is clean and clear, insisted that we should keep that principle in view, Judge Douglas will have it that I want a negro wife. He never can be brought to understand that there is any middle ground on this subject. I have lived until my fiftieth year, and have never had a negro woman either for a slave or a wife, and I think I can live fifty centuries, for that matter, without having had one for either. I maintain that you may take Judge Douglas's quotations from my Chicago speech, and from my Charleston speech, and the Galesburgh speech,—in his speech of to-day,—and compare them over, and I am willing to trust them with you upon his proposition that they show rascality or double-dealing. I deny that they do.

The Judge does not seem at all disposed to have peace, but I find he is disposed to have a personal warfare with me. He says that my oath would not be taken against the bare word of Charles H. Lanphier or Thomas L. Harris. Well, that is altogether a matter of opinion. It is certainly not for me to vaunt my word against oaths of these gentlemen, but I will tell Judge Douglas again the facts upon which I *"dared"* to say they proved a forgery. I pointed out at Galesburgh that the publication of these resolutions in the Illinois *State Register* could not have been the result of accident, as the proceedings of that meeting bore unmistakable evidence of being done by a man who *knew* it was a forgery; that it was a publication partly taken from the real proceedings of the Convention, and partly from the proceedings of a convention at another place,—which showed that he had the real proceedings before him, and taking one part of the resolutions, he threw out another part, and substituted false and fraudulent ones in their stead. I pointed that out to him, and also that his friend Lanphier, who was editor of the *Register* at that time and now is, must have known how it was done. Now, whether *he* did it, or got some friend to do it for him, I could not tell, but he certainly knew all about it. I pointed out to Judge Douglas that in his Freeport speech he had promised to *investigate* that matter. Does he now say he did not make that promise? I have a right to ask *why he did not keep it.* I call upon him to tell here to-day why he did not keep that promise. That fraud has been traced up so that it lies between him, Harris, and Lanphier. There is little room for escape for Lanphier. Lanphier is doing the Judge good service, and Douglas desires his word to be taken for the truth. He desires Lanphier to be taken as authority in what he states in his newspaper. He desires Harris to be taken as a man of vast credibility; and when this thing lies among them, they will not press it to show where the guilt really belongs. Now, as he has said that he would investigate it, and implied that he would tell us the result of his investigation, I demand of him to tell why he did not investigate it, if he did not; and if he did, *why he won't tell the result.* I call upon him for that.

This is the third time that Judge Douglas has assumed that he learned about these resolutions by Harris's attempting to use them against Norton on the floor of Congress. I tell Judge Douglas the public records of the country show that *he* himself attempted it upon Trumbull a month before Harris tried them on Norton; that Harris had the opportunity of *learning it from him,* rather than he from Harris. I now ask his attention to that part of the record on the case. My friends, I am not disposed to detain you longer in regard to that matter.

I am told that I still have five minutes left. There is another matter I wish to call attention to. He says, when he discovered there was a mistake in that case, he came forward magnanimously, without my calling his attention to it, and explained it. I will tell you how he became so magnanimous. When the newspapers of our side had discovered and published it, and put it beyond his power to deny it, then he came forward and made a virtue of necessity by acknowledging it. Now he argues that all the point there was in those resolutions, although never passed at Springfield, is retained by their being passed at other localities. Is that true? He said I had a hand in passing them, in his opening speech,—that I was in the convention and helped to pass them. Do the resolutions touch me at all? It strikes me there is some difference between holding a man responsible for an act which he *has not* done and holding him responsible for an act that he *has* done. You will judge whether there is any difference in the *"spots."* And he has taken credit for great magnanimity in coming forward and acknowledging what is proved on him beyond even the capacity of Judge Douglas to deny; and he has more capacity in that way than any other living man.

Then he wants to know why I won't withdraw the charge in regard to a conspiracy to make slavery national, as he has withdrawn the one he made. May it please his worship, I will withdraw it *when it is proven false on me as that was proven false on him.* I will add a little more than that. I will withdraw it whenever a reasonable man shall be brought to believe that the charge is not true. I have asked Judge Douglas's attention to certain matters of fact tending to prove the charge of a conspiracy to nationalize slavery, and he says he convinces me that this is all untrue because Buchanan was not in the country at that time, and because the Dred Scott case had not then got into the Supreme Court; and he says that I say the *Democratic* owners of Dred Scott got up the case. I never did say that. I defy Judge Douglas to show that I ever said so, *for I never uttered it*. [One of Mr. Douglas's reporters gesticulated affirmatively at Mr. Lincoln.] I don't care if your hireling does say I did, I tell you myself that *I never said the "Democratic" owners of Dred Scott got up the case.* I have never pretended to know whether Dred Scott's owners were Democrats, or Abolitionists, or Freesoilers or Border Ruffians. I have said that there is evidence about the case tending to show that it was a made-up case, for the purpose of getting that decision. I have said that that evidence was very strong in the fact that when Dred Scott was declared to be a slave, the owner of him made him free, showing that he had had the case tried and the question settled for such use as could be made of that decision; he cared nothing about the property thus declared to be his by that decision. But my time is out, and I can say no more.

# The Last Joint Debate, at Alton

*October 15, 1858*

### MR. DOUGLAS'S OPENING SPEECH

LADIES AND GENTLEMEN: It is now nearly four months since the canvass between Mr. Lincoln and myself commenced. On the 16th of June the Republican Convention assembled at Springfield and nominated Mr. Lincoln as their candidate for the United States Senate, and he, on that occasion, delivered a speech in which he laid down what he understood to be the Republican creed, and the platform on which he proposed to stand during the contest. The principal points in that speech of Mr. Lincoln's were: First, that this government could not endure permanently divided into free and slave States, as our fathers made it; that they must all become free or all become slave; all become one thing, or all become the other,—otherwise this Union could not continue to exist. I give you his opinions almost in the identical language he used. His second proposition was a crusade against the Supreme Court of the United States because of the Dred Scott decision, urging as an especial reason for his opposition to that decision that it deprived the negroes of the rights and benefits of that clause in the Constitution of the United States which guarantees to the citizens of each State all the rights, privileges, and immunities of the citizens of the several States. On the 10th of July I returned home, and delivered a speech to the people of Chicago, in which I announced it to be my purpose to appeal to the people of Illinois to sustain the course I had pursued in Congress. In that speech I joined issue with Mr. Lincoln on the points which he had presented. Thus there was an issue clear and distinct made up between us on these two propositions laid down in the speech of Mr. Lincoln at Springfield, and controverted by me in my reply to him at Chicago. On the next day, the 11th of July, Mr. Lincoln replied to me at Chicago, explaining at some length and reaffirming the positions which he had taken in his Springfield speech. In that Chicago speech he even went further than he had before, and uttered sentiments in regard to the negro being on an equality with the white man. He adopted in support of this position the argument which Lovejoy and Codding and other Abolition lecturers had made familiar in the northern and central portions of the State: to wit, that the Declaration of Independence having declared all men free and equal, by divine law, also that negro equality was an inalienable right, of which they could not be deprived. He insisted, in that speech, that the Declaration of Independence included the negro in the clause asserting that all men were created equal, and went so far as to say that if one man was allowed to take the position that it did not include the negro, others might take the position that it did not include other men. He said that all these distinctions between this man and that man, this race and the other race, must be discarded, and we must all stand by the Declaration of Independence, declaring that all men were created equal.

The issue thus being made up between Mr. Lincoln and myself on three points, we went before the people of the State. During the following seven weeks, between the Chicago speeches and our first meeting at Ottawa, he and I addressed large assemblages of the people in many of the central counties. In my speeches I confined myself closely to those three positions which he had taken, controverting his proposition that this Union could not exist as our fathers made it, divided into free and slave States, controverting his proposition of a crusade against the Supreme Court because of the Dred Scott decision, and controverting his proposition that the Declaration of Independence included and meant the negroes as well as the white men, when it declared all men to be created equal. I supposed at that time that these propositions constituted a distinct issue between us, and that the opposite positions we had taken upon them we would be willing to be held to in every part of the State. I never intended to waver one hair's breadth from that issue either in the north or the south, or wherever I should address the people of Illinois. I hold that when the time arrives that I cannot proclaim my political creed in the same terms, not only in the northern, but the southern part of Illinois, not only in the Northern, but the Southern States, and wherever the American flag waves over American soil, that then there must be something wrong in that creed; so long as we live under a common Constitution, so long as we live in a confederacy of sovereign and equal States, joined together as one for certain purposes, that any political creed is radically wrong which cannot be proclaimed in every State and every section of that Union, alike. I took up Mr. Lincoln's three propositions in my several speeches, analyzed them, and pointed out what I believed to be the radical errors contained in them. First, in regard to his doctrine that this government was in violation of the law of God, which says that a house divided against itself cannot stand, I repudiated it as a slander upon the immortal framers of our Constitution. I then said, I have often repeated, and now again assert, that in my opinion our government can endure forever, divided into free and slave States as our fathers made it,—each State having the right to prohibit, abolish, or sustain slavery, just as it pleases. This government was made upon the great basis of the sovereignty of the States, the right of each State to regulate its own domestic institutions to suit itself; and that right was conferred with the understanding and expectation that, inasmuch as each locality had separate interests, each locality must have different and distinct local and domestic institutions, corresponding to its wants and interests. Our fathers knew when they made the government that the laws and institutions which were well adapted to the Green Mountains of Vermont were unsuited to the rice plantations of South Carolina. They knew then, as well as we know now, that the laws and institutions which would be well adapted to the beautiful prairies of Illinois would not be suited to the mining regions of California. They knew that in a republic as broad as this, having such a variety of soil, climate, and interest, there must necessarily be a corresponding variety of local laws,—the policy and institutions of each State adapted to its condition and wants. For this reason this Union was established on the right of each State to do as it pleased on the question of slavery, and every other question; and the various States were not allowed to complain of, much less interfere with, the policy of their neighbors.

Suppose the doctrine advocated by Mr. Lincoln and the Abolitionists of this day had prevailed when the Constitution was made, what would have been the result? Imagine for a moment that Mr. Lincoln had been a member of the Convention that framed the Constitution of the United States, and that when its members were about to sign that wonderful document, he had arisen in that Convention as he did at Springfield this summer, and, addressing himself to the President, had said: "A house divided against itself cannot stand; this government divided into free and slave States cannot endure, they must all be free or all be slave; they must all be one thing, or all the other, otherwise, it is a violation of the law of God, and cannot continue to exist";—suppose Mr. Lincoln had convinced that body of sages that that doctrine was sound, what would have been the result? Remember that the Union was then composed of thirteen States, twelve of which were slaveholding, and one free. Do you think that the one free State would have outvoted the twelve slaveholding States, and thus have secured the abolition of slavery? On the other hand, would not the twelve slaveholding States have outvoted the one free State, and thus have fastened slavery, by a constitutional provision, on every foot of the American Republic forever? You see that if this Abolition doctrine of Mr. Lincoln had prevailed when the government was made, it would have established slavery as a permanent institution in all the States, whether they wanted it or not; and the question for us to determine in Illinois now, as one of the free States, is whether or not we are willing, having become the majority section, to enforce a doctrine on the minority which we would have resisted with our heart's blood had it been attempted on us when we were in a minority. How has the South lost her power as the majority section in this Union, and how have the free States gained it, except under the operation of that principle which declares the right of the people of each State and each Territory to form and regulate their domestic institutions in their own way? It was under that principle that slavery was abolished in New Hampshire, Rhode Island, Connecticut, New York, New Jersey, and Pennsylvania; it was under that principle that one half of the slaveholding States became free; it was under that principle that the number of free States increased until, from being one out of twelve States, we have grown to be the majority of States of the whole Union, with the power to control the House of Representatives and Senate, and the power, consequently, to elect a President by Northern votes, without the aid of a Southern State. Having obtained this power under the operation of that great principle, are you now prepared to abandon the principle and declare that merely because we have the power you will wage a war against the Southern States and their institutions until you force them to abolish slavery everywhere?

After having pressed these arguments home on Mr. Lincoln for seven weeks, publishing a number of my speeches, we met at Ottawa in joint discussion, and he then began to crawfish a little, and let himself down. I there propounded certain questions to him. Amongst others, I asked him whether he would vote for the admission of any more slave States, in the event the people wanted them. He would not answer. I then told him that if he did not answer the question there, I would renew it at Freeport, and would then trot him down into Egypt, and again put it to him. Well, at Freeport, knowing that the next joint discussion took place in Egypt, and being in dread of it, he did answer my question in regard to no more slave States in a mode which he hoped would be satisfactory to me, and accomplish the object he had in view. I will show you what his answer was. After saying that he was not pledged to the Republican doctrine of "no more slave States," he declared:

> I state to you freely, frankly, that I should be exceedingly sorry to ever be put in the position of having to pass upon that question. I should be exceedingly glad to know that there never would be another slave State admitted into this Union.

Here permit me to remark, that I do not think the people will ever force him into a position against his will. He went on to say:

But I must add, in regard to this, that if slavery shall be kept out of the Territory during the Territorial existence of any one given Territory, and then the people should, having a fair chance and a clear field, when they come to adopt a constitution, if they should do the extraordinary thing of adopting a slave constitution uninfluenced by the actual presence of the institution among them, I see no alternative, if we own the country, but we must admit it into the Union.

That answer Mr. Lincoln supposed would satisfy the old-line Whigs, composed of Kentuckians and Virginians, down in the southern part of the State. Now, what does it amount to? I desired to know whether he would vote to allow Kansas to come into the Union with slavery or not, as her people desired. He would not answer, but in a roundabout way said that if slavery should be kept out of a Territory during the whole of its Territorial existence, and then the people, when they adopted a State Constitution, asked admission as a slave State, he supposed he would have to let the State come in. The case I put to him was an entirely different one. I desired to know whether he would vote to admit a State if Congress had not prohibited slavery in it during its Territorial existence, as Congress never pretended to do under Clay's Compromise measures of 1850. He would not answer, and I have not yet been able to get an answer from him. I have asked him whether he would vote to admit Nebraska if her people asked to come in as a State with a constitution recognizing slavery, and he refused to answer. I have put the question to him with reference to New Mexico, and he has not uttered a word in answer. I have enumerated the Territories, one after another, putting the same question to him with reference to each, and he has not said, and will not say, whether, if elected to Congress, he will vote to admit any Territory now in existence with such a constitution as her people may adopt. He invents a case which does not exist, and cannot exist under this government, and answers it; but he will not answer the question I put to him in connection with any of the Territories now in existence. The contract we entered into with Texas when she entered the Union obliges us to allow four States to be formed out of the old State, and admitted with or without slavery, as the respective inhabitants of each may determine. I have asked Mr. Lincoln three times in our joint discussions whether he would vote to redeem that pledge, and he has never yet answered. He is as silent as the grave on the subject. He would rather answer as to a state of the case which will never arise than commit himself by telling what he would do in a case which would come up for his action soon after his election to Congress. Why can he not say whether he is willing to allow the people of each State to have slavery or not as they please, and to come into the Union, when they have the requisite population, as a slave or a free State as they decide? I have no trouble in answering the question. I have said everywhere, and now repeat it to you, that if the people of Kansas want a slave State they have a right, under the Constitution of the United States, to form such a State, and I will let them come into the Union with slavery or without, as they determine. If the people of any other Territory desire slavery, let them have it. If they do not want it, let them prohibit it. It is their business, not mine. It is none of our business in Illinois whether Kansas is a free State or a slave State. It is none of your business in Missouri whether Kansas shall adopt slavery or reject it. It is the business of her people, and none of yours. The people of Kansas have as much right to decide that question for themselves as you have in Missouri to decide it for yourselves, or we in Illinois to decide it for ourselves.

And here I may repeat what I have said in every speech I have made in Illinois, that I fought the Lecompton Constitution to its death not because of the slavery clause in it, but because it was not the act and deed of the people of Kansas. I said then in Congress, and I say now, that if the people of Kansas want a slave State, they have a right to have it. If they wanted the Lecompton Constitution, they had a right to have it. I was opposed to that constitution because I did not believe that it was the act and deed of the people, but, on the contrary, the act of a small, pitiful minority acting in the name of the majority. When at last it was determined to send that constitution back to the people, and, accordingly, in August last, the question of admission under it was submitted to a popular vote, the citizens rejected it by nearly ten to one, thus showing conclusively that I was right when I said that the Lecompton Constitution was not the act and deed of the people of Kansas, and did not embody their will.

I hold that there is no power on earth, under our system of government, which has the right to force a constitution upon an unwilling people. Suppose that there had been a majority of ten to one in favor of slavery in Kansas, and suppose there had been an Abolition President and an Abolition Administration, and by some means the Abolitionists succeeded in forcing an Abolition constitution upon those slaveholding people, would the people of the South have submitted to that act for an instant? Well, if you of the South would not have submitted to it a day, how can you, as fair, honorable, and honest men, insist on putting a slave constitution on a people who desire a free State? Your safety and ours depend upon both of us acting in good faith, and living up to that great principle which asserts the right of every people to form and regulate their domestic institutions to suit themselves, subject only to the Constitution of the United States.

Most of the men who denounced my course on the Lecompton question objected to it, not because I was not right, but because they thought it expedient at that time, for the sake of keeping the party together, to do wrong. I never knew the Democratic party to violate any one of its principles, out of policy or expediency, that it did not pay the debt with sorrow. There is no safety or success for our party unless we always do right, and trust the consequences to God and the people. I chose not to depart from principle for the sake of expediency on the Lecompton question, and I never intend to do it on that or any other question.

But I am told that I would have been all right if I had only voted for the English bill after Lecompton was killed. You know a general pardon was granted to all political offenders on the Lecompton question, provided they would only vote for the English bill. I did not accept the benefits of that pardon, for the reason that I had been right in the course I had pursued, and hence did not require any forgiveness. Let us see how the result has been worked out. English brought in his bill referring the Lecompton Constitution back to the people, with the provision that if it was rejected, Kansas should be kept out of the Union until she had the full ratio of population required for a member of Congress,—thus in effect declaring that if the people of Kansas would only consent to come into the Union under the Lecompton Constitution, and have a slave State when they did not want it, they should be admitted with a population of 35,000; but that if they were so obstinate as to insist upon having just such a constitution as they thought best, and to desire admission as a free State, then they should be kept out until they had 93,420 inhabitants. I then said, and I now repeat to you, that whenever Kansas has people enough for a slave State she has people enough for a free State. I was and am willing to adopt the rule that no State shall ever come into the Union until she has the full ratio of population for a member of Congress, provided that rule is made uniform. I made that proposition in the Senate last winter, but a majority of the senators would not agree to it; and I then said to them, If you will not adopt the general rule, I will not consent to make an exception of Kansas.

I hold that it is a violation of the fundamental principles of this government to throw the weight of Federal power into the scale, either in favor of the free or the slave States. Equality among all the States of this Union is a fundamental principle in our political system. We have no more right to throw the weight of the Federal Government into the scale in favor of the slaveholding than the free States, and least of all should our friends in the South consent for a moment that Congress should withhold its powers either way when they know that there is a majority against them in both Houses of Congress.

Fellow-citizens, how have the supporters of the English bill stood up to their pledges not to admit Kansas until she obtained a population of 93,420 in the event she rejected the Lecompton Constitution? How? The newspapers inform us that English himself, whilst conducting his canvass for re-election, and in order to secure it, pledged himself to his constituents that if returned he would disregard his own bill and vote to admit Kansas into the Union with such population as she might have when she made application. We are informed that every Democratic candidate for Congress in all the States where elections have recently been held was pledged against the English bill, with perhaps one or two exceptions. Now, if I had only done as these anti-Lecompton men who voted for the English bill in Congress, pledging themselves to refuse to admit Kansas if she refused to become a slave State until she had a population of 93,420, and then returned to their people, forfeited their pledge, and made a new pledge to admit Kansas at any time she applied, without regard to population, I would have had no trouble. You saw the whole power and patronage of the Federal Government wielded in Indiana, Ohio, and Pennsylvania to re-elect anti-Lecompton men to Congress who voted against Lecompton, then voted for the English bill, and then denounced the English bill, and pledged themselves to their people to disregard it. My sin consists in not having given a pledge, and then in not having afterward forfeited it. For that reason, in this State, every postmaster, every route agent, every collector of the ports, and every Federal office-holder forfeits his head the moment he expresses a preference for the Democratic candidates against Lincoln and his Abolition associates. A Democratic Administration which we helped to bring into power deems it consistent with its fidelity to principle and its regard to duty to wield its power in this State in behalf of the Republican Abolition candidates in every county and every Congressional District against the Democratic party. All I have to say in reference to the matter is, that if that Administration have not regard enough for principle, if they are not sufficiently attached to the creed of the Democratic party, to bury forever their personal hostilities in order to succeed in carrying out our glorious principles, I have. I have no personal difficulty with Mr. Buchanan or his Cabinet. He chose to make certain recommendations to Congress, as he had a right to do, on the Lecompton question. I could not vote in favor of them. I had as much right to judge for myself how I should vote as he had how he should recommend. He undertook to say to me, "If you do not vote as I tell you I will take off the heads of your friends." I replied to him, "You did not elect me. I represent Illinois, and I am accountable to Illinois, as my constituency, and to God; but not to the President or to any other power on earth."

And now this warfare is made on me because I would not surrender my convictions of duty, because I would not abandon my constituency, and receive the orders of the executive authorities how I should vote in the Senate of the United States. I hold that an attempt to control the Senate on the part of the Executive is subversive of the principles of our Constitution. The Executive department is independent of the Senate, and the Senate is independent of the President. In matters of legislation the President has a veto on the action of the Senate, and in appointments and treaties the Senate has a veto on the President. He has no more right to tell me how I shall vote on his appointments than I have to tell him whether he shall veto or approve a bill that the Senate has passed. Whenever you recognize the right of the Executive to say to a senator, "Do this, or I will take off the heads of your friends," you convert this government from a republic into a despotism. Whenever you recognize the right of a President to say to a member of Congress, "Vote as I tell you, or I will bring a power to bear against you at home which will crush you," you destroy the independence of the representative, and convert him into a tool of Executive power. I resisted this invasion of the constitutional rights of a senator, and I intend to resist it as long as I have a voice to speak or a vote to give. Yet Mr. Buchanan cannot provoke me to abandon one iota of Democratic principles out of revenge or hostility to his course. I stand by the platform of the Democratic party, and by its organization, and support its nominees. If there are any who choose to bolt, the fact only shows that they are not as good Democrats as I am.

My friends, there never was a time when it was as important for the Democratic party, for all national men, to rally and stand together, as it is to-day. We find all sectional men giving up past differences and continuing the one question of slavery; and when we find sectional men thus uniting, we should unite to resist them and their treasonable designs. Such was the case in 1850, when Clay left the quiet and peace of his home, and again entered upon public life to quell agitation and restore peace to a distracted Union. Then we Democrats, with Cass at our head, welcomed Henry Clay, whom the whole nation regarded as having been preserved by God for the times. He became our leader in that great fight, and we rallied around him the same as the Whigs rallied around old Hickory in 1832 to put down nullification. Thus you see that whilst Whigs and Democrats fought fearlessly in old times about banks, the tariff, distribution, the specie circular, and the sub-treasury, all united as a band of brothers when the peace, harmony, or integrity of the Union was imperiled. It was so in 1850, when Abolitionism had even so far divided this country. North and South, as to endanger the peace of the Union; Whigs and Democrats united in establishing

the Compromise measures of that year and restoring tranquillity and good feeling. These measures passed on the joint action of the two parties. They rested on
the great principle that the people of each State and each Territory should be left
perfectly free to form and regulate their domestic institutions to suit themselves.
You Whigs and we Democrats justified them in that principle. In 1854, when it
became necessary to organize the Territories of Kansas and Nebraska, I brought
forward the bill on the same principle. In the Kansas-Nebraska Bill you find
it declared to be the true intent and meaning of the act not to legislate slavery
into any State or Territory, nor to exclude it therefrom, but to leave the people
thereof perfectly free to form and regulate their domestic institutions in their
own way. I stand on that same platform in 1858 that I did in 1850, 1854, and
1856. The Washington *Union,* pretending to be the organ of the Administration,
in the number of the 5th of this month devotes three columns and a half to
establish these propositions: first, that Douglas, in his Freeport speech, held the
same doctrine that he did in his Nebraska Bill in 1854; second, that in 1854
Douglas justified the Nebraska Bill upon the ground that it was based upon the
same principle as Clay's Compromise measures of 1850. The *Union* thus proved
that Douglas was the same in 1858 that he was in 1856, 1854, and 1850, and
consequently argued that he was never a Democrat. Is it not funny that I was
never a Democrat? There is no pretence that I have changed a hair's breadth.
The *Union* proves by my speeches that I explained the Compromise measures of
1850 just as I do now, and that I explained the Kansas and Nebraska Bill in 1854
just as I did in my Freeport speech, and yet says that I am not a Democrat, and
cannot be trusted, because I have not changed during the whole of that time. It
has occurred to me that in 1854 the author of the Kansas and Nebraska Bill was
considered a pretty good Democrat. It has occurred to me that in 1856, when I
was exerting every nerve and every energy for James Buchanan, standing on the
same platform then that I do now, that I was a pretty good Democrat. They now
tell me that I am not a Democrat, because I assert that the people of a Territory,
as well as those of a State, have the right to decide for themselves whether slavery
can or cannot exist in such Territory. Let me read what James Buchanan said on
that point when he accepted the Democratic nomination for the presidency in
1856. In his letter of acceptance, he used the following language:

> The recent legislation of Congress respecting domestic slav-
> ery, derived as it has been from the original and pure fountain
> of legitimate political power, the will of the majority, promises
> ere long to allay the dangerous excitement. This legislation is

founded upon principles as ancient as free government itself, and, in accordance with them, has simply declared that the people of a Territory, like those of a State, shall decide for themselves whether slavery shall or shall not exist within their limits.

Dr. Hope will there find my answer to the question he propounded to me before I commenced speaking. Of course, no man will consider it an answer who is outside of the Democratic organization, bolts Democratic nominations, and indirectly aids to put Abolitionists into power over Democrats. But whether Dr. Hope considers it an answer or not, every fair-minded man will see that James Buchanan has answered the question, and has asserted that the people of a Territory, like those of a State, shall decide for themselves whether slavery shall or shall not exist within their limits. I answer specifically if you want a further answer, and say that while, under the decision of the Supreme Court, as recorded in the opinion of Chief Justice Taney, slaves are property like all other property, and can be carried into any Territory of the United States the same as any other description of property, yet when you get them there they are subject to the local law of the Territory just like all other property. You will find in a recent speech delivered by that able and eloquent statesman Hon. Jefferson Davis, at Bangor, Maine, that he took the same view of this subject that I did in my Freeport speech. He there said:

> If the inhabitants of any Territory should refuse to enact such laws and police regulations as would give security to their property or to his, it would be rendered more or less valueless in proportion to the difficulties of holding it without such protection. In the case of property in the labor of man, or what is usually called slave property, the insecurity would be so great that the owner could not ordinarily retain it. Therefore, though the right would remain, the remedy being withheld, it would follow that the owner would be practically debarred, by the circumstances of the case, from taking slave property into a Territory where the sense of the inhabitants was opposed to its introduction. So much for the oft-repeated fallacy of forcing slavery upon any community.

You will also find that the distinguished Speaker of the present House of Representatives, Hon. Jas. L. Orr, construed the Kansas and Nebraska Bill in this same way in 1856, and also that great intellect of the South, Alex. H. Stephens, put the same construction upon it in Congress that I did in my Freeport speech. The whole South are rallying to the support of the doctrine that if the people of a Territory want slavery, they have a right to have it, and if they do not want it, that no power on earth can force it upon them. I hold that there is no principle on earth more sacred to all the friends of freedom than that which says that no institution, no law, no constitution, should be forced on an unwilling people contrary to their wishes; and I assert that the Kansas and Nebraska Bill contains that principle. It is the great principle contained in that bill. It is the principle on which James Buchanan was made President. Without that principle, he never would have been made President of the United States. I will never violate or abandon that doctrine, if I have to stand alone. I have resisted the blandishments and threats of power on the one side, and seduction on the other, and have stood immovably for that principle, fighting for it when assailed by Northern mobs, or threatened by Southern hostility. I have defended it against the North and the South, and I will defend it against whoever assails it, and I will follow it wherever its logical conclusions lead me. I say to you that there is but one hope, one safety for this country, and that is to stand immovably by that principle which declares the right of each State and each Territory to decide these questions for themselves. This government was founded on that principle, and must be administered in the same sense in which it was founded.

But the Abolition party really think that under the Declaration of Independence the negro is equal to the white man, and that negro equality is an inalienable right conferred by the Almighty, and hence that all human laws in violation of it are null and void. With such men it is no use for me to argue. I hold that the signers of the Declaration of Independence had no reference to negroes at all when they declared all men to be created equal. They did not mean negroes, nor the savage Indians, nor the Feejee Islanders, nor any other barbarous race. They were speaking of white men. They alluded to men of European birth and European descent,—to white men, and to none others,—when they declared that doctrine. I hold that this government was established on the white basis. It was established by white men for the benefit of white men and their posterity forever, and should be administered by white men, and none others. But it does not follow by any means, that merely because the negro is not a citizen, and merely because he is not our equal, that, therefore, he should be a slave. On the contrary, it does follow that we ought to extend to the negro race, and to all other dependent races, all the rights, all the privileges, and all the immunities which they can exercise consistently with the safety of society. Humanity requires that we should give them all these privileges;

Christianity commands that we should extend those privileges to them. The question then arises. What are those privileges, and what is the nature and extent of them? My answer is, that that is a question which each State must answer for itself. We in Illinois have decided it for ourselves. We tried slavery, kept it up for twelve years, and, finding that it was not profitable, we abolished it for that reason, and became a free State. We adopted in its stead the policy that a negro in this State shall not be a slave and shall not be a citizen. We have a right to adopt that policy. For my part, I think it is a wise and sound policy for us. You in Missouri must judge for yourselves whether it is a wise policy for you. If you choose to follow our example, very good; if you reject it, still well,—it is your business, not ours. So with Kentucky. Let Kentucky adopt a policy to suit herself. If we do not like it we will keep away from it; and if she does not like ours, let her stay at home, mind her own business, and let us alone. If the people of all the States will act on that great principle, and each State mind its own business, attend to its own affairs, take care of its own negroes, and not meddle with its neighbors, then there will be peace between the North and the South, the East and the West, throughout the whole Union.

Why can we not thus have peace? Why should we thus allow a sectional party to agitate this country, to array the North against the South, and convert us into enemies instead of friends, merely that a few ambitious men may ride into power on a sectional hobby? How long is it since these ambitious Northern men wished for a sectional organization? Did any one of them dream of a sectional party as long as the North was the weaker section and the South the stronger? Then all were opposed to sectional parties; but the moment the North obtained the majority in the House and Senate by the admission of California, and could elect a President without the aid of Southern votes, that moment ambitious Northern men formed a scheme to excite the North against the South, and make the people be governed in their votes by geographical lines, thinking that the North, being the stronger section, would outvote the South, and consequently they, the leaders, would ride into office on a sectional hobby. I am told that my hour is out. It was very short.

## Mr. Lincoln's Reply

LADIES AND GENTLEMEN: I have been somewhat, in my own mind, complimented by a large portion of Judge Douglas's speech,—I mean that portion which he devotes to the controversy between himself and the present Administration. This is the seventh time Judge Douglas and myself have met in these joint discussions, and he has been gradually improving in regard to his war with the Administration. At Quincy, day before yesterday, he was a little more severe upon the Administration than I had heard him upon any occasion, and I took pains to compliment him for it. I then told him to give it to them with all the power he had; and as some of them were present, I told them I would be very much obliged if they would *give it to him* in about the same way. I take it he has now vastly improved upon the attack he made then upon the Administration. I flatter myself he has really taken my advice on this subject. All I can say now is to re-commend to him and to them what I then commended,—to prosecute the war against one another in the most vigorous manner. I say to them again: "Go it, husband!—Go it, bear!"

There is one other thing I will mention before I leave this branch of the discussion,—although I do not consider it much of my business, anyway. I refer to that part of the Judge's remarks where he undertakes to involve Mr. Buchanan in an inconsistency. He reads something from Mr. Buchanan, from which he undertakes to involve him in an inconsistency; and he gets something of a cheer for having done so. I would only remind the Judge that while he is very valiantly fighting for the Nebraska Bill and the repeal of the Missouri Compromise, it has been but a little while since he was the *valiant advocate* of the Missouri Compromise. I want to know if Buchanan has not as much right to be inconsistent as Douglas has. Has Douglas the *exclusive right,* in this country, of being *on all sides of all questions?* Is nobody allowed that high privilege but himself? Is he to have an entire *monopoly* on that subject?

So far as Judge Douglas addressed his speech to me, or so far as it was about me, it is my business to pay some attention to it. I have heard the Judge state two or three times what he has stated to-day, that in a speech which I made at Springfield, Illinois, I had in a very especial manner complained that the Supreme Court in the Dred Scott case had decided that a negro could never be a citizen of the United States. I have omitted by some accident heretofore to analyze this statement, and it is required of me to notice it now. In point of fact it is *untrue.* I never have complained *especially* of the Dred Scott decision because it held that a negro could not be a citizen, and the Judge is always wrong when he says I ever did so complain of it. I have the speech here, and I will thank him or any of his friends to show where I said that a negro should be a citizen, and complained especially of the Dred Scott decision because it declared he could not be one. I have done no such thing; and Judge Douglas, so persistently insisting that I have done so, has strongly impressed me with the belief of a predetermination on his part to misrepresent me. He could not get his foundation for insisting that I was in favor of this negro equality anywhere else as well as he could by assuming that untrue proposition. Let me tell this audience what is true in regard to that matter; and the means by which they may correct me if I do not tell them truly is by a recurrence to the speech itself. I spoke of the Dred Scott decision in my Springfield speech, and I was then endeavoring to prove that the Dred Scott decision was a portion of a system or scheme to make slavery national in this country. I pointed out what things had been decided by the court. I mentioned as a fact that they had decided that a negro could not be a citizen; that they had done so, as I supposed, to deprive the negro, under all circumstances, of the remotest possibility of ever becoming a citizen and claiming the rights of a citizen of the United States under a certain clause of the Constitution. I stated that, without making any complaint of it at all. I then went on and stated the other points decided in the case; namely, that the bringing of a negro into the State of Illinois and holding him in slavery for two years here was a matter in regard to which they would not decide whether it would make him free or not; that they decided the further point that taking him into a United States Territory where slavery was prohibited by Act of Congress did not make him free, because that Act of Congress, as they held, was unconstitutional. I mentioned these three things as making up the points decided in that case. I mentioned them in a lump, taken in connection with the introduction of the Nebraska Bill, and the amendment of Chase, offered at the time, declaratory of the right of the people of the Territories to *exclude slavery*, which was voted down by the friends of the bill. I mentioned all these things together, as evidence tending to prove a combination and conspiracy to make the institution of slavery national. In that connection and in that way I mentioned the decision on the point that a negro could not be a citizen, and in no other connection.

Out of this Judge Douglas builds up his beautiful fabrication of my purpose to introduce a perfect social and political equality between the white and black races. His assertion that I made an "especial objection" (that is his exact language) to the decision on this account is untrue in point of fact.

Now, while I am upon this subject, and as Henry Clay has been alluded to, I desire to place myself, in connection with Mr. Clay, as nearly right before this people as may be. I am quite aware what the Judge's object is here by all these allusions. He knows that we are before an audience having strong sympathies southward, by relationship, place of birth, and so on. He desires to place me in an extremely Abolition attitude. He read upon a former occasion, and alludes, without reading, to-day to a portion of a speech which I delivered in Chicago. In his quotations from that speech, as he has made them upon former occasions, the extracts were taken in such a way as, I suppose, brings them within the definition of what is called *garbling*,—taking portions of a speech which, when taken by themselves, do not present the entire sense of the speaker as expressed at the time. I propose, therefore, out of that same speech, to show how one portion of it which he skipped over (taking an extract before and an extract after) will give a different idea, and the true idea I intended to convey. It will take me some little time to read it, but I believe I will occupy the time that way.

You have heard him frequently allude to my controversy with him in regard to the Declaration of Independence. I confess that I have had a struggle with Judge Douglas on that matter, and I will try briefly to place myself right in regard to it on this occasion. I said—and it is between the extracts Judge Douglas has taken from this speech, and put in his published speeches:

> It may be argued that there are certain conditions that make necessities and impose them upon us, and to the extent that a necessity is imposed upon a man he must submit to it. I think that was the condition in which we found ourselves when we established this government. We had slaves among us, we could not get our Constitution unless we permitted them to remain in slavery, we could not secure the good we did secure if we grasped for more; and having by necessity submitted to that much, it does not destroy the principle that is the charter of our liberties. Let the charter remain as our standard.

Now, I have upon all occasions declared as strongly as Judge Douglas against the disposition to interfere with the existing institution of slavery. You hear me read it from the same speech from which he takes garbled extracts for the purpose of proving upon me a disposition to interfere with the institution of slavery, and establish a perfect social and political equality between negroes and white people.

Allow me while upon this subject briefly to present one other extract from a speech of mine, more than a year ago, at Springfield, in discussing this very same question, soon after Judge Douglas took his ground that negroes were not included in the Declaration of Independence:

> I think the authors of that notable instrument intended to include *all* men, but they did not mean to declare all men equal *in all respects*. They did not mean to say all men were equal in color, size, intellect, moral development, or social capacity. They defined with tolerable distinctness in what they did consider all men created equal,—equal in certain inalienable rights,

among which are life, liberty, and the pursuit of happiness. This they said, and this they meant. They did not mean to assert the obvious untruth that all were then actually enjoying that equality, or yet that they were about to confer it immediately upon them. In fact they had no power to confer such a boon. They meant simply to declare the *right,* so that the *enforcement* of it might follow as fast as circumstances should permit.

They meant to set up a standard maxim for free society which should be familiar to all,—constantly looked to, constantly labored for, and even, though never perfectly attained, constantly approximated, and thereby constantly spreading and deepening its influence, and augmenting the happiness and value of life to all people, of all colors, everywhere.

There again are the sentiments I have expressed in regard to the Declaration of Independence upon a former occasion,—sentiments which have been put in print and read wherever anybody cared to know what so humble an individual as myself chose to say in regard to it.

At Galesburgh, the other day, I said, in answer to Judge Douglas, that three years ago there never had been a man, so far as I knew or believed, in the whole world, who had said that the Declaration of Independence did not include negroes in the term "all men." I reassert it to-day. I assert that Judge Douglas and all his friends may search the whole records of the country, and it will be a matter of great astonishment to me if they shall be able to find that one human being three years ago had ever uttered the astounding sentiment that the term "all men" in the Declaration did not include the negro. Do not let me be misunderstood. I know that more than three years ago there were men who, finding this assertion constantly in the way of their schemes to bring about the ascendency and perpetuation of slavery, *denied the truth of it.* I know that Mr. Calhoun and all the politicians of his school denied the truth of the Declaration. I know that it ran along in the mouth of some Southern men for a period of years, ending at last in that shameful, though rather forcible, declaration of Pettit of Indiana, upon the floor of the United States Senate, that the Declaration of Independence was in that respect "a self-evident lie," rather than a self-evident truth. But I say, with a perfect knowledge of all this hawking at the Declaration without directly attacking it, that three years ago there never had lived a man who had ventured to assail it in the sneaking way of pretending to believe it, and then asserting it did not include the negro. I believe the first man who ever said it was Chief Justice Taney in the

Dred Scott case, and the next to him was our friend Stephen A. Douglas. And now it has become the catchword of the entire party. I would like to call upon his friends everywhere to consider how they have come in so short a time to view this matter in a way so entirely different from their former belief; to ask whether they are not being borne along by an irresistible current,—whither, they know not.

In answer to my proposition at Galesburgh last week, I see that some man in Chicago has got up a letter, addressed to the Chicago *Times,* to show, as he professes, that somebody *had* said so before; and he signs himself "An Old-Line Whig," if I remember correctly. In the first place, I would say he *was not* an old-line Whig. I am somewhat acquainted with old-line Whigs from the origin to the end of that party; I became pretty well acquainted with them, and I know they always had some sense, whatever else you could ascribe to them. I know there never was one who had not more sense than to try to show by the evidence he produces that some men had, prior to the time I named, said that negroes were not included in the term "all men" in the Declaration of Independence. What is the evidence he produces? I will bring forward *his* evidence, and let you see what *he* offers by way of showing that somebody more than three years ago had said negroes were not included in the Declaration. He brings forward part of a speech from Henry Clay,—*the* part of *the* speech of Henry Clay which I used to bring forward to prove precisely the contrary. I guess we are surrounded to some extent to-day by the old friends of Mr. Clay, and they will be glad to hear anything from that authority. While he was in Indiana a man presented a petition to liberate his negroes, and he (Mr. Clay) made a speech in answer to it, which I suppose he carefully wrote out himself and caused to be published. I have before me an extract from that speech which constitutes the evidence this pretended "Old-Line Whig" at Chicago brought forward to show that Mr. Clay didn't suppose the negro was included in the Declaration of Independence. Hear what Mr. Clay said:

> And what is the foundation of this appeal to me in Indiana to liberate the slaves under my care in Kentucky? It is a general declaration in the act announcing to the world the independence of the thirteen American colonies, that all men are created equal. Now, as an abstract principle, *there is no doubt of the truth of that declaration*; and it is desirable, *in the original construction of society and in organized societies*, to keep it in view as a great fundamental principle. But, then, I apprehend that in no society that ever did exist, or ever shall be formed, was or can the equality asserted among the members of the human race be practically enforced

and carried out. There are portions, large portions,—women, minors, insane, culprits, transient sojourners,—that will always probably remain subject to the government of another portion of the community.

That declaration, whatever may be the extent of its import, was made by the delegations of the thirteen States. In most of them slavery existed, and had long existed, and was established by law. It was introduced and forced upon the colonies by the paramount law of England. Do you believe that in making that declaration the States that concurred in it intended that it should be tortured into a virtual emancipation of all the slaves within their respective limits? Would Virginia and other Southern States have ever united in a declaration which was to be interpreted into an abolition of slavery among them? Did any one of the thirteen colonies entertain such a design or expectation? To impute such a secret and unavowed purpose, would be to charge a political fraud upon the noblest band of patriots that ever assembled in council,—a fraud upon the Confederacy of the Revolution; a fraud upon the union of those States whose Constitution not only recognized the lawfulness of slavery, but permitted the importation of slaves from Africa until the year 1808.

This is the entire quotation brought forward to prove that somebody previous to three years ago had said the negro was not included in the term "all men" in the Declaration. How does it do so? In what way has it a tendency to prove that? Mr. Clay says *it is true as an abstract principle* that all men are created equal, but that we cannot practically apply it in all cases. He illustrates this by bringing forward the cases of females, minors, and insane persons, with whom it cannot be enforced; but he says it is true as an abstract principle in the organization of society as well as in organized society and it should be kept in view as a fundamental principle. Let me read a few words more before I add some comments of my own. Mr. Clay says, a little further on:

I desire no concealment of my opinions in regard to the institution of slavery. I look upon it as a great evil, and deeply lament that we have derived it from the parental government and from our ancestors. I wish every slave in the United States was in the country of his ancestors. But here they are, and the

> question is, How can they be best dealt with? If a state of nature existed, and we were about to lay the foundations of society, *no man would be more strongly opposed than I should be to incorporate the institution of slavery among its elements.*

Now, here in this same book, in this same speech, in this same extract, brought forward to prove that Mr. Clay held that the negro was not included in the Declaration of Independence, is no such statement on his part, but the declaration *that it is a great fundamental truth* which should be constantly kept in view in the organization of society and in societies already organized. But if I say a word about it; if I attempt, as Mr. Clay said all good men ought to do, to keep it in view; if, in this "organized society," I ask to have the public eye turned upon it; if I ask, in relation to the organization of new Territories, that the public eye should be turned upon it,—forthwith I am vilified as you hear me to-day. What have I done that I have not the license of Henry Clay's illustrious example here in doing? Have I done aught that I have not his authority for, while maintaining that in organizing new Territories and societies this fundamental principle should be regarded, and in organized society holding it up to the public view and recognizing what *he* recognized as the great principle of free government?

And when this new principle—this new proposition that no human being ever thought of three years ago—is brought forward, *I combat it* as having an evil tendency, if not an evil design. I combat it as having a tendency to dehumanize the negro, to take away from him the right of ever striving to be a man. I combat it as being one of the thousand things constantly done in these days to prepare the public mind to make property, and nothing but property, of the *negro in all the States of this Union.*

But there is a point that I wish, before leaving this part of the discussion, to ask attention to. I have read and I repeat the words of Henry Clay:

> I desire no concealment of my opinions in regard to the institution of slavery. I look upon it as a great evil, and deeply lament that we have derived it from the parental government and from our ancestors. I wish every slave in the United States was in the country of his ancestors. But here they are, and the question is, How can they best be dealt with? If a state of nature existed, and we were about to lay the foundations of society, no man would be more strongly opposed than I should be to incorporate the institution of slavery among its elements.

The principle upon which I have insisted in this canvass is in relation to laying the foundations of new societies. I have never sought to apply these principles to the old States for the purpose of abolishing slavery in those States. It is nothing but a miserable perversion of what I *have* said, to assume that I have declared Missouri, or any other slave State, shall emancipate her slaves; I have proposed no such thing. But when Mr. Clay says that in laying the foundations of society in our Territories where it does not exist, he would be opposed to the introduction of slavery as an element, I insist that we have *his warrant*—his license—for insisting upon the exclusion of that element which he declared in such strong and emphatic language *was most hateful to him.*

Judge Douglas has again referred to a Springfield speech in which I said "a house divided against itself cannot stand." The Judge has so often made the entire quotation from that speech that I can make it from memory. I used this language:

> We are now far into the fifth year since a policy was initiated with the avowed object and confident promise of putting an end to the slavery agitation. Under the operation of this policy, that agitation has not only not ceased, but has constantly augmented. In my opinion it will not cease until a crisis shall have been reached and passed. "A house divided against itself cannot stand." I believe this government cannot endure permanently, half slave and half free. I do not expect the house to fall, but I do expect it will cease to be divided. It will become all one thing, or all the other. Either the opponents of slavery will arrest the further spread of it, and place it where the public mind shall rest in the belief that it is in the course of ultimate extinction, or its advocates will push it forward till it shall become alike lawful in all the States,—old as well as new, North as well as South.

That extract and the sentiments expressed in it have been extremely offensive to Judge Douglas. He has warred upon them as Satan wars upon the Bible. His perversions upon it are endless. Here now are my views upon it in brief:

I said we were now far into the fifth year since a policy was initiated with the avowed object and confident promise of putting an end to the slavery agitation. Is it not so? When that Nebraska Bill was brought forward four years ago last January, was it not for the "avowed object" of putting an end to the slavery agitation? We were to have no more agitation in Congress; it was all to be banished to the Territories. By the way, I will remark here that, as Judge Douglas is very fond of complimenting Mr. Crittenden in these days, Mr. Crittenden has said there was a falsehood in that whole business, for there was *no slavery agitation at that time to allay.* We were for a little while *quiet* on the troublesome thing, and that very allaying plaster of Judge Douglas's stirred it up again. But was it not understood or intimated with the "confident promise" of putting an end to the slavery agitation? Surely it was. In every speech you heard Judge Douglas make, until he got into this "imbroglio," as they call it, with the Administration about the Lecompton Constitution, every speech on that Nebraska Bill was full of his felicitations that we were *just at the end* of the slavery agitation. The last tip of the last joint of the old serpent's tail was just drawing out of view. But has it proved so? I have asserted that under that policy that agitation "has not only not ceased, but has constantly augmented." When was there ever a greater agitation in Congress than last winter? When was it as great in the country as to-day?

There was a collateral object in the introduction of that Nebraska policy, which was to clothe the people of the Territories with a superior degree of self-government, beyond what they had ever had before. The first object and the main one of conferring upon the people a higher degree of "self-government" is a question of fact to be determined by you in answer to a single question. Have you ever heard or known of a people anywhere on earth who had as little to do as, in the first instance of its use, the people of Kansas had with this same right of "self-government"? In its main policy and in its collateral object, *it has been nothing but a living, creeping lie from the time of its introduction till to-day.*

I have intimated that I thought the agitation would not cease until a crisis should have been reached and passed. I have stated in what way I thought it would be reached and passed. I have said that it might go one way or the other. We might, by arresting the further spread of it, and placing it where the fathers originally placed it, put it where the public mind should rest in the belief that it was in the course of ultimate extinction. Thus the agitation may cease. It may be pushed forward until it shall become alike lawful in all the States, old as well as new, North as well as South. I have said, and I repeat, my wish is that the further spread of it may be arrested, and that it may be placed where the public mind shall rest in the belief that it is in the course of ultimate extinction. I have expressed that as my wish. I entertain the opinion, upon evidence sufficient to my mind, that the fathers of this government placed that institution where the public mind *did* rest in the belief that it was in the course of ultimate extinction. Let me ask why they made provision that the source of slavery—the African slave-trade—should be cut off at the end of twenty years? Why did they make provision that in all the new territory we owned at that time slavery should be forever inhibited? Why stop its spread in one direction, and cut off its source in another, if they did not look to its being placed in the course of its ultimate extinction?

Again: the institution of slavery is only mentioned in the Constitution of the United States two or three times, and in neither of these cases does the word "slavery" or "negro race" occur; but covert language is used each time, and for a purpose full of significance. What is the language in regard to the prohibition of the African slave-trade? It runs in about this way: "The migration or importation of such persons as any of the States now existing shall think proper to admit, shall not be prohibited by the Congress prior to the year one thousand eight hundred and eight."

The next allusion in the Constitution to the question of slavery and the black race is on the subject of the basis of representation, and there the language used is:

> Representatives and direct taxes shall be apportioned among the several States which may be included within this Union, according to their respective numbers, which shall be determined by adding to the whole number of free persons, including those bound to service for a term of years, and excluding Indians not taxed,—three-fifths of all other persons.

It says "persons," not slaves, not negroes; but this "three-fifths" can be applied to no other class among us than the negroes.

Lastly, in the provision for the reclamation of fugitive slaves, it is said: "No person held to service or labor in one State, under the laws thereof, escaping into another, shall in consequence of any law or regulation therein be discharged from such service or labor, but shall be delivered up, on claim of the party to whom such service or labor may be due." There again there is no mention of the word "negro" or of slavery. In all three of these places, being the only allusions to slavery in the instrument, covert language is used. Language is used not suggesting that slavery existed or that the black race were among us. And I understand the contemporaneous history of those times to be that covert language was used with a purpose, and that purpose was that in our Constitution, which it was hoped and is still hoped will endure forever,—when it should be read by intelligent and patriotic men, after the institution of slavery had passed from among us,—there should be nothing on the face of the great charter of liberty suggesting that such a thing as negro slavery had ever existed among us. This is part of the evidence that the fathers of the government expected and intended the institution of slavery to come to an end. They expected and intended that it should be in the course of ultimate extinction. And when I say that I desire to see the further spread of it arrested, I only say I desire to see that done which the fathers have first done. When I say I desire to see it placed where the public mind will rest in the belief that it is in the course of ultimate extinction, I only say I desire to see it placed where they placed it. It is not true that our fathers, as Judge Douglas assumes, made this government part slave and part free. Understand the sense in which he puts it. He assumes that slavery is a rightful thing within itself,—was introduced by the framers of the Constitution. The exact truth is, that they found the institution existing among us, and they left it as they found it. But in making the government they left this institution with many clear marks of disapprobation upon it. They found slavery among them, and they left it among them because of the difficulty—the absolute impossibility—of its immediate removal. And when Judge Douglas asks me why we cannot let it remain part slave and part free, as the fathers of the government made it, he asks a question based upon an assumption which is itself a falsehood; and I turn upon him and ask him the question, when the policy that the fathers of the government had adopted in relation to this element among us was the best policy in the world, the only wise policy, the only policy that we can ever safely continue upon that will ever give us peace, unless this dangerous element masters us all and becomes a national institution,—*I turn upon him and ask him why he could not leave it alone.* I turn and ask him why he was driven to the necessity of introducing a *new policy* in regard to it. He has himself said he introduced a new policy. He said so in his speech on the 22d of March of the present year, 1858. I ask him why he could not let it remain where our fathers placed it. I ask, too, of Judge Douglas and his friends why we shall not again place this institution upon the basis on which the fathers left it. I ask you, when he infers that I am in favor of setting the free and slave States at war, when the institution was placed in that attitude by those who made the Constitution, *did they make any war?* If we had no war out of it when thus placed, wherein is the ground of belief that we shall have war out of it if we return to that policy? Have we had any peace upon this matter springing from any other basis? I maintain that we have not. I have proposed nothing more than a return to the policy of the fathers.

I confess, when I propose a certain measure of policy, it is not enough for me that I do not intend anything evil in the result, but it is incumbent on me to show that it has not a *tendency* to that result. I have met Judge Douglas in that point of view. I have not only made the declaration that I do not *mean* to produce a conflict between the States, but I have tried to show by fair reasoning, and I think I have shown to the minds of fair men, that I propose nothing but what has a most peaceful tendency. The quotation that I happened to make in that Springfield Speech, that "a house divided against itself cannot stand," and which has proved so offensive to the Judge, was part and parcel of the same thing. He tries to show that variety in the domestic institutions of the different States is necessary and indispensable. I do not dispute it. I have no controversy with Judge Douglas about that. I shall very readily agree with him that it would be foolish for us to insist upon having a cranberry law here in Illinois, where we have no cranberries, because they have a cranberry law in Indiana, where they have cranberries. I should insist that it would be exceedingly wrong in us to deny to Virginia the right to enact oyster laws, where they have oysters, because we want no such laws here. I understand, I hope, quite as well as Judge Douglas or anybody else, that the variety in the soil and climate and face of the country, and consequent variety in the industrial pursuits and productions of a country, require systems of law conforming to this variety in the natural features of the country. I understand quite as well as Judge Douglas that if we here raise a barrel of flour more than we want, and the Louisianians raise a barrel of sugar more than they want, it is of mutual advantage to exchange. That produces commerce, brings us together, and makes us better friends. We like one another the more for it. And I understand as well as Judge Douglas, or anybody else, that these mutual accommodations are the cements which bind together the different parts of this Union; that instead of being a thing to "divide the house,"—figuratively expressing the Union,—they tend to sustain it; they are the props of the house, tending always to hold it up.

But when I have admitted all this, I ask if there is any parallel between these things and this institution of slavery? I do not see that there is any parallel at all between them. Consider it. When have we had any difficulty or quarrel amongst ourselves about the cranberry laws of Indiana, or the oyster laws of Virginia, or the pine-lumber laws of Maine, or the fact that Louisiana produces sugar, and Illinois flour? When have we had any quarrels over these things? When have we had perfect peace in regard to this thing which I say is an element of discord in this Union? We have sometimes had peace, but when was it? It was when the institution of slavery remained quiet where it was. We have had difficulty and turmoil whenever it has made a struggle to spread itself where it was not. I ask, then, if experience does not speak in thunder-tones telling us that the policy which has given peace to the country heretofore, being returned to, gives the greatest promise of peace again. You may say, and Judge Douglas has intimated the same thing, that all this difficulty in regard to the institution of slavery is the mere agitation of office-seekers and ambitious Northern politicians. He thinks we want to get "his place," I suppose. I agree that there are office-seekers amongst us. The Bible says somewhere that we are desperately selfish. I think we would have discovered that fact without the Bible. I do not claim that I am any less so than the average of men, but I do claim that I am not more selfish than Judge Douglas.

But is it true that all the difficulty and agitation we have in regard to this institution of slavery spring from office-seeking, from the mere ambition of politicians? Is that the truth? How many times have we had danger from this question? Go back to the day of the Missouri Compromise. Go back to the Nullification question, at the bottom of which lay this same slavery question. Go back to the time of the annexation of Texas. Go back to the troubles that led to the Compromise of 1850. You will find that every time, with the single exception of the Nullification question, they sprung from an endeavor to spread this institution. There never was a party in the history of this country, and there probably never will be, of sufficient strength to disturb the general peace of the country. Parties themselves may be divided and quarrel on minor questions, yet it extends not beyond the parties themselves. But does *not* this question make a disturbance outside of political circles? Does it not enter into the churches and rend them asunder? What divided the great Methodist Church into two parts, North and South? What has raised this constant disturbance in every Presbyterian General Assembly that meets? What disturbed the Unitarian Church in this very city two years ago? What has jarred and shaken the great American Tract Society recently, not yet splitting it, but sure to divide it in the end? Is it not this same mighty, deep-seated power that somehow operates on the minds of men, exciting and stirring them up in every avenue of society,—in politics, in religion, in literature, in morals, in all the manifold relations of life? Is this the work of politicians? Is that irresistible power, which for fifty years has shaken the government and agitated the people, to be stilled and subdued by pretending that it is an exceedingly simple thing, and we ought not to talk about it? If you will get everybody else to stop talking about it, I assure you I will quit before they have half done so. But where is the philosophy or statesmanship which assumes that you can quiet that disturbing element in our society which has disturbed us for more than half a century, which has been the only serious danger that has threatened our institutions,—I say, where is the philosophy or the statesmanship based on the assumption that we are to quit talking about it, and that the public mind is all at once to cease being agitated by it? Yet this is the policy here in the North that Douglas is advocating,—that we are to care nothing about it! I ask you if it is not a false philosophy. Is it not a false statesmanship that undertakes to build up a system of policy upon the basis of caring nothing about *the very thing that everybody does care the most about*—a thing which all experience has shown we care a very great deal about?

The Judge alludes very often in the course of his remarks to the exclusive right which the States have to decide the whole thing for themselves. I agree with him very readily that the different States have that right. He is but fighting a man of straw when he assumes that I am contending against the right of the States to do as they please about it. Our controversy with him is in regard to the new Territories. We agree that when the States come in as States they have the right and the power to do as they please. We have no power as citizens of the free States, or in our Federal capacity as members of the Federal Union through the General Government, to disturb slavery in the States where it exists. We profess constantly that we have no more inclination than belief in the power of the government to disturb it; yet we are driven constantly to defend ourselves from the assumption that we are warring upon the rights of the *States*. What I insist upon is, that the new Territories shall be kept free from it while in the Territorial condition. Judge Douglas assumes that we have no interest in them,—that we have no right whatever to interfere. I think we have some interest. I think that as white men we have. Do we not wish for an outlet for our surplus population, if I may so express myself? Do we not feel an interest in getting to that outlet with such institutions as we would like to have prevail there? If *you* go to the Territory opposed to slavery, and another man comes upon the same ground with his slave, upon the assumption that the things are equal, it turns out that he has the equal right all his way, and you have no part of it your way. If he goes in and makes it a slave Territory, and by consequence a slave State, is it not time that those who desire to have it a free State were on equal ground? Let me suggest it in a different way. How many Democrats are there about here ["A thousand"] who have left slave States and come into the free State of Illinois to get rid of the institution of slavery? [Another voice: "A thousand and one."] I reckon there are a thousand and one. I will ask you, if the policy you are now advocating had prevailed when this country was in a Territorial condition, where would you have gone to get rid of it? Where would you have found your free State or Territory to go to? And when hereafter, for any cause, the people in this place shall desire to find new homes, if they wish to be rid of the institution, where will they find the place to go to?

Now, irrespective of the moral aspect of this question as to whether there is a right or wrong in enslaving a negro, I am still in favor of our new Territories being in such a condition that white men may find a home,—may find some spot where they can better their condition; where they can settle upon new soil and better their condition in life. I am in favor of this, not merely (I must say it here as I have elsewhere) for our own people who are born amongst us, but as an outlet for *free white people everywhere*—the world over—in which Hans, and

Baptiste, and Patrick, and all other men from all the world, may find new homes and better their conditions in life.

I have stated upon former occasions, and I may as well state again, what I understand to be the real issue in this controversy between Judge Douglas and myself. On the point of my wanting to make war between the free and the slave States, there has been no issue between us. So, too, when he assumes that I am in favor of introducing a perfect social and political equality between the white and black races. These are false issues, upon which Judge Douglas has tried to force the controversy. There is no foundation in truth for the charge that I maintain either of these propositions. The real issue in this controversy—the one pressing upon every mind—is the sentiment on the part of one class that looks upon the institution of slavery *as a wrong*, and of another class that *does not* look upon it as a wrong. The sentiment that contemplates the institution of slavery in this country as a wrong is the sentiment of the Republican party. It is the sentiment around which all their actions, all their arguments, circle, from which all their propositions radiate. They look upon it as being a moral, social, and political wrong; and while they contemplate it as such, they nevertheless have due regard for its actual existence among us, and the difficulties of getting rid of it in any satisfactory way, and to all the constitutional obligations thrown about it. Yet, having a due regard for these, they desire a policy in regard to it that looks to its not creating any more danger. They insist that it should, as far as may be, *be treated* as a wrong; and one of the methods of treating it as a wrong is to *make provision that it shall grow no larger*. They also desire a policy that looks to a peaceful end of slavery at some time, as being wrong. These are the views they entertain in regard to it as I understand them; and all their sentiments, all their arguments and propositions, are brought within this range. I have said, and I repeat it here, that if there be a man amongst us who does not think that the institution of slavery is wrong in any one of the aspects of which I have spoken, he is misplaced, and ought not to be with us. And if there be a man amongst us who is so impatient of it as a wrong as to disregard its actual presence among us and the difficulty of getting rid of it suddenly in a satisfactory way, and to disregard the constitutional obligations thrown about it, that man is misplaced if he is on our platform. We disclaim sympathy with him in practical action. He is not placed properly with us.

On this subject of treating it as a wrong, and limiting its spread, let me say a word. Has anything ever threatened the existence of this Union save and except this very institution of slavery? What is it that we hold most dear amongst us? Our own liberty and prosperity. What has ever threatened our liberty and prosperity, save and except this institution of slavery? If this is true, how do you propose to improve the condition of things by enlarging slavery,—by spreading it out and making it bigger? You may have a wen or cancer upon your person, and not be able to cut it out, lest you bleed to death; but surely it is no way to cure it, to engraft it and spread it over your whole body. That is no proper way of treating what you regard a wrong. You see this peaceful way of dealing with it as a wrong,—restricting the spread of it, and not allowing it to go into new countries where it has not already existed. That is the peaceful way, the old-fashioned way, the way in which the fathers themselves set us the example.

On the other hand, I have said there is a sentiment which treats it as *not* being wrong. That is the Democratic sentiment of this day. I do not mean to say that every man who stands within that range positively asserts that it is right. That class will include all who positively assert that it is right, and all who, like Judge Douglas, treat it as indifferent and do not say it is either right or wrong. These two classes of men fall within the general class of those who do not look upon it as a wrong. And if there be among you anybody who supposes that he, as a Democrat, can consider himself "as much opposed to slavery as anybody," I would like to reason with him. You never treat it as a wrong. What other thing that you consider as a wrong do you deal with as you deal with that? Perhaps you *say* it is wrong, *but your leader never does, and you quarrel with anybody who says it is wrong.* Although you pretend to say so yourself, you can find no fit place to deal with it as a wrong. You must not say anything about it in the free States, *because it is not here.* You must not say anything about it in the slave States, *because it is there.* You must not say anything about it in the pulpit, because that is religion, and has nothing to do with it. You must not say anything about it in politics, *because that will disturb the security* of *"my place."* There is no place to talk about it as being a wrong, although you say yourself it is a wrong. But, finally, you will screw yourself up to the belief that if the people of the slave States should adopt a system of gradual emancipation on the slavery question, you would be in favor of it. You would be in favor of it. You say that is getting it in the right place, and you would be glad to see it succeed. But you are deceiving yourself. You all know that Frank Blair and Gratz Brown, down there in St. Louis, undertook to introduce that system in Missouri. They fought as valiantly as they could for the system of gradual emancipation which you pretend you would be glad to see succeed. Now, I will bring you to the test. After a hard fight they were beaten, and when the news came over here, you threw up your hats and *hurrahed for Democracy.* More than that, take all the argument made in favor of the system you have proposed, and it carefully excludes the idea that there is anything wrong in the institution of slavery. The arguments to sustain that policy carefully exclude it. Even here to-day you heard Judge Douglas quarrel with me because I uttered a wish that it might sometime come to an end. Although Henry Clay could say he wished every slave in the United States was in the country of his ancestors, I am denounced by those pretending to respect Henry Clay for uttering a wish that it might sometime, in some peaceful way, come to an end. The Democratic policy in regard to that institution will not tolerate the merest breath, the slightest hint, of the least degree of wrong about it. Try it by some of Judge Douglas's arguments. He says he "don't care whether it is voted up or voted down" in the Territories. I do not care myself, in dealing with that expression, whether it is intended to be expressive of his individual sentiments on the subject, or only of the national policy he desires to have established. It is alike valuable for my purpose. Any man can say that who does not see anything wrong in slavery; but no man can logically say it who does see a wrong in it, because no man can logically say he don't care whether a wrong is voted up or voted down. He may say he don't care whether an indifferent thing is voted up or down, but he must logically have a choice between a right thing and a wrong thing. He contends that whatever community wants slaves has a right to have them. So they have, if it is not a wrong. But if it is a wrong, he cannot say people have a right to do wrong. He says that upon the score of equality slaves should be allowed to go in a new Territory, like other property. This is strictly logical if there is no difference between it and other property. If it and other property are equal, this argument is entirely logical. But if you insist that one is wrong and the other right, there is no use to institute a comparison between right and wrong. You may turn over everything in the Democratic policy from beginning to end, whether in the shape it takes on the statute book, in the shape it takes in the Dred Scott decision, in the shape it takes in conversation, or the shape it takes in short maxim-like arguments,—it everywhere carefully excludes the idea that there is anything wrong in it.

That is the real issue. That is the issue that will continue in this country when these poor tongues of Judge Douglas and myself shall be silent. It is the eternal struggle between these two principles—right and wrong—throughout the world. They are the two principles that have stood face to face from the beginning of time, and will ever continue to struggle. The one is the common right of humanity, and the other the divine right of kings. It is the same principle in whatever shape it develops itself. It is the same spirit that says, "You work and toil and earn bread, and I'll eat it." No matter in what shape it comes, whether from the mouth of a king who seeks to bestride the people of his own nation and live by the fruit of their labor, or from one race of men as an apology for enslaving another race, it is the same tyrannical principle. I was glad to express my gratitude at Quincy, and I re-express it here, to Judge Douglas,—*that he looks to no end of the institution of slavery*. That will help the people to see where the struggle really is. It will hereafter place with us all men who really do wish the wrong may have an end. And whenever we can get rid of the fog which obscures the real question, when we can get Judge Douglas and his friends to avow a policy looking to its perpetuation,—we can get out from among that class of men and bring them to the side of those who treat it as a wrong. Then there will soon be an end of it, and that end will be its "ultimate extinction." Whenever the issue can be distinctly made, and all extraneous matter thrown out so that men can fairly see the real difference between the parties, this controversy will soon be settled, and it will be done peaceably too. There will be no war, no violence. It will be placed again where the wisest and best men of the world placed it. Brooks of South Carolina once declared that when this Constitution was framed its framers did not look to the institution existing until this day. When he said this, I think he stated a fact that is fully borne out by the history of the times. But he also said they were better and wiser men than the men of these days, yet the men of these days had experience which they had not, and by the invention of the cotton-gin it became a necessity in this country that slavery should be perpetual. I now say that, willingly or unwillingly, purposely or without purpose, Judge Douglas has been the most prominent instrument in changing the position of the institution of slavery,—which the fathers of the government expected to come to an end ere this,—*and putting it upon Brooks's cotton-gin basis*; placing it where he openly confesses he has no desire there shall ever be an end of it.

I understand I have ten minutes yet. I will employ it in saying something about this argument Judge Douglas uses, while he sustains the Dred Scott decision, that the people of the Territories can still somehow exclude slavery. The first thing I ask attention to is the fact that Judge Douglas constantly said, before the decision, that whether they could or not, *was a question for the Supreme Court*. But after the court had made the decision he virtually says it is *not* a question for the Supreme Court, but for the people. And how is it he tells us they can exclude it? He says it needs "police regulations," and that admits of "unfriendly legislation." Although it is a right established by the Constitution of the United States to take a slave into a Territory of the United States and hold him as property, yet unless the Territorial Legislature will give friendly legislation, and more especially if they adopt unfriendly legislation, they can practically exclude him. Now, without meeting this proposition as a matter of fact, I pass to consider the real constitutional obligation. Let me take the gentleman who looks me in the face before me, and let us suppose that he is a member of the Territorial Legislature. The first thing he will do will be to swear that he will support the Constitution of the United States. His neighbor by his side in the Territory has slaves and needs Territorial legislation to enable him to enjoy that constitutional right. Can he withhold the legislation which his neighbor needs for the enjoyment of a right which is fixed in his favor in the Constitution of the United States which he has sworn to support? Can he withhold it without violating his oath? And, more especially, can he pass unfriendly legislation to violate his oath? Why, this is a *monstrous* sort of talk about the Constitution of the United States! *There has never been as outlandish or lawless a doctrine from the mouth of any respectable man on earth.* I do not believe it is a constitutional right to hold slaves in a Territory of the United States. I believe the decision was improperly made and I go for reversing it. Judge Douglas is furious against those who go for reversing a decision. But he is for legislating it out of all force while the law itself stands. I repeat that there has never been so monstrous a doctrine uttered from the mouth of a respectable man.

I suppose most of us (I know it of myself) believe that the people of the Southern States are entitled to a Congressional Fugitive Slave law,—that is a right fixed in the Constitution. But it cannot be made available to them without Congressional legislation. In the Judge's language, it is a "barren right," which needs legislation before it can become efficient and valuable to the persons to whom it is guaranteed. And as the right is constitutional, I agree that the legislation shall be granted to it,—and that not that we like the institution of slavery. We profess to have no taste for running and catching niggers,—at least, I profess no taste for that job at all. Why then do I yield support to a Fugitive Slave law? Because I do not understand that the Constitution, which guarantees that right, can be supported without it. And if I believed that the right to hold a slave in a Territory was equally fixed in the Constitution with the right to reclaim fugitives, I should be bound to give it the legislation necessary to support it. I say that no man can deny his obligation to give the necessary legislation to support slavery in a Territory, who believes it is a constitutional right to have it there. No man can, who does not give the Abolitionists an argument to deny the obligation enjoined by the Constitution to enact a Fugitive State law. Try it now. It is the strongest Abolition argument ever made. I say if that Dred Scott decision is correct, then the right to hold slaves in a Territory is equally a constitutional right with the right of a slaveholder to have his runaway returned. No one can show the distinction between them. The one is express, so that we cannot deny it. The other is construed to be in the Constitution, so that he who believes the decision to be correct believes in the right. And the man who argues that by unfriendly legislation, in spite of that constitutional right, slavery may be driven from the Territories, can-

not avoid furnishing an argument by which Abolitionists may deny the obligation to return fugitives, and claim the power to pass laws unfriendly to the right
of the slaveholder to reclaim his fugitive. I do not know how such an argument
may strike a popular assembly like this, but I defy anybody to go before a body of
men whose minds are educated to estimating evidence and reasoning, and show
that there is an iota of difference between the constitutional right to reclaim a
fugitive and the constitutional right to hold a slave, in a Territory, provided this
Dred Scott decision is correct, I defy any man to make an argument that will
justify unfriendly legislation to deprive a slaveholder of his right to hold his slave
in a Territory, that will not equally, in all its length, breadth, and thickness, furnish an argument for nullifying the Fugitive Slave law. Why, there is not such an
Abolitionist in the nation as Douglas, after all!

## MR. DOUGLAS'S REJOINDER

Mr. Lincoln has concluded his remarks by saymg that there is not such an
Abolitionist as I am in all America. If he could make the Abolitionists of Illinois
believe that, he would not have much show for the Senate. Let him make the
Abolitionists believe the truth of that statement, and his political back is broken.

His first criticism upon me is the expression of his hope that the war of the
Administration will be prosecuted against me and the Democratic party of this
State with vigor. He wants that war prosecuted with vigor; I have no doubt of
it. His hopes of success and the hopes of his party depend solely upon it. They
have no chance of destroying the Democracy of this State except by the aid of
Federal patronage. He has all the Federal office-holders here as his allies, running
separate tickets against the Democracy to divide the party, although the leaders
all intend to vote directly the Abolition ticket, and only leave the greenhorns to
vote this separate ticket who refuse to go into the Abolition camp. There is something really refreshing in the thought that Mr. Lincoln is in favor of prosecuting
one war vigorously. It is the first war that I ever knew him to be in favor of prosecuting. It is the first war that I ever knew him to believe to be just or constitutional. When the Mexican War was being waged, and the American army was
surrounded by the enemy in Mexico, he thought that war was unconstitutional,
unnecessary, and unjust. He thought it was not commenced on the right *spot*.

When I made an incidental allusion of that kind in the joint discussion
over at Charleston some weeks ago, Lincoln, in replying, said that I, Douglas,
had charged him with voting against supplies for the Mexican War, and then he
reared up, full length, and swore that he never voted against the supplies; that
it was a slander; and caught hold of Ficklin, who sat on the stand, and said,

"Here, Ficklin, tell the people that it is a lie." Well, Ficklin, who had served in Congress with him, stood up and told them all that he recollected about it. It was that when George Ashmun, of Massachusetts, brought forward a resolution declaring the war unconstitutional, unnecessary and unjust, that Lincoln had voted for it. "Yes," said Lincoln, "I did." Thus he confessed that he voted that the war was wrong, that our country was in the wrong, and consequently that the Mexicans were in the right; but charged that I had slandered him by saying that he voted against the supplies. I never charged him with voting against the supplies in my life, because I knew that he was not in Congress when they were voted. The war was commenced on the 13th day of May, 1846, and on that day we appropriated in Congress ten millions of dollars and fifty thousand men to prosecute it. During the same session we voted more men and more money, and at the next session we voted more men and more money, so that by the time Mr. Lincoln entered Congress we had enough men and enough money to carry on the war, and had no occasion to vote for any more. When he got into the House, being opposed to the war, and not being able to stop the supplies, because they had all gone forward, all he could do was to follow the lead of Corwin, and prove that the war was not begun on the right spot, and that it was unconstitutional, unnecessary, and wrong. Remember, too, that this he did after the war had been begun. It is one thing to be opposed to the declaration of a war, another and very different thing to take sides with the enemy against your own country after the war has been commenced. Our army was in Mexico at the time, many battles had been fought; our citizens, who were defending the honor of their country's flag, were surrounded by the daggers, the guns, and the poison of the enemy. Then it was that Corwin made his speech in which he declared that the American soldiers ought to be welcomed by the Mexicans with bloody hands and hospitable graves; then it was that Ashmun and Lincoln voted in the House of Representatives that the war was unconstitutional and unjust; and Ashmun's resolution, Corwin's speech, and Lincoln's vote were sent to Mexico and read at the head of the Mexican army, to prove to them that there was a Mexican party in the Congress of the United States who were doing all in their power to aid them. That a man who takes sides with the common enemy against his own country in time of war should rejoice in a war being made on me now, is very natural. And, in my opinion, no other kind of a man would rejoice in it.

Mr. Lincoln has told you a great deal to-day about his being an old-line Clay Whig. Bear in mind that there are a great many old Clay Whigs down in this region. It is more agreeable, therefore, for him to talk about the old Clay Whig party than it is for him to talk Abolitionism. We did not hear much about the old Clay Whig party up in the Abolition districts. How much of an old-line Henry Clay Whig was he? Have you read General Singleton's speech at Jacksonville? You know that General Singleton was for twenty-five years the confidential friend of Henry Clay in Illinois, and he testified that in 1847, when the Constitutional Convention of this State was in session, the Whig members were invited to a Whig caucus at the house of Mr. Lincoln's brother-in-law, where Mr. Lincoln proposed to throw Henry Clay overboard and take up General Taylor in his place, giving as his reason that if the Whigs did not take up General Taylor the Democrats would. Singleton testifies that Lincoln in that speech urged as another reason for throwing Henry Clay overboard that the Whigs had fought long enough for principle and ought to begin to fight for success. Singleton also testifies that Lincoln's speech did have the effect of cutting Clay's throat, and that he (Singleton) and others withdrew from the caucus in indignation. He further states that when they got to Philadelphia to attend the National Convention of the Whig party, that Lincoln was there, the bitter and deadly enemy of Clay, and that he tried to keep him (Singleton) out of the Convention because he insisted on voting for Clay, and Lincoln was determined to have Taylor. Singleton says that Lincoln rejoiced with very great joy when he found the mangled remains of the murdered Whig statesman lying cold before him. Now, Mr. Lincoln tells you that he is an old-line Clay Whig! General Singleton testifies to the facts I have narrated, in a public speech which has been printed and circulated broadcast over the State for weeks, yet not a lisp have we heard from Mr. Lincoln on the subject, except that he is an old Clay Whig.

What part of Henry Clay's policy did Lincoln ever advocate? He was in Congress in 1848–9, when the Wilmot Proviso warfare disturbed the peace and harmony of the country, until it shook the foundation of the Republic from its centre to its circumference. It was that agitation that brought Clay forth from his retirement at Ashland again to occupy his seat in the Senate of the United States, to see if he could not, by his great wisdom and experience, and the renown of his name, do something to restore peace and quiet to a disturbed country. Who got up that sectional strife that Clay had to be called upon to quell? I have heard Lincoln boast that he voted forty-two times for the Wilmot Proviso, and that he would have voted as many times more if he could. Lincoln is the man, in connection with Seward, Chase, Giddings, and other Abolitionists, who got up that strife that I helped Clay to put down. Henry Clay came back to the Senate in 1849, and saw that he must do something to restore peace to the country. The Union Whigs and the Union Democrats welcomed him, the moment he arrived, as the man for the occasion. We believed that he, of all men on earth, had been preserved by Divine Providence to guide us out of our difficulties, and we Democrats rallied under Clay then, as you Whigs in Nullification time rallied under the banner of old Jackson, forgetting party when the country was in danger, in order that we might have a country first, and parties afterwards.

And this reminds me that Mr. Lincoln told you that the slavery question was the only thing that ever disturbed the peace and harmony of the Union. Did not Nullification once raise its head and disturb the peace of this Union in 1832? Was that the slavery question, Mr. Lincoln? Did not disunion raise its monster head during the last war with Great Britain? Was that the slavery question, Mr. Lincoln? The peace of this country has been disturbed three times, once during the war with Great Britain, once on the tariff question, and once on the slavery question. His argument, therefore, that slavery is the only question that has ever created dissension in the Union falls to the ground. It is true that agitators are enabled now to use this slavery question for the purpose of sectional strife. He admits that in regard to all things else, the principle that I advocate, making each State and Territory free to decide for itself, ought to prevail. He instances the cranberry laws and the oyster laws, and he might have gone through the whole list with the same effect. I say that all these laws are local and domestic, and that local and domestic concerns should be left to each State and each Territory to manage for itself. If agitators would acquiesce in that principle, there never would be any danger to the peace and harmony of the Union.

Mr. Lincoln tries to avoid the main issue by attacking the truth of my proposition that our fathers made this government divided into free and slave States, recognizing the right of each to decide all its local questions for itself. Did they not thus make it? It is true that they did not establish slavery in any of the States, or abolish it in any of them; but finding thirteen States, twelve of which were slave and one free, they agreed to form a government uniting them together as they stood, divided into free and slave States, and to guarantee forever to each State the right to do as it pleased on the slavery question. Having thus made the government, and conferred this right upon each State forever, I assert that this government can exist as they made it, divided into free and slave States, if any one State chooses to retain slavery. He says that he looks forward to a time when slavery shall be abolished everywhere. I look forward to a time when each State shall be allowed to do as it pleases. If it chooses to keep slavery forever, it is not my business, but its own; if it chooses to abolish slavery, it is its own business,— not mine. I care more for the great principle of self-government, the right of the people to rule, than I do for all the negroes in Christendom. I would not endanger the perpetuity of this Union, I would not blot out the great inalienable rights of the white man, for all the negroes that ever existed. Hence, I say, let us maintain this government on the principles that our fathers made it, recognizing the right of each State to keep slavery as long as its people determine, or to abolish it when they please. But Mr. Lincoln says that when our fathers made this government they did not look forward to the state of things now existing, and therefore he thinks the doctrine was wrong; and he quotes Brooks of South Carolina to prove that our fathers then thought that probably slavery would be abolished by each State acting for itself before this time. Suppose they did; suppose they did not foresee what has occurred,—does that change the principles of our government? They did not, probably, foresee the telegraph that transmits intelligence by lightning, nor did they foresee the railroads that now form the bonds of union between the different States, or the thousand mechanical inventions that have elevated mankind. But do these things change the principles of the government? Our fathers, I say, made this government on the principle of the right of each State to do as it pleases in its own domestic affairs, subject to the Constitution, and allowed the people of each to apply to every new change of circumstances such remedy as they may see fit to improve their condition. This right they have for all time to come.

Mr. Lincoln went on to tell you that he does not at all desire to interfere with slavery in the States where it exists, nor does his party. I expected him to say that down here. Let me ask him, then, how he expects to put slavery in the course of ultimate extinction everywhere, if he does not intend to interfere with it in the States where it exists? He says that he will prohibit it in all Territories, and the inference is, then, that unless they make free States out of them he will keep them out of the Union; for, mark you, he did not say whether or not he would vote to admit Kansas with slavery or not, as her people might apply (he forgot that, as usual, etc.): he did not say whether or not he was in favor of bringing the Territories now in existence into the Union on the principle of Clay's Compromise measures on the slavery question. I told you that he would not. His idea is that he will prohibit slavery in all the Territories and thus force them all to become free States, surrounding the slave States with a cordon of free States, and hemming them in, keeping the slaves confined to their present limits whilst they go on multiplying, until the soil on which they live will no longer feed them, and he will thus be able to put slavery in a course of ultimate extinction by starvation. He will extinguish slavery in the Southern States as the French general exterminated the Algerines when he smoked them out. He is going to extinguish slavery by surrounding the slave States, hemming in the slaves, and starving them out of existence, as you smoke a fox out of his hole. He intends to do that in the name of humanity and Christianity, in order that we may get rid of the terrible crime and sin entailed upon our fathers of holding slaves. Mr. Lincoln makes out that line of policy, and appeals to the moral sense of justice and to the Christian feeling of the community to sustain him. He says that any man who holds to the contrary doctrine is in the position of the king who claimed to govern by divine right. Let us examine for a moment and see what principle it was that overthrew the divine right of George the Third to govern us. Did not these colonies rebel because the British Parliament had no right to pass laws concerning our property and domestic and private institutions without our consent? We demanded that the British Government should not pass such laws unless they gave us representation in the body passing them; and this the British Government insisting on doing, we went to war, on the principle that the home government should not control and govern distant colonies without giving them a representation. Now, Mr. Lincoln proposes to govern the Territories without giving them a representation, and calls on Congress to pass laws controlling their property and domestic concerns without their consent and against their will. Thus, he asserts for his party the identical principle asserted by George III and the Tories of the Revolution.

I ask you to look into these things, and then tell me whether the Democracy or the Abolitionists are right. I hold that the people of a Territory, like those of a State (I use the language of Mr. Buchanan in his Letter of Acceptance), have the right to decide for themselves whether slavery shall or shall not exist within their limits. The point upon which Chief Justice Taney expresses his opinion is simply this, that slaves, being property, stand on an equal footing with other property, and consequently that the owner has the same right to carry that property into a Territory that he has any other, subject to the same conditions. Suppose that one of your merchants was to take fifty or one hundred thousand dollars' worth of liquors to Kansas. He has a right to go there, under that decision; but when he gets there he finds the Maine liquor law in force, and what can he do with his property after he gets it there? He cannot sell it, he cannot use it; it is subject to the local law, and that law is against him, and the best thing he can do with it is to bring it back into Missouri or Illinois and sell it. If you take negroes to Kansas, as Colonel Jefferson Davis said in his Bangor speech, from which I have quoted to-day, you must take them there subject to the local law. If the people want the institution of slavery, they will protect and encourage it; but if they do not want it, they will withhold that protection, and the absence of local legislation protecting slavery excludes it as completely as a positive prohibition. You slaveholders of Missouri might as well understand, what you know practically, that you cannot carry slavery where the people do not want it. All you have a right to ask is that the people shall do as they please: if they want slavery, let them have it; if they do not want it, allow them to refuse to encourage it.

My friends, if, as I have said before, we will only live up to this great fundamental principle, there will be peace between the North and the South. Mr. Lincoln admits that, under the Constitution, on all domestic questions, except slavery, we ought not to interfere with the people of each State. What right have we to interfere with slavery any more than we have to interfere with any other question? He says that this slavery question is now the bone of contention. Why? Simply because agitators have combined in all the free States to make war upon it. Suppose the agitators in the States should combine in one half of the Union to make war upon the railroad system of the other half? They would thus be driven to the same sectional strife. Suppose one section makes war upon any other peculiar institution of the opposite section, and the same strife is produced. The only remedy and safety is that we shall stand by the Constitution as our fathers made it, obey the laws as they are passed, while they stand the proper test, and sustain the decisions of the Supreme Court and the constituted authorities.

# LATER ADDRESSES, SPEECHES, *and* WRITINGS

# Lecture on Discoveries, Inventions, and Improvements

We have all heard of Young America. He is the most *current* youth of the age. Some think him conceited, and arrogant; but has he not reason to entertain a rather extensive opinion of himself? Is he not the inventor and owner of the *present,* and sole hope of the *future?* Men, and things, everywhere, are ministering unto him. Look at his apparel, and you shall see cotton fabrics from Manchester and Lowell; flax-linen from Ireland; wool-cloth from Spain; silk from France; furs from the Arctic region; with a buffalo-robe from the Rocky Mountains, as a general out-sider. At his table, besides plain bread and meat made at home, are sugar from Louisiana; coffee and fruits from the tropics; salt from Turk's Island; fish from New-foundland; tea from China, and spices from the Indies. The whale of the Pacific furnishes his candle-light; he has a diamond-ring from Brazil; a gold-watch from California, and a spanish cigar from Havana. He not only has a present supply of all these, and much more; but thousands of hands are engaged in producing fresh supplies, and other thousands, in bringing them to him. The iron horse is panting, and impatient, to carry him everywhere in no time; and the lightening stands ready harnessed to take and bring his tidings in a trifle less than no time. He owns a large part of the world, by right of possessing it; and all the rest by right of *wanting* it, and *intending* to have it. As Plato had for the immortality of the soul, so Young America has "a pleasing hope—a fond desire—a longing after" territory. He has a great passion—a perfect rage—for the "*new*"; particularly new men for office, and the new earth mentioned in the revelations, in which, being no more sea, there must be about three times as much land as in the present. He is a great friend of humanity; and his desire for land is not self-ish, but merely an impulse to extend the area of freedom. He is very anxious to fight for the liberation of enslaved nations and colonies, provided, always, they *have* land, and have *not* any liking for his interference. As to those who have no land, and would be glad of help from any quarter, he considers *they* can afford to wait a few hundred years longer. In knowledge he is particularly rich. He knows all that can possibly be known; inclines to believe in spiritual rappings, and is the unquestioned inventor of "*Manifest Destiny.*" His horror is for all that is old, particularly "Old Fogy"; and if there be any thing old which he can endure, it is only old whiskey and old tobacco.

If the said Young America really is, as he claims to be, the owner of all present, it must be admitted that he has considerable advantage of Old Fogy. Take, for instance, the first of all fogies, father Adam. There he stood, a very perfect physical man, as poets and painters inform us; but he must have been very ignorant, and simple in his habits. He had had no sufficient time to learn much by observation; and he had no near neighbors to teach him anything. No part of his breakfast had been brought from the other side of the world; and it is quite probable, he had no conception of the world having any other side. In all these things, it is very plain, he was no equal of Young America; the most that can be said is, that *according to his chance* he may have been quite as much of a man as his very self-complaisant descendant. Little as was what he knew, let the Youngster discard all he has learned from others, and then show, if he can, any advantage on his side. In the way of *land* and *live stock*, Adam was quite in the ascendant. He had dominion over all the earth, and all the living things upon, and round about it. The land has been sadly divided out since; but never fret, Young America will *re-annex* it.

The great difference between Young America and Old Fogy, is the result of *Discoveries, Inventions,* and *Improvements*. These, in turn, are the result of *observation, reflection* and *experiment*. For instance, it is quite certain that ever since water has been boiled in covered vessels, men have seen the lids of the vessels rise and fall a little, with a sort of fluttering motion, by force of the steam; but so long as this was not specially observed, and reflected and experimented upon, it came to nothing. At length however, after many thousand years, some man observes this long-known effect of hot water lifting a pot-lid, and begins a train of reflection upon it. He says, "Why, to be sure, the force that lifts the pot-lid will lift any thing else, which is no heavier than the pot-lid." "And, as man has much hard fighting to do, can not this hot-water power be made to help him?" He has become a little excited on the subject, and he fancies he hears a voice answering "Try me." He does try it; and the *observation, reflection,* and *trial* gives to the world the control of that tremendous, and now well known agent, called steam-power. This is not the actual history in detail, but the general principle.

But was this first inventor of the application of steam, wiser or more ingenious than those who had gone before him? Not at all. Had he not learned much of them, he never would have succeeded—probably, never would have thought of making the attempt. To be fruitful in invention, it is indispensable to have a *habit* of observation and reflection; and this *habit*, our steam friend acquired, no doubt, from those who, to him, were old fogies. But for the difference in *habit* of observation, why did yankees, almost instantly, discover gold in California, which had been trodden upon, and overlooked by indians and Mexican greasers, for centuries? Gold-mines are not the only mines overlooked in the same way. There are more mines above the Earth's surface than below it. All nature—the whole world, material, moral, and intellectual,—is a mine; and, in Adam's day, it was a wholly unexplored mine. Now, it was the destined work of Adam's race to develop, by discoveries, inventions, and improvements, the hidden treasures of this mine. But Adam had nothing to turn his attention to the work. If he should do anything in the way of invention, he had first to invent the art of invention— the *instance* at least, if not the *habit* of observation and reflection. As might be expected he seems not to have been a very observing man at first; for it appears he went about naked a considerable length of time, before he ever noticed that obvious fact. But when he did observe it, the observation was not lost upon him; for it immediately led to the first of all inventions, of which we have any direct account—*the fig-leaf apron.*

The inclination to exchange thoughts with one another is probably an original impulse of our nature. If I be in pain I wish to let you know it, and to ask your sympathy and assistance; and my pleasurable emotions also, I wish to communicate to, and share with you. But to carry on such communication, some *instrumentality* is indispensable. Accordingly speech—articulate sounds rattled off from the tongue—was used by our first parents, and even by Adam, before the creation of Eve. He gave names to the animals while she was still a bone in his side; and he broke out quite volubly when she first stood before him, the best present of his maker. From this it would appear that speech was not an invention of man, but rather the direct gift of his Creator. But whether Divine gift, or invention, it is still plain that if a mode of communication had been left to invention, *speech* must have been the first, from the superior adaptation to the end, of the organs of speech, over every other means within the whole range of nature. Of the organs of speech the tongue is the principal; and if we shall test it, we shall find the capacities of the tongue, in the utterance of articulate sounds, absolutely wonderful. You can count from one to one hundred, quite distinctly in about forty seconds. In doing this two hundred and eighty three distinct sounds or syllables are uttered, being seven to each second; and yet there shall be enough difference between every two, to be easily recognized by the ear of the hearer. What other *signs* to represent *things* could possibly be produced so rapidly? or, even, if ready made, could be *arranged* so rapidly to express the sense? *Motions* with the hands are no adequate substitute. *Marks* for the recognition of the eye—*writing*—although a wonderful auxiliary for speech, is no worthy substitute for it. In addition to the more slow and laborious process of getting up a communication in writing, the materials—pen, ink, and paper—are not always at hand. But one always has his tongue with him, and the breath of his life is the ever-ready material with which it works. Speech, then, by enabling different individuals to interchange thoughts, and thereby to combine their powers of observation and reflection, greatly facilitates useful discoveries and inventions. What one observes, and would himself infer nothing from, he tells to another, and that other at once sees a valuable hint in it. A result is thus reached which neither *alone* would have arrived at.

And this reminds me of what I passed unnoticed before, that the very first invention was a joint operation, Eve having shared with Adam the getting up of the apron. And, indeed, judging from the fact that sewing has come down to our times as "woman's work" it is very probable she took the leading part; he, perhaps, doing no more than to stand by and thread the needle. That proceeding may be reckoned as the mother of all "Sewing societies"; and the first and most perfect "world's fair" all inventions and all inventors then in the world, being on the spot.

But speech alone, valuable as it ever has been, and is, has not advanced the condition of the world much. This is abundantly evident when we look at the degraded condition of all those tribes of human creatures who have no considerable additional means of communicating thoughts. *Writing*—the art of communicating thoughts to the mind, through the eye—is the great invention of the world. Great is the astonishing range of analysis and combination which necessarily underlies the most crude and general conception of it—great, very great in enabling us to converse with the dead, the absent, and the unborn, at all distances of time and of space; and great, not only in its direct benefits, but greatest help, to all other inventions. Suppose the art, with all conception of it, were this day lost to the world, how long, think you, would it be, before Young America could get up the letter A. with any adequate notion of using it to advantage? The precise period at which writing was invented, is not known; but it certainly was as early as the time of Moses; from which we may safely infer that it's inventors were very old fogies.

Webster, at the time of writing his Dictionary, speaks of the English Language as then consisting of seventy or eighty thousand words. If so, the language in which the five books of Moses were written must, at that time, now thirty-three or -four hundred years ago, have consisted of at least one quarter as many, or, twenty thousand. When we remember that words are *sounds* merely, we shall conclude that the idea of representing those sounds by *marks*, so that whoever should at any time after see the marks, would understand what sounds they meant, was a bold and ingenious conception, not likely to occur to one man in a million, in the run of a thousand years. And, when it did occur, a distinct mark for each word, giving twenty thousand different marks first to be learned, and afterwards remembered, would follow as the second thought, and would present such a difficulty as would lead to the conclusion that the whole thing was impracticable. But the *necessity* still would exist; and we may readily suppose that the idea was conceived, and lost, and reproduced, and dropped, and taken up again and again, until at last the thought of dividing sounds into parts, and making a mark, not to represent a whole sound, but only a part of one, and then of combining those marks, not very many in number, upon principles of permutation, so as to represent any and all of the whole twenty thousand words, and even any additional number was somehow conceived and pushed into practice. This was the invention of *phonetic* writing, as distinguished from the clumsy picture writing of some of the nations. That it was difficult of conception and execution, is apparent, as well by the foregoing reflections, as the fact that so many tribes of men have come down from Adam's time to our own without ever having possessed it. It's utility may be conceived, by the reflection that, to *it* we owe everything which distinguishes us from savages. Take it from us, and the Bible, all history, all science, all government, all commerce, and nearly all social intercourse go with it.

The great activity of the tongue, in articulating sounds, has already been mentioned; and it may be of some passing interest to notice the wonderful power of the *eye*, in conveying ideas to the mind from writing. Take the same example of the numbers from *one* to *one hundred*, written down, and you can run your eye over the list, and be assured that every number is in it, in about one half the time it would require to pronounce the words with the voice; and not only so, but you can, in the same short time, determine whether every word is spelled correctly, by which it is evident that every separate letter, amounting to eight hundred and sixty-four, has been recognized, and reported to the mind, within the incredibly short space of twenty seconds, or one third of a minute.

I have already intimated my opinion that in the world's history, certain inventions and discoveries occurred, of peculiar value, on account of their great efficiency in facilitating all other inventions and discoveries. Of these were the art of writing and of printing—the discovery of America, and the introduction of Patent-laws. The date of the first, as already stated, is unknown; but it certainly was as much as fifteen hundred years before the Christian era; the second—printing—came in 1436, or nearly three thousand years after the first. The others followed more rapidly—the discovery of America in 1492, and the first patent laws in 1624. Though not apposite to my present purpose, it is but justice to the fruitfulness of that period, to mention two other important events—the Lutheran Reformation in 1517, and, still earlier, the invention of negroes, or, of the present mode of using them, in 1434. But, to return to the consideration of printing, it is plain that it is but the *other* half—and in real utility, the *better* half—of writing; and that both together are but the assistants of speech in the communication of thoughts between man and man. When man was possessed of speech alone, the chances of invention, discovery, and improvement were very limited; but by the introduction of each of these, they were greatly multiplied. When writing was invented, any important observation, likely to lead to a discovery, had at least a chance of being written down, and consequently, a better chance of never being forgotten; and of being seen, and reflected upon, by a much greater number of persons; and thereby the chances of a valuable hint being caught, proportionately augmented. By this means the observation of a single individual might lead to an important invention, years, and even centuries after he was dead. In one word, by means of writing, the seeds of invention were more permanently preserved, and more widely sown. And yet, for three thousand years during which printing remained undiscovered after writing was in use, it was only a small portion of the people who could write, or read writing; and consequently the field of invention, though much extended, still continued very limited. At length printing came. It gave ten thousand copies of any written matter, quite as cheaply as ten were given before; and consequently a thousand minds were brought into the field where there was but one before. This was a great *gain*; and history shows a great *change* corresponding to it, in point of time. I will venture to consider *it* the true termination of that period called "the dark ages." Discoveries, inventions, and improvements followed rapidly, and have been increasing their rapidity ever since. The effects could not come, all at once. It required time to bring them out; and they are still coming. The *capacity* to read, could not be multiplied as fast as the *means* of reading. Spelling-books just began to go into the hands of the children; but the teachers were not very numerous, or very competent; so that it is safe to infer they did not advance so speedily as they do now-a-days. It is very probable— almost certain—that the great mass of men, at that time, were utterly unconscious, that their *conditions*, or their *minds* were capable of improvement. They not only looked upon the educated few as superior beings; but they supposed themselves to be naturally incapable of rising to equality. To emancipate the mind from this false and under estimate of itself, is the great task which printing came into the world to perform. It is difficult for us, *now* and *here,* to conceive how strong this slavery of the mind was; and how long it did, of necessity, take, to break it's shackles, and to get a habit of freedom of thought, established. It is, in this connection, a curious fact that a new country is most favorable—almost necessary—to the emancipation of thought, and the consequent advancement of civilization and the arts. The human family originated as is thought, somewhere in Asia, and have worked their way principally Westward. Just now, in civilization, and the arts, the people of Asia are entirely behind those of Europe; those of the East of Europe behind those of the West of it; while we, here in America, *think* we discover, and invent, and improve, faster than any of them. *They* may think this is arrogance; but they can not deny that Russia has called on us to show her how to build steam-boats and railroads—while in the older parts of Asia they scarcely know that such things as S.Bs & RR.s. exist. In anciently inhabited countries, the dust of ages—a real downright old-fogyism—seems to settle upon, and smother the intellect and energies of man. It is in this view that I have mentioned the discovery of America as an event greatly favoring and facilitating useful discoveries and inventions.

Next came the Patent laws. These began in England in 1624; and, in this country, with the adoption of our constitution. Before then, any man might instantly use what another man had invented; so that the inventor had no special advantage from his invention. The patent system changed this; secured to the inventor, for a limited time, the exclusive use of his invention; and thereby added the fuel of *interest* to the *fire* of genius, in the discovery and production of new and useful things.

*February 11, 1859*

# Speech at Chicago, Illinois

I understand that you have to-day rallied around your principles and they have again triumphed in the city of Chicago. I am exceedingly happy to meet you under such cheering auspices on this occasion—the first on which I have appeared before an audience since the campaign of last year. It is unsuitable to enter into a lengthy discourse, as is quite apparent, at a moment like this. I shall therefore detain you only a very short while.

It gives me peculiar pleasure to find an opportunity under such favorable circumstances to return my thanks for the gallant support that you of the city of Chicago and of Cook County gave to the cause in which we were all engaged in the late momentous struggle in Illinois. And while I am at it, I will through you thank all the Republicans of the State for the earnest devotion and glorious support they gave to the cause.

I am resolved not to deprive myself of the pleasure of believing, now, and so long as I live, that all those who, while we were in that contest, professed to be the friends of the cause, were really and truly so—that we are all really brothers in the work, with no false hearts among us.

For myself I am also gratified that during that canvass and since, however disappointing its termination, there was among my party friends so little fault found in me as to the manner in which I bore my part. I hardly dared hope to give as high a degree of satisfaction as it has since been my pleasure to believe I did in the part I bore in the contest.

I remember in that canvass but one instance of dissatisfaction with my course, and I allude to that, not for the purpose of reviving any matter of dispute or producing any unpleasant feeling, but in order to help get rid of the point upon which that matter of disagreement or dissatisfaction arose. I understand that in some speeches I made I said something, or was supposed to have said something, that some very good people, as I really believe them to be, commented upon unfavorably, and said that rather than support one holding such sentiments as I had expressed, the real friends of liberty could afford to wait awhile. I don't want to say anything that shall excite unkind feeling, and I mention this simply to suggest that I am afraid of the effect of that sort of argument. I do not doubt that it comes from good men, but I am afraid of the result upon organized action where great results are in view, if any of us allow ourselves to seek out minor or separate points on which there may be difference of views as to policy and right, and let them keep us from uniting in action upon a great principle in a cause on which we all agree; or are deluded into the belief that all can be brought to consider alike and agree upon every minor point before we unite and press forward in organization, asking the coöperation of all good men in that resistance to the extension of slavery upon which we all agree. I am afraid that such methods would result in keeping the friends of liberty waiting longer than we ought to. I say this for the purpose of suggesting that we consider whether it would not be better and wiser, so long as we all agree that this matter of slavery is a moral, political and social wrong, and ought to be treated as a wrong, not to let anything minor or subsidiary to that main principle and purpose make us fail to coöperate.

One other thing, and that again I say in no spirit of unkindness. There was a question amongst Republicans all the time of the canvass of last year, and it has not quite ceased yet, whether it was not the true and better policy for the Republicans to make it their chief object to reëlect Judge Douglas to the Senate of the United States. Now, I differed with those who thought that the true policy, but I have never said an unkind word of any one entertaining that opinion. I believe most of them were as sincerely the friends of our cause as I claim to be myself; yet I thought they were mistaken, and I speak of this now for the purpose of justifying the course that I took and the course of those who supported me. In what I say now there is no unkindness even towards Judge Douglas. I have believed, that in the Republican situation in Illinois, if we, the Republicans of this State, had made Judge Douglas our candidate for the Senate of the United States last year and had elected him, there would to-day be no Republican party in this Union. I believed that the principles around which we have rallied and organized that party would live; they will live under all circumstances, while we will die. They would reproduce another party in the future. But in the meantime all the labor that has been done to build up the present Republican party would be entirely lost, and perhaps twenty years of time, before we would again have formed around that principle as solid, extensive, and formidable an organization as we have, standing shoulder to shoulder to-night in harmony and strength around the Republican banner.

It militates not at all against this view to tell us that the Republicans could make something in the State of New York by electing to Congress John B. Haskin, who occupied a position similar to Judge Douglas, or that they could make something by electing Hickman, of Pennsylvania, or Davis, of Indiana. I think it likely that they could and do make something by it; but it is false logic to assume that for that reason anything could be gained by us in electing Judge Douglas in Illinois. And for this reason: It is no disparagement to these men, Hickman and Davis, to say that individually they were comparatively small men, and the Republican party could take hold of them, use them, elect them, absorb them, expel them, or do whatever it pleased with them, and the Republican organization be in no wise shaken. But it is not so with Judge Douglas. Let the Republican party of Illinois dally with Judge Douglas; let them fall in behind him and make him their candidate, and they do not absorb him; he absorbs them. They would come out at the end all Douglas men, all claimed by him as having indorsed every one of his doctrines upon the great subject with which the whole nation is engaged at this hour—that the question of negro slavery is simply a question of dollars and cents; that the Almighty has drawn a line across the continent, on one side of which labor—the cultivation of the soil—must always be performed by slaves. It would be claimed that we, like him, do not care whether slavery is voted up or voted down. Had we made him our candidate and given him a great majority, we should have never heard an end of declarations by him that we had indorsed all these dogmas. Try it by an example.

You all remember that at the last session of Congress there was a measure introduced in the Senate by Mr. Crittenden, which proposed that the pro-slavery Lecompton constitution should be left to a vote to be taken in Kansas, and if it and slavery were adopted Kansas should be at once admitted as a slave State. That same measure was introduced into the House by Mr. Montgomery, and therefore got the name of the Crittenden-Montgomery bill; and in the House of Representatives the Republicans all voted for it under the peculiar circumstances in which they found themselves placed. You may remember also that the New York *Tribune*, which was so much in favor of our electing Judge Douglas to the Senate of the United States, has not yet got through the task of defending the Republican party, after that one vote in the House of Representatives, from the charge of having gone over to the doctrine of popular sovereignty. Now, just how long would the New York *Tribune* have been in getting rid of the charge that the Republicans had abandoned their principles, if we had taken up Judge Douglas, adopted all his doctrines and elected him to the Senate, when the single vote upon that one point so confused and embarrassed the position of the Republicans that it has kept the *Tribune* one entire year arguing against the effect of it?

This much being said on that point, I wish now to add a word that has a bearing on the future. The Republican principle, the profound central truth that slavery is wrong and ought to be dealt with as a wrong, though we are always to remember the fact of its actual existence amongst us and faithfully observe all the constitutional guarantees—the unalterable principle never for a moment to be lost sight of that it is a wrong and ought to be dealt with as such, cannot advance at all upon Judge Douglas' ground—that there is a portion of the country in which slavery must always exist; that he does not care whether it is voted up or voted down, as it is simply a question of dollars and cents. Whenever, in any compromise or arrangement or combination that may promise some temporary advantage, we are led upon that ground, then and there the great living principle upon which we have organized as a party is surrendered. The proposition now in our minds that this thing is wrong being once driven out and surrendered, then the institution of slavery necessarily becomes national.

One or two words more of what I did not think of when I arose. Suppose it is true that the Almighty has drawn a line across this continent, on the south side of which part of the people will hold the rest as slaves; that the Almighty ordered this; that it is right, unchangeably right, that men ought there to be held as slaves, and that their fellow men will always have the right to hold them as slaves. I ask you, this once admitted, how can you believe that it is not right for us, or for them coming here, to hold slaves on this other side of the line? Once we come to acknowledge that it is right, that it is the law of the Eternal Being, for slavery to exist on one side of that line, have we any sure ground to object to slaves being held on the other side? Once admit the position that a man rightfully holds another man as property on one side of the line, and you must, when it suits his convenience to come to the other side, admit that he has the same right to hold his property there. Once admit Judge Douglas's proposition and we must all finally give way. Although we may not bring ourselves to the idea that it is to our interest to have slaves in this Northern country, we shall soon bring ourselves to admit that, while we may not want them, if any one else does he has the moral right to have them. Step by step—south of the Judge's moral climate line in the States, then in the Territories everywhere, and then in all the States—it is thus that Judge Douglas would lead us inevitably to the nationalization of slavery. Whether by his doctrine of squatter sovereignty, or by the ground taken by him in his recent speeches in Memphis and through the South,—that wherever the climate makes it the interest of the inhabitants to encourage slave property, they will pass a slave code—whether it is covertly nationalized, by Congressional legislation, or by the Dred Scott decision, or by the sophistical and misleading doctrine he has last advanced, the same goal is inevitably reached by the one or the other device. It is only travelling to the same place by different roads.

In this direction lies all the danger that now exists to the Republican cause. I take it that so far as concerns forcibly establishing slavery in the Territories by Congressional legislation, or by virtue of the Dred Scott decision, that day has passed. Our only serious danger is that we shall be led upon this ground of

Judge Douglas, on the delusive assumption that it is a good way of whipping our opponents, when in fact, it is a way that leads straight to final surrender. The Republican party should not dally with Judge Douglas when it knows where his proposition and his leadership would take us, nor be disposed to listen to it because it was best somewhere else to support somebody occupying his ground. That is no just reason why we ought to go over to Judge Douglas, as we were called upon to do last year. Never forget that we have before us this whole matter of the right or wrong of slavery in this Union, though the immediate question is as to its spreading out into new Territories and States.

I do not wish to be misunderstood upon this subject of slavery in this country. I suppose it may long exist, and perhaps the best way for it to come to an end peaceably is for it to exist for a length of time. But I say that the spread and strengthening and perpetuation of it is an entirely different proposition. There we should in every way resist it as a wrong, treating it as a wrong, with the fixed idea that it must and will come to an end. If we do not allow ourselves to be allured from the strict path of our duty by such a device as shifting our ground and throwing ourselves into the rear of a leader who denies our first principle, denies that there is an absolute wrong in the institution of slavery, then the future of the Republican cause is safe and victory is assured. You Republicans of Illinois have deliberately taken your ground; you have heard the whole subject discussed again and again; you have stated your faith, in platforms laid down in a State Convention, and in a National Convention; you have heard and talked over and considered it until you are now all of opinion that you are on a ground of unquestionable right. All you have to do is to keep the faith, to remain steadfast to the right, to stand by your banner. Nothing should lead you to leave your guns. Stand together, ready, with match in hand. Allow nothing to turn you to the right or to the left. Remember how long you have been in setting out on the true course; how long you have been in getting your neighbors to understand and believe as you now do. Stand by your principles; stand by your guns; and victory complete and permanent is sure at the last.

*March 1, 1859*

# Speech at Columbus, Ohio

FELLOW-CITIZENS OF THE STATE OF OHIO:

I cannot fail to remember that I appear for the first time before an audience in this now great State—an audience that is accustomed to hear such speakers as Corwin, and Chase, and Wade, and many other renowned men; and, remembering this, I feel that it will be well for you, as for me, that you should not raise your expectations to that standard to which you would have been justified in raising them had one of these distinguished men appeared before you. You would perhaps be only preparing a disappointment for yourselves, and, as a consequence of your disappointment, mortification to me. I hope, therefore, that you will commence with very moderate expectations; and perhaps, if you will give me your attention, I shall be able to interest you to a moderate degree.

Appearing here for the first time in my life, I have been somewhat embarrassed for a topic by way of introduction to my speech; but I have been relieved from that embarrassment by an introduction which the Ohio *Statesman* newspaper gave me this morning. In this paper I have read an article, in which, among other statements, I find the following:

> In debating with Senator Douglas during the memorable contest of last fall, Mr. Lincoln declared in favor of negro suffrage, and attempted to defend that vile conception against the Little Giant.

I mention this now, at the opening of my remarks, for the purpose of making three comments upon it. The first I have already announced—it furnishes me an introductory topic; the second is to show that the gentleman is mistaken; thirdly, to give him an opportunity to correct it. (A voice—"That he won't do.")

In the first place, in regard to this matter being a mistake. I have found that it is not entirely safe, when one is misrepresented under his very nose, to allow the misrepresentation to go uncontradicted. I therefore propose, here at the outset, not only to say that this is a misrepresentation, but to show conclusively that it is so; and you will bear with me while I read a couple of extracts from that very "memorable" debate with Judge Douglas last year, to which this newspaper refers. In the first pitched battle which Senator Douglas and myself had, at the town of

Ottawa, I used the language which I will now read. Having been previously reading an extract, I continued as follows:

> Now, gentlemen, I don't want to read at any greater length, but this is the true complexion of all I have ever said in regard to the institution of slavery and the black race. This is the whole of it, and anything that argues me into his idea of perfect social and political equality with the negro, is but a specious and fantastic arrangement of words, by which a man can prove a horse chestnut to be a chestnut horse. I will say here, while upon this subject, that I have no purpose directly or indirectly to interfere with the institution of slavery in the States where it exists. I believe I have no lawful right to do so and I have no inclination to do so. I have no purpose to introduce political and social equality between the white and the black races. There is a physical difference between the two which in my judgment will probably forbid their ever living together upon the footing of perfect equality; and inasmuch as it becomes a necessity that there must be a difference, I, as well as Judge Douglas, am in favor of the race to which I belong, having the superior position. I have never said anything to the contrary, but I hold that notwithstanding all this, there is no reason in the world why the negro is not entitled to all the natural rights enumerated in the Declaration of Independence, the right to life, liberty, and the pursuit of happiness. I hold that he is as much entitled to these as the white man. I agree with Judge Douglas, he is not my equal in many respects—certainly not in color, perhaps not in moral or intellectual endowments. But in the right to eat the bread, without leave of anybody else, which his own hand earns, *he is my equal and the equal of Judge Douglas and the equal of every living man.*

Upon a subsequent occasion, when the reason for making a statement like this recurred, I said:

> While I was at the hotel to-day an elderly gentleman called upon me to know whether I was really in favor of producing perfect equality between the negroes and white people. While I had not proposed to myself on this occasion to say much on that sub-

ject, yet, as the question was asked me I thought I would occupy perhaps five minutes in saying something in regard to it. I will say then that I am not, nor ever have been in favor of bringing about in any way the social and political equality of the white and black races—that I am not, nor ever have been in favor of making voters or jurors of negroes, nor of qualifying them to hold office, or intermarry with the white people; and I will say in addition to this that there is a physical difference between the white and black races which I believe will forever forbid the two races living together on terms of social and political equality. And inasmuch as they cannot so live, while they do remain together there must be the position of superior and inferior, and I as much as any other man am in favor of having the superior position assigned to the white race. I say upon this occasion I do not perceive that because the white man is to have the superior position, the negro should be denied everything. I do not understand that because I do not want a negro woman for a slave, I must necessarily want her for a wife. My understanding is that I can just let her alone. I am now in my fiftieth year, and I certainly never have had a black woman for either a slave or a wife. So it seems to me quite possible for us get along without making either slaves or wives of negroes. I will add to this that I have never seen to my knowledge a man, woman or child, who was in favor of producing perfect equality, social and political, between negroes and white men. I recollect of but one distinguished instance that I ever heard of so frequently as to be satisfied of its correctness—and that is the case of Judge Douglas' old friend, Colonel Richard M. Johnson. I will also add to the remarks I have made, (for I am not going to enter at large upon this subject,) that I have never had the least apprehension that I or my friends would marry negroes, if there was no law to keep them from it; but as Judge Douglas and his friends seem to be in great apprehension that they might, if there were no law to keep them from it, I give him the most solemn pledge that I will to the very last stand by the law of the State, which forbids the marrying of white people with negroes.

There, my friends, you have briefly what I have, upon former occasions, said upon the subject to which this newspaper, to the extent of its ability, [laughter] has drawn the public attention. In it you not only perceive as a probability that in that contest I did not at any time say I was in favor of negro suffrage, but the absolute proof that twice—once substantially and once expressly—I declared against it. Having shown you this, there remains but a word of comment upon that newspaper article. It is this: that I presume the editor of that paper is an honest and truth-loving man, [a voice—"that's a great mistake,"] and that he will be greatly obliged to me for furnishing him thus early an opportunity to correct the misrepresentation he has made, before it has run so long that malicious people can call him a liar. [Laughter and applause.]

The Giant himself has been here recently. [Laughter.] I have seen a brief report of his speech. If it were otherwise unpleasant to me to introduce the subject of the negro as a topic for discussion, I might be somewhat relieved by the fact that he dealt exclusively in that subject while he was here. I shall, therefore, without much hesitation or diffidence, enter upon this subject.

The American people, on the first day of January, 1854, found the African slave trade prohibited by a law of Congress. In a majority of the states of this Union, they found African slavery, or any other sort of slavery, prohibited by State constitutions. They also found a law existing, supposed to be valid, by which slavery was excluded from almost all the territory the United States then owned. This was the condition of the country, with reference to the institution of slavery, on the 1st of January, 1854. A few days after that, a bill was introduced into Congress, which ran through its regular course in the two branches of the National Legislature, and finally passed into a law in the month of May, by which the act of Congress prohibiting slavery from going into the territories of the United States was repealed. In connection with the law itself, and, in fact, in the terms of the law, the then existing prohibition was not only repealed, but there was a declaration of a purpose on the part of Congress never thereafter to exercise any power that they might have, real or supposed, to prohibit the extension or spread of slavery. This was a very great change; for the law thus repealed was of more than thirty years' standing. Following rapidly upon the heels of this action of Congress, a decision of the Supreme Court is made, by which it is declared that Congress, if it desires to prohibit the spread of slavery into the territories, has no constitutional power to do so. Not only so, but that decision lays down principles, which, if pushed to their logical conclusion—I say pushed to their logical conclusion—would decide that the constitutions of free States, forbidding slavery, are themselves unconstitutional. Mark me, I do not say the judge said this, and let no man say I affirm the judge used these words; but I only say it is my opinion that what they did say, if pressed to its logical conclusion, will inevitably result thus. [Cries of "Good! good!"]

Looking at these things, the Republican party, as I understand its principles and policy, believe that there is great danger of the institution of slavery being spread out and extended, until it is ultimately made alike lawful in all the States of this Union; so believing, to prevent that incidental and ultimate consummation, is the original and chief purpose of the Republican organization. I say "chief purpose" of the Republican organization; for it is certainly true that if the national House shall fall into the hands of the Republicans, they will have to attend to all the other matters of national housekeeping, as well as this. The chief and real purpose of the Republican party is eminently conservative. It proposes nothing save and except to restore this government to its original tone in regard to this element of slavery, and there to maintain it, looking for no further change, in reference to it, than that which the original framers of the government themselves expected and looked forward to.

The chief danger to this purpose of the Republican party is not just now the revival of the African slave trade, or the passage of a Congressional slave code, or the declaring of a second Dred Scott decision, making slavery lawful in all the States. These are not pressing us just now. They are not quite ready yet. The authors of these measures know that we are too strong for them; but they will be upon us in due time, and we will be grappling with them hand to hand, if they are not now headed off. They are not now the chief danger to the purpose of the Republican organization; but the most imminent danger that now threatens that purpose is that insidious Douglas Popular Sovereignty. This is the miner and sapper. While it does not propose to revive the African slave trade, nor to pass a slave code, nor to make a second Dred Scott decision, it is preparing us for the onslaught and charge of these ultimate enemies when they shall be ready to come on and the word of command for them to advance shall be given. I say this Douglas Popular Sovereignty—for there is a broad distinction, as I now understand it, between that article and a genuine popular sovereignty.

I believe there is a genuine popular sovereignty. I think a definition of genuine popular sovereignty, in the abstract, would be about this: That each man shall do precisely as he pleases with himself, and with all those things which exclusively concern him. Applied to government, this principle would be, that a general government shall do all those things which pertain to it, and all the local governments shall do precisely as they please in respect to those matters which exclusively concern them. I understand that this government of the United States, under which we live, is based upon this principle; and I am misunderstood if it is supposed that I have any war to make upon that principle.

Now, what is Judge Douglas' Popular Sovereignty? It is, as a principle, no other than that, if one man chooses to make a slave of another man, neither that other man nor anybody else has a right to object. [Cheers and laughter.] Applied in government, as he seeks to apply it, it is this: If, in a new territory into which a few people are beginning to enter for the purpose of making their homes, they choose to either exclude slavery from their limits, or to establish it there, however one or the other may affect the persons to be enslaved, or the infinitely greater number of persons who are afterward to inhabit that territory, or the other members of the families of communities, of which they are but an incipient member, or the general head of the family of States as parent of all—however their action may affect one or the other of these, there is no power or right to interfere. That is Douglas' popular sovereignty applied.

He has a good deal of trouble with his popular sovereignty. His explanations explanatory of explanations explained are interminable. [Laughter.] The most lengthy, and, as I suppose, the most maturely considered of his long series of explanations, is his great essay in Harper's Magazine. [Laughter.] I will not attempt to enter on any very thorough investigation of his argument, as there made and presented. I will nevertheless occupy a good portion of your time here in drawing your attention to certain points in it. Such of you as may have read this document will have perceived that the Judge, early in the document, quotes from two persons as belonging to the Republican party, without naming them, but who can readily be recognized as being Gov. Seward of New York and myself. It is true, that exactly fifteen months ago this day, I believe, I for the first time expressed a sentiment upon this subject, and in such a manner that it should get into print, that the public might see it beyond the circle of my hearers; and my expression of it at that time is the quotation that Judge Douglas makes. He has not made the quotation with accuracy, but justice to him requires me to say that it is sufficiently accurate not to change its sense.

The sense of that quotation condensed is this—that this slavery element is a durable element of discord among us, and that we shall probably not have perfect peace in this country with it until it either masters the free principle in our government, or is so far mastered by the free principle as for the public mind to rest in the belief that it is going to its end. This sentiment, which I now express in this way, was, at no great distance of time, perhaps in different language, and in connection with some collateral ideas, expressed by Gov. Seward. Judge Douglas has been so much annoyed by the expression of that sentiment that he has constantly, I believe, in almost all his speeches since it was uttered, been referring to it. I find he alluded to it in his speech here, as well as in the copy-right essay. [Laughter.] I do not now enter upon this for the purpose of making an elaborate argument to show that we were right in the expression of that sentiment. In other words,

I shall not stop to say all that might properly be said upon this point; but I only ask your attention to it for the purpose of making one or two points upon it.

If you will read the copy-right essay, you will discover that Judge Douglas himself says a controversy between the American Colonies and the government of Great Britain began on the slavery question in 1699, and continued from that time until the Revolution; and, while he did not say so, we all know that it has continued with more or less violence ever since the Revolution.

Then we need not appeal to history, to the declaration of the framers of the government, but we know from Judge Douglas himself that slavery began to be an element of discord among the white people of this country as far back as 1699, or one hundred and sixty years ago, or five generations of men—counting thirty years to a generation. Now it would seem to me that it might have occurred to Judge Douglas, or anybody who had turned his attention to these facts, that there was something in the nature of that thing, Slavery, somewhat durable for mischief and discord. [Laughter.]

There is another point I desire to make in regard to this matter, before I leave it. From the adoption of the constitution down to 1820 is the precise period of our history when we had comparative peace upon this question—the precise period of time when we came nearer to having peace about it than any other time of that entire one hundred and sixty years, in which he says it began, or of the eighty years of our own constitution. Then it would be worth our while to stop and examine into the probable reason of our coming nearer to having peace then than at any other time. This was the precise period of time in which our fathers adopted, and during which they followed a policy restricting the spread of slavery, and the whole Union was acquiescing in it. The whole country looked forward to the ultimate extinction of the institution. It was when a policy had been adopted and was prevailing, which led all just and right-minded men to suppose that slavery was gradually coming to an end, and that they might be quiet about it, watching it as it expired. I think Judge Douglas might have perceived that too, and whether he did or not, it is worth the attention of fair-minded men, here and else where, to con-sider whether that is not the truth of the case. If he had looked at these two facts, that this matter has been an element of discord for one hundred and sixty years among this people, and that the only comparative peace we have had about it was when that policy prevailed in this government, which he now wars upon, he might then, perhaps, have been brought to a more just appreciation of what I said fifteen months ago—that "a house divided against itself cannot stand. I believe that this government cannot endure permanently half slave and half free. I do not expect the house to fall. I do not expect the Union to dissolve; but I do expect it will cease to be divided. It will become all one thing or all the other. Either the opponents of slavery will arrest the further spread of it, and place it where the public mind will rest in the belief that it is in the course of ultimate extinction; or its advocates will push it forward, until it shall become alike lawful in all the States, old as well as new, north as well as south." That was my sentiment at that time. In connection with it, I said, "we are now, far into the fifth year, since a policy was inaugurated with the avowed object and confident promise of putting an end to slavery agitation. Under the operation of the policy, that agitation has not only not ceased, but has constantly augmented." I now say to you here that we are advanced still farther into the sixth year since that policy of Judge Douglas—that Popular Sovereignty of his, for quieting the Slavery question—was made the national policy. Fifteen months more have been added since I uttered that sentiment, and I call upon you, and all other right-minded men, to say whether that fifteen months have belied or corroborated my words. ["Good, good! that's the truth!"]

While I am here upon this subject, I cannot but express gratitude that this true view of this element of discord among us—as I believe it is—is attracting more and more attention. I do not believe that Gov. Seward uttered that sentiment because I had done so before, but because he reflected upon this subject and saw the truth of it. Nor do I believe, because Gov. Seward or I uttered it, that Mr. Hickman of Pennsylvania, in different language, since that time, has declared his belief in the utter antagonism which exists between the principles of liberty and slavery. You see we are multiplying. [Applause and laughter.] Now, while I am speaking of Hickman, let me say, I know but little about him. I have never seen him, and know scarcely anything about the man; but I will say this much of him: Of all the Anti-Lecompton Democracy that have been brought to my notice, he alone has the true, genuine ring of the metal. And now, without endorsing anything else he has said, I will ask this audience to give three cheers for Hickman. [The audience responded with three rousing cheers for Hickman.]

Another point in the copy-right essay to which I would ask your attention, is rather a feature to be extracted from the whole thing, than from any express declaration of it at any point. It is a general feature of that document, and indeed, of all of Judge Douglas' discussions of this question, that the territories of the United States and the States of this Union are exactly alike—that there is no difference between them at all—that the constitution applies to the territories precisely as it does to the States—and that the United States Government, under the constitution, may not do in a State what it may not do in a territory, and what it must do in a state, it must do in a territory. Gentlemen, is that a true view of the case? It is necessary for this squatter sovereignty; but is it true?

Let us consider. What does it depend upon? It depends altogether upon the proposition that the States must, without the interference of the general government, do all those things that pertain *exclusively* to themselves—that are local in their nature, that have no connection with the general government. After Judge Douglas has established this proposition, which nobody disputes or ever has disputed, he proceeds to assume, without proving it, that slavery is one of those little, unimportant, trivial matters which are of just about as much consequence as the question would be to me, whether my neighbor should raise horned cattle or plant tobacco (laughter); that there is no moral question about it, but that it is altogether a matter of dollars and cents; that when a new territory is opened for settlement, the first man who goes into it may plant there a thing which, like the Canada thistle, or some other of those pests of the soil, cannot be dug out by the millions of men who will come thereafter; that it is one of those little things that is so trivial in its nature that it has no effect upon anybody save the few men who first plant upon the soil; that it is not a thing which in any way affects the family of communities composing these States, nor any way endangers the general government. Judge Douglas ignores altogether the very well known fact, that we have never had a serious menace to our political existence, except it sprang from this thing which he chooses to regard as only upon a par with onions and potatoes. [Laughter.]

Turn it, and contemplate it in another view. He says, that according to his Popular Sovereignty, the general government may give to the territories governors, judges, marshals, secretaries, and all the other chief men to govern them, but they must not touch upon this other question. Why? The question of who shall be governor of a territory for a year or two, and pass away, without his track being left upon the soil, or an act which he did for good or for evil being left behind, is a question of vast national magnitude. It is so much opposed in its nature to locality, that the nation itself must decide it; while this other matter of planting slavery upon a soil—a thing which once planted can not be eradicated by the succeeding millions who have as much right there as the first comers or if eradicated, not without infinite difficulty and a long struggle—he considers the power to prohibit it, as one of these little, local, trivial things that the nation ought not to say a word about; that it affects nobody save the few men who are there.

Take these two things and consider them together, present the question of planting a State with the Institution of slavery by the side of a question of who shall be Governor of Kansas for a year or two, and is there a man here,—is there a man on earth, who would not say the that Governor question is the little one, and the slavery question is the great one? I ask any honest Democrat if the small, the local, and the trivial and temporary question is not, who shall be Governor?

While the durable, the important and the mischievous one is, shall this soil be planted with slavery?

This is an idea, I suppose, which has arisen in Judge Douglas' mind from his peculiar structure. I suppose the institution of slavery really looks small to him. He is so put up by nature that a lash upon his back would hurt him, but a lash upon anybody else's back does not hurt him. [Laughter.] That is the build of the man, and consequently he looks upon the matter of slavery in this unimportant light.

Judge Douglas ought to remember when he is endeavoring to force this policy upon the American people that while he is put up in that way a good many are not. He ought to remember that there was once in this country a man by the name of Thomas Jefferson, supposed to be a Democrat—a man whose principles and policy are not very prevalent among Democrats to-day, it is true; but that man did not take exactly this view of the insignificance of the element of slavery which our friend Judge Douglas does. In contemplation of this thing, we all know he was led to exclaim: "I tremble for my country when I remember that God is just!" We know how he looked upon it when he thus expressed himself. There was danger to this country—danger of the avenging justice of God in that little unimportant popular sovereignty question of Judge Douglas. He supposed there was a question of God's eternal justice wrapped up in the enslaving of any race of men, or any man, and that those who did so braved the arm of Jehovah— that when a nation thus dared the Almighty, every friend of that nation had cause to dread His wrath. Choose ye between Jefferson and Douglas as to what is the true view of this element among us. [Applause.]

There is another little difficulty about this matter of treating the Territories and States alike in all things, to which I ask your attention, and I shall leave this branch of the case. If there is no difference between them, why not make the Territories States at once? What is the reason that Kansas was not fit to come into the Union when it was organized into a Territory, in Judge Douglas's view? Can any of you tell any reason why it should not have come into the Union at once? They are fit, as he thinks, to decide upon the slavery question—the largest and most important with which they could possibly deal—what could they do by coming into the Union that they are not fit to do, according to his view, by staying out of it? Oh, they are not fit to sit in Congress and decide upon the rates of postage, or questions of *ad valorem* or specific duties on foreign goods, or live oak timber contracts (laughter); they are not fit to decide these vastly important matters, which are national in their import, but they are fit, "from the jump," to decide this little negro question. But, gentlemen, the case is too plain; I occupy too much time on this head, and I pass on.

Near the close of the copyright essay, the Judge, I think, comes very near kicking his own fat into the fire (laughter). I did not think, when I commenced these remarks, that I would read from that article, but I now believe I will:

> This exposition of the history of these measures, shows conclusively that the authors of the Compromise Measures of 1850 and of the Kansas-Nebraska act of 1854, as well as the members of the Continental Congress of 1774, and the founders of our system of government subsequent to the Revolution, regarded the people of the Territories and Colonies as political communities which were entitled to a free and exclusive power of legislation in their Provincial legislatures, where their representation could alone be preserved, in all cases of taxation and internal polity.

When the Judge saw that putting in the word "slavery" would contradict his own history, he put in what he knew would pass as synonymous with it: "internal polity." Whenever we find *that* in one of his speeches, the substitute is used in this manner; and I can tell you the reason. It would be too bald a contradiction to say slavery, but "internal polity" is a general phrase, which would pass in some quarters, and which he hopes will pass with the reading community for the same thing.

> This right pertains to the people collectively, as a law-abiding and peaceful community, and not in the isolated individuals who may wander upon the public domain in violation of the law. It can only be exercised where there are inhabitants sufficient to constitute a government, and capable of performing its various functions and duties, a fact to be ascertained and determined by—

Who do you think? Judge Douglas says "By Congress!" [Laughter.]

> Whether the number shall be fixed at ten, fifteen, or twenty thousand inhabitants does not affect the principle.

Now I have only a few comments to make. Popular Sovereignty, by his own words, does not pertain to the few persons who wander upon the public domain in violation of law. We have his words for that. When it does pertain to them, is when they are sufficient to be formed into an organized political community, and he fixes the minimum for that at 10,000, and the maximum at 20,000. Now I would like to know what is to be done with the 9,000? Are they all to be treated, until they are large enough to be organized into a political community, as wanderers upon the public land in violation of law? And if so treated and driven out, at what point of time would there ever be ten thousand? (Great laughter.) If they were not driven out, but remained there as trespassers upon the public land in violation of the law, can they establish slavery there? No,—the judge says Popular Sovereignty don't pertain to them then. Can they exclude it then? No, Popular Sovereignty don't pertain to them then. I would like to know, in the case covered by the Essay, what condition the people of the Territory are in before they reach the number of ten thousand?

But the main point I wish to ask attention to is, that the question as to when they shall have reached a sufficient number to be formed into a regular organized community, is to be decided "by Congress." Judge Douglas says so. Well, gentlemen, that is about all we want. [Here some one in the crowd made a remark inaudible to the reporter, whereupon Mr. Lincoln continued.] No; that is all the Southerners want. That is what all those who are for slavery want. They do not want Congress to prohibit slavery from coming into the new territories, and they do not want Popular Sovereignty to hinder it; and as Congress is to say when they are ready to be organized, all that the south has to do is to get Congress to hold off. Let Congress hold off until they are ready to be admitted as a State, and the south has all it wants in taking slavery into and planting it in all the territories that we now have, or hereafter may have. In a word, the whole thing, at a dash of the pen, is at last put in the power of Congress; for if they do not have this Popular Sovereignty until Congress organizes them, I ask if it at last does not come from Congress? If, at last, it amounts to anything at all, Congress gives it to them. I submit this rather for your reflection than for comment. After all that is said, at last by a dash of the pen, everything that has gone before is undone, and he puts the whole question under the control of Congress. After fighting through more than three hours, if you undertake to read it, he at last places the whole matter under the control of that power which he had been contending against, and arrives at a result directly contrary to what he had been laboring to do. He at last leaves the whole matter to the control of Congress.

There are two main objects, as I understand it, of this Harper's Magazine essay. One was to show, if possible, that the men of our revolutionary times were in favor of his popular sovereignty; and the other was to show that the Dred Scott Decision had not entirely squelched out this popular sovereignty. I do not propose, in regard to this argument drawn from the history of former times, to

enter into a detailed examination of the historical statements he has made. I have
the impression that they are inaccurate in a great many instances. Sometimes in
positive statement but very much more inaccurate by the suppression of statements that really belong to the history. But I do not propose to affirm that this
is so to any very great extent; or to enter into a very minute examination of his
historical statements. I avoid doing so upon this principle—that if it were important for me to pass out of this lot in the least period of time possible and I came
to that fence and saw by a calculation of my known strength and agility that I
could clear it at a bound, it would be folly for me to stop and consider whether
I could or not crawl through a crack. [Laughter.] So I say of the whole history,
contained in his essay, where he endeavored to link the men of the revolution to
popular sovereignty. It only requires an effort to leap out of it—a single bound
to be entirely successful. If you read it over you will find that he quotes here
and there from documents of the revolutionary times, tending to show that the
people of the colonies were desirous of regulating their own concerns in their
own way; that the British Government should not interfere; that at one time they
struggled with the British Government to be permitted to exclude the African
slave trade; if not directly, to be permitted to exclude it indirectly by taxation
sufficient to discourage and destroy it. From these and many things of this sort,
Judge Douglas argues that they were in favor of the people of our own territories
excluding slavery if they wanted to, or planting it there if they wanted to, doing
just as they pleased from the time they settled upon the territory. Now, however
his history may apply, and whatever of his argument there may be that is sound
and accurate or unsound and inaccurate, if we can find out what these men did
themselves do upon this very question of slavery in the territories, does it not
end the whole thing? If, after all this labor and effort to show that the men of
the revolution were in favor of his popular sovereignty and his mode of dealing
with slavery in the territories, we can show that these very men took hold of that
subject, and dealt with it, we can see for ourselves *how* they dealt with it. It is not
a matter of argument or inference, but we know what they thought about it.

It is precisely upon that part of the history of the country, that one important omission is made by Judge Douglas. He selects parts of the history of the
United States upon the subject of slavery, and treats it as the whole, omitting
from his historical sketch the legislation of Congress in regard to the admission
of Missouri, by which the Missouri Compromise was established, and slavery
excluded from a country half as large as the present United States. All this is left
out of his history, and in nowise alluded to by him, so far as I remember, save
once, when he makes a remark, that upon his principle the Supreme Court were

authorized to pronounce a decision that the act called the Missouri Compromise was unconstitutional. All that history has been left out. But this part of the history of the country was not made by the men of the Revolution.

There was another part of our political history made by the very men who were the actors in the Revolution, which has taken the name of the ordinance of '87. Let me bring that history to your attention. In 1784, I believe, this same Mr. Jefferson drew up an ordinance for the government of the country upon which we now stand; or rather a frame or draft of an ordinance for the government of this country, here in Ohio; our neighbors in Indiana; us who live in Illinois; our neighbors in Wisconsin and Michigan. In that ordinance, drawn up not only for the government of that territory, but for the territories south of the Ohio River, Mr. Jefferson expressly provided for the prohibition of slavery. Judge Douglas says, and perhaps is right, that that provision was lost from that ordinance. I believe that is true. When the vote was taken upon it, a majority of all present in the Congress of the Confederation voted for it; but there were so many absentees that those voting for it did not make the clear majority necessary, and it was lost. But three years after that the Congress of the Confederation were together again, and they adopted a new ordinance for the government of this northwest territory, not contemplating territory south of the river, for the States owning that territory had hitherto refrained from giving it to the general Government; hence, they made the ordinance to apply only to what the Government owned. In that, the provision excluding slavery *was inserted and passed unanimously,* or at any rate it passed and became a part of the law of the land. Under that ordinance we live. First here in Ohio you were a territory, then an enabling act was passed authorizing you to form a constitution and State government, provided it was republican and not in conflict with the ordinance of '87. When you framed your constitution and presented it for admission, I think you will find the legislation upon the subject will show that, "whereas you had formed a constitution that was republican and not in conflict with the ordinance of '87," therefore you were admitted upon equal footing with the original States. The same process in a few years was gone through with in Indiana, and so with Illinois, and the same substantially with Michigan and Wisconsin.

Not only did that ordinance prevail, but it was constantly looked to whenever a step was taken by a new Territory to become a State. Congress always turned their attention to it, and in all their movements upon this subject, they traced their course by that ordinance of '87. When they admitted new States they advertised them of this ordinance as a part of the legislation of the country. They did so because they had traced the ordinance of '87 throughout the history of this country. Begin with the men of the Revolution, and go down for sixty entire years, and until the last scrap of that territory comes into the Union in the form of the State of Wisconsin—everything was made to conform with the ordinance of '87 excluding slavery from that vast extent of country.

I omitted to mention in the right place that the Constitution of the United States was in process of being framed when that ordinance was made by the Congress of the Confederation; and one of the first acts of Congress itself under the new Constitution itself was to give force to that ordinance by putting power to carry it out in the hands of the new officers under the Constitution, in place of the old ones who had been legislated out of existence by the change in the government from the Confederation to the Constitution. Not only so, but I believe Indiana once or twice, if not Ohio, petitioned the general government for the privilege of suspending that provision and allowing them to have slaves. A report made by Mr. Randolph of Virginia, himself a slaveholder, was directly against it, and the action was to refuse them the privilege of violating the ordinance of '87.

This period of history which I have run over briefly is, I presume, as familiar to most of this assembly as any other part of the history of our country. I suppose that few of my hearers are not as familiar with that part of history as I am, and I only mention it to recall your attention to it at this time. And hence I ask how extraordinary a thing it is that a man who has occupied a position upon the floor of the Senate of the United States, who is now in his third term, and who looks to see the government of this whole country fall into his own hands, pretending to give a truthful and accurate history of the slavery question in this country, should so entirely ignore the whole of that portion of our history—the most important of all. Is it not a most extraordinary spectacle that a man should stand up and ask for any confidence in his statements, who sets out as he does with portions of history calling upon the people to believe that it is a true and fair representation, when the leading part, and controlling feature of the whole history, is carefully suppressed?

But the mere leaving out is not the most remarkable feature of this most remarkable essay. His proposition is to establish that the leading men of the revolution were for his great principle of non-intervention by the government in the question of slavery in the territories; while history shows that they decided in the cases actually brought before them, in exactly the contrary way, and he knows it. Not only did they so decide at that time, but they stuck to it during sixty years, through thick and thin, as long as there was one of the revolutionary heroes upon the stage of political action. Through their whole course, from first to last, they clung to freedom. And now he asks the community to believe that the men of the revolution were in favor of his great principle, when we have the naked history that they themselves dealt with this very subject matter of his principle, and utterly repudiated his principle, acting upon a precisely contrary ground. It is as impudent and absurd as if a prosecuting attorney should stand up before a jury, and ask them to convict A as the murderer of B, while B was walking alive before them. [Cheers and laughter.]

I say again, if Judge Douglas asserts that the men of the Revolution acted upon principles by which, to be consistent with themselves, they ought to have adopted his popular sovereignty, then, upon a consideration of his own argument, he had a right to make you believe that they understood the principles of government, but misapplied them—that he has arisen to enlighten the world as to the just application of this principle. He has a right to try to persuade you that he understands their principles better than they did, and therefore he will apply them now, not as they did, but as they ought to have done. He has a right to go before the community, and try to convince them of this; but he has no right to attempt to impose upon any one the belief that these men themselves approved of his great principle. There are two ways of establishing a proposition. One is by trying to demonstrate it upon reason; and the other is, to show that great men in former times have thought so and so, and thus to pass it by the weight of pure authority. Now, if Judge Douglas will demonstrate somehow that this is popular sovereignty—the right of one man to make a slave of another, without any right in that other, or any one else, to object—demonstrate it as Euclid demonstrated propositions—there is no objection. But when he conies forward, seeking to carry a principle by bringing to it the authority of men who themselves utterly repudiate that principle, I ask that he shall not be permitted to do it. [Applause.]

I see, in the Judge's speech here, a short sentence in these words, "Our fathers, when they formed this government under which we live, understood this question just as well and even better than we do now." That is true; I stick to that. (Great cheers and laughter.) I will stand by Judge Douglas in that to the bitter end. (Renewed laughter.) And now, Judge Douglas, come and stand by me, and truthfully show how they acted, understanding it better than we do. All I ask of you, Judge Douglas, is to stick to the proposition that the men of the revolution understood this subject better than we do now, *and with that better understanding they acted better than you are trying to act now.* [Applause and laughter.]

I wish to say something now in regard to the Dred Scott decision, as dealt with by Judge Douglas. In that "memorable debate," between Judge Douglas and myself last year, the Judge thought fit to commence a process of catechising me, and at Freeport I answered his questions, and propounded some to him. Among others propounded to him was one that I have here now. The substance, as I remember it, is, "Can the people of a United States territory, under the Dred Scott decision, in any lawful way, against the wish of any citizen of the United States, exclude slavery from its limits, prior to the formation of a State Constitution?" He answered that they could lawfully exclude slavery from the United States territories, notwithstanding the Dred Scott decision. There was something about that answer that has probably been a trouble to the Judge ever since. [Laughter.]

The Dred Scott decision expressly gives every citizen of the United States a right to carry his slaves into the United States' Territories. And now there was some inconsistency in saying that the decision was right and saying too, that the people of the Territory could lawfully drive slavery out again. When all the trash, the words, the collateral matter, was cleared away from it; all the chaff was fanned out of it, it was a bare absurdity—*no less than a thing may lie lawfully driven away from where it has a lawful right to be.* [Cheers and laughter.] Clear it of all the verbiage, and that is the naked truth of his proposition—that a thing may be lawfully driven from the place where it has a lawful right to stay. Well, it was because the Judge couldn't help seeing this, that he has had so much trouble with it; and what I want to ask your especial attention to, just now, is to remind you, if you have not noticed the fact, that the Judge does not any longer say that the people can exclude slavery. He does not say so in the copyright essay; he did not say so in the speech that he made here, and so far as I know, since his re-election to the Senate, he has never said, as he did at Freeport, that the people of the Territories can exclude slavery. He desires that you, who wish the territories to remain free, should believe that he stands by that position, but he does not say it himself. He escapes to some extent the absurd position I have stated by changing his language entirely. What he says now is something different in language, and we will consider whether it is not different in sense too. It is now that the Dred Scott decision, or rather the Constitution under that decision, does not carry slavery into the Territories beyond the power of the people of the Territories *to control it as other property.* He does not say the people can drive it out, but they can control it as other property. The language is different, we should consider whether the sense is different. Driving a horse out of this lot, is too plain a proposition to be mistaken about; it is putting him on the other side of the fence. [Laughter.] Or it might be a sort of exclusion of him from the lot if you were to kill him and let the worms devour him; but neither of these things is the same as "controlling him as other property." That would be to feed him, to pamper him, to ride him, to use and abuse him, to make the most money out of him "as other property"; but, please you, what do the men who are in favor of slavery want more than this? [Laughter and applause.] What do they really want, other than that slavery being in the Territories, shall be controlled as other property. [Renewed applause.]

If they want anything else, I do not comprehend it. I ask your attention to this, first for the purpose of pointing out the change of ground the Judge has made; and, in the second place, the importance of the change—that that change is not such as to give you gentlemen who want his popular sovereignty the power to exclude the institution or drive it out at all. I know the Judge sometimes squints at the argument that in controlling it as other property by unfriendly legislation they may control it to death, as you might in the case of a horse, perhaps, feed him so lightly and ride him so much that he would die. [Cheers and laughter.] But when you come to legislative control, there is something more to be attended to. I have no doubt, myself, that if the people of territories should undertake to control slave property as other property—that is, control it in such a way that it would be the most valuable as property, and make it bear its just proportion in the way of burdens as property—really deal with it as property—the Supreme Court of the United States will say, "God speed you and amen." But I undertake to give the opinion, at least, that if the territories attempt by any direct legislation to drive the man with his slave out of the territory, or to decide that his slave is free because of his being taken in there, or to tax him to such an extent that he cannot keep him there, the Supreme Court will unhesitatingly decide all such legislation unconstitutional, as long as that Supreme Court is constructed as the Dred Scott Supreme Court is. The first two things they have already decided, except that there is a little quibble among the lawyers between the words *dicta* and decision. They have already decided a negro can not be made free by territorial legislation.

What is that Dred Scott decision? Judge Douglas labors to show that it is one thing, while I think it is altogether different. It is a long opinion, but it is all embodied in this short statement: "The Constitution of the United States forbids Congress to deprive a man of his property, without due process of law; the right of property in slaves is distinctly and expressly affirmed in that Constitution; therefore, if Congress shall undertake to say that a man's slave is no longer his slave, when he crosses a certain line into a territory, that is depriving him of his property without due process of law, and is unconstitutional." There is the whole Dred Scott decision. They add that if Congress cannot do so itself, Congress can not confer any power to do so, and hence any effort by the Territorial Legislature to do either of these things is absolutely decided against. It is a foregone conclusion by that court.

Now, as to this indirect mode by "unfriendly legislation," all lawyers here will readily understand that such a proposition can not be tolerated for a moment, because a legislature can not indirectly do that which it can not accomplish directly. Then I say any legislation to control this property, as property, for its benefit as property, would be hailed by this Dred Scott Supreme Court, and fully sustained; but any legislation driving slave property out, or destroying it as property, directly or indirectly, will most assuredly, by that court, be held unconstitutional.

Judge Douglas says if the Constitution carries slavery into the territories, beyond the power of the people of the territories to control it as other property, then it follows logically that every one who swears to support the Constitution of the United States, must give that support to that property which it needs. And if the Constitution carries slavery into the territories, beyond the power of the people to control it as other property, then it also carries it into the States, because the Constitution is the supreme law of the land. Now, gentlemen, if it were not for my excessive modesty, I would say that I told that very thing to Judge Douglas quite a year ago. This argument is here in print, and if it were not for my modesty, as I said, I might call your attention to it. If you read it, you will find that I not only made that argument, but made it better than he has made it since. [Laughter.]

There is, however, this difference. I say now, and said then, there is no sort of question that the Supreme Court *has* decided that it is the right of the slaveholder to take his slave and hold him in the territory; and saying this, Judge Douglas himself admits the conclusion. He says if that is so, this consequence will follow; and because this consequence would follow, his argument is, the decision cannot, therefore, be that way—"that would spoil my popular sovereignty, and it cannot be possible that this great principle has been squelched out in this extraordinary way. It might be, if it were not for the extraordinary consequences of spoiling my humbug." [Cheers and laughter.]

Another feature of the Judge's argument about the Dred Scott case is, an effort to show that that decision deals altogether in declarations of negatives; that the constitution does not affirm anything as expounded by the Dred Scott decision, but it only declares a want of power—a total absence of power, in reference to the territories. It seems to be his purpose to make the whole of that decision to result in a mere negative declaration of a want of power in Congress to do anything in relation to this matter in the territories. I know the opinion of the Judges states that there is a total absence of power; but that is, unfortunately, not all it states; for the Judges add that the right of property in a slave is distinctly and expressly affirmed in the constitution. It does not stop at saying that the right of property in a slave is recognized in the constitution, is declared to exist somewhere in the constitution, but says it is *affirmed* in the constitution. Its language is equivalent to saying that it is embodied and so woven into that instrument that it cannot be detached without breaking the constitution itself. In a word, it is part of the constitution.

Douglas is singularly unfortunate in his effort to make out that decision to be altogether negative, when the express language at the vital part is that this is distinctly affirmed in the Constitution. I think myself, and I repeat it here, that this decision does not merely carry slavery into the Territories, but by its logical conclusion it carries it into the States in which we live. One provision of that Constitution is, that it shall be the supreme law of the land—I do not quote the language—any Constitution or law of any State to the contrary notwithstanding. This Dred Scott decision says that the right of property in a slave is affirmed in that Constitution, which is the supreme law of the land, any State Constitution or law notwithstanding. Then I say that to destroy a thing which is distinctly affirmed and supported by the supreme law of the land, even by a State Constitution or law, is a violation of that supreme law and there is no escape from it. In my judgment there is no avoiding that result, save that the American people shall see that Constitutions are better construed than our Constitution is construed in that decision. They must take care that it is more faithfully and truly carried out than it is there expounded.

I must hasten to a conclusion. Near the beginning of my remarks, I said that this insidious Douglas popular sovereignty is the measure that now threatens the purpose of the Republican party, to prevent slavery from being nationalized in the United States. I propose to ask your attention for a little while to some propositions in affirmance of that statement. Take it just as it stands, and apply it as a principle; extend and apply that principle elsewhere and consider where it will lead you. I now put this proposition that Judge Douglas' popular sovereignty applied will re-open the African slave trade; and I will demonstrate it by any variety of ways in which you can turn the subject or look at it.

The judge says that the people of the territories have the right, by his principle, to have slaves, if they want them. Then I say that the people in Georgia have the right to buy slaves in Africa, if they want them, and I defy any man on earth to show any distinction between the two things—to show that the one is either more wicked or more unlawful; to show, on original principles, that one is better or worse than the other; or to show by the constitution, that one differs a whit from the other. He will tell me, doubtless, that there is no constitutional provision against people taking slaves into the new territories, and I tell him that there is equally no constitutional provision against buying slaves in Africa. He will tell you that a people, in the exercise of popular sovereignty, ought to do as they please about that thing, and have slaves if they want them; and I tell you that the people of Georgia are as much entitled to popular sovereignty and to buy slaves in Africa, if they want them, as the people of the territory are to have slaves if they want them. I ask any man, dealing honestly with himself, to point out a distinction.

I have recently seen a letter of Judge Douglas', in which, without stating that to be the object, he doubtless endeavors, to make a distinction between the two. He says he is unalterably opposed to the repeal of the laws against the African Slave trade. And why? He then seeks to give a reason that would not apply to his popular sovereignty in the territories. What is that reason? "The abolition of the African slave trade is a compromise of the constitution." I deny it. There is no truth in the proposition that the abolition of the African slave trade is a compromise of the constitution. No man can put his finger on anything in the constitution, or on the line of history which shows it. It is a mere barren assertion, made simply for the purpose of getting up a distinction between the revival of the African slave trade and his "great principle."

At the time the constitution of the United States was adopted, it was expected that the slave trade would be abolished. I should assert, and insist upon that, if Judge Douglas denied it. But I know that it was equally expected that slavery would be excluded from the territories and I can show by history, that in regard to these two things, public opinion was exactly alike, while in regard to positive action, there was more done in the Ordinance of '87, to resist the spread of slavery than was ever done to abolish the foreign slave trade. Lest I be misunderstood, I say again that at the time of the formation of the constitution, public expectation was that the slave trade would be abolished, but no more so than the spread of slavery in the territories should be restrained. They stand alike, except that in the Ordinance of '87 there was a mark left by public opinion showing that it was more committed against the spread of slavery in the territories than against the foreign slave trade.

Compromise! What word of compromise was there about it. Why, the public sense was then in favor of the abolition of the slave trade; but there was at the time a very great commercial interest involved in it and extensive capital in that branch of trade. There were doubtless the incipient stages of improvement in the South in the way of farming, dependent on the slave trade, and they made a proposition to Congress to abolish the trade after allowing it twenty years, a sufficient time for the capital and commerce engaged in it to be transferred to other channels. They made no provision that it should be abolished in twenty years; I do not doubt that they expected it would be; but they made no bargain about it. The public sentiment left no doubt in the minds of any that it would be done away. I repeat, there is nothing in the history of those times in favor of that matter being a *compromise* of the Constitution. It was the public expectation at the time, manifested in a thousand ways, that the spread of slavery should also be restricted.

Then I say if this principle is established, that there is no wrong in slavery, and whoever wants it has a right to have it, is a matter of dollars and cents, a sort of question as to how they shall deal with brutes, that between us and the negro here there is no sort of question, but at the South the question is between the negro and the crocodile. That is all. It is a mere matter of policy; there is a perfect right according to interest to do just as you please—when this is done, where this doctrine prevails, the miners and sappers will have formed public opinion for the slave trade. They will be ready for Jeff Davis and Stephens and other leaders of that company, to sound the bugle for the revival of the slave trade, for the second Dred Scott decision, for the flood of slavery to be poured over the free States, while we shall be here tied down and helpless and run over like sheep.

It is to be a part and parcel of this same idea, to say to men who want to adhere to the Democratic party, who have always belonged to that party, and are only looking about for some excuse to stick to it, but nevertheless hate slavery, that Douglas' Popular Sovereignty is as good a way as any to oppose slavery. They allow themselves to be persuaded easily in accordance with their previous dispositions, into this belief, that it is about as good a way of opposing slavery as any, and we can do that without straining our old party ties or breaking up old political associations. We can do so without being called negro worshipers. We can do that without being subjected to the jibes and sneers that are so readily thrown out in place of argument where no argument can be found; so let us stick to this Popular Sovereignty—this insidious Popular Sovereignty. Now let me call your attention to one thing that has really happened, which shows this gradual and steady debauching of public opinion, this course of preparation for the revival of the slave trade, for the territorial slave code, and the new Dred Scott decision that is to carry slavery into the free States. Did you ever five years ago, hear of anybody in the world saying that the negro had no share in the Declaration of National Independence; that it did not mean negroes at all; and when "all men" were spoken of, negroes were not included?

I am satisfied that five years ago that proposition was not put upon paper by any living being anywhere. I have been unable at any time to find a man in an audience who would declare that he had ever known of anybody saying so five years ago. But last year there was not a Douglas popular sovereign in Illinois who did not say it. Is there one in Ohio but declares his firm belief that the Declaration of Independence did not mean negroes at all? I do not know how this is; I have not been here much; but I presume you are very much alike everywhere. Then I suppose that all now express the belief that the Declaration of Independence never did mean negroes. I call upon one of them to say that he said it five years ago.

If you think that now, and did not think it then, the next thing that strikes me is to remark that there has been a *change* wrought in you [laughter and applause], and a very significant change it is, being no less than changing the negro, in your estimation, from the rank of a man to that of a brute. They are taking him down, and placing him, when spoken of, among reptiles and crocodiles, as Judge Douglas himself expresses it.

Is not this change wrought in your minds a very important change? Public opinion in this country is everything. In a nation like ours this popular sovereignty and squatter sovereignty have already wrought a change in the public mind to the extent I have stated. There is no man in this crowd who can contradict it.

Now, if you are opposed to slavery honestly, as much as anybody I ask you to note that fact, and the like of which is to follow, to be plastered on, layer after layer, until very soon you are prepared to deal with the negro everywhere as with the brute. If public sentiment has not been debauched already to this point, a new turn of the screw in that direction is all that is wanting; and this is constantly being done by the teachers of this insidious popular sovereignty. You need but one or two turns further until your minds, now ripening under these teachings will be ready for all these things, and you will receive and support, or submit to, the slave trade, revived with all its horrors; a slave code enforced in our territories, and a new Dred Scott decision to bring slavery up into the very heart of the free North. This, I must say, is but carrying out those words prophetically spoken by Mr. Clay, many, many years ago. I believe more than thirty years when he told an audience that if they repress all tendencies to liberty and ultimate emancipation, they must go back to the era of our independence and muzzle the cannon which thundered its annual joyous return on the Fourth of July; they must blow out the moral lights around us; they must penetrate the human soul and eradicate the love of liberty; but until they did these things, and others eloquently enumerated by him, they could not repress all tendencies to ultimate emancipation.

I ask attention to the fact that in a pre-eminent degree these popular sovereigns are at this work; blowing out the moral lights around us; teaching that the negro is no longer a man but a brute; that the Declaration has nothing to do with him; that he ranks with the crocodile and the reptile; that man, with body and soul, is a matter of dollars and cents. I suggest to this portion of the Ohio Republicans, or Democrats if there be any present, the serious consideration of this fact, that there is now going on among you a steady process of debauching public opinion on this subject. With this, my friends, I bid you adieu.

*September 16, 1859*

# Speech at Cincinnati, Ohio

My fellow-citizens of the State of Ohio:

This is the first time in my life that I have appeared before an audience in so great a city as this. I therefore—though I am no longer a young man—make this appearance under some degree of embarrassment. But, I have found that when one is embarrassed, usually the shortest way to get through with it is to quit talking or thinking about it, and go at something else. (Applause.)

I understand that you have had recently with you, my very distinguished friend, Judge Douglas, of Illinois, (laughter) and I understand, without having had an opportunity, (not greatly sought to be sure,) of seeing a report of the speech, that he made here, that he did me the honor to mention my humble name. I suppose that he did so for the purpose of making some objection to some sentiment at some time expressed by me. I should expect, it is true, that Judge Douglas had reminded you, or informed you, if you had never before heard it, that I had once in my life declared it as my opinion that this government cannot "endure permanently half slave and half free; that a house divided against itself cannot stand," and, as I had expressed it, I did not expect the house to fall; that I did not expect the Union to be dissolved; but, that I did expect that it would cease to be divided; that it would become all one thing or all the other, that either the opponents of Slavery would arrest the further spread of it, and place it where the public mind would rest in the belief that it was in the course of ultimate extinction; or the friends of Slavery will push it forward until it becomes alike lawful in all the States, old or new, Free as well as Slave. I did, fifteen months ago, express that opinion, and upon many occasions Judge Douglas has denounced it, and has greatly, intentionally or unintentionally, misrepresented my purpose in the expression of that opinion.

I presume, without having seen a report of his speech, that he did so here. I presume that he alluded also to that opinion in different language, having been expressed at a subsequent time by Governor Seward of New York, and that he took the two in a lump and denounced them; that he tried to point out that there was something couched in this opinion which led to the making of an entire uniformity of the local institutions of the various States of the Union, in utter disregard of the different States, which in their nature would seem to require a variety of institutions, and a variety of laws, conforming to the differences in the nature of the different States.

Not only so; I presume he insisted that this was a declaration of war between the Free and Slave States—that it was the sounding to the onset of continual war between the different States, the Slave and Free States.

This charge, in this form, was made by Judge Douglas on, I believe, the 9th of July, 1858, in Chicago, in my hearing. On the next evening, I made some reply to it. I informed him that many of the inferences he drew from that expression of mine were altogether foreign to any purpose entertained by me, and in so far as he should ascribe those inferences to me, as my purpose, he was entirely mistaken; and in so far as he might argue that whatever might be my purpose, actions, conforming to my views, would lead to these results, he might argue and establish if he could; but, so far as purposes were concerned, he was totally mistaken as to me.

When I made that reply to him—when I told him, on the question of declaring war between the different States of the Union, that I had not said I did not expect any peace upon this question until Slavery was exterminated; that I had only said I expected peace when that institution was put where the public mind should rest in the belief that it was in course of ultimate extinction; that I believed from the organization of our government, until a very recent period of time, the institution had been placed and continued upon such a basis; that we had had comparative peace upon that question through a portion of that period of time, only because the public mind rested in that belief in regard to it, and that when we returned to that position in relation to that matter, I supposed we should again have peace as we previously had. I assured him, as I now assure you, that I neither then had, nor have, or ever had, any purpose in any way of interfering with the institution of Slavery, where it exists. [Long continued applause.] I believe we have no power, under the Constitution of the United States; or rather under the form of government under which we live, to interfere with the institution of Slavery, or any other of the institutions of our sister States, be they Free or Slave States. [Cries of "Good," and applause.] I declared then and I now re-declare, that I have as little inclination to so interfere with the institution of Slavery where it now exists, through the instrumentality of the general Government, or any other instrumentality, as I believe we have no power to do so. [A voice—"You're right."] I accidentally used this expression: I had no purpose of entering into the Slave States to disturb the institution of Slavery! So, upon the first occasion that Judge Douglas got an opportunity to reply to me, he passed by the whole body of what I had said upon that subject, and seized upon the particular expression of mine, that I had no purpose of entering into the Slave States to disturb the institution of Slavery! "Oh, no," said he, "he (Lincoln) won't enter into the Slave States to disturb the institution of Slavery; he is too prudent a man to do such a thing as that; he only means that he will go on to the line between the Free and Slave States, and shoot over at them. [Laughter.] This is all he means to do. He means to do them all the harm he can, to disturb them all he can, in such a way as to keep his own hide in perfect safety." [Laughter.]

Well, now, I did not think, at that time, that that was either a very dignified or very logical argument; but so it was, I had to get along with it as well as I could.

It has occurred to me here to-night, that if I ever do shoot over the line at the people on the other side of the line into a Slave State, and purpose to do so, keeping my skin safe, that I have now about the best chance I shall ever have. [Laughter and applause.] I should not wonder that there are some Kentuckians about this audience; we are close to Kentucky; and whether that be so or not, we are on elevated ground, and by speaking distinctly, I should not wonder if some of the Kentuckians would hear me on the other side of the river. [Laughter.] For that reason I propose to address a portion of what I have to say to the Kentuckians.

I say, then, in the first place, to the Kentuckians, that I am what they call, as I understand it, a "Black Republican." (Applause and laughter.) I think Slavery is wrong, morally, and politically. I desire that it should be no further spread in these United States, and I should not object if it should gradually terminate in the whole Union. (Applause.) While I say this for myself, I say to you, Kentuckians, that I understand you differ radically with me upon this proposition; that you believe Slavery is a good thing; that Slavery is right; that it ought to be extended and perpetuated in this Union. Now, there being this broad difference between us, I do not pretend in addressing myself to you, Kentuckians, to attempt proselyting you; that would be a vain effort. I do not enter upon it. I only propose to try to show you that you ought to nominate for the next Presidency, at Charleston, my distinguished friend Judge Douglas. [Applause.] In all that there is a difference between you and him, I understand he is as sincerely for you, and more wisely for you, than you are for yourselves. [Applause.] I will try to demonstrate that proposition. Understand now, I say that I believe he is as sincerely for you, and more wisely for you, than you are for yourselves.

What do you want more than anything else to make successful your views of Slavery,—to advance the outspread of it, and to secure and perpetuate the nationality of it? What do you want more than anything else? What is needed absolutely? What is indispensable to you? Why! if I may be allowed to answer the question, it is to retain a hold upon the North—it is to retain support and strength from the Free States. If you can get this support and strength from the

Free States, you can succeed. If you do not get this support and this strength from the Free States, you are in the minority, and you are beaten at once.

If that proposition be admitted,—and it is undeniable, then the next thing I say to you, is that Douglas of all the men in this nation is the only man that affords you any hold upon the Free States; that no other man can give you any strength in the Free States. This being so, if you doubt the other branch of the proposition, whether he is for you—whether he is really for you as I have expressed it, I propose asking your attention for awhile to a few facts.

The issue between you and me, understand, is that I think Slavery is wrong, and ought not to be outspread, and you think it is right and ought to be extended and perpetuated. (A voice, "oh, Lord.") That is my Kentuckian I am talking to now. (Applause.)

I now proceed to try to show you that Douglas is as sincerely for you and more wisely for you than you are for yourselves.

In the first place we know that in a Government like this, in a Government of the people, where the voice of all the men of the country, substantially enter into the execution,—or administration rather—of the Government—in such a Government, what lies at the bottom of all of it, is public opinion. I lay down the proposition, that Douglas is not only the man that promises you in advance a hold upon the North, and support in the North, but that he constantly moulds public opinion to your ends; that in every possible way he can, he constantly moulds the public opinion of the North to your ends; and if there are a few things in which he seems to be against you—a few things which he says that appear to be against you, and a few that he forbears to say which you would like to have him say—you ought to remember that the saying of the one, or the forbearing to say the other, would loose his hold upon the North, and, by consequence, would lose his capacity to serve you. (A voice—"That is so.")

Upon this subject of moulding public opinion, I call your attention to the fact—for a well-established fact it is—that the Judge never says your institution of Slavery is wrong; he never says it is right, to be sure, but he never says it is wrong. [Laughter.] There is not a public man in the United States, I believe, with the exception of Senator Douglas, who has not, at some time in his life, declared his opinion whether the thing is right or wrong; but, Senator Douglas never declares it is wrong. He leaves himself at perfect liberty to do all in your favor which he would be hindered from doing if he were to declare the thing to be wrong. On the contrary, he takes all the chances that he has for inveigling the sentiment of the North, opposed to Slavery, into your support, by never saying it is right. [Laughter.] This you ought to set down to his credit. [Laughter.] You ought to give him full credit for this much, little though it be, in comparison to the whole which he does for you.

Some other things I will ask your attention to. He said upon the floor of the United States Senate, and he has repeated it as I understand, a great many times, that he does not care whether Slavery is "voted up or voted down." This again shows you, or ought to show you, if you would reason upon it, that he does not believe it to be wrong, for a man may say, when he sees nothing wrong in a thing, that he does not care whether it be voted up or voted down, but no man can logically say that he cares not whether a thing goes up or goes down, which to him appears to be wrong. You therefore have a demonstration in this, that to Douglas' mind your favorite institution which you would have spread out, and made perpetual, is no wrong.

Another thing he tells you, in a speech made at Memphis in Tennessee, shortly after the canvass in Illinois, last year. He there distinctly told the people, that there was a "line drawn by the Almighty across this continent, on the one side of which the soil must always be cultivated by slaves," that he did not pretend to know exactly where that line was, [laughter and applause,] but that there was such a line. I want to ask your attention to that proposition again; that there is one portion of this continent where the Almighty has designed the soil shall always be culti-vated by slaves; that its being cultivated by slaves at that place is right; that it has the direct sympathy and authority of the Almighty. Whenever you can get these Northern audiences to adopt the opinion that Slavery is right on the other side of the Ohio; whenever you can get them, in pursuance of Douglas' views, to adopt that sentiment, they will very readily make the other argument, which is perfectly logical, that that which is right on that side of the Ohio, cannot be wrong on this, [laughter;] and that if you have that property on that side of the Ohio, under the seal and stamp of the Almighty, when by any means it escapes over here, it is wrong to have constitutions and laws, "to devil" you about it. So Douglas is moulding the public opinion of the North, first to say that the thing is right in your State over the Ohio river, and hence to say that that which is right there is not wrong here, [at this moment the cannon was fired; to the great injury of sundry panes of glass in the vicinity,] and that all laws and constitutions here, recognizing it as being wrong, are themselves wrong, and ought to be repealed and abrogated. He will tell you, men of Ohio, that if you choose here to have laws against Slavery it is in conformity to the idea that your climate is not suited to it, that your climate is not suited to slave labor, and therefore you have constitutions and laws against it.

Let us attend to that argument for a little while and see if it be sound. You do not raise sugar cane—[except the new fashioned sugar cane, and you won't raise that long] but they do raise it in Louisiana. You don't raise it in Ohio because you can't raise it profitably, because the climate don't suit it. [Here again the cannon interrupted. Its report was followed by another fall of window glass.] They do raise it in Louisiana because there it is profitable. Now, Douglas will tell you that is precisely the Slavery question. That they do have slaves there because they are profitable, and you don't have them here because they are not profitable. If that is so, then it leads to dealing with the one precisely as with the other. Is there then anything in the constitution or laws of Ohio against raising sugar cane? Have you found it necessary to put any such provision in your law? Surely not! No man desires to raise sugar cane in Ohio; but, if any man did desire to do so, you would say it was a tyrannical law that forbid his doing so, and whenever you shall agree with Douglas, whenever your minds are brought to adopt his argument, as surely you will have reached the conclusion, that although Slavery is not profitable in Ohio, if any man wants it, it is wrong to him not to let him have it.

In this matter Judge Douglas is preparing the public mind for you of Kentucky, to make perpetual that good thing in your estimation, about which you and I differ.

In this connection let me ask your attention to another thing. I believe it is safe to assert that five years ago, no living man had expressed the opinion that the negro had no share in the Declaration of Independence. Let me state that again: five years ago no living man had expressed the opinion that the negro had no share in the Declaration of Independence. If there is in this large audience any man who ever knew of that opinion being put upon paper as much as five years ago, I will be obliged to him now or at a subsequent time to show it.

If that be true I wish you then to note the next fact; that within the space of five years Senator Douglas, in the argument of this question, has got his entire party, so far as I know, without exception, to join in saying that the negro has no share in the Declaration of Independence. If there be now in all these United States, one Douglas man that does not say this, I have been unable upon any occasion to scare him up. Now if none of you said this five years ago, and all of you say it now, that is a matter that you Kentuckians ought to note. That is a vast change in the Northern public sentiment upon that question.

Of what tendency is that change? The tendency of that change is to bring the public mind to the conclusion that when men are spoken of, the negro is not meant; that when negroes are spoken of, brutes alone are contemplated. That change in public sentiment has already degraded the black man in the estimation of Douglas and his followers from the condition of a man of some sort, and assigned him to the condition of a brute. Now, you Kentuckians ought to give

Douglas credit for this. That is the largest possible stride that can be made in regard to the perpetuation of your thing of Slavery.

A VOICE: "Speak to Ohio men, and not to Kentuckians!"

MR. LINCOLN: I beg permission to speak as I please. (Laughter.)

In Kentucky, perhaps, in many of the Slave States certainly, you are trying to establish the rightfulness of Slavery by reference to the Bible. You are trying to show that slavery existed in the Bible times by Divine ordinance. Now Douglas is wiser than you, for your own benefit, upon that subject. Douglas knows that whenever you establish that Slavery was right by the Bible, it will occur that that Slavery was the Slavery of the *white* man—of men without reference to color— and he knows very well that you may entertain that idea in Kentucky as much as you please, but you will never win any Northern support upon it. He makes a wiser argument for you; he makes the argument that the slavery of the *black* man, the slavery of the man who has a skin of a different color from your own, is right. He thereby brings to your support Northern voters who could not for a moment be brought by your own argument of the Bible-right of slavery. Will you not give him credit for that? Will you not say that in this matter he is more wisely for you than you are for yourselves.

Now having established with his entire party this doctrine—having been entirely successful in that branch of his efforts in your behalf; he is ready for another.

At this same meeting at Memphis, he declared that while in all contests between the negro and the white man, he was for the white man, but that in all questions between the negro and the crocodile he was for the negro. (Laughter.) He did not make that declaration accidentally at Memphis. He made it a great many times in the canvass in Illinois last year, (though I don't know that it was reported in any of his speeches there,) but he frequently made it. I believe he repeated it at Columbus, and I should not wonder if he repeated it here. It is, then, a deliberate way of expressing himself upon that subject. It is a matter of mature deliberation with him thus to express himself upon that point of his case. It therefore requires some deliberate attention.

The first inference seems to be that if you do not enslave the negro you are wronging the white man in some way or other, and that whoever is opposed to the negro being enslaved is in some way or other against the white man. Is not that a falsehood? If there was a necessary conflict between the white man and the negro, I should be for the white man as much as Judge Douglas; but I say there is no such necessary conflict. I say that there is room enough for us all to be free, (loud manifestations of applause,) and that it not only does not wrong the white man that the negro should be free, but it positively wrongs the mass of the white men that the negro should be enslaved; that the mass of white men are really injured by the effect of slave labor in the vicinity of the fields of their own labor. (Applause.)

But I do not desire to dwell upon this branch of the question more than to say that this assumption of his is false, and I do hope that that fallacy will not long prevail in the minds of intelligent white men. At all events, you Kentuckians ought to thank Judge Douglas for it. It is for your benefit it is made.

The other branch of it is, that in a struggle between the negro and the crocodile, he is for the negro. Well, I don't know that there is any struggle between the negro and the crocodile, either. (Laughter.) I suppose that if a crocodile (or as we old Ohio river boatmen used to call them, alligators) should come across a white man, he would kill him if he could, and so he would a negro. But what, at last, is this proposition? I believe it is a sort of proposition in proportion, which may be stated thus: As the negro is to the white man, so is the crocodile to the negro, and as the negro may rightfully treat the crocodile as a beast or reptile, so the white man may rightfully treat the negro as a beast or a reptile. (Applause.) That is really the "knip" of all that argument of his.

Now, my brother Kentuckians, who believe in this, you ought to thank Judge Douglas for having put that in a much more taking way than any of yourselves have done. (Applause.)

Again, Douglas' *great principle*, "Popular Sovereignty," as he calls it, gives you, by natural consequence, the revival of the Slavetrade whenever you want it. If you question this, listen a while, consider a while, what I shall advance in support of that proposition.

He says that it is the sacred right of the man who goes into the Territories, to have Slavery if he wants it. Grant that for argument's sake. Is it not the sacred right of the man that don't go there equally to buy slaves in Africa, if he wants them? Can you point out the difference? The man who goes into the Territories of Kansas and Nebraska, or any other new Territory, with the sacred right of taking a slave there which belongs to him, would certainly have no more right to take one there than I would who own no slave, but who would desire to buy one and take him there. You will not say—you, the friends of Douglas—but that the man who does not own a slave, has an equal right to buy one and take him to the Territory, as the other does?

A VOICE: "I want to ask a question. Don't foreign nations interfere with the Slave-trade?"

MR. LINCOLN: Well! I understand it to be a principle of Democracy to whip foreign nations whenever they interfere with us. (Laughter and applause.)

A VOICE: "I only asked for information. I am a Republican myself."

MR. LINCOLN: You and I will be on the best terms in the world, but I do not wish to be diverted from the point I was trying to press.

I say that Douglas's Popular Sovereignty, establishing a sacred right in the people, if you please, if carried to its logical conclusion, gives equally the sacred right to the people of the States or the Territories themselves to buy slaves, wherever they can buy them cheapest; and if any man can show a distinction, I should like to hear him try it. If any man can show how the people of Kansas have a better right to slaves because they want them, than the people of Georgia have to buy them in Africa, I want him to do it. I think it cannot be done. If it is "Popular Sovereignty" for the people to have slaves because they want them, it is Popular Sovereignty for them to buy them in Africa, because they desire to do so.

I know that Douglas has recently made a little effort—not seeming to notice that he had a different theory—has made an effort to get rid of that. He has written a letter addressed to somebody, I believe, who resides in Iowa, declaring his opposition to the repeal of the laws that prohibit the African Slave Trade. He bases his opposition to such repeal upon the ground that these laws are themselves one of the compromises of the Constitution of the United States. Now it would be very interesting to see Judge Douglas or any of his friends turn to the Constitution of the United States and point out that compromise, to show where there is any compromise in the Constitution or provision in the Constitution, express or implied, by which the Administrators of that Constitution are under any obligation to repeal the African Slave-trade. I know, or at least I think I know, that the framers of that Constitution did expect that the African Slave-trade would be abolished at the end of twenty years, to which time their prohibition against its being abolished extended. I think there is abundant contemporaneous history to show that the framers of the Constitution expected it to be abolished. But while they so expected, they gave nothing for that expectation, and they put no provision in the Constitution requiring it should be so abolished. The migration or importation of such persons as the States shall see fit to admit shall not be prohibited, but a certain tax might be levied upon such importation. But what was to be done after that time? The Constitution is as silent about that, as it is silent personally about myself. There is absolutely nothing in it about that subject—there is only the expectation of the framers of the Constitution that the Slave-trade would be abolished at the end of that time and they expected it would be abolished, owing to public sentiment, before that time, and they put that provision in, in order that it should not be abolished before that time, for reasons which I suppose they thought to be sound ones, but which I will not now try to enumerate before you.

But while they expected the Slave-trade would be abolished at that time, they expected that the spread of Slavery into the new Territories should also be restricted. It is as easy to prove that the framers of the Constitution of the United States, expected that Slavery should be prohibited from extending into the new Territories, as it is to prove that it was expected that the Slave-trade should be abolished. Both these things were expected. One was no more expected than the other, and one was no more a compromise of the Constitution than the other. There was nothing said in the Constitution in regard to the spread of Slavery into the Territory. I grant that, but there was something very important said about it by the same generation of men in the adoption of the old Ordinance of '87, through the influence of which you here in Ohio, our neighbors in Indiana, we in Illinois, our neighbors in Michigan and Wisconsin are happy, prosperous, teeming millions of free men. (Continued applause.) That generation of men, though not to the full extent members of the Convention that framed the Constitution, were to some extent members of that Convention, holding seats, at the same time in one body and the other, so that if there was any compromise on either of these subjects, the strong evidence is that that compromise was in favor of the restriction of Slavery from the new territories.

But Douglas says that he is unalterably opposed to the repeal of those laws; because, in his view, it is a compromise of the Constitution. You Kentuckians, no doubt, are somewhat offended with that! You ought not to be! You ought to be patient! You ought to know that if he said less than that, he would lose the power of "lugging" the Northern States to your support. Really, what you would push him to do would take from him his entire power to serve you. And you ought to remember how long, by precedent, Judge Douglas holds himself obliged to stick by compromises. You ought to remember that by the time you yourselves think you are ready to inaugurate measures for the revival of the African Slave-trade that sufficient time will have arrived by precedent, for Judge Douglas to break through that compromise. He says now nothing more strong than he said in 1849 when he declared in favor of the Missouri Compromise— that precisely four years and a quarter after he declared that compromise to be a sacred thing, which "no ruthless hand would ever dare to touch," he, himself, brought forward the measure, ruthlessly to destroy it. (A voice—"hit him again!" Applause.) By a mere calculation of time it will only be four years more until he is ready to take back his profession about the sacredness of the Compromise abolishing the slave trade. Precisely as soon as you are ready to have his services in that direction, by fair calculation you may be sure of having them. (Applause and laughter.)

But you remember and set down to Judge Douglas' debit, or discredit, that he, last year, said the people of the Territories can, in spite of the Dred Scott decision, exclude your slaves from those territories; that he declared by "unfriendly legislation," the extension of your property into the new Territories may be cut off in the teeth of the decision of the Supreme Court of the United States.

He assumed that position at Freeport on the 27th of August, 1858. He said that the people of the Territories can exclude Slavery in so many words. You ought, however, to bear in mind that he has never said it since. (Laughter.) You may hunt in every speech that he has since made, and he has never used that expression once. He has never seemed to notice that he is stating his views differently from what he did then; but, by some sort of accident, he has always really stated it differently. He has always since then declared that "the Constitution does not carry Slavery into the Territories of the United States beyond the power of the people legally to control it, as other property." Now, there is a difference in the language used upon that former occasion and in this latter day. There may or may not be a difference in the meaning, but it is worth while considering whether there is not also a difference in meaning.

What is it to exclude? Why, it is to drive it out. It is in some way to put it out of the Territory. It is to force it across the line, or change its character, so that as property it is out of existence. But what is the controlling of it "as other property?" Is controlling it as other property the same thing as destroying it, or driving it away? I should think not. I should think the controlling of it as other property would be just about what you in Kentucky should want. I understand the controlling of property means the controlling of it for the benefit of the owner of it. While I have no doubt the Supreme Court of the United States would say "God speed" to any of the Territorial legislatures that should thus control slave property, they would sing quite a different tune if by the pretense of controlling it they were to undertake to pass laws which virtually excluded it, and that upon a very well known principle to all lawyers, that what a legislature cannot directly do, it cannot do by indirection; that as, the legislature has not the power to drive slaves out, they have no power by indirection, by tax or by imposing burdens in any way on that property, to effect the same end, and that any attempt to do so would be held by the Dred Scott Court unconstitutional.

Douglas is not willing to stand by his first proposition that they can exclude it, because we have seen that that proposition amounts to nothing more nor less than the naked absurdity, that you may lawfully drive out that which has a lawful right to remain. He admitted at first that the slave might be lawfully taken into the Territories under the Constitution of the United States, and yet asserted that he might be lawfully driven out. That being the proposition, it is the absurdity I have stated. He is not willing to stand in the face of that direct, naked and impudent absurdity; he has, therefore, modified his language into that of being *"controlled as other property."*

The Kentuckians don't like this in Douglas! I will tell you where it will go. He now swears by the Court. He was once a leading man in Illinois to break down a Court, because it had made a decision he did not like. But he now not only swears by the Court, the courts having got to working for you, but he denounces all men that do not swear by the Courts, as unpatriotic, as bad citizens. When one of these acts of unfriendly legislation shall impose such heavy burdens as to, in effect, destroy property in slaves in a Territory and show plainly enough that there can be no mistake in the purpose of the Legislature to make them so burdensome, this same Supreme Court will decide that law to be unconstitutional, and he will be ready to say for your benefit, "I swear by the Court; I give it up"; and while that is going on he has been getting all his men to swear by the Courts, and to give it up with him. In this again he serves you faithfully, and as I say, more wisely than you serve yourselves.

Again! I have alluded in the beginning of these remarks to the fact, that Judge Douglas has made great complaint of my having expressed the opinion that this Government "cannot endure permanently half slave and half free." He has complained of Seward for using different language, and declaring that there is an "irrepressible conflict" between the principles of free and slave labor.

(A voice—"He says it is not original with Seward. That is original with Lincoln.")

I will attend to that immediately, sir. Since that time, Hickman, of Pennsylvania expressed the same sentiment. He has never denounced Mr. Hickman: why? There is a little chance, notwithstanding that opinion in the mouth of Hickman, that he may yet be a Douglas man. That is the difference! It is not unpatriotic to hold that opinion, if a man is a Douglas man.

But neither I nor Seward, nor Hickman, is entitled to the enviable or unenviable distinction of having first expressed that idea. That same idea was expressed by the Richmond *Enquirer* in Virginia, in 1856; quite two years before it was expressed by the first of us. And while Douglas was pluming himself, that in his conflict with my humble self, last year, he had "squelched out" that fatal heresy, as he delighted to call it, and had suggested that if he only had had a chance to be in New York and meet Seward he would have "squelched" it there also, it never occurred to him to breathe a word against Pryor. I don't think that you can discover that Douglas ever talked of going to Virginia to "squelch" out that idea there.

No. More than that. That same Roger A. Pryor was brought to Washington City and made the editor of the *par excellence* Douglas paper, after making use of that expression, which, in us, is so unpatriotic and heretical. From all this, my Kentucky friends may see that this opinion is heretical in his view only when it is expressed by men suspected of a desire that the country shall all become free and not when expressed by those fairly known to entertain the desire that the whole country shall become slave. When expressed by that class of men, it is in no wise offensive to him. In this again, my friends of Kentucky, you have Judge Douglas with you.

There is another reason why you Southern people ought to nominate Douglas at your convention at Charleston. That reason is the wonderful capacity of the man; [laughter] the power he has of doing what would seem to be impossible. Let me call your attention to one of these apparently impossible things.

Douglas had three or four very distinguished men of the most extreme anti-slavery views of any men in the Republican party, expressing their desire for his re-election to the Senate last year. That would, of itself, have seemed to be a little wonderful, but that wonder is heightened when we see that Wise of Virginia, a man exactly opposed to them, a man who believes in the Divine right of slavery, was also expressing his desire that Douglas should be re-elected, that another man that may be said to be kindred to Wise, Mr. Breckinridge, the Vice President, and of your own State, was also agreeing with the anti-slavery men in the North; that Douglas ought to be re-elected. Still, to heighten the wonder, a Senator from Kentucky, whom I have always loved with an affection as tender and endearing as I have ever loved any man; who was opposed to the anti-slavery men for reasons which seemed sufficient to him, and equally opposed to Wise and Breckinridge, was writing letters into Illinois to secure the re-election of Douglas. Now that all these conflicting elements should be brought, while at dagger's points, with one another, to support him, is a feat that is worthy for you to note and consider. It is quite probable, that each of these classes of men thought by the re-election of Douglas, their peculiar views would gain something, it is probable that the anti-slavery men thought their views would gain something that Wise and Breckinridge thought so too, as regards their opinions, that Mr. Crittenden thought that his views would gain something, although he was opposed to both these other men. It is probable that each and all of them thought that they were using Douglas, and it is yet an unsolved problem whether he was not using them all. If he was, then it is for you to consider whether that power to perform wonders, is one for you lightly to throw away.

There is one other thing that I will say to you in this relation. It is but my opinion, I give it to you without a fee. It is my opinion that it is for you to take him or be defeated; and that if you do take him you may be beaten. You will surely be beaten if you do not take him. We, the Republicans and others forming the Opposition of the country, intend to "stand by our guns," to be patient and firm, and in the long run to beat you whether you take him or not. [Applause.] We know that before we fairly beat you, we have to beat you both together. We know that you are "all of a feather," [loud applause,] and that we have to beat you altogether, and we expect to do it. [Applause] We don't intend to be very impatient about it. We mean to be as deliberate and calm about it as it is possible to be, but as firm and resolved, as it is possible for men to be. When we do as we say, beat you, you perhaps want to know what we will do with you. [Laughter]

I will tell you, so far as I am authorized to speak for the Opposition, what we mean to do with you. We mean to treat you as near as we possibly can, like Washington, Jefferson and Madison treated you. [Cheers] We mean to leave you alone, and in no way to interfere with your institution; to abide by all and every compromise of the constitution, and, in a word, coming back to the original proposition, to treat you, so far as degenerated men (if we have degenerated) may, according to the examples of those noble fathers—Washington, Jefferson and Madison. [Applause] We mean to remember that you are as good as we; that there is no difference between us other than the difference of circumstances. We mean to recognise and bear in mind always that you have as good hearts in your bosoms as other people, or as we claim to have, and treat you accordingly. We mean to marry your girls when we have a chance—the white ones I mean— [laughter] and I have the honor to inform you that I once did have a chance in that way. [A voice, "Good for you," and applause]

I have told you what we mean to do. I want to know, now, when that thing takes place, what you mean to do. I often hear it intimated that you mean to divide the Union whenever a Republican, or anything like it, is elected President of the United States. [A voice, "That is so."] "That is so," one of them says. I wonder if he is a Kentuckian? [A voice, "He is a Douglas man."] Well, then, I want to know what you are going to do with your half of it? [Applause and laughter] Are you going to split the Ohio down through, and push your half off a piece? Or are you going to keep it right alongside of us outrageous fellows? Or are you going to build up a wall some way between your country and ours, by which that moveable property of yours can't come over here any more, to the danger of your losing it? Do you think you can better yourselves on that subject, by leaving us here under no obligation whatever to return those specimens of your moveable property that come hither? You have divided the Union because we would not do right with you as you think, upon that subject; when we cease to be under obligations to do anything for you, how much better off do you think you will be? Will you make war upon us and kill us all? Why, gentlemen, I think you are as gallant and as brave men as live; that you can fight as bravely in a good cause, man for man, as any other people living; that you have shown yourselves capable of this upon various occasions; but, man for man, you are not better than we are, and there are not so many of you as there are of us. [Loud cheering.] You will never make much of a hand at whipping us. If we were fewer in numbers than you, I think that you could whip us; if we were equal it would likely be a drawn battle; but being inferior in numbers, you will make nothing by attempting to master us.

But perhaps I have addressed myself as long, or longer, to the Kentuckians than I ought to have done inasmuch as I have said that whatever course you take we intend in the end to beat you. I propose to address a few remarks to our friends by way of discussing with them the best means of keeping that promise, that I have in good faith made. [Long continued applause.]

It may appear a little episodical for me to mention the topic of which I shall speak now. It is a favorite proposition of Douglas' that the interference of the General Government, through the Ordinance of '87, or through any other act of the General Government, never has made or ever can make a Free State; that the Ordinance of '87 did not make Free States of Ohio, Indiana or Illinois. That these States are free upon his "great principle" of Popular Sovereignty, because the people of those several States have chosen to make them so. At Columbus, and probably here, he undertook to compliment the people that they themselves have made the State of Ohio free and that the Ordinance of '87 was not entitled in any degree to divide the honor with them. I have no doubt that the people of the State of Ohio did make her free according to their own will and judgment, but let the facts be remembered.

In 1802, I believe, it was you who made your first constitution, with the clause prohibiting slavery, and you did it I suppose very nearly unanimously, but you should bear in mind that you—speaking of you as one people—that you did so unembarrassed by the actual presence of the institution amongst you; that you made it a Free State, not with the embarrassment upon you of already having among you many slaves, which if they had been here, and you had sought to make a Free State, you would not know what to do with. If they had been among you, embarrassing difficulties, most probably, would have induced you to tolerate a slave constitution instead of a free one, as indeed these very difficulties have constrained every people on this continent who have adopted slavery.

Pray what was it that made you free? What kept you free? Did you not find your country free when you came to decide that Ohio should be a Free State? It is important to enquire by what reason you found it so? Let us take an illustration between the States of Ohio and Kentucky. Kentucky is separated by this river Ohio, not a mile wide. A portion of Kentucky, by reason of the course of the Ohio, is further north than this portion of Ohio in which we now stand. Kentucky is entirely covered with slavery—Ohio is entirely free from it. What made that difference? Was it climate? No! A portion of Kentucky was further north than this portion of Ohio. Was it soil? No! There is nothing in the soil of the one more favorable to slave labor than the other. It was not climate or soil that caused one side of the line to be entirely covered with slavery and the other side free of it. What was it? Study over it. Tell us, if you can, in all the range of conjecture, if there be anything you can conceive of that made that difference, other than that there was no law of any sort keeping it out of Kentucky? while the Ordinance of '87 kept it out of Ohio. If there is any other reason than this, I confess that it is wholly beyond my power to conceive of it. This, then, I offer to combat the idea that that ordinance has never made any State free.

I don't stop at this illustration. I come to the State of Indiana; and what I have said as between Kentucky and Ohio I repeat as between Indiana and Kentucky; it is equally applicable. One additional argument is applicable also to Indiana. In her Territorial condition she more than once petitioned Congress to abrogate the ordinance entirely, or at least so far as to suspend its operation for a time, in order that they should exercise the "Popular Sovereignty" of having slaves if they wanted them. The men then controlling the General Government, imitating the men of the Revolution, refused Indiana that privilege. And so we have the evidence that Indiana supposed she could have slaves, if it were not for that ordinance that she besought Congress to put that barrier out of the way; that Congress refused to do so, and it all ended at last in Indiana being a Free State. Tell me not, then, that the Ordinance of '87 had nothing to do with making Indiana a free state, when we find some men chafing against and only restrained by that barrier.

Come down again to our State of Illinois. The great Northwest Territory including Ohio, Indiana, Illinois, Michigan and Wisconsin, was acquired, first I believe by the British Government, in part at least, from the French. Before the establishment of our independence, it became a part of Virginia, enabling Virginia afterwards to transfer it to the general government. There were French settlements in what is now Illinois, and at the same time there were French settlements in what is now Missouri—in the tract of country that was not purchased till about 1803. In these French settlements negro slavery had existed for many years—perhaps more than a hundred, if not as much as two hundred years—at Kaskaskia in Illinois, and at St. Genevieve, or Cape Girardeau, perhaps, in Missouri. The number of slaves was not very great, but there was about the same number in each place. They were there when we acquired the Territory. There was no effort made to break up the relation of master and slave and even the Ordinance of 1787 was not so enforced as to destroy that slavery in Illinois; nor did the Ordinance apply to Missouri at all.

What I want to ask your attention to, at this point, is that Illinois and Missouri came into the Union about the same time, Illinois in the latter part of 1818, and Missouri, after a struggle, I believe some time in 1820. They had been filling up with American people about the same period of time; their progress enabling them to come into the Union at about the same time. At the end of that ten years, in which they had been so preparing, (for it was about that period of time) the number of slaves in Illinois had actually decreased; while in Missouri, beginning with very few, at the end of that ten years, there were about ten thousand. This being so, and it being remembered that Missouri and Illinois are, to a certain extent, in the same parallel of latitude—that the Northern half of Missouri and the Southern half of Illinois are in the same parallel of latitude—so that climate would have the same effect upon one as upon the other, and that in the soil there is no material difference so far as bears upon the question of slavery being settled upon one or the other—there being none of those natural causes to produce a difference in filling them, and yet there being a broad difference in their filling up, we are led again to inquire what was the cause of that difference.

It is most natural to say that in Missouri there was no law to keep that country from filling up with slaves, while in Illinois there was the Ordinance of '87. The Ordinance being there, slavery decreased during that ten years—the Ordinance not being in the other, it increased from a few to ten thousand. Can anybody doubt the reason of the difference?

I think all these facts most abundantly prove that my friend Judge Douglas' proposition, that the Ordinance of '87 or the national restriction of slavery, never had a tendency to make a Free State, is a fallacy—a proposition without the shadow or substance of truth about it.

Douglas sometimes says that all the States (and it is part of this same proposition I have been discussing) that have become free, have become so upon his "great principle"—that the State of Illinois itself came into the Union as a slave State, and that the people upon the "great principle" of Popular Sovereignty have since made it a Free State. Allow me but a little while to state to you what facts there are to justify him in saying that Illinois came into the Union as a Slave State.

I have mentioned to you that there were a few old French slaves there. They numbered, I think, one or two hundred. Besides that there had been a Territorial law for indenturing black persons. Under that law, in violation of the Ordinance of '87, but without any enforcement of the Ordinance to overthrow the system, there had been a small number of slaves introduced as indentured persons. Owing to this the clause for the prohibition of slavery, was slightly modified. Instead of running like yours, that neither slavery nor involuntary servitude, except for crime of which the party shall have been duly convicted, should exist in the State, they said that neither slavery nor involuntary servitude should thereafter be introduced, and that the children of indentured servants should be born free; and nothing was said about the few old French slaves. Out of this fact, that the clause for prohibiting slavery was modified because of the actual presence of it, Douglas asserts again and again that Illinois came into the Union as a Slave State. How far the facts sustain the conclusion that he draws, it is for intelligent and impartial men to decide. I leave it with you with these remarks, worthy of being remembered, that that little thing, those few indentured servants being there, was of itself sufficient to modify a Constitution made by a people ardently desiring to have a free Constitution; showing the power of the actual presence of the institution of slavery to prevent any people, however anxious to make a Free State, from making it perfectly so.

I have been detaining you longer perhaps than I ought to do. [Long and repeated cries of "go on."]

I am in some doubt whether to introduce another topic upon which I could talk awhile. [Cries of "Go on," and "Give us it."] It is this then. Douglas' Popular Sovereignty as a principle, is simply this: If one man chooses to make a slave of another man, neither that other man or anybody else has a right to object. [Cheers and laughter.] Apply it to government, as he seeks to apply it and it is this—if, in a new Territory, into which a few people are beginning to enter for the purpose of making their homes, they choose to either exclude slavery from their limits, or to establish it there, however one or the other may affect the persons to be enslaved, or the infinitely greater number of persons who are afterwards to inhabit that Territory, or the other members of the family of communities, of which they are but an incipient member, or the general head of the family of states as parent of all—however their action may affect one or the other of these, there is no power or right to interfere. That is Douglas' Popular sovereignty in the world. I think a definition of popular sovereignty, in the abstract, would be about this—that each man shall do precisely as he pleases with himself, and with all those things which exclusively concern him. Applied in government, this principle would be, that a general government shall do all those things which pertain to it, and all the local governments shall do precisely as they please in respect to those matters which exclusively concern them.

Douglas looks upon slavery as so insignificant that the people must decide that question for themselves, and yet they are not fit to decide who shall be their Governor, Judge or secretary, or who shall be any of their officers. These are vast national matters in his estimation but the little matter in his estimation, is that of planting slavery there. That is purely of local interest, which nobody should be allowed to say a word about. [Applause.]

Labor is the great source from which nearly all, if not all, human comforts and necessities are drawn. There is a difference in opinion about the elements of labor in society. Some men assume that there is a necessary connection between capital and labor, and that connection draws within it the whole of the labor of the community. They assume that nobody works unless capital excites them to work. They begin next to consider what is the best way. They say that there are but two ways; one is to hire men and to allure them to labor by their consent; the other is to buy the men and drive them to it, and that is slavery. Having assumed that, they proceed to discuss the question of whether the laborers themselves are better off in the condition of slaves or of hired laborers, and they usually decide that they are better off in the condition of slaves.

In the first place, I say, that the whole thing is a mistake. That there is a certain relation between capital and labor, I admit. That it does exist, and rightfully exists, I think is true. That men who are industrious, and sober, and honest in the pursuit of their own interests should after a while accumulate capital, and after that should be allowed to enjoy it in peace, and also if they should choose when they have accumulated it to use it to save themselves from actual labor and hire other people to labor for them is right. In doing so they do not wrong the man they employ, for they find men who have not of their own land to work upon, or shops to work in, and who are benefited by working for others, hired laborers, receiving their capital for it. Thus a few men that own capital, hire a few others, and these establish the relation of capital and labor rightfully. A relation of which I make no complaint. But I insist that that relation after all does not embrace more than one-eighth of the labor of the country. At least seven-eighths of the labor is done without relation to it. Take the State of Ohio. Out of eight bushels of wheat, seven are raised by those men who labor for themselves, aided by their boys grown to manhood, neither being hired nor hiring, but literally laboring upon their own hook, asking no favor of capital, of hired laborer, or slave. That is the true condition of the larger portion of all the labor done in this community, or that should be the condition of labor in well-regulated communities of agriculturists. Thus much for that part of the subject.

Again: The assumption that the slave is in a better condition than the hired laborer, includes the further assumption that he who is once a hired laborer always remains a hired laborer; that there is a certain class of men who remain through life in a dependent condition. Then they endeavor to point out that when they get old, they have no kind masters to take care of them, and that they fall dead in the traces, with the harness of actual labor upon their backs. In point of fact that is a false assumption. There is no such thing as a man who is a hired laborer, of a necessity, always remaining in his early condition. The general rule is otherwise. I know it is so, and I will tell you why. When at an early age, I was myself a hired laborer, at twelve dollars per month; and therefore I do know that there is not always the necessity for actual labor because once there was propriety in being so. My understanding of the hired laborer is this: A young man finds himself of an age to be dismissed from parental control; he has for his capital nothing, save two strong bands that God has given him, a heart willing to labor, and a freedom to choose the mode of his work and the manner of his employment; he has got no soil nor shop, and he avails himself of the opportunity of hiring himself to some man who has capital to pay him a fair day's wages for a fair day's work. He is benefited by availing himself of that privilege: He works industriously, he behaves soberly, and the result of a year or two's labor is a surplus of capital. Now he buys land on his own hook; he settles, marries, begets sons and daughters, and in course of time he has enough capital to hire some new beginner.

In this same way every member of the whole community benefits and improves his condition. That is the true condition of labor in the world, and it breaks up the saying of these men that there is a class of men chained down throughout life to labor for another.

There is no such case unless he be of that confiding, and leaning disposition that makes it preferable for him to choose that course, or unless he be a vicious man, who, by reason of his vice, is, in some way prevented from improving his condition, or else he be a singularly unfortunate man. There is no such thing as a man being bound down in a free country through his life as a laborer. This progress by which the poor, honest, industrious, and resolute man raises himself, that he may work on his own account and hire somebody else, is that progress that human nature is entitled to, is that improvement in condition that is intended to be secured by those institutions under which we live, is the great principle for which this Government was really formed. Our Government was not established that one man might do with himself as he pleases, and with another man too.

I hold that if there is any one thing that can be proved to be the will of God by external nature around us without reference to revelation, it is the proposition that whatever any one man earns with his hands and by the sweat of his brow, he shall enjoy in peace. I say that whereas God Almighty has given every man one mouth to be fed, and one pair of hands adapted to furnish food for that mouth, if anything can be proved to be the will of Heaven, it is proved by this fact, that that mouth is to be fed by those hands, without being interfered with by any other man who has also his mouth to feed and his hands to labor with. I hold if the Almighty had ever made a set of men that should do all of the eating and none of the work, he would have made them with mouths only and no hands; and if he had ever made another class that he intended should do all the work and none of the eating, he would have made them without mouths and with all hands. But inasmuch as he has not chosen to make man in that way, if anything is proved, it is that those hands and mouths are to be co-operative through life and not to be interfered with. That they are to go forth and improve their condition as I have been trying to illustrate, is the inherent right given to mankind directly by the Maker.

In the exercise of this right you must have room. In the filling up of countries, it turns out after a while that we get so thick that we have not quite room enough for the exercise of that right, and we desire to go somewhere else. Where shall we go to? Where shall you go to escape from over-population and competition? To those new Territories which belong to us, which are God-given for that purpose. If, then, you will go to those Territories that you may improve your condition, you have a right to keep them in the best condition for those going into them, and can they make that natural advance in their condition if they find the institution of slavery planted there?

My good friends, let me ask you a question—you who have come from Virginia or Kentucky, to get rid of this thing of slavery—let me ask you what headway would you have made in getting rid of it, if by Popular Sovereignty you found slavery on that soil which you looked for to be free when you got there? You would not have made much headway if you had found slavery already here, if you had to sit down to your labor by the side of the unpaid workman.

I say, then, that it is due to yourselves as voters, as owners of the new Territories, that you shall keep those Territories free, in the best condition for all such of your gallant sons as may choose to go there.

I do not desire to elaborate this branch of the general subject of political discussion at this time further. I did not think I would get upon this topic at all, and I have detained you already too long in its discussion.

I have taken upon myself in the name of some of you to say, that we expect upon these principles to ultimately beat them. In order to do so, I think we want and must have a national policy in regard to the institution of slavery, that acknowledges and deals with that institution as being wrong. (Loud cheering) Whoever desires the prevention of the spread of slavery and the nationalization of that institution, yields all, when he yields to any policy that either recognizes slavery as being right, or as being an indifferent thing. Nothing will make you successful but setting up a policy which shall treat the thing as being wrong. When I say this, I do not mean to say that this general government is charged with the duty of redressing or preventing all the wrongs in the world; but I do think that it is charged with the duty of preventing and redressing all wrongs which are wrongs to itself. This government is expressly charged with the duty of providing for the general welfare. We believe that the spreading out and perpetuity of the institution of slavery impairs the general welfare. We believe—nay, we know, that that is the only thing that has ever threatened the perpetuity of the Union itself. The only thing which has ever menaced the destruction of the government under which we live, is this very thing. To repress this thing, we think is providing for the general welfare. Our friends in Kentucky differ from us. We need not make our argument for them, but we who think it is wrong in all its relations, or in some of them at least, must decide as to our own actions, and our own course, upon our own judgment.

I say that we must not interfere with the institution of slavery in the states where it exists, because the constitution forbids it, and the general welfare does not require us to do so. We must not withhold an efficient fugitive slave law because the constitution requires us, as I understand it, not to withhold such a law. But we must prevent the outspreading of the institution, because neither the constitution nor general welfare requires us to extend it. We must prevent the revival of the African slave trade and the enacting by Congress of a territorial slave code. We must prevent each of these things being done by either Congresses or courts. The people of these United States are the rightful masters of both Congresses and courts (Applause) not to overthrow the constitution, but to overthrow the men who pervert that constitution. (Applause.)

To do these things we must employ instrumentalities. We must hold conventions; we must adopt platforms if we conform to ordinary custom; we must nominate candidates, and we must carry elections. In all these things, I think that we ought to keep in view our real purpose, and in none do anything that stands adverse to our purpose. If we shall adopt a platform that fails to recognize or express our purpose, or elect a man that declares himself inimical to our purpose, we not only take nothing by our success, but we tacitly admit that we act upon no other principle than a desire to have "the loaves and fishes," by which, in the end our apparent success is really an injury to us.

I know that it is very desirable with me, as with everybody else, that all the elements of the Opposition shall unite in the next Presidential election and in all future time. I am anxious that that should be, but there are things seriously to be considered in relation to that matter. If the terms can be arranged, I am in favor of the Union. But suppose we shall take up some man and put him upon one end or the other of the ticket, who declares himself against us in regard to the prevention of the spread of slavery—who turns up his nose and says he is tired of hearing anything about it, who is more against us than against the enemy, what will be the issue? Why he will get no slave states after all—he has tried that already until being beat is the rule for him. If we nominate him upon that ground, he will not carry a slave state; and not only so, but that portion of our men who are high strung upon the principle we really fight for, will not go for him, and he won't get a single electoral vote anywhere except, perhaps, in the state of Maryland. There is no use in saying to us that we are stubborn and obstinate, because we won't do some such thing as this. We cannot do it. We cannot get our men to vote it. I speak by the card, that we cannot give the state of Illinois in such case by fifty thousand. We would be flatter down than the "Negro Democracy" themselves have the heart to wish to see us.

After saying this much, let me say a little on the other side. There are plenty of men in the slave states that are altogether good enough for me to be either President or Vice President, provided they will profess their sympathy with our purpose, and will place themselves on the ground that our men, upon principle, can vote for them. There are scores of them, good men in their character for intelligence and talent and integrity. If such a one will place himself upon the right ground I am for his occupying one place upon the next Republican or Opposition ticket. [Applause] I will heartily go for him. But, unless he does so place himself, I think it a matter of perfect nonsense to attempt to bring about a union upon any other basis; that if a union be made, the elements will scatter so that there can be no success for such a ticket, nor anything like success. The good old maxims of the Bible are applicable, and truly applicable to human affairs, and in this as in other things, we may say here that he who is not for us is against us; he who gathereth not with us scattereth. [Applause] I should be glad to have some of the many good, and able, and noble men of the south to place themselves where we can confer upon them the high honor of an election upon one or the other end of our ticket. It would do my soul good to do that thing.

It would enable us to teach them that inasmuch as we select one of their own number to carry out our principles, we are free from the charge that we mean more than we say.

But, my friends I have detained you much longer than I expected to do. I believe I may do myself the compliment to say that you have stayed and heard me with great patience, for which I return you my most sincere thanks.

*September 17, 1859*

# Address Before the Wisconsin State Agricultural Society, Milwaukee, Wisconsin

MEMBERS OF THE AGRICULTURAL SOCIETY AND CITIZENS OF WISCONSIN:

Agricultural Fairs are becoming an institution of the country; they are useful in more ways than one; they bring us together, and thereby make us better acquainted, and better friends than we otherwise would be. From the first appearance of man upon the earth, down to very recent times, the words *"stranger"* and *"enemy"* were *quite* or *almost,* synonymous. Long after civilized nations had defined robbery and murder as high crimes, and had affixed severe punishments to them, when practiced among and upon their own people respectively, it was deemed no offence, but even meritorious, to rob, and murder, and enslave *strangers,* whether as nations or as individuals. Even yet, this has not totally disappeared. The man of the highest moral cultivation, in spite of all which abstract principle can do, likes him whom he *does* know, much better than him whom he does *not* know. To correct the evils, great and small, which spring from want of sympathy, and from positive enmity, among *strangers,* as nations, or as individuals, is one of the highest functions of civilization. To this end our Agricultural Fairs contribute in no small degree. They make more pleasant, and more strong, and more durable, the bond of social and political union among us. Again, if, as Pope declares, "happiness is our being's end and aim," our Fairs contribute much to that end and aim, as occasions of recreation—as holidays. Constituted as man is, he has positive need of occasional recreation; and whatever can give him this, associated with virtue and advantage, and free from vice and disadvantage, is a positive good. Such recreation our Fairs afford. They are a present pleasure, to be followed by no pain, as a consequence; they are a present pleasure, making the future more pleasant.

But the chief use of agricultural fairs is to aid in improving the great calling of *agriculture*, in all it's departments, and minute divisions—to make mutual exchange of agricultural discovery, information, and knowledge; so that, at the end, *all* may know every thing, which may have been known to but *one,* or to but a *few,* at the beginning—to bring together especially all which is supposed to not be generally known, because of recent discovery, or invention.

And not only to bring together, and to impart all which has been *accidentally* discovered or invented upon ordinary motive; but, by exciting emulation, for premiums, and for the pride and honor of success—of triumph, in some sort—to stimulate that discovery and invention into extraordinary activity. In this, these

Fairs are kindred to the patent clause in the Constitution of the United States; and to the department, and practical system, based upon that clause.

One feature, I believe, of every fair, is a regular *address*. The Agricultural Society of the young, prosperous, and soon to be, great State of Wisconsin, has done me the high honor of selecting me to make that address upon this occasion—an honor for which I make my profound, and grateful acknowledgement.

I presume I am not expected to employ the time assigned me, in the mere flattery of the farmers, as a class. My opinion of them is that, in proportion to numbers, they are neither better nor worse than other people. In the nature of things they are more numerous than any other class; and I believe there really are more attempts at flattering them than any other; the reason of which I cannot perceive, unless it be that they can cast more votes than any other. On reflection, I am not quite sure that there is not cause of suspicion against you, in selecting me, in some sort a politician, and in no sort a farmer, to address you.

But farmers, being the most numerous class, it follows that their interest is the largest interest. It also follows that that interest is most worthy of all to be cherished and cultivated—that if there be inevitable conflict between that interest and any other, that other should yield.

Again, I suppose it is not expected of me to impart to you much specific information on Agriculture. You have no reason to believe, and do not believe, that I possess it—if that were what you seek in this address, any one of your own number, or class, would be more able to furnish it.

You, perhaps, do expect me to give some general interest to the occasion; and to make some general suggestions, on practical matters. I shall attempt nothing more. And in such suggestions by me, quite likely very little will be new to you, and a large part of the rest possibly already known to be erroneous.

My first suggestion is an inquiry as to the effect of greater *thoroughness* in all the departments of Agriculture than now prevails in the North-West—perhaps I might say in America. To speak entirely within bounds, it is known that fifty bushels of wheat, or one hundred bushels of Indian corn can be produced from an acre. Less than a year ago I saw it stated that a man, by extraordinary care and labor, had produced of wheat, what was equal to two hundred bushels from an acre. But take fifty of wheat, and one hundred of corn, to be the *possibility*, and compare with it the actual crops of the country. Many years ago I saw it stated in a Patent Office Report that eighteen bushels was the average crop throughout the wheat growing region of the United States; and this year an intelligent farmer of Illinois, assured me that he did not believe the land harvested in that State this season, had yielded more than an average of eight bushels to the acre. The brag crop I heard of in our vicinity was two thousand bushels from ninety acres. Many crops were thrashed, producing no more than three bushels to the acre; much was cut, and then abandoned as not worth threshing; and much was abandoned as not worth cutting. As to Indian corn, and, indeed, most other crops, the case has not been much better. For the last four years I do not believe the ground planted with corn in Illinois, has produced an average of twenty bushels to the acre. It is true, that heretofore we have had better crops, with no better cultivators; but I believe it is also true that the soil has never been pushed up to one-half of its capacity.

What would be the effect upon the farming interest, to push the soil up to something near its full capacity? Unquestionably it will take more labor to produce *fifty* bushels from an acre, than it will to produce *ten* bushels from the same acre. But will it take more labor to produce fifty bushels from *one* acre, than from *five*? Unquestionably, thorough cultivation will require more labor to the *acre*; but will it require more to the *bushel*? If it should require just as *much* to the bushel, there are some *probable*, and several *certain,* advantages in favor of the thorough practice. It is probable it would develope those unknown causes, or develope unknown cures for those causes, which of late years have cut down our crops below their former average. It is almost certain, I think, that in the deeper plowing, analysis of soils, experiments with manures, and varieties of seeds, observance of seasons, and the like, these causes would be found. It is certain that thorough cultivation would spare half or more than half, the cost of land, simply because the same product would be got from half, or from less than half the quantity of land. This proposition is self-evident, and can be made no plainer by repetitions or illustrations. The cost of land is a great item, even in new countries; and constantly grows greater and greater, in comparison with other items, as the country grows older.

It also would spare a large proportion of the making and maintaining of inclosures—the same, whether these inclosures should be hedges, ditches, or fences. This again, is a heavy item—heavy at first, and heavy in its continual demand for repairs. I remember once being greatly astonished by an apparently authentic exhibition of the proportion the cost of inclosures bears to all the other expenses of the farmer; though I can not remember exactly what that proportion was. Any farmer, if he will, can ascertain it in his own case, for himself.

Again, a great amount of "locomotion" is spared by thorough cultivation. Take fifty bushels of wheat, ready for the harvest, standing upon a *single* acre, and it can be harvested in any of the known ways, with less than half the labor which would be required if it were spread over *five* acres. This would be true, if cut by the old hand sickle; true, to a greater extent if by the scythe and cradle; and to a still greater extent, if by the machines now in use. These machines are chiefly valuable, as a means of substituting animal power for the power of men in this branch of farm work. In the highest degree of perfection yet reached in applying the horse power to harvesting, fully nine-tenths of the power is expended by the animal in carrying himself and dragging the machine over the field, leaving certainly not more than one-tenth to be applied directly to the only end of the whole operation—the gathering in the grain, and clipping of the straw. When grain is very thin on the ground, it is always more or less intermingled with weeds, chess and the like, and a large part of the power is expended in cutting these. It is plain that when the crop is very thick upon the ground, the larger proportion of the power is directly applied to gathering in and cutting it; and the smaller, to that which is totally useless as an end. And what I have said of harvesting is true, in a greater or less degree of mowing, plowing, gathering in of crops generally, and, indeed, of almost all farm work.

The effect of thorough cultivation upon the farmer's own mind, and, in reaction through his mind, back upon his business, is perhaps quite equal to any other of its effects. Every man is proud of what he does *well*; and no man is proud of what he does *not* do well. With the former, his heart is in his work; and he will do twice as much of it with less fatigue. The latter performs a little imperfectly, looks at it in disgust, turns from it, and imagines himself exceedingly tired. The little he has done, comes to nothing, for want of finishing.

The man who produces a good full crop will scarcely ever let any part of it go to waste. He will keep up the enclosure about it, and allow neither man nor beast to trespass upon it. He will gather it in due season and store it in perfect security. Thus he labors with satisfaction, and saves himself the whole fruit of his labor. The other, starting with no purpose for a full crop, labors less, and with less satisfaction; allows his fences to fall, and cattle to trespass; gathers not in due season, or not at all. Thus the labor he has performed, is wasted away, little by little, till in the end, he derives scarcely anything from it.

The ambition for broad acres leads to poor farming, even with men of energy. I scarcely ever knew a mammoth farm to sustain itself; much less to return a profit upon the outlay. I have more than once known a man to spend a respectable fortune upon one; fail and leave it; and then some man of more modest aims, get a small fraction of the ground, and make a good living upon it. Mammoth farms are like tools or weapons, which are too heavy to be handled. Ere long they are thrown aside, at a great loss.

The successful application of *steam power*, to farm work is a *desideratum*— especially a Steam Plow. It is not enough, that a machine operated by steam, will really plow. To be successful, it must, all things considered, plow *better* than can be done with animal power. It must do all the work as well, and *cheaper;* or more *rapidly,* so as to get through more perfectly *in season;* or in some way afford an advantage over plowing with animals, else it is no success. I have never seen a machine intended for a Steam Plow. Much praise, and admiration, are bestowed upon some of them; and they may be, for aught I know, already successful; but I have not perceived the demonstration of it. I have thought a good deal, in an abstract way, about a Steam Plow. That one which shall be so contrived as to apply the larger proportion of its power to the cutting and turning the soil, and the smallest, to the moving itself over the field, will be the best one. A very small stationary engine would draw a large gang of plows through the ground from a short distance to itself; but when it is not stationary, but has to move along like a horse, dragging the plows after it, it must have additional power to carry itself; and the difficulty grows by what is intended to overcome it; for what adds power also adds size, and weight to the machine, thus increasing again, the demand for power. Suppose you should construct the machine so as to cut a succession of short furrows, say a rod in length, transversely to the course the machine is locomoting, something like the shuttle in weaving. In such case the whole machine would move North only the width of a furrow, while in length, the furrow would be a rod from East to West. In such case, a very large proportion of the power, would be applied to the actual plowing. But in this, too, there would be a difficulty, which would be the getting of the plow *into,* and *out of,* the ground, at the ends of all these short furrows.

I believe, however, ingenious men will, if they have not already, overcome the difficulty I have suggested. But there is still another, about which I am less sanguine. It is the supply of *fuel,* and especially of *water,* to make steam. Such supply is clearly practicable, but can the expense of it be borne? Steamboats live upon the water, and find their fuel at stated places. Steam mills, and other stationary steam machinery, have their stationary supplies of fuel and water. Railroad locomotives have their regular wood and water station. But the steam plow is less fortunate. It does not live upon the water; and if it be once at a water station, it will work away from it, and when it gets away can not return, without leaving its work, at a great expense of its time and strength. It will occur that a wagon and horse team might be employed to supply it with fuel and water; but this, too, is expensive; and the question recurs, "can the expense be borne?" When this is added to all other expenses, will not the plowing cost more than in the old way?

It is to be hoped that the steam plow will be finally successful, and if it shall be, *"thorough cultivation"*—putting the soil to the top of its capacity—producing the largest crop possible from a given quantity of ground—will be most favorable to it. Doing a large amount of work upon a small quantity of ground, it will be, as nearly as possible, stationary while working, and as free as possible from locomotion; thus expending its strength as much as possible upon its work, and as little as possible in travelling. Our thanks, and something more substantial than thanks, are due to every man engaged in the effort to produce a successful steam plow. Even the unsuccessful will bring something to light, which, in the hands of others, will contribute to the final success. I have not pointed out difficulties, in order to discourage, but in order that being seen, they may be the more readily overcome.

The world is agreed that *labor* is the source from which human wants are mainly supplied. There is no dispute upon this point. From this point, however, men immediately diverge. Much disputation is maintained as to the best way of applying and controlling the labor element. By some it is assumed that labor is available only in connection with capital—that nobody labors, unless somebody else, owning capital, somehow, by the use of that capital, induces him to do it. Having assumed this, they proceed to consider whether it is best that capital shall *hire* laborers, and thus induce them to work by their own consent; or *buy* them, and drive them to it without their consent. Having proceeded so far they naturally conclude that all laborers are necessarily either *hired* laborers, or *slaves*. They further assume that whoever is once a *hired* laborer, is fatally fixed in that condition for life; and thence again that his condition is as bad as, or worse than that of a slave. This is the *"mud-sill"* theory.

But another class of reasoners hold the opinion that there is no *such* relation between capital and labor, as assumed; and that there is no such thing as a freeman being fatally fixed for life, in the condition of a hired laborer, that both these assumptions are false, and all inferences from them groundless. They hold that labor is prior to, and independent of, capital; that, in fact, capital is the fruit of labor, and could never have existed if labor had not *first* existed—that labor can exist without capital, but that capital could never have existed without labor. Hence they hold that labor is the superior—greatly the superior—of capital.

They do not deny that there is, and probably always will be, *a* relation between labor and capital. The error, as they hold, is in assuming that the *whole* labor of the world exists within that relation. A few men own capital; and that few avoid labor themselves, and with their capital, hire, or buy, another few to labor for them. A large majority belong to neither class—neither work for others, nor have others working for them. Even in all our slave States, except South Carolina, a majority of the whole people of all colors, are neither slaves nor masters. In these Free States, a large majority are neither *hirers* nor *hired*. Men, with their families—wives, sons and daughters—work for themselves, on their farms, in their houses and in their shops, taking the whole product to themselves, and asking no favors of capital on the one hand, nor of hirelings or slaves on the other. It is not forgotten that a considerable number of persons mingle their own labor with capital; that is, labor with their own hands, and also buy slaves or hire freemen to labor for them; but this is only a *mixed*, and not a *distinct* class. No principle stated is disturbed by the existence of this mixed class. Again, as has already been said, the opponents of the *"mud-sill"* theory insist that there is not, of necessity, any such thing as the free hired laborer being fixed to that condition for life. There is demonstration for saying this. Many independent men, in this assembly, doubtless a few years ago were hired laborers. And their case is almost if not quite the general rule.

The prudent, penniless beginner in the world, labors for wages awhile, saves a surplus with which to buy tools or land, for himself; then labors on his own account another while, and at length hires another new beginner to help him. This, say its advocates, is *free* labor—the just and generous, and prosperous system, which opens the way for all—gives hope to all, and energy, and progress, and improvement of condition to all. If any continue through life in the condition of the hired laborer, it is not the fault of the system, but because of either a dependent nature which prefers it, or improvidence, folly, or singular misfortune. I have said this much about the elements of labor generally, as introductory to the consideration of a new phase which that element is in process of assuming. The old general rule was that *educated* people did not perform manual labor. They managed to eat their bread, leaving the toil of producing it to the uneducated. This was not an insupportable evil to the working bees, so long as the class of drones remained very small. But *now,* especially in these free States, nearly all are educated—quite too nearly all, to leave the labor of the uneducated, in any wise adequate to the support of the whole. It follows from this that henceforth educated people must labor. Otherwise, education itself would become a positive and intolerable evil. No country can sustain, in idleness, more than a small percentage of its numbers. The great majority must labor at something productive. From these premises the problem springs, "How can *labor* and *education* be the most satisfactorily combined?"

By the *"mud-sill"* theory it is assumed that labor and education are incompatible; and any practical combination of them impossible. According to that theory, a blind horse upon a tread-mill, is a perfect illustration of what a laborer should be—all the better for being blind, that he could not tread out of place, or kick understandingly. According to that theory, the education of laborers, is not only useless, but pernicious, and dangerous. In fact, it is, in some sort, deemed a misfortune that laborers should have heads at all. Those same heads are regarded as explosive materials, only to be safely kept in damp places, as far as possible from that peculiar sort of fire which ignites them. A Yankee who could invent a strong *handed* man without a head would receive the everlasting gratitude of the "mud-sill" advocates.

But Free Labor says "no!" Free Labor argues that, as the Author of man makes every individual with one head and one pair of hands, it was probably intended that heads and hands should cooperate as friends; and that that particular head, should direct and control that particular pair of hands. As each man has one mouth to be fed, and one pair of hands to furnish food, it was probably intended that that particular pair of hands should feed that particular mouth— that each head is the natural guardian, director, and protector of the hands and mouth inseparably connected with it; and that being so, every head should be cultivated, and improved, by whatever will add to its capacity for performing its charge. In one word Free Labor insists on universal education.

I have so far stated the opposite theories of *"Mud-Sill"* and "Free Labor" without declaring any preference of my own between them. On an occasion like this I ought not to declare any. I suppose, however, I shall not be mistaken, in assuming as a fact, that the people of Wisconsin prefer free labor, with its natural companion, education.

This leads to the further reflection, that no other human occupation opens so wide a field for the profitable and agreeable combination of labor with cultivated thought, as agriculture. I know of nothing so pleasant to the mind, as the discovery of anything which is at once *new* and *valuable*—nothing which so lightens and sweetens toil, as the hopeful pursuit of such discovery. And how vast, and how varied a field is agriculture, for such discovery. The mind, already trained to thought, in the country school, or higher school, cannot fail to find there an exhaustless source of profitable enjoyment. Every blade of grass is a study; and to produce two, where there was but one, is both a profit and a pleasure. And not grass alone; but soils, seeds, and seasons—hedges, ditches, and fences, draining, droughts, and irrigation—plowing, hoeing, and harrowing—reaping, mowing, and threshing—saving crops, pests of crops, diseases of crops, and what will prevent or cure them—implements, utensils, and machines, their relative merits, and how to improve them—hogs, horses, and cattle—sheep, goats, and poultry—trees, shrubs, fruits, plants, and flowers—the thousand things of which these are specimens—each a world of study within itself.

In all this, book-learning is available. A capacity, and taste, for reading, gives access to whatever has already been discovered by others. It is the key, or one of the keys, to the already solved problems. And not only so. It gives a relish, and facility, for successfully pursuing the yet unsolved ones. The rudiments of science, are available, and highly valuable. Some knowledge of Botany assists in dealing with the vegetable world—with all growing crops. Chemistry assists in the analysis of soils, selection, and application of manures, and in numerous other ways. The mechanical branches of Natural Philosophy, are ready help in almost everything; but especially in reference to implements and machinery.

The thought recurs that education—cultivated thought—can best be combined with agricultural labor, or any labor, on the principle of *thorough* work— that careless, half performed, slovenly work, makes no place for such combination. And thorough work, again, renders sufficient, the smallest quantity of ground to each man. And this again, conforms to what must occur in a world less inclined to wars, and more devoted to the arts of peace, than heretofore. Population must increase rapidly—more rapidly than in former times—and ere long the most valuable of all arts, will be the art of deriving a comfortable subsistence from the smallest area of soil. No community whose every member possesses this art, can ever be the victim of oppression in any of its forms. Such community will be alike independent of crowned-kings, money-kings, and land-kings.

But, according to your programme, the awarding of premiums awaits the closing of this address. Considering the deep interest necessarily pertaining to that performance, it would be no wonder if I am already heard with some impatience. I will detain you but a moment longer. Some of you will be successful, and such will need but little philosophy to take them home in cheerful spirits; others will be disappointed, and will be in a less happy mood. To such, let it be said, "Lay it not too much to heart." Let them adopt the maxim, "Better luck next time;" and then, by renewed exertion, make that better luck for themselves.

And by the successful, and the unsuccessful, let it be remembered, that while occasions like the present, bring their sober and durable benefits, the exultations and mortifications of them, are but temporary; that the victor shall soon be the vanquished, if he relax in his exertion; and that the vanquished this year, may be victor the next, in spite of all competition.

It is said an Eastern monarch once charged his wise men to invent him a sentence, to be ever in view, and which should be true and appropriate in all times and situations. They presented him the words: *"And this, too, shall pass away."* How much it expresses! How chastening in the hour of pride!—how consoling in the depths of affliction! "And this, too, shall pass away." And yet let us hope it is not quite true. Let us hope, rather, that by the best cultivation of the physical world, beneath and around us; and the intellectual and moral world within us, we shall secure an individual, social, and political prosperity and happiness, whose course shall be onward and upward, and which, while the earth endures, shall not pass away.

*September 30, 1859*

# Address at the Cooper Union, New York City

Mr. President and Fellow-Citizens of New York:

The facts with which I shall deal this evening are mainly old and familiar; nor is there anything new in the general use I shall make of them. If there shall be any novelty, it will be in the mode of presenting the facts, and the inferences and observations following that presentation.

In his speech last autumn, at Columbus, Ohio, as reported in *The New-York Times*, Senator Douglas said:

*"Our fathers, when they framed the Government under which we live, understood this question just as well, and even better, than we do now."*

I fully indorse this, and I adopt it as a text for this discourse. I so adopt it because it furnishes a precise and an agreed starting point for a discussion between Republicans and that wing of the Democracy headed by Senator Douglas. It simply leaves the inquiry: *"What was the understanding those fathers had of the question mentioned?"*

What is the frame of Government under which we live?

The answer must be: "The Constitution of the United States." That Constitution consists of the original, framed in 1787, (and under which the present government first went into operation,) and twelve subsequently framed amendments, the first ten of which were framed in 1789.

Who were our fathers that framed the Constitution? I suppose the "thirty-nine" who signed the original instrument may be fairly called our fathers who framed that part of the present Government. It is almost exactly true to say they framed it, and it is altogether true to say they fairly represented the opinion and sentiment of the whole nation at that time. Their names, being familiar to nearly all, and accessible to quite all, need not now be repeated.

I take these "thirty-nine" for the present, as being "our fathers who framed the Government under which we live."

What is the question which, according to the text, those fathers understood "just as well, and even better than we do now?"

It is this: Does the proper division of local from federal authority, or anything in the Constitution, forbid *our Federal Government* to control as to slavery in *our Federal Territories?*

Upon this, Senator Douglas holds the affirmative, and Republicans the negative. This affirmation and denial form an issue; and this issue—this question—is precisely what the text declares our fathers understood "better than we."

Let us now inquire whether the "thirty-nine," or any of them, ever acted upon this question; and if they did, how they acted upon it—how they expressed that better understanding?

In 1784, three years before the Constitution—the United States then owning the Northwestern Territory, and no other, the Congress of the Confederation had before them the question of prohibiting slavery in that Territory; and four of the "thirty-nine," who afterward framed the Constitution, were in that Congress, and voted on that question. Of these, Roger Sherman, Thomas Mifflin, and Hugh Williamson voted for the prohibition, thus showing that, in their understanding, no line dividing local from federal authority, nor anything else, properly forbade the Federal Government to control as to slavery in federal territory. The other of the four—James M'Henry—voted against the prohibition, showing that, for some cause, he thought it improper to vote for it.

In 1787, still before the Constitution, but while the Convention was in session framing it, and while the Northwestern Territory still was the only territory owned by the United States, the same question of prohibiting slavery in the territory again came before the Congress of the Confederation; and two more of the "thirty-nine" who afterward signed the Constitution, were in that Congress, and voted on the question. They were William Blount and William Few; and they both voted for the prohibition—thus showing that, in their understanding, no line dividing local from federal authority, nor anything else, properly forbade the Federal Government to control as to slavery in federal territory. This time the prohibition became a law, being part of what is now well known as the Ordinance of '87.

The question of federal control of slavery in the territories, seems not to have been directly before the Convention which framed the original Constitution; and hence it is not recorded that the "thirty-nine," or any of them, while engaged on that instrument, expressed any opinion on that precise question.

In 1789, by the first Congress which sat under the Constitution, an act was passed to enforce the Ordinance of '87, including the prohibition of slavery in the Northwestern Territory. The bill for this act was reported by one of the "thirty-nine," Thomas Fitzsimmons, then a member of the House of Representatives from Pennsylvania. It went through all its stages without a word of opposition, and finally passed both branches without yeas and nays, which is equivalent to a unanimous passage. In this Congress there were sixteen of the thirty-nine fathers who framed the original Constitution. They were John Langdon, Nicholas Gilman, Wm. S. Johnson, Roger Sherman, Robert Morris, Thos. Fitzsimmons,

William Few, Abraham Baldwin, Rufus King, William Paterson, George Clymer, Richard Bassett, George Read, Pierce Butler, Daniel Carroll, James Madison.

This shows that, in their understanding, no line dividing local from federal authority, nor anything in the Constitution, properly forbade Congress to prohibit slavery in the federal territory; else both their fidelity to correct principle, and their oath to support the Constitution, would have constrained them to oppose the prohibition.

Again, George Washington, another of the "thirty-nine," was then President of the United States, and, as such approved and signed the bill; thus completing its validity as a law, and thus showing that, in his understanding, no line dividing local from federal authority, nor anything in the Constitution, forbade the Federal Government, to control as to slavery in federal territory.

No great while after the adoption of the original Constitution, North Carolina ceded to the Federal Government the country now constituting the State of Tennessee; and a few years later Georgia ceded that which now constitutes the States of Mississippi and Alabama. In both deeds of cession it was made a condition by the ceding States that the Federal Government should not prohibit slavery in the ceded territory. Besides this, slavery was then actually in the ceded country. Under these circumstances, Congress, on taking charge of these countries, did not absolutely prohibit slavery within them. But they did interfere with it—take control of it—even there, to a certain extent. In 1798, Congress organized the Territory of Mississippi. In the act of organization, they prohibited the bringing of slaves into the Territory, from any place without the United States, by fine, and giving freedom to slaves so bought. This act passed both branches of Congress without yeas and nays. In that Congress were three of the "thirty-nine" who framed the original Constitution. They were John Langdon, George Read and Abraham Baldwin. They all, probably, voted for it. Certainly they would have placed their opposition to it upon record, if, in their understanding, any line dividing local from federal authority, or anything in the Constitution, properly forbade the Federal Government to control as to slavery in federal territory.

In 1803, the Federal Government purchased the Louisiana country. Our former territorial acquisitions came from certain of our own States; but this Louisiana country was acquired from a foreign nation. In 1804, Congress gave a territorial organization to that part of it which now constitutes the State of Louisiana. New Orleans, lying within that part, was an old and comparatively large city. There were other considerable towns and settlements, and slavery was extensively and thoroughly intermingled with the people. Congress did not, in the Territorial Act, prohibit slavery; but they did interfere with it—take control of it—in a more marked and extensive way than they did in the case of Mississippi. The substance of the provision therein made, in relation to slaves, was:

*First.* That no slave should be imported into the territory from foreign parts.

*Second.* That no slave should be carried into it who had been imported into the United States since the first day of May, 1798.

*Third.* That no slave should be carried into it, except by the owner, and for his own use as a settler; the penalty in all the cases being a fine upon the violator of the law, and freedom to the slave.

This act also was passed without yeas and nays. In the Congress which passed it, there were two of the "thirty-nine." They were Abraham Baldwin and Jonathan Dayton. As stated in the case of Mississippi, it is probable they both voted for it. They would not have allowed it to pass without recording their opposition to it, if, in their understanding, it violated either the line properly dividing local from federal authority, or any provision of the Constitution.

In 1819–20, came and passed the Missouri question. Many votes were taken, by yeas and nays, in both branches of Congress, upon the various phases of the general question. Two of the "thirty-nine"—Rufus King and Charles Pinckney—were members of that Congress. Mr. King steadily voted for slavery prohibition and against all compromises, while Mr. Pinckney as steadily voted against slavery prohibition and against all compromises. By this, Mr. King showed that, in his understanding, no line dividing local from federal authority, nor anything in the Constitution, was violated by Congress prohibiting slavery in federal territory; while Mr. Pinckney, by his votes, showed that, in his understanding, there was some sufficient reason for opposing such prohibition in that case.

The cases I have mentioned are the only acts of the "thirty-nine," or of any of them, upon the direct issue, which I have been able to discover.

To enumerate the persons who thus acted, as being four in 1784, two in 1787, seventeen in 1789, three in 1798, two in 1804, and two in 1819–20—there would be thirty of them. But this would be counting John Langdon, Roger Sherman, William Few, Rufus King, and George Read each twice, and Abraham Baldwin, three times. The true number of those of the "thirty-nine" whom I have shown to have acted upon the question, which, by the text, they understood better than we, is twenty-three, leaving sixteen not shown to have acted upon it in any way.

Here, then, we have twenty-three out of our thirty-nine fathers "who framed the Government under which we live," who have, upon their official responsibility and their corporal oaths, acted upon the very question which the text affirms they "understood just as well, and even better than we do now;" and twenty-one of them—a clear majority of the whole "thirty-nine"—so acting upon it as to make them guilty of gross political impropriety and willful perjury, if, in their under-standing, any proper division between local and federal authority, or anything in the Constitution they had made themselves, and sworn to support, forbade the Federal Government to control as to slavery in the federal territories. Thus the twenty-one acted; and, as actions speak louder than words, so actions, under such responsibility, speak still louder.

Two of the twenty-three voted against Congressional prohibition of slavery in the federal territories, in the instances in which they acted upon the question. But for what reasons they so voted is not known. They may have done so because they thought a proper division of local from federal authority, or some provision or principle of the Constitution, stood in the way; or they may, without any such question, have voted against the prohibition, on what appeared to them to be suf-ficient grounds of expediency. No one who has sworn to support the Constitution, can conscientiously vote for what he understands to be an unconstitutional mea-sure, however expedient he may think it; but one may and ought to vote against a measure which he deems constitutional, if, at the same time, he deems it inexpe-dient. It, therefore, would be unsafe to set down even the two who voted against the prohibition, as having done so because, in their understanding, any proper division of local from federal authority, or anything in the Constitution, forbade the Federal Government to control as to slavery in federal territory.

The remaining sixteen of the "thirty-nine," so far as I have discovered, have left no record of their understanding upon the direct question of federal control of slavery in the federal territories. But there is much reason to believe that their understanding upon that question would not have appeared different from that of their twenty-three compeers, had it been manifested at all.

For the purpose of adhering rigidly to the text, I have purposely omitted whatever understanding may have been manifested by any person, however distin-guished, other than the thirty-nine fathers who framed the original Constitution; and, for the same reason, I have also omitted whatever understanding may have been manifested by any of the "thirty-nine" even, on any other phase of the general question of slavery. If we should look into their acts and declarations on those other phases, as the foreign slave trade, and the morality and policy of slavery generally, it would appear to us that on the direct question of federal control of slavery in federal territories, the sixteen, if they had acted at all, would probably have acted just as the twenty-three did. Among that sixteen were several of the most noted anti-slavery men of those times—as Dr. Franklin, Alexander Hamilton and Gouverneur Morris—while there was not one now known to have been otherwise, unless it may be John Rutledge, of South Carolina.

The sum of the whole is, that of our thirty-nine fathers who framed the original Constitution, twenty-one—a clear majority of the whole—certainly understood that no proper division of local from federal authority, nor any part of the Constitution, forbade the Federal Government to control slavery in the federal territories; while all the rest probably had the same understanding. Such, unquestionably, was the understanding of our fathers who framed the original Constitution; and the text affirms that they understood the question "better than we."

But, so far, I have been considering the understanding of the question manifested by the framers of the original Constitution. In and by the original instrument, a mode was provided for amending it; and, as I have already stated, the present frame of "the Government under which we live" consists of that original, and twelve amendatory articles framed and adopted since. Those who now insist that federal control of slavery in federal territories violates the Constitution, point us to the provisions which they suppose it thus violates; and, as I understand, that all fix upon provisions in these amendatory articles, and not in the original instrument. The Supreme Court, in the Dred Scott case, plant themselves upon the fifth amendment, which provides that no person shall be deprived of "life, liberty or property without due process of law;" while Senator Douglas and his peculiar adherents plant themselves upon the tenth amendment, providing that "the powers not delegated to the United States by the Constitution" "are reserved to the States respectively, or to the people."

Now, it so happens that these amendments were framed by the first Congress which sat under the Constitution—the identical Congress which passed the act already mentioned, enforcing the prohibition of slavery in the Northwestern Territory. Not only was it the same Congress, but they were the identical, same individual men who, at the same session, and at the same time within the session, had under consideration, and in progress toward maturity, these Constitutional amendments, and this act prohibiting slavery in all the territory the nation then owned. The Constitutional amendments were introduced before, and passed after the act enforcing the Ordinance of '87; so that, during the whole pendency of the act to enforce the Ordinance, the Constitutional amendments were also pending.

The seventy-six members of that Congress, including sixteen of the framers of the original Constitution, as before stated, were preeminently our fathers who framed that part of "the Government under which we live," which is now claimed as forbidding the Federal Government to control slavery in the federal territories.

Is it not a little presumptuous in any one at this day to affirm that the two things which that Congress deliberately framed, and carried to maturity at the same time, are absolutely inconsistent with each other? And does not such affirmation become impudently absurd when coupled with the other affirmation from the same mouth, that those who did the two things, alleged to be inconsistent, understood whether they really were inconsistent better than we—better than he who affirms that they are inconsistent?

It is surely safe to assume that the thirty-nine framers of the original Constitution, and the seventy-six members of the Congress which framed the amendments thereto, taken together, do certainly include those who may be fairly called "our fathers who framed the Government under which we live." And so assuming, I defy any man to show that any one of them ever, in his whole life, declared that, in his understanding, any proper division of local from federal authority, or any part of the Constitution, forbade the Federal Government to control as to slavery in the federal territories. I go a step further. I defy any one to show that any living man in the whole world ever did, prior to the beginning of the present century, (and I might almost say prior to the beginning of the last half of the present century,) declare that, in his understanding, any proper division of local from federal authority, or any part of the Constitution, forbade the Federal Government to control as to slavery in the federal territories. To those who now so declare, I give, not only "our fathers who framed the Government under which we live," but with them all other living men within the century in which it was framed, among whom to search, and they shall not be able to find the evidence of a single man agreeing with them.

Now, and here, let me guard a little against being misunderstood. I do not mean to say we are bound to follow implicitly in whatever our fathers did. To do so, would be to discard all the lights of current experience—to reject all progress—all improvement. What I do say is, that if we would supplant the opinions and policy of our fathers in any case, we should do so upon evidence so conclusive, and argument so clear, that even their great authority, fairly considered and weighed, cannot stand; and most surely not in a case whereof we ourselves declare they understood the question better than we.

If any man at this day sincerely believes that a proper division of local from federal authority, or any part of the Constitution, forbids the Federal Government to control as to slavery in the federal territories, he is right to say so, and to enforce his position by all truthful evidence and fair argument which he can. But he has no right to mislead others, who have less access to history, and less leisure to study it, into the false belief that "our fathers, who framed the Government under which we live," were of the same opinion—thus substituting falsehood and deception for truthful evidence and fair argument. If any man at this day sincerely believes "our fathers who framed the Government under which we live," used and applied principles, in other cases, which ought to have led them to understand that a proper division of local from federal authority or some part of the Constitution, forbids the Federal Government to control as to slavery in the federal territories, he is right to say so. But he should, at the same time, brave the responsibility of declaring that, in his opinion, he understands their principles better than they did themselves; and especially should he not shirk that responsibility by asserting that they "understood the question just as well, and even better, than we do now."

But enough! *Let all who believe that "our fathers, who framed the Government under which we live, understood this question just as well, and even better, than we do now," speak as they spoke, and act as they acted upon it. This is all Republicans ask—all Republicans desire—in relation to slavery. As those fathers marked it, so let it be again marked, as an evil not to be extended, but to be tolerated and protected only because of and so far as its actual presence among us makes that toleration and protection a necessity. Let all the guaranties those fathers gave it, be, not grudgingly, but fully and fairly maintained.* For this Republicans contend, and with this, so far as I know or believe, they will be content.

And now, if they would listen—as I suppose they will not—I would address a few words to the Southern people.

I would say to them:—You consider yourselves a reasonable and a just people; and I consider that in the general qualities of reason and justice you are not inferior to any other people. Still, when you speak of us Republicans, you do so only to denounce us a reptiles, or, at the best, as no better than outlaws. You will grant a hearing to pirates or murderers, but nothing like it to "Black Republicans." In all your contentions with one another, each of you deems an unconditional condemnation of "Black Republicanism" as the first thing to be attended to. Indeed, such condemnation of us seems to be an indispensable prerequisite—license, so to speak—among you to be admitted or permitted to speak at all. Now, can you, or not, be prevailed upon to pause and to consider whether this is quite just to us, or even to yourselves? Bring forward your charges and specifications, and then be patient long enough to hear us deny or justify.

You say we are sectional. We deny it. That makes an issue; and the burden of proof is upon you. You produce your proof; and what is it? Why, that our party has no existence in your section—gets no votes in your section. The fact is substantially true; but does it prove the issue? If it does, then in case we should, without change of principle, begin to get votes in your section, we should thereby cease to be sectional. You cannot escape this conclusion; and yet, are you willing to abide by it? If you are, you will probably soon find that we have ceased to be sectional, for we shall get votes in your section this very year. You will then begin to discover, as the truth plainly is, that your proof does not touch the issue. The fact that we get no votes in your section, is a fact of your making, and not of ours. And if there be fault in that fact, that fault is primarily yours, and remains until you show that we repel you by some wrong principle or practice. If we do repel you by any wrong principle or practice, the fault is ours; but this brings you to where you ought to have started—to a discussion of the right or wrong of our principle. If our principle, put in practice, would wrong your section for the bene-fit of ours, or for any other object, then our principle, and we with it, are sectional, and are justly opposed and denounced as such. Meet us, then, on the question of whether our principle, put in practice, would wrong your section; and so meet us as if it were possible that something may be said on our side. Do you accept the challenge? No! Then you really believe that the principle which "our fathers who framed the Government under which we live" thought so clearly right as to adopt it, and indorse it again and again, upon their official oaths, is in fact so clearly wrong as to demand your condemnation without a moment's consideration.

Some of you delight to flaunt in our faces the warning against sectional parties given by Washington in his Farewell Address. Less than eight years before Washington gave that warning, he had, as President of the United States, approved and signed an act of Congress, enforcing the prohibition of slavery in the Northwestern Territory, which act embodied the policy of the Government upon that subject up to and at the very moment he penned that warning; and about one year after he penned it, he wrote La Fayette that he considered that prohibition a wise measure, expressing in the same connection his hope that we should at some time have a confederacy of free States.

Bearing this in mind, and seeing that sectionalism has since arisen upon this same subject, is that warning a weapon in your hands against us, or in our hands against you? Could Washington himself speak, would he cast the blame of that sectionalism upon us, who sustain his policy, or upon you who repudiate it? We respect that warning of Washington, and we commend it to you, together with his example pointing to the right application of it.

But you say you are conservative—eminently conservative—while we are revolutionary, destructive, or something of the sort. What is conservatism? Is it not adherence to the old and tried, against the new and untried? We stick to, con-tend for, the identical old policy on the point in controversy which was adopted by "our fathers who framed the Government under which we live;" while you with one accord reject, and scout, and spit upon that old policy, and insist upon substituting something new. True, you disagree among yourselves as to what that substitute shall be. You are divided on new propositions and plans, but you are unanimous in rejecting and denouncing the old policy of the fathers. Some of you are for reviving the foreign slave trade; some for a Congressional Slave-Code for the Territories; some for Congress forbidding the Territories to prohibit Slavery within their limits; some for maintaining Slavery in the Territories through the judiciary; some for the "gur-reat pur-rinciple" that "if one man would enslave another, no third man should object," fantastically called "Popular Sovereignty;" but never a man among you is in favor of federal prohibition of slavery in federal territories, according to the practice of "our fathers who framed the Government under which we live." Not one of all your various plans can show a precedent or an advocate in the century within which our Government originated. Consider, then, whether your claim of conservatism for yourselves, and your charge or destructiveness against us, are based on the most clear and stable foundations.

Again, you say we have made the slavery question more prominent than it formerly was. We deny it. We admit that it is more prominent, but we deny that we made it so. It was not we, but you, who discarded the old policy of the fathers. We resisted, and still resist, your innovation; and thence comes the greater prominence of the question. Would you have that question reduced to its former proportions? Go back to that old policy. What has been will be again, under the same conditions. If you would have the peace of the old times, readopt the precepts and policy of the old times.

You charge that we stir up insurrections among your slaves. We deny it; and what is your proof? Harper's Ferry! John Brown!! John Brown was no Republican; and you have failed to implicate a single Republican in his Harper's Ferry enterprise. If any member of our party is guilty in that matter, you know it or you do not know it. If you do know it, you are inexcusable for not designating the man and proving the fact. If you do not know it, you are inexcusable for asserting it, and especially for persisting in the assertion after you have tried and failed to make the proof. You need to be told that persisting in a charge which one does not know to be true, is simply malicious slander.

Some of you admit that no Republican designedly aided or encouraged the Harper's Ferry affair; but still insist that our doctrines and declarations necessarily lead to such results. We do not believe it. We know we hold to no doctrine, and make no declaration, which were not held to and made by "our fathers who framed the Government under which we live." You never dealt fairly by us in relation to this affair. When it occurred, some important State elections were near at hand, and you were in evident glee with the belief that, by charging the blame upon us, you could get an advantage of us in those elections. The elections came, and your expectations were not quite fulfilled. Every Republican man knew that, as to himself at least, your charge was a slander, and he was not much inclined by it to cast his vote in your favor. Republican doctrines and declarations are accompanied with a continual protest against any interference whatever with your slaves, or with you about your slaves. Surely, this does not encourage them to revolt. True, we do, in common with "our fathers, who framed the Government under which we live," declare our belief that slavery is wrong; but the slaves do not hear us declare even this. For anything we say or do, the slaves would scarcely know there is a Republican party. I believe they would not, in fact, generally know it but for your misrepresentations of us, in their hearing. In your political contests among yourselves, each faction charges the other with sympathy with Black Republicanism; and then, to give point to the charge, defines Black Republicanism to simply be insurrection, blood and thunder among the slaves.

Slave insurrections are no more common now than they were before the Republican party was organized. What induced the Southampton insurrection, twenty-eight years ago, in which, at least, three times as many lives were lost as at Harper's Ferry? You can scarcely stretch your very elastic fancy to the conclusion that Southampton was "got up by Black Republicanism." In the present state of things in the United States, I do not think a general, or even a very extensive slave insurrection, is possible. The indispensable concert of action cannot be attained. The slaves have no means of rapid communication; nor can incendiary freemen, black or white, supply it. The explosive materials are everywhere in parcels; but there neither are, nor can be supplied, the indispensable connecting trains.

Much is said by Southern people about the affection of slaves for their masters and mistresses; and a part of it, at least, is true. A plot for an uprising could scarcely be devised and communicated to twenty individuals before some one of them, to save the life of a favorite master or mistress, would divulge it. This is the rule; and the slave revolution in Hayti was not an exception to it, but a case occurring under peculiar circumstances. The gunpowder plot of British history, though not connected with slaves, was more in point. In that case, only about twenty were admitted to the secret; and yet one of them, in his anxiety to save a friend, betrayed the plot to that friend, and, by consequence, averted the calamity. Occasional poisonings from the kitchen, and open or stealthy assassinations in the field, and local revolts extending to a score or so, will continue to occur as the natural results of slavery; but no general insurrection of slaves, as I think, can happen in this country for a long time. Whoever much fears, or much hopes for such an event, will be alike disappointed.

In the language of Mr. Jefferson, uttered many years ago, "It is still in our power to direct the process of emancipation, and deportation, peaceably, and in such slow degrees, as that the evil will wear off insensibly; and their places be, *pari passu*, filled up by free white laborers. If, on the contrary, it is left to force itself on, human nature must shudder at the prospect held up."

Mr. Jefferson did not mean to say, nor do I, that the power of emancipation is in the Federal Government. He spoke of Virginia; and, as to the power of emancipation, I speak of the slaveholding States only. The Federal Government, however, as we insist, has the power of restraining the extension of the institution—the power to insure that a slave insurrection shall never occur on any American soil which is now free from slavery.

John Brown's effort was peculiar. It was not a slave insurrection. It was an attempt by white men to get up a revolt among slaves, in which the slaves refused to participate. In fact, it was so absurd that the slaves, with all their ignorance, saw plainly enough it could not succeed. That affair, in its philosophy, corresponds with the many attempts, related in history, at the assassination of kings and emperors. An enthusiast broods over the oppression of a people till he fancies himself commissioned by Heaven to liberate them. He ventures the attempt, which ends in little else than his own execution. Orsini's attempt on Louis Napoleon, and John Brown's attempt at Harper's Ferry were, in their philosophy, precisely the same. The eagerness to cast blame on old England in the one case, and on New England in the other, does not disprove the sameness of the two things.

And how much would it avail you, if you could, by the use of John Brown, Helper's Book, and the like, break up the Republican organization? Human action can be modified to some extent, but human nature cannot be changed. There is a judgment and a feeling against slavery in this nation, which cast at least a million and a half of votes. You cannot destroy that judgment and feeling—that sentiment—by breaking up the political organization which rallies around it. You can scarcely scatter and disperse an army which has been formed into order in the face of your heaviest fire; but if you could, how much would you gain by forcing the sentiment which created it out of the peaceful channel of the ballot-box, into some other channel? What would that other channel probably be? Would the number of John Browns be lessened or enlarged by the operation?

But you will break up the Union rather than submit to a denial of your Constitutional rights.

That has a somewhat reckless sound; but it would be palliated, if not fully justified, were we proposing, by the mere force of numbers, to deprive you of some right, plainly written down in the Constitution. But we are proposing no such thing.

When you make these declarations, you have a specific and well-understood allusion to an assumed Constitutional right of yours, to take slaves into the federal territories, and to hold them there as property. But no such right is specifically written in the Constitution. That instrument is literally silent about any such right. We, on the contrary, deny that such a right has any existence in the Constitution, even by implication.

Your purpose, then, plainly stated, is that you will destroy the Government, unless you be allowed to construe and enforce the Constitution as you please, on all points in dispute between you and us. You will rule or ruin in all events.

This, plainly stated, is your language. Perhaps you will say the Supreme Court has decided the disputed Constitutional question in your favor. Not quite so. But waiving the lawyer's distinction between dictum and decision, the Court have decided the question for you in a sort of way. The Court have substantially said, it is your Constitutional right to take slaves into the federal territories, and to hold them there as property. When I say the decision was made in a sort of way, I mean it was made in a divided Court, by a bare majority of the Judges, and they not quite agreeing with one another in the reasons for making it; that it is so made as that its avowed supporters disagree with one another about its meaning, and that it was mainly based upon a mistaken statement of fact—the statement in the opinion that "the right of property in a slave is distinctly and expressly affirmed in the Constitution."

An inspection of the Constitution will show that the right of property in a slave is not "*distinctly* and *expressly* affirmed" in it. Bear in mind, the Judges do not pledge their judicial opinion that such right is *impliedly* affirmed in the Constitution; but they pledge their veracity that it is "*distinctly* and *expressly*" affirmed there—"distinctly," that is, not mingled with anything else—"expressly," that is, in words meaning just that, without the aid of any inference, and susceptible of no other meaning.

If they had only pledged their judicial opinion that such right is affirmed in the instrument by implication, it would be open to others to show that neither the word "slave" nor "slavery" is to be found in the Constitution, nor the word "property" even, in any connection with language alluding to the things slave, or slavery; and that wherever in that instrument the slave is alluded to, he is called a "person;"—and wherever his master's legal right in relation to him is alluded to, it is spoken of as "service or labor which may be due,"—as a debt payable in service or labor. Also, it would be open to show, by contemporaneous history, that this mode of alluding to slaves and slavery, instead of speaking of them, was employed on purpose to exclude from the Constitution the idea that there could be property in man.

To show all this, is easy and certain.

When this obvious mistake of the Judges shall be brought to their notice, is it not reasonable to expect that they will withdraw the mistaken statement, and reconsider the conclusion based upon it?

And then it is to be remembered that "our fathers, who framed the Government under which we live"—the men who made the Constitution—decided this same Constitutional question in our favor, long ago—decided it without division among themselves, when making the decision; without division among themselves about the meaning of it after it was made, and, so far as any evidence is left, without basing it upon any mistaken statement of facts.

Under all these circumstances, do you really feel yourselves justified to break up this Government, unless such a court decision as yours is, shall be at once submitted to as a conclusive and final rule of political action? But you will not abide the election of a Republican president! In that supposed event, you say, you will destroy the Union; and then, you say, the great crime of having destroyed it will be upon us! That is cool. A highwayman holds a pistol to my ear, and mutters through his teeth, "Stand and deliver, or I shall kill you, and then you will be a murderer!"

To be sure, what the robber demanded of me—my money—was my own; and I had a clear right to keep it; but it was no more my own than my vote is my own; and the threat of death to me, to extort my money, and the threat of destruction to the Union, to extort my vote, can scarcely be distinguished in principle.

A few words now to Republicans. *It is exceedingly desirable that all parts of this great Confederacy shall be at peace, and in harmony, one with another. Let us Republicans do our part to have it so. Even though much provoked, let us do nothing through passion and ill temper. Even though the southern people will not so much as listen to us, let us calmly consider their demands, and yield to them if, in our deliberate view of our duty, we possibly can.* Judging by all they say and do, and by the subject and nature of their controversy with us, let us determine, if we can, what will satisfy them.

Will they be satisfied if the Territories be unconditionally surrendered to them? We know they will not. In all their present complaints against us, the Territories are scarcely mentioned. Invasions and insurrections are the rage now. Will it satisfy them, if, in the future, we have nothing to do with invasions and insurrections? We know it will not. We so know, because we know we never had anything to do with invasions and insurrections; and yet this total abstaining does not exempt us from the charge and the denunciation.

The question recurs, what will satisfy them? Simply this: We must not only let them alone, but we must, somehow, convince them that we do let them alone. This, we know by experience, is no easy task. We have been so trying to convince them from the very beginning of our organization, but with no success. In all our platforms and speeches we have constantly protested our purpose to let them alone; but this has had no tendency to convince them. Alike unavailing to convince them, is the fact that they have never detected a man of us in any attempt to disturb them.

These natural, and apparently adequate means all failing, what will convince them? This, and this only: cease to call slavery *wrong*, and join them in calling it *right*. And this must be done thoroughly—done in *acts* as well as in *words*. Silence will not be tolerated—we must place ourselves avowedly with them. Senator Douglas's new sedition law must be enacted and enforced, suppressing all declarations that slavery is wrong, whether made in politics, in presses, in pulpits, or in private. We must arrest and return their fugitive slaves with greedy pleasure. We must pull down our Free State constitutions. The whole atmosphere must be disinfected from all taint of opposition to slavery, before they will cease to believe that all their troubles proceed from us.

I am quite aware they do not state their case precisely in this way. Most of them would probably say to us, "Let us alone, *do* nothing to us, and *say* what you please about slavery." But we do let them alone—have never disturbed them—so that, after all, it is what we say, which dissatisfies them. They will continue to accuse us of doing, until we cease saying.

I am also aware they have not, as yet, in terms, demanded the overthrow of our Free-State Constitutions. Yet those Constitutions declare the wrong of slavery, with more solemn emphasis, than do all other sayings against it; and when all these other sayings shall have been silenced, the overthrow of these Constitutions will be demanded, and nothing be left to resist the demand. It is nothing to the contrary, that they do not demand the whole of this just now. Demanding what they do, and for the reason they do, they can voluntarily stop nowhere short of this consummation. Holding, as they do, that slavery is morally right, and socially elevating, they cannot cease to demand a full national recognition of it, as a legal right, and a social blessing.

Nor can we justifiably withhold this, on any ground save our conviction that slavery is wrong. If slavery is right, all words, acts, laws, and constitutions against it, are themselves wrong, and should be silenced, and swept away. If it is right, we cannot justly object to its nationality—its universality; if it is wrong, they cannot justly insist upon its extension—its enlargement. All they ask, we could readily grant, if we thought slavery right; all we ask, they could as readily grant, if they thought it wrong. Their thinking it right, and our thinking it wrong, is the precise fact upon which depends the whole controversy. Thinking it right, as they do, they are not to blame for desiring its full recognition, as being right; but, thinking it wrong, as we do, can we yield to them? Can we cast our votes with their view, and against our own? In view of our moral, social, and political responsibilities, can we do this?

Wrong as we think slavery is, we can yet afford to let it alone where it is, because that much is due to the necessity arising from its actual presence in the nation; but can we, while our votes will prevent it, allow it to spread into the National Territories, and to overrun us here in these Free States? If our sense of duty forbids this, then let us stand by our duty, fearlessly and effectively. Let us be diverted by none of those sophistical contrivances wherewith we are so industriously plied and belabored—contrivances such as groping for some middle ground between the right and the wrong, vain as the search for a man who should be neither a living man nor a dead man—such as a policy of "don't care" on a question about which all true men do care—such as Union appeals beseeching true Union men to yield to Disunionists, reversing the divine rule, and calling, not the sinners, but the righteous to repentance—such as invocations to Washington, imploring men to unsay what Washington said, and undo what Washington did.

Neither let us be slandered from our duty by false accusations against us, nor frightened from it by menaces of destruction to the Government nor of dungeons to ourselves. LET US HAVE FAITH THAT RIGHT MAKES MIGHT, AND IN THAT FAITH, LET US, TO THE END, DARE TO DO OUR DUTY AS WE UNDERSTAND IT.

*February 27, 1860*

# Speech at New Haven, Connecticut

MR. PRESIDENT AND FELLOW-CITIZENS OF NEW HAVEN:

If the Republican party of this nation shall ever have the national house entrusted to its keeping, it will be the duty of that party to attend to all the affairs of national housekeeping. Whatever matters of importance may come up, whatever difficulties may arise in the way of its administration of the government, that party will then have to attend to. It will then be compelled to attend to other questions, besides this question which now assumes an overwhelming importance—the question of Slavery. It is true that in the organization of the Republican party this question of Slavery was more important than any other; indeed, so much more important has it become that no other national question can even get a hearing just at present. The old question of tariff—a matter that will remain one of the chief affairs of national housekeeping to all time—the question of the management of financial affairs; the question of the disposition of the public domain—how shall it be managed for the purpose of getting it well settled, and of making there the homes of a free and happy people—these will remain open and require attention for a great while yet, and these questions will have to be attended to by whatever party has the control of the government. Yet, just now, they cannot even obtain a hearing, and I do not purpose to detain you upon these topics, or what sort of hearing they should have when opportunity shall come.

For, whether we will or not, the question of Slavery is *the* question, the all absorbing topic of the day. It is true that all of us—and by that I mean, not the Republican party alone, but the whole American people, here and elsewhere—all of us wish this question settled—wish it out of the way. It stands in the way, and prevents the adjustment, and the giving of necessary attention to other questions of national housekeeping. The people of the whole nation agree that this question ought to be settled, and yet it is not settled. And the reason is that they are not yet agreed *how* it shall be settled. All wish it done, but some wish one way and some another, and some a third, or fourth, or fifth; different bodies are pulling in different directions, and none of them having a decided majority, are able to accomplish the common object.

In the beginning of the year 1854 a new policy was inaugurated with the avowed object and confident promise that it would entirely and forever put an end to the Slavery agitation. It was again and again declared that under this policy, when once successfully established, the country would be forever rid of this whole question. Yet under the operation of that policy this agitation has not only not ceased, but it has been constantly augmented. And this too, although, from the day of its introduction, its friends, who promised that it would wholly end all agitation, constantly insisted, down to the time that the Lecompton bill was introduced, that it was working admirably, and that its inevitable tendency was to remove the question forever from the politics of the country. Can you call to mind any Democratic speech, made after the repeal of the Missouri Compromise, down to the time of the Lecompton bill, in which it was not predicted that the Slavery agitation was just at an end; that "the abolition excitement was played out," "the Kansas question was dead," "they have made the most they can out of this question and it is now forever settled." But since the Lecompton bill no Democrat, within my experience, has ever pretended that he could see the end. That cry has been dropped. They themselves do not pretend, now, that the agitation of this subject has come to an end yet. [Applause.]

The truth is, that this question is one of national importance, and we cannot help dealing with it: we must do something about it, whether we will or not. We cannot avoid it; the subject is one we cannot avoid considering; we can no more avoid it than a man can live without eating. It is upon us; it attaches to the body politic as much and as closely as the natural wants attach to our natural bodies. Now I think it important that this matter should be taken up in earnest, and really settled. And one way to bring about a true settlement of the question is to understand its true magnitude.

There have been many efforts to settle it. Again and again it has been fondly hoped that it was settled, but every time it breaks out afresh, and more violently than ever. It was settled, our fathers hoped, by the Missouri Compromise, but it did not stay settled. Then the compromises of 1850 were declared to be a full and final settlement of the question. The two great parties, each in National Convention, adopted resolutions declaring that the settlement made by the Compromise of 1850 was a finality—that it would last forever. Yet how long before it was unsettled again! It broke out again in 1854, and blazed higher and raged more furiously than ever before, and the agitation has not rested since.

These repeated settlements must have some fault about them. There must be some inadequacy in their very nature to the purpose for which they were designed. We can only speculate as to where that fault—that inadequacy, is, but we may perhaps profit by past experience.

I think that one of the causes of these repeated failures is that our best and greatest men have greatly underestimated the size of this question. They have constantly brought forward small cures for great sores—plasters too small to cover the wound. That is one reason that all settlements have proved so temporary—so evanescent. [Applause.]

Look at the magnitude of this subject! One sixth of our population, in round numbers—not quite one sixth, and yet more than a seventh,—about one sixth of the whole population of the United States are slaves! The owners of these slaves consider them property. The effect upon the minds of the owners is that of property, and nothing else—it induces them to insist upon all that will favorably affect its value as property, to demand laws and institutions and a public policy that shall increase and secure its value, and make it durable, lasting and universal. The effect on the minds of the owners is to persuade them that there is no wrong in it. The slaveholder does not like to be considered a mean fellow, for holding that species of property, and hence he has to struggle within himself and sets about arguing himself into the belief that Slavery is right. The property influences his mind. The dissenting minister, who argued some theological point with one of the established church, was always met by the reply, "I can't see it so." He opened the Bible, and pointed him to a passage, but the orthodox minister replied, "I can't see it so." Then he showed him a single word—"Can you see that?" "Yes, I see it," was the reply. The dissenter laid a guinea over the word and asked, "Do you see it now?" [Great laughter.] So here. Whether the owners of this species of property do really see it as it is, it is not for me to say, but if they do, they see it as it is through 2,000,000,000 of dollars, and that is a pretty thick coating. [Laughter.] Certain it is, that they do not see it as we see it. Certain it is, that this two thousand million of dollars, invested in this species of property, all so concentrated that the mind can grasp it at once—this immense pecuniary interest, has its influence upon their minds.

But here in Connecticut and at the North Slavery does not exist, and we see it through no such medium. To us it appears natural to think that slaves are human beings; *men,* not property; that some of the things, at least, stated about men in the Declaration of Independence apply to them as well as to us. [Applause.] I say, we think, most of us, that this Charter of Freedom applies to the slave as well as to ourselves, that the class of arguments put forward to batter down that idea, are also calculated to break down the very idea of a free government, even for white men, and to undermine the very foundations of free society. [Continued applause.] We think Slavery a great moral wrong, and while we do not claim the right to touch it where it exists, we wish to treat it as a wrong in the Territories, where our votes will reach it. We think that a respect for ourselves, a regard for future generations and for the God that made us, require that we put down this wrong where our votes will properly reach it. We think that species of labor an injury to free white men—in short, we think Slavery a great moral, social and political evil, tolerable only because, and so far as its actual existence makes it necessary to tolerate it, and that beyond that, it ought to be treated as a wrong.

Now these two ideas, the property idea that Slavery is right, and the idea that it is wrong, come into collision, and do actually produce that irrepressible conflict which Mr. Seward has been so roundly abused for mentioning. The two ideas conflict, and must conflict.

Again, in its political aspect, does anything in any way endanger the perpetuity of this Union but that single thing, Slavery? Many of our adversaries are anxious to claim that they are specially devoted to the Union, and take pains to charge upon us hostility to the Union. Now we claim that we are the only true Union men, and we put to them this one proposition: What ever endangered this Union, save and except Slavery? Did any other thing ever cause a moment's fear? All men must agree that this thing alone has ever endangered the perpetuity of the Union. But if it was threatened by any other influence, would not all men say that the best thing that could be done, if we could not or ought not to destroy it, would be at least to keep it from growing any larger? Can any man believe that the way to save the Union is to extend and increase the only thing that threatens the Union, and to suffer it to grow bigger and bigger? [Great applause.]

Whenever this question shall be settled, it must be settled on some philosophical basis. No policy that does not rest upon some philosophical public opinion can be permanently maintained. And hence, there are but two policies in regard to Slavery that can be at all maintained. The first, based on the property view that Slavery is right, conforms to that idea throughout, and demands that we shall do everything for it that we ought to do if it were right. We must sweep away all opposition, for opposition to the right is wrong; we must agree that Slavery is right, and we must adopt the idea that property has persuaded the owner to believe—that Slavery is morally right and socially elevating. This gives a philosophical basis for a permanent policy of encouragement.

The other policy is one that squares with the idea that Slavery is wrong, and it consists in doing everything that we ought to do if it is wrong. Now, I don't wish to be misunderstood, nor to leave a gap down to be misrepresented, even. I don't mean that we ought to attack it where it exists. To me it seems that if we were to form a government anew, in view of the actual presence of Slavery we should find it necessary to frame just such a government as our fathers did; giving to the slaveholder the entire control where the system was established, while we possessed the power to restrain it from going outside those limits. [Applause.] From the necessities of the case we should be compelled to form just such a government as our blessed fathers gave us; and, surely, if they have so made it, that adds another reason why we should let Slavery alone where it exists.

If I saw a venomous snake crawling in the road, any man would say I might seize the nearest stick and kill it; but if I found that snake in bed with my children, that would be another question. [Laughter.] I might hurt the children more than the snake, and it might bite them. [Applause.] Much more, if I found it in bed with my neighbor's children, and I had bound myself by a solemn compact not to meddle with his children under any circumstances, it would become me to let that particular mode of getting rid of the gentleman alone. [Great laughter.] But if there was a bed newly made up, to which the children were to be taken, and it was proposed to take a batch of young snakes and put them there with them, I take it no man would say there was any question how I ought to decide! [Prolonged applause and cheers.]

That is just the case! The new Territories are the newly made bed to which our children are to go, and it lies with the nation to say whether they shall have snakes mixed up with them or not. It does not seem as if there could be much hesitation what our policy should be! [Applause.]

Now I have spoken of a policy based on the idea that Slavery is wrong, and a policy based upon the idea that it is right. But an effort has been made for a policy that shall treat it as neither right or wrong. It is based upon utter indifference. Its leading advocate has said "I don't care whether it be voted up or down." [Laughter.] "It is merely a matter of dollars and cents." "The Almighty has drawn a line across this continent, on one side of which all soil must forever be cultivated by slave labor, and on the other by free;" "when the struggle is between the white man and the negro, I am for the white man; when it is between the negro and the crocodile, I am for the negro." Its central idea is indifference. It holds that it makes no more difference to us whether the Territories become free or slave States, than whether my neighbor stocks his farm with horned cattle or puts it into tobacco. All recognize this policy, the plausible sugar-coated name of which is *"popular sovereignty."* [Laughter.]

This policy chiefly stands in the way of a permanent settlement of the question. I believe there is no danger of its becoming the permanent policy of the country, for it is based on a public indifference. There is nobody that "don't care." ALL THE PEOPLE DO CARE! one way or the other. [Great applause.] I do not charge that its author, when he says he "don't care," states his individual opinion; he only expresses his policy for the government. I understand that he has never said, as an individual, whether he thought Slavery right or wrong—and he is the only man in the nation that has not! Now such a policy may have a temporary run;

it may spring up as necessary to the political prospects of some gentleman; but it is utterly baseless; the people are not indifferent; and it can therefore have no durability or permanence.

But suppose it could! Then it could be maintained only by a public opinion that shall say "we don't care." There must be a change in public opinion, the public mind must be so far debauched as to square with this policy of caring not at all. The people must come to consider this as "merely a question of dollars and cents," and to believe that in some places the Almighty has made Slavery necessarily eternal. This policy can be brought to prevail if the people can be brought round to say honestly "we don't care;" if not, it can never be maintained. It is for you to say whether that can be done. [Applause.]

You are ready to say it cannot, but be not too fast! Remember what a long stride has been taken since the repeal of the Missouri Compromise! Do you know of any Democrat, of either branch of the party—do you know one who declares that he believes that the Declaration of Independence has any application to the negro? Judge Taney declares that it has not, and Judge Douglas even vilifies me personally and scolds me roundly for saying that the Declaration applies to all men, and that negroes are men. [Cheers.] Is there a Democrat here who does not deny that the Declaration applies to a negro? Do any of you know of one? Well, I have tried before perhaps fifty audiences, some larger and some smaller than this, to find one such Democrat, and never yet have I found one who said I did not place him right in that. I must assume that Democrats hold that, and now, *not one of these Democrats can show that he said that five years ago!* [Applause.] I venture to defy the whole party to produce one man that ever uttered the belief that the Declaration did not apply to negroes, before the repeal of the Missouri Compromise! Four or five years ago we all thought negroes were men, and that when *"all men"* were named, negroes were included. But *the whole Democratic party has deliberately taken negroes from the class of men and put them in the class of brutes.* [Applause.] Turn it as you will, it is simply the truth! Don't be too hasty then in saying that the people cannot be brought to this new doctrine, but note that long stride. One more as long completes the journey, from where negroes are estimated as men to where they are estimated as mere brutes—as rightful property!

That saying, "in the struggle between the white man and the negro," &c., which I know came from the same source as this policy—that saying marks another step. There is a falsehood wrapped up in that statement. "In the struggle between the white man and the negro" assumes that there is a struggle, in which either the white man must enslave the negro or the negro must enslave the white. There is no such struggle! It is merely an ingenious falsehood, to degrade and brutalize the negro. Let each let the other alone, and there is no struggle about it. If it was like two wrecked seamen on a narrow plank, when each must push the other off or drown himself, I would push the negro off or a white man either, but it is not; the plank is large enough for both. [Applause.] This good earth is plenty broad enough for white man and negro both, and there is no need of either pushing the other off. [Continued applause.]

So that saying, "in the struggle between the negro and the crocodile," &c., is made up from the idea that down where the crocodile inhabits a white man can't labor; it must be nothing else but crocodile or negro; if the negro does not the crocodile must possess the earth; [laughter;] in that case he declares for the negro. The meaning of the whole is just this: As a white man is to a negro, so is a negro to a crocodile; and as the negro may rightfully treat the crocodile, so may the white man rightfully treat the negro. This very dear phrase coined by its author, and so dear that he deliberately repeats it in many speeches, has a tendency to still further brutalize the negro, and to bring public opinion to the point of utter indifference whether men so brutalized are enslaved or not. When that time shall come, if ever, I think that policy to which I refer may prevail. But I hope the good freemen of this country will never allow it to come, and until then the policy can never be maintained.

Now consider the effect of this policy. We in the States are not to care whether Freedom or Slavery gets the better, but the people in the Territories may care. They are to decide, and they may think what they please; it is a matter of dollars and cents! But are not the people of the Territories detailed from the States? If this feeling of indifference—this absence of moral sense about the question—prevails in the States, will it not be carried into the Territories? Will not every man say, "I don't care, it is nothing to me?" If any one comes that wants Slavery, must they not say, "I don't care whether Freedom or Slavery be voted up or voted down?" It results at last in nationalizing the institution of Slavery. Even if fairly carried out, that policy is just as certain to nationalize Slavery as the doctrine of Jeff Davis himself. These are only two roads to the same goal, and "popular sovereignty" is just as sure and almost as short as the other. [Applause.]

What we want, and all we want, is to have with us the men who think slavery wrong. But those who say they hate slavery, and are opposed to it, but yet act with the Democratic party—where are they? Let us apply a few tests. You say that you think slavery is wrong, but you denounce all attempts to restrain it. Is there anything else that you think wrong, that you are not willing to deal with as a wrong? Why are you so careful, so tender of this one wrong and no other? [Laughter.] You will not let us *do* a single thing as if it was wrong; there is no place where you will allow it to be even *called* wrong! We must not call it wrong in the Free States, because it is *not* there, and we must not call it wrong in the Slave States because it *is* there; we must not call it wrong in politics because that is bringing morality into politics, and we must not call it wrong in the pulpit because that is bringing politics into religion; we must not bring it into the Tract Society or the other societies, because those are such unsuitable places, and there is no single place, according to you, where this wrong thing can properly be called wrong! [Continued laughter and applause.]

Perhaps you will plead that if the people of Slave States should themselves set on foot an effort for emancipation, you would wish them success, and bid them God-speed. Let us test that! In 1858, the emancipation party of Missouri, with Frank Blair at their head, tried to get up a movement for that purpose, and having started a party contested the State. Blair was beaten, apparently if not truly, and when the news came to Connecticut, you, who knew that Frank Blair was taking hold of this thing by the right end, and doing the only thing that you say can properly be done to remove this wrong—did you bow your heads in sorrow because of that defeat? Do you, any of you, know one single Democrat that showed sorrow over that result? Not one! On the contrary every man threw up his hat, and hallooed at the top of his lungs, "hooray for Democracy!" [Great laughter and applause.]

Now, gentlemen, *the Republicans desire to place this great question of slavery on the very basis on which our fathers placed it, and no other.* [Applause.] It is easy to demonstrate that "our Fathers, who framed this government under which we live," looked on Slavery as wrong, and so framed it and everything about it as to square with the idea that it was wrong, so far as the necessities arising from its existence permitted. In forming the Constitution they found the slave trade existing; capital invested in it; fields depending upon it for labor, and the whole system resting upon the importation of slave-labor. They therefore did not prohibit the slave trade at once, but they gave the power to prohibit it after twenty years. Why was this? What other foreign trade did they treat in that way? Would they have done this if they had not thought slavery wrong?

Another thing was done by some of the same men who framed the Constitution, and afterwards adopted as their own act by the first Congress held under that Constitution, of which many of the framers were members; they prohibited the spread of Slavery into Territories. Thus the same men, the framers of the Constitution, cut off the supply and prohibited the spread of Slavery, and both acts show conclusively that they considered that the thing was wrong.

If additional proof is wanting it can be found in the phraseology of the Constitution. When men are framing a supreme law and chart of government, to secure blessings and prosperity to untold generations yet to come, they use language as short and direct and plain as can be found, to express their meaning. In all matters but this of Slavery the framers of the Constitution used the very clearest, shortest, and most direct language. But the Constitution alludes to Slavery three times without mentioning it once! The language used becomes ambiguous, roundabout, and mystical. They speak of the "immigration of persons," and mean the importation of slaves, but do not say so. In establishing a basis of representation they say "all other persons," when they mean to say slaves—why did they not use the shortest phrase? In providing for the return of fugitives they say "persons held to service or labor." If they had said slaves it would have been plainer, and less liable to misconstruction. Why didn't they do it. We cannot doubt that it was done on purpose. Only one reason is possible, and that is supplied us by one of the framers of the Constitution—and it is not possible for man to conceive of any other—they expected and desired that the system would come to an end, and meant that when it did, the Constitution should not show that there ever had been a slave in this good free country of ours! [Great applause.]

I will dwell on that no longer. I see the signs of the approaching triumph of the Republicans in the bearing of their political adversaries. A great deal of their war with us now-a-days is mere bushwhacking. [Laughter.] At the battle of Waterloo, when Napoleon's cavalry had charged again and again upon the unbroken squares of British infantry, at last they were giving up the attempt, and going off in disorder, when some of the officers in mere vexation and complete despair fired their pistols at those solid squares. The Democrats are in that sort of extreme desperation; it is nothing else. [Laughter.] I will take up a few of these *arguments*.

There is "THE IRREPRESSIBLE CONFLICT." [Applause.] How they rail at Seward for that saying! They repeat it constantly; and although the proof has been thrust under their noses again and again, that almost every good man since the formation of our government has uttered that same sentiment, from Gen. Washington, who "trusted that we should yet have a confederacy of Free States," with Jefferson, Jay, Monroe, down to the latest days, yet they refuse to notice that at all, and persist in railing at Seward for saying it. Even Roger A. Pryor, editor of the Richmond Enquirer, uttered the same sentiment in almost the same language, and yet so little offence did it give the Democrats that he was sent for to Washington to edit the States—the Douglas organ there, while Douglas goes into hydrophobia and spasms of rage because Seward dared to repeat it. [Great applause.] This is what I call bushwhacking, a sort of argument that they must know any child can see through.

Another is JOHN BROWN! [Great laughter.] You stir up insurrections, you invade the South! John Brown! Harper's Ferry! Why, John Brown was not a Republican! You have never implicated a single Republican in that Harper's Ferry enterprise. We tell you that if any member of the Republican party is guilty in that matter, you know it or you do not know it. If you do know it, you are inexcusable not to designate man and prove the fact. If you do not know it, you are inexcusable to assert it, and especially to persist in the assertion after you have tried and failed to make the proof. You need not be told that persisting in a charge which one does not know to be true is simply malicious slander. Some of you admit that no Republican designedly aided or encouraged the Harper's Ferry affair; but still insist that our doctrines and declarations necessarily lead to such results. We do not believe it. We know we hold to no doctrines, and make no declarations, which were not held to and made by our fathers who framed the Government under which we live, and we cannot see how declarations that were patriotic when they made them are villainous when we make them. You never dealt fairly by us in relation to that affair—and I will say frankly that I know of nothing in your character that should lead us to suppose that you would. You had just been soundly thrashed in elections in several States, and others were soon to come. You rejoiced at the occasion, and only were troubled that there were not three times as many killed in the affair. You were in evident glee—there was no sorrow for the killed nor for the peace of Virginia disturbed—you were rejoicing that by charging Republicans with this thing you might get an advantage of us in New York, and the other States. You pulled that string as tightly as you could, but your very generous and worthy expectations were not quite fulfilled. [Laughter.] Each Republican knew that the charge was a slander as to himself at least, and was not inclined by it to cast his vote in your favor. It was mere bushwhacking, because you had nothing else to do. You are still on that track, and I say, go on! If you think you can slander a woman into loving you or a man into voting for you, try it till you are satisfied! [Tremendous applause.]

Another specimen of this bushwhacking, that "shoe strike." [Laughter.] Now be it understood that I do not pretend to know all about the matter. I am merely going to speculate a little about some of its phases. And at the outset, *I am glad to see that a system of labor prevails in New England under which laborers CAN strike* when they want to [Cheers,] where they are not obliged to work under all circumstances, and are not tied down and obliged to labor whether you pay them or not! [Cheers.] I *like* the system which lets a man quit when he wants to, and wish it might prevail everywhere. [Tremendous applause.] One of the reasons why I am opposed to Slavery is just here. What is the true condition of the laborer? I take it that it is best for all to leave each man free to acquire property as fast as he can. Some will get wealthy. I don't believe in a law to prevent a man from getting rich; it would do more harm than good. So while we do not propose any war upon capital, we do wish to allow the humblest man an equal chance to get rich with everybody else. [Applause.] When one starts poor, as most do in the race of life, free society is such that he knows he can better his condition; he knows that there is no fixed condition of labor, for his whole life. I am not ashamed to confess that twenty five years ago I was a hired laborer, mauling rails, at work on a flat-boat—just what might happen to any poor man's son! [Applause.] I want every man to have the chance—and I believe a black man is entitled to it—in which he *can* better his condition—when he may look forward and hope to be a hired laborer this year and the next, work for himself afterward, and finally to hire men to work for him! That is the true system. Up here in New England, you have a soil that scarcely sprouts black-eyed beans, and yet where will you find wealthy men so wealthy, and poverty so rarely in extremity? There is not another such place on earth! [Cheers.] I desire that if you get too thick here, and find it hard to better your condition on this soil, you may have a chance to strike and go somewhere else, where you may not be degraded, nor have your family corrupted by forced rivalry with negro slaves. I want you to have a clean bed, and no snakes in it! [Cheers.] Then you can better your condition, and so it may go on and on in one ceaseless round so long as man exists on the face of the earth! [Prolonged applause.]

Now, to come back to this shoe strike,—if, as the Senator from Illinois asserts, this is caused by withdrawal of Southern votes, consider briefly how you will meet the difficulty. You have done nothing, and have protested that you have done nothing, to injure the South. And yet, to get back the shoe trade, you must leave off doing something that you are now doing. What is it? You must stop thinking slavery wrong! Let your institutions be wholly changed; let your State Constitutions be subverted, glorify slavery, and so you will get back the shoe trade—for what? You have brought owned labor with it to compete with your own labor, to underwork you, and to degrade you! Are you ready to get back the trade on those terms?

But the statement is not correct. You have not lost that trade; orders were never better than now! Senator Mason, a Democrat, comes into the Senate in homespun, a proof that the dissolution of the Union has actually begun! but orders are the same. Your factories have not struck work, neither those where they make anything for coats, nor for pants, nor for shirts, nor for ladies' dresses. Mr. Mason has not reached the manufacturers who ought to have made him a coat and pants! To make his proof good for anything he should have come into the Senate barefoot! (Great laughter.)

Another bushwhacking contrivance; simply that, nothing else! I find a good many people who are very much concerned about the loss of Southern trade. Now either these people are sincere or they are not. (Laughter.) I will speculate a little about that. If they are sincere, and are moved by any real danger of the loss of Southern trade, they will simply get their names on the white list, and then, instead of persuading Republicans to do likewise, they will be glad to keep you away! Don't you see they thus shut off competition? They would not be whispering around to Republicans to come in and share the profits with them. But if they are not sincere, and are merely trying to fool Republicans out of their votes, they will grow very anxious about *your* pecuniary prospects; they are afraid you are going to get broken up and ruined; they did not care about Democratic votes—*Oh no, no, no!* You must judge which class those belong to whom you meet; I leave it to you to determine from the facts.

Let us notice some more of the stale charges against Republicans. You say we are sectional. We deny it. That makes an issue; and the burden of proof is upon you. You produce your proof; and what is it? Why, that our party has no existence in your section—gets no votes in your section. The fact is substantially true; but does it prove the issue? If it does, then in case we should, without change of principle, begin to get votes in your section, we should thereby cease to be sectional. You cannot escape this conclusion; and yet, are you willing to abide by it? If you are, you will probably soon find that we have ceased to be sectional, for we shall get votes in your section this very year. [Applause.] The fact that we get no votes in your section is a fact of your making, and not of ours. And if there be fault in that fact, that fault is primarily yours, and remains so until you show that we repel you by some wrong principle or practice. If we do repel you by any wrong principle or practice, the fault is ours; but this brings you to where you ought to have started—to a discussion of the right or wrong of our principle. If our principle, put in practice, would wrong your section for the benefit of ours, or for any other object, then our principle, and we with it, are sectional, and are justly opposed and denounced as such. Meet us, then, on the question of whether our principle, put in practice, would wrong your section; and so meet it as if it were possible that something may be said on our side. Do you accept the challenge? No? Then you really believe that the principle which our fathers who framed the Government under which we live thought so clearly right as to adopt it, and indorse it again and again, upon their official oaths, is, in fact, so clearly wrong as to demand your condemnation without a moment's consideration.

Some of you delight to flaunt in our faces the warning against sectional parties given by Washington in his Farewell address. Less than eight years before Washington gave that warning, he had, as President of the United States, approved and signed an act of Congress, enforcing the prohibition of Slavery in the northwestern Territory, which act embodied the policy of Government upon that subject, up to and at the very moment he penned that warning; and about one year after he penned it he wrote LaFayette that he considered that prohibition a wise measure, expressing in the same connection his hope that we should some time have a confederacy of Free States.

Bearing this in mind, and seeing that sectionalism has since arisen upon this same subject, is that warning a weapon in your hands against us, or in our hands against you? Could Washington himself speak, would he cast the blame of that sectionalism upon us, who sustain his policy, or upon you who repudiate it? We respect that warning of Washington, and we commend it to you, together with his example pointing to the right application of it. [Applause.]

But you say you are conservative—eminently conservative—while we are revolutionary, destructive, or something of the sort. What is conservatism? Is it not adherenece to the old and tried, against the new and untried? We stick to, contend for, the identical old policy on the point in controversy which was adopted by our fathers who framed the Government under which we live; while you with one accord reject, and scout, and spit upon that old policy, and insist upon substituting something new. True, you disagree among yourselves as to what that substitute shall be. You have considerable variety of new propositions and plans, but you are unanimous in rejecting and denouncing the old policy of the fathers. Some of you are for reviving the foreign slave-trade; some for a Congressional Slave-Code for the Territories; some for Congress forbidding the Territories to prohibit Slavery within their limits; some for maintaining Slavery in the Territories through the Judiciary; some for the "gur-reat pur-rin-ciple" that "if one man would enslave another, no third man should object," fantastically called "Popular Sovereignty;" [great laughter,] but never a man among you in favor of Federal prohibition of Slavery in Federal Territories, according to the practice of our fathers who framed the Government under which we live. Not one of all your various plans can show a precedent or an advocate in the century within which our Government originated. And yet you draw yourselves up and say "We are eminently conservative!" [Great laughter.]

It is exceedingly desirable that all parts of this great Confederacy shall be at peace, and in harmony, one with another. Let us Republicans do our part to have it so. Even though much provoked, let us do nothing through passion and ill temper. Even though the Southern people will not so much as listen to us, let us calmly consider their demands, and yield to them if, in our deliberate view of our duty, we possibly can. Judging by all they say and do, and by the subject and nature of their controversy with us, let us determine, if we can, what will satisfy them?

Will they be satisfied if the Territories be unconditionally surrendered to them? We know they will not. In all their present complaints against us, the Territories are scarcely mentioned. Invasions and insurrections are the rage now. Will it satisfy them if, in the future, we have nothing to do with invasions and insurrections? We know it will not. We so know because we know we never had anything to do with invasions and insurrections; and yet this total abstaining does not exempt us from the charge and the denunciation.

The question recurs, what will satisfy them? Simply this: we must not only let them alone, but we must, somehow, convince them that we do let them alone. [Applause.] This, we know by experience, is no easy task. We have been so trying to convince them, from the very beginning of our organization, but with no success. In all our platforms and speeches, we have constantly protested our purpose to let them alone; but this has had no tendency to convince them. Alike unavailing to convince them is the fact that they have never detected a man of us in any attempt to disturb them.

These natural and apparently adequate means all failing, what will convince them? This, and this only; cease to call slavery *wrong*, and join them in calling it *right*. And this must be done thoroughly—done in *acts* as well as in *words*. Silence will not be tolerated—we must place ourselves avowedly with them. Douglas's new sedition law must be enacted and enforced, suppressing all delcarations that Slavery is wrong, whether made in politics, in presses, in pulpits, or in private. We must arrest and return their fugitive slaves with greedy pleasure. We must pull down our Free State Constitutions. The whole atmosphere must be disinfected of all taint of opposition to Slavery, before they will cease to believe that all their troubles proceed from us. So long as we call Slavery wrong, whenever a slave runs away they will overlook the obvious fact that he ran because he was oppressed, and declare he was stolen off. Whenever a master cuts his slaves with the lash, and they cry out under it, he will overlook the obvious fact that the negroes cry out because they are hurt, and insist that they were *put up to it by some rascally abolitionist*. [Great laughter.]

I am quite aware that they do not state their case precisely in this way. Most of them would probably say to us, "Let us alone, do nothing to us, and say what you please about Slavery." But we do let them alone—have never disturbed them—so that, after all, it is what we say, which dissatisfies them. They will continue to accuse us of doing, until we cease saying.

I am also aware they have not, as yet, in terms, demanded the overthrow of our Free State Constitutions. Yet those Constitutions declare the wrong of Slavery, with more solemn emphasis than do all other sayings against it; and when all these other sayings shall have been silenced, the overthrow of these Constitutions will be demanded, and nothing be left to resist the demand. It is nothing to the contrary, that they do not demand the whole of this just now. Demanding what they do, and for the reason they do, they can voluntarily stop nowhere short of this consummation. Holding as they do, that Slavery is morally right, and socially elevating, they cannot cease to demand a full national recognition of it, as a legal right, and a social blessing.

Nor can we justifiably withhold this, on any ground save our conviction that Slavery is wrong. If Slavery is right, all words, acts, laws, and Constitutions against it, are themselves wrong, and should be silenced, and swept away. If it is right, we cannot justly object to its nationality—its universality; if it is wrong, they cannot justly insist upon its extension—its enlargement. All they ask, we could as readily grant, if we thought it wrong. Their thinking it right, and our thinking it wrong, is the precise fact upon which depends the whole controversy. Thinking it right as they do, they are not to blame for desiring its full recognition, as being right; but, thinking it wrong, as we do, can we yield to them? Can we cast our votes with their view, and against our own? In view of our moral, social, and political responsibilities, can we do this?

Wrong as we think Slavery is, we can yet afford to let it alone where it is, because that much is due to the necessity arising from its actual presence in the nation; but can we, while our votes will prevent it, allow it to spread into the National Territories, and to overrun us here in these Free States?

If our sense of duty forbids this, then let us stand by our duty, fearlessly and effectively. Let us be diverted by none of those sophistical contrivances wherewith we are so industriously plied and belabored—contrivances such as groping for some middle ground between the right and the wrong, vain as the search for a man who should be neither a living man nor a dead man—such as a policy of "don't care" on a question about which all true men do care—such as Union appeals beseeching true Union men to yield to Disunionists, reversing the divine rule, and calling, not the sinners, but the righteous to repentance—such as invocations of Washington, imploring men to unsay what Washington did.

Neither let us be slandered from our duty by false accusations against us, nor frightened from it by menaces of destruction to the Government, nor of dungeons to ourselves. Let us have faith that right makes might; and in that faith, let us, to the end, dare to do our duty, as we understand it.

*March 6, 1860*

# Speech at Indianapolis, Indiana

It is not possible, in my journey to the national capital, to address assemblies like this which may do me the great honor to meet me as you have done, but very briefly. I should be entirely worn out if I were to attempt it. I appear before you now to thank you for this very magnificent welcome which you have given me, and still more for the very generous support which your State recently gave to the political cause of the whole country, and the whole world. [Applause.] Solomon has said, that there is a time to keep silence. [Renewed and deafening applause.] * * * * * We know certain that they mean the same thing while using the same words now, and it perhaps would be as well if they would keep silence.

The words "coercion" and "invasion" are in great use about these days. Suppose we were simply to try if we can, and ascertain what, is the meaning of these words. Let us get, if we can, the exact definitions of these words—not from dictionaries, but from the men who constantly repeat them—what things they mean to express by the words. What, then, is "coercion"? What is "invasion"? Would the marching of an army into South California, for instance, without the consent of her people, and in hostility against them, be coercion or invasion? I very frankly say, I think it would be invasion, and it would be coercion too, if the people of that country were forced to submit. But if the Government, for instance, but simply insists upon holding its own forts, or retaking those forts which belong to it—[cheers,]—or the enforcement of the laws of the United States in the collection of duties upon foreign importations,—[renewed cheers,]—or even the withdrawal of the mails from those portions of the country where the mails themselves are habitually violated; would any or all of these things be coercion? Do the lovers of the Union contend that they will resist coercion or invasion of any State, understanding that any or all of these would be coercing or invading a State? If they do, then it occurs to me that the means for the preservation of the Union they so greatly love, in their own estimation, is of a very thin and airy character. [Applause.] If sick, they would consider the little pills of the homeopathist as already too large for them to swallow. In their view, the Union, as a family relation, would not be anything like a regular marriage at all, but only as a sort of free-love arrangement,—[laughter,]—to be maintained on what that sect calls passionate attraction. [Continued laughter.] But, my friends, enough of this.

What is the particular sacredness of a State? I speak not of that position which is given to a State in and by the Constitution of the United States, for that all of us agree to—we abide by; but that position assumed, that a State can carry with it out of the Union that which it holds in sacredness by virtue of its connection with the Union. I am speaking of that assumed right of a State, as a primary principle, that the Constitution should rule all that is less than itself, and ruin all that is bigger than itself. [Laughter.] But, I ask, wherein does consist that right? If a State, in one instance, and a county in another, should be equal in extent of territory, and equal in the number of people, wherein is that State any better than the county? Can a change of name change the right? By what principle of original right is it that one-fiftieth or one-ninetieth of a great nation, by calling themselves a State, have the right to break up and ruin that nation as a matter of original principle? Now, I ask the question—I am not deciding any-thing—[laughter,]—and with the request that you will think somewhat upon that subject and decide for yourselves, if you choose, when you get ready,—where is the mysterious, original right, from principle, for a certain district of country with inhabitants, by merely being called a State, to play tyrant over all its own citizens, and deny the authority of everything greater than itself. [Laughter.] I say I am deciding nothing, but simply giving something for you to reflect upon; and, with having said this much, and having declared, in the start, that I will make no long speeches, I thank you again for this magnificent welcome, and bid you an affectionate farewell. [Cheers.]

*February 11, 1861*

# Speech to Germans at Cincinnati, Ohio

MR. CHAIRMAN: I thank you and those whom you represent, for the compliment you have paid me, by tendering me this address. In so far as there is an allusion to our present national difficulties, which expresses, as you have said, the views of the gentlemen present, I shall have to beg pardon for not entering fully upon the questions, which the address you have now read, suggests.

I deem it my duty—a duty which I owe to my constituents—to you, gentlemen, that I should wait until the last moment, for a development of the present national difficulties, before I express myself decidedly what course I shall pursue. I hope, then, not to be false to anything that you have to expect of me.

I agree with you, Mr. Chairman, that the working men are the basis of all governments, for the plain reason that they are the most numerous, and as you added that those were the sentiments of the gentlemen present, representing not only the working class, but citizens of other callings than those of the mechanic, I am happy to concur with you in these sentiments, not only of the native born citizens, but also of the Germans and foreigners from other countries.

Mr. Chairman, I hold that while man exists, it is his duty to improve not only his own condition, but to assist in ameliorating mankind; and therefore, without entering upon the details of the question, I will simply say, that I am for those means which will give the greatest good to the greatest number.

In regard to the Homestead Law, I have to say that in so far as the Government lands can be disposed of, I am in favor of cutting up the wild lands into parcels, so that every poor man may have a home.

In regard to the Germans and foreigners, I esteem them no better than other people, nor any worse. [Cries of good.] It is not my nature, when I see a people borne down by the weight of their shackles—the oppression of tyranny—to make their life more bitter by heaping upon them greater burdens; but rather would I do all in my power to raise the yoke, than to add anything that would tend to crush them.

Inasmuch as our country is extensive and new, and the countries of Europe are densely populated, if there are any abroad who desire to make this the land of their adoption, it is not in my heart to throw aught in their way, to prevent them from coming to the United States.

Mr. Chairman, and Gentlemen, I will bid you an affectionate farewell.

*February 12, 1861*

# Speech in Independence Hall, Philadelphia, Pennsylvania

Mr. Cuyler:

I am filled with deep emotion at finding myself standing here in the place where were collected together the wisdom, the patriotism, the devotion to principle, from which sprang the institutions under which we live. You have kindly suggested to me that in my hands is the task of restoring peace to our distracted country. I can say in return, sir, that all the political sentiments I entertain have been drawn, so far as I have been able to draw them, from the sentiments which originated, and were given to the world from this hall in which we stand. I have never had a feeling politically that did not spring from the sentiments embodied in the Declaration of Independence. (Great cheering.) I have often pondered over the dangers which were incurred by the men who assembled here and adopted that Declaration of Independence—I have pondered over the toils that were endured by the officers and soldiers of the army, who achieved that Independence. (Applause.) I have often inquired of myself, what great principle or idea it was that kept this Confederacy so long together. It was not the mere matter of the separation of the colonies from the mother land; but something in that Declaration giving liberty, not alone to the people of this country, but hope to the world for all future time. (Great applause.) It was that which gave promise that in due time the weights should be lifted from the shoulders of all men, and that *all* should have an equal chance. (Cheers.) This is the sentiment embodied in that Declaration of Independence.

Now, my friends, can this country be saved upon that basis? If it can, I will consider myself one of the happiest men in the world if I can help to save it. If it can't be saved upon that principle, it will be truly awful. But, if this country cannot be saved without giving up that principle—I was about to say I would rather be assassinated on this spot than to surrender it. (Applause.)

Now, in my view of the present aspect of affairs, there is no need of bloodshed and war. There is no necessity for it. I am not in favor of such a course, and I may say in advance, there will be no blood shed unless it be forced upon the Government. The Government will not use force unless force is used against it. (Prolonged applause and cries of "That's the proper sentiment.")

My friends, this is a wholly unprepared speech. I did not expect to be called upon to say a word when I came here—I supposed I was merely to do something towards raising a flag. I may, therefore, have said something indiscreet, (cries of "no, no"), but I have said nothing but what I am willing to live by, and, in the pleasure of Almighty God, die by.

*February 22, 1861*

# PRESIDENTIAL SPEECHES, WRITINGS, *and* PROCLAMATIONS

# First Inaugural Address

FELLOW CITIZENS OF THE UNITED STATES:

In compliance with a custom as old as the government itself, I appear before you to address you briefly, and to take, in your presence, the oath prescribed by the Constitution of the United States, to be taken by the President "before he enters on the execution of his office."

I do not consider it necessary, at present, for me to discuss those matters of administration about which there is no special anxiety, or excitement.

Apprehension seems to exist among the people of the Southern States, that by the accession of a Republican Administration, their property and their peace, and personal security, are to be endangered. There has never been any reasonable cause for such apprehension. Indeed, the most ample evidence to the contrary has all the while existed, and been open to their inspection. It is found in nearly all the published speeches of him who now addresses you. I do but quote from one of those speeches when I declare that "I have no purpose, directly or indirectly, to interfere with the institution of slavery in the States where it exists. I believe I have no lawful right to do so, and I have no inclination to do so." Those who nominated and elected me did so with full knowledge that I had made this, and many similar declarations, and had never recanted them. And more than this, they placed in the platform, for my acceptance, and as a law to themselves, and to me, the clear and emphatic resolution which I now read:

"*Resolved,* That the maintenance inviolate of the rights of the States, and especially the right of each State to order and control its own domestic institutions according to its own judgment exclusively, is essential to that balance of power on which the perfection and endurance of our political fabric depend; and we denounce the lawless invasion by armed force of the soil of any State or Territory, no matter under what pretext, as among the gravest of crimes."

I now reiterate these sentiments: and in doing so, I only press upon the public attention the most conclusive evidence of which the case is susceptible, that the property, peace and security of no section are to be in anywise endangered by the now incoming Administration. I add too, that all the protection which, consistently with the Constitution and the laws, can be given, will be cheerfully given to all the States when lawfully demanded, for whatever cause—as cheerfully to one section, as to another.

There is much controversy about the delivering up of fugitives from service or labor. The clause I now read is as plainly written in the Constitution as any other of its provisions:

"No person held to service or labor in one State, under the laws thereof, escaping into another, shall, in consequence of any law or regulation therein, be discharged from such service or labor, but shall be delivered up on claim of the party to whom such service or labor may be due."

It is scarcely questioned that this provision was intended by those who made it, for the reclaiming of what we call fugitive slaves; and the intention of the law-giver is the law. All members of Congress swear their support to the whole Constitution—to this provision as much as to any other. To the proposition, then, that slaves whose cases come within the terms of this clause "shall be delivered up," their oaths are unanimous. Now, if they would make the effort in good temper, could they not with nearly equal unanimity, frame and pass a law, by means of which to keep good that unanimous oath?

There is some difference of opinion whether this clause should be enforced by national or by state authority; but surely that difference is not a very material one. If the slave is to be surrendered, it can be of but little consequence to him, or to others, by which authority it is done. And should any one, in any case, be content that his oath shall go unkept, on a merely unsubstantial controversy as to *how* it shall be kept?

Again, in any law upon this subject, ought not all the safeguards of liberty known in civilized and humane jurisprudence to be introduced, so that a free man be not, in any case, surrendered as a slave? And might it not be well, at the same time, to provide by law for the enforcement of that clause in the Constitution which guarranties that "The citizens of each State shall be entitled to all privileges and immunities of citizens in the several States?"

I take the official oath to-day, with no mental reservations, and with no purpose to construe the Constitution or laws, by any hypercritical rules. And while I do not choose now to specify particular acts of Congress as proper to be enforced, I do suggest, that it will be much safer for all, both in official and private stations, to conform to, and abide by, all those acts which stand unrepealed, than to violate any of them, trusting to find impunity in having them held to be unconstitutional.

It is seventy-two years since the first inauguration of a President under our national Constitution. During that period fifteen different and greatly distinguished citizens, have, in succession, administered the executive branch of the government. They have conducted it through many perils; and, generally with great success. Yet, with all this scope for precedent, I now enter upon the same task for the brief constitutional term of four years, under great and peculiar difficulty. A disruption of the Federal Union heretofore only menaced, is now formidably attempted.

I hold, that in contemplation of universal law, and of the Constitution, the Union of these States is perpetual. Perpetuity is implied, if not expressed, in the fundamental law of all national governments. It is safe to assert that no government proper, ever had a provision in its organic law for its own termination. Continue to execute all the express provisions of our national Constitution, and the Union will endure forever—it being impossible to destroy it, except by some action not provided for in the instrument itself.

Again, if the United States be not a government proper, but an association of States in the nature of contract merely, can it, as a contract, be peaceably unmade, by less than all the parties who made it? One party to a contract may violate it— break it, so to speak; but does it not require all to lawfully rescind it?

Descending from these general principles, we find the proposition that, in legal contemplation, the Union is perpetual, confirmed by the history of the Union itself. The Union is much older than the Constitution. It was formed in fact, by the Articles of Association in 1774. It was matured and continued by the Declaration of Independence in 1776. It was further matured and the faith of all the then thirteen States expressly plighted and engaged that it should be perpetual, by the Articles of Confederation in 1778. And finally, in 1787, one of the declared objects for ordaining and establishing the Constitution, was "*to form a more perfect union.*"

But if the destruction of the Union, by one or by a part only, of the States, be lawfully possible, the Union is *less* perfect than before the Constitution, having lost the vital element of perpetuity.

It follows from these views that no State, upon its own mere motion, can lawfully get out of the Union,—that *resolves* and *ordinances* to that effect are legally void; and that acts of violence, within any State or States, against the authority of the United States, are insurrectionary or revolutionary, according to circumstances.

I therefore consider that, in view of the Constitution and the laws, the Union is unbroken; and, to the extent of my ability, I shall take care, as the Constitution itself expressly enjoins upon me, that the laws of the Union be faithfully executed in all the States. Doing this I deem to be only a simple duty on my part; and I shall perform it, so far as practicable, unless my rightful masters, the American people, shall withhold the requisite means, or, in some authoritative manner, direct the contrary. I trust this will not be regarded as a menace, but only as the declared purpose of the Union that it *will* constitutionally defend, and maintain itself.

In doing this there needs to be no bloodshed or violence; and there shall be none, unless it be forced upon the national authority. The power confided to me, will be used to hold, occupy, and possess the property, and places belonging to the government, and to collect the duties and imposts; but beyond what may be necessary for these objects, there will be no invasion—no using of force against, or among the people anywhere. Where hostility to the United States, in any interior locality, shall be so great and universal, as to prevent competent resident citizens from holding the Federal offices, there will be no attempt to force obnoxious strangers among the people for that object. While the strict legal right may exist in the government to enforce the exercise of these offices, the attempt to do so would be so irritating, and so nearly impracticable with all, that I deem it better to forego, for the time, the uses of such offices.

The mails, unless repelled, will continue to be furnished in all parts of the Union. So far as possible, the people everywhere shall have that sense of perfect security which is most favorable to calm thought and reflection. The course here indicated will be followed, unless current events, and experience, shall show a modification, or change, to be proper, and in every case and exigency, my best discretion will be exercised, according to circumstances actually existing, and with a view and a hope of a peaceful solution of the national troubles, and the restoration of fraternal sympathies and affections.

That there are persons in one section, or another who seek to destroy the Union at all events, and are glad of any pretext to do it, I will neither affirm or deny; but if there be such, I need address no word to them. To those, however, who really love the Union, may I not speak?

Before entering upon so grave a matter as the destruction of our national fabric, with all its benefits, its memories, and its hopes, would it not be wise to ascertain precisely why we do it? Will you hazard so desperate a step, while there is any possibility that any portion of the ills you fly from, have no real existence? Will you, while the certain ills you fly to, are greater than all the real ones you fly from? Will you risk the commission of so fearful a mistake?

All profess to be content in the Union, if all constitutional rights can be maintained. Is it true, then, that any right, plainly written in the Constitution, has been denied? I think not. Happily the human mind is so constituted, that no party can reach to the audacity of doing this. Think, if you can, of a single instance in which a plainly written provision of the Constitution has ever been denied. If, by the mere force of numbers, a majority should deprive a minority of any clearly written constitutional right, it might, in a moral point of view, justify revolution—certainly would, if such right were a vital one. But such is not our case. All the vital rights of minorities, and of individuals, are so plainly assured to them, by affirmations and negations, guarranties and prohibitions, in the Constitution, that controversies never arise concerning them. But no organic law can ever be framed with a provision specifically applicable to every question which may occur in practical administration. No foresight can anticipate, nor any document of reasonable length contain express provisions for all possible questions. Shall fugitives from labor be surrendered by national or State authority? The Constitution does not expressly say. *May* Congress prohibit slavery in the territories? The Constitution does not expressly say. *Must* Congress protect slavery in the territories? The Constitution does not expressly say.

From questions of this class spring all our constitutional controversies, and we divide upon them into majorities and minorities. If the minority will not acquiesce, the majority must, or the government must cease. There is no other alternative; for continuing the government, is acquiescence on one side or the other. If a minority, in such case, will secede rather than acquiesce, they make a precedent which, in turn, will divide and ruin them; for a minority of their own will secede from them, whenever a majority refuses to be controlled by such minority. For instance, why may not any portion of a new confederacy, a year or two hence, arbitrarily secede again, precisely as portions of the present Union now claim to secede from it. All who cherish disunion sentiments, are now being educated to the exact temper of doing this. Is there such perfect identity of interests among the States to compose a new Union, as to produce harmony only, and prevent renewed secession?

Plainly, the central idea of secession, is the essence of anarchy. A majority, held in restraint by constitutional checks, and limitations, and always changing easily, with deliberate changes of popular opinions and sentiments, is the only true sovereign of a free people. Whoever rejects it, does, of necessity, fly to anarchy or to despotism. Unanimity is impossible; the rule of a minority, as a permanent arrangement, is wholly inadmissible; so that, rejecting the majority principle, anarchy, or despotism in some form, is all that is left.

I do not forget the position assumed by some, that constitutional questions are to be decided by the Supreme Court; nor do I deny that such decisions must be binding in any case, upon the parties to a suit, as to the object of that suit, while they are also entitled to very high respect and consideration, in all paralel cases, by all other departments of the government. And while it is obviously possible that such decision may be erroneous in any given case, still the evil effect following it, being limited to that particular case, with the chance that it may be over-ruled and never become a precedent for other cases, can better be borne than could the evils of a different practice. At the same time the candid citizen must confess that if the policy of the government, upon vital questions, affecting the whole people, is to be irrevocably fixed by decisions of the Supreme Court, the instant they are made, in ordinary litigation between parties, in personal actions, the people will have ceased, to be their own rulers, having, to that extent, practically resigned their government, into the hands of that eminent tribunal. Nor is there, in this view, any assault upon the court, or the judges. It is a duty, from which they may not shrink, to decide cases properly brought before them; and it is no fault of theirs, if others seek to turn their decisions to political purposes.

One section of our country believes slavery is *right*, and ought to be extended, while the other believes it is *wrong*, and ought not to be extended. This is the only substantial dispute. The fugitive-slave clause of the Constitution, and the law for the suppression of the foreign slave trade, are each as well enforced, perhaps, as any law can ever be in a community where the moral sense of the people imperfectly supports the law itself. The great body of the people abide by the dry legal obligation in both cases, and a few break over in each. This, I think, cannot be perfectly cured; and it would be worse in both cases *after* the separation of the sections, than before. The foreign slave trade, now imperfectly suppressed, would be ultimately revived without restriction, in one section; while fugitive slaves, now only partially surrendered, would not be surrendered at all, by the other.

Physically speaking, we cannot separate. We cannot remove our respective sections from each other, nor build an impassable wall between them. A husband and wife may be divorced, and go out of the presence, and beyond the reach of each other; but the different parts of our country cannot do this. They cannot but remain face to face; and intercourse, either amicable or hostile, must continue between them. Is it possible then to make that intercourse more advantageous, or more satisfactory, *after* separation than *before*? Can aliens make treaties easier than friends can make laws? Can treaties be more faithfully enforced between aliens, than laws can among friends? Suppose you go to war, you cannot fight always; and when, after much loss on both sides, and no gain on either, you cease fighting, the identical old questions, as to terms of intercourse, are again upon you.

This country, with its institutions, belongs to the people who inhabit it. Whenever they shall grow weary of the existing government, they can exercise their *constitutional* right of amending it, or their *revolutionary* right to dismember or overthrow it. I cannot be ignorant of the fact that many worthy, and patriotic citizens are desirous of having the national constitution amended. While I make no recommendation of amendments, I fully recognize the rightful authority of the people over the whole subject, to be exercised in either of the modes prescribed in the instrument itself; and I should, under existing circumstances, favor, rather than oppose, a fair opportunity being afforded the people to act upon it.

I will venture to add that, to me, the convention mode seems preferable, in that it allows amendments to originate with the people themselves, instead of only permitting them to take, or reject, propositions, originated by others, not especially chosen for the purpose, and which might not be precisely such, as they would wish to either accept or refuse. I understand a proposed amendment to the Constitution—which amendment, however, I have not seen, has passed Congress, to the effect that the federal government, shall never interfere with the domestic institutions of the States, including that of persons held to service. To avoid misconstruction of what I have said, I depart from my purpose not to speak of particular amendments, so far as to say that, holding such a provision to now be implied constitutional law, I have no objection to its being made express, and irrevocable.

The Chief Magistrate derives all his authority from the people, and they have conferred none upon him to fix terms for the separation of the States. The people themselves can do this also if they choose; but the executive, as such, has nothing to do with it. His duty is to administer the present government, as it came to his hands, and to transmit it, unimpaired by him, to his successor.

Why should there not be a patient confidence in the ultimate justice of the people? Is there any better, or equal hope, in the world? In our present differences, is either party without faith of being in the right? If the Almighty Ruler of Nations, with his eternal truth and justice, be on your side of the North, or on yours of the South, that truth, and that justice, will surely prevail, by the judgment of this great tribunal, the American people.

By the frame of the government under which we live, this same people have wisely given their public servants but little power for mischief; and have, with equal wisdom, provided for the return of that little to their own hands at very short intervals.

While the people retain their virtue, and vigilance, no administration, by any extreme of wickedness or folly, can very seriously injure the government, in the short space of four years.

My countrymen, one and all, think calmly and *well*, upon this whole subject. Nothing valuable can be lost by taking time. If there be an object to *hurry* any of you, in hot haste, to a step which you would never take *deliberately*, that object will be frustrated by taking time; but no good object can be frustrated by it. Such of you as are now dissatisfied, still have the old Constitution unimpaired, and, on the sensitive point, the laws of your own framing under it; while the new administration will have no immediate power, if it would, to change either. If it were admitted that you who are dissatisfied, hold the right side in the dispute, there still is no single good reason for precipitate action. Intelligence, patriotism, Christianity, and a firm reliance on Him, who has never yet forsaken this favored land, are still competent to adjust, in the best way, all our present difficulty.

In *your* hands, my dissatisfied fellow countrymen, and not in *mine*, is the momentous issue of civil war. The government will not assail *you*. You can have no conflict, without being yourselves the aggressors. *You* have no oath registered in Heaven to destroy the government, while *I* shall have the most solemn one to "preserve, protect and defend" it.

I am loth to close. We are not enemies, but friends. We must not be enemies. Though passion may have strained, it must not break our bonds of affection. The mystic chords of memory, stretching from every battle-field, and patriot grave, to every living heart and hearthstone, all over this broad land, will yet swell the chorus of the Union, when again touched, as surely they will be, by the better angels of our nature.

*March 4, 1861*

# Message to Congress in Special Session

Fellow-citizens of the Senate and House of Representatives:

Having been convened on an extraordinary occasion, as authorized by the Constitution, your attention is not called to any ordinary subject of legislation.

At the beginning of the present Presidential term, four months ago, the functions of the Federal Government were found to be generally suspended within the several States of South Carolina, Georgia, Alabama, Mississippi, Louisiana, and Florida, excepting only those of the Post Office Department.

Within these States, all the Forts, Arsenals, Dock-yards, Custom-houses, and the like, including the movable and stationary property in, and about them, had been seized, and were held in open hostility to this Government, excepting only Forts Pickens, Taylor, and Jefferson, on, and near the Florida coast, and Fort Sumter, in Charleston harbor, South Carolina. The Forts thus seized had been put in improved condition; new ones had been built; and armed forces had been organized, and were organizing, all avowedly with the same hostile purpose.

The Forts remaining in the possession of the Federal government, in, and near, these States, were either besieged or menaced by warlike preparations; and especially Fort Sumter was nearly surrounded by well-protected hostile batteries, with guns equal in quality to the best of its own, and outnumbering the latter as perhaps ten to one. A disproportionate share, of the Federal muskets and rifles, had somehow found their way into these States, and had been seized, to be used against the government. Accumulations of the public revenue, lying within them, had been seized for the same object. The Navy was scattered in distant seas; leaving but a very small part of it within the immediate reach of the government. Officers of the Federal Army and Navy, had resigned in great numbers; and, of those resigning, a and large proportion had taken up arms against the government. Simultaneously, and in connection, with all this, the purpose to sever the Federal Union, was openly avowed. In accordance with this purpose, an ordinance had been adopted in each of these States, declaring the States, respectively, to be separated from the National Union. A formula for instituting a combined government of these states had been promulgated; and this illegal organization, in the character of confederate States was already invoking recognition, aid, and intervention, from Foreign Powers.

Finding this condition of things, and believing it to be an imperative duty upon the incoming Executive, to prevent, if possible, the consummation of such attempt to destroy the Federal Union, a choice of means to that end became indispensable. This choice was made; and was declared in the Inaugural address. The policy chosen looked to the exhaustion of all peaceful measures, before a resort to any stronger ones. It sought only to hold the public places and property, not already wrested from the Government, and to collect the revenue; relying for the rest, on time, discussion, and the ballot-box. It promised a continuance of the mails, at government expense, to the very people who were resisting the government; and it gave repeated pledges against any disturbance to any of the people, or any of their rights. Of all that which a president might constitutionally, and justifiably, do in such a case, everything was foreborne, without which, it was believed possible to keep the government on foot.

On the 5th of March, (the present incumbent's first full day in office) a letter of Major Anderson, commanding at Fort Sumter, written on the 28th of February, and received at the War Department on the 4th of March, was, by that Department, placed in his hands. This letter expressed the professional opinion of the writer, that re-inforcements could not be thrown into that Fort within the time for his relief, rendered necessary by the limited supply of provisions, and with a view of holding possession of the same, with a force of less than twenty thousand good, and well-disciplined men. This opinion was concurred in by all the officers of his command; and their *memoranda* on the subject, were made enclosures of Major Anderson's letter. The whole was immediately laid before Lieutenant General Scott, who at once concurred with Major Anderson in opinion. On reflection, however, he took full time, consulting with other officers, both of the Army and the Navy; and, at the end of four days, came reluctantly, but decidedly, to the same conclusion as before. He also stated at the same time that no such sufficient force was then at the control of the Government, or could be raised, and brought to the ground, within the time when the provisions in the Fort would be exhausted. In a purely military point of view, this reduced the duty of the administration, in the case, to the mere matter of getting the garrison safely out of the Fort.

It was believed, however, that to so abandon that position, under the circumstances, would be utterly ruinous; that the *necessity* under which it was to be done, would not be fully understood—that, by many, it would be construed as a part of a *voluntary* policy—that, at home, it would discourage the friends of the Union, embolden its adversaries, and go far to insure to the latter, a recognition abroad— that, in fact, it would be our national destruction consummated. This could not be allowed. Starvation was not yet upon the garrison; and ere it would be reached, *Fort Pickens* might be reinforced. This last, would be a clear indication of *policy*, and would better enable the country to accept the evacuation of Fort Sumter, as a military *necessity.* An order was at once directed to be sent for the landing of the troops from the Steamship Brooklyn, into Fort Pickens. This order could not go by land, but must take the longer, and slower route by sea. The first return news from the order was received just one week before the fall of Fort Sumter. The news itself was, that the officer commanding the Sabine, to which vessel the troops had been transferred from the Brooklyn, acting upon some *quasi* armistice of the late administration, (and of the existence of which, the present administration, up to the time the order was despatched, had only too vague and uncertain rumors, to fix attention) had refused to land the troops. To now re-inforce Fort Pickens, before a crisis would be reached at Fort Sumter was impossible—rendered so by the near exhaustion of provisions in the latter-named Fort. In precaution against such a conjuncture, the government had, a few days before, commenced preparing an expedition, as well adapted as might be, to relieve Fort Sumter, which expedition was intended to be ultimately used, or not, according to circumstances. The strongest anticipated case, for using it, was now presented; and it was resolved to send it forward. As had been intended, in this contingency, it was also resolved to notify the Governor of South Carolina, that he might expect an attempt would be made to provision the Fort; and that, if the attempt should not be resisted, there would be no effort to throw in men, arms, or ammunition, without further notice, or in case of an attack upon the Fort. This notice was accordingly given; whereupon the Fort was attacked, and bombarded to its fall, without even awaiting the arrival of the provisioning expedition.

It is thus seen that the assault upon, and reduction of, Fort Sumter, was, in no sense, a matter of self defence on the part of the assailants. They well knew that the garrison in the Fort could, by no possibility, commit aggression upon them. They knew—they were expressly notified—that the giving of bread to the few brave and hungry men of the garrison, was all which would on that occasion be attempted, unless themselves, by resisting so much, should provoke more. They knew that this Government desired to keep the garrison in the Fort, not to assail them, but merely to maintain visible possession, and thus to preserve the Union from actual, and immediate dissolution—trusting, as herein-before stated, to time, discussion, and the ballot-box, for final adjustment; and they assailed, and reduced the Fort, for precisely the reverse object—to drive out the visible authority of the Federal Union, and thus force it to immediate dissolution.

That this was their object, the Executive well understood; and having said to them in the inaugural address, "You can have no conflict without being yourselves the aggressors," he took pains, not only to keep this declaration good, but also to keep the case so free from the power of ingenious sophistry, as that the world should not be able to misunderstand it. By the affair at Fort Sumter, with its surrounding circumstances, that point was reached. Then, and thereby, the assailants of the Government, began the conflict of arms, without a gun in sight, or in expectancy, to return their fire, save only the few in the Fort, sent to that harbor, years before, for their own protection, and still ready to give that protection, in whatever was lawful. In this act, discarding all else, they have forced upon the country, the distinct issue: "Immediate dissolution, or blood."

And this issue embraces more than the fate of these United States. It presents to the whole family of man, the question, whether a constitutional republic, or a democracy—a government of the people, by the same people—can, or cannot, maintain its territorial integrity, against its own domestic foes. It presents the question, whether discontented individuals, too few in numbers to control administration, according to organic law, in any case, can always, upon the pretences made in this case, or on any other pretences, or arbitrarily, without any pretence, break up their Government, and thus practically put an end to free government upon the earth. It forces us to ask: "Is there, in all republics, this inherent, and fatal weakness?" "Must a government, of necessity, be too *strong* for the liberties of its own people, or too *weak* to maintain its own existence?"

So viewing the issue, no choice was left but to call out the war power of the Government; and so to resist force, employed for its destruction, by force, for its preservation.

The call was made; and the response of the country was most gratifying; surpassing, in unanimity and spirit, the most sanguine expectation. Yet none of the States commonly called Slave-states, except Delaware, gave a Regiment through regular State organization. A few regiments have been organized within some others of those states, by individual enterprise, and received into the government service. Of course the seceded States, so called, (and to which Texas had been joined about the time of the inauguration,) gave no troops to the cause of the Union. The border States, so called, were not uniform in their actions; some of them being almost *for* the Union, while in others—as Virginia, North Carolina, Tennessee, and Arkansas—the Union sentiment was nearly repressed, and silenced. The course taken in Virginia was the most remarkable—perhaps the most important. A convention, elected by the people of that State, to consider this very question of disrupting the Federal Union, was in session at the capital of Virginia when Fort Sumter fell. To this body the people had chosen a large majority of *professed* Union men. Almost immediately after the fall of Sumter, many members of that majority went over to the original disunion minority, and, with them, adopted an ordinance for withdrawing the State from the Union. Whether this change was wrought by their great approval of the assault upon Sumter, or their great resentment at the government's resistance to that assault, is not definitely known. Although they submitted the ordinance, for ratification, to a vote of the people, to be taken on a day then somewhat more than a month distant, the convention, and the Legislature, (which was also in session at the same time and place) with leading men of the State, not members of either, immediately commenced acting, as if the State were already out of the Union. They pushed military preparations vigorously forward all over the state. They seized the United States Armory at Harper's Ferry, and the Navy-yard at Gosport, near Norfolk. They received—perhaps invited—into their state, large bodies of troops, with their warlike appointments, from the so-called seceded States. They formally entered into a treaty of temporary alliance, and co-operation with the so-called "Confederate States," and sent members to their Congress at Montgomery. And, finally, they permitted the insurrectionary government to be transferred to their capital at Richmond.

The people of Virginia have thus allowed this giant insurrection to make its nest within her borders; and this government has no choice left but to deal with it, *where* it finds it. And it has the less regret, as the loyal citizens have, in due form, claimed its protection. Those loyal citizens, this government is bound to recognize, and protect, as being Virginia.

In the border States, so called—in fact, the middle states—there are those who favor a policy which they call "armed neutrality"—that is, an arming of those states to prevent the Union forces passing one way, or the disunion, the other, over their soil. This would be disunion completed. Figuratively speaking, it would be the building of an impassable wall along the line of separation. And yet, not quite an impassable one; for, under the guise of neutrality, it would tie the hands of the Union men, and freely pass supplies from among them, to the insurrectionists, which it could not do as an open enemy. At a stroke, it would take all the trouble off the hands of secession, except only what proceeds from the external blockade. It would do for the disunionists that which, of all things, they most desire—feed them well, and give them disunion without a struggle of their own. It recognizes no fidelity to the Constitution, no obligation to maintain the Union; and while very many who have favored it are, doubtless, loyal citizens, it is, nevertheless, treason in effect.

Recurring to the action of the government, it may be stated that, at first, a call was made for seventy-five thousand militia; and rapidly following this, a proclamation was issued for closing the ports of the insurrectionary districts by proceedings in the nature of Blockade. So far all was believed to be strictly legal.

At this point the insurrectionists announced their purpose to enter upon the practice of privateering.

Other calls were made for volunteers, to serve three years, unless sooner discharged; and also for large additions to the regular Army and Navy. These measures, whether strictly legal or not, were ventured upon, under what appeared to be a popular demand, and a public necessity; trusting, then as now, that Congress would readily ratify them. It is believed that nothing has been done beyond the constitutional competency of Congress.

Soon after the first call for militia, it was considered a duty to authorize the Commanding General, in proper cases, according to his discretion, to suspend the privilege of the writ of habeas corpus; or, in other words, to arrest, and detain, without resort to the ordinary processes and forms of law, such individuals as he might deem dangerous to the public safety. This authority has purposely been exercised but very sparingly. Nevertheless, the legality and propriety of what has been done under it, are questioned; and the attention of the country has been called to the proposition that one who is sworn to "take care that the laws be faithfully executed," should not himself violate them. Of course some consideration was given to the questions of power, and propriety, before this matter was acted upon. The whole of the laws which were required to be faithfully executed, were being resisted, and failing of execution, in nearly one-third of the States. Must they be allowed to finally fail of execution, even had it been perfectly clear, that by the use of the means necessary to their execution, some single law, made in such extreme tenderness of the citizen's liberty, that practically, it relieves more of the guilty, than of the innocent, should, to a very limited extent, be violated? To state the question more directly, are all the laws, *but one*, to go unexecuted, and the government itself go to pieces, lest that one be violated? Even in such a case, would not the official oath be broken, if the government should be overthrown, when it was believed that disregarding the single law, would tend to preserve it? But it was not believed that this question was presented. It was not believed that any law was violated. The provision of the Constitution that "The privilege of the writ of habeas corpus, shall not be suspended unless when, in cases of rebellion or invasion, the public safety may require it," is equivalent to a provision—is a provision—that such privilege may be suspended when, in cases of rebellion, or invasion, the public safety *does* require it. It was decided that we have a case of rebellion, and that the public safety does require the qualified suspension of the privilege of the writ which was authorized to be made. Now it is insisted that Congress, and not the Executive, is vested with this power. But the Constitution itself, is silent as to which, or who, is to exercise the power; and as the provision was plainly made for a dangerous emergency, it cannot be believed the framers of the instrument intended, that in every case, the danger should run its course, until Congress could be called together; the very assembling of which might be prevented, as was intended in this case, by the rebellion.

No more extended argument is now offered; as an opinion, at some length, will probably be presented by the Attorney General. Whether there shall be any legislation upon the subject, and if any, what, is submitted entirely to the better judgment of Congress.

The forbearance of this government had been so extraordinary, and so long continued, as to lead some foreign nations to shape their action as if they supposed the early destruction of our national Union was probable. While this, on discovery, gave the Executive some concern, he is now happy to say that the sovereignty, and rights of the United States, are now everywhere practically respected by foreign powers; and a general sympathy with the country is manifested throughout the world.

The reports of the Secretaries of the Treasury, War, and the Navy, will give the information in detail deemed necessary, and convenient for your deliberation, and action; while the Executive, and all the Departments, will stand ready to supply omissions, or to communicate new facts, considered important for you to know.

It is now recommended that you give the legal means for making this contest a short, and a decisive one; that you place at the control of the government, for the work, at least four hundred thousand men, and four hundred millions of dollars. That number of men is about one tenth of those of proper ages within the regions where, apparently, *all* are willing to engage; and the sum is less than a twentythird part of the money value owned by the men who seem ready to devote the whole. A debt of six hundred millions of dollars *now*, is a less sum per head, than was the debt of our revolution, when we came out of that struggle; and the money value in the country now, bears even a greater proportion to what it was *then*, than does the population. Surely each man has as strong a motive *now*, to *preserve* our liberties, as each had *then*, to *establish* them.

A right result, at this time, will be worth more to the world, than ten times the men, and ten times the money. The evidence reaching us from the country, leaves no doubt, that the material for the work is abundant; and that it needs only the hand of legislation to give it legal sanction, and the hand of the Executive to give it practical shape and efficiency. One of the greatest perplexities of the government, is to avoid receiving troops faster than it can provide for them. In a word, the people will save their government, if the government itself, will do its part, only indifferently well.

It might seem, at first thought, to be of little difference whether the present movement at the South be called "secession" or "rebellion." The movers, however, well understand the difference. At the beginning, they knew they could never raise their treason to any respectable magnitude, by any name which implies *violation* of law. They knew their people possessed as much of moral sense, as much of devotion to law and order, and as much pride in, and reverence for, the history, and government, of their common country, as any other civilized, and patriotic people. They knew they could make no advancement directly in the teeth of these strong and noble sentiments. Accordingly they commenced by an insidious debauching of the public mind. They invented an ingenious sophism, which, if conceded, was followed by perfectly logical steps, through all the incidents, to the complete destruction of the Union. The sophism itself is, that any state of the Union may, *consistently* with the national Constitution, and therefore *lawfully,* and *peacefully,* withdraw from the Union, without the consent of the Union, or of any other state. The little disguise that the supposed right is to be exercised only for just cause, themselves to be the sole judge of its justice, is too thin to merit any notice.

With rebellion thus sugar-coated, they have been drugging the public mind of their section for more than thirty years; and, until at length, they have brought many good men to a willingness to take up arms against the government the day *after* some assemblage of men have enacted the farcical pretence of taking their State out of the Union, who could have been brought to no such thing the day *before*.

This sophism derives much—perhaps the whole—of its currency, from the assumption, that there is some omnipotent, and sacred supremacy, pertaining to a *State*—to each State of our Federal Union. Our States have neither more, nor less power, than that reserved to them, in the Union, by the Constitution—no one of them ever having been a State *out* of the Union. The original ones passed into the Union even *before* they cast off their British colonial dependence; and the new ones each came into the Union directly from a condition of dependence, excepting Texas. And even Texas, in its temporary independence, was never designated a State. The new ones only took the designation of States, on coming into the Union, while that name was first adopted for the old ones, in, and by, the Declaration of Independence. Therein the "United Colonies" were declared to be "Free and Independent States"; but, even then, the object plainly was not to declare their independence of *one another,* or of the *Union*; but directly the contrary, as their mutual pledge, and their mutual action, before, at the time, and afterwards, abundantly show. The express plighting of faith, by each and all of the original thirteen, in the Articles of Confederation, two years later, that the

Union shall be perpetual, is most conclusive. Having never been States, either in substance, or in name, *outside* of the Union, whence this magical omnipotence of "State rights," asserting a claim of power to lawfully destroy the Union itself? Much is said about the "sovereignty" of the States; but the word, even, is not in the national Constitution; nor, as is believed, in any of the State constitutions. What is a "sovereignty," in the political sense of the term? Would it be far wrong to define it "A political community, without a political superior"? Tested by this, no one of our States, except Texas, ever was a sovereignty. And even Texas gave up the character on coming into the Union; by which act, she acknowledged the Constitution of the United States, and the laws and treaties of the United States made in pursuance of the Constitution, to be, for her, the supreme law of the land. The States have their *status* IN the Union, and they have no other *legal status*. If they break from this, they can only do so against law, and by revolution. The Union, and not themselves separately, procured their independence, and their liberty. By conquest, or purchase, the Union gave each of them, whatever of independence, and liberty, it has. The Union is older than any of the States; and, in fact, it created them as States. Originally, some dependent colonies made the Union; and, in turn, the Union threw off their old dependence, for them, and made them States, such as they are. Not one of them ever had a State constitution, independent of the Union. Of course, it is not forgotten that all the new States framed their constitutions, before they entered the Union; nevertheless, dependent upon, and preparatory to, coming into the Union.

Unquestionably the States have the powers, and rights, reserved to them in, and by the National Constitution; but among these, surely, are not included all conceivable powers, however mischievous, or destructive; but, at most, such only, as were known in the world, at the time, as governmental powers; and certainly, a power to destroy the government itself, had never been known as a governmental—as a merely administrative power. This relative matter of National power, and State rights, as a principle, is no other than the principle of *generality*, and *locality*. Whatever concerns the whole, should be confided to the whole—to the general government; while, whatever concerns *only* the State, should be left exclusively, to the State. This is all there is of original principle about it. Whether the National Constitution, in defining boundaries between the two, has applied the principle with exact accuracy, is not to be questioned. We are all bound by that defining, without question.

What is now combatted, is the position that secession is *consistent* with the Constitution—is *lawful*, and *peaceful*. It is not contended that there is any express law for it; and nothing should ever be implied as law, which leads to unjust, or absurd consequences. The nation purchased, with money, the countries out of which several of these States were formed. Is it just that they shall go off without leave, and without refunding? The nation paid very large sums, (in the aggregate, I believe, nearly a hundred millions) to relieve Florida of the aboriginal tribes. Is it just that she shall now be off without consent, or without making any return? The nation is now in debt for money applied to the benefit of these so-called seceding States, in common with the rest. Is it just, either that creditors shall go unpaid, or the remaining States pay the whole? A part of the present national debt was contracted to pay the old debts of Texas. Is it just that she shall leave, and pay no part of this herself?

Again, if one State may secede, so may another; and when all shall have seceded, none is left to pay the debts. Is this quite just to creditors? Did we notify them of this sage view of ours, when we borrowed their money? If we now recognize this doctrine, by allowing the seceders to go in peace, it is difficult to see what we can do, if others choose to go, or to extort terms upon which they will promise to remain.

The seceders insist that our Constitution admits of secession. They have assumed to make a National Constitution of their own, in which, of necessity, they have either *discarded,* or *retained,* the right of secession, as they insist, it exists in ours. If they have discarded it, they thereby admit that, on principle, it ought not to be in ours. If they have retained it, by their own construction of ours they show that to be consistent they must secede from one another, whenever they shall find it the easiest way of settling their debts, or effecting any other selfish, or unjust object. The principle itself is one of disintegration, and upon which no government can possibly endure.

If all the States, save one, should assert the power to *drive* that one out of the Union, it is presumed the whole class of seceder politicians would at once deny the power, and denounce the act as the greatest outrage upon State rights. But suppose that precisely the same act, instead of being called "driving the one out," should be called "the seceding of the others from that one," it would be exactly what the seceders claim to do; unless, indeed, they make the point, that the one, because it is a minority, may rightfully do, what the others, because they are a majority, may not rightfully do. These politicians are subtle, and profound, on the rights of minorities. They are not partial to that power which made the Constitution, and speaks from the preamble, calling itself "We, the People."

It may well be questioned whether there is, to-day, a majority of the legally qualified voters of any State, except perhaps South Carolina, in favor of disunion. There is much reason to believe that the Union men are the majority in many, if not in every other one, of the so-called seceded States. The contrary has not been demonstrated in any one of them. It is ventured to affirm this, even of Virginia and Tennessee; for the result of an election, held in military camps, where the bayonets are all on one side of the question voted upon, can scarcely be considered as demonstrating popular sentiment. At such an election, all that large class who are, at once, *for* the Union, and *against* coercion, would be coerced to vote against the Union.

It may be affirmed, without extravagance, that the free institutions we enjoy, have developed the powers, and improved the condition, of our whole people, beyond any example in the world. Of this we now have a striking, and an impressive illustration. So large an army as the government has now on foot, was never before known, without a soldier in it, but who had taken his place there, of his own free choice. But more than this: there are many single Regiments whose members, one and another, possess full practical knowledge of all the arts, sciences, professions, and whatever else, whether useful or elegant, is known in the world; and there is scarcely one, from which there could not be selected, a President, a Cabinet, a Congress, and perhaps a Court, abundantly competent to administer the government itself. Nor do I say this is not true, also, in the army of our late friends, now adversaries, in this contest; but if it is, so much better the reason why the government, which has conferred such benefits on both them and us, should not be broken up. Whoever, in any section, proposes to abandon such a government, would do well to consider, in deference to what principle it is, that he does it—what better he is likely to get in its stead—whether the substitute will give, or be intended to give, so much of good to the people. There are some foreshadowings on this subject. Our adversaries have adopted some Declarations of Independence; in which, unlike the good old one, penned by Jefferson, they omit the words "all men are created equal." Why? They have adopted a temporary national constitution, in the preamble of which, unlike our good old one, signed by Washington, they omit "We, the People," and substitute "We, the deputies of the sovereign and independent States." Why? Why this deliberate pressing out of view, the rights of men, and the authority of the people?

This is essentially a People's contest. On the side of the Union, it is a struggle for maintaining in the world, that form, and substance of government, whose leading object is, to elevate the condition of men—to lift artificial weights from all shoulders—to clear the paths of laudable pursuit for all—to afford all, an unfettered start, and a fair chance, in the race of life. Yielding to partial, and temporary departures, from necessity, this is the leading object of the government for whose existence we contend.

I am most happy to believe that the plain people understand, and appreciate this. It is worthy of note, that while in this, the government's hour of trial, large numbers of those in the Army and Navy, who have been favored with the offices, have resigned, and proved false to the hand which had pampered them, not one common soldier, or common sailor is known to have deserted his flag.

Great honor is due to those officers who remain true, despite the example of their treacherous associates; but the greatest honor, and most important fact of all, is the unanimous firmness of the common soldiers, and common sailors. To the last man, so far as known, they have successfully resisted the traitorous efforts of those, whose commands, but an hour before, they obeyed as absolute law. This is the patriotic instinct of the plain people. They understand, without an argument, that destroying the government, which was made by Washington, means no good to them.

Our popular government has often been called an experiment. Two points in it, our people have already settled—the successful *establishing*, and the successful *administering* of it. One still remains—its successful *maintenance* against a formidable internal attempt to overthrow it. It is now for them to demonstrate to the world, that those who can fairly carry an election, can also suppress a rebellion—that ballots are the rightful, and peaceful, successors of bullets; and that when ballots have fairly, and constitutionally, decided, there can be no successful appeal, back to bullets; that there can be no successful appeal, except to ballots themselves, at succeeding elections. Such will be a great lesson of peace; teaching men that what they cannot take by an election, neither can they take it by a war—teaching all, the folly of being the beginners of a war.

Lest there be some uneasiness in the minds of candid men, as to what is to be the course of the government, towards the Southern States, *after* the rebellion shall have been suppressed, the Executive deems it proper to say, it will be his purpose then, as ever, to be guided by the Constitution, and the laws; and that he probably will have no different understanding of the powers, and duties of the Federal government, relatively to the rights of the States, and the people, under the Constitution, than that expressed in the inaugural address.

He desires to preserve the government, that it may be administered for all, as it was administered by the men who made it. Loyal citizens everywhere, have the right to claim this of their government; and the government has no right to withhold, or neglect it. It is not perceived that, in giving it, there is any coercion, any conquest, or any subjugation, in any just sense of those terms.

The Constitution provides, and all the States have accepted the provision, that "The United States shall guarantee to every State in this Union a republican form of government." But, if a State may lawfully go out of the Union, having done so, it may also discard the republican form of government; so that to prevent its going out, is an indispensable *means,* to the end, of maintaining the guaranty mentioned; and when an *end* is lawful and obligatory, the indispensable means to it, are also lawful, and obligatory.

It was with the deepest regret that the Executive found the duty of employing the war-power, in defence of the government, forced upon him. He could but perform this duty, or surrender the existence of the government. No compromise, by public servants, could, in this case, be a cure; not that compromises are not often proper, but that no popular government can long survive a marked precedent, that those who carry an election, can only save the government from immediate destruction, by giving up the main point, upon which the people gave the election. The people themselves, and not their servants, can safely reverse their own deliberate decisions. As a private citizen, the Executive could not have consented that these institutions shall perish; much less could he, in betrayal of so vast, and so sacred a trust, as these free people had confided to him. He felt that he had no moral right to shrink; nor even to count the chances of his own life, in what might follow. In full view of his great responsibility, he has, so far, done what he has deemed his duty. You will now, according to your own judgment, perform yours. He sincerely hopes that your views, and your action, may so accord with his, as to assure all faithful citizens, who have been disturbed in their rights, of a certain, and speedy restoration to them, under the Constitution, and the laws.

And having thus chosen our course, without guile, and with pure purpose, let us renew our trust in God, and go forward without fear, and with manly hearts.

*July 4, 1861*

# Annual Message to Congress, 1861

Fellow Citizens of the Senate and House of Representatives:

In the midst of unprecedented political troubles, we have cause of great gratitude to God for unusual good health, and most abundant harvests.

You will not be surprised to learn that, in the peculiar exigencies of the times, our intercourse with foreign nations has been attended with profound solicitude, chiefly turning upon our own domestic affairs.

A disloyal portion of the American people have, during the whole year, been engaged in an attempt to divide and destroy the Union. A nation which endures factious domestic division, is exposed to disrespect abroad; and one party, if not both, is sure, sooner or later, to invoke foreign intervention.

Nations, thus tempted to interfere, are not always able to resist the counsels of seeming expediency, and ungenerous ambition, although measures adopted under such influences seldom fail to be unfortunate and injurious to those adopting them.

The disloyal citizens of the United States who have offered the ruin of our country, in return for the aid and comfort which they have invoked abroad, have received less patronage and encouragement than they probably expected. If it were just to suppose, as the insurgents have seemed to assume, that foreign nations, in this case, discarding all moral, social, and treaty obligations, would act solely, and selfishly, for the most speedy restoration of commerce, including, especially, the acquisition of cotton, those nations appear, as yet, not to have seen their way to their object more directly, or clearly, through the destruction, than through the preservation, of the Union. If we could dare to believe that foreign nations are actuated by no higher principle than this, I am quite sure a sound argument could be made to show them that they can reach their aim more readily, and easily, by aiding to crush this rebellion, than by giving encouragement to it.

The principal lever relied on by the insurgents for exciting foreign nations to hostility against us, as already intimated, is the embarrassment of commerce. Those nations, however, not improbably, saw from the first, that it was the Union which made as well our foreign, as our domestic, commerce. They can scarcely have failed to perceive that the effort for disunion produces the existing difficulty; and that one strong nation promises more durable peace, and a more extensive, valuable and reliable commerce, than can the same nation broken into hostile fragments.

It is not my purpose to review our discussions with foreign states, because whatever might be their wishes, or dispositions, the integrity of our country, and the stability of our government, mainly depend, not upon them, but on the loyalty, virtue, patriotism, and intelligence of the American people. The correspondence itself, with the usual reservations, is herewith submitted.

I venture to hope it will appear that we have practiced prudence, and liberality towards foreign powers, averting causes of irritation; and, with firmness, maintaining our own rights and honor.

Since, however, it is apparent that here, as in every other state, foreign dangers necessarily attend domestic difficulties, I recommend that adequate and ample measures be adopted for maintaining the public defences on every side. While, under this general recommendation, provision for defending our sea-coast line readily occurs to the mind, I also, in the same connexion, ask the attention of Congress to our great lakes and rivers. It is believed that some fortifications and depots of arms and munitions, with harbor and navigation improvements, all at well selected points upon these, would be of great importance to the national defence and preservation. I ask attention to the views of the Secretary of War, expressed in his report, upon the same general subject.

I deem it of importance that the loyal regions of East Tennessee and western North Carolina should be connected with Kentucky, and other faithful parts of the Union, by railroad. I therefore recommend, as a military measure, that Congress provide for the construction of such road, as speedily as possible. Kentucky, no doubt, will co-operate, and, through her legislature, make the most judicious selection of a line. The northern terminus must connect with some existing railroad; and whether the route shall be from Lexington, or Nicholasville, to the Cumberland Gap; or from Lebanon to the Tennessee line, in the direction of Knoxville; or on some still different line, can easily be determined. Kentucky and the general government co-operating, the work can be completed in a very short time; and when done, it will be not only of vast present usefulness, but also a valuable permanent improvement, worth its cost in all the future.

Some treaties, designed chiefly for the interests of commerce, and having no grave political importance, have been negotiated, and will be submitted to the Senate for their consideration.

Although we have failed to induce some of the commercial powers to adopt a desirable melioration of the rigor of maritime war, we have removed all obstructions from the way of this humane reform, except such as are merely of temporary and accidental occurrence.

I invite your attention to the correspondence between her Britannic Majesty's minister accredited to this government, and the Secretary of State, relative to the detention of the British ship Perthshire in June last, by the United States steamer Massachusetts, for a supposed breach of the blockade. As this detention was occasioned by an obvious misapprehension of the facts, and as justice requires that we should commit no belligerent act not founded in strict right, as sanctioned by public law, I recommend that an appropriation be made to satisfy the reasonable demand of the owners of the vessel for her detention.

I repeat the recommendation of my predecessor, in his annual message to Congress in December last, in regard to the disposition of the surplus which will probably remain after satisfying the claims of American citizens against China, pursuant to the awards of the commissioners under the act of the 3rd of March, 1859. If, however, it should not be deemed advisable to carry that recommendation into effect, I would suggest that authority be given for investing the principal, over the proceeds of the surplus referred to, in good securities, with a view to the satisfaction of such other just claims of our citizens against China as are not unlikely to arise hereafter in the course of our extensive trade with that Empire.

By the act of the 5th of August last, Congress authorized the President to instruct the commanders of suitable vessels to defend themselves against, and to capture pirates. This authority has been exercised in a single instance only. For the more effectual protection of our extensive and valuable commerce, in the eastern seas especially, it seems to me that it would also be advisable to authorize the commanders of sailing vessels to re-capture any prizes which pirates might make of United States vessels and their cargoes, and the consular courts, now established by law in eastern countries, to adjudicate the cases, in the event that this should not be objected to by the local authorities.

If any good reason exists why we should persevere longer in withholding our recognition of the independence and sovereignty of Hayti and Liberia, I am unable to discern it. Unwilling, however, to inaugurate a novel policy in regard to them without the approbation of Congress, I submit for your consideration the expediency of an appropriation for maintaining a chargé d'affaires near each of those new states. It does not admit of doubt that important commercial advantages might be secured by favorable commercial treaties with them.

The operations of the treasury during the period which has elapsed since your adjournment have been conducted with signal success. The patriotism of the people has placed at the disposal of the government the large means demanded by the public exigencies. Much of the national loan has been taken by citizens of the industrial classes, whose confidence in their country's faith, and zeal for their country's deliverance from present peril, have induced them to contribute to the support of the government the whole of their limited acquisitions. This fact imposes peculiar obligations to economy in disbursement and energy in action.

The revenue from all sources, including loans, for the financial year ending on the 30th June, 1861, was eighty six million, eight hundred and thirty five thousand, nine hundred dollars, and twenty seven cents, ($86,835,900.27,) and the expenditures for the same period, including payments on account of the public debt, were eighty four million, five hundred and seventy eight thousand, eight hundred and thirty four dollars and forty seven cents, ($84,578,834.47;) leaving a balance in the treasury, on the 1st July, of two million, two hundred and fifty seven thousand, sixty five dollars and eighty cents, ($2,257,065.80.) For the first quarter of the financial year, ending on the 30th September, 1861, the receipts from all sources, including the balance of first of July, were $102,532,509.27, and the expenses $98,239,733.09; leaving a balance on the 1st of October, 1861, of $4,292,776.18.

Estimates for the remaining three quarters of the year, and for the financial year 1863, together with his views of ways and means for meeting the demands contemplated by them, will be submitted to Congress by the Secretary of the Treasury. It is gratifying to know that the expenditures made necessary by the rebellion are not beyond the resources of the loyal people, and to believe that the same patriotism which has thus far sustained the government will continue to sustain it till Peace and Union shall again bless the land.

I respectfully refer to the report of the Secretary of War for information respecting the numerical strength of the army, and for recommendations having in view an increase of its efficiency and the well being of the various branches of the service intrusted to his care. It is gratifying to know that the patriotism of the people has proved equal to the occasion, and that the number of troops tendered greatly exceeds the force which Congress authorized me to call into the field.

I refer with pleasure to those portions of his report which make allusion to the creditable degree of discipline already attained by our troops, and to the excellent sanitary condition of the entire army.

The recommendation of the Secretary for an organization of the militia upon a uniform basis, is a subject of vital importance to the future safety of the country, and is commended to the serious attention of Congress.

The large addition to the regular army, in connexion with the defection that has so considerably diminished the number of its officers, gives peculiar importance to his recommendation for increasing the corps of cadets to the greatest capacity of the Military Academy.

By mere omission, I presume, Congress has failed to provide chaplains for hospitals occupied by volunteers. This subject was brought to my notice, and I was induced to draw up the form of a letter, one copy of which, properly addressed, has been delivered to each of the persons, and at the dates respectively named and stated, in a schedule, containing also the form of the letter, marked A, and herewith transmitted.

These gentlemen, I understand, entered upon the duties designated, at the times respectively stated in the schedule, and have labored faithfully therein ever since. I therefore recommend that they be compensated at the same rate as chaplains in the army. I further suggest that general provision be made for chaplains to serve at hospitals, as well as with regiments.

The report of the Secretary of the Navy presents in detail the operations of that branch of the service, the activity and energy which have characterized its administration, and the results of measures to increase its efficiency and power. Such have been the additions, by construction and purchase, that it may almost be said a navy has been created and brought into service since our difficulties commenced.

Besides blockading our extensive coast, squadrons larger than ever before assembled under our flag have been put afloat and performed deeds which have increased our naval renown.

I would invite special attention to the recommendation of the Secretary for a more perfect organization of the navy by introducing additional grades in the service.

The present organization is defective and unsatisfactory, and the suggestions submitted by the department will, it is believed, if adopted, obviate the difficulties alluded to, promote harmony, and increase the efficiency of the navy.

There are three vacancies on the bench of the Supreme Court—two by the decease of Justices Daniel and McLean, and one by the resignation of Justice Campbell. I have so far forborne making nominations to fill these vacancies for reasons which I will now state. Two of the outgoing judges resided within the States now overrun by revolt; so that if successors were appointed in the same localities, they could not now serve upon their circuits; and many of the most competent men there, probably would not take the personal hazard of accepting to serve, even here, upon the supreme bench. I have been unwilling to throw all the appointments northward, thus disabling myself from doing justice to the south on the return of peace; although I may remark that to transfer to the north one which has heretofore been in the south, would not, with reference to territory and population, be unjust.

During the long and brilliant judicial career of Judge McLean his circuit grew into an empire—altogether too large for any one judge to give the courts therein more than a nominal attendance—rising in population from one million four hundred and seventy-thousand and eighteen, in 1830, to six million one hundred and fifty-one thousand four hundred and five, in 1860.

Besides this, the country generally has outgrown our present judicial system. If uniformity was at all intended, the system requires that all the States shall be accommodated with circuit courts, attended by supreme judges, while, in fact, Wisconsin, Minnesota, Iowa, Kansas, Florida, Texas, California, and Oregon, have never had any such courts. Nor can this well be remedied without a change of the system; because the adding of judges to the Supreme Court, enough for the accommodation of all parts of the country, with circuit courts, would create a court altogether too numerous for a judicial body of any sort. And the evil, if it be one, will increase as new States come into the Union. Circuit courts are useful, or they are not useful. If useful, no State should be denied them; if not useful, no State should have them. Let them be provided for all, or abolished as to all.

Three modifications occur to me, either of which, I think, would be an improvement upon our present system. Let the Supreme Court be of convenient number in every event. Then, first, let the whole country be divided into circuits of convenient size, the supreme judges to serve in a number of them corresponding to their own number, and independent circuit judges be provided for all the rest. Or, secondly, let the supreme judges be relieved from circuit duties, and circuit judges provided for all the circuits. Or, thirdly, dispense with circuit courts altogether, leaving the judicial functions wholly to the district courts and an independent Supreme Court.

I respectfully recommend to the consideration of Congress the present condition of the statute laws, with the hope that Congress will be able to find an easy remedy for many of the inconveniences and evils which constantly embarrass those engaged in the practical administration of them. Since the organization of the government, Congress has enacted some five thousand acts and joint resolutions, which fill more than six thousand closely printed pages, and are scattered through many volumes. Many of these acts have been drawn in haste and without sufficient caution, so that their provisions are often obscure in themselves, or in conflict with each other, or at least so doubtful as to render it very difficult for even the best informed persons to ascertain precisely what the statute law really is.

It seems to me very important that the statute laws should be made as plain and intelligible as possible, and be reduced to as small a compass as may consist with the fullness and precision of the will of the legislature and the perspicuity of its language. This, well done, would, I think, greatly facilitate the labors of those whose duty it is to assist in the administration of the laws, and would be a lasting benefit to the people, by placing before them, in a more accessible and intelligible form, the laws which so deeply concern their interests and their duties.

I am informed by some whose opinions I respect, that all the acts of Congress now in force, and of a permanent and general nature, might be revised and re-written, so as to be embraced in one volume (or at most, two volumes) of ordinary and convenient size. And I respectfully recommend to Congress to consider of the subject, and, if my suggestion be approved, to devise such plan as to their wisdom shall seem most proper for the attainment of the end proposed.

One of the unavoidable consequences of the present insurrection is the entire suppression, in many places, of all the ordinary means of administering civil justice by the officers and in the forms of existing law. This is the case, in whole or in part, in all the insurgent States; and as our armies advance upon and take possession of parts of those States, the practical evil becomes more apparent. There are no courts nor officers to whom the citizens of other States may apply for the enforcement of their lawful claims against citizens of the insurgent States; and there is a vast amount of debt constituting such claims. Some have estimated it as high as two hundred million dollars, due, in large part, from insurgents, in open rebellion, to loyal citizens who are, even now, making great sacrifices in the discharge of their patriotic duty to support the government.

Under these circumstances, I have been urgently solicited to establish, by military power, courts to administer summary justice in such cases. I have thus far declined to do it, not because I had any doubt that the end proposed—the collection of the debts—was just and right in itself, but because I have been unwilling to go beyond the pressure of necessity in the unusual exercise of power. But the powers of Congress I suppose are equal to the anomalous occasion, and therefore I refer the whole matter to Congress, with the hope that a plan may be devised for the administration of justice in all such parts of the insurgent States and Territories as may be under the control of this government, whether by a voluntary return to allegiance and order or by the power of our arms. This, however, not to be a permanent institution, but a temporary substitute, and to cease as soon as the ordinary courts can be re-established in peace.

It is important that some more convenient means should be provided, if possible, for the adjustment of claims against the government, especially in view of their increased number by reason of the war. It is as much the duty of government to render prompt justice against itself, in favor of citizens, as it is to administer the same, between private individuals. The investigation and adjudication of claims, in their nature belong to the judicial department; besides it is apparent that the attention of Congress, will be more than usually engaged, for some time to come, with great national questions. It was intended, by the organization of the court of claims, mainly to remove this branch of business from the halls of Congress; but while the court has proved to be an effective, and valuable means of investigation, it in great degree fails to effect the object of its creation, for want of power to make its judgments final.

Fully aware of the delicacy, not to say the danger, of the subject, I commend to your careful consideration whether this power of making judgments final, may not properly be given to the court, reserving the right of appeal on questions of law to the Supreme Court, with such other provisions as experience may have shown to be necessary.

I ask attention to the report of the Postmaster General, the following being a summary statement of the condition of the department:

The revenue from all sources during the fiscal year ending June 30, 1861, including the annual permanent appropriation of seven hundred thousand dollars ($700,000) for the transportation of "free mail matter," was nine million, forty nine thousand, two hundred and ninety six dollars and forty cents ($9,049,296.40) being about two per cent. less than the revenue for 1860.

The expenditures were thirteen million, six hundred and six thousand, seven hundred and fifty nine dollars and eleven cents. ($13,606,759.11) showing a decrease of more than eight per cent. as compared with those of the previous year, and leaving an excess of expenditure over the revenue for the last fiscal year of four million, five hundred and fifty seven thousand, four hundred and sixty two dollars and seventy one cents ($4,557,462.71.)

The gross revenue for the year ending June 30, 1863, is estimated at an increase of four per cent. on that of 1861, making eight million, six hundred and eighty three thousand dollars ($8,683,000) to which should be added the earnings of the department in carrying free matter, viz: seven hundred thousand dollars ($700,000.) making nine million, three hundred and eighty three thousand dollars, ($9,383,000.)

The total expenditures for 1863 are estimated at $12,528,000, leaving an estimated deficiency of $3,145,000, to be supplied from the treasury, in addition to the permanent appropriation.

The present insurrection shows, I think, that the extension of this District across the Potomac river, at the time of establishing the capital here, was eminently wise, and consequently that the relinquishment of that portion of it which lies within the State of Virginia was unwise and dangerous. I submit for your consideration the expediency of regaining that part of the District, and the restoration of the original boundaries thereof, through negotiations with the State of Virginia.

The report of the Secretary of the Interior, with the accompanying documents, exhibits the condition of the several branches of the public business pertaining to that department. The depressing influences of the insurrection have been especially felt in the operations of the Patent and General Land Offices. The cash receipts from the sales of public lands during the past year have exceeded the expenses of our land system only about $200,000. The sales have been entirely suspended in the southern States, while the interruptions to the business of the country, and the diversion of large numbers of men from labor to military service, have obstructed settlements in the new States and Territories of the northwest.

The receipts of the Patent Office have declined in nine months about $100,000, rendering a large reduction of the force employed necessary to make it self sustaining.

The demands upon the Pension Office will be largely increased by the insurrection. Numerous applications for pensions, based upon the casualties of the existing war, have already been made. There is reason to believe that many who are now upon the pension rolls and in receipt of the bounty of the government, are in the ranks of the insurgent army, or giving them aid and comfort. The Secretary of the Interior has directed a suspension of the payment of the pensions of such persons upon proof of their disloyalty. I recommend that Congress authorize that officer to cause the names of such persons to be stricken from the pension rolls.

The relations of the government with the Indian tribes have been greatly disturbed by the insurrection, especially in the southern superintendency and in that of New Mexico. The Indian country south of Kansas is in the possession of insurgents from Texas and Arkansas. The agents of the United States appointed since the 4th. of March for this superintendency have been unable to reach their posts, while the most of those who were in office before that time have espoused the insurrectionary cause, and assume to exercise the powers of agents by virtue of commissions from the insurrectionists. It has been stated in the public press that a portion of those Indians have been organized as a military force, and are attached to the army of the insurgents. Although the government has no official information upon this subject, letters have been written to the Commissioner of Indian Affairs by several prominent chiefs, giving assurance of their loyalty to the United States, and expressing a wish for the presence of federal troops to protect them. It is believed that upon the repossession of the country by the federal forces the Indians will readily cease all hostile demonstrations, and resume their former relations to the government.

Agriculture, confessedly the largest interest of the nation, has, not a department, nor a bureau, but a clerkship only, assigned to it in the government. While it is fortunate that this great interest is so independent in its nature as to not have demanded and extorted more from the government, I respectfully ask Congress to consider whether something more cannot be given voluntarily with general advantage.

Annual reports exhibiting the condition of our agriculture, commerce, and manufactures would present a fund of information of great practical value to the country. While I make no suggestion as to details, I venture the opinion that an agricultural and statistical bureau might profitably be organized.

The execution of the laws for the suppression of the African slave trade, has been confided to the Department of the Interior. It is a subject of gratulation that the efforts which have been made for the suppression of this inhuman traffic, have been recently attended with unusual success. Five vessels being fitted out for the slave trade have been seized and condemned. Two mates of vessels engaged in the trade, and one person in equipping a vessel as a slaver, have been convicted and subjected to the penalty of fine and imprisonment, and one captain, taken with a cargo of Africans on board his vessel, has been convicted of the highest grade of offence under our laws, the punishment of which is death.

The Territories of Colorado, Dakotah and Nevada, created by the last Congress, have been organized, and civil administration has been inaugurated therein under auspices especially gratifying, when it is considered that the leaven of treason was found existing in some of these new countries when the federal officers arrived there.

The abundant natural resources of these Territories, with the security and protection afforded by organized government, will doubtless invite to them a large immigration when peace shall restore the business of the country to its accustomed channels. I submit the resolutions of the legislature of Colorado, which evidence the patriotic spirit of the people of the Territory. So far the authority of the United States has been upheld in all the Territories, as it is hoped it will be in the future. I commend their interests and defence to the enlightened and generous care of Congress.

I recommend to the favorable consideration of Congress the interests of the District of Columbia. The insurrection has been the cause of much suffering and sacrifice to its inhabitants, and as they have no representative in Congress, that body should not overlook their just claims upon the government.

At your late session a joint resolution was adopted authorizing the President to take measures for facilitating a proper representation of the industrial interests of the United States at the exhibition of the industry of all nations to be holden at

London in the year 1862. I regret to say I have been unable to give personal attention to this subject,—a subject at once so interesting in itself, and so extensively and intimately connected with the material prosperity of the world. Through the Secretaries of State and of the Interior a plan, or system, has been devised, and partly matured, and which will be laid before you.

Under and by virtue of the act of Congress entitled "An act to confiscate property used for insurrectionary purposes," approved August, 6, 1861, the legal claims of certain persons to the labor and service of certain other persons have become forfeited; and numbers of the latter, thus liberated, are already dependent on the United States, and must be provided for in some way. Besides this, it is not impossible that some of the States will pass similar enactments for their own benefit respectively, and by operation of which persons of the same class will be thrown upon them for disposal. In such case I recommend that Congress provide for accepting such persons from such States, according to some mode of valuation, in lieu, *pro tanto*, of direct taxes, or upon some other plan to be agreed on with such States respectively; that such persons, on such acceptance by the general government, be at once deemed free; and that, in any event, steps be taken for colonizing both classes, (or the one first mentioned, if the other shall not be brought into existence,) at some place, or places, in a climate congenial to them. It might be well to consider, too,—whether the free colored people already in the United States could not, so far as individuals may desire, be included in such colonization.

To carry out the plan of colonization may involve the acquiring of territory, and also the appropriation of money beyond that to be expended in the territorial acquisition. Having practiced the acquisition of territory for nearly sixty years, the question of constitutional power to do so is no longer an open one with us. The power was questioned at first by Mr. Jefferson, who, however, in the purchase of Louisiana, yielded his scruples on the plea of great expediency. If it be said that the only legitimate object of acquiring territory is to furnish homes for white men, this measure effects that object; for the emigration of colored men leaves additional room for white men remaining or coming here. Mr. Jefferson, however, placed the importance of procuring Louisiana more on political and commercial grounds than on providing room for population.

On this whole proposition,—including the appropriation of money with the acquisition of territory, does not the expediency amount to absolute necessity— that, without which the government itself cannot be perpetuated? The war continues. In considering the policy to be adopted for suppressing the insurrection, I have been anxious and careful that the inevitable conflict for this purpose shall not degenerate into a violent and remorseless revolutionary struggle. I have, therefore, in every case, thought it proper to keep the integrity of the Union prominent as the primary object of the contest on our part, leaving all questions which are not of vital military importance to the more deliberate action of the legislature.

In the exercise of my best discretion I have adhered to the blockade of the ports held by the insurgents, instead of putting in force, by proclamation, the law of Congress enacted at the late session, for closing those ports.

So, also, obeying the dictates of prudence, as well as the obligations of law, instead of transcending, I have adhered to the act of Congress to confiscate property used for insurrectionary purposes. If a new law upon the same subject shall be proposed, its propriety will be duly considered.

The Union must be preserved, and hence, all indispensable means must be employed. We should not be in haste to determine that radical and extreme measures, which may reach the loyal as well as the disloyal, are indispensable.

The inaugural address at the beginning of the Administration, and the message to Congress at the late special session, were both mainly devoted to the domestic controversy out of which the insurrection and consequent war have sprung. Nothing now occurs to add or subtract, to or from, the principles or general purposes stated and expressed in those documents.

The last ray of hope for preserving the Union peaceably, expired at the assault upon Fort Sumter; and a general review of what has occurred since may not be unprofitable. What was painfully uncertain then, is much better defined and more distinct now; and the progress of events is plainly in the right direction. The insurgents confidently claimed a strong support from north of Mason and Dixon's line; and the friends of the Union were not free from apprehension on the point. This, however, was soon settled definitely and on the right side. South of the line, noble little Delaware led off right from the first. Maryland was made to *seem* against the Union. Our soldiers were assaulted, bridges were burned, and railroads torn up, within her limits; and we were many days, at one time, without the ability to bring a single regiment over her soil to the capital. Now, her bridges and railroads are repaired and open to the government; she already gives seven regiments to the cause of the Union and none to the enemy; and her people, at a regular election, have sustained the Union, by a larger majority, and a larger aggregate vote than they ever before gave to any candidate, or any question. Kentucky, too, for some time in doubt, is now decidedly, and, I think, unchangeably, ranged on the side of the Union. Missouri is comparatively quiet; and I believe cannot again be overrun by the insurrectionists. These three States of Maryland, Kentucky, and Missouri, neither of which would promise a single soldier at first, have now an aggregate of not less than forty thousand in the field, for the Union; while, of their citizens, certainly not more than a third of that number, and they of doubtful whereabouts, and doubtful existence, are in arms against it. After a somewhat bloody struggle of months, winter closes on the Union people of western Virginia, leaving them masters of their own country.

An insurgent force of about fifteen hundred, for months dominating the narrow peninsular region, constituting the counties of Accomac and Northampton, and known as eastern shore of Virginia, together with some contiguous parts of Maryland, have laid down their arms; and the people there have renewed their allegiance to, and accepted the protection of, the old flag. This leaves no armed insurrectionist north of the Potomac, or east of the Chesapeake.

Also we have obtained a footing at each of the isolated points, on the southern coast, of Hatteras, Port Royal, Tybee Island, near Savannah, and Ship Island; and we likewise have some general accounts of popular movements, in behalf of the Union, in North Carolina and Tennessee.

These things demonstrate that the cause of the Union is advancing steadily and certainly southward.

Since your last adjournment, Lieutenant General Scott has retired from the head of the army. During his long life, the nation has not been unmindful of his merit; yet, on calling to mind how faithfully, ably and brilliantly he has served the country, from a time far back in our history, when few of the now living had been born, and thenceforward continually, I cannot but think we are still his debtors. I submit, therefore, for your consideration, what further mark of recognition is due to him, and to ourselves, as a grateful people.

With the retirement of General Scott came the executive duty of appointing, in his stead, a general-in-chief of the army. It is a fortunate circumstance that neither in council nor country was there, so far as I know, any difference of opinion as to the proper person to be selected. The retiring chief repeatedly expressed his judgment in favor of General McClellan for the position; and in this the nation seemed to give a unanimous concurrence. The designation of General McClellan is therefore in considerable degree, the selection of the Country as well as of the Executive; and hence there is better reason to hope there will be given him, the confidence, and cordial support thus, by fair implication, promised, and without which, he cannot, with so full efficiency, serve the country.

It has been said that one bad general is better than two good ones; and the saying is true, if taken to mean no more than that an army is better directed by a single mind, though inferior, than by two superior ones, at variance, and cross-purposes with each other.

And the same is true, in all joint operations wherein those engaged, *can* have none but a common end in view, and *can* differ only as to the choice of means. In a storm at sea, no one on board *can* wish the ship to sink; and yet, not unfrequently, all go down together, because too many will direct, and no single mind can be allowed to control.

It continues to develop that the insurrection is largely, if not exclusively, a war upon the first principle of popular government—the rights of the people. Conclusive evidence of this is found in the most grave and maturely considered public documents, as well as in the general tone of the insurgents. In those documents we find the abridgement of the existing right of suffrage and the denial to the people of all right to participate in the selection of public officers, except the legislative boldly advocated, with labored arguments to prove that large control of the people in government, is the source of all political evil. Monarchy itself is sometimes hinted at as a possible refuge from the power of the people.

In my present position, I could scarcely be justified were I to omit raising a warning voice against this approach of returning despotism.

It is not needed, nor fitting here, that a general argument should be made in favor of popular institutions; but there is one point, with its connexions, not so hackneyed as most others, to which I ask a brief attention. It is the effort to place *capital* on an equal footing with, if not above *labor,* in the structure of government. It is assumed that labor is available only in connexion with capital; that nobody labors unless somebody else, owning capital, somehow by the use of it, induces him to labor. This assumed, it is next considered whether it is best that capital shall *hire* laborers, and thus induce them to work by their own consent, or *buy* them, and drive them to it without their consent. Having proceeded so far, it is naturally concluded that all laborers are either *hired* laborers, or what we call slaves. And further it is assumed that whoever is once a hired laborer, is fixed in that condition for life.

Now, there is no such relation between capital and labor as assumed; nor is there any such thing as a free man being fixed for life in the condition of a hired laborer. Both these assumptions are false, and all inferences from them are groundless.

Labor is prior to, and independent of, capital. Capital is only the fruit of labor, and could never have existed if labor had not first existed. Labor is the superior of capital, and deserves much the higher consideration. Capital has its rights, which are as worthy of protection as any other rights. Nor is it denied that there is, and probably always will be, a relation between labor and capital, producing mutual benefits. The error is in assuming that the whole labor of community exists within that relation. A few men own capital, and that few avoid labor themselves, and, with their capital, hire or buy another few to labor for them. A large majority belong to neither class—neither work for others, nor have others working for them. In most of the southern States, a majority of the whole people of all colors are neither slaves nor masters; while in the northern a large majority are neither hirers nor hired. Men with their families—wives, sons, and daughters—work for themselves, on their farms, in their houses, and in their shops, taking the whole product to themselves, and asking no favors of capital on the one hand, nor of hired laborers or slaves on the other. It is not forgotten that a considerable number of persons mingle their own labor with capital—that is, they labor with their own hands, and also buy or hire others to labor for them; but this is only a mixed, and not a distinct class. No principle stated is disturbed by the existence of this mixed class.

Again: as has already been said, there is not, of necessity, any such thing as the free hired laborer being fixed to that condition for life. Many independent men everywhere in these States, a few years back in their lives, were hired laborers. The prudent, penniless beginner in the world, labors for wages awhile, saves a surplus with which to buy tools or land for himself; then labors on his own account another while, and at length hires another new beginner to help him. This is the just, and generous, and prosperous system, which opens the way to all—gives hope to all, and consequent energy, and progress, and improvement of condition to all. No men living are more worthy to be trusted than those who toil up from poverty—none less inclined to take, or touch, aught which they have not honestly earned. Let them beware of surrendering a political power which they already possess, and which, if surrendered, will surely be used to close the door of advancement against such as they, and to fix new disabilities and burdens upon them, till all of liberty shall be lost.

From the first taking of our national census to the last are seventy years; and we find our population at the end of the period eight times as great as it was at the beginning. The increase of those other things which men deem desirable has been even greater. We thus have at one view, what the popular principle applied to government, through the machinery of the States and the Union, has produced in a given time; and also what, if firmly maintained, it promises for the future. There are already among us those, who, if the Union be preserved, will live to see it contain two hundred and fifty millions. The struggle of today, is not altogether for today—it is for a vast future also. With a reliance on Providence, all the more firm and earnest, let us proceed in the great task which events have devolved upon us.

*December 3, 1861*

# Message to Congress

Fellow-citizens of the Senate, and House of Representatives,

I recommend the adoption of a Joint Resolution by your honorable bodies which shall be substantially as follows:

"Resolved that the United States ought to co-operate with any state which may adopt gradual abolishment of slavery, giving to such state pecuniary aid, to be used by such state in it's discretion, to compensate for the inconveniences public and private, produced by such change of system"

If the proposition contained in the resolution does not meet the approval of Congress and the country, there is the end; but if it does command such approval, I deem it of importance that the states and people immediately interested, should be at once distinctly notified of the fact, so that they may begin to consider whether to accept or reject it. The federal government would find it's highest interest in such a measure, as one of the most efficient means of self-preservation. The leaders of the existing insurrection entertain the hope that this government will ultimately be forced to acknowledge the independence of some part of the disaffected region, and that all the slave states North of such part will then say "the Union, for which we have struggled, being already gone, we now choose to go with the Southern section." To deprive them of this hope, substantially ends the rebellion; and the initiation of emancipation completely deprives them of it, as to all the states initiating it. The point is not that *all* the states tolerating slavery would very soon, if at all, initiate emancipation; but that, while the offer is equally made to all, the more Northern shall, by such initiation, make it certain to the more Southern, that in no event, will the former ever join the latter, in their proposed confederacy. I say "initiation" because, in my judgment, gradual, and not sudden emancipation, is better for all. In the mere financial, or pecuniary view, any member of Congress, with the census-tables and Treasury-reports before him, can readily see for himself how very soon the current expenditures of this war would purchase, at fair valuation, all the slaves in any named State. Such a proposition, on the part of the general government, sets up no claim of a right, by federal authority, to interfere with slavery within state limits, referring, as it does, the absolute control of the subject, in each case, to the state and it's people, immediately interested. It is proposed as a matter of perfectly free choice with them.

In the annual message last December, I thought fit to say "The Union must be preserved; and hence all indispensable means must be employed." I said this, not hastily, but deliberately. War has been made, and continues to be, an indispensable means to this end. A practical re-acknowledgement of the national authority would render the war unnecessary, and it would at once cease. If, however, resistance continues, the war must also continue; and it is impossible to foresee all the incidents, which may attend and all the ruin which may follow it. Such as may seem indispensable, or may obviously promise great efficiency towards ending the struggle, must and will come.

The proposition now made, though an offer only, I hope it may be esteemed no offence to ask whether the pecuniary consideration tendered would not be of more value to the States and private persons concerned, than are the institution, and property in it, in the present aspect of affairs.

While it is true that the adoption of the proposed resolution would be merely initiatory, and not within itself a practical measure, it is recommended in the hope that it would soon lead to important practical results. In full view of my great responsibility to my God, and to my country, I earnestly beg the attention of Congress and the people to the subject.

*March 6, 1862*

# Annual Message to Congress, 1862

Fellow-citizens of the Senate and House of Representatives:

Since your last annual assembling another year of health and bountiful harvests has passed. And while it has not pleased the Almighty to bless us with a return of peace, we can but press on, guided by the best light He gives us, trusting that in His own good time, and wise way, all will yet be well.

The correspondence touching foreign affairs which has taken place during the last year is herewith submitted, in virtual compliance with a request to that effect, made by the House of Representatives near the close of the last session of Congress.

If the condition of our relations with other nations is less gratifying than it has usually been at former periods, it is certainly more satisfactory than a nation so unhappily distracted as we are, might reasonably have apprehended. In the month of June last there were some grounds to expect that the maritime powers which, at the beginning of our domestic difficulties, so unwisely and unnecessarily, as we think, recognized the insurgents as a belligerent, would soon recede from that position, which has proved only less injurious to themselves, than to our own country. But the temporary reverses which afterwards befell the national arms, and which were exaggerated by our own disloyal citizens abroad have hitherto delayed that act of simple justice.

The civil war, which has so radically changed for the moment, the occupations and habits of the American people, has necessarily disturbed the social condition, and affected very deeply the prosperity of the nations with which we have carried on a commerce that has been steadily increasing throughout a period of half a century. It has, at the same time, excited political ambitions and apprehensions which have produced a profound agitation throughout the civilized world. In this unusual agitation we have forborne from taking part in any controversy between foreign states, and between parties or factions in such states. We have attempted no propagandism, and acknowledged no revolution. But we have left to every nation the exclusive conduct and management of its own affairs. Our struggle has been, of course, contemplated by foreign nations with reference less to its own merits, than to its supposed, and often exaggerated effects and consequences resulting to those nations themselves. Nevertheless, complaint on the part of this government, even if it were just, would certainly be unwise.

The treaty with Great Britain for the suppression of the slave trade has been put into operation with a good prospect of complete success. It is an occasion of special pleasure to acknowledge that the execution of it, on the part of Her Majesty's government, has been marked with a jealous respect for the authority of the United States, and the rights of their moral and loyal citizens.

The convention with Hanover for the abolition of the stade dues has been carried into full effect, under the act of Congress for that purpose.

A blockade of three thousand miles of sea-coast could not be established, and vigorously enforced, in a season of great commercial activity like the present, without committing occasional mistakes, and inflicting unintentional injuries upon foreign nations and their subjects.

A civil war occurring in a country where foreigners reside and carry on trade under treaty stipulations, is necessarily fruitful of complaints of the violation of neutral rights. All such collisions tend to excite misapprehensions, and possibly to produce mutual reclamations between nations which have a common interest in preserving peace and friendship. In clear cases of these kinds I have, so far as possible, heard and redressed complaints which have been presented by friendly powers. There is still, however, a large and an augmenting number of doubtful cases upon which the government is unable to agree with the governments whose protection is demanded by the claimants. There are, moreover, many cases in which the United States, or their citizens, suffer wrongs from the naval or military authorities of foreign nations, which the governments of those states are not at once prepared to redress. I have proposed to some of the foreign states, thus interested, mutual conventions to examine and adjust such complaints. This proposition has been made especially to Great Britain, to France, to Spain, and to Prussia. In each case it has been kindly received, but has not yet been formally adopted.

I deem it my duty to recommend an appropriation in behalf of the owners of the Norwegian bark Admiral P. Tordenskiold, which vessel was, in May, 1861, prevented by the commander of the blockading force off Charleston from leaving that port with cargo, notwithstanding a similar privilege had, shortly before, been granted to an English vessel. I have directed the Secretary of State to cause the papers in the case to be communicated to the proper committees.

Applications have been made to me by many free Americans of African descent to favor their emigration, with a view to such colonization as was contemplated in recent acts of Congress. Other parties, at home and abroad—some from interested motives, others upon patriotic considerations, and still others influenced by philanthropic sentiments—have suggested similar measures; while, on the other hand, several of the Spanish-American republics have protested against the sending of such colonies to their respective territories. Under these circumstances, I have declined to move any such colony to any state, without first obtaining the consent of its government, with an agreement on its part to receive and protect such emigrants in all the rights of freemen; and I have, at the same time, offered to the several states situated within the tropics, or having colonies there, to negotiate with them, subject to the advice and consent of the Senate, to favor the voluntary emigration of persons of that class to their respective territories, upon conditions which shall be equal, just, and humane. Liberia and Hayti are, as yet, the only countries to which colonists of African descent from here, could go with certainty of being received and adopted as citizens; and I regret to say such persons, contemplating colonization, do not seem so willing to migrate to those countries, as to some others, nor so willing as I think their interest demands. I believe, however, opinion among them, in this respect, is improving; and that, ere long, there will be an augmented, and considerable migration to both these countries, from the United States.

The new commercial treaty between the United States and the Sultan of Turkey has been carried into execution.

A commercial and consular treaty has been negotiated, subject to the Senate's consent, with Liberia; and a similar negotiation is now pending with the republic of Hayti. A considerable improvement of the national commerce is expected to result from these measures.

Our relations with Great Britain, France, Spain, Portugal, Russia, Prussia, Denmark, Sweden, Austria, the Netherlands, Italy, Rome, and the other European states, remain undisturbed. Very favorable relations also continue to be maintained with Turkey, Morocco, China and Japan.

During the last year there has not only been no change of our previous relations with the independent states of our own continent, but, more friendly sentiments than have heretofore existed, are believed to be entertained by these neighbors, whose safety and progress, are so intimately connected with our own. This statement especially applies to Mexico, Nicaragua, Costa Rica, Honduras, Peru, and Chile.

The commission under the convention with the republic of New Granada closed its session, without having audited and passed upon, all the claims which were submitted to it. A proposition is pending to revive the convention, that it may be able to do more complete justice. The joint commission between the United States and the republic of Costa Rica has completed its labors and submitted its report.

I have favored the project for connecting the United States with Europe by an Atlantic telegraph, and a similar project to extend the telegraph from San Francisco, to connect by a Pacific telegraph with the line which is being extended across the Russian empire.

The Territories of the United States, with unimportant exceptions, have remained undisturbed by the civil war, and they are exhibiting such evidence of prosperity as justifies an expectation that some of them will soon be in a condition to be organized as States, and be constitutionally admitted into the federal Union.

The immense mineral resources of some of those Territories ought to be developed as rapidly as possible. Every step in that direction would have a tendency to improve the revenues of the government, and diminish the burdens of the people. It is worthy of your serious consideration whether some extraordinary measures to promote that end cannot be adopted. The means which suggests itself as most likely to be effective, is a scientific exploration of the mineral regions in those Territories, with a view to the publication of its results at home and in foreign countries—results which cannot fail to be auspicious.

The condition of the finances will claim your most diligent consideration. The vast expenditures incident to the military and naval operations required for the suppression of the rebellion, have hitherto been met with a promptitude, and certainty, unusual in similar circumstances, and the public credit has been fully maintained. The continuance of the war, however, and the increased disbursements made necessary by the augmented forces now in the field, demand your best reflections as to the best modes of providing the necessary revenue, without injury to business and with the least possible burdens upon labor.

The suspension of specie payments by the banks, soon after the commencement of your last session, made large issues of United States notes unavoidable. In no other way could the payment of the troops, and the satisfaction of other just demands, be so economically, or so well provided for. The judicious legislation of Congress, securing the receivability of these notes for loans and internal duties, and making them a legal tender for other debts, has made them an universal currency; and has satisfied, partially, at least, and for the time, the long felt want of an uniform circulating medium, saving thereby to the people, immense sums in discounts and exchanges.

A return to specie payments, however, at the earliest period compatible with due regard to all interests concerned, should ever be kept in view. Fluctuations in the value of currency are always injurious, and to reduce these fluctuations to the lowest possible point will always be a leading purpose in wise legislation. Convertibility, prompt and certain convertibility into coin, is generally acknowledged to be the best and surest safeguard against them; and it is extremely doubtful whether a circulation of United States notes, payable in coin, and sufficiently large for the wants of the people, can be permanently, usefully and safely maintained.

Is there, then, any other mode in which the necessary provision for the public wants can be made, and the great advantages of a safe and uniform currency secured?

I know of none which promises so certain results, and is, at the same time, so unobjectionable, as the organization of banking associations, under a general act of Congress, well guarded in its provisions. To such associations the government might furnish circulating notes, on the security of United States bonds deposited in the treasury. These notes, prepared under the supervision of proper officers, being uniform in appearance and security, and convertible always into coin, would at once protect labor against the evils of a vicious currency, and facilitate commerce by cheap and safe exchanges.

A moderate reservation from the interest on the bonds would compensate the United States for the preparation and distribution of the notes and a general supervision of the system, and would lighten the burden of that part of the public debt employed as securities. The public credit, moreover, would be greatly improved, and the negotiation of new loans greatly facilitated by the steady market demand for government bonds which the adoption of the proposed system would create.

It is an additional recommendation of the measure, of considerable weight, in my judgment, that it would reconcile, as far as possible, all existing interests, by the opportunity offered to existing institutions to reorganize under the act, substituting only the secured uniform national circulation for the local and various circulation, secured and unsecured, now issued by them.

The receipts into the treasury from all sources, including loans and balance from the preceding year, for the fiscal year ending on the 30th June, 1862, were $583,885,247.06, of which sum $49,056,397.62 were derived from customs; $1,795,331.73 from the direct tax; from public lands $152,203.77; from miscellaneous sources, $931,787.64; from loans in all forms, $529,692,460.50. The remainder, $2,257,065.80, was the balance from last year.

The disbursements during the same period were for congressional, executive, and judicial purposes, $5,939,009.29; for foreign intercourse, $1,339,710.35; for miscellaneous expenses, including the mints, loans, post office deficiencies, collection of revenue, and other like charges, $14,129,771.50; for expenses under the Interior Department, $3,102,985.52; under the War Department, $394,368,407.36; under the Navy Department, $42,674,569.69; for interest on public debt, $13,190,324.45; and for payment of public debt, including reimbursement of temporary loan, and redemptions, $96,096,922.09; making an aggregate of $570,841,700.25; and leaving a balance in the treasury on the first day of July, 1862, of $13,043,546.81.

It should be observed that the sum of $96,096,922.09, expended for reimbursements and redemption of public debt, being included also in the loans made, may be properly deducted, both from receipts and expenditures, leaving the actual receipts for the year $487,788,324.97; and the expenditures, $474,744,778.16.

Other information on the subject of the finances will be found in the report of the Secretary of the Treasury, to whose statements and views I invite your most candid and considerate attention.

The reports of the Secretaries of War, and of the Navy, are herewith transmitted. These reports, though lengthy, are scarcely more than brief abstracts of the very numerous and extensive transactions and operations conducted through those departments. Nor could I give a summary of them here, upon any principle, which would admit of its being much shorter than the reports themselves. I therefore content myself with laying the reports before you, and asking your attention to them.

It gives me pleasure to report a decided improvement in the financial condition of the Post Office Department, as compared with several preceding years. The receipts for the fiscal year 1861 amounted to $8,349,296.40, which embraced the revenue from all the States of the Union for three quarters of that year. Notwithstanding the cessation of revenue from the so-called seceded States during the last fiscal year, the increase of the correspondence of the loyal States has been sufficient to produce a revenue during the same year of $8,299,820.90, being only $50,000 less than was derived from all the States of the Union during the previous year. The expenditures show a still more favorable result. The amount expended in 1861 was $13,606,759.11. For the last year the amount has been reduced to $11,125,364.13, showing a decrease of about $2,481,000 in the expenditures as compared with the preceding year and about $3,750,000 as compared with the fiscal year 1860. The deficiency in the department for the previous year was $4,551,966.98. For the last fiscal year it was reduced to $2,112,814.57. These favorable results are in part owing to the cessation of mail service in the insurrectionary States, and in part to a careful review of all expenditures in that department in the interest of economy. The efficiency of the postal service, it is believed, has also been much improved. The Postmaster General has also opened a correspondence, through the Department of State, with foreign governments, proposing a convention of postal representatives for the purpose of simplifying the rates of foreign postage, and to expedite the foreign mails. This proposition, equally important to our adopted citizens, and to the commercial interests of this country, has been favorably entertained, and agreed to, by all the governments from whom replies have been received.

I ask the attention of Congress to the suggestions of the Postmaster General in his report respecting the further legislation required, in his opinion, for the benefit of the postal service.

The Secretary of the Interior reports as follows in regard to the public lands:

"The public lands have ceased to be a source of revenue. From the 1st July, 1861, to the 30th September, 1862, the entire cash receipts from the sale of lands were $137,476.26—a sum much less than the expenses of our land system during the same period. The homestead law, which will take effect on the 1st of January next, offers such inducements to settlers, that sales for cash cannot be expected, to an extent sufficient to meet the expenses of the General Land Office, and the cost of surveying and bringing the land into market."

The discrepancy between the sum here stated as arising from the sales of the public lands, and the sum derived from the same source as reported from the Treasury Department arises, as I understand, from the fact that the periods of time, though apparently, were not really, coincident at the beginning point—the Treasury report including a considerable sum now, which had previously been reported from the Interior—sufficiently large to greatly overreach the sum derived from the three months now reported upon by the Interior, and not by the Treasury.

The Indian tribes upon our frontiers have, during the past year, manifested a spirit of insubordination, and, at several points, have engaged in open hostilities against the white settlements in their vicinity. The tribes occupying the Indian country south of Kansas, renounced their allegiance to the United States, and entered into treaties with the insurgents. Those who remained loyal to the United States were driven from the country. The chief of the Cherokees has visited this city for the purpose of restoring the former relations of the tribe with the United States. He alleges that they were constrained, by superior force, to enter into treaties with the insurgents, and that the United States neglected to furnish the protection which their treaty stipulations required.

In the month of August last the Sioux Indians, in Minnesota, attacked the settlements in their vicinity with extreme ferocity, killing, indiscriminately, men, women, and children. This attack was wholly unexpected, and, therefore, no means of defence had been provided. It is estimated that not less than eight hundred persons were killed by the Indians, and a large amount of property was destroyed. How this outbreak was induced is not definitely known, and suspicions, which may be unjust, need not to be stated. Information was received by the Indian bureau, from different sources, about the time hostilities were commenced, that a simultaneous attack was to be made upon the white settlements by all the tribes between the Mississippi river and the Rocky mountains. The State of Minnesota has suffered great injury from this Indian war. A large portion of her territory has been depopulated, and a severe loss has been sustained by the destruction of property. The people of that State manifest much anxiety for the removal of the tribes beyond the limits of the State as a guarantee against future hostilities. The Commissioner of Indian Affairs will furnish full details. I submit for your especial consideration whether our Indian system shall not be remodelled. Many wise and good men have impressed me with the belief that this can be profitably done.

I submit a statement of the proceedings of commissioners, which shows the progress that has been made in the enterprise of constructing the Pacific railroad. And this suggests the earliest completion of this road, and also the favorable action of Congress upon the projects now pending before them for enlarging the capacities of the great canals in New York and Illinois, as being of vital, and rapidly increasing importance to the whole nation, and especially to the vast interior region hereinafter to be noticed at some greater length. I purpose having prepared and laid before you at an early day some interesting and valuable statistical information upon this subject. The military and commercial importance of enlarging the Illinois and Michigan canal, and improving the Illinois river, is presented in the report of Colonel Webster to the Secretary of War, and now transmitted to Congress. I respectfully ask attention to it.

To carry out the provisions of the act of Congress of the 15th of May last, I have caused the Department of Agriculture of the United States to be organized.

The Commissioner informs me that within the period of a few months this department has established an extensive system of correspondence and exchanges, both at home and abroad, which promises to effect highly beneficial results in the development of a correct knowledge of recent improvements in agriculture, in the introduction of new products, and in the collection of the agricultural statistics of the different States.

Also that it will soon be prepared to distribute largely seeds, cereals, plants and cuttings, and has already published, and liberally diffused, much valuable information in anticipation of a more elaborate report, which will in due time be furnished, embracing some valuable tests in chemical science now in progress in the laboratory.

The creation of this department was for the more immediate benefit of a large class of our most valuable citizens; and I trust that the liberal basis upon which it has been organized will not only meet your approbation, but that it will realize, at no distant day, all the fondest anticipations of its most sanguine friends, and become the fruitful source of advantage to all our people.

On the twenty-second day of September last a proclamation was issued by the Executive, a copy of which is herewith submitted.

In accordance with the purpose expressed in the second paragraph of that paper, I now respectfully recall your attention to what may be called "compensated emancipation."

A nation may be said to consist of its territory, its people, and its laws. The territory is the only part which is of certain durability. "One generation passeth away, and another generation cometh, but the earth abideth forever." It is of the first importance to duly consider, and estimate, this ever-enduring part. That portion of the earth's surface which is owned and inhabited by the people of the United States, is well adapted to be the home of one national family; and it is not well adapted for two, or more. Its vast extent, and its variety of climate and productions, are of advantage, in this age, for one people, whatever they might have been in former ages. Steam, telegraphs, and intelligence, have brought these, to be an advantageous combination, for one united people.

In the inaugural address I briefly pointed out the total inadequacy of disunion, as a remedy for the differences between the people of the two sections. I did so in language which I cannot improve, and which, therefore, I beg to repeat:

"One section of our country believes slavery is *right*, and ought to be extended, while the other believes it is *wrong,* and ought not to be extended. This is the only substantial dispute. The fugitive slave clause of the Constitution, and the law for the suppression of the foreign slave trade, are each as well enforced, perhaps, as any law can ever be in a community where the moral sense of the people imperfectly supports the law itself. The great body of the people abide by the dry legal obligation in both cases, and a few break over in each. This, I think, cannot be perfectly cured; and it would be worse in both cases *after* the separation of the sections, than before. The foreign slave trade, now imperfectly suppressed, would be ultimately revived without restriction in one section; while fugitive slaves, now only partially surrendered, would not be surrendered at all by the other.

"Physically speaking, we cannot separate. We cannot remove our respective sections from each other, nor build an impassable wall between them. A husband and wife may be divorced, and out of the presence, and beyond the reach of each other; but the different parts of our country cannot do this. They cannot but remain face to face; and intercourse, either amicable or hostile, must continue between them. Is it possible, then, to make that intercourse more advantageous, or more satisfactory, *after* separation than *before*? Can aliens make treaties, easier than friends can make laws? Can treaties be more faithfully enforced between aliens, than laws can among friends? Suppose you go to war, you cannot fight always; and when, after much loss on both sides, and no gain on either, you cease fighting, the identical old questions, as to terms of intercourse, are again upon you."

There is no line, straight or crooked, suitable for a national boundary, upon which to divide. Trace through, from east to west, upon the line between the free and slave country, and we shall find a little more than one-third of its length are rivers, easy to be crossed, and populated, or soon to be populated, thickly upon both sides; while nearly all its remaining length, are merely surveyor's lines, over which people may walk back and forth without any consciousness of their presence. No part of this line can be made any more difficult to pass, by writing it down on paper, or parchment, as a national boundary. The fact of separation, if it comes, gives up, on the part of the seceding section, the fugitive slave clause, along with all other constitutional obligations upon the section seceded from, while I should expect no treaty stipulation would ever be made to take its place.

But there is another difficulty. The great interior region, bounded east by the Alleghanies, north by the British dominions, west by the Rocky mountains, and south by the line along which the culture of corn and cotton meets, and which includes part of Virginia, part of Tennessee, all of Kentucky, Ohio, Indiana, Michigan, Wisconsin, Illinois, Missouri, Kansas, Iowa, Minnesota and the Territories of Dakota, Nebraska, and part of Colorado, already has above ten millions of people, and will have fifty millions within fifty years, if not prevented by any political folly or mistake. It contains more than one-third of the country owned by the United States—certainly more than one million of square miles. Once half as populous as Massachusetts already is, it would have more than seventy-five millions of people. A glance at the map shows that, territorially speaking, it is the great body of the republic. The other parts are but marginal borders to it, the magnificent region sloping west from the rocky mountains to the Pacific, being the deepest, and also the richest, in undeveloped resources. In the production of provisions, grains, grasses, and all which proceed from them, this great interior region is naturally one of the most important in the world. Ascertain from the statistics the small proportion of the region which has, as yet, been brought into cultivation, and also the large and rapidly increasing amount of its products, and we shall be overwhelmed with the magnitude of the prospect presented. And yet this region has no sea-coast, touches no ocean anywhere. As part of one nation, its people now find, and may forever find, their way to Europe by New York, to South America and Africa by New Orleans, and to Asia by San

Francisco. But separate our common country into two nations, as designed by the present rebellion, and every man of this great interior region is thereby cut off from some one or more of these outlets, not, perhaps, by a physical barrier, but by embarrassing and onerous trade regulations.

And this is true, *wherever* a dividing, or boundary line, may be fixed. Place it between the now free and slave country, or place it south of Kentucky, or north of Ohio, and still the truth remains, that none south of it, can trade to any port or place north of it, and none north of it, can trade to any port or place south of it, except upon terms dictated by a government foreign to them. These outlets, east, west, and south, are indispensable to the well-being of the people inhabiting, and to inhabit, this vast interior region. *Which* of the three may be the best, is no proper question. All, are better than either, and all, of right, belong to that people, and to their successors forever. True to themselves, they will not ask *where* a line of separation shall be, but will vow, rather, that there shall be no such line. Nor are the marginal regions less interested in these communications to, and through them, to the great outside world. They too, and each of them, must have access to this Egypt of the West, without paying toll at the crossing of any national boundary.

Our national strife springs not from our permanent part; not from the land we inhabit; not from our national homestead. There is no possible severing of this, but would multiply, and not mitigate, evils among us. In all its adaptations and aptitudes, it demands union, and abhors separation. In fact, it would, ere long, force reunion, however much of blood and treasure the separation might have cost.

Our strife pertains to ourselves—to the passing generations of men; and it can, without convulsion, be hushed forever with the passing of one generation.

In this view, I recommend the adoption of the following resolution and articles amendatory to the Constitution of the United States:

*"Resolved by the Senate and House of Representatives of the United States of America in Congress assembled,* (two thirds of both houses concurring,) That the following articles be proposed to the legislatures (or conventions) of the several States as amendments to the Constitution of the United States, all or any of which articles when ratified by three-fourths of the said legislatures (or conventions) to be valid as part or parts of the said Constitution, viz:

"Article —.

"Every State, wherein slavery now exists, which shall abolish the same therein, at any time, or times, before the first day of January, in the year of our Lord one thousand and nine hundred, shall receive compensation from the United States as follows, to wit:

"The President of the United States shall deliver to every such State, bonds of the United States, bearing interest at the rate of —— per cent, per annum, to an amount equal to the aggregate sum of ⎯⎯⎯ for each slave shown to have been therein, by the eighth census of the United States, said bonds to be delivered to such State by instalments, or in one parcel, at the completion of the abolishment, accordingly as the same shall have been gradual, or at one time, within such State; and interest shall begin to run upon any such bond, only from the proper time of its delivery as aforesaid. Any State having received bonds as aforesaid, and afterwards reintroducing or tolerating slavery therein, shall refund to the United States the bonds so received, or the value thereof, and all interest paid thereon.

"Article —.

"All slaves who shall have enjoyed actual freedom by the chances of the war, at any time before the end of the rebellion, shall be forever free; but all owners of such, who shall not have been disloyal, shall be compensated for them, at the same rates as is provided for States adopting abolishment of slavery, but in such way, that no slave shall be twice accounted for.

"Article —.

"Congress may appropriate money, and otherwise provide, for colonizing free colored persons, with their own consent, at any place or places without the United States."

I beg indulgence to discuss these proposed articles at some length. Without slavery the rebellion could never have existed; without slavery it could not continue.

Among the friends of the Union there is great diversity, of sentiment, and of policy, in regard to slavery, and the African race amongst us. Some would perpetuate slavery; some would abolish it suddenly, and without compensation; some would abolish it gradually, and with compensation; some would remove the freed people from us, and some would retain them with us; and there are yet other minor diversities. Because of these diversities, we waste much strength in struggles among ourselves. By mutual concession we should harmonize, and act together. This would be compromise; but it would be compromise among the friends, and not with the enemies of the Union. These articles are intended to embody a plan of such mutual concessions. If the plan shall be adopted, it is assumed that emancipation will follow, at least, in several of the States.

As to the first article, the main points are: first, the emancipation; secondly, the length of time for consummating it—thirty-seven years; and thirdly, the compensation.

The emancipation will be unsatisfactory to the advocates of perpetual slavery; but the length of time should greatly mitigate their dissatisfaction. The time spares both races from the evils of sudden derangement—in fact, from the necessity of any derangement—while most of those whose habitual course of thought will be disturbed by the measure will have passed away before its consummation. They will never see it. Another class will hail the prospect of emancipation, but will deprecate the length of time. They will feel that it gives too little to the now living slaves. But it really gives them much. It saves them from the vagrant destitution which must largely attend immediate emancipation in localities where their numbers are very great; and it gives the inspiring assurance that their posterity shall be free forever. The plan leaves to each State, choosing to act under it, to abolish slavery now, or at the end of the century, or at any intermediate time, or by degrees, extending over the whole or any part of the period; and it obliges no two states to proceed alike. It also provides for compensation, and generally the mode of making it. This, it would seem, must further mitigate the dissatisfaction of those who favor perpetual slavery, and especially of those who are to receive the compensation. Doubtless some of those who are to pay, and not to receive will object. Yet the measure is both just and economical. In a certain sense the liberation of slaves is the destruction of property—property acquired by descent, or by purchase, the same as any other property. It is no less true for having been often said, that the people of the south are not more responsible for the original introduction of this property, than are the people of the north; and when it is remembered how unhesitatingly we all use cotton and sugar, and share the profits of dealing in them, it may not be quite safe to say, that the south has been more responsible than the north for its continuance. If then, for a common object, this property is to be sacrificed is it not just that it be done at a common charge?

And if, with less money, or money more easily paid, we can preserve the benefits of the Union by this means, than we can by the war alone, is it not also economical to do it? Let us consider it then. Let us ascertain the sum we have expended in the war since compensated emancipation was proposed last March, and consider whether, if that measure had been promptly accepted, by even some of the slave States, the same sum would not have done more to close the war, than has been otherwise done. If so the measure would save money, and, in that view, would be a prudent and economical measure. Certainly it is not so easy to pay *something* as it is to pay *nothing*; but it is easier to pay a *large* sum than it is to pay a larger one. And it is easier to pay any sum *when* we are able, than it is to pay it *before* we are able. The war requires large sums, and requires them at once. The aggregate sum necessary for compensated emancipation, of course, would be large. But it would require no ready cash; nor the bonds even, any faster than the emancipation progresses. This might not, and probably would not, close before the end of the thirty-seven years. At that time we shall probably have a hundred millions of people to share the burden, instead of thirty one millions, as now. And not only so, but the increase of our population may be expected to continue for a long time after that period, as rapidly as before; because our territory will not have become full. I do not state this inconsiderately. At the same ratio of increase which we have maintained, on an average, from our first national census, in 1790, until that of 1860, we should, in 1900, have a population of 103,208,415. And why may we not continue that ratio far beyond that period? Our abundant room—our broad national homestead—is our ample resource. Were our territory as limited as are the British Isles, very certainly our population could not expand as stated. Instead of receiving the foreign born, as now, we should be compelled to send part of the native born away. But such is not our condition. We have two millions nine hundred and sixty-three thousand square miles. Europe has three millions and eight hundred thousand, with a population averaging seventy-three and one-third persons to the square mile. Why may not our country, at some time, average as many? Is it less fertile? Has it more waste surface, by mountains, rivers, lakes, deserts, or other causes? Is it inferior to Europe in any natural advantage? If, then, we are, at some time, to be as populous as Europe, how soon? As to when this *may* be, we can judge by the past and the present; as to when it *will* be, if ever, depends much on whether we maintain the Union. Several of our States are already above the average of Europe—seventy three and a third to the square mile. Massachusetts has 157; Rhode Island, 133; Connecticut, 99; New York and New Jersey, each, 80; also two other great States, Pennsylvania and Ohio, are not far below, the former having 63, and the latter 59. The States already above the European average, except New York, have increased in as rapid a ratio, since passing that point, as ever before; while no one of them is equal to some other parts of our country, in natural capacity for sustaining a dense population.

Taking the nation in the aggregate, and we find its population and ratio of increase, for the several decennial periods, to be as follows:—

| 1790 | 3,929,827 | | |
|------|-----------|------|------|
| 1800 | 5,305,937 | 35.02 per cent. | {ratio of increase |
| 1810 | 7,239,814 | 36.45 | " |
| 1820 | 9,638,131 | 33.13 | " |
| 1830 | 12,866,020 | 33.49 | " |
| 1840 | 17,069,453 | 32.67 | " |
| 1850 | 23,191,876 | 35.87 | " |
| 1860 | 31,443,790 | 35.58 | " |

This shows an average decennial increase of 34.60 per cent. in population through the seventy years from our first, to our last census yet taken. It is seen that the ratio of increase, at no one of these seven periods, is either two per cent. below, or two per cent. above, the average; thus showing how inflexible, and, consequently, how reliable, the law of increase, in our case, is. Assuming that it will continue, gives the following results:—

| 1870 | 42,323,341 | 1910 | 138,918,526 |
|------|-----------|------|-------------|
| 1880 | 56,967,216 | 1920 | 186,984,335 |
| 1890 | 76,677,872 | 1930 | 251,680,914 |
| 1900 | 103,208,415 | | |

These figures show that our country *may* be as populous as Europe now is, at some point between 1920 and 1930—say about 1925—our territory, at seventy-three and a third persons to the square mile, being of capacity to contain 217,186,000.

And we *will* reach this, too, if we do not ourselves relinquish the chance, by the folly and evils of disunion, or by long and exhausting war springing from the only great element of national discord among us. While it cannot be foreseen exactly how much one huge example of secession, breeding lesser ones indefinitely, would retard population, civilization, and prosperity, no one can doubt that the extent of it would be very great and injurious.

The proposed emancipation would shorten the war, perpetuate peace, insure this increase of population, and proportionately the wealth of the country. With these, we should pay all the emancipation would cost, together with our other debt, easier than we should pay our other debt, without it. If we had allowed our old national debt to run at six per cent. per annum, simple interest, from the end of our revolutionary struggle until to day, without paying anything on either principal or interest, each man of us would owe less upon that debt now, than each man owed upon it then; and this because our increase of men, through the whole period, has been greater than six per cent.; has run faster than the interest upon the debt. Thus, time alone relieves a debtor nation, so long as its population increases faster than unpaid interest accumulates on its debt.

This fact would be no excuse for delaying payment of what is justly due; but it shows the great importance of time in this connexion—the great advantage of a policy by which we shall not have to pay until we number a hundred millions, what, by a different policy, we would have to pay now, when we number but thirty one millions. In a word, it shows that a dollar will be much harder to pay for the war, than will be a dollar for emancipation on the proposed plan. And then the latter will cost no blood, no precious life. It will be a saving of both.

As to the second article, I think it would be impracticable to return to bondage the class of persons therein contemplated. Some of them, doubtless, in the property sense, belong to loyal owners; and hence, provision is made in this article for compensating such.

The third article relates to the future of the freed people. It does not oblige, but merely authorizes, Congress to aid in colonizing such as may consent. This ought not to be regarded as objectionable, on the one hand, or on the other, in so much as it comes to nothing, unless by the mutual consent of the people to be deported, and the American voters, through their representatives in Congress.

I cannot make it better known than it already is, that I strongly favor colonization. And yet I wish to say there is an objection urged against free colored persons remaining in the country, which is largely imaginary, if not sometimes malicious.

It is insisted that their presence would injure, and displace white labor and white laborers. If there ever could be a proper time for mere catch arguments, that time surely is not now. In times like the present, men should utter nothing for which they would not willingly be responsible through time and in eternity. Is it true, then, that colored people can displace any more white labor, by being free, than by remaining slaves? If they stay in their old places, they jostle no white laborers; if they leave their old places, they leave them open to white laborers. Logically, there is neither more nor less of it. Emancipation, even without deportation, would probably enhance the wages of white labor, and, very surely, would not reduce them. Thus, the customary amount of labor would still have to be performed; the freed people would surely not do more than their old proportion of it, and very probably, for a time, would do less, leaving an increased part to white laborers, bringing their labor into greater demand, and, consequently, enhancing the wages of it. With deportation, even to a limited extent, enhanced wages to white labor is mathematically certain. Labor is like any other commodity in the market—increase the demand for it, and you increase the price of it. Reduce the supply of black labor, by colonizing the black laborer out of the country, and, by precisely so much, you increase the demand for, and wages of, white labor.

But it is dreaded that the freed people will swarm forth, and cover the whole land? Are they not already in the land? Will liberation make them any more numerous? Equally distributed among the whites of the whole country, and there would be but one colored to seven whites. Could the one, in any way, greatly disturb the seven? There are many communities now, having more than one free colored person, to seven whites; and this, without any apparent consciousness of evil from it. The District of Columbia, and the States of Maryland and Delaware, are all in this condition. The District has more than one free colored to six whites; and yet, in its frequent petitions to Congress, I believe it has never presented the presence of free colored persons as one of its grievances. But why should emancipation south, send the free people north? People, of any color, seldom run, unless there be something to run from. *Heretofore* colored people, to some extent, have fled north from bondage; and *now,* perhaps, from both bondage and destitution. But if gradual emancipation and deportation be adopted, they will have neither to flee from. Their old masters will give them wages at least until new laborers can be procured; and the freed men, in turn, will gladly give their labor for the wages, till new homes can be found for them, in congenial climes, and with people of their own blood and race. This proposition can be trusted on the mutual interests involved. And, in any event, cannot the north decide for itself, whether to receive them?

Again, as practice proves more than theory, in any case, has there been any irruption of colored people northward, because of the abolishment of slavery in this District last spring?

What I have said of the proportion of free colored persons to the whites, in the District, is from the census of 1860, having no reference to persons called contrabands, nor to those made free by the act of Congress abolishing slavery here.

The plan consisting of these articles is recommended, not but that a restoration of the national authority would be accepted without its adoption.

Nor will the war, nor proceedings under the proclamation of September 22, 1862, be stayed because of the *recommendation* of this plan. Its timely *adoption,* I doubt not, would bring restoration and thereby stay both.

And, notwithstanding this plan, the recommendation that Congress provide by law for compensating any State which may adopt emancipation, before this plan shall have been acted upon, is hereby earnestly renewed. Such would be only an advance part of the plan, and the same arguments apply to both.

This plan is recommended as a means, not in exclusion of, but additional to, all others for restoring and preserving the national authority throughout the Union. The subject is presented exclusively in its economical aspect. The plan would, I am confident, secure peace more speedily, and maintain it more permanently, than can be done by force alone; while all it would cost, considering amounts, and manner of payment, and times of payment, would be easier paid than will be the additional cost of the war, if we rely solely upon force. It is much—very much—that it would cost no blood at all.

The plan is proposed as permanent constitutional law. It cannot become such without the concurrence of, first, two-thirds of Congress, and, afterwards, three-fourths of the States. The requisite three-fourths of the States will necessarily include seven of the Slave states. Their concurrence, if obtained, will give assurance of their severally adopting emancipation, at no very distant day, upon the new constitutional terms. This assurance would end the struggle now, and save the Union forever.

I do not forget the gravity which should characterize a paper addressed to the Congress of the nation by the Chief Magistrate of the nation. Nor do I forget that some of you are my seniors, nor that many of you have more experience than I, in the conduct of public affairs. Yet I trust that in view of the great responsibility resting upon me, you will perceive no want of respect to yourselves, in any undue earnestness I may seem to display.

Is it doubted, then, that the plan I propose, if adopted, would shorten the war, and thus lessen its expenditure of money and of blood? Is it doubted that it would restore the national authority and national prosperity, and perpetuate both indefinitely? Is it doubted that we here—Congress and Executive—can secure its adoption? Will not the good people respond to a united, and earnest appeal from us? Can we, can they, by any other means, so certainly, or so speedily, assure these vital objects? We can succeed only by concert. It is not "can *any* of us *imagine* better?" but "can we *all* do better?" Object whatsoever is possible, still the question recurs "can we do better?" The dogmas of the quiet past, are inadequate to the stormy present. The occasion is piled high with difficulty, and we must rise with the occasion. As our case is new, so we must think anew, and act anew. We must disenthrall ourselves, and then we shall save our country.

Fellow-citizens, *we* cannot escape history. We of this Congress and this administration, will be remembered in spite of ourselves. No personal significance, or insignificance, can spare one or another of us. The fiery trial through which we pass, will light us down, in honor or dishonor, to the latest generation. We *say* we are for the Union. The world will not forget that we say this. We know how to save the Union. The world knows we do know how to save it. We—even *we here*—hold the power, and bear the responsibility. In *giving* freedom to the *slave,* we *assure* freedom to the *free*—honorable alike in what we give, and what we preserve. We shall nobly save, or meanly lose, the last best, hope of earth. Other means may succeed; this could not fail. The way is plain, peaceful, generous, just—a way which, if followed, the world will forever applaud, and God must forever bless.

*December 1, 1862*

# Opinion on the Admission of West Virginia into the Union

The consent of the Legislature of Virginia is constitutionally necessary to the bill for the admission of West-Virginia becoming a law. A body claiming to be such Legislature has given it's consent. We can not well deny that it is such, unless we do so upon the outside knowledge that the body was chosen at elections, in which a majority of the qualified voters of Virginia did not participate. But it is a universal practice in the popular elections in all these states, to give no legal consideration whatever to those who do not choose to vote, as against the effect of the votes of those, who do choose to vote. Hence it is not the qualified voters, but the qualified voters, *who choose to vote,* that constitute the political power of the state. Much less than to non-voters, should any consideration be given to those who did not vote, *in this case*: because it is also matter of outside knowledge, that they were not merely neglectful of their rights under, and duty to, this government, but were also engaged in open rebellion against it. Doubtless among these non-voters were some Union men whose voices were smothered by the more numerous secessionists; but we know too little of their number to assign them any appreciable value. Can this government stand, if it indulges constitutional constructions by which men in open rebellion against it, are to be accounted, man for man, the equals of those who maintain their loyalty to it? Are they to be accounted even better citizens, and more worthy of consideration, than those who merely neglect to vote? If so, their treason against the constitution, enhances their constitutional value! Without braving these absurd conclusions, we can not deny that the body which consents to the admission of West-Virginia, is the Legislature of Virginia. I do not think the plural form of the words "Legislatures" and "States" in the phrase of the constitution "without the consent of the Legislatures of the States concerned &c" has any reference to the *new* State concerned. That plural form sprang from the contemplation of two or more old States contributing to form a new one. The idea that the new state was in danger of being admitted without its own consent, was not provided against, because it was not thought of, as I conceive. It is said, the devil takes care of his own. Much more should a good spirit—the spirit of the Constitution and the Union—take care of it's own. I think it can not do less, and live.

But is the admission into the Union, of West-Virginia, expedient. This, in my general view, is more a question for Congress, than for the Executive. Still I do not evade it. More than on anything else, it depends on whether the admission or rejection of the new state would under all the circumstances tend the more strongly to the restoration of the national authority throughout the Union. That which helps most in this direction is the most expedient at this time. Doutless those in remaining Virginia would return to the Union, so to speak, less reluctantly without the division of the old state than with it; but I think we could not save as much in this quarter by rejecting the new state, as we should lose by it in West-Virginia. We can scarcely dispense with the aid of West-Virginia in this struggle; much less can we afford to have her against us, in congress and in the field. Her brave and good men regard her admission into the Union as a matter of life and death. They have been true to the Union under very severe trials. We have so acted as to justify their hopes; and we can not fully retain their confidence, and co-operation, if we seem to break faith with them. In fact, they could not do so much for us, if they would.

Again, the admission of the new state, turns that much slave soil to free; and thus, is a certain, and irrevocable encroachment upon the cause of the rebellion.

The division of a State is dreaded as a precedent. But a measure made expedient by a war, is no precedent for times of peace. It is said that the admission of West-Virginia, is secession, and tolerated only because it is our secession. Well, if we call it by that name, there is still difference enough between secession against the constitution, and secession in favor of the constitution.

I believe the admission of West-Virginia into the Union is expedient.

*c. late December 1862*

# The Emancipation Proclamation

By the President of the United States of America:
A Proclamation.

Whereas, on the twenty-second day of September, in the year of our Lord one thousand eight hundred and sixty two, a proclamation was issued by the President of the United States, containing, among other things, the following, towit:

> That on the first day of January, in the year of our Lord one thousand eight hundred and sixty-three, all persons held as slaves within any State or designated part of a State, the people whereof shall then be in rebellion against the United States, shall be then, thenceforward, and forever free; and the Executive Government of the United States, including the military and naval authority thereof, will recognize and maintain the freedom of such persons and will do no act or acts to repress such persons, or any of them, in any efforts they may make for their actual freedom.

> That the executive will, on the first day of January aforesaid, by proclamation, designate the States and parts of States, if any, in which the people thereof, respectively, shall then be in rebellion against the United States; and the fact that any State, or the people thereof, shall on that day be, in good faith, represented in the Congress of the United States by members chosen thereto at elections wherein a majority of the qualified voters of such States shall have participated, shall, in the absence of strong countervailing testimony, be deemed conclusive evidence that such State, and the people thereof, are not then in rebellion against the United States.

Now, therefore, I, Abraham Lincoln, President of the United States, by virtue of the power in me vested as Commander-in-Chief, of the Army and Navy of the United States in time of actual armed rebellion against the authority and government of the United States, and as a fit and necessary war measure for supressing said rebellion, do, on this first day of January, in the year of our Lord one thousand eight hundred and sixty three, and in accordance with my purpose so to do publicly proclaimed for the full period of one hundred days, from the first day above mentioned, order and designate as the States and parts of States wherein the people thereof respectively, are this day in rebellion against the United States, the following, towit:

Arkansas, Texas, Louisiana, (except the parishes of St. Bernard, Palquemines, Jefferson, St. Johns, St. Charles, St. James, Ascension, Assumption, Terrebonne, Lafourche, St. Mary, St. Martin, and Orleans, including the city of New Orleans) Mississippi, Alabama, Florida, Georgia, South-Carolina, North-Carolina, and Virginia (except the fortyeight counties designated as West Virginia, and also the counties of Berkley, Accomac, Northampton, Elizabeth-City, York, Princess Ann, and Norfolk, including the cities of Norfolk & Portsmouth); and which excepted parts are, for the present, left precisely as if this proclamation were not issued.

And by virtue of the power and for the purpose aforesaid, I do order and declare that all persons held as slaves within said designated States, and parts of States, are, and henceforward shall be free; and that the Executive government of the United States, including the military and naval authorities thereof, will recognize and maintain the freedom of said persons.

And I hereby enjoin upon the people so declared to be free to abstain from all violence, unless in necessary self-defence; and I recommend to them that, in all case when allowed, they labor faithfully for reasonable wages.

And I further declare and make known, that such persons of suitable condition, will be received into the armed service of the United States to garrison forts, positions, stations, and other places, and to man vessels of all sorts in said service.

And upon this act, sincerely believed to be an act of justice, warranted by the Constitution, upon military necessity, I invoke the considerate judgment of mankind, and the gracious favor of Almighty God.

In witness whereof, I have hereunto set my hand and caused the seal of the United States to be affixed.

Done at the City of Washington, this first day of January, in the year of our Lord one thousand eight hundred and sixty-three, and of the Independence of the United States of America the eighty-seventh.

By the President:                                    ABRAHAM LINCOLN
    WILLIAM H. SEWARD, Secretary of State

# To the Workingmen of Manchester, England

To the workingmen of Manchester:

I have the honor to acknowledge the receipt of the address and resolutions which you sent me on the eve of the new year.

When I came, on the fourth day of March, 1861, through a free and constitutional election, to preside in the government of the United States, the country was found at the verge of civil war. Whatever might have been the cause, or whosoever the fault, one duty paramount to all others was before me, namely, to maintain and preserve at once the Constitution and the integrity of the federal republic. A conscientious purpose to perform this duty is a key to all the measures of administration which have been, and to all which will hereafter be pursued. Under our frame of government, and my official oath, I could not depart from this purpose if I would. It is not always in the power of governments to enlarge or restrict the scope of moral results which follow the policies that they may deem it necessary for the public safety, from time to time, to adopt.

I have understood well that the duty of self-preservation rests solely with the American people. But I have at the same time been aware that favor or disfavor of foreign nations might have a material influence in enlarging or prolonging the struggle with disloyal men in which the country is engaged. A fair examination of history has seemed to authorize a belief that the past actions and influences of the United States were generally regarded as having been beneficent towards mankind. I have therefore reckoned upon the forbearance of nations. Circumstances, to some of which you kindly allude, induced me especially to expect that if justice and good faith should be practiced by the United States, they would encounter no hostile influence on the part of Great Britain. It is now a pleasant duty to acknowledge the demonstration you have given of your desire that a spirit of peace and amity toward this country may prevail in the councils of your Queen, who is respected and esteemed in your own country only more than she is by the kindred nation which has its home on this side of the Atlantic.

I know and deeply deplore the sufferings which the workingmen at Manchester and in all Europe, are called to endure in this crisis. It has been often and studiously represented that the attempt to overthrow this government, which was built upon the foundation of human rights, and to substitute for it one which should rest exclusively on the basis of human slavery, was likely to obtain the favor of Europe.

Through the actions of our disloyal citizens the workingmen of Europe have been subjected to a severe trial, for the purpose of forcing their sanction to that attempt. Under the circumstances, I cannot but regard your decisive utterances upon the question as an instance of sublime Christian heroism which has not been surpassed in any age or in any country. It is, indeed, an energetic and reinspiring assurance of the inherent power of truth and of the ultimate and universal triumph of justice, humanity, and freedom. I do not doubt that the sentiments you have expressed will be sustained by your great nation, and, on the other hand, I have no hesitation in assuring you that they will excite admiration, esteem, and the most reciprocal feelings of friendship among the American people. I hail this interchange of sentiment, therefore, as an augury that, whatever else may happen, whatever misfortune may befall your country or my own, the peace and friendship which now exist between the two nations will be, as it shall be my desire to make them, perpetual.

*January 19, 1863*

# Opinion on the Draft

It is at all times proper that misunderstanding between the public and the public servant should be avoided; and this is far more important now, than in times of peace and tranquility. I therefore address you without searching for a precedent upon which to do so. Some of you are sincerely devoted to the republican institutions, and territorial integrity of our country, and yet are opposed to what is called the draft, or conscription.

At the beginning of the war, and ever since, a variety of motives pressing, some in one direction and some in the other, would be presented to the mind of each man physically fit for a soldier, upon the combined effect of which motives, he would, or would not, voluntarily enter the service. Among these motives would be patriotism, political bias, ambition, personal courage, love of adventure, want of employment, and convenience, or the opposites of some of these.

We already have, and have had in the service, as appears, substantially all that can be obtained upon this voluntary weighing of motives. And yet we must somehow obtain more, or relinquish the original object of the contest, together with all the blood and treasure already expended in the effort to secure it. To meet this necessity the law for the draft has been enacted. You who do not wish to be soldiers, do not like this law. This is natural; nor does it imply want of patriotism. Nothing can be so just, and necessary, as to make us like it, if it is disagreeable to us. We are prone, too, to find false arguments with which to excuse ourselves for opposing such disagreeable things. In this case those who desire the rebellion to succeed, and others who seek reward in a different way, are very active in accommodating us with this class of arguments. They tell us the law is unconstitutional. It is the first instance, I believe, in which the power of congress to do a thing has ever been questioned, in a case when the power is given by the constitution in express terms. Whether a power can be implied, when it is not expressed, has often been the subject of controversy; but this is the first case in which the degree of effrontery has been ventured upon, of denying a power which is plainly and distinctly written down in the constitution. The constitution declares that "The congress shall have power . . . To raise and support armies; but no appropriation of money to that use shall be for a longer term than two years." The whole scope of the conscription act is "to raise and support armies." There is nothing else in it. It makes no appropriation of money; and hence the money clause just quoted, is not touched by it. The case simply is the constitution provides that the congress shall have power to raise and support armies; and, by this act, the congress has exercised the power to raise and support armies. This is the whole of it. It is a law made in litteral pursuance of this part of the United States Constitution; and another part of the same constitution declares that "This constitution, and the laws made in pursuance thereof . . . shall be the supreme law of the land, and the judges in every state shall be bound thereby, anything in the constitution or laws of any state to the contrary notwithstanding."

Do you admit that the power is given to raise and support armies, and yet insist that by this act congress has not exercised the power in a constitutional mode?—has not done the thing, in the right way? Who is to judge of this? The constitution gives congress the power, but it does not prescribe the mode, or expressly declare who shall prescribe it. In such case congress must prescribe the mode, or relinquish the power. There is no alternative. Congress could not exercise the power to do the thing, if it had not the power of providing a way to do it, when no way is provided by the constitution for doing it. In fact congress would not have the power to raise and support armies, if even by the constitution, it were left to the option of any other, or others, to give or withhold the only mode of doing it. If the constitution had prescribed a mode, congress could and must follow that mode; but as it is, the mode necessarily goes to congress, with the power expressly given. The power is given fully, completely, unconditionally. It is not a power to raise armies *if* State authorities consent; nor *if* the men to compose the armies are entirely willing; but it is a power to raise and support armies given to congress by the constitution, without an if.

It is clear that a constitutional law may not be expedient or proper. Such would be a law to raise armies when no armies were needed. But this is not such. The republican institutions, and territorial integrity of our country can not be maintained without the further raising and supporting of armies. There can be no army without men. Men can be had only voluntarily, or involuntarily. We have ceased to obtain them voluntarily; and to obtain them involuntarily, is the draft— the conscription. If you dispute the fact, and declare that men can still be had voluntarily in sufficient numbers prove the assertion by yourselves volunteering in such numbers, and I shall gladly give up the draft. Or if not a sufficient number, but any one of you will volunteer, he for his single self, will escape all the horrors of the draft; and will thereby do only what each one of at least a million of his manly brethren have already done. Their toil and blood have been given as much for you as for themselves. Shall it all be lost rather than you too, will bear your part?

I do not say that all who would avoid serving in the war, are unpatriotic; but I do think every patriot should willingly take his chance under a law made with great care in order to secure entire fairness. This law was considered, discussed, modified, and amended, by congress, at great length, and with much labor; and was finally passed, by both branches, with a near approach to unanimity. At last, it may not be exactly such as any one man out of congress, or even in congress, would have made it. It has been said, and I believe truly, that the constitution itself is not altogether such as any one of it's framers would have preferred. It was the joint work of all; and certainly the better that it was so.

Much complaint is made of that provision of the conscription law which allows a drafted man to substitute three hundred dollars for himself; while, as I believe, none is made of that provision which allows him to substitute another man for himself. Nor is the three hundred dollar provision objected to for unconstitutionality; but for inequality—for favoring the rich against the poor. The substitution of men is the provision if any, which favors the rich to the exclusion of the poor. But this being a provision in accordance with an old and well known practice, in the raising of armies, is not objected to. There would have been great objection if that provision had been omitted. And yet being in, the money provision really modifies the inequality which the other introduces. It allows men to escape the service, who are too poor to escape but for it. Without the money provision, competition among the more wealthy might, and probably would, raise the price of substitutes above three hundred dollars, thus leaving the man who could raise only three hundred dollars, no escape from personal service. True, by the law as it is, the man who can not raise so much as three hundred dollars, nor obtain a personal substitute for less, can not escape; but he can come quite as near escaping as he could if the money provision were not in the law. To put it another way, is an unobjectionable law which allows only the man to escape who can pay a thousand dollars, made objectionable by adding a provision that any one may escape who can pay the smaller sum of three hundred dollars? This is the exact difference at this point between the present law and all former draft laws. It is true that by this law a somewhat larger number will escape than could under a law allowing personal substitutes only; but each additional man thus escaping will be a poorer man than could have escaped by the law in the other form. The money provision enlarges the class of exempts from actual service simply by admitting poorer men into it. How, then can the money provision be a wrong to the poor man? The inequality complained of pertains in greater degree to the substitution of men, and is really modified and lessened by the money provision. The inequality could only be perfectly cured by sweeping both provisions away. This being a great innovation, would probably leave the law more distasteful than it now is.

The principle of the draft, which simply is involuntary, or enforced service, is not new. It has been practiced in all ages of the world. It was well known to the framers of our constitution as one of the modes of raising armies, at the time they placed in that instrument the provision that "the congress shall have power to raise and support armies." It had been used, just before, in establishing our independence; and it was also used under the constitution in 1812. Wherein is the peculiar hardship now? Shall we shrink from the necessary means to maintain our free government, which our grand-fathers employed to establish it, and our own fathers have already employed once to maintain it? Are we degenerate? Has the manhood of our race run out?

Again, a law may be both constitutional and expedient, and yet may be administered in an unjust and unfair way. This law belongs to a class, which class is composed of those laws whose object is to distribute burthens or benefits on the principle of equality. No one of these laws can ever be practically administered with that exactness which can be conceived of in the mind. A tax law, the principle of which is that each owner shall pay in proportion to the value of his property, will be a dead letter, if no one can be compelled to pay until it can be shown that every other one pay at all—even in unequal proportion. Again the United States House of representatives is constituted on the principle that each member is sent by the same number of people that each other one is sent by; and yet in practice no two of the whole number, much less the whole number, are ever sent by precisely the same number of constituents. The Districts can not be made precisely equal in population at first, and if they could, they would become unequal in a single day, and much more so in the ten years, which the Districts, once made, are to continue. They can not be re-modelled every day; nor, without too much expence and labor, even every year.

This sort of difficulty applies in full force, to the practical administration of the draft law. In fact the difficulty is greater in the case of the draft law. First, it starts with all the inequality of the congressional Districts; but these are based on entire population, while the draft is based upon those only who are fit for soldiers, and such may not bear the same proportion to the whole in one District, that they do in another. Again, the facts must be ascertained, and credit given, for the unequal numbers of soldiers which have already gone from the several Districts. In all these points errors will occur in spite of the utmost fidelity. The government is bound to administer the law with such an approach to exactness as is usual in analogous cases, and as entire good faith and fidelity will reach. If so great departures as to be inconsistent with such good faith and fidelity, or great departures occurring in any way, be pointed out, they shall be corrected; and any agent shown to have caused such departures intentionally, shall be dismissed.

With these views, and on these principles, I feel bound to tell you it is my purpose to see the draft law faithfully executed.

c. *mid-September 1863*

# Proclamation of Thanksgiving

By the President of the United States of America:
A Proclamation.

The year that is drawing towards its close, has been filled with the blessings of fruitful fields and healthful skies. To these bounties, which are so constantly enjoyed that we are prone to forget the source from which they come, others have been added, which are of so extraordinary a nature, that they cannot fail to penetrate and soften even the heart which is habitually insensible to the ever watchful providence of Almighty God. In the midst of a civil war of unequalled magnitude and severity, which has sometimes seemed to foreign States to invite and provoke their aggression, peace has been preserved with all nations, order has been maintained, the laws have been respected and obeyed, and harmony has prevailed everywhere except in the theatre of military conflict; while that theatre has been greatly contracted by the advancing armies and navies of the Union. Needful diversions of wealth and of strength from the fields of peaceful industry to the national defence, has not arrested the plough, the shuttle or the ship; the axe has enlarged the borders of our settlements, and the mines, as well of iron and coal as of the precious metals, have yielded even more abundantly than heretofore. Population has steadily increased, notwithstanding the waste that has been made in the camp, the siege and the battle-field; and the country, rejoicing in the consciousness of augmented strength and vigor, is permitted to expect continuance of years with large increase of freedom. No human counsel hath devised nor hath any mortal hand worked out these great things. They are the gracious gifts of the Most High God, who, while dealing with us in anger for our sins, hath nevertheless remembered mercy. It has seemed to me fit and proper that they should be solemnly, reverently and gratefully acknowledged as with one heart and voice by the whole American People. I do therefore invite my fellow citizens in every part of the United States, and also those who are at sea and those who are sojourning in foreign lands, to set apart and observe the last Thursday of November next, as a day of Thanksgiving and Praise to our beneficent Father who dwelleth in the Heavens. And I recommend to them that while offering up the ascriptions justly due to Him for such singular deliverances and blessings, they do also, with humble penitence for our national perverseness and disobedience, commend to His tender care all those who have become widows, orphans, mourners or sufferers in the lamentable civil strife in which we are unavoidably engaged, and fervently implore the interposition of the Almighty Hand to heal the wounds of the nation and to restore it as soon as may be consistent with Divine purposes to the full enjoyment of peace, harmony, tranquillity, and Union.

In testimony whereof, I have hereunto set my hand and caused the Seal of the United States to be affixed.

Done at the city of Washington, this Third day of October, in the year of our Lord one thousand eight hundred and sixty-three, and of the Independence of the United States the Eighty-eighth.

By the President:                                    Abraham Lincoln

William H. Seward, Secretary of State

*October 3, 1863*

# The Gettysburg Address

*Delivered at the dedication of the Cemetery at Gettysburg*

Four score and seven years ago our fathers brought forth upon this continent, a new nation, conceived in Liberty, and dedicated to the proposition that all men are created equal.

Now we are engaged in a great civil war, testing whether that nation, or any nation so conceived and so dedicated, can long endure. We are met on a great battle-field of that war. We have come to dedicate a portion of that field, as a final resting place for those who here gave their lives that that nation might live. It is altogether fitting and proper that we should do this.

But, in a larger sense, we can not dedicate—we can not consecrate—we can not hallow—this ground. The brave men, living and dead, who struggled here, have consecrated it, far above our poor power to add or detract. The world will little note, nor long remember what we say here, but it can never forget what they did here. It is for us the living, rather, to be dedicated here to the unfinished work which they who fought here have thus far so nobly advanced. It is rather for us to be here dedicated to the great task remaining before us—that from these honored dead we take increased devotion to that cause for which they gave the last full measure of devotion—that we here highly resolve that these dead shall not have died in vain—that this nation, under God, shall have a new birth of freedom—and that government of the people, by the people, for the people, shall not perish from the earth.

*November 19, 1863*

# Annual Message to Congress, 1863

Fellow citizens of the Senate and House of Representatives:

Another year of health, and of sufficiently abundant harvests has passed. For these, and especially for the improved condition of our national affairs, our renewed, and profoundest gratitude to God is due.

We remain in peace and friendship with foreign powers.

The efforts of disloyal citizens of the United States to involve us in foreign wars, to aid an inexcusable insurrection, have been unavailing. Her Britannic Majesty's government, as was justly expected, have exercised their authority to prevent the departure of new hostile expeditions from British ports. The Emperor of France has, by a like proceeding, promptly vindicated the neutrality which he proclaimed at the beginning of the contest. Questions of great intricacy and importance have arisen out of the blockade, and other belligerent operations, between the government and several of the maritime powers, but they have been discussed, and, as far as was possible, accommodated in a spirit of frankness, justice, and mutual good will. It is especially gratifying that our prize courts, by the impartiality of their adjudications, have commanded the respect and confidence of maritime powers.

The supplemental treaty between the United States and Great Britain for the suppression of the African slave trade, made on the 17th. day of February last, has been duly ratified, and carried into execution. It is believed that, so far as American ports and American citizens are concerned, that inhuman and odious traffic has been brought to an end.

I shall submit, for the consideration of the Senate, a convention for the adjustment of possessory claims in Washington Territory, arising out of the treaty of the 15th. June, 1846, between the United States and Great Britain, and which have been the source of some disquiet among the citizens of that now rapidly improving part of the country.

A novel and important question, involving the extent of the maritime jurisdiction of Spain in the waters which surround the island of Cuba, has been debated without reaching an agreement, and it is proposed in an amicable spirit to refer it to the arbitrament of a friendly power. A convention for that purpose will be submitted to the Senate.

I have thought it proper, subject to the approval of the Senate, to concur with the interested commercial powers in an arrangement for the liquidation of the

Scheldt dues upon the principles which have been heretofore adopted in regard to the imposts upon navigation in the waters of Denmark.

The long pending controversy between this government and that of Chili touching the seizure at Sitana, in Peru, by Chilian officers, of a large amount in treasure belonging to citizens of the United States, has been brought to a close by the award of His Majesty, the King of the Belgians, to whose arbitration the question was referred by the parties. The subject was thoroughly and patiently examined by that justly respected magistrate, and although the sum awarded to the claimants may not have been as large as they expected, there is no reason to distrust the wisdom of his Majesty's decision. That decision was promptly complied with by Chili, when intelligence in regard to it reached that country.

The joint commission, under the act of the last session, for carrying into effect the convention with Peru on the subject of claims, has been organized at Lima, and is engaged in the business intrusted to it.

Difficulties concerning inter-oceanic transit through Nicaragua are in course of amicable adjustment.

In conformity with principles set forth in my last annual message, I have received a representative from the United States of Colombia, and have accredited a minister to that republic.

Incidents occurring in the progress of our civil war have forced upon my attention the uncertain state of international questions, touching the rights of foreigners in this country and of United States citizens abroad. In regard to some governments these rights are at least partially defined by treaties. In no instance, however, is it expressly stipulated that, in the event of civil war, a foreigner residing in this country, within the lines of the insurgents, is to be exempted from the rule which classes him as a belligerent, in whose behalf the government of his country cannot expect any privileges or immunities distinct from that character. I regret to say, however, that such claims have been put forward, and, in some instances, in behalf of foreigners who have lived in the United States the greater part of their lives.

There is reason to believe that many persons born in foreign countries, who have declared their intention to become citizens, or who have been fully naturalized, have evaded the military duty required of them by denying the fact, and thereby throwing upon the government the burden of proof. It has been found difficult or impracticable to obtain this proof from the want of guides to the proper sources of information. These might be supplied by requiring clerks of courts, where declarations of intention may be made or naturalizations effected, to send, periodically, lists of the names of the persons naturalized, or declaring their intention to become citizens, to the Secretary of the Interior, in whose department those names might be arranged and printed for general information.

There is also reason to believe that foreigners frequently become citizens of the United States for the sole purpose of evading duties imposed by the laws of their native countries, to which, on becoming naturalized here, they at once repair, and though never returning to the United States, they still claim the interposition of this government as citizens. Many altercations and great prejudices have heretofore arisen out of this abuse. It is therefore, submitted to your serious consideration. It might be advisable to fix a limit, beyond which no Citizen of the United States residing abroad may claim the interposition of his government.

The right of suffrage has often been assumed and exercised by aliens, under pretences of naturalization, which they have disavowed when drafted into the military service. I submit the expediency of such an amendment of the law as will make the fact of voting an estoppel against any plea of exemption from military service, or other civil obligation, on the ground of alienage.

In common with other western powers, our relations with Japan have been brought into serious jeopardy, through the perverse opposition of the hereditary aristocracy of the empire, to the enlightened and liberal policy of the Tycoon designed to bring the country into the society of nations. It is hoped, although not with entire confidence, that these difficulties may be peacefully overcome. I ask your attention to the claim of the Minister residing there for the damages he sustained in the destruction by fire of the residence of the legation at Yedo.

Satisfactory arrangements have been made with the Emperor of Russia, which, it is believed, will result in effecting a continuous line of telegraph through that empire from our Pacific coast.

I recommend to your favorable consideration the subject of an international telegraph across the Atlantic ocean; and also of a telegraph between this capital and the national forts along the Atlantic seaboard and the Gulf of Mexico. Such communications, established with any reasonable outlay, would be economical as well as effective aids to the diplomatic, military, and naval service.

The consular system of the United States, under the enactments of the last Congress, begins to be self-sustaining; and there is reason to hope that it may become entirely so, with the increase of trade which will ensue whenever peace is restored. Our ministers abroad have been faithful in defending American rights. In protecting commercial interests, our Consuls have necessarily had to encounter increased labors and responsibilities, growing out of the war. These they have, for the most part, met and discharged with zeal and efficiency. This acknowledgment justly includes those Consuls who, residing in Morocco, Egypt, Turkey,

Japan, China, and other oriental countries, are charged with complex functions and extraordinary powers.

The condition of the several organized Territories is generally satisfactory, although Indian disturbances in New Mexico have not been entirely suppressed. The mineral resources of Colorado, Nevada, Idaho, New Mexico, and Arizona are proving far richer than has been heretofore understood. I lay before you a communication on this subject from the governor of New Mexico. I again submit to your consideration the expediency of establishing a system for the encouragement of immigration. Although this source of national wealth and strength is again flowing with greater freedom than for several years before the insurrection occurred, there is still a great deficiency of laborers in every field of industry, especially in agriculture and in our mines, as well of iron and coal as of the precious metals. While the demand for labor is thus increased here, tens of thousands of persons, destitute of remunerative occupation, are thronging our foreign consulates, and offering to emigrate to the United States if essential, but very cheap, assistance can be afforded them. It is easy to see that, under the sharp discipline of civil war, the nation is beginning a new life. This noble effort demands the aid, and ought to receive the attention and support of the government.

Injuries, unforseen by the government and unintended, may, in some cases, have been inflicted on the subjects or citizens of foreign countries, both at sea and on land, by persons in the service of the United States. As this government expects redress from other powers when similar injuries are inflicted by persons in their service upon citizens of the United States, we must be prepared to do justice to foreigners. If the existing judicial tribunals are inadequate to this purpose, a special court may be authorized, with power to hear and decide such claims of the character referred to as may have arisen under treaties and the public law. Conventions for adjusting the claims by joint commission have been proposed to some governments, but no definitive answer to the proposition has yet been received from any.

In the course of the session I shall probably have occasion to request you to provide indemnification to claimants where decrees of restitution have been rendered, and damages awarded by admiralty courts; and in other cases where this government may be acknowledged to be liable in principle, and where the amount of that liability has been ascertained by an informal arbitration.

The proper officers of the treasury have deemed themselves required, by the law of the United States upon the subject, to demand a tax upon the incomes of foreign consuls in this country. While such a demand may not, in strictness, be in derogation of public law, or perhaps of any existing treaty between the United States and a foreign country, the expediency of so far modifying the act as to exempt from tax the income of such consuls as are not citizens of the United States, derived from the emoluments of their office, or from property not situated in the United States, is submitted to your serious consideration. I make this suggestion upon the ground that a comity which ought to be reciprocated exempts our Consuls, in all other countries, from taxation to the extent thus indicated. The United States, I think, ought not to be exceptionally illiberal to international trade and commerce.

The operations of the treasury during the last year have been successfully conducted. The enactment by Congress of a national banking law has proved a valuable support of the public credit; and the general legislation in relation to loans has fully answered the expectations of its favorers. Some amendments may be required to perfect existing laws; but no change in their principles or general scope is believed to be needed.

Since these measures have been in operation, all demands on the treasury, including the pay of the army and navy, have been promptly met and fully satisfied. No considerable body of troops, it is believed, were ever more amply provided, and more liberally and punctually paid; and it may be added that by no people were the burdens incident to a great war ever more cheerfully borne.

The receipts during the year from all sources, including loans and the balance in the treasury at its commencement, were $901,125,674.86, and the aggregate disbursements $895,796,630.65, leaving a balance on the 1st. July, 1863, of $5,329,044.21. Of the receipts there were derived from customs, $69,059,642.40; from internal revenue, $37,640,787.95; from direct tax, $1,485,103.61; from lands, $167,617.17; from miscellaneous sources, $3,046,615.35; and from loans, $776,682,361.57; making the aggregate, $901,125,674.86. Of the disbursements there were for the civil service, $23,253,922.08; for pensions and Indians, $4,216,520.79; for interest on public debt, $24,729,846.51; for the War Department, $599,298,600.83; for the Navy Department, $63,211,105.27; for payment of funded and temporary debt, $181,086,635.07; making the aggregate, $895,796,630.65, and leaving the balance of $5,329,044.21. But the payment of funded and temporary debt, having been made from moneys borrowed during the year, must be regarded as merely nominal payments, and the moneys borrowed to make them as merely nominal receipts; and their amount, $181,086,635.07, should therefore be deducted both from receipts and disbursements. This being done, there remains as actual receipts $720,039,039.79; and the actual disbursements, $714,709,995.58, leaving the balance as already stated.

The actual receipts and disbursements for the first quarter, and the estimated receipts and disbursements for the remaining three quarters, of the current fiscal year, 1864, will be shown in detail by the report of the Secretary of the Treasury, to which I invite your attention. It is sufficient to say here that it is not believed that actual results will exhibit a state of the finances less favorable to the country than the estimates of that officer heretofore submitted; while it is confidently expected that at the close of the year both disbursements and debt will be found very considerably less than has been anticipated.

The report of the Secretary of War is a document of great interest. It consists of—

1. The military operations of the year, detailed in the report of the general-in-chief.

2. The organization of colored persons into the war service.

3. The exchange of prisoners, fully set forth in the letter of General Hitchcock.

4. The operations under the act for enrolling and calling out the national forces, detailed in the report of the provost marshal general.

5. The organization of the invalid corps; and

6. The operation of the several departments of the quartermaster general, commissary general, paymaster general, chief of engineers, chief of ordnance, and surgeon general.

It has appeared impossible to make a valuable summary of this report except such as would be too extended for this place, and hence I content myself by asking your careful attention to the report itself.

The duties devolving on the naval branch of the service during the year, and throughout the whole of this unhappy contest, have been discharged with fidelity and eminent success. The extensive blockade has been constantly increasing in efficiency, as the navy has expanded; yet on so long a line it has so far been impossible to entirely suppress illicit trade. From returns received at the Navy Department, it appears that more than one thousand vessels have been captured since the blockade was instituted, and that the value of prizes already sent in for adjudication amounts to over thirteen millions of dollars.

The naval force of the United States consists at this time of five hundred and eighty-eight vessels, completed and in the course of completion, and of these seventy-five are iron-clad or armored steamers. The events of the war give an increased interest and importance to the navy which will probably extend beyond the war itself.

The armored vessels in our navy completed and in service, or which are under contract and approaching completion, are believed to exceed in number those of any other power. But while these may be relied upon for harbor defence and coast service, others of greater strength and capacity will be necessary for cruising purposes, and to maintain our rightful position on the ocean.

The change that has taken place in naval vessels and naval warfare, since the introduction of steam as a motive-power for ships-of-war, demands either a corresponding change in some of our existing navy yards, or the establishment of new ones, for the construction and necessary repair of modern naval vessels. No inconsiderable embarrassment, delay, and public injury have been experienced from the want of such governmental establishments. The necessity of such a navy yard, so furnished, at some suitable place upon the Atlantic seaboard, has on repeated occasions been brought to the attention of Congress by the Navy Department, and is again presented in the report of the Secretary which accompanies this communication. I think it my duty to invite your special attention to this subject, and also to that of establishing a yard and depot for naval purposes upon one of the western rivers. A naval force has been created on those interior waters, and under many disadvantages, within little more than two years, exceeding in numbers the whole naval force of the country at the commencement of the present administration. Satisfactory and important as have been the performances of the heroic men of the navy at this interesting period, they are scarcely more wonderful than the success of our mechanics and artisans in the production of war vessels which has created a new form of naval power.

Our country has advantages superior to any other nation in our resources of iron and timber, with inexhaustible quantities of fuel in the immediate vicinity of both, and all available and in close proximity to navigable waters. Without the advantage of public works the resources of the nation have been developed and its power displayed in the construction of a navy of such magnitude which has, at the very period of its creation, rendered signal service to the Union.

The increase of the number of seamen in the public service, from seven thousand five hundred men, in the spring of 1861, to about thirty four thousand at the present time has been accomplished without special legislation, or extraordinary bounties to promote that increase. It has been found, however, that the operation of the draft, with the high bounties paid for army recruits, is beginning to affect injuriously the naval service, and will, if not corrected, be likely to impair its efficiency, by detaching seamen from their proper vocation and inducing them to enter the Army. I therefore respectfully suggest that Congress might aid both the army and naval services by a definite provision on this subject, which would at the same time be equitable to the communities more especially interested.

I commend to your consideration the suggestions of the Secretary of the Navy in regard to the policy of fostering and training seamen, and also the education of officers and engineers for the naval service. The Naval Academy is rendering signal service in preparing midshipmen for the highly responsible duties which in after life they will be required to perform. In order that the country should not be deprived of the proper quota of educated officers, for which legal provision has been made at the naval school, the vacancies caused by the neglect or omission to make nominations from the States in insurrection have been filled by the Secretary of the Navy.

The school is now more full and complete than at any former period, and in every respect to the favorable consideration of Congress.

During the past fiscal year the financial condition of the Post office Department has been one of increasing prosperity, and I am gratified in being able to state that the actual postal revenue has nearly equalled the entire expenditures; the latter amounting to $11,314,206.84, and the former to $11,163,789.59, leaving a deficiency of but $150,417.25. In 1860, the year immediately preceding the rebellion the deficiency amounted to $5,656,705.49, the postal receipts of that year being $2,645,722.19 less than those of 1863. The decrease since 1860 in the annual amount of transportation has been only about 25 per cent, but the annual expenditure on account of the same has been reduced 35 per cent. It is manifest, therefore, that the Post Office Department may become self-sustaining in a few years, even with the restoration of the whole service.

The international conference of postal delegates from the principal countries of Europe and America, which was called at the suggestion of the Postmaster General, met at Paris on the 11th of May last, and concluded its deliberations on the 8th of June. The principles established by the conference as best adapted to facilitate postal intercourse between nations, and as the basis of future postal conventions, inaugurate a general system of uniform international charges, at reduced rates of postage, and cannot fail to produce beneficial results.

I refer you to the report of the Secretary of the Interior, which is herewith laid before you, for useful and varied information in relation to the public lands, Indian affairs, patents, pensions, and other matters of public concern pertaining to his department.

The quantity of land disposed of during the last and the first quarter of the present fiscal years was three million eight hundred and forty one thousand five hundred and forty nine acres, of which one hundred and sixty one thousand nine hundred and eleven acres were sold for cash, one million four hundred and fifty six thousand five hundred and fourteen acres were taken up under the homestead law, and the residue disposed of under laws granting lands for military bounties, for railroad and other purposes. It also appears that the sale of the public lands is largely on the increase.

It has long been a cherished opinion of some of our wisest statesmen that the people of the United States had a higher and more enduring interest in the early settlement and substantial cultivation of the public lands than in the amount of direct revenue to be derived from the sale of them. This opinion has had a controlling influence in shaping legislation upon the subject of our national domain. I may cite, as evidence of this, the liberal measures adopted in reference to actual settlers; the grant to the States of the overflowed lands within their limits in order to their being reclaimed and rendered fit for cultivation; the grants to railway companies of alternate sections of land upon the contemplated lines of their roads which, when completed, will so largely multiply the facilities for reaching our distant possessions. This policy has received its most signal and beneficent illustration in the recent enactment granting homesteads to actual settlers.

Since the first day of January last the before-mentioned quantity of one million four hundred and fifty-six thousand five hundred and fourteen acres of land have been taken up under its provisions. This fact and the amount of sales furnish gratifying evidence of increasing settlement upon the public lands, notwithstanding the great struggle in which the energies of the nation have been engaged, and which has required so large a withdrawal of our citizens from their accustomed pursuits. I cordially concur in the recommendation of the Secretary of the Interior suggesting a modification of the act in favor of those engaged in the military and naval service of the United States. I doubt not that Congress will cheerfully adopt such measures as will, without essentially changing the general features of the system, secure to the greatest practicable extent, its benefits to those who have left their homes in the defence of the country in this arduous crisis.

I invite your attention to the views of the Secretary as to the propriety of raising by appropriate legislation a revenue from the mineral lands of the United States.

The measures provided at your last session for the removal of certain Indian tribes have been carried into effect. Sundry treaties have been negotiated which will, in due time, be submitted for the constitutional action of the Senate. They contain stipulations for extinguishing the possessory rights of the Indians to large and valuable tracts of land. It is hoped that the effect of these treaties will result in the establishment of permanent friendly relations with such of these tribes as have been brought into frequent and bloody collision with our outlying settlements and emigrants.

Sound policy and our imperative duty to these wards of the government demand our anxious and constant attention to their material well-being, to their progress in the arts of civilization, and, above all, to that moral training which, under the blessing of Divine Providence, will confer upon them the elevated and sanctifying influences, the hopes and consolation of the Christian faith.

I suggested in my last annual message the propriety of remodelling our Indian system. Subsequent events have satisfied me of its necessity. The details set forth in the report of the Secretary evince the urgent need for immediate legislative action.

I commend the benevolent institutions, established or patronized by the government in this District, to your generous and fostering care.

The attention of Congress, during the last session, was engaged to some extent with a proposition for enlarging the water communication between the Mississippi river and the northeastern seaboard, which proposition, however, failed for the time. Since then, upon a call of the greatest respectability a convention has been held at Chicago upon the same subject, a summary of whose views is contained in a memorial addressed to the President and Congress, and which I now have the honor to lay before you. That this interest is one which, ere long, will force its own way, I do not entertain a doubt, while it is submitted entirely to your wisdom as to what can be done now. Augmented interest is given to this subject by the actual commencement of work upon the Pacific railroad, under auspices so favorable to rapid progress and completion. The enlarged navigation becomes a palpable need to the great road.

I transmit the second annual report of the Commissioner of the Department of Agriculture, asking your attention to the developments in that vital interest of the nation.

When Congress assembled a year ago the war had already lasted nearly twenty months, and there had been many conflicts on both land and sea, with varying results.

The rebellion had been pressed back into reduced limits; yet the tone of public feeling and opinion, at home and abroad, was not satisfactory. With other signs, the popular elections, then just past, indicated uneasiness among ourselves, while amid much that was cold and menacing the kindest words coming from Europe were uttered in accents of pity, that we were too blind to surrender a hopeless cause. Our commerce was suffering greatly by a few armed vessels built upon and furnished from foreign shores, and we were threatened with such additions from the same quarter as would sweep our trade from the sea and raise our blockade. We had failed to elicit from European governments anything hopeful upon this subject. The preliminary emancipation proclamation, issued in September, was running its assigned period to the beginning of the new year. A month later the final proclamation came, including the announcement that colored men of suitable condition would be received into the war service. The policy of emancipation, and of employing black soldiers, gave to the future a new aspect, about which hope, and fear, and doubt contended in uncertain conflict. According to our political system, as a matter of civil administration, the general government had no lawful power to effect emancipation in any State, and for a long time it had been hoped that the rebellion could be suppressed without resorting to it as a military measure. It was all the while deemed possible that the necessity for it might come, and that if it should, the crisis of the contest would then be presented. It came, and as was anticipated, it was followed by dark and doubtful days. Eleven months having now passed, we are permitted to take another review. The rebel borders are pressed still further back, and by the complete opening of the Mississippi the country domi-nated by the rebellion is divided into distinct parts, with no practical communi-cation between them. Tennessee and Arkansas have been substantially cleared of insurgent control, and influential citizens in each, owners of slaves and advocates of slavery at the beginning of the rebellion, now declare openly for emancipation in their respective States. Of those States not included in the emancipation procla-mation, Maryland, and Missouri, neither of which three years ago would tolerate any restraint upon the extension of slavery into new territories, only dispute now as to the best mode of removing it within their own limits.

Of those who were slaves at the beginning of the rebellion, full one hundred thousand are now in the United States military service, about one-half of which number actually bear arms in the ranks; thus giving the double advantage of taking so much labor from the insurgent cause, and supplying the places which otherwise must be filled with so many white men. So far as tested, it is difficult to say they are not as good soldiers as any. No servile insurrection, or tendency to violence or cruelty, has marked the measures of emancipation and arming the blacks. These measures have been much discussed in foreign countries, and contemporary with such discussion the tone of public sentiment there is much improved. At home the same measures have been fully discussed, supported, criticised, and denounced, and the annual elections following are highly encour-aging to those whose official duty it is to bear the country through this great trial. Thus we have the new reckoning. The crisis which threatened to divide the friends of the Union is past.

Looking now to the present and future, and with reference to a resumption of the national authority within the States wherein that authority has been sus-pended, I have thought fit to issue a proclamation, a copy of which is herewith transmitted. On examination of this proclamation it will appear, as is believed, that nothing is attempted beyond what is amply justified by the Constitution. True, the form of an oath is given, but no man is coerced to take it. The man is only promised a pardon in case he voluntarily takes the oath. The Constitution authorizes the Executive to grant or withhold the pardon at his own absolute discretion; and this includes the power to grant on terms, as is fully established by judicial and other authorities.

It is also proffered that if, in any of the States named, a State government shall be, in the mode prescribed, set up, such government shall be recognized and guarantied by the United States, and that under it the State shall, on the constitutional conditions, be protected against invasion and domestic violence. The constitutional obligation of the United States to guaranty to every State in the Union a republican form of government, and to protect the State, in the cases stated, is explicit and full. But why tender the benefits of this provision only to a State government set up in this particular way? This section of the Constitution contemplates a case wherein the element within a State, favorable to republican government, in the Union, may be too feeble for an opposite and hostile element external to, or even within the State; and such are precisely the cases with which we are now dealing.

An attempt to guaranty and protect a revived State government, constructed in whole, or in preponderating part, from the very element against whose hostility and violence it is to be protected, is simply absurd. There must be a test by which to separate the opposing elements, so as to build only from the sound; and that test is a sufficiently liberal one, which accepts as sound whoever will make a sworn recantation of his former unsoundness.

But if it be proper to require, as a test of admission to the political body, an oath of allegiance to the Constitution of the United States, and to the Union under it, why also to the laws and proclamations in regard to slavery? Those laws and proclamations were enacted and put forth for the purpose of aiding in the suppression of the rebellion. To give them their fullest effect, there had to be a pledge for their maintenance. In my judgment they have aided, and will further aid, the cause for which they were intended. To now abandon them would be not only to relinquish a lever of power, but would also be a cruel and an astounding breach of faith. I may add at this point, that while I remain in my present position I shall not attempt to retract or modify the emancipation proclamation; nor shall I return to slavery any person who is free by the terms of that proclamation, or by any of the acts of Congress. For these and other reasons it is thought best that support of these measures shall be included in the oath; and it is believed the Executive may lawfully claim it in return for pardon and restoration of forfeited rights, which he has clear constitutional power to withhold altogether, or grant upon the terms which he shall deem wisest for the public interest. It should be observed, also, that this part of the oath is subject to the modifying and abrogating power of legislation and supreme judicial decision.

The proposed acquiescence of the national Executive in any reasonable temporary State arrangement for the freed people is made with the view of possibly modifying the confusion and destitution which must, at best, attend all classes by a total revolution of labor throughout whole States. It is hoped that the already deeply afflicted people in those States may be somewhat more ready to give up the cause of their affliction, if, to this extent, this vital matter be left to themselves; while no power of the national Executive to prevent an abuse is abridged by the proposition.

The suggestion in the proclamation as to maintaining the political framework of the States on what is called reconstruction, is made in the hope that it may do good without danger of harm. It will save labor and avoid great confusion.

But why any proclamation now upon this subject? This question is beset with the conflicting views that the step might be delayed too long or be taken too soon. In some States the elements for resumption seem ready for action, but remain inactive, apparently for want of a rallying point—a plan of action. Why shall A adopt the plan of B, rather than B that of A? And if A and B should agree, how can they know but that the general government here will reject their plan? By the proclamation a plan is presented which may be accepted by them as a rallying point, and which they are assured in advance will not be rejected here. This may bring them to act sooner than they otherwise would.

The objections to a premature presentation of a plan by the national Executive consists in the danger of committals on points which could be more safely left to further developments. Care has been taken to so shape the document as to avoid embarrassments from this source. Saying that, on certain terms, certain classes will be pardoned, with rights restored, it is not said that other classes, or other terms, will never be included. Saying that reconstruction will be accepted if presented in a specified way, it is not said it will never be accepted in any other way.

The movements, by State action, for emancipation in several of the States, not included in the emancipation proclamation, are matters of profound gratulation. And while I do not repeat in detail what I have hertofore so earnestly urged upon this subject, my general views and feelings remain unchanged; and I trust that Congress will omit no fair opportunity of aiding these important steps to a great consummation.

In the midst of other cares, however important, we must not lose sight of the fact that the war power is still our main reliance. To that power alone can we look, yet for a time, to give confidence to the people in the contested regions, that the insurgent power will not again overrun them. Until that confidence shall be established, little can be done anywhere for what is called reconstruction. Hence our chiefest care must still be directed to the army and navy, who have thus far borne their harder part so nobly and well. And it may be esteemed fortunate that in giving the greatest efficiency to these indispensable arms, we do also honorably recognize the gallant men, from commander to sentinel, who compose them, and to whom, more than to others, the world must stand indebted for the home of freedom disenthralled, regenerated, enlarged, and perpetuated.

*December 8, 1863*

# Proclamation of Amnesty and Reconstruction

By the President of the United States of America:

A Proclamation.

Whereas, in and by the Constitution of the United States, it is provided that the President "shall have power to grant reprieves and pardons for offences against the United States, except in cases of impeachment"; and

Whereas a rebellion now exists whereby the loyal State governments of several States have for a long time been subverted, and many persons have committed and are now guilty of treason against the United States; and

Whereas, with reference to said rebellion and treason, laws have been enacted by Congress declaring forfeitures and confiscation of property and liberation of slaves, all upon terms and conditions therein stated, and also declaring that the President was thereby authorized at any time thereafter, by proclamation, to extend to persons who may have participated in the existing rebellion, in any State or part thereof, pardon and amnesty, with such exceptions and at such times and on such conditions as he may deem expedient for the public welfare; and

Whereas the congressional declaration for limited and conditional pardon accords with well-established judicial exposition of the pardoning power; and

Whereas, with reference to said rebellion, the President of the United States has issued several proclamations, with provisions in regard to the liberation of slaves; and

Whereas it is now desired by some persons heretofore engaged in said rebellion to resume their allegiance to the United States, and to reinaugurate loyal State governments within and for their respective States; therefore,

I, Abraham Lincoln, President of the United States, do proclaim, declare, and make known to all persons who have, directly or by implication, participated in the existing rebellion, except as hereinafter excepted, that a full pardon is hereby granted to them and each of them, with restoration of all rights of property, except as to slaves, and in property cases where rights of third parties shall have intervened, and upon the condition that every such person shall take and subscribe an oath, and thenceforward keep and maintain said oath inviolate; and which oath shall be registered for permanent preservation, and shall be of the tenor and effect following, to wit:

"I, ———, do solemnly swear, in presence of Almighty God, that I will henceforth faithfully support, protect and defend the Constitution of the United States, and the union of the States thereunder; and that I will, in like manner, abide by and faithfully support all acts of Congress passed during the existing rebellion with reference to slaves, so long and so far as not repealed, modified or held void by Congress, or by decision of the Supreme Court; and that I will, in like manner, abide by and faithfully support all proclamations of the President made during the existing rebellion having reference to slaves, so long and so far as not modified or declared void by decision of the Supreme Court. So help me God."

The persons excepted from the benefits of the foregoing provisions are all who are, or shall have been, civil or diplomatic officers or agents of the so-called confederate government; all who have left judicial stations under the United States to aid the rebellion; all who are, or shall have been, military or naval officers of said so-called confederate government above the rank of colonel in the army, or of lieutenant in the navy; all who left seats in the United States Congress to aid the rebellion; all who resigned commissions in the army or navy of the United States, and afterwards aided the rebellion; and all who have engaged in any way in treating colored persons or white persons, in charge of such, otherwise than lawfully as prisoners of war, and which persons may have been found in the United States service, as soldiers, seamen, or in any other capacity.

And I do further proclaim, declare, and make known, that whenever, in any of the States of Arkansas, Texas, Louisiana, Mississippi, Tennessee, Alabama, Georgia, Florida, South Carolina, and North Carolina, a number of persons, not less than one-tenth in number of the votes cast in such State at the Presidential election of the year of our Lord one thousand eight hundred and sixty, each having taken the oath aforesaid and not having since violated it, and being a qualified voter by the election law of the State existing immediately before the so-called act of secession, and excluding all others, shall re-establish a State government which shall be republican, and in no wise contravening said oath, such shall be recognized as the true government of the State, and the State shall receive thereunder the benefits of the constitutional provision which declares that "The United States shall guaranty to every State in this union a republican form of government, and shall protect each of them against invasion; and, on application of the legislature, or the executive, (when the legislature cannot be convened,) against domestic violence."

And I do further proclaim, declare, and make known that any provision which may be adopted by such State government in relation to the freed people of such State, which shall recognize and declare their permanent freedom, provide for their education, and which may yet be consistent, as a temporary arrangement, with their present condition as a laboring, landless, and homeless class, will not be objected to by the national Executive. And it is suggested as not improper, that, in constructing a loyal State government in any State, the name of the State, the boundary, the subdivisions, the constitution, and the general code of laws, as before the rebellion, be maintained, subject only to the modifications made necessary by the conditions hereinbefore stated, and such others, if any, not contravening said conditions, and which may be deemed expedient by those framing the new State government.

To avoid misunderstanding, it may be proper to say that this proclamation, so far as it relates to State governments, has no reference to States wherein loyal State governments have all the while been maintained. And for the same reason, it may be proper to further say that whether members sent to Congress from any State shall be admitted to seats, constitutionally rests exclusively with the respective Houses, and not to any extent with the Executive. And still further, that this proclamation is intended to present the people of the States wherein the national authority has been suspended, and loyal State governments have been subverted, a mode in and by which the national authority and loyal State governments may be re-established within said States, or in any of them; and, while the mode presented is the best the Executive can suggest, with his present impressions, it must not be understood that no other possible mode would be acceptable.

Given under my hand at the city, of Washington, the 8th. day of December, A.D. one thousand eight hundred and sixty-three, and of the independence of the United States of America the eighty-eighth.

By the President:                                          ABRAHAM LINCOLN

WILLIAM H. SEWARD, Secretary of State

*December 8, 1863*

# Lecture on Liberty at the Sanitary Fair in Baltimore, Maryland

Ladies and Gentlemen—

Calling to mind that we are in Baltimore, we can not fail to note that the world moves. Looking upon these many people, assembled here, to serve, as they best may, the soldiers of the Union, it occurs at once that three years ago, the same soldiers could not so much as pass through Baltimore. The change from then till now, is both great, and gratifying. Blessings on the brave men who have wrought the change, and the fair women who strive to reward them for it.

But Baltimore suggests more than could happen within Baltimore. The change within Baltimore is part only of a far wider change. When the war began, three years ago, neither party, nor any man, expected it would last till now. Each looked for the end, in some way, long ere to-day. Neither did any anticipate that domestic slavery would be much affected by the war. But here we are; the war has not ended, and slavery has been much affected—how much needs not now to be recounted. So true is it that man proposes, and God disposes.

But we can see the past, though we may not claim to have directed it; and seeing it, in this case, we feel more hopeful and confident for the future.

The world has never had a good definition of the word liberty, and the American people, just now, are much in want of one. We all declare for liberty; but in using the same *word* we do not all mean the same *thing*. With some the word liberty may mean for each man to do as he pleases with himself, and the product of his labor; while with others the same word may mean for some men to do as they please with other men, and the product of other men's labor. Here are two, not only different, but incompatible things, called by the same name— liberty. And it follows that each of the things is, by the respective parties, called by two different and incompatible names—liberty and tyranny.

The shepherd drives the wolf from the sheep's throat, for which the sheep thanks the shepherd as a *liberator*, while the wolf denounces him for the same act, as the destroyer of liberty, especially as the sheep was a black one. Plainly, the sheep and the wolf are not agreed upon a definition of the word liberty; and precisely the same difference prevails to-day among us human creatures, even in the North, and all professing to love liberty. Hence we behold the processes by which thousands are daily passing from under the yoke of bondage, hailed by some as the advance of liberty, and bewailed by others as the destruction of all liberty. Recently, as it seems, the people of Maryland have been doing something to define liberty; and thanks to them that, in what they have done, the wolf's dictionary, has been repudiated.

It is not very becoming for one in my position to make speeches at great length; but there is another subject upon which I feel that I ought to say a word. A painful rumor, true I fear, has reached us, of the massacre, by the rebel forces, at Fort Pillow, in the West end of Tennessee, on the Mississippi river, of some three hundred colored soldiers and white officers, who had just been overpowered by their assailants. There seems to be some anxiety in the public mind whether the government is doing it's duty to the colored soldier, and to the service, at this point. At the beginning of the war, and for some time, the use of colored troops was not contemplated; and how the change of purpose was wrought, I will not now take time to explain. Upon a clear conviction of duty I resolved to turn that element of strength to account; and I am responsible for it to the American people, to the christian world, to history, and on my final account to God. Having determined to use the negro as a soldier, there is no way but to give him all the protection given to any other soldier. The difficulty is not in stating the principle, but in practically applying it. It is a mistake to suppose the government is indifferent to this matter, or is not doing the best it can in regard to it. We do not to-day *know* that a colored soldier, or white officer commanding colored soldiers, has been massacred by the rebels when made a prisoner. We fear it, believe it, I may say, but we do not *know* it. To take the life of one of their prisoners, on the assumption that they murder ours, when it is short of certainty that they do murder ours, might be too serious, too cruel a mistake. We are having the Fort-Pillow affair thoroughly investigated; and such investigation will probably show conclusively how the truth is. If, after all that has been said, it shall turn out that there has been no massacre at Fort-Pillow, it will be almost safe to say there has been none, and will be none elsewhere. If there has been the massacre of three hundred there, or even the tenth part of three hundred, it will be conclusively proved; and being so proved, the retribution shall as surely come. It will be matter of grave consideration in what exact course to apply the retribution; but in the supposed case, it must come.

*April 18, 1864*

# Speech at the Great Central Sanitary Fair, Philadelphia, Pennsylvania

I suppose that this toast was intended to open the way for me to say something. [Laughter.] War, at the best, is terrible, and this war of ours, in its magnitude and in its duration, is one of the most terrible. It has deranged business, totally in many localities, and partially in all localities. It has destroyed property, and ruined homes; it has produced a national debt and taxation unprecedented, at least in this country. It has carried mourning to almost every home, until it can almost be said that the "heavens are hung in black." Yet it continues, and several relieving coincidents have accompanied it from the very beginning, which have not been known, as I understood, or have any knowledge of, in any former wars in the history of the world. The Sanitary Commission, with all its benevolent labors, the Christian Commission, with all its Christian and benevolent labors, and the various places, arrangements, so to speak, and institutions, have contributed to the comfort and relief of the soldiers. You have two of these places in this city—the Cooper-Shop and Union Volunteer Refreshment Saloons. [Great applause and cheers.] And lastly, these fairs, which, I believe, began only in last August, if I mistake not, in Chicago; then at Boston, at Cincinnati, Brooklyn, New York, at Baltimore, and those at present held at St. Louis, Pittsburg, and Philadelphia. The motive and object that lie at the bottom of all these are most worthy; for, say what you will, after all the most is due to the soldier, who takes his life in his hands and goes to fight the battles of his country. [Cheers.] In what is contributed to his comfort when he passes to and fro, and in what is contributed to him when he is sick and wounded, in whatever shape it comes, whether from the fair and tender hand of woman, or from any other source, is much, very much; but, I think there is still that which has as much value to him—he is not forgotten. [Cheers.] Another view of these various institutions is worthy of consideration, I think; they are voluntary contributions, given freely, zealously, and earnestly, on top of all the disturbances of business, the taxation and burdens that the war has imposed upon us, giving proof that the national resources are not at all exhausted, [cheers;] that the national spirit of patriotism is even stronger than at the commencement of the rebellion.

It is a pertinent question often asked in the mind privately, and from one to the other, when is the war to end? Surely I feel as deep an interest in this question as any other can, but I do not wish to name a day, or month, or a year when it is to end. I do not wish to run any risk of seeing the time come, without our being ready for the end, and for fear of disappointment, because the time had come and not the end. We accepted this war for an object, a worthy object, and the war will end when that object is attained. Under God, I hope it never will until that time. [Great cheering.] Speaking of the present campaign, General Grant is reported to have said, I am going through on this line if it takes all summer. [Cheers.] This war has taken three years; it was begun or accepted upon the line of restoring the national authority over the whole national domain, and for the American people, as far as my knowledge enables me to speak, I say we are going through on this line if it takes three years more. [Cheers.] My friends, I did not know but that I might be called upon to say a few words before I got away from here, but I did not know it was coming just here. [Laughter.] I have never been in the habit of making predictions in regard to the war, but I am almost tempted to make one.—If I were to hazard it, it is this: That Grant is this evening, with General Meade and General Hancock, of Pennsylvania, and the brave officers and soldiers with him, in a position from whence he will never be dislodged until Richmond is taken [loud cheering], and I have but one single proposition to put now, and, perhaps, I can best put it in form of an interrogative. If I shall discover that General Grant and the noble officers and men under him can be greatly facilitated in their work by a sudden pouring forward of men and assistance, will you give them to me? [Cries of "yes."] Then, I say, stand ready, for I am watching for the chance. [Laughter and cheers.] I thank you, gentlemen.

*June 16, 1864*

# Address to the 164<sup>th</sup> Ohio Regiment

SOLDIERS—

You are about to return to your homes and your friends, after having, as I learn, performed in camp a comparatively short term of duty in this great contest. I am greatly obliged to you, and to all who have come forward at the call of their country. I wish it might be more generally and universally understood what the country is now engaged in. We have, as all will agree, a free Government, where every man has a right to be equal with every other man. In this great struggle, this form of Government and every form of human right is endangered if our enemies succeed. There is more involved in this contest than is realized by every one. There is involved in this struggle the question whether your children and my children shall enjoy the privileges we have enjoyed. I say this in order to impress upon you, if you are not already so impressed, that no small matter should divert us from our great purpose. There may be some irregularities in the practical application of our system. It is fair that each man shall pay taxes in exact proportion to the value of his property; but if we should wait before collecting a tax to adjust the taxes upon each man in exact proportion with every other man, we should never collect any tax at all. There may be mistakes made sometimes; things may be done wrong, while the officers of the Government do all they can to prevent mistakes. But I beg of you, as citizens of this great Republic, not to let your minds be carried off from the great work we have before us. This struggle is too large for you to be diverted from it by any small matter. When you return to your homes, rise up to the height of a generation of men worthy of a free Government, and we will carry out the great work we have commenced. I return to you my sincere thanks, soldiers, for the honor you have done me this afternoon.

*August 18, 1864*

# Address to the 166<sup>th</sup> Ohio Regiment

I suppose you are going home to see your families and friends. For the services you have done in this great struggle in which we are engaged I present you sincere thanks for myself and the country. I almost always feel inclined, when I say anything to soldiers, to impress upon them in a few brief remarks the importance of success in this contest. It is not merely for to-day, but for all time to come that we should perpetuate for our children's children this great and free government, which we have enjoyed all our lives. I beg you to remember this, not merely for my sake, but for yours. I happen temporarily to occupy this big White House. I am a living witness that any one of your children may look to come here as my father's child has. It is in order that each one of you may have through this free government which we have enjoyed, an open field and a fair chance for your industry, enterprise and intelligence; that you may all have equal privileges in the race of life, with all its desirable human aspirations. It is for this the struggle should be maintained, that we may not lose our birthright—not only for one, but for two or three years. The nation is worth fighting for, to secure such an inestimable jewel.

*August 22, 1864*

# Address to the 148ᵗʰ Ohio Regiment

SOLDIERS OF THE 148ᵀᴴ OHIO:

I am most happy to meet you on this occasion. I understand that it has been your honorable privilege to stand, for a brief period, in the defense of your country, and that now you are on your way to your homes. I congratulate you, and those who are waiting to bid you welcome home from the war; and permit me, in the name of the people, to thank you for the part you have taken in this straggle for the life of the nation. You are soldiers of the Republic, everywhere honored and respected. Whenever I appear before a body of soldiers, I feel tempted to talk to them of the nature of the struggle in which we are engaged. I look upon it as an attempt on the one hand to overwhelm and destroy the national existence, while, on our part, we are striving to maintain the government and institutions or our fathers, to enjoy them ourselves, and transmit them to our children and our children's children forever.

To do this the constitutional administration of our government must be sustained, and I beg of you not to allow your minds or your hearts to be diverted from the support of all necessary measures for that purpose, by any miserable picayune arguments addressed to your pockets, or inflammatory appeals made to your passions and your prejudices.

It is vain and foolish to arraign this man or that for the part he has taken, or has not taken, and to hold the government responsible for his acts. In no administration can there be perfect equality of action and uniform satisfaction rendered by all. But this government must be preserved in spite of the acts of any man or set of men. It is worthy your every effort. Nowhere in the world is presented a government of so much liberty and equality. To the humblest and poorest amongst us are held out the highest privileges and positions. The present moment finds me at the White House, yet there is as good a chance for your children as there was for my father's.

Again I admonish you not to be turned from your stern purpose of defending your beloved country and its free institutions by any arguments urged by ambitious and designing men, but to stand fast for the Union and the old flag. Soldiers, I bid you God-speed to your homes.

*August 31, 1864*

# Response to a Serenade

It has long been a grave question whether any government, not *too* strong for the liberties of its people, can be strong *enough* to maintain its existence, in great emergencies.

On this point the present rebellion brought our republic to a severe test, and a presidential election occurring in regular course during the rebellion added not a little to the strain. If the loyal people, *united*, were put to the utmost of their strength by the rebellion, must they not fail when *divided*, and partially paralyzed, by a political war among themselves?

But the election was a necessity.

We can not have free government without elections; and if the rebellion could force us to forego, or postpone a national election, it might fairly claim to have already conquered and ruined us. The strife of the election is but human-nature practically applied to the facts of the case. What has occurred in this case, must ever recur in similar cases. Human-nature will not change. In any future great national trial, compared with the men of this, we will have as weak, and as strong; as silly and as wise; as bad and good. Let us, therefore, study the incidents of this, as philosophy to learn wisdom from, and none of them as wrongs to be revenged.

But the election, along with its incidental, and undesirable strife, has done good too. It has demonstrated that a people's government can sustain a national election, in the midst of a great civil war. Until now it has not been known to the world that this was a possibility. It shows also how *sound,* and how *strong* we still are. It shows that, even among the candidates of the same party, he who is most devoted to the Union, and most opposed to treason, can receive most of the people's votes. It shows also, to the extent yet known, that we have more men now, than we had when the war began. Gold is good in its place; but living, brave, patriotic men, are better than gold.

But the rebellion continues; and now that the election is over, may not all, having a common interest, re-unite in a common effort, to save our common country? For my own part I have striven, and shall strive to avoid placing any obstacle in the way. So long as I have been here I have not willingly planted a thorn in any man's bosom.

While I am deeply sensible to the high compliment of a re-election; and duly grateful, as I trust, to Almighty God for having directed my countrymen to a right conclusion, as I think, for their own good, it adds nothing to my satisfaction that any other man may be disappointed by the result.

May I ask those who have not differed with me, to join with me, in this same spirit towards those who have?

And now, let me close by asking three hearty cheers for our brave soldiers and seamen and their gallant and skilful commanders.

*November 10, 1864*

# Annual Message to Congress, 1864

Fellow-citizens of the Senate and House of Representatives:

Again the blessings of health and abundant harvests claim our profoundest gratitude to Almighty God.

The condition of our foreign affairs is reasonably satisfactory.

Mexico continues to be a theatre of civil war. While our political relations with that country have undergone no change, we have, at the same time, strictly maintained neutrality between the belligerents.

At the request of the states of Costa Rica and Nicaragua, a competent engineer has been authorized to make a survey of the river San Juan and the port of San Juan. It is a source of much satisfaction that the difficulties which for a moment excited some political apprehensions, and caused a closing of the inter-oceanic transit route, have been amicably adjusted, and that there is a good prospect that the route will soon be reopened with an increase of capacity and adaptation. We could not exaggerate either the commercial or the political importance of that great improvement.

It would be doing injustice to an important South American state not to acknowledge the directness, frankness, and cordiality with which the United States of Colombia have entered into intimate relations with this government. A claims convention has been constituted to complete the unfinished work of the one which closed its session in 1861.

The new liberal constitution of Venezuela having gone into effect with the universal acquiescence of the people, the government under it has been recognized, and diplomatic intercourse with it has opened in a cordial and friendly spirit. The long-deferred Aves Island claim has been satisfactorily paid and discharged.

Mutual payments have been made of the claims awarded by the late joint commission for the settlement of claims between the United States and Peru. An earnest and cordial friendship continues to exist between the two countries, and such efforts as were in my power have been used to remove misunderstanding and avert a threatened war between Peru and Spain.

Our relations are of the most friendly nature with Chile, the Argentine Republic, Bolivia, Costa Rica, Paraguay, San Salvador, and Hayti.

During the past year no differences of any kind have arisen with any of those republics, and, on the other hand, their sympathies with the United States are constantly expressed with cordiality and earnestness.

The claim arising from the seizure of the cargo of the brig Macedonian in 1821 has been paid in full by the government of Chile.

Civil war continues in the Spanish part of San Domingo, apparently without prospect of an early close.

Official correspondence has been freely opened with Liberia, and it gives us a pleasing view of social and political progress in that Republic. It may be expected to derive new vigor from American influence, improved by the rapid disappearance of slavery in the United States.

I solicit your authority to furnish to the republic a gunboat at moderate cost, to be reimbursed to the United States by instalments. Such a vessel is needed for the safety of that state against the native African races; and in Liberian hands it would be more effective in arresting the African slave trade than a squadron in our own hands. The possession of the least organized naval force would stimulate a generous ambition in the republic, and the confidence which we should manifest by furnishing it would win forbearance and favor towards the colony from all civilized nations.

The proposed overland telegraph between America and Europe, by the way of Behring's Straits and Asiatic Russia, which was sanctioned by Congress at the last session, has been undertaken, under very favorable circumstances, by an association of American citizens, with the cordial good-will and support as well of this government as of those of Great Britain and Russia. Assurances have been received from most of the South American States of their high appreciation of the enterprise, and their readiness to co-operate in constructing lines tributary to that world-encircling communication. I learn, with much satisfaction, that the noble design of a telegraphic communication between the eastern coast of America and Great Britain has been renewed with full expectation of its early accomplishment.

Thus it is hoped that with the return of domestic peace the country will be able to resume with energy and advantage its former high career of commerce and civilization.

Our very popular and estimable representative in Egypt died in April last. An unpleasant altercation which arose between the temporary incumbent of the office and the government of the Pacha resulted in a suspension of intercourse. The evil was promptly corrected on the arrival of the successor in the consulate, and our relations with Egypt, as well as our relations with the Barbary powers, are entirely satisfactory.

The rebellion which has so long been flagrant in China, has at last been suppressed, with the co-operating good offices of this government, and of the other western commercial states. The judicial consular establishment there has become very difficult and onerous, and it will need legislative revision to adapt it to the extension of our commerce, and to the more intimate intercourse which has been instituted with the government and people of that vast empire. China seems to be accepting with hearty good-will the conventional laws which regulate commercial and social intercourse among the western nations.

Owing to the peculiar situation of Japan, and the anomalous form of its government, the action of that empire in performing treaty stipulations is inconstant and capricious. Nevertheless, good progress has been effected by the western powers, moving with enlightened concert. Our own pecuniary claims have been allowed, or put in course of settlement, and the inland sea has been reopened to commerce. There is reason also to believe that these proceedings have increased rather than diminished the friendship of Japan towards the United States.

The ports of Norfolk, Fernandina, and Pensacola have been opened by proclamation. It is hoped that foreign merchants will now consider whether it is not safer and more profitable to themselves, as well as just to the United States, to resort to these and other open ports, than it is to pursue, through many hazards, and at vast cost, a contraband trade with other ports which are closed, if not by actual military occupation, at least by a lawful and effective blockade.

For myself, I have no doubt of the power and duty of the Executive, under the law of nations, to exclude enemies of the human race from an asylum in the United States. If Congress should think that proceedings in such cases lack the authority of law, or ought to be further regulated by it, I recommend that provision be made for effectually preventing foreign slave traders from acquiring domicile and facilities for their criminal occupation in our country.

It is possible that, if it were a new and open question, the maritime powers, with the lights they now enjoy, would not concede the privileges of a naval belligerent to the insurgents of the United States, destitute, as they are, and always have been, equally of ships-of-war and of ports and harbors. Disloyal emissaries have been neither less assiduous nor more successful during the last year than they were before that time in their efforts, under favor of that privilege, to embroil our country in foreign wars. The desire and determination of the governments of the maritime states to defeat that design are believed to be as sincere as, and cannot be more earnest than our own. Nevertheless, unforeseen political difficulties have arisen, especially in Brazilian and British ports, and on the northern boundary of the United States, which have required, and are likely to continue to require, the practice of constant vigilance, and a just and conciliatory spirit on the part of the United States as well as of the nations concerned and their governments.

Commissioners have been appointed under the treaty with Great Britain on the adjustment of the claims of the Hudson's Bay and Puget's Sound Agricultural Companies, in Oregon, and are now proceeding to the execution of the trust assigned to them.

In view of the insecurity of life and property in the region adjacent to the Canadian border, by reason of recent assaults and depredations committed by inimical and desperate persons, who are harbored there, it has been thought proper to give notice that after the expiration of six months, the period conditionally stipulated in the existing arrangement with Great Britain, the United States must hold themselves at liberty to increase their naval armament upon the lakes, if they shall find that proceeding necessary. The condition of the border will necessarily come into consideration in connection with the question of continuing or modifying the rights of transit from Canada through the United States, as well as the regulation of imposts, which were temporarily established by the reciprocity treaty of the 5th of June, 1854.

I desire, however, to be understood, while making this statement, that the Colonial authorities of Canada are not deemed to be intentionally unjust or unfriendly towards the United States; but, on the contrary, there is every reason to expect that, with the approval of the imperial government, they will take the necessary measures to prevent new incursions across the border.

The act passed at the last session for the encouragement of emigration has, so far as was possible, been put into operation. It seems to need amendment which will enable the officers of the government to prevent the practice of frauds against the immigrants while on their way and on their arrival in the ports, so as to secure them here a free choice of avocations and places of settlement. A liberal disposition towards this great national policy is manifested by most of the European States, and ought to be reciprocated on our part by giving the immigrants effective national protection. I regard our emigrants as one of the principal replenishing streams which are appointed by Providence to repair the ravages of internal war, and its wastes of national strength and health. All that is necessary is to secure the flow of that stream in its present fullness, and to that end the government must, in every way, make it manifest that it neither needs nor designs to impose involuntary military service upon those who come from other lands to cast their lot in our country.

The financial affairs of the government have been successfully administered during the last year. The legislation of the last session of Congress has beneficially affected the revenues, although sufficient time has not yet elapsed to experience the full effect of several of the provisions of the acts of Congress imposing increased taxation.

The receipts during the year, from all sources, upon the basis of warrants signed by the Secretary of the Treasury, including loans and the balance in the treasury on the first day of July, 1863, were $1,394,796,007.62; and the aggregate disbursements, upon the same basis, were $1,298,056,101.89, leaving a balance in the treasury, as shown by warrants, of $96,739,905.73.

Deduct from these amounts the amount of the principal of the public debt redeemed, and the amount of issues in substitution therefor, and the actual cash operations of the treasury were: receipts, $884,076,646.57; disbursements $865,234,087.86; which leaves a cash balance in the treasury of $18,842,558.71. Of the receipts, there were derived from customs, $102,316,152.99; from lands, $588,333.29; from direct taxes, $475,648.96; from internal revenue, $109,741,134.10; from miscellaneous sources, $47,511,448.10; and from loans applied to actual expenditures, including former balance, $623,443,929.13.

There were disbursed, for the civil service, $27,505,599.46; for pensions and Indians, $7,517,930.97; for the War Department $690,791,842.97; for the Navy Department $85,733,292.77; for interest of the public debt $53,685,421.69;— making an aggregate of $865,234,087.86, and leaving a balance in the treasury of $18,842,558.71, as before stated.

For the actual receipts and disbursements for the first quarter, and the estimated receipts and disbursements for the three remaining quarters of the current fiscal year, and the general operations of the treasury in detail, I refer you to the report of the Secretary of the Treasury. I concur with him in the opinion that the proportion of moneys required to meet the expenses consequent upon the war derived from taxation should be still further increased; and I earnestly invite your attention to this subject, to the end that there may be such additional legislation as shall be required to meet the just expectations of the Secretary.

The public debt on the first day of July last, as appears by the books of the treasury, amounted to $1,740,690,489.49. Probably, should the war continue for another year, that amount may be increased by not far from five hundred millions. Held as it is, for the most part, by our own people, it has become a substantial branch of national, though private, property. For obvious reasons, the more nearly this property can be distributed among all the people the better. To favor such general distribution, greater inducements to become owners might, perhaps, with good effect, and without injury, be presented to persons of limited means. With this view, I suggest whether it might not be both competent and expedient for Congress to provide that a limited amount of some future issue of public securities might be held by any bona fide purchaser exempt from taxation, and from seizure for debt, under such restrictions and limitations as might be necessary to guard against abuse of so important a privilege. This would enable every prudent person to set aside a small annuity against a possible day of want.

Privileges like these would render the possession of such securities, to the amount limited, most desirable to every person of small means who might be able to save enough for the purpose. The great advantage of citizens being creditors as well as debtors, with relation to the public debt, is obvious. Men readily perceive that they cannot be much oppressed by a debt which they owe to themselves.

The public debt on the first day of July last, although somewhat exceeding the estimate of the Secretary of the Treasury made to Congress at the commencement of the last session, falls short of the estimate of that officer made in the preceding December, as to its probable amount at the beginning of this year, by the sum of $3,995,097.31. This fact exhibits a satisfactory condition and conduct of the operations of the Treasury.

The national banking system is proving to be acceptable to capitalists and to the people. On the twenty-fifth day of November five hundred and eighty-four national banks had been organized, a considerable number of which were conversions from State banks. Changes from State systems to the national system are rapidly taking place, and it is hoped that, very soon, there will be in the United States, no banks of issue not authorized by Congress, and no bank-note circulation not secured by the government. That the government and the people will derive great benefit from this change in the banking systems of the country can hardly be questioned. The national system will create a reliable and permanent influence in support of the national credit, and protect the people against losses in the use of paper money. Whether or not any further legislation is advisable for the suppression of State bank issues, it will be for Congress to determine. It seems quite clear that the treasury cannot be satisfactorily conducted unless the government can exercise a restraining power over the bank-note circulation of the country.

The report of the Secretary of War and the accompanying documents will detail the campaigns of the armies in the field since the date of the last annual message, and also the operations of the several administrative bureaus of the War Department during the last year. It will also specify the measures deemed essential for the national defence, and to keep up and supply the requisite military force.

The report of the Secretary of the Navy presents a comprehensive and satisfactory exhibit of the affairs of that Department and of the naval service. It is a subject of congratulation and laudable pride to our countrymen that a navy of such vast proportions has been organized in so brief a period, and conducted with so much efficiency and success.

The general exhibit of the navy, including vessels under construction on the 1st. of December, 1864, shows a total of 671 vessels, carrying 4,610 guns, and of 510,396 tons, being an actual increase during the year, over and above all losses by shipwreck or in battle, of 83 vessels, 167 guns, and 42,427 tons.

The total number of men at this time in the naval service, including officers, is about 51,000.

There have been captured by the navy during the year 324 vessels, and the whole number of naval captures since hostilities commenced is 1,379, of which 267 are steamers.

The gross proceeds arising from the sale of condemned prize property, thus far reported, amount to $14,396,250.51. A large amount of such proceeds is still under adjudication and yet to be reported.

The total expenditures of the Navy Department of every description, including the cost of the immense squadrons that have been called into existence from the 4th of March, 1861, to the 1st. of November, 1864, are $238,647,262.35.

Your favorable consideration is invited to the various recommendations of the Secretary of the Navy, especially in regard to a navy yard and suitable establishment for the construction and repair of iron vessels, and the machinery and armature for our ships, to which reference was made in my last annual message.

Your attention is also invited to the views expressed in the report in relation to the legislation of Congress at its last session in respect to prize on our inland waters.

I cordially concur in the recommendation of the Secretary as to the propriety of creating the new rank of vice-admiral in our naval service.

Your attention is invited to the report of the Postmaster General for a detailed account of the operations and financial condition of the Post Office Department.

The postal revenues for the year ending June 30, 1864, amounted to $12,438,253.78 and the expenditures to $12,644,786.20; the excess of expenditures over receipts being $206,652.42.

The views presented by the Postmaster General on the subject of special grants by the government in aid of the establishment of new lines of ocean mail steamships and the policy he recommends for the development of increased commercial intercourse with adjacent and neighboring countries, should receive the careful consideration of Congress.

It is of noteworthy interest that the steady expansion of population, improvement and governmental institutions over the new and unoccupied portions of our country have scarcely been checked, much less impeded or destroyed, by our great civil war, which at first glance would seem to have absorbed almost the entire energies of the nation.

The organization and admission of the State of Nevada has been completed in conformity with law, and thus our excellent system is firmly established in the mountains, which once seemed a barren and uninhabitable waste between the Atlantic States and those which have grown up on the coast of the Pacific ocean.

The territories of the Union are generally in a condition of prosperity and rapid growth. Idaho and Montana, by reason of their great distance and the interruption of communication with them by Indian hostilities, have been only partially organized; but it is understood that these difficulties are about to disappear, which will permit their governments, like those of the others, to go into speedy and full operation.

As intimately connected with, and promotive of, this material growth of the nation, I ask the attention of Congress to the valuable information and important recommendations relating to the public lands, Indian affairs, the Pacific railroad, and mineral discoveries contained in the report of the Secretary of the Interior, which is herewith transmitted, and which report also embraces the subjects of patents, pensions and other topics of public interest pertaining to his department.

The quantity of public land disposed of during the five quarters ending on the 30th of September last was 4,221,342 acres, of which 1,538,614 acres were entered under the homestead law. The remainder was located with military land warrants, agricultural scrip certified to States for railroads, and sold for cash. The cash received from sales and location fees was $1,019,446.

The income from sales during the fiscal year, ending June 30, 1864, was $678,007.21, against $136,077.95 received during the preceding year. The aggregate number of acres surveyed during the year has been equal to the quantity disposed of; and there is open to settlement about 133,000,000 acres of surveyed land.

The great enterprise of connecting the Atlantic with the Pacific States by railways and telegraph lines has been entered upon with a vigor that gives assurance of success, notwithstanding the embarrassments arising from the prevailing high prices of materials and labor. The route of the main line of the road has been definitely located for one hundred miles westward from the initial point at Omaha City, Nebraska, and a preliminary location of the Pacific railroad of California has been made from Sacramento eastward to the great bend of the Truckee river in Nevada.

Numerous discoveries of gold, silver and cinnabar mines have been added to the many heretofore known and the country occupied by the Sierra Nevada and Rocky mountains, and the subordinate ranges, now teems with enterprising labor, which is richly remunerative. It is believed that the product of the mines of precious metals in that region has, during the year, reached, if not exceeded, one hundred millions in value.

It was recommended in my last annual message that our Indian system be remodelled. Congress, at its last session, acting upon the recommendation, did provide for reorganizing the system in California, and it is believed that under the present organization the management of the Indians there will be attended with reasonable success. Much yet remains to be done to provide for the proper government of the Indians in other parts of the country to render it secure for the advancing settler, and to provide for the welfare of the Indian. The Secretary reiterates his recommendations, and to them the attention of Congress is invited.

The liberal provisions made by Congress for paying pensions to invalid soldiers and sailors of the republic, and to the widows, orphans, and dependent mothers of those who have fallen in battle, or died of disease contracted, or of wounds received in the service of their country, have been diligently administered. There have been added to the pension, rolls, during the year ending the 30th day of June last, the names of 16,770 invalid soldiers, and of 271 disabled seamen, making the present number of army invalid pensioners 22,767, and of navy invalid pensioners 712.

Of widows, orphans and mothers, 22,198 have been placed on the army pension rolls, and 248 on the navy rolls. The present number of army pensioners of this class is 25,433, and of navy pensioners 793. At the beginning of the year the number of revolutionary pensioners was 1,430; only twelve of them were soldiers, of whom seven have since died. The remainder are those who, under the law, receive pensions because of relationship to revolutionary soldiers. During the year ending the 30th of June, 1864, $4,504,616.92 have been paid to pensioners of all classes.

I cheerfully commend to your continued patronage the benevolent institutions of the District of Columbia which have hitherto been established or fostered by Congress, and respectfully refer, for information concerning them, and in relation to the Washington aqueduct, the Capitol and other matters of local interest, to the report of the Secretary.

The Agricultural Department, under the supervision of its present energetic and faithful head, is rapidly commending itself to the great and vital interest it was created to advance. It is peculiarly the people's department, in which they feel more directly concerned than in any other. I commend it to the continued attention and fostering care of Congress.

The war continues. Since the last annual message all the important lines and positions then occupied by our forces have been maintained, and our arms have steadily advanced; thus liberating the regions left in rear, so that Missouri,

Kentucky, Tennessee and parts of other States have again produced reasonably fair crops.

The most remarkable feature in the military operations of the year is General Sherman's attempted march of three hundred miles directly through the insurgent region. It tends to show a great increase of our relative strength that our General-in-Chief should feel able to confront and hold in check every active force of the enemy, and yet to detach a well-appointed large army to move on such an expedition. The result not yet being known, conjecture in regard to it is not here indulged.

Important movements have also occurred during the year to the effect of moulding society for durability in the Union. Although short of complete success, it is much in the right direction, that twelve thousand citizens in each of the States of Arkansas and Louisiana have organized loyal State governments with free constitutions, and are earnestly struggling to maintain and administer them. The movements in the same direction, more extensive, though less definite in Missouri, Kentucky and Tennessee, should not be overlooked. But Maryland presents the example of complete success. Maryland is secure to Liberty and Union for all the future. The genius of rebellion will no more claim Maryland. Like another foul spirit, being driven out, it may seek to tear her, but it will woo her no more.

At the last session of Congress a proposed amendment of the Constitution abolishing slavery throughout the United States, passed the Senate, but failed for lack of the requisite two-thirds vote in the House of Representatives. Although the present is the same Congress, and nearly the same members, and without questioning the wisdom or patriotism of those who stood in opposition, I venture to recommend the reconsideration and passage of the measure at the present session. Of course the abstract question is not changed; but an intervening election shows, almost certainly, that the next Congress will pass the measure if this does not. Hence there is only a question of *time* as to when the proposed amendment will go to the States for their action. And as it is to so go, at all events, may we not agree that the sooner the better? It is not claimed that the election has imposed a duty on members to change their views or their votes, any further than, as an additional element to be considered, their judgment may be affected by it. It is the voice of the people now, for the first time, heard upon the question. In a great national crisis, like ours, unanimity of action among those seeking a common end is very desirable—almost indispensable. And yet no approach to such unanimity is attainable, unless some deference shall be paid to the will of the majority, simply because it is the will of the majority. In this case the common end is the maintenance of the Union; and, among the means to secure that end, such will, through the election, is most clearly declared in favor of such constitutional amendment.

The most reliable indication of public purpose in this country is derived through our popular elections. Judging by the recent canvass and its result, the purpose of the people, within the loyal States, to maintain the integrity of the Union, was never more firm, nor more nearly unanimous, than now. The extraordinary calmness and good order with which the millions of voters met and mingled at the polls, give strong assurance of this. Not only all those who supported the Union ticket, so called, but a great majority of the opposing party also, may be fairly claimed to entertain, and to be actuated by, the same purpose. It is an unanswerable argument to this effect, that no candidate for any office whatever, high or low, has ventured to seek votes on the avowal that he was for giving up the Union. There have been much impugning of motives, and much heated controversy as to the proper means and best mode of advancing the Union cause; but on the distinct issue of Union or no Union, the politicians have shown their instinctive knowledge that there is no diversity among the people. In affording the people the fair opportunity of showing, one to another and to the world, this firmness and unanimity of purpose, the election has been of vast value to the national cause.

The election has exhibited another fact not less valuable to be known—the fact that we do not approach exhaustion in the most important branch of national resources—that of living men. While it is melancholy to reflect that the war has filled so many graves, and carried mourning to so many hearts, it is some relief to know that, compared with the surviving, the fallen have been so few. While corps, and divisions, and brigades, and regiments have formed, and fought, and dwindled, and gone out of existence, a great majority of the men who composed them are still living. The same is true of the naval service. The election returns prove this. So many voters could not else be found. The States regularly holding elections, both now and four years ago, to wit, California, Connecticut, Delaware, Illinois, Indiana, Iowa, Kentucky, Maine, Maryland, Massachusetts, Michigan, Minnesota, Missouri, New Hampshire, New Jersey, New York, Ohio, Oregon, Pennsylvania, Rhode Island, Vermont, West Virginia, and Wisconsin cast 3,982,011 votes now, against 3,870,222 cast then, showing an aggregate now of 3,982,011. To this is to be added 33,762 cast now in the new States of Kansas and Nevada, which States did not vote in 1860, thus swelling the aggregate to 4,015,773 and the net increase during the three years and a half of war to 145,551. A table is appended showing particulars. To this again should be added the number of all soldiers in the field from Massachusetts, Rhode Island, New Jersey, Delaware, Indiana, Illinois, and California, who, by the laws of those States, could not vote away from their homes, and which number cannot be less than 90,000. Nor yet is this all. The number in organized Territories is triple now what it was four years ago, while thousands, white and black, join us as the national arms press back the insurgent lines. So much is shown, affirmatively and negatively, by the election. It is not material to inquire *how* the increase has been produced, or to show that it would have been *greater* but for the war, which is probably true. The important fact remains demonstrated, that we have *more* men *now* than we had when the war *began*; that we are not exhausted, nor in process of exhaustion; that we are *gaining* strength, and may, if need be, maintain the contest indefinitely. This as to men. Material resources are now more complete and abundant than ever.

The national resources, then, are unexhausted, and, as we believe, inexhaustible. The public purpose to re-establish and maintain the national authority is unchanged, and, as we believe, unchangeable. The manner of continuing the effort remains to choose. On careful consideration of all the evidence accessible it seems to me that no attempt at negotiation with the insurgent leader could result in any good. He would accept nothing short of severance of the Union—precisely what we will not and cannot give. His declarations to this effect are explicit and oft-repeated. He does not attempt to deceive us. He affords us no excuse to deceive ourselves. He cannot voluntarily reaccept the Union; we cannot voluntarily yield it. Between him and us the issue is distinct, simple, and inflexible. It is an issue which can only be tried by war, and decided by victory. If we yield, we are beaten; if the Southern people fail him, he is beaten. Either way, it would be the victory and defeat following war. What is true, however, of him who heads the insurgent cause, is not necessarily true of those who follow. Although he cannot reaccept the Union, they can. Some of them, we know, already desire peace and reunion. The number of such may increase. They can, at any moment, have peace simply by laying down their arms and submitting to the national authority under the Constitution. After so much, the government could not, if it would, maintain war against them. The loyal people would not sustain or allow it. If questions should remain, we would adjust them by the peaceful means of legislation, conference, courts, and votes, operating only in constitutional and lawful channels. Some certain, and other possible, questions are, and would be, beyond the Executive power to adjust; as, for instance, the admission of members into Congress, and whatever might require the appropriation of money. The Executive power itself would be greatly diminished by the cessation of actual war. Pardons and remissions of forfeitures, however, would still be within Executive control. In what spirit and temper this control would be exercised can be fairly judged of by the past.

A year ago general pardon and amnesty, upon specified terms, were offered to all, except certain designated classes; and, it was, at the same time, made known that the excepted classes were still within contemplation of special clemency. During the year many availed themselves of the general provision, and many more would, only that the signs of bad faith in some led to such precautionary measures as rendered the practical process less easy and certain. During the same time also special pardons have been granted to individuals of the excepted classes, and no voluntary application has been denied. Thus, practically, the door has been, for a full year, open to all, except such as were not in condition to make free choice—that is, such as were in custody or under constraint. It is still so open to all. But the time may come—probably will come—when public duty shall demand that it be closed; and that, in lieu, more rigorous measures than heretofore shall be adopted.

In presenting the abandonment of armed resistance to the national authority on the part of the insurgents, as the only indispensable condition to ending the war on the part of the government, I retract nothing heretofore said as to slavery. I repeat the declaration made a year ago, that "while I remain in my present position I shall not attempt to retract or modify the emancipation proclamation, nor shall I return to slavery any person who is free by the terms of that proclamation, or by any of the Acts of Congress." If the people should, by whatever mode or means, make it an Executive duty to re-enslave such persons, another, and not I, must be their instrument to perform it.

In stating a single condition of peace, I mean simply to say that the war will cease on the part of the government, whenever it shall have ceased on the part of those who began it.

*December 6, 1864*

# Second Inaugural Address

FELLOW COUNTRYMEN:

At this second appearing to take the oath of the presidential office, there is less occasion for an extended address than there was at the first. Then a statement, somewhat in detail, of a course to be pursued, seemed fitting and proper. Now, at the expiration of four years, during which public declarations have been constantly called forth on every point and phase of the great contest, which still absorbs the attention, and engrosses the energies of the nation, little that is new could be presented. The progress of our arms, upon which all else chiefly depends, is as well known to the public as to myself; and it is, I trust, reasonably satisfactory and encouraging to all. With high hope for the future, no prediction in regard to it is ventured.

On the occasion corresponding to this four years ago, all thoughts were anxiously directed to an impending civil-war. All dreaded it—all sought to avert it. While the inaugural address was being delivered from this place, devoted altogether to *saving* the Union without war, insurgent agents were in the city seeking to *destroy* it without war—seeking to dissolve the Union, and divide effects, by negotiation. Both parties deprecated war; but one of them would *make* war rather than let the nation survive; and the other would *accept* war rather than let it perish. And the war came.

One eighth of the whole population were colored slaves, not distributed generally over the Union, but localized in the Southern part of it. These slaves constituted a peculiar and powerful interest. All knew that this interest was, somehow, the cause of the war. To strengthen, perpetuate, and extend this interest was the object for which the insurgents would rend the Union, even by war; while the government claimed no right to do more than to restrict the territorial enlargement of it. Neither party expected for the war, the magnitude, or the duration, which it has already attained. Neither anticipated that the *cause* of the conflict might cease with, or even before, the conflict itself should cease. Each looked for an easier triumph, and a result less fundamental and astounding. Both read the same Bible, and pray to the same God; and each invokes His aid against the other. It may seem strange that any men should dare to ask a just God's assistance in wringing their bread from the sweat of other men's faces; but let us judge not that we be not judged. The prayers of both could not be answered; that of neither has been answered fully. The Almighty has His own purposes. "Woe unto the world because of offences! for it must needs be that offences come; but woe to that man by whom the offence cometh!" If we shall suppose that American Slavery is one of those offences which, in the providence of God, must needs come, but which, having continued through His appointed time, He now wills to remove, and that He gives to both North and South, this terrible war, as the woe due to those by whom the offence came, shall we discern therein any departure from those divine attributes which the believers in a Living God always ascribe to Him? Fondly do we hope—fervently do we pray—that this mighty scourge of war may speedily pass away. Yet, if God wills that it continue, until all the wealth piled by the bondman's two hundred and fifty years of unrequited toil shall be sunk, and until every drop of blood drawn by the lash, shall be paid by another drawn with the sword, as was said three thousand years ago, so still it must be said "the judgments of the Lord are true and righteous altogether"

With malice toward none; with charity for all; with firmness in the right, as God gives us to see the right, let us strive on to finish the work we are in; to bind up the nation's wounds; to care for him who shall have borne the battle, and for his widow, and his orphan—to do all which may achieve and cherish a just, and lasting peace, among ourselves, and with all nations.

*March 4, 1865*

# Address to the 140<sup>th</sup> Indiana Regiment

Fellow Citizens—

It will be but a very few words that I shall undertake to say. I was born in Kentucky, raised in Indiana and lived in Illinois. (Laughter.) And now I am here, where it is my business to care equally for the good people of all the States. I am glad to see an Indiana regiment on this day able to present the captured flag to the Governor of Indiana. (Applause.) I am not disposed, in saying this, to make a distinction between the States, for all have done equally well. (Applause.) There are but few views or aspects of this great war upon which I have not said or written something whereby my own opinions might be known. But there is one—the recent attempt of our erring brethren, as they are sometimes called—(laughter)—to employ the negro to fight for them. I have neither written nor made a speech on that subject, because that was their business, not mine; and if I had a wish upon the subject I had not the power to introduce it, or make it effective. The great question with them was, whether the negro, being put into the army, would fight for them. I do not know, and therefore cannot decide. (Laughter.) They ought to know better than we. I have in my lifetime heard many arguments why the negroes ought to be slaves; but if they fight for those who would keep them in slavery it will be a better argument than any I have yet heard. (Laughter and applause.) He who will fight for that ought to be a slave. (Applause.) They have concluded at last to take one out of four of the slaves, and put them in the army; and that one out of the four who will fight to keep the others in slavery ought to be a slave himself unless he is killed in a fight. (Applause.) While I have often said that all men ought to be free, yet would I allow those colored persons to be slaves who want to be; and next to them those white people who argue in favor of making other people slaves. (Applause.) I am in favor of giving an opportunity to such white men to try it on for themselves. (Applause.) I will say one thing in regard to the negro being employed to fight for them. I do know he cannot fight and stay at home and make bread too—(laughter and applause)—and as one is about as important as the other to them, I don't care which they do. (Renewed applause.) I am rather in favor of having them try them as soldiers. (Applause.) They lack one vote of doing that, and I wish I could send my vote over the river so that I might cast it in favor of allowing the negro to fight. (Applause.) But they cannot fight and work both. We must now see the bottom of the enemy's resources. They will stand out as long as they can, and if the negro will fight for them, they must allow him to fight. They have drawn upon their last branch of resources. (Applause.) And we can now see the bottom. (Applause.) I am glad to see the end so near at hand. (Applause.) I have said now more than I intended, and will therefore bid you goodby.

*March 17, 1865*

# Speech on Reconstruction, Washington, D.C.

We meet this evening, not in sorrow, but in gladness of heart. The evacuation of Petersburg and Richmond, and the surrender of the principal insurgent army, give hope of a righteous and speedy peace whose joyous expression can not be restrained. In the midst of this, however, He, from Whom all blessings flow, must not be forgotten. A call for a national thanksgiving is being prepared, and will be duly promulgated. Nor must those whose harder part gives us the cause of rejoicing, be overlooked. Their honors must not be parcelled out with others. I myself, was near the front, and had the pleasure of transmitting much of the good news to you; but no part of the honor, for plan or execution, is mine. To Gen. Grant, his skilful officers, and brave men, all belongs. The gallant Navy stood ready, but was not in reach to take active part.

By these recent successes the re-inauguration of the national authority—reconstruction—which has had a large share of thought from the first, is pressed much more closely upon our attention. It is fraught with great difficulty. Unlike a case of war between independent nations, there is no authorized organ for us to treat with. No one man has authority to give up the rebellion for any other man. We simply must begin with, and mould from, disorganized and discordant elements. Nor is it a small additional embarrassment that we, the loyal people, differ among ourselves as to the mode, manner, and measure of reconstruction.

As a general rule, I abstain from reading the reports of attacks upon myself, wishing not to be provoked by that to which I cannot properly offer an answer. In spite of this precaution, however, it comes to my knowledge that I am much censured for some supposed agency in setting up, and seeking to sustain, the new State Government of Louisiana. In this I have done just so much as, and no more than, the public knows. In the Annual Message of Dec. 1863 and the accompanying Proclamation, I presented *a* plan of reconstruction (as the phrase goes) which, I promised, if adopted by any State, should be acceptable to, and sustained by, the Executive government of the nation. I distinctly stated that this was not the only plan which might possibly be acceptable; and I also distinctly protested that the Executive claimed no right to say when, or whether members should be admitted to seats in Congress from such States. This plan was, in advance, submitted to the then Cabinet, and distinctly approved by every member of it. One of them suggested that I should then, and in that connection, apply the Emancipation Proclamation to the theretofore excepted parts of Virginia and Louisiana; that I should drop the suggestion about apprenticeship for freed-people, and that I should omit the protest against my own power, in regard to the admission of members to Congress; but even he approved every part and parcel of the plan which has since been employed or touched by the action of Louisiana. The new constitution of Louisiana, declaring emancipation for the whole State, practically applies the Proclamation to the part previously excepted. It does not adopt apprenticeship for freed-people; and it is silent, as it could not well be otherwise, about the admission of members to Congress. So that, as it applies to Louisiana, every member of the Cabinet fully approved the plan. The message went to Congress, and I received many commendations of the plan, written and verbal; and not a single objection to it, from any professed emancipa-tionist, came to my knowledge, until after the news reached Washington that the people of Louisiana had begun to move in accordance with it. From about July 1862, I had corresponded with different persons, supposed to be interested, seek-ing a reconstruction of a State government for Louisiana. When the Message of 1863, with the plan before mentioned, reached New-Orleans, Gen. Banks wrote me that he was confident that the people, with his military co-operation, would reconstruct, substantially on that plan. I wrote him, and some of them to try it; they tried it, and the result is known. Such only has been my agency in getting up the Louisiana government. As to sustaining it, my promise is out, as before stated. But, as bad promises are better broken than kept, I shall treat this as a bad promise, and break it, whenever I shall be convinced that keeping it is adverse to the public interest. But I have not yet been so convinced.

I have been shown a letter on this subject, supposed to be an able one, in which the writer expresses regret that my mind has not seemed to be definitely fixed upon the question whether the seceded States, so called, are in the Union or out of it. It would perhaps, add astonishment to his regret, were he to learn that since I have found professed Union men endeavoring to answer that ques-tion, I have *purposely* forborne any public expression upon it. As appears to me that question has not been, nor yet is, a practically material one, and that any discussion of it, while it thus remains practically immaterial, could have no effect other than the mischievous one of dividing our friends. As yet, whatever it may become, that question is bad, as the basis of a controversy, and good for nothing at all—a merely pernicious abstraction.

We all agree that the seceded States, so called, are out of their proper practi-cal relation with the Union; and that the sole object of the government, civil and military, in regard to those States is to again get them into their proper practical relation. I believe that it is not only possible, but in fact, easier, to do this, without deciding, or even considering, whether these states have ever been out of the Union, than with it. Finding themselves safely at home, it would be utterly immaterial whether they had been abroad. Let us all join in doing the acts necessary to restoring the proper practical relations between these states and the Union; and each forever after, innocently indulge his own opinion whether, in doing the acts, he brought the States from without, into the Union, or only gave them proper assistance, they never having been out of it.

The amount of constituency, so to speak, on which the Louisiana government rests, would be more satisfactory to all, if it contained fifty, thirty, or even twenty thousand, instead of only about twelve thousand, as it does. It is also unsatisfactory to some that the elective franchise is not given to the colored man. I would myself prefer that it were now conferred on the very intelligent, and on those who serve our cause as soldiers. Still the question is not whether the Louisiana government, as it stands, is quite all that is desirable. The question is "Will it be wiser to take it as it is, and help to improve it; or to reject, and disperse it? "Can Louisiana be brought into proper practical relation with the Union *sooner* by *sustaining*, or by *discarding* her new State Government?"

Some twelve thousand voters in the heretofore slave-state of Louisiana have sworn allegiance to the Union, assumed to be the rightful political power of the State, held elections, organized a State government, adopted a free-state constitution, giving the benefit of public schools equally to black and white, and empowering the Legislature to confer the elective franchise upon the colored man. This Legislature has already voted to ratify the constitutional amendment recently passed by Congress, abolishing slavery throughout the nation. These twelve thousand persons are thus fully committed to the Union, and to perpetual freedom in the state—committed to the very things, and nearly all things the nation wants—and they ask the nations recognition, and it's assistance to make good their committal. Now, if we reject, and spurn them, we do our utmost to disorganize and disperse them. We in effect say to the white men "You are worthless, or worse—we will neither help you, nor be helped by you." To the blacks we say "This cup of liberty which these, your old masters, hold to your lips, we will dash from you, and leave you to the chances of gathering the spilled and scattered contents in some vague and undefined when, where, and how." If this course, discouraging and paralyzing both white and black, has any tendency to bring Louisiana into proper practical relations with the Union, I have, so far, been unable to perceive it. If, on the contrary, we recognize, and sustain the new government of Louisiana the converse of all this is made true. We encourage the hearts, and nerve the arms of twelve thousand to adhere to their work, and argue for it, and proselyte for it, and fight for it, and feed it, and grow it, and ripen it to a complete success. The colored man too, in seeing all united for him, is inspired with vigilance, and energy, and daring, to the same end. Grant that he desires the elective franchise, will he not attain it sooner by saving the already advanced steps towards it, than by running backward over them? Concede that the new government of Louisiana is only to what it should be as the egg is to the fowl, we shall sooner have the fowl by hatching the egg than by smashing it? Again, if we reject Louisiana, we also reject one vote in favor of the proposed amendment to the national constitution. To meet this proposition, it has been argued that no more than three fourths of those States which have not attempted secession are necessary to validly ratify the amendment. I do not commit myself against this, further than to say that such a ratification would be questionable, and sure to be persistently questioned; while a ratification by three fourths of all the States would be unquestioned and unquestionable.

I repeat the question. "Can Louisiana be brought into proper practical relation with the Union *sooner* by *sustaining* or by *discarding* her new State Government?

What has been said of Louisiana will apply to other States. And yet so great peculiarities pertain to each state; and such important and sudden changes occur in the same state; and, withal, so new and unprecedented is the whole case, that no exclusive, and inflexible plan can safely be prescribed as to details and collaterals. Such exclusive, and inflexible plan, would surely become a new entanglement. Important principles may, and must, be inflexible.

In the present "*situation*" as the phrase goes, it may be my duty to make some new announcement to the people of the South. I am considering, and shall not fail to act, when satisfied that action will be proper.

*April 11, 1865*

# LETTERS

# To George Robertson

The volume you left for me has been received. I am really grateful for the honor of your kind remembrance, as well as for the book. The partial reading I have already given it, has afforded me much of both pleasure and instruction. It was new to me that the exact question which led to the Missouri compromise, had arisen before it arose in regard to Missouri; and that you had taken so prominent a part in it. Your short, but able and patriotic speech on that occasion, has not been improved upon since, by those holding the same views; and, with all the lights you then had, the views you took appear to me as very reasonable.

You are not a friend of slavery in the abstract. In that speech you spoke of *"the peaceful extinction of slavery"* and used other expressions indicating your belief that the thing was, at some time, to have an end. Since then we have had thirty six years of experience; and this experience has demonstrated, I think, that there is no peaceful extinction of slavery in prospect for us. The signal failure of Henry Clay, and other good and great men, in 1849, to effect any thing in favor of gradual emancipation in Kentucky, together with a thousand other signs, extinguishes that hope utterly. On the question of liberty, as a principle, we are not what we have been. When we were the political slaves of King George, and wanted to be free, we called the maxim that "all men are created equal" a self evident truth; but now when we have grown fat, and have lost all dread of being slaves ourselves, we have become so greedy to be *masters* that we call the same maxim "a self-evident lie." The fourth of July has not quite dwindled away; it is still a great day—*for burning fire-crackers!!!*

That spirit which desired the peaceful extinction of slavery, has itself become extinct, with the *occasion,* and the *men* of the Revolution. Under the impulse of that occasion, nearly half the states adopted systems of emancipation at once; and it is a significant fact, that not a single state has done the like since. So far as peaceful, voluntary emancipation is concerned, the condition of the negro slave in America, scarcely less terrible to the contemplation of a free mind, is now as fixed and hopeless of change for the better, as that of the lost souls of the finally impenitent. The Autocrat of all the Russias will resign his crown, and proclaim his subjects free republicans sooner than will our American masters voluntarily give up their slaves.

Our political problem now is "Can we, as a nation, continue together *permanently—forever*—half slave, and half free?" The problem is too mighty for me. May God, in his mercy, superintend the solution.

*August 15, 1855*

# To Joshua F. Speed

You know what a poor correspondent I am. Ever since I received your very agreeable letter of the 22nd. of May I have been intending to write you in answer to it. You suggest that in political action now, you and I would differ. I suppose we would; not quite so much, however, as you may think. You know I dislike slavery, and you fully admit the abstract wrong of it. So far there is no cause of difference. But you say that sooner than yield your legal right to the slave—especially at the bidding of those who are not themselves interested, you would see the Union dissolved. I am not aware that *any one* is bidding you, yield that right; very certainly *I* am not. I leave that matter entirely to yourself. I also acknowledge *your* rights and *my* obligations, under the constitution, in regard to your slaves. I confess I hate to see the poor creatures hunted down, and caught, and carried back to their stripes, and unrewarded toils; but I bite my lip and keep quiet. In 1841 you and I had together a tedious low-water trip, on a Steam Boat from Louisville to St. Louis. You may remember, as I well do, that from Louisville to the mouth of the Ohio, there were, on board, ten or a dozen slaves, shackled together with irons. That sight was a continued torment to me; and I see something like it every time I touch the Ohio, or any other slave-border. It is hardly fair for you to assume, that I have no interest in a thing which has, and continually exercises, the power of making me miserable. You ought rather to appreciate how much the great body of the Northern people do crucify their feelings, in order to maintain their loyalty to the constitution and the Union.

I do oppose the extension of slavery, because my judgment and feeling, so prompt me, and I am under no obligation to the contrary. If for this you and I must differ, differ we must. You say if you were President, you would send an army and hang the leaders of the Missouri outrages upon the Kansas elections; still, if Kansas fairly votes herself a slave state, she must be admitted, or the Union must be dissolved. But how if she votes herself a slave state *unfairly*—that is, by the very means for which you say you would hang men? Must she still be admitted, or the Union dissolved? That will be the phase of the question when it first becomes a practical one. In your assumption that there may be a *fair* decision of the slavery question in Kansas, I plainly see you and I would differ about the Nebraska-law. I look upon that enactment not as a *law*, but as *violence* from the beginning. It was conceived in violence, passed in violence, is maintained in violence, and is being executed in violence. I say it was *conceived* in violence, because the destruction of the Missouri Compromise, under the circumstances, was nothing less than violence. It was *passed* in violence, because it could not have passed at all but for the votes of many members, in violent disregard of the known will of their constituents. It is *maintained* in violence because the elections since, clearly demand it's repeal, and this demand is openly disregarded. *You* say men ought to be hung for the way they are executing the law; and *I* say that the way it is being executed is quite as good as any of its antecedents. It is being executed in the precise way which was intended from the first; else why does no Nebraska man express astonishment or condemnation? Poor Reeder is the only public man who has been silly enough to believe that any thing like fairness was ever intended; and he has been bravely undeceived.

That Kansas will form a Slave constitution, and, with it will ask to be admitted into the Union, I take to be already a settled question; and so settled by the very means you so pointedly condemn. By every principle of law, ever held by any court, North or South, every negro taken to Kansas is free; yet in utter disregard of this—in the spirit of violence merely—that beautiful Legislature gravely passes a law to hang men who shall venture to inform a negro of his legal rights. This is the substance and real object of the law. If, like Haman, they should hang upon the gallows of their own building, I shall not be among the mourners for their fate.

In my humble sphere, I shall advocate the restoration of the Missouri Compromise, so long as Kansas remains a territory; and when, by all these foul means, it seeks to come into the Union as a Slave-state, I shall oppose it. I am very loth, in any case, to withhold my assent to the enjoyment of property *acquired*, or *located*, in good faith; but I do not admit that *good faith*, in taking a negro to Kansas, to be held in slavery, is a *possibility* with any man. Any man who has sense enough to be the controller of his own property, has too much sense to misunderstand the outrageous character of this whole Nebraska business. But I digress. In my opposition to the admission of Kansas I shall have some company; but we may be beaten. If we are, I shall not, on that account, attempt to dissolve the Union. I think it probable, however, we shall be beaten. Standing as a unit among yourselves, you can, directly, and indirectly, bribe enough of our men to carry the day—as you could on the open proposition to establish monarchy. Get hold of some man in the North, whose position and ability is such, that he can make the support of your measure—whatever it may be—a *democratic party necessity*, and the thing is done. *Apropos* of this, let me tell you an anecdote. Douglas introduced the Nebraska bill in January. In February afterwards, there was a call session of the Illinois Legislature. Of the one hundred members composing the two branches of that body, about seventy were democrats. These latter held a caucus, in which the Nebraska bill was talked of, if not formally discussed. It was thereby discovered that just three, and no more, were in favor of the measure. In a day or two Douglas' orders came on to have resolutions passed approving the bill; and they were passed by large majorities!!! The truth of this is vouched for by a bolting democratic member. The masses too, democratic as well as whig, were even, nearer unanimous against it; but as soon as the party necessity of supporting it, became apparent, the way the democracy began to see the *wisdom* and *justice* of it, was perfectly astonishing.

You say that if Kansas fairly votes herself a free state, as a christian you will rather rejoice at it. All decent slave-holders *talk* that way; and I do not doubt their candor. But they never *vote* that way. Although in a private letter, or conversation, you will express your preference that Kansas should be free, you would vote for no man for Congress who would say the same thing publicly. No such man could be elected from any district in a slave-state. You think Stringfellow and Co ought to be hung; and yet, at the next presidential election you will vote for the exact type and representative of Stringfellow. The slave-breeders and slave-traders, are a small, odious and detested class, among you; and yet in politics, they dictate the course of all of you, and are as completely your masters, as you are the masters of your own negroes.

You inquire where I now stand. That is a disputed point. I think I am a whig; but others say there are no whigs, and that I am an abolitionist. When I was at Washington I voted for the Wilmot Proviso as good as forty times, and I never heard of any one attempting to unwhig me for that. I now do no more than oppose the *extension* of slavery.

I am not a Know-Nothing. That is certain. How could I be? How can any one who abhors the oppression of negroes, be in favor of degrading classes of white people? Our progress in degeneracy appears to me to be pretty rapid. As a nation, we began by declaring that "*all men are created equal.*" We now practically read it "all men are created equal *except negroes.*" When the Know-Nothings get control, it will read "all men are created equal, except negroes, *and foreigners, and catholics.*" When it comes to this I shall prefer emigrating to some country where they make no pretence of loving liberty—to Russia, for instance, where despotism can be taken pure, and without the base alloy of hypocrisy.

Mary will probably pass a day or two in Louisville in October. My kindest regards to Mrs. Speed. On the leading subject of this letter, I have more of her sympathy than I have of yours.

*August 24, 1855*

# To James N. Brown

I do not perceive how I can express myself, more plainly, than I have done in the foregoing extracts. In four of them I have expressly disclaimed all intention to bring about social and political equality between the white and black races, and, in all the rest, I have done the same thing by clear implication.

I have made it equally plain that I think the negro is included in the word "men" used in the Declaration of Independence.

I believe the declaration that "all men are created equal" is the great fundamental principle upon which our free institutions rest; that negro slavery is violative of that principle; but that, by our frame of government, that principle has not been made one of legal obligation; that by our frame of government, the States which have slavery are to retain it, or surrender it at their own pleasure; and that all others—individuals, free-states and national government—are constitutionally bound to leave them alone about it.

I believe our government was thus framed because of the *necessity* springing from the actual presence of slavery, when it was framed.

That such necessity does not exist in the territories, where slavery is not present.

In his Mendenhall speech Mr. Clay says

"Now, as an abstract principle, there is no doubt of the truth of that declaration (all men created equal) and it is desireable, in the original construction of society, and in organized societies, to keep it in view, as a great fundamental principle"

Again, in the same speech Mr. Clay says:

"If a state of nature existed, and we were about to lay the foundations of society, no man would be more strongly opposed than I should to incorporate the institutions of slavery among it's elements."

Exactly so. In our new free territories, a state of nature *does* exist. In them Congress lays the foundations of society; and, in laying those foundations, I say, with Mr. Clay, it is desireable that the declaration of the equality of all men shall be kept in view, as a great fundamental principle; and that Congress, which lays the foundations of society, should, like Mr. Clay, be strongly opposed to the incorporation of slavery among it's elements.

But it does not follow that social and political equality between whites and blacks, *must* be incorporated, because slavery must *not*. The declaration does not so require.

*October 18, 1858*

## To W. H. Wells

Yours of the 3rd. Inst. is just received. I regret to say that the joint discussions between Judge Douglas and myself have been published in no shape except in the first newspaper reports; and that I have no copy of them, or even of the single one at Freeport, which I could send you. By dint of great labor since the election, I have got together a nearly, (not quite) complete single set to preserve myself. I shall preserve your address, and if I can, in a reasonable time, lay my hand on an old paper containing the Freeport discussion, I will send it to you.

All dallying with Douglas by Republicans, who are such at heart, is, at the very least, time, and labor lost; and all such, who so dally with him, will yet bite their lips in vexation for their own folly. His policy, which rigourously excludes all idea of there being any *wrong* in slavery, does lead inevitably to the nationalization of the Institution; and all who deprecate that consummation, and yet are seduced into his support, do but cut their own throats. True, Douglas *has* opposed the administration on one measure, and yet *may* on some other; but while he upholds the Dred Scott decision, declares that he cares not whether slavery be voted down or voted up; that it is simply a question of dollars and cents, and that the Almighty has drawn a line on one side of which labor *must* be performed by slaves; to support him or Buchanan, is simply to reach the same goal by only slightly different roads.

*January 8, 1859*

## To Henry L. Pierce and Others

Your kind note inviting me to attend a Festival in Boston, on the 13th. Inst. in honor of the birth-day of Thomas Jefferson, was duly received. My engagements are such that I can not attend.

Bearing in mind that about seventy years ago, two great political parties were first formed in this country, that Thomas Jefferson was the head of one of them, and Boston the headquarters of the other, it is both curious and interesting that those supposed to descend politically from the party opposed to Jefferson, should now be celebrating his birth-day in their own original seat of empire, while those claiming political descent from him have nearly ceased to breathe his name everywhere.

Remembering too, that the Jefferson party was formed upon their supposed superior devotion to the *personal* rights of men, holding the rights of *property* to be secondary only, and greatly inferior, and assuming that the so-called democracy of to-day, are the Jefferson, and their opponents, the anti-Jefferson parties, it will be equally interesting to note how completely the two have changed hands as to the principle upon which they were originally supposed to be divided.

The democracy of to-day hold the *liberty* of one man to be absolutely nothing, when in conflict with another man's right of *property*. Republicans, on the contrary, are for both the *man* and the *dollar*; but in cases of conflict, the man *before* the dollar.

I remember being once much amused at seeing two partially intoxicated men engaged in a fight with their great-coats on, which fight, after a long, and rather harmless contest, ended in each having fought himself *out* of his own coat, and *into* that of the other. If the two leading parties of this day are really identical with the two in the days of Jefferson and Adams, they have performed the same feat as the two drunken men.

But soberly, it is now no child's play to save the principles of Jefferson from total overthrow in this nation.

One would state with great confidence that he could convince any sane child that the simpler propositions of Euclid are true; but, nevertheless, he would fail, utterly, with one who should deny the definitions and axioms. The principles of Jefferson are the definitions and axioms of free society. And yet they are denied, and evaded, with no small show of success. One dashingly calls them "glittering generalities"; another bluntly calls them "self-evident lies"; and still others insidiously argue that they apply to "superior races."

These expressions, differing in form, are identical in object and effect—the supplanting the principles of free government, and restoring those of classification, caste, and legitimacy. They would delight a convocation of crowned heads plotting against the people. They are the van-guard—the miners, and sappers—of returning despotism. We must repulse them, or they will subjugate us.

This is a world of compensation; and he who would *be* no slave, must consent to *have* no slave. Those who deny freedom to others, deserve it not for themselves; and, under a just God, cannot long retain it.

All honor to Jefferson—to the man who, in the concrete pressure of a struggle for national independence by a single people, had the coolness, forecast, and capacity to introduce into a mere revolutionary document, an abstract truth, applicable to all men and all times, and so to embalm it there, that to-day, and in all coming days, it shall be a rebuke and a stumbling-block to the very harbingers of re-appearing tyranny and oppression.

*April 6, 1859*

# To Salmon P. Chase

Yours of the 13th. Inst. is received. You say you would be glad to have my views. Although I think congress has constitutional authority to enact a Fugitive Slave law, I have never elaborated an opinion upon the subject. My view has been, and is, simply this: The U.S. constitution says the fugitive slave *"shall be delivered up"* but it does not expressly say *who* shall deliver him up. Whatever the constitution says *"shall be done"* and has omitted saying who shall do it, the government established by that constitution, *ex vi termini*, is vested with the power of doing; and congress is, by the constitution, expressly empowered to make all laws which shall be necesary and proper for carrying into execution all powers vested by the constitution in the government of the United States. This would be my view, on a simple reading of the constitution; and it is greatly strengthened by the historical fact that the constitution was adopted, in great part, in order to get a government which could execute it's own behests, in contradistinction to that under the Articles of confederation, which depended, in many respects, upon the States, for its' execution; and the other fact that one of the earliest congresses, under the constitution, did enact a Fugitive Slave law.

But I did not write you on this subject, with any view of discussing the constitutional question. My only object was to impress you with what I believe is true, that the introduction of a proposition for repeal of the Fugitive Slave law, into the next Republican National convention, will explode the convention and the party. Having turned your attention to the point, I wish to do no more.

*June 20, 1859*

# To O. P. Hall, J. R. Fullinwider, and W. F. Correll

Your letter, in which among other things, you ask "what I meant when I said this Union could not stand half slave and half free—and also what I meant when I said a house divided against itself could not stand" is received, and I very cheerfully answer it as plainly as I may be able. You misquote, to some material extent, what I did say; which induces me to think you have not, very carefully read the speech in which the expressions occur which puzzle you to understand. For this reason and because the language I used is as plain as I can make it, I now quote at length the whole paragraph in which the expressions which puzzle you occur. It is as follows: "We are now far into the fifth year since a policy was initiated with the avowed object, and confident promise of putting an end to slavery agitation. Under the operation of that policy that agitation has not only not ceased but constantly augmented. I believe it will not cease until a crisis shall have been reached, and passed. A house divided against itself can not stand. I believe this government can not endure *permanently,* half slave, and half free. I do not expect the Union to be dissolved; I do not expect the house to fall; but I do expect it will cease to be divided. It will become all one thing, or all the other. Either the opponents of slavery will arrest the further spread of it, and place it where the public mind shall rest in the belief that it is in course of ultimate extinction; or it's advocates will push it forward till it will become alike lawful in all the states, old as well as new, North, as well as South."

That is the whole paragraph; and it puzzles me to make my meaning plainer. Look over it carefully, and conclude I meant all I said and did not mean anything I did not say, and you will have my meaning. Douglas attacked me upon this, saying it was a declaration of war between the slave and the free states. You will perceive I said no such thing, and I assure you I thought of no such thing.

If I had said "I believe this government can not *last always*, half slave and half free" would you understand it any better than you do? "Endure permanently" and "last always" have exactly the same meaning.

If you, or any of you, will state to me some meaning which you suppose I had, I can, and will instantly tell you whether that was my meaning.

*February 14, 1860*

# To Horace Greeley

I have just read yours of the 19th. addressed to myself through the New-York Tribune. If there be in it any statements, or assumptions of fact, which I may know to be erroneous, I do not, now and here, controvert them. If there be in it any inferences which I may believe to be falsely drawn, I do not now and here, argue against them. If there be perceptable in it an impatient and dictatorial tone, I waive it in deference to an old friend, whose heart I have always supposed to be right.

As to the policy I "seem to be pursuing" as you say, I have not meant to leave any one in doubt.

I would save the Union. I would save it the shortest way under the Constitution. The sooner the national authority can be restored; the nearer the Union will be "the Union as it was." If there be those who would not save the Union, unless they could at the same time *save* slavery, I do not agree with them. If there be those who would not save the Union unless they could at the same time *destroy* slavery, I do not agree with them. My paramount object in this struggle *is* to save the Union, and is *not* either to save or destroy slavery. If I could save the Union without freeing *any* slave I would do it, and if I could save it by freeing *all* the slaves I would do it; and if I could do it by freeing some and leaving others alone I would also do that. What I do about slavery, and the colored race, I do because I believe it helps to save this Union; and what I forbear, I forbear because I do *not* believe it would help to save the Union. I shall do *less* whenever I shall believe what I am doing hurts the cause, and I shall do *more* whenever I shall believe doing more will help the cause. I shall try to correct errors when shown to be errors; and I shall adopt new views so fast as they shall appear to be true views.

I have here stated my purpose according to my view of *official* duty; and I intend no modification of my oft-expressed *personal* wish that all men every where could be free.

*August 22, 1862*

# To Andrew Johnson

I am told you have at least *thought* of raising a negro military force. In my opinion the country now needs no specific thing so much as some man of your ability, and position, to go to this work. When I speak of your position, I mean that of an eminent citizen of a slave-state, and himself a slaveholder. The colored population is the great *available* and yet *unavailed* of, force for restoring the Union. The bare sight of fifty thousand armed, and drilled black soldiers upon the banks of the Mississippi, would end the rebellion at once. And who doubts that we can present that sight, if we but take hold in earnest? If you *have* been thinking of it please do not dismiss the thought.

*March 26, 1863*

# To Erastus Corning and Others

Your letter of May 19th, inclosing the resolutions of a public meeting held at Albany, N.Y., on the 16th. of the same month, was received several days ago.

The resolutions, as I understand them, are resolvable into two propositions—first, the expression of a purpose to sustain the cause of the Union, to secure peace through victory, and to support the Administration in every constitutional and lawful measure to suppress the Rebellion; and secondly, a declaration of censure upon the Administration for supposed unconstitutional action, such as the making of military arrests. And, from the two propositions, a third is deduced, which is, that the gentlemen composing the meeting are resolved on doing their part to maintain our common government and country, despite the folly or wickedness, as they may conceive, of any Administration. This position is eminently patriotic, and as such I thank the meeting and congratulate the nation for it. My own purpose is the same; so that the meeting and myself have a common object, and can have no difference, except in the choice of means or measures for effecting that object.

And here I ought to close this paper, and would close it, if there were no apprehension that more injurious consequences than any merely personal to myself might follow the censures systematically cast upon me for doing what, in my view of duty, I could not forbear. The resolutions promise to support me in every constitutional and lawful measure to suppress the Rebellion; and I have not knowingly employed, nor shall knowingly employ, any other. But the meeting, by their resolutions, assert and argue that certain military arrests, and proceedings following them, for which I am ultimately responsible, are unconstitutional. I think they are not. The resolutions quote from the Constitution the definition of treason, and also the limiting safeguards and guarantees therein provided for the citizen on trials for treason, and on his being held to answer for capital or otherwise infamous crimes, and, in criminal prosecutions, his right to a speedy and public trial by an impartial jury. They proceed to resolve "that these safeguards of the rights of the citizen against the pretentions of arbitrary power, were intended more *especially* for his protection in times of civil commotion." And, apparently to demonstrate the proposition, the resolutions proceed: "They were secured substantially to the English people *after* years of protracted civil war, and were adopted into our Constitution at the *close* of the Revolution." Would not the demonstration have been better if it could have been truly said that these safeguards had been adopted and applied *during* the civil wars and *during* our Revolution, instead of *after* the one and at the *close* of the other? I, too, am devotedly for them *after* civil war, and *before* civil war, and at all times "except when, in cases of rebellion or invasion, the public Safety may require" their suspension. The resolutions proceed to tell us that these safeguards "have stood the test of seventy-six years of trial, under our republican system, under circumstances which show that, while they constitute the foundation of all free government, they are the elements of the enduring stability of the Republic." No one denies that they have so stood the test up to the beginning of the present Rebellion, if we except a certain occurrence at New-Orleans; nor does any one question that they will stand the same test much longer after the Rebellion closes. But these provisions of the Constitution have no application to the case we have in hand, because the arrests complained of were not made for treason—that is, not for *the* treason defined in the Constitution, and upon the conviction of which the punishment is death—nor yet were they made to hold persons to answer for any capital or otherwise infamous crimes; nor were the proceedings following, in any constitutional or legal sense, "criminal prosecutions." The arrests were made on totally different grounds, and the proceedings following accorded with the grounds of the arrests. Let us consider the real case with which we are dealing, and apply to it the parts of the Constitution plainly made for such cases.

Prior to my installation here, it had been inculcated that any State had a lawful right to secede from the national Union, and that it would be expedient to exercise the right whenever the devotees of the doctrine should fail to elect a President to their own liking. I was elected contrary to their liking; and, accordingly, so far as it was legally possible, they had taken seven States out of the Union, had seized many of the United States forts, and had fired upon the United States flag, all before I was inaugurated, and, of course, before I had done any official act whatever. The Rebellion thus began soon ran into the present Civil War; and, in certain respects, it began on very unequal terms between the parties. The insurgents had been preparing for it more than thirty years, while the Government had taken no steps to resist them. The former had carefully considered all the means which could be turned to their account. It undoubtedly was a well-pondered reliance with them that, in their own unrestricted efforts to destroy Union, Constitution, and law, all together, the Government would, in great degree, be restrained by the same Constitution and law, from arresting their progress. Their sympathizers pervaded all departments of the Government, and nearly all communities of the people. From this material, under cover of "liberty of speech," "liberty of the press," and "habeas corpus," they hoped to keep on foot amongst us a most efficient corps of spies, informers, suppliers, and aiders and abettors of their cause in a thousand ways. They knew that in times such as they were inaugurating, by the Constitution itself, the "habeas corpus" might be suspended; but they also knew they had friends who would make a question as to *who was to suspend it*; meanwhile, their spies and others might remain at large to help on their cause. Or, if, as has happened, the Executive should suspend the writ, without ruinous waste of time, instances of arresting innocent persons might occur, as are always likely to occur in such cases; and then a clamor could be raised in regard to this, which might be, at least, of some service to the insurgent cause. It needed no very keen perception to discover this part of the enemies' programme, so soon as, by open hostilities, their machinery was fairly put in motion. Yet, thoroughly imbued with a reverence for the guaranteed rights of individuals, I was slow to adopt the strong measures which by degrees I have been forced to regard as being within the exceptions of the Constitution, and as indispensable to the public safety. Nothing is better known to history than that courts of justice are utterly incompetent to such cases. Civil courts are organized chiefly for trials of individuals, or, at most, a few individuals acting in concert; and this in quiet times, and on charges of crimes well defined in the law. Even in times of peace, bands of horse-thieves and robbers frequently grow too numerous and powerful for the ordinary courts of justice. But what comparison, in numbers have such bands ever borne to the insurgent sympathizers, even in many of the loyal States? Again: a jury too frequently has at least one member more ready to hang the panel than to hang the traitor. And yet, again, he who dissuades one man from volunteering, or induces one soldier to desert, weakens the Union cause as much as he who kills a Union soldier in battle. Yet this dissuasion or inducement may be so conducted as to be no defined crime of which any civil court would take cognizance.

Ours is a case of rebellion—so called by the resolutions before me—in fact, a clear, flagrant, and gigantic case of rebellion; and the provision of the Constitution that "the privilege of the writ of habeas corpus shall not be suspended, unless when, in cases of rebellion or invasion, the public safety may require it," is *the* provision which specially applies to our present case. This provision plainly attests the understanding of those who made the Constitution, that ordinary courts of justice are inadequate to "cases of rebellion"—attests their purpose that, in such cases, men may be held in custody whom the courts, acting on ordinary rules, would discharge. Habeas corpus does not discharge men who are proved to be guilty of defined crime; and its suspension is allowed by the Constitution on purpose that men may be arrested and held who can not be proved to be guilty of defined crime, "when, in cases of rebellion or invasion, the public safety may require it." This is precisely our present case—a case of rebellion, wherein the public safety *does* require the suspension. Indeed, arrests by process of courts, and arrests in cases of rebellion, do not proceed altogether upon the same basis. The former is directed at the small per centage of ordinary and continuous perpetration of crime; while the latter is directed at sudden and extensive uprisings against the Government, which at most, will succeed or fail in no great length of time. In the latter case, arrests are made, not so much for what has been done, as for what probably would be done. The latter is more for the preventive and less for the vindictive than the former. In such cases, the purposes of men are much more easily understood than in cases of ordinary crime. The man who stands by and says nothing when the peril of his Government is discussed, cannot be misunderstood. If not hindered, he is sure to help the enemy; much more, if he talks ambiguously—talks for his country with "buts" and "ifs" and "ands." Of how little value the constitutional provision I have quoted will be rendered, if arrests shall never be made until defined crimes shall have been committed, may be illustrated by a few notable examples. Gen. John C. Breckinridge, Gen. Robert E. Lee, Gen. Joseph E. Johnston, Gen. John B. Magruder, Gen. William B. Preston, Gen. Simon B. Buckner, and Commodore Franklin Buchanan, now occupying the very highest places in the Rebel war service, were all within the power of the Government since the Rebellion began, and were nearly as well known to be traitors then as now. Unquestionably if we had seized and held them, the insurgent cause would be much weaker. But no one of them had then committed any crime defined in the law. Every one of them, if arrested, would have been discharged on *habeas corpus* were the writ allowed to operate. In view of these and similar cases, I think the time not unlikely to come when I shall be blamed for having made too few arrests rather than too many.

By the third resolution, the meeting indicate their opinion that military arrests may be constitutional in localities where rebellion actually exists, but that such arrests are unconstitutional in localities where rebellion or insurrection does *not* actually exist. They insist that such arrests shall not be made "outside of the lines of necessary military occupation, and the scenes of insurrection." Inasmuch, however, as the Constitution itself makes no such distinction, I am unable to believe that there *is* any such constitutional distinction. I concede that the class of arrests complained of can be constitutional only when, in cases of rebellion or invasion, the public safety may require them; and I insist that in such cases, they are constitutional *wherever* the public safety does require them; as well in places to which they may prevent the Rebellion extending as in those where it may be already prevailing; as well where they may restrain mischievous interference with the raising and supplying of armies to suppress the Rebellion, as where the Rebellion may actually be; as well where they may restrain the enticing men out of the army, as where they would prevent mutiny in the army; equally constitutional at all places where they will conduce to the public safety, as against the dangers of rebellion or invasion. Take the particular case mentioned by the meeting. It is asserted, in substance, that Mr. Vallandigham was, by a military commander, seized and tried "for no other reason than words addressed to a public meeting, in criticism of the course of the Administration, and in condemnation of the Military orders of that General." Now, if there be no mistake about this; if this assertion is the truth and the whole truth; if there was no other reason for the arrest, then I concede that the arrest was wrong. But the arrest, as I understand, was made for a very different reason. Mr. Vallandigham avows his hostility to the War on the part of the Union; and his arrest was made because he was laboring, with some effect, to prevent the raising of troops; to encourage desertions from the army; and to leave the Rebellion without an adequate military force to suppress it. He was not arrested because he was damaging the political prospects of the Administration, or the personal interests of the Commanding General, but because he was damaging the Army, upon the existence and vigor of which the life of the Nation depends. He was warring upon the Military, and this gave the Military constitutional jurisdiction to lay hands upon him. If Mr. Vallandigham was not damaging the military power of the country, then his arrest was made on mistake of fact, which I would be glad to correct on reasonably satisfactory evidence.

I understand the meeting, whose resolutions I am considering, to be in favor of suppressing the Rebellion by military force—by armies. Long experience has shown that armies cannot be maintained unless desertion shall be punished by the severe penalty of death. The case requires, and the law and the Constitution sanction, this punishment. Must I shoot a simple-minded soldier boy who deserts, while I must not touch a hair of a wily agitator who induces him to desert? This is none the less injurious when effected by getting a father, or brother, or friend, into a public meeting, and there working upon his feelings till he is persuaded to write the soldier boy that he is fighting in a bad cause, for a wicked Administration of a contemptible Government, too weak to arrest and punish him if he shall desert. I think that in such a case to silence the agitator, and save the boy is not only constitutional, but withal a great mercy.

If I be wrong on this question of constitutional power, my error lies in believing that certain proceedings are constitutional when, in cases of rebellion or invasion, the public safety requires them, which would not be constitutional when, in absence of rebellion or invasion, the public safety does *not* require them: in other words, that the Constitution is not, in its application, in all respects the same, in cases of rebellion or invasion involving the public safety, as it is in time of profound peace and public security. The Constitution itself makes the distinction; and I can no more be persuaded that the Government can constitutionally take no strong measure, in time of rebellion, because it can be shown that the same could not be lawfully taken in time of peace, than I can be persuaded that a particular drug is not good medicine for a sick man, because it can be shown not to be good food for a well one. Nor am I able to appreciate the danger apprehended by the meeting that the American people will, by means of military arrests during the Rebellion, lose the right of Public Discussion, the Liberty of Speech and the Press, the Law of Evidence, Trial by Jury, and Habeas Corpus, throughout the indefinite peaceful future which I trust lies before them, any more than I am able to believe that a man could contract so strong an appetite for emetics during temporary illness as to persist in feeding upon them through the remainder of his healthful life.

In giving the resolutions that earnest consideration which you request of me, I cannot overlook the fact that the meeting speak as "Democrats." Nor can I, with full respect for their known intelligence, and the fairly presumed deliberation with which they prepared their resolutions, be permitted to suppose that this occurred by accident, or in any way other than that they preferred to designate themselves "Democrats" rather than "American citizens." In this time of national peril, I would have preferred to meet you upon a level one step higher than any party platform; because I am sure that, from such more elevated position, we could do better battle for the country we all love than we possibly can from those lower ones where, from the force of habit, the prejudices of the past, and selfish hopes of the future, we are sure to expend much of our ingenuity and strength in finding fault with, and aiming blows at each other. But, since you have denied me this, I will yet be thankful, for the country's sake, that not all Democrats have done so. He on whose discretionary judgment Mr. Vallandigham was arrested and tried is a Democrat, having no old party affinity with me; and the judge who rejected the constitutional view expressed in these resolutions, by refusing to discharge Mr. Vallandigham on habeas corpus, is a Democrat of better days than these, having received his judicial mantle at the hands of President Jackson. And still more, of all those Democrats who are nobly exposing their lives and shedding their blood on the battle-field, I have learned that many approve the course taken with Mr. Vallandigham, while I have not heard of a single one condemning it. I cannot assert that there are none such. And the name of President Jackson recalls an instance of pertinent history: After the battle of New-Orleans, and while the fact that the treaty of peace had been concluded was well known in the city, but before official knowledge of it had arrived, Gen. Jackson still maintained martial or military law. Now, that it could be said the war was over, the clamor against martial law, which had existed from the first, grew more furious. Among other things, a Mr. Louiallier published a denunciatory newspaper article. Gen. Jackson arrested him. A lawyer by the name of Morel procured the United States Judge Hall to order a writ of habeas corpus to release Mr. Louiallier. Gen. Jackson arrested both the lawyer and the judge. A Mr. Hollander ventured to say of some part of the matter that "it was a dirty trick." Gen. Jackson arrested him. When the officer undertook to serve the writ of habeas corpus, Gen. Jackson took it from him, and sent him away with a copy. Holding the judge in custody a few days, the General sent him beyond the limits of his encampment, and set him at liberty, with an order to remain till the ratification of peace should be regularly announced, or until the British should have left the Southern coast. A day or two more elapsed, the ratification of the treaty of peace was regularly announced, and the judge and others were fully liberated. A few days more, and the judge called Gen. Jackson into court and fined him $1,000 for having arrested him and the others named. The General paid the fine, and there the matter rested for nearly thirty years, when Congress refunded principal and interest. The late Senator Douglas, then in the House of Representatives, took a leading part in the debates, in which the constitutional question was much discussed. I am not prepared to say whom the journals would show to have voted for the measure.

It may be remarked: First, that we had the same Constitution then as now; secondly, that we then had a case of invasion, and that now we have a case of rebellion; and, thirdly, that the permanent right of the People to Public Discussion, the Liberty of Speech and the Press, the Trial by Jury, the Law of Evidence, and the Habeas Corpus, suffered no detriment whatever by that conduct of Gen. Jackson, or its subsequent approval by the American Congress.

And yet, let me say that in my own discretion, I do not know whether I would have ordered the arrest of Mr. Vallandigham. While I can not shift the responsibility from myself, I hold that, as a general rule, the commander in the field is the better judge of the necessity in any particular case. Of course, I must practice a general directory and revisory power in the matter.

One of the resolutions expresses the opinion of the meeting that arbitrary arrests will have the effect to divide and distract those who should be united in suppressing the Rebellion, and I am specifically called on to discharge Mr. Vallandigham. I regard this as, at least, a fair appeal to me on the expediency of exercising a Constitutional power which I think exists. In response to such appeal, I have to say, it gave me pain when I learned that Mr. Vallandigham had been arrested—that is, I was pained that there should have seemed to be a necessity for arresting him—and that it will afford me great pleasure to discharge him so soon as I can, by any means, believe the public safety will not suffer by it. I further say that, as the war progress, it appears to me, opinion, and action, which were in great confusion at first, take shape, and fall into more regular channels, so that the necessity for strong dealing with them gradually decreases. I have every reason to desire that it would cease altogether, and far from the least is my regard for the opinions and wishes of those who, like the meeting at Albany, declare their purpose to sustain the Government in every constitutional and lawful measure to suppress the Rebellion. Still, I must continue to do so much as may seem to be required by the public safety.

*June 12, 1863*

# To James C. Conkling

Your letter inviting me to attend a mass-meeting of unconditional Union-men, to be held at the capital of Illinois, on the 3d day of September, has been received.

It would be very agreeable for me, to thus meet my old friends, at my own home; but I can not, just now, be absent from here, so long as a visit there, would require.

The meeting is to be of all those who maintain unconditional devotion to the Union; and I am sure that my old political friends will thank me for tendering, as I do, the nation's gratitude to those other noble men, whom no partizan malice, or partizan hope, can make false to the nation's life.

There are those who are dissatisfied with me. To such, I would say: You desire peace; and you blame me that we do not have it. But how can we attain it? There are but three conceivable ways. First, to suppress the rebellion by force of arms. This I am trying to do. Are you for it? If you are, so far we are agreed. If you are not for it, a second way is, to give up the Union. I am against this. Are you for it? If you are, you should say so plainly. If you are not for *force*, nor yet for *dissolution*, there only remains some imaginable *compromise*. I do not believe that any compromise, embracing the maintenance of the Union, is now possible. All I learn, leads to a directly opposite belief. The strength of the rebellion, is its military—its army. That army dominates all the country, and all the people, within its range. Any offer of terms made by any man or men within that range, in opposition to that army, is simply nothing for the present; because such man or men, have no power whatever to enforce their side of a compromise, if one were made with them. To illustrate—Suppose refugees from the South, and peace men of the North, get together in convention, and frame and proclaim a compromise embracing a restoration of the Union; in what way can that compromise be used to keep Lee's army out of Pennsylvania? Meade's army can keep Lee's army out of Pennsylvania, and, I think, can ultimately drive it out of existence. But no paper compromise, to which the controllers of Lee's army are not agreed, can, at all, affect that army. In an effort at such compromise we should waste time, which the enemy would improve to our disadvantage; and that would be all. A compromise, to be effective, must be made either with those who control the rebel army, or with the people first liberated from the domination of that army, by the success of our own army. Now allow me to assure you, that no word or intimation, from that rebel army, or from any of the men controlling it, in relation to any peace compromise, has ever come to my knowledge or belief. All charges and insinuations to the contrary, are deceptive and groundless. And I promise you, that if any such proposition shall hereafter come, it shall not be rejected, and kept a secret from you. I freely acknowledge myself to be the servant of the people, according to the bond of service—the United States Constitution; and that, as such, I am responsible to them.

But, to be plain, you are dissatisfied with me about the negro. Quite likely there is a difference of opinion between you and myself upon that subject. I certainly wish that all men could be free, while I suppose you do not. Yet I have neither adopted, nor proposed any measure, which is not consistent with even your view, provided you are for the Union. I suggested compensated emancipation; to which you replied you wished not to be taxed to buy negroes. But I had not asked you to be taxed to buy negroes, except in such way, as to save you from greater taxation to save the Union exclusively by other means.

You dislike the emancipation proclamation; and, perhaps, would have it retracted. You say it is unconstitutional—I think differently. I think the constitution invests its commander-in-chief, with the law of war, in time of war. The most that can be said, if so much, is, that slaves are property. Is there—has there ever been—any question that by the law of war, property, both of enemies and friends, may be taken when needed? And is it not needed whenever taking it, helps us, or hurts the enemy? Armies, the world over, destroy enemies' property when they cannot use it; and even destroy their own to keep it from the enemy. Civilized belligerents do all in their power to help themselves, or hurt the enemy, except a few things regarded as barbarous or cruel. Among the exceptions are the massacre of vanquished foes, and non-combatants, male and female.

But the proclamation, as law, either is valid, or is not valid. If it is not valid, it needs no retraction. If it is valid, it can not be retracted, any more than the dead can be brought to life. Some of you profess to think its retraction would operate favorably for the Union. Why better *after* the retraction, than *before* the issue? There was more than a year and a half of trial to suppress the rebellion before the proclamation issued, the last one hundred days of which passed under an explicit notice that it was coming, unless averted by those in revolt, returning to their allegiance. The war has certainly progressed as favorably for us, since the issue of the proclamation as before. I know as fully as one can know the opinions of others, that some of the commanders of our armies in the field who have given us our most important successes, believe the emancipation policy, and the use of colored troops, constitute the heaviest blow yet dealt to the rebellion; and that, at least one of those important successes, could not have been achieved when it was, but for the aid of black soldiers. Among the commanders who hold these views are some who have never had any affinity with what is called abolitionism, or with republican party politics; but who hold them purely as military opinions. I submit these opinions as being entitled to some weight against the objections, often urged, that emancipation, and arming the blacks, are unwise as military measures, and were not adopted, as such, in good faith.

You say that you will not fight to free negroes. Some of them seem willing to fight for you; but, no matter. Fight you, then, exclusively, to save the Union. I issued the proclamation on purpose to aid you in saving the Union. Whenever you shall have conquered all resistance to the Union, if I shall urge you to continue fighting, it will be an apt time, then, for you to declare you will not fight to free negroes.

I thought that in your struggle for the Union, to whatever extent the negroes should cease helping the enemy, to that extent it weakened the enemy in his resistance to you. Do you think differently? I thought that whatever negroes can be got to do as soldiers, leaves just so much less for white soldiers to do, in saving the Union. Does it appear otherwise to you? But negroes, like other people, act upon motives. Why should they do any thing for us, if we will do nothing for them? If they stake their lives for us, they must be prompted by the strongest motive— even the promise of freedom. And the promise being made, must be kept.

The signs look better. The Father of Waters again goes unvexed to the sea. Thanks to the great North-West for it. Nor yet wholly to them. Three hundred miles up, they met New England, Empire, Key-Stone, and Jersey, hewing their way right and left. The Sunny South too, in more colors than one, also lent a hand. On the spot, their part of the history was jotted down in black and white. The job was a great national one; and let none be banned who bore an honorable part in it. And while those who have cleared the great river may well be proud, even that is not all. It is hard to say that anything has been more bravely, and well done, than at Antietam, Murfreesboro, Gettysburg, and on many fields of lesser note. Nor must Uncle Sam's Web-feet be forgotten. At all the watery margins they have been present. Not only on the deep sea, the broad bay, and the rapid river, but also up the narrow muddy bayou, and wherever the ground was a little damp, they have been, and made their tracks. Thanks to all. For the great republic—for the principle it lives by, and keeps alive—for man's vast future—thanks to all.

Peace does not appear so distant as it did. I hope it will come soon, and come to stay; and so come as to be worth the keeping in all future time. It will then have been proved that, among free men, there can be no successful appeal from the ballot to the bullet; and that they who take such appeal are sure to lose their case, and pay the cost. And then, there will be some black men who can remember that, with silent tongue, and clenched teeth, and steady eye, and well-poised bayonet, they have helped mankind on to this great consummation; while, I fear, there will be some white ones, unable to forget that, with malignant heart, and deceitful speech, they have strove to hinder it.

Still let us not be over-sanguine of a speedy final triumph. Let us be quite sober. Let us diligently apply the means, never doubting that a just God, in his own good time, will give us the rightful result.

*August 26, 1863*

# To Edwin M. Stanton

On principle I dislike an oath which requires a man to swear he has not done wrong. It rejects the Christian principle of forgiveness on terms of repentance. I think it is enough if the man does no wrong *hereafter*.

*February 5, 1864*

# To Albert G. Hodges

You ask me to put in writing the substance of what I verbally said the other day, in your presence, to Governor Bramlette and Senator Dixon. It was about as follows:

"I am naturally anti-slavery. If slavery is not wrong, nothing is wrong. I can not remember when I did not so think, and feel. And yet I have never understood that the Presidency conferred upon me an unrestricted right to act officially upon this judgment and feeling. It was in the oath I took that I would, to the best of my ability, preserve, protect, and defend the Constitution of the United States. I could not take the office without taking the oath. Nor was it my view that I migh take an oath to get power, and break the oath in using the power. I understood, too, that in ordinary civil administration this oath even forbade me to practically indulge my primary abstract judgment on the moral question of slavery. I had publicly declared this many times, and in many ways. And I aver that, to this day, I have done no official act in mere deference to my abstract judgment and feeling on slavery. I did understand however, that my oath to preserve the constitution to the best of my ability, imposed upon me the duty of preserving, by every indispensable means, that government—that nation—of which that constitution was the organic law. Was it possible to lose the nation and yet preserve the constitution? By general law life *and* limb must be protected; yet often a limb must be amputated to save a life; but a life is never wisely given to save a limb. I felt that measures, otherwise unconstitutional, might become lawful, by becoming indispensable to the preservation of the constitution, through the preservation of the nation. Right or wrong, I assumed this ground, and now avow it. I could not feel that, to the best of my ability, I had even tried to preserve the constitution, if, to save slavery, or any minor matter, I should permit the wreck of government, country, and Constitution all together. When, early in the war, Gen. Fremont attempted military emancipation, I forbade it, because I did not then think it an indispensable necessity. When a little later, Gen. Cameron, then Secretary of War, suggested the arming of the blacks, I objected, because I did not yet think it an indispensable necessity. When, still later, Gen. Hunter attempted military emancipation, I again forbade it, because I did not yet think the indispensable necessity had come. When, in March, and May, and July 1862 I made earnest, and successive appeals to the border states to favor compensated emancipation, I believed the indispensable necessity for military emancipation, and arming the blacks would come, unless averted by that measure. They declined the proposition; and I was, in my best judgment, driven to the alternative of either surrendering the Union, and with it, the Constitution, or of laying strong hand upon the colored element. I chose the latter. In choosing it, I hoped for greater gain than loss; but of this, I was not entirely confident. More than a year of trial now shows no loss by it in our foreign relations, none in our home popular sentiment, none in our white military force,—no loss by it any how or any where. On the contrary, it shows a gain of quite a hundred and thirty thousand soldiers, seamen, and laborers. These are palpable facts, about which, as facts, there can be no cavilling. We have the men; and we could not have had them without the measure.

"And now let any Union man who complains of the measure, test himself by writing down in one line that he is for subduing the rebellion by force of arms; and in the next, that he is for taking these hundred and thirty thousand men from the Union side, and placing them where they would be but for the measure he condemns. If he can not face his case so stated, it is only because he can not face the truth."

I add a word which was not in the verbal conversation. In telling this tale I attempt no compliment to my own sagacity. I claim not to have controlled events, but confess plainly that events have controlled me. Now, at the end of three years struggle the nation's condition is not what either party, or any man devised, or expected. God alone can claim it. Whither it is tending seems plain. If God now wills the removal of a great wrong, and wills also that we of the North as well as you of the South, shall pay fairly for our complicity in that wrong, impartial history will find therein new cause to attest and revere the justice and goodness of God.

*April 4, 1864*

## To Charles D. Robinson

To me it seems plain that saying re-union and abandonment of slavery would be considered, if offered, is not saying that nothing *else* or *less* would be considered, if offered. But I will not stand upon the mere construction of language. It is true, as you remind me, that in the Greeley letter of 1862, I said: "If I could save the Union without freeing any slave I would do it; and if I could save it by freeing all the slaves I would do it; and if I could save it by freeing some, and leaving others alone I would also do that." I continued in the same letter as follows: "What I do about slavery and the colored race, I do because I believe it helps to save the Union; and what I forbear I forbear because I do not believe it would help to save the Union. I shall do less whenever I shall believe what I am doing hurts the cause; and I shall do more whenever I shall believe doing more will help the cause." All this I said in the utmost sincerity; and I am as true to the whole of it now, as when I first said it. When I afterwards proclaimed emancipation, and employed colored soldiers, I only followed the declaration just quoted from the Greeley letter that "I shall do *more* whenever I shall believe *doing* more will help the cause" The way these measures were to help the cause, was not to be by magic, or miracles, but by inducing the colored people to come bodily over from the rebel side to ours. On this point, nearly a year ago, in a letter to Mr. Conkling, made public at once, I wrote as follows: "But negroes, like other people, act upon motives. Why should they do anything for us if we will do nothing for them? If they stake their lives for us they must be prompted by the strongest motive—even the promise of freedom.

And the promise, being made, must be kept." I am sure you will not, on due reflection, say that the promise being made, must be *broken* at the first opportunity. I am sure you would not desire me to say, or to leave an inference, that I am ready, whenever convenient, to join in re-enslaving those who shall have served us in consideration of our promise. As matter of morals, could such treachery by any possibility, escape the curses of Heaven, or of any good man? As matter of policy, to *announce* such a purpose, would ruin the Union cause itself. All recruiting of colored men would instantly cease, and all colored men now in our service, would instantly desert us. And rightfully too. Why should they give their lives for us, with full notice of our purpose to betray them? Drive back to the support of the rebellion the physical force which the colored people now give, and promise us, and neither the present, nor any coming, administration, *can* save the Union. Take from us, and give to the enemy, the hundred and thirty, forty, or fifty thousand colored persons now serving us as soldiers, seamen, and laborers, and we can not longer maintain the contest. The party who could elect a President on a War & Slavery Restoration platform, would, of necessity, lose the colored force; and that force being lost, would be as powerless to save the Union as to do any other impossible thing. It is not a question of sentiment or taste, but one of physical force, which may be measured and estimated, as horse-power, and steam power, are measured, and estimated. And by measurement, it is more than we can lose, and live. Nor can we, by discarding it, get a white force in place of it. There is a witness in every white mans bosom that he would rather go to the war having the negro to help him, than to help the enemy against him. It is not the giving of one class for another. It is simply giving a large force to the enemy, for *nothing* in return.

In addition to what I have said, allow me to remind you that no one, having control of the rebel armies, or, in fact, having any influence whatever in the rebellion, has offered, or intimated a willingness to, a restoration of the Union, in any event, or on any condition whatever. Let it be constantly borne in mind that no such offer has been made or intimated. Shall we be weak enough to allow the enemy to distract us with an abstract question which he himself refuses to present as a practical one? In the Conkling letter before mentioned, I said: "Whenever you shall have conquered all resistance to the Union, if I shall urge you to continue fighting, it will be an apt time *then* to declare that you will not fight to free negroes." I repeat this now. If Jefferson Davis wishes, for himself, or for the benefit of his friends at the North, to know what I would do if he were to offer peace and re-union, saying nothing about slavery, let him try me.

*August 17, 1864*

# To Isaac M. Schermerhorn
### (Unfinished Draft of Letter)

Yours inviting me to attend a Union Mass Meeting at Buffalo is received. Much is being said about peace; and no man desires peace more ardently than I. Still I am yet unprepared to give up the Union for a peace which, so achieved, could not be of much duration. The preservation of our Union was *not* the sole avowed object for which the war was commenced. It was commenced for precisely the reverse object—*to destroy our Union.* The insurgents commenced it by firing upon the *Star of the West,* and on Fort Sumter, and by other similar acts. It is true, however, that the administration accepted the war thus commenced, for the sole avowed object of preserving our Union; and it is not true that it has since been, or will be, prosecuted by this administration, for any other object. In declaring this, I only declare what I can know, and do know to be true, and what no other man can know to be false.

In taking the various steps which have led to my present position in relation to the war, the public interest, and my private interest, have been perfectly parallel, because in no other way could I serve myself so well, as by truly serving the Union. The whole field has been open to me, where to choose. No place-hunting necessity has been upon me urging me to seek a position of antagonism to some other man, irrespective of whether such position might be favorable or unfavorable to the Union.

Of course I may err in judgment, but my present position in reference to the rebellion is the result of my best judgment, and, according to that best judgment, it is the only position upon which any Executive can or could save the Union. Any substantial departure from it insures the success of the rebellion. An armistice—a cessation of hostilities—is the end of the struggle, and the insurgents would be in peaceable possession of all that has been struggled for. Any different policy in regard to the colored man, deprives us of his help, and this is more than we can bear. We can not spare the hundred and forty or fifty thousand now serving us as soldiers, seamen, and laborers. This is not a question of sentiment or taste, but one of physical force, which may be measured and estimated as horse-power and Steam-power are measured and estimated. Keep it, and you can save the Union. Throw it away, and the Union goes with it. Nor is it possible for any administration to retain the service of these people with the express or implied understanding that, upon the first convenient occasion, they are to be re-enslaved. It *can* not be; and it *ought* not to be.

*September 12, 1864*

## To Henry W. Hoffman

A convention of Maryland has framed a new constitution for the State; a public meeting is called for this evening, at Baltimore, to aid in securing its ratification by the people; and you ask a word from me, for the occasion. I presume the only feature of the instrument, about which there is serious controversy, is that which provides for the extinction of slavery. It needs not to be a secret, and I presume it is no secret, that I wish success to this provision. I desire it on every consideration. I wish all men to be free. I wish the material prosperity of the already free which I feel sure the extinction of slavery would bring. I wish to see, in process of disappearing, that only thing which ever could bring this nation to civil war. I attempt no argument. Argument upon the question is already exhausted by the abler, better informed, and more immediately interested sons of Maryland herself. I only add that I shall be gratified exceedingly if the good people of the State shall, by their votes, ratify the new constitution.

*October 10, 1864*

## To Mrs. Lydia Bixby

I have been shown in the files of the War Department a statement of the Adjutant General of Massachusetts, that you are the mother of five sons who have died gloriously on the field of battle.

I feel how weak and fruitless must be any words of mine which should attempt to beguile you from the grief of a loss so overwhelming. But I cannot refrain from tendering to you the consolation that may be found in the thanks of the Republic they died to save.

I pray that our Heavenly Father may assuage the anguish of your bereavement, and leave you only the cherished memory of the loved and lost, and the solemn pride that must be yours, to have laid so costly a sacrifice upon the altar of Freedom.

*November 21, 1864*